# Lecture Notes of the Institute for Computer Sciences, Social Informatics and Telecommunications Engineering 682

The LNICST series publishes ICST's conferences, symposia and workshops.

LNICST reports state-of-the-art results in areas related to the scope of the Institute.

The type of material published includes

- Proceedings (published in time for the respective event)
- Other edited monographs (such as project reports or invited volumes)

LNICST topics span the following areas:

- General Computer Science
- E-Economy
- E-Medicine
- Knowledge Management
- Multimedia
- Operations, Management and Policy
- Social Informatics
- Systems

Mohammed Zafar Ali Khan · Anuradha Sundru ·
Sreenivasa Rao Ekkurthi · Nishu Gupta
Editors

# Advanced Technologies in Electronics, Communications and Signal Processing

Second EAI International Conference, ICATECS 2026
Hyderabad, India, January 30–31, 2026
Proceedings

Springer

*Editors*
Mohammed Zafar Ali Khan
Indian Institute of Technology Hyderabad
Hyderabad, Andhra Pradesh, India

Anuradha Sundru
National Institute of Technology
Warangal, Andhra Pradesh, India

Sreenivasa Rao Ekkurthi
Vasavi College of Engineering
Hyderabad, Andhra Pradesh, India

Nishu Gupta
VTT Technical Research Centre of Finland Ltd.
Oulu, Finland

ISSN 1867-8211 ISSN 1867-822X (electronic)
Lecture Notes of the Institute for Computer Sciences, Social Informatics and Telecommunications Engineering
ISBN 978-3-032-29698-6 ISBN 978-3-032-29699-3 (eBook)
https://doi.org/10.1007/978-3-032-29699-3



This Springer imprint is published by the registered company Springer Nature Switzerland AG
The registered company address is: Gewerbestrasse 11, 6330 Cham, Switzerland

# Preface

We are delighted to introduce the proceedings of the second edition of the International Conference on Advanced Technologies in Electronics, Communications and Signal Processing (2nd EAI ICATECS), powered by the European Alliance for Innovation (EAI), and hosted by the Electronics and Communication Engineering department, Vasavi College of Engineering, Hyderabad, India, during 30–31 January 2026 in hybrid mode. This conference brought together researchers, developers, and practitioners from around the world who are leveraging and developing intelligent computing systems and cyber-physical systems to make communication smarter, faster, less expensive, and more accessible in bundles. The theme of the 2nd EAI ICATECS was "Harnessing the power of various technologies of electronics to achieve relevant sustainable development goals".

The technical program of the conference comprised 30 full papers, presented in hybrid mode by registered authors across six technical sessions and six tracks. The conference tracks were: Track 1: Wireless Communications & Signal Processing; Track 2: Electronic Systems; Track 3: Embedded and Machine Learning Approaches; Track 4: Biomedical and Computing Systems; Track 5: Communication Networks; Track 6: Electronics in Health Care. These papers were selected from 116 submissions. Each submission was reviewed following a double-blind process with a minimum of 3 reviews per paper. Apart from high-quality technical paper presentations, the technical program also featured four keynote speeches from eminent speakers, namely K. Srinivas, ASL, DRDO, India; Nishu Gupta, VTT Technical Research Centre of Finland Ltd., Finland; Sandeep Chaturvedi, GAETEC – DRDO, India; and Ramam Akkipeddi, Singapore Institute of Technology, Singapore.

We sincerely appreciate the continuous guidance and extended support of the Conference Chair, Mohammed Zafar Ali Khan, IIT Hyderabad, whose deep involvement helped the conference to proceed smoothly. It was also a great pleasure to work with the excellent organizing committee, chaired by Nishu Gupta, for their hard work in organizing and supporting the conference. In particular, we also appreciate the technical program committee, which coordinated and completed the peer-review process of technical papers and framed a well-designed technical program. We are also grateful to Conference Manager Stella Dao for her support and to all the authors who submitted their papers to the 2nd EAI ICATECS.

We sincerely appreciate the management and administration of Vasavi College of Engineering, Hyderabad, India, for their support as the main host Institute of the 2nd EAI ICATECS. We strongly believe that this conference provided a forum for researchers, developers, and practitioners to discuss the scientific and technological aspects of advanced electronics, communications, and signal processing. We also expect that future editions of the EAI ICATECS conferences will be as successful and stimulating as indicated by the contributions presented in this volume.

Mohammed Zafar Ali Khan
S. Anuradha
E. Sreenivasa Rao
Nishu Gupta

# Organization

## Steering Committee

| | |
|---|---|
| P. Ramamohan Rao | Vasavi Academy of Education, India |
| V. M. Parthasarathi | Vasavi Academy of Education, India |
| P. Balaji | Vasavi Academy of Education, India |
| S. V. Ramana | Vasavi College of Engineering, India |
| E. Sreenivasa Rao | Vasavi College of Engineering, India |

## Organizing Committee

### General Chair

| | |
|---|---|
| Mohammed Zafar Ali Khan | Indian Institute of Technology Hyderabad, India |

### General Co-chair

| | |
|---|---|
| Arun Prakash | Motilal Nehru National Institute of Technology Allahabad, India |

### Organizing Chair

| | |
|---|---|
| Nishu Gupta | VTT Technical Research Centre of Finland Ltd., Oulu, Finland |

### Organizing Co-chair

| | |
|---|---|
| Prakash Pareek | Vishnu Institute of Technology, India |

### Program Chairs

| | |
|---|---|
| S. Anuradha | National Institute of Technology Warangal, India |
| E. Sreenivasa Rao | Vasavi College of Engineering, India |

## Technical Program Committee Chair

| | |
|---|---|
| D. M. K. Chaitanya | Vasavi College of Engineering, India |

## Sponsorship and Exhibit Chair

| | |
|---|---|
| K. Deepti | Vasavi College of Engineering, India |

## Local Chair

| | |
|---|---|
| Srilakshmi Aouthu | Vasavi College of Engineering, India |

## Workshops Chair

| | |
|---|---|
| P. V. Ramana | Lightspeed Photonics Pte. Ltd, Singapore |

## Publicity and Social Media Chair

| | |
|---|---|
| K. Veera Swamy | Vasavi College of Engineering, India |

## Publications Chairs

| | |
|---|---|
| E. Sreenivasa Rao | Vasavi College of Engineering, India |
| D. M. K. Chaitanya | Vasavi College of Engineering, India |
| Nishu Gupta | VTT Technical Research Centre of Finland Ltd., Finland |

## Web Chair

| | |
|---|---|
| Vamsi Krishna Palukuru | CoreIoT Technologies Ltd., Finland |

## Posters and PhD Track Chair

| | |
|---|---|
| Bhaskar Choubey | Universität Siegen, Germany |

## Panels Chair

| | |
|---|---|
| Azremi Abdullah Al-Hadi | Universiti Malaysia Perlis, Malaysia |

### Demos Chair

| | |
|---|---|
| Arun Kumar | Vasavi College of Engineering, India |

### Tutorials Chair

| | |
|---|---|
| Ramam Akkipeddi | Singapore Institute of Technology, Singapore |

## Technical Program Committee

| | |
|---|---|
| Arun Kumar | Vasavi College of Engineering, India |
| D. M. K. Chaitanya | Vasavi College of Engineering, India |
| D. Ramakrishna | Osmania University, India |
| D. Sashank Kulkarni | Mathworks, India |
| E. Sreenivasa Rao | Vasavi College of Engineering, India |
| K. Krishna Kishore | Vasavi College of Engineering, India |
| K. Samba Siva Rao | RCI, India |
| K. Veera Swamy | Vasavi College of Engineering, India |
| L. Anjaneyulu | National Institute of Technology Warangal, India |
| N. Bheema Rao | National Institute of Technology Warangal, India |
| P. Chandrasekhar Reddy | Jawaharlal Nehru Technological University, Hyderabad, India |
| P. Koti Lakshmi | Osmania University, India |
| P. Naveen Kumar | Osmania University, India |
| Patri Sreehari Rao | National Institute of Technology Warangal, India |
| Sandeep Chaturvedi | GAETEC, India |
| Srinivas Talabattula | Indian Institute of Science, India |

# Contents

## Electronic Systems



## Embedded and Machine Learning Approaches

# Wireless Communications and Signal Processing

# An Efficient, Secure and Leveraging IoT Based Hypothermia Diagnosing and Monitoring System for Climbers with Smart Jacket

V. Vijayasaro[1](✉), Niveathasaro Vijayaregunathan[2], Santhosh Kumar Allemki[1], Vishal Walia[3], Harpreet Kaur[4], and Banavathu Ramyasree[1]

[1] Department of ECE, Guru Nanak institute of Technology Hyderabad, Hyderabad, India
viji.saro17@gmail.com
[2] Department of ECE, School of Engineering, Mohan Babu University, Kotala, India
[3] Department of ECE, Guru Nanak University Hyderabad, Hyderabad, India
[4] ECE department, UIET, GNU Guru Nanak University, Hyderabad, India

**Abstract.** The primary focus of this paper is to identify a gadget which will identify hypothermia Condition to 2-wheeler riders. Our proposed research will develop a health monitoring device using Wireless Body Area Network (WBAN) and embedded into climbing jackets. The device will not be cumbersome to climbers since they can use it during the climb. It consists of a heating sensor, pulse sensor as well as temperature sensor. The treatment of different ailments such as stroke, heart diseases and hyperthermia among others has been revolutionized by the pace with which communications, particularly the wireless Communications and Technology have been developed to monitor the bio functions of a patient. This device will be connected with the smartphone of the user with the Bluetooth connection so that he could see his physical condition, alter the temperature of the heating element, and create a climbing team. Based on the result of the experiment, the device is capable of detecting the indicators of hypothermia and informing the user and mountaineer teams about the indicators. This helps climbers to react faster to hypothermia and lowers the amount of deaths that are related to this condition.

**Keywords:** Smart Jackets · Internet of Things (IOT) · Detection · Bluetooth · wireless Communications

## 1 Introduction

Hypothermia is the most prevalent health problems that are being reported in India where excessive heat loss occurs in the body that causes an extreme cold body temperature. Due to it, the body temperature drops to below 35 o C and it changes the consciousness that can cause death [1]. Climbers who do things in cold temperature and strong winds experience more hypothermia . Wet clothes are the main predisposing factor in hypothermia and it


M. Zafar Ali Khan et al. (Eds.): ICATECS 2025, LNICST 682, pp. 3–13, 2027.
https://doi.org/10.1007/978-3-032-29699-3_1

is not possible that a trekking individual should be aware of his or her body temperature or their colleagues body temperature as to whether it is on the normal range or it is below normal range [2].

This concept can assist in reducing the death rate by 7–10% since it can be used to promise safety to pedestrians. Presently, the death toll of highway accidents in India constitutes 20% of the death rate in India. This is because the work of a four-wheeler car is built on an impact with a thing or two other cars. This system is fitted on the back of the jacket [3].

The two-wheeler accidents have mushroomed over the past year [4]. As the said populations increase, the number of accidents is on the increase as well as road congestion has increased these days. This new technology will be installed in the airbag jacket and has the ability of reducing the extent of injuries caused by frontal collisions.

The airbag system has been fitted in nearly all the body parts that were affected such as heads, shoulders and ribs. A control board is used and sensors to operate these Airbags. The two situations, in which the system is activated, are the calculation of the angle difference and the issue of the two bikes colliding or any other accident involving a bike and an object [5].

The embedded systems is the calculated machine that does not have a particular job that it is focused on. The embedded software is also known as firmware. The desktop or the laptop can be utilized in different tasks such as playing a game, word processor, accounting, software development etc. In the embedded systems technologies there is standard fixed software on the other hand [6].

The embedded systems technologies have performed a considerable task, but it cannot be programmed to different purposes. The embedded systems also possess a significant number of weaknesses such as limited resources and reduced storage space [7]. It lacks space to store secondary storage also such as CDROM and the floppy disk. Embedded systems technologies are not a convenient one to use in any activity with a time limit since the deadlines are very strict in the real time systems and it may result in catastrophic occurrence in case of failure to achieve the right timeline [8].

Embedded systems are not that powerful. This means that since many embedded devices have to operate on a battery, they need to be very low power consuming. Other embedded systems however have to operate in very harsh environments such as very high humidity and temperatures. In an effortless way, the Internet of Things system is revolutionizing various industries by connecting embedded systems to the internet in order to gather data. The IoT is widely used in the smart house where, among other things, it may be remotely used to control a thermostat and a surveillance camera to be even more automated and economical [9].

In the medical field, IoT has been applied in remote patient monitoring to monitor critical signs of health in real-time using interconnected devices to enhance the care of the patient. Smart cities use IoT to regulate the management of traffic and garbage. Precision farming is a significant field in agriculture as it maximizes the use of resources [10]. IoT is applied in industrial automation to enhance the efficiency of the operations by means of predictive maintenance and real-time monitoring of machinery. The IoT finds application in connected vehicles to navigate with and track a fleet as well as in retail applications such as smart shelves that track inventory levels. In general, the IoT systems are the dominant elements in any contemporary life and offer radical solutions in healthcare, transport, farming, and urban administration that result in smarter living environments [11] (Fig. 1).

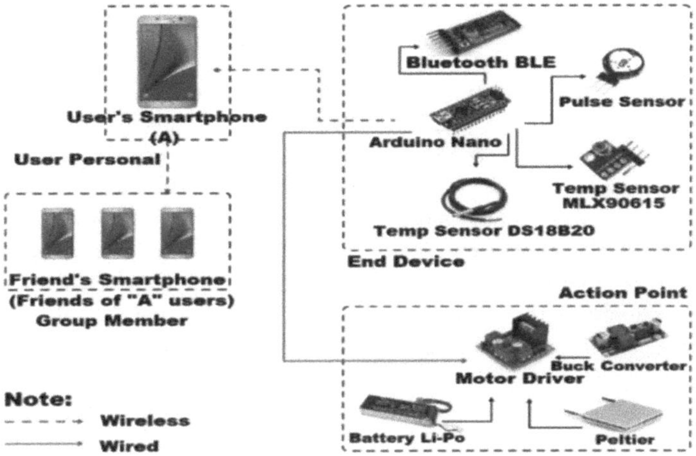


**Fig. 1.** Sample Hardware Architecture

This paper employed information from heart rate and temperature sensors as markers to assess the climber's physical health. The climber health code was obtained by processing the data from the two sensors to provide an output value. Wireless data transfer was accomplished through a Bluetooth communication network.

## 2 Literature Survey

Some of the technologies that trigger brain hypothermia have been studied in the various studies. Cojocaru et al. [12] have developed a brain hypothermia-inducing device, a non-invasive device that is used in stroke and hypothermia treatment. This technology attempted to develop a better method of reducing the body temperature by incorporating Peltier elements on the basis of thermal energy in the helmet. The device feature is used in cooperation with an electric pump to create a closed circuit in which water circulates in a coolant.

This system employs Peltier thermos cooling elements as a cooling system and they are fitted in a helmet. The hot side of the Peltier is cooled with the water circulating that further enhances the cooling of the system and working time [13]. The temperature of the patient in four locations is measured using A Raspberry Pi and a temperature sensor (NTC), and Arduino controller is utilized to control the process of the device functioning and a Peltier main cooling element is implemented. The temperature is based on the value of NTC resistance and the near value of the known resistor to get a voltage divider.

A non-invasive approach of controlling the brain temperature was created by Giuliani et al. [14] who produced a cooling compression collar that was made of a plastic outer part. In order to utilize this device the patient must wear a cooling collar around his/her neck which lowers the temperature and pressure exerted to the arteries supplying the brain of the patient. The device is expected to control the reduction of blood temperature with the help of the arteries connected to the head of the patient. The device is turned on and the cooling process takes place at a certain period of time which is determined by the temperature-regulating collar.

WBAN sensor nodes in the long run gather biological signal information of the patient. The information is wirelessly transmitted to the server where it is stored to be analyzed at a later time and used as a reference point to make a crucial decision. To increase the life time of the network sensor nodes ought to use specific communication techniques to conserve power [15]. It is directed at chilling the skull and lowering the temperature in the brain. This system is applied to wrap the front and back of the head in order to cool it. The material that fills the holes in the helmet is referred to as crystal. In order to prepare the crystal component, so that it could be gel-like, prior to the experiment, the helmet is moistened in water. It is applied on the patient, and in a period of four hours, it has been stored at 15 °C. The drawback of this helmet is that one can shave the head successfully [16].

Another warming device in case of hypothermia. This is then stuffed into a single and easy to wear heating jacket.

1. Software Development and Integration.

Has a mobile app that regulates and monitors data, delivers notifications and switches on heater. One can move around temperature and design aspects, which make it easier to use. There are also algorithms which enable detection of the abnormality and relevant response implementation.

2. Testing and Calibration

Test and calibration entails robustness to contravening circumstances of the instrument, relative to the instrument accuracy and dependability. The environmental testing will reveal what other factors can influence the performance and usability in different temperatures and user feedback will enhance functionality and usability.

3. Real Time Monitoring and Deployment.

This allows the users to monitor the performance of the extreme cliff and motorbike riding conditions with ease. The deployment is on when completed.

## 3 Methodology

The climber should be aware of the signs of hypothermia disease in order to provide handling more efficiently and promptly. This study created a software and hardware tool that intends to make it easier to identify and treat hypothermia. They would mount the hardware gadgets on a climbing. The climber should be aware of the signs of hypothermia disease in order to provide handling more efficiently and promptly. In order to make the diagnosis and treatment of hypothermia disease easier, this research developed a hardware and software tool.

The main objective of the paper as follows

1. The creation and deployment of a wearable jacket prototype system that uses sensors and a heating element to detect hypothermia and administer first therapy.
2. A case study planning and implementation involving the demonstration of the relevance and practicality of wearable jacket sensors to climbing.
3. Using Wi-Fi Direct technology, climbers on the same network can share information about their physical states and receive real-time hypothermia feedback from the system without needing to connect to the internet.

Temperature and pulse sensors were employed, and the Arduino Nano served as the device's sensor data processing hub. The MLX90615 body temperature sensor is employed in the gadget; it uses infrared technology to measure temperature without requiring physical touch.

Regarding the heart sensor, the XD-58C sensor pulse will be applied to the climber's fingertip in order to detect the heart beats per minute. Additionally, a TEC-12706 Peltier heating element is included with this gadget. The motor driver that controls the temperature will be connected to the Peltier. The gadget has Bluetooth built in, which allows the climber's Android smartphone to receive sensor data. Bluetooth v4.0, which is compatible with low energy technologies, was utilized in this study (Fig. 2).

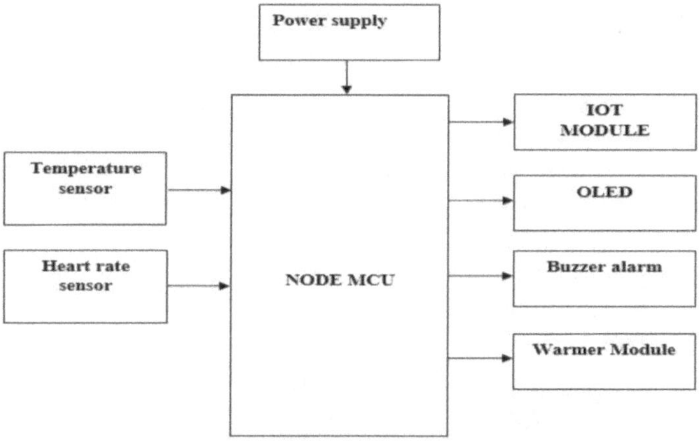


**Fig. 2.** Block Diagram of proposed system

This section describes the block diagram of IOT-based smart jackets of cyclists. In this case, the central component of the processor is the Node MCU. On the foundations of ESP8266 Wi-Fi System on Chip, Node MCU is an open-source programming board specifically designed to be used in the Internet of Things (IoT) applications. It contains 16 digital I/O pins, 1 analog input pin, a 32-bit RISC CPU, and it supports SPI, I2C and UART communication protocols. Node MCU would work well with battery-powered equipment because it is compact and consumes very little energy; it can be programmed via Python, Lua, or the Arduino IDE, which makes it approachable to both inexperienced and experienced developers.

Having the capability to connect to different networks or act as a hotspot with the built-in Wi-Fi, a plethora of applications can be found, one of them being home automation, environmental monitoring, and smart agriculture. Finally, Node MCU is fun and highly adaptable, and thus a highly suitable option when prototyping and creating IoT solutions.

## 3.1 Node MCU ESP8266

The ESP8266 Node MCU is a smart development platform and a firmware that is designed to use in the Internet of Things (IoT) and which executes the Lua scripting language. It is a development board, which is built around ESP8266 build-in Wi-Fi SoC by Espressif Systems, and is based on ESP-12. This board has several pads that have various specification functions such as some power pads including Micro-USB that is Usb Transformation feeding pin, 3.3 V that is ringing power input, GND and Vin which are ground and external power port respectively. The control pins are reset connectors (EN, RST), an analog bus (A0), which is used to measure the voltage in the range between 0 and 3.3 V, and general-purpose I/O pins, named as GPIO, in arrange (GPIO1 to GPIO16). It also supports communication of SPI type with four pins and serial communication with UART interfaces having UART0 to do general functions and UART1 to Upload firmware. The I2C protocol is also known to be supported by the board although the pin mapping in question needs to be confirmed since it has internal mappings.

The computer unit is present in the Node MCU ESP8266 and has a Tensilica 32-bit RISC CPU (Xtensa LX106) and targets the 3.3 V operating voltage and a 7 V to 12 V input voltage range. It also has a variety of peripherals such as 16 digital I/O pins, 1 analog input pin, 1 UART, 1 SPI and 1 I2C bus. It has a 4 MB flash and 64Kb SRAM memory and operates at 80Mhz, Inside it has PCB antenna, PCB Antenna and wireless communication (Figs. 3 and 4).

**Fig. 3.** ESP2866 Node MCU

## 3.2 Heart Rate Sensor(HW827)

Applications for the Hall effect sensor HW 827 include linear position sensing, rotational sensing, and speed detection. It detects magnetic fields. The Hall effect, which states that a conductor subjected to a magnetic field injected at a specific angle experiences a

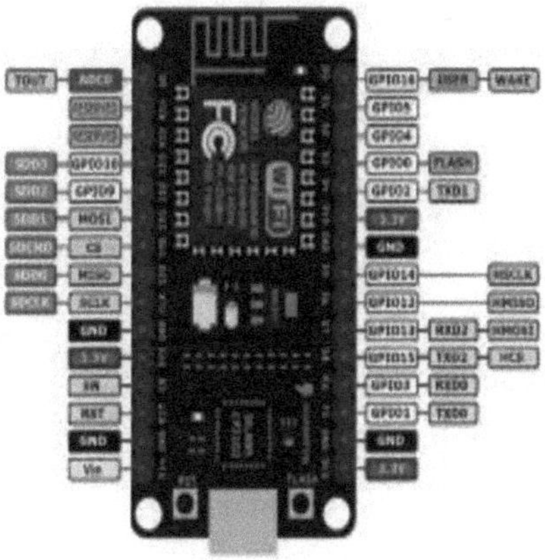

**Fig. 4.** Pinout Diagram of Node MCU

potential difference across it, is the basis for this sensor. The HW 827 is advised for use in consumer, industrial, and automotive electronics because of its excellent precision and sensitivity. It can be used in a variety of settings, including battery-operated devices where reliable and effective magnetic field detection is required, thanks to its compact size, durability, and low power consumption (Fig. 5).

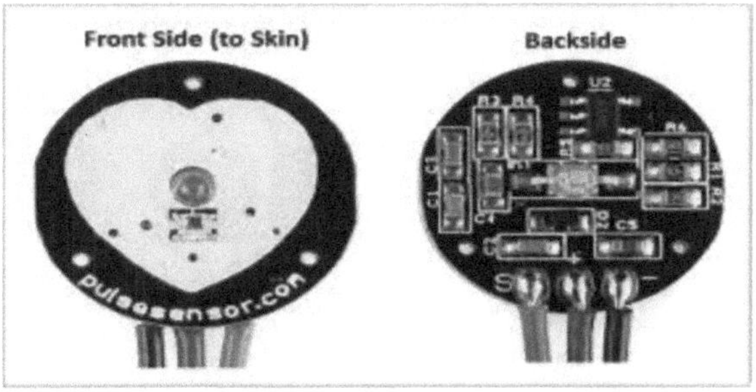


**Fig. 5.** HW827 Sensor

### 3.3 Temperature Sensor(MLX90614)

The MLX90614 is a small size device and is trusted in areas such as medical thermometers, HVAC equipment, and industrial process surveillance. Since it relies on non-contact techniques, it is ideal for use in situations where measurement of the temperature of moving or hard to reach objects is necessary (Fig. 6).

### 3.4 OLED Organic Light Emitting Diodes

The 1.3 OLED display that uses the SH1106 chip is a graphic LCD with a dot resolution of 128x64 pixels. This OLED display accepts a voltage supply of between 3.3 V and

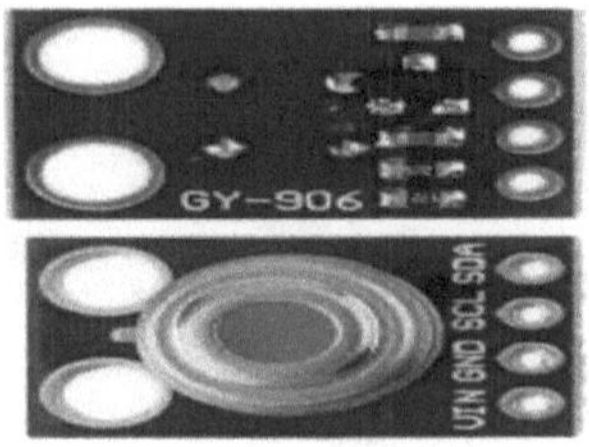


**Fig. 6.** MLX90614 Sensor

5 V, which is ideal for many 3.3 V or 5 V microcontrollers. According to your project requirements, the display is available in two variants which are the OLED 1.3 I2C WHITE and the OLED 1.3 I2C BLUE. We will instead make use of the I2C interface, which allows us to connect the OLED display to the microcontroller in a much easier fashion with fewer wires and therefore less pins. There's no need for a voltage regulating circuit because the OLED can be connected through the microcontroller. The OLED has the same operation voltage as the microcontroller which ranges from 3.3–5 V.

The overall current consumption is very low at only 8 mA during display operation, and thus have low power consumption. The PCB Size is small (33.7 mm x 35.5 mm) and makes the board fit into a project that requires space-constrained designs. In our project, we will make use of this OLED display to show graphical or text information. The I2C protocol will be used for effective communication with the microcontroller, and we will implement proper libraries to control output from the display (Figs. 7 and 8).

**Fig. 7.** Diagram of OLED display

### 3.5 Implementation

The circuit diagram that describes the features of the paper and identifies each module demonstrate the way to develop in implementation monitoring system. The unit of processing is the microcontroller node MCU V3. It consists of a circuit comprising TR1, which produces AC voltage, rectified by BR1 and then controlled by the 7805 voltage regulator U2 to produce a circuit that draws 5 V DC. It also has a smoothing capacitor C1 and an LED, D1 in that order to stabilize power and provide an indication respectively.

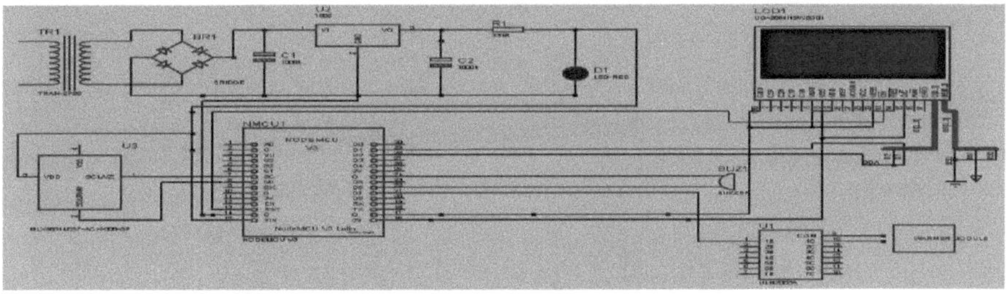

Fig. 8. Interfacing between Node MCU and sensors

## 4 Process and Requirements

One of the modern monitoring systems is Thing Speak, which consists of a platform providing services that depend entirely on the Internet of Things (IoT) [8]. The fact that the system can store and show data and information distinguishes it. Data processing and visualization by means of MATLAB or other tools is also possible. Figure is a visualization of the output of the cloud of the smart jacket (Fig. 9).

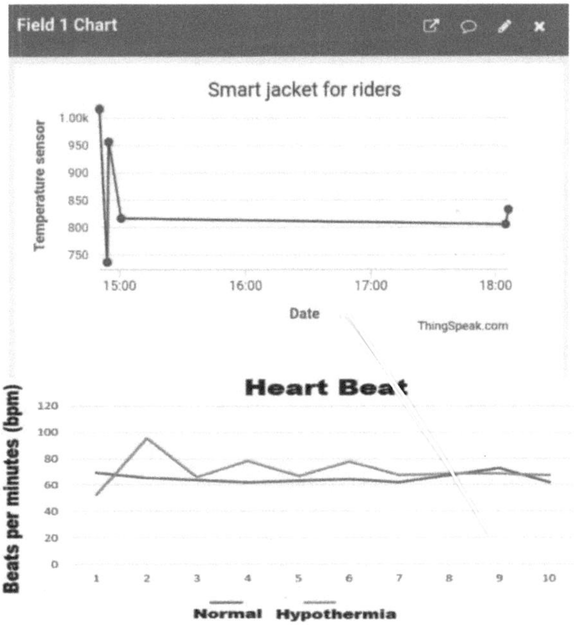


Fig. 9. output in the cloud

### 4.1 Prototype

The prototype showcases a scalable design for applications such as safety gear or environmental monitoring, emphasizing reliability, simplicity, and IoT connectivity for real-time data sharing and alerts (Fig. 10).

**Fig. 10.** Prototype Diagram

## 5 Conclusion and Future Work

The smart jacket combines temperature monitoring, heart rate tracking, and IoT connectivity to improve safety and comfort. Its proactive design aims to prevent hypothermia and enhance climber and rider safety through real-time data sharing and alerts. By transitioning safety gear from reactive to proactive, this technology not only reduces risks but also improves the overall experience of outdoor and motorcycling activities. Future developments could include integrating advanced AI algorithms for predictive health monitoring, cloud-based data analytics for broader safety insights, and enhanced materials for greater comfort and durability. Such innovations will further solidify the role of smart jackets as indispensable tools for safety and connectivity.

## References

1. Pivoto, D.G.S., de Figueiredo, F.A.P., Cavdar, C., Tejerina, G.R.d.L., Mendes, L.L.: A comprehensive survey of machine learning applied to resource allocation in wireless communications. IEEE Commun. Surv. Tutor. **28** (2026). https://doi.org/10.1109/COMST.2025.3552370
2. Kim, Y., Su Park, Y., Gyu Lee, H., Baek, D.: Designing cost-effective battery-less energy harvesting for intermittent wireless communication. IEEE Access **13** (2025). https://doi.org/10.1109/ACCESS.2025.3606514

3. Song, H., Chung, J.M.: Next-generation wireless communication technologies for improved disaster response and management. ETRI J. **47**(3) (2025). https://doi.org/10.4218/etrij.2024-0546
4. Hasan, S., Sjoberg, K., Wallin, P.: Wireless communication in underground mining teleoperation: a systematic review. IEEE Access **13** (2025). https://doi.org/10.1109/ACCESS.2025.3563138
5. Zhan, H., et al.: Review for wireless communication technology based on digital encoding metasurfaces. Opto-Electron. Adv. **8**(7) (2025). https://doi.org/10.29026/oea.2025.240315
6. Zhao, W., et al.: Quantum computing in wireless communications and networking: a tutorial-cum-survey. IEEE Commun. Surv. Tutor. **27**(4) (2025). https://doi.org/10.1109/COMST.2024.3502762
7. Meenu, L., Aiswarya, S., Menon, K.A.U., Sreedevi, K.M.: Experimental investigation to analyze the electromagnetic radiation exposure from wireless communication devices. J. Hazard. Mater. Adv. **17** (2025). https://doi.org/10.1016/j.hazadv.2024.100548
8. Huang, Y., Shen, Y., Wang, J.: From Terahertz Imaging to Terahertz Wireless Communications (2023). https://doi.org/10.1016/j.eng.2022.06.023.
9. Yan, J., Zhang, X., Zhu, N., Qin, Y., Yang, G.: High-performance triboelectric nanogenerators boosted by synergistically aligned piezoelectric/conductive composite nanofibers. Polym. Compos. **46**(4) (2025). https://doi.org/10.1002/pc.29165
10. Sahil, K., Suman, A., Rishi, J., Ranjan, A., Ray, R.: IND-AIR-life saving jacket for workplace environment. IJIRT **11**(11) (2025)
11. Azhan, N.A.: Evaluating the effectiveness of a CDIO-based smart safety jacket for deaf users: fashion technology education. Int. J. Educ. Psychol. Couns. **10**(60) (2025). https://doi.org/10.35631/ijepc.1060059
12. Sarkar, S.: Smart life safety jacket for rescuers. Int. J. Disaster Risk Manag. **7**(1) (2025). https://doi.org/10.18485/ijdrm.2025.7.1.21
13. P, S.V., M, J.P.K., Patil, A.B., H, M.D.: Smart Soilder Jacket. Int. J. Sci. Res. Eng. Manag. **09**(12) (2025). https://doi.org/10.55041/ijsrem54871
14. Jawaharlalnehru, M., Begum, Y.A., Ajeeth, A., Nitheesh, N., Krishnan, N.Y., Murali, A.: IoT-based smart helmet and jacket for real-time safety monitoring in construction site. In: Proceedings of 7th International Conference on Inventive Material Science and Applications, ICIMA 2025 (2025). https://doi.org/10.1109/ICIMA64861.2025.11074111
15. Sah, P.K., Das, A.M., Jayan, L., Gaayathri, R.R., Vijayan, L.: AlpineShield: advanced smart jacket for mountaineer safety. In: Proceedings of 8th International Conference on Inventive Computation Technologies, ICICT 2025 (2025). https://doi.org/10.1109/ICICT64420.2025.11004707
16. Raghuvanshi, A., Parikh, P., Shah, P.: Integrated smart helmet and jacket system for enhanced worker safety and health monitoring in hazardous environments. Int. J. Novel Res. Dev. **10**(2) (2025)

# AquaRefine: Adaptive Color Transformer for Underwater Image Restoration

M. Puja Sree[1], N. Satish[1], P. Sasi Kiran[1], M. Sai Durga Prasad[1], K. N. Prakash[1(✉)], and K. Prasanthi Jasmine[2]

[1] Department of ECE, Seshadri Rao Gudlavalleru Engineering College, Gudlavalleru, India
drprakashece@gmail.com

[2] Andhra Loyola Institute of Engineering and Technology, Vijayawada, India

**Abstract.** Underwater visual data typically experience color degradation due to the physical processes of scattering of light. As a consequence, image contrast is reduced, important details become unclear, and color inconsistencies arise, adversely affecting applications such as segmentation, object detection, and recognition. To overcome these issues, a transformer-based framework named AquaRefine is designed for adaptive and efficient underwater image enhancement. The architecture is built around three complementary modules: a Channel-Aware Cross Interaction block that captures long-range relationships through channel-focused attention; a Gated Spatial Feed Modulator that refines spatial and semantic cues via gated feature control; and a Dual-Stream Adaptive Fusion block that merges multi-scale information for balanced color and structure restoration. These components collectively improve perceptual clarity, texture continuity, and color fidelity while maintaining low computational overhead. The model adapts well to varied water conditions and illumination levels, preserving stable enhancement even under severe visibility loss. Its computationally efficient architecture allows practical deployment on real-time and resource-constrained platforms. Comprehensive evaluations conducted on standard benchmarks indicate that AquaRefine achieves superior performance compared to existing transformer-based methods in terms of both quantitative measures and perceptual quality.

**Keywords:** Underwater image restoration · Transformers · Color correction · Channel-focused attention · Gated spatial feed modulator

## 1 Introduction

Underwater imaging serves as an important tool in fields such as marine ecology, archaeological investigation, surveillance, and autonomous navigation. Imagery collected by remotely operated or autonomous underwater vehicles offers valuable information for applications including biodiversity analysis, coral reef evaluation, habitat characterization, and object inspection. In contrast to land-based


M. Zafar Ali Khan et al. (Eds.): ICATECS 2025, LNICST 682, pp. 14–26, 2027.
https://doi.org/10.1007/978-3-032-29699-3_2

scenes, however, underwater environments are strongly affected by the longer wavelengths diminish rapidly, while shorter wavelengths persist, resulting in noticeable color distortion, reduced contrast, and a hazy visual appearance. These degradations conceal fine structural features and considerably weaken the performance of subsequent computer vision processes such as segmentation, recognition, and depth estimation.

Existing image enhancement techniques depend on handcrafted priors or pixel-level heuristics, such as contrast stretching [7], histogram equalization [16], and dark-channel dehazing [2]. Although these methods are computationally lightweight, they typically assume uniform illumination and a constant scattering model, limiting their adaptability to complex and spatially varying underwater conditions. Retinex-based and color-compensation approaches [5,26,29] partially correct chromatic distortions but frequently introduce color over-enhancement or loss of fine textures, especially in regions with uneven lighting or strong turbidity. Moreover, such methods often fail to generalize to different water types or camera devices, making them less suitable for autonomous deployments in dynamic marine environments.

With the progress of deep learning, learning-based enhancement methods [4,10,18,21] have achieved significant success by modeling complex nonlinear relationships between degraded underwater images and their restored counterparts. Nevertheless, traditional networks are limited by their localized behavior, which hinder their capability to model long-range contextual relationships and maintain consistent global color representation. Transformer-based architectures [22,23,28] have shown promising results in image restoration through their self-attention mechanisms, enabling them to learn context-aware global relationships. Nevertheless, most existing transformer models are computationally intensive and often designed for general restoration tasks, making them less efficient and less adaptive for underwater enhancement, where color distortions and scattering effects vary widely across depth and scene composition. Additionally, their reliance on dense attention computation hinders real-time performance and interpretability, both of which are crucial for embedded and field-deployed underwater systems.

To address these challenges, **AquaRefine**, a lightweight transformer framework is proposed. The proposed model is both efficient and adaptive, focusing on accurate color restoration and structural consistency under diverse underwater conditions. AquaRefine introduces three key modules: a Channel-Aware Cross Interaction (CACI) block that captures long-range dependencies through channel-wise attention with minimal overhead, a Gated Spatial Feed Modulator (GSFM) that refines semantic and spatial representations via gated feature modulation, and a Dual-Stream Adaptive Fusion (DSAF) block that selectively integrates multi-scale contextual cues to ensure balanced color correction and texture recovery. Together, these modules enable the network to learn contextually relevant representations while preserving fine details, maintaining strong balance in interpretability, generalization, and computational efficiency.

The overall contributions of this work are:

- A compact transformer-based framework for underwater image enhancement is proposed, named AquaRefine, that jointly models global attention and localized refinement.
- Channel-Aware Cross Interaction (CACI) block is proposed to efficiently capture cross-channel dependencies, enabling structure-preserving and color-consistent enhancement.
- Gated Spatial Feed Modulator (GSFM) is introduced for spatial and semantic refinement through gated modulation, and a Dual-Stream Adaptive Fusion (DSAF) block for context-aware multi-scale feature integration.

Experiments conducted on standard underwater datasets validate that AquaRefine achieves superior quantitative performance and perceptually natural results while maintaining low computational cost.

## 2 Related Work

Early efforts in underwater image enhancement (UIE) primarily relied on traditional image processing methods guided by manually defined assumptions. Hitam *et al.* [7] improved underwater visibility by combining adaptive histogram equalization with contrast adjustment in the RGB and HSV colour domains. Fu *et al.* [5] introduced a Retinex-oriented model that incorporated image layer separation and colour correction to achieve more stable illumination normalization. Drews *et al.* [2] modified the dark-channel prior for underwater conditions through transmission map estimation to reduce haze artifacts. Zhang *et al.* [29] carried out colour compensation in the CIELab space by aligning luminance and chromatic statistics with reference exemplars. Later, Zhang *et al.* [30] proposed a strategy for addressing channel-specific attenuation by selecting the least degraded channel as a baseline and adjusting the remaining channels prior to histogram balancing. Wang *et al.* [26] utilized saliency-based fusion combined with edge enhancement to recover weakened RGB components, while Wang *et al.* [24] applied the Segment Anything Model to partition foreground and background regions, enabling region-dependent colour adjustment and refinement of high-frequency details. Although these techniques are computationally light and simple to implement, they depend on idealized optical assumptions such as uniform illumination and constant attenuation, which restrict their effectiveness in complex and diverse underwater environments.

The development of deep learning initiated a major transition toward data-driven underwater restoration approaches [3]. Islam *et al.* [10] and Fabbri *et al.* [4] employed conditional generative adversarial networks to learn end-to-end mappings from degraded inputs to enhanced outputs. Liu *et al.* [18] designed a twin adversarial contrastive framework that leverages object-level cues to jointly improve structural integrity and colour quality. Sharma *et al.* [21] proposed an attention-driven multi-scale network capable of performing both enhancement and super-resolution in a unified manner, while Zhao *et al.* [31] explored interactions in the wavelet domain to achieve frequency-consistent detail recovery. Even though these learning-based models surpass classical pipelines, they frequently

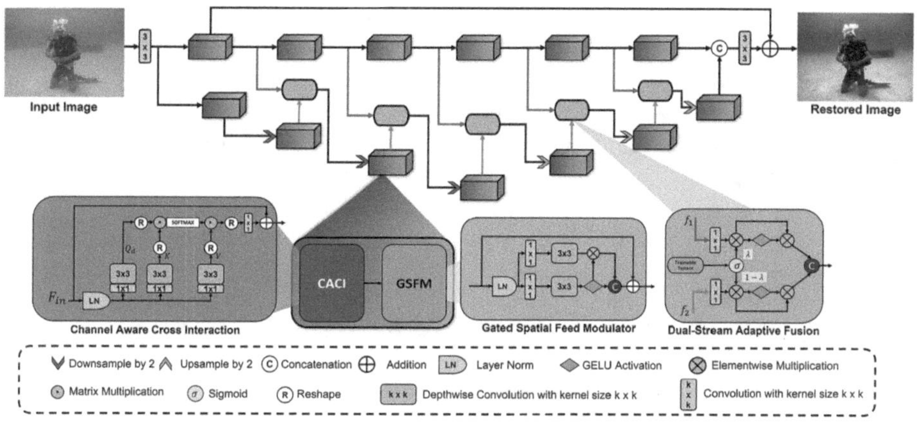


**Fig. 1.** Architectural representation of the proposed AquaRefine.

encounter difficulties when dealing with strong colour attenuation and depth-varying degradations. Wang *et al.* [25] further cast the enhancement problem within a reinforcement learning formulation by integrating a residual-attention encoder with a perceptually guided reward optimized using proximal policy optimization.

In recent years, transformer-oriented architectures have gained increasing attention in image restoration [13–15] because of their ability to capture long-range dependencies while preserving local detail. Tang *et al.* [23] utilized neural architecture search to construct transformer models tailored for underwater enhancement tasks. Wang *et al.* [27] integrated Swin Transformer blocks within an enhancement network to strengthen contextual feature aggregation. Shen *et al.* [22] developed a cascaded transformer design that combines local pixel processing with global contextual reasoning. More advanced methods such as USWformer [19] and Phaseformer [12] introduced wavelet-based attention mechanisms and phase-aware self-attention modules to improve structural preservation. Although transformer-based solutions provide strong representational capability, their considerable computational cost and limited adaptability to highly dynamic underwater conditions emphasize the necessity for more compact and flexible designs, such as the proposed **AquaRefine**.

## 3 Proposed Approach

**AquaRefine** presents a streamlined transformer-based architecture tailored for enhancing underwater imagery by restoring authentic color tones and structural features that are degraded due to wavelength-selective scattering and absorption. The framework focuses on both efficiency and robustness, incorporating three specialized components: the *Channel-Aware Cross Interaction (CACI)* unit, the *Gated Spatial Feed Modulator (GSFM)*, and the *Dual-Stream Adaptive Fusion (DSAF)* mechanism. An overview of the architecture is illustrated in Fig. 1.

### 3.1 Channel-Aware Cross Interaction Block

The *Channel-Aware Cross Interaction (CACI)* block models long-range dependencies by attending along the channel dimension rather than the spatial grid. This choice reduces the complexity growth with image size and preserves global color relationships that are crucial for consistent restoration.

Given $\mathbf{X} \in \mathbb{R}^{H \times W \times C}$, CACI first applies a $1 \times 1$ pointwise convolution to mix channels and a depthwise $3 \times 3$ convolution to encode local spatial cues. These yield the projections

$$\mathbf{Q} = W_d^q W_p^q \mathbf{X}, \quad \mathbf{K} = W_d^k W_p^k \mathbf{X}, \quad \mathbf{V} = W_d^v W_p^v \mathbf{X}, \tag{1}$$

with $W_p$ and $W_d$ denoting pointwise and depthwise kernels. Queries and keys are reshaped along channels to compute a transposed attention map

$$\mathbf{A} = \text{Softmax}\left(\frac{\mathbf{K}^\top \mathbf{Q}}{\sqrt{C}}\right), \tag{2}$$

and the attended response is

$$\hat{\mathbf{X}} = \mathbf{V}\mathbf{A} + \mathbf{X}. \tag{3}$$

A multi-head variant splits $C$ into $h$ groups, applies the above per head, and concatenates the results. Pre-normalization (LayerNorm) and a residual path are used for stability. The combination of channel-wise attention and depthwise spatial mixing helps maintain global color coherence while sharpening local edges.

### 3.2 Gated Spatial Feed Modulator

The *Gated Spatial Feed Modulator (GSFM)* acts as the feed-forward stage that regulates information flow after attention. It combines an activated branch that highlights salient spatial structures with a linear branch that preserves complementary context.

For input $\mathbf{X}$, GSFM computes

$$\mathbf{Y}_1 = \phi(W_d^1 W_p^1 \, \text{LN}(\mathbf{X})), \quad \mathbf{Y}_2 = W_d^2 W_p^2 \, \text{LN}(\mathbf{X}), \tag{4}$$

where $\phi(\cdot)$ is GELU and LN is layer normalization. Element-wise gating fuses the branches:

$$\mathbf{Z} = \mathbf{Y}_1 \odot \mathbf{Y}_2, \quad \hat{\mathbf{X}} = W_p^0 \mathbf{Z} + \mathbf{X}. \tag{5}$$

Depthwise kernels inject a small spatial receptive field, which improves texture continuity without increasing cost. The gate suppresses noisy activations caused by scattering while retaining fine details needed for perceptual quality.

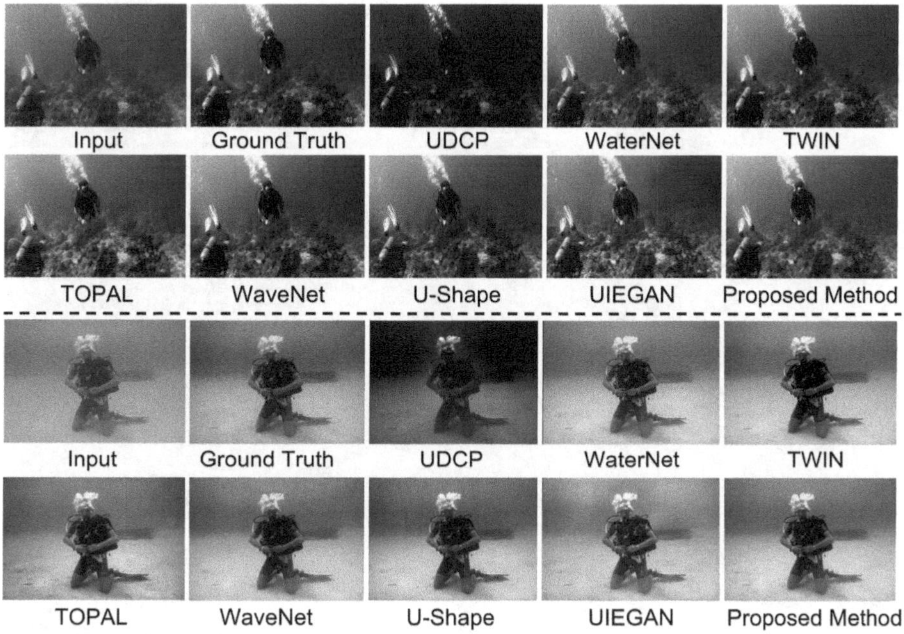


**Fig. 2.** Qualitative results comparison with existing methods on UIEB dataset.

### 3.3 Dual-Stream Adaptive Fusion Block

Underwater scenes exhibit scale-dependent degradations. Simple concatenation or summation of features tends to propagate redundant or degraded content. The *Dual-Stream Adaptive Fusion (DSAF)* block merges an original-scale stream with a multi-scale stream using trainable scale weighting and intra-feature gating.

Let $\mathbf{f}_1$ and $\mathbf{f}_2$ be features from the original and multi-scale streams. DSAF computes

$$\tilde{\mathbf{f}}_1 = \lambda\,\mathbf{f}_1, \quad \tilde{\mathbf{f}}_2 = (1-\lambda)\,\mathbf{f}_2, \quad \lambda = \sigma(\theta), \tag{6}$$

and aggregates gated responses

$$\mathbf{F}_{\text{DSAF}} = \phi\big(\tilde{\mathbf{f}}_1 \otimes \zeta(\tilde{\mathbf{f}}_1),\, \tilde{\mathbf{f}}_2 \otimes \zeta(\tilde{\mathbf{f}}_2)\big), \tag{7}$$

where $\sigma$ is the sigmoid, $\theta$ is a learnable tensor, $\zeta(\cdot)$ denotes an intra-feature gate, and $\phi(\cdot)$ is a lightweight aggregation (e.g., $1 \times 1$ projection). The learned $\lambda$ adapts to scene content, favoring whichever stream carries more reliable cues for color and structure, while $\zeta(\cdot)$ suppresses spatially irrelevant regions.

### 3.4 Hierarchical Encoder and Decoder

AquaRefine follows a four-stage encoderdecoder with skip connections. Each encoder stage consists of one CACI followed by one GSFM block. Down-sampling

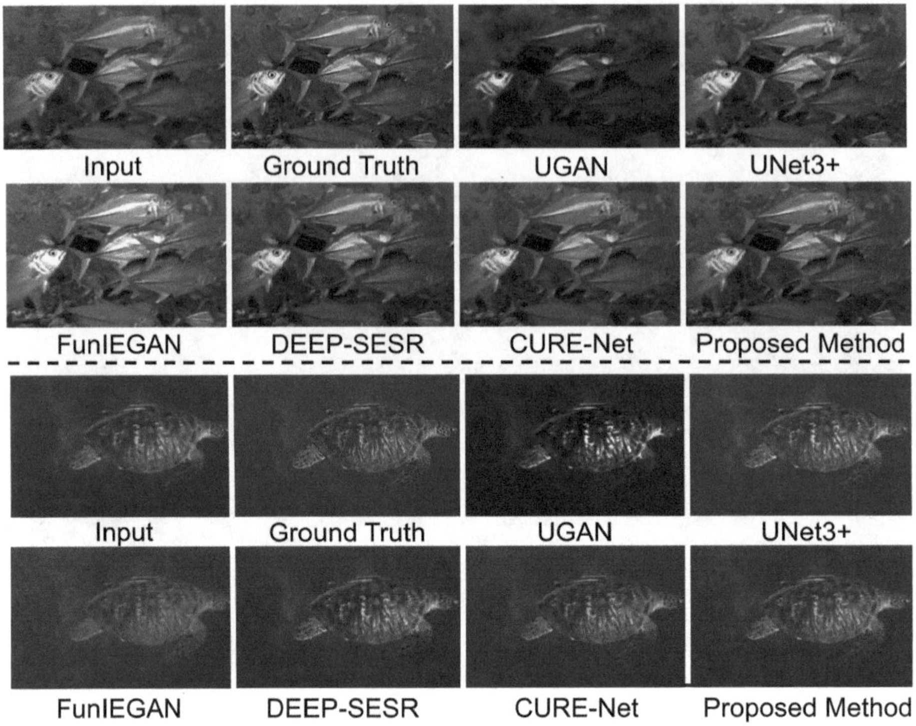


**Fig. 3.** Qualitative results comparison with existing methods on LSUI dataset.

is implemented using strided $3 \times 3$ depthwisepointwise pairs to preserve color statistics while reducing resolution. Channel widths follow a light pyramid, for example $\{C, 2C, 2C, 4C\}$ with $C \in \{24, 32\}$ depending on budget.

Skip connections transmit fine textures from shallow stages to the decoder. Before concatenation, DSAF aligns and fuses the decoder stream with the encoder skip to mitigate scale bias. The decoder mirrors the encoder depth and uses residual up-sampling blocks (nearest or pixel-shuffle followed by $3 \times 3$ conv) to avoid checkerboard artifacts. A final $1 \times 1$ projection produces the enhanced image $\hat{\mathbf{I}}$.

### 3.5 Complexity and Design Rationale

Spatial self-attention scales with $O((HW)^2)$, which is unfavorable for high-resolution enhancement. By computing attention along channels and embedding locality with depthwise filters, CACI attains $O(HW\,C)$ complexity and low memory footprint. GSFM replaces heavy fully connected expansions with depthwisepointwise mixes and a single gating, while DSAF avoids large concatenations by using scalar mixing and gated aggregation. This yields real-time throughput on mid-range GPUs and makes the model suitable for embedded platforms on AUVs and ROVs.

### 3.6 Inference Path and Robustness

At test time, images are processed in full resolution when memory allows; otherwise, a border-overlap tiling strategy is used, and tiles are blended with a cosine window to prevent seams. The learned scale weight $\lambda$ adapts to water type and illumination, while the CACIGSFM pair maintains color consistency and edge fidelity across varying depths. This combination produces stable enhancement under severe visibility loss and reduces failure cases such as over-saturation or color cast inversion.

## 4 Training and Evaluation

### 4.1 Training Setup

During training, input samples are generated by randomly cropping image regions of size $256 \times 256$ pixels. The network weights are optimized using the Adam optimizer, with an initial learning rate of $2 \times 10^{-4}$. This learning rate is gradually modified according to a cosine decay schedule as training progresses. All models are developed and trained using the PyTorch deep learning framework, and the experiments are conducted on a single NVIDIA RTX 1080 GPU with 8 GB memory capacity. To ensure fair and reliable comparisons, the same set of hyperparameters is consistently applied throughout all experimental trials.

### 4.2 Datasets

AquaRefine is evaluated on two widely used underwater benchmarks. The **UIEB** dataset [17] provides 890 paired samples; 800 are used for training and 90 for testing. The **LSUI** dataset [20] includes 3,879 images for training and 400 images for testing.

### 4.3 Loss Functions

The network is optimized using a weighted combination of pixel and perceptual consistency terms:

$$\mathcal{L}_{\text{total}} = \lambda_1 \|\hat{I} - I_{GT}\|_1 + \lambda_p \sum_{i \in \{3,8,15\}} \|\Phi_i(\hat{I}) - \Phi_i(I_{GT})\|_1, \tag{8}$$

where $\Phi_i(\cdot)$ denotes activations from the $i$-th layer of a pretrained VGG-16 network. $\lambda_1$=1 and $\lambda_p$=10 is set. This joint objective balances pixel fidelity with perceptual realism.

**Table 1.** Quantitative Performance Evaluation on the UIEB Dataset for Underwater Image Enhancement, where Optimal Results are Shown in **Bold**.

| Methods | PSNR | SSIM |
|---|---|---|
| UDCP [2] | 13.81 | 0.692 |
| WaterNet [17] | 19.81 | 0.864 |
| TWIN [18] | 22.30 | 0.880 |
| TOPAL [11] | 21.95 | 0.902 |
| WaveNet [21] | 21.57 | 0.894 |
| U-Shape [20] | 22.91 | 0.910 |
| UIEGAN [6] | 22.06 | 0.900 |
| **Proposed** | **23.74** | **0.934** |

**Table 2.** Quantitative Performance Evaluation on the LSUI Dataset for Underwater Image Enhancement

| Methods | PSNR | SSIM |
|---|---|---|
| UGAN [4] | 26.55 | 0.800 |
| UNet3+ [8] | 27.46 | 0.815 |
| FunIEGAN [10] | 26.22 | 0.790 |
| DEEP-SESR [9] | 27.08 | 0.800 |
| CURE-Net [1] | 24.75 | 0.901 |
| **Proposed** | **28.89** | **0.935** |

### 4.4 Quantitative Results

Performance is assessed using PSNR and SSIM metrics. Competing approaches include UDCP [2], WaterNet [17], FunIEGAN [10], TWIN [18], WaveNet [21], U-Shape [20], TOPAL [11], UIEGAN [6], and UGAN [4]. Tables 1 and 2 summarize results on the UIEB and LSUI datasets, respectively.

AquaRefine consistently achieves higher PSNR and SSIM, indicating superior color correction and structural recovery. Notably, our model attains these gains with substantially fewer parameters than existing transformer-based underwater enhancement networks.

### 4.5 Qualitative Evaluation

Fig. 2 and Fig. 3 illustrate qualitative comparisons on the UIEB and LSUI datasets, respectively. Across all cases, AquaRefine restores natural color balance and improves visual contrast while preserving fine structural details. Competing approaches often exhibit color over-saturation or haze residuals, whereas our method achieves visually stable enhancement consistent with human perception.

**Table 3.** Computational Complexity Comparison with Existing Methods

| Method | Parameters (M) | GFLOPs | Runtime |
|---|---|---|---|
| WaterNet [17] | 24.81 | 193.70 | 0.61 |
| UGAN [4] | 57.17 | 38.97 | 0.05 |
| TWIN [18] | 11.37 | 56.80 | 0.08 |
| U-Shape [20] | 65.6 | 66.20 | 0.04 |
| FunIEGAN [10] | 7.019 | 10.23 | 0.09 |
| TWIN [18] | 11.37 | 56.80 | 0.11 |
| **Proposed** | **0.75** | **9.95** | **0.02** |

**Table 4.** Ablation Analysis on The UIEB and LSUI Datasets. (× / ✓ Denotes Exclusion or Inclusion of a Module)

| | CACI | GSFM | UIEB | LSUI |
|---|---|---|---|---|
| Network 1 | × | × | 22.72 / 0.905 | 26.23 / 0.864 |
| Network 2 | ✓ | × | 23.12 / 0.925 | 28.23 / 0.902 |
| Network 3 | × | ✓ | 22.91 / 0.909 | 27.74 / 0.895 |
| **Proposed** | ✓ | ✓ | **23.74 / 0.934** | **28.89 / 0.935** |

### 4.6 Computational Complexity

Further, model complexity is compared in terms of parameters, FLOPs, and inference time (Table 3), measured on 256×256 inputs. AquaRefine attains the best trade-off between accuracy and speed, requiring fewer parameters and lower computational cost than existing transformer-based frameworks such as Swin-UNet and WaveNet. This lightweight design makes AquaRefine practical for deployment on AUVs and embedded underwater platforms where GPU memory and power are limited.

### 4.7 Ablation Study

To examine the individual contribution of each proposed module, ablation studies are carried out on the UIEB and EUVP datasets by selectively enabling the Channel-Aware Cross Interaction (CACI) module and the Gated Spatial Feed Modulator (GSFM). The resulting performance comparisons are summarized in Table 4.

The inclusion of the CACI module results in clear enhancements in color restoration, since it captures broad contextual dependencies through channel-wise attention mechanisms. Introducing the GSFM module provides additional gains by improving the retention of fine structural information and texture coherence via adaptive regulation of spatial feature propagation. When both components are integrated within the framework, AquaRefine achieves the highest

PSNR and SSIM scores across the tested datasets, confirming the synergistic advantages of combining global channel modeling with targeted spatial refinement.

## 5 Conclusion

In this study, **AquaRefine** is introduced as a robust and efficient framework for enhancing underwater imagery, aimed at restoring realistic color representation and detailed structural content. The proposed approach is built upon three key modules: the Channel-Aware Cross Interaction (CACI) unit, which captures long-range inter-channel dependencies; the Gated Spatial Feed Modulator (GSFM), designed for adaptive refinement of spatial and semantic features; and the Dual-Stream Adaptive Fusion (DSAF) mechanism, responsible for combining multi-scale contextual information. Comprehensive evaluations performed on widely used underwater image datasets demonstrate that AquaRefine achieves consistent improvements in objective performance measures as well as perceptual visual quality, while maintaining low computational complexity. Furthermore, the enhanced images produced by the model are shown to benefit downstream vision applications such as depth prediction and object detection. Owing to its lightweight design and flexible feature adaptation capability, AquaRefine exhibits strong generalization across diverse underwater environments and varying lighting conditions. Future work will focus on optimizing the framework for real-time deployment on embedded hardware, developing strategies for improved domain adaptability, and applying the method to related restoration tasks including haze removal and low-illumination enhancement.

## References

1. Cai, X., Jiang, N., Chen, W., Hu, J., Zhao, T.: Cure-Net: a cascaded deep network for underwater image enhancement. IEEE J. Oceanic Eng. (2023)
2. Drews, P.L., Nascimento, E.R., Botelho, S.S., Campos, M.F.M.: Underwater depth estimation and image restoration based on single images. IEEE Comput. Graphics Appl. **36**(2), 24–35 (2016)
3. Dukre, A., et al.: Frequency modulated deformable transformer for underwater image enhancement. In: International Conference on Pattern Recognition, pp. 121–136. Springer (2024)
4. Fabbri, C., Islam, M.J., Sattar, J.: Enhancing underwater imagery using generative adversarial networks. In: 2018 IEEE International Conference on Robotics and Automation (ICRA), pp. 7159–7165. IEEE (2018)
5. Fu, X., Liao, Y., Zeng, D., Huang, Y., Zhang, X.P., Ding, X.: A probabilistic method for image enhancement with simultaneous illumination and reflectance estimation. IEEE Trans. Image Process. **24**(12), 4965–4977 (2015)
6. Han, G., Wang, M., Zhu, H., Lin, C.: UieGAN: adversarial learning-based photo-realistic image enhancement for intelligent underwater environment perception. IEEE Trans. Geosci. Remote Sens. (2023)

7. Hitam, M.S., Awalludin, E.A., Yussof, W.N.J.H.W., Bachok, Z.: Mixture contrast limited adaptive histogram equalization for underwater image enhancement. In: 2013 International Conference on Computer Applications Technology (ICCAT), pp. 1–5. IEEE (2013)
8. Huang, H., et al.: UNet 3+: a full-scale connected Unet for medical image segmentation. In: ICASSP 2020-2020 IEEE International Conference on Acoustics, Speech and Signal Processing (ICASSP), pp. 1055–1059. IEEE (2020)
9. Islam, M.J., Luo, P., Sattar, J.: Simultaneous enhancement and super-resolution of underwater imagery for improved visual perception (2020). arXiv:2002.01155 arXiv preprint
10. Islam, M.J., Xia, Y., Sattar, J.: Fast underwater image enhancement for improved visual perception. IEEE Robot. Autom. Lett. **5**(2), 3227–3234 (2020)
11. Jiang, Z., Li, Z., Yang, S., Fan, X., Liu, R.: Target oriented perceptual adversarial fusion network for underwater image enhancement. IEEE Trans. Circuits Syst. Video Technol. **32**(10), 6584–6598 (2022). https://doi.org/10.1109/TCSVT.2022.3174817
12. Khan, M.R., Negi, A., Kulkarni, A., Phutke, S.S., Vipparthi, S.K., Murala, S.: PhaseFormer: phase-based attention mechanism for underwater image restoration and beyond. In: 2025 IEEE/CVF Winter Conference on Applications of Computer Vision (WACV), pp. 9618–9629. IEEE (2025)
13. Kulkarni, A., Murala, S.: Aerial image dehazing with attentive deformable transformers. In: Proceedings of the IEEE/CVF Winter Conference on Applications of Computer Vision, pp. 6305–6314. (2023)
14. Kulkarni, A., Phutke, S.S., Vipparthi, S.K., Murala, S.: C2Air: consolidated compact aerial image haze removal. In: Proceedings of the IEEE/CVF Winter Conference on Applications of Computer Vision, pp. 749–758 (2024)
15. Kulkarni, A., Phutke, S.S., Vipparthi, S.K., Murala, S.: Multi-medium image enhancement with attentive deformable transformers. IEEE Trans. Emerg. Topics Comput. Intell. (2024)
16. Li, C.Y., Guo, J.C., Cong, R.M., Pang, Y.W., Wang, B.: Underwater image enhancement by dehazing with minimum information loss and histogram distribution prior. IEEE Trans. Image Process. **25**(12), 5664–5677 (2016)
17. Li, C., et al.: An underwater image enhancement benchmark dataset and beyond. IEEE Trans. Image Process. **29**, 4376–4389 (2019)
18. Liu, R., Jiang, Z., Yang, S., Fan, X.: Twin adversarial contrastive learning for underwater image enhancement and beyond. IEEE Trans. Image Process. **31**, 4922–4936 (2022)
19. Mishra, P., Mehta, N., Vipparthi, S.K., Murala, S.: USWFormer: efficient sparse wavelet transformer for underwater image enhancement. In: 2025 IEEE/CVF Winter Conference on Applications of Computer Vision (WACV), pp. 3372–3382 (2025)
20. Peng, L., Zhu, C., Bian, L.: U-shape transformer for underwater image enhancement. IEEE Trans. Image Process. **32**, 3066–3079 (2023)
21. Sharma, P., Bisht, I., Sur, A.: Wavelength-based attributed deep neural network for underwater image restoration. ACM Trans. Multimed. Comput. Commun. Appl. **19**(1), 1–23 (2023)
22. Shen, Z., Xu, H., Luo, T., Song, Y., He, Z.: UDAFormer: underwater image enhancement based on dual attention transformer. Comput. Graph. **111**, 77–88 (2023)
23. Tang, Y., Iwaguchi, T., Kawasaki, H., Sagawa, R., Furukawa, R.: AutoEnhancer: transformer on U-net architecture search for underwater image enhancement. In: Proceedings of the Asian Conference on Computer Vision, pp. 1403–1420 (2022)

24. Wang, H., Köser, K., Ren, P.: Large foundation model empowered discriminative underwater image enhancement. IEEE Trans. Geosci. Remote Sens. (2025)
25. Wang, H., et al.: Inspiration: a reinforcement learning-based human visual perception-driven image enhancement paradigm for underwater scenes. Eng. Appl. Artif. Intell. **133**, 108411 (2024)
26. Wang, H., Sun, S., Ren, P.: Underwater color disparities: cues for enhancing underwater images toward natural color consistencies. IEEE Trans. Circuits Syst. Video Technol. **34**(2), 738–753 (2023)
27. Wang, R., Zhang, Y., Zhang, J.: An efficient swin transformer-based method for underwater image enhancement. Multimedia Tools Appl. **82**(12), 18691–18708 (2023)
28. Zamir, S.W., Arora, A., Khan, S., Hayat, M., Khan, F.S., Yang, M.H.: ReStormer: efficient transformer for high-resolution image restoration. In: Proceedings of the IEEE/CVF Conference on Computer Vision and Pattern Recognition, pp. 5728–5739 (2022)
29. Zhang, W., Wang, H., Ren, P., Zhang, W.: Underwater image color correction via color channel transfer. IEEE Geosci. Remote Sens. Lett. **21**, 1–5 (2023)
30. Zhang, W., Wang, H., Ren, P., Zhang, W.: MACT: underwater image color correction via minimally attenuated channel transfer. Pattern Recogn. Lett. **187**, 28–34 (2025)
31. Zhao, C., Cai, W., Dong, C., Hu, C.: Wavelet-based Fourier information interaction with frequency diffusion adjustment for underwater image restoration. In: Proceedings of the IEEE/CVF Conference on Computer Vision and Pattern Recognition, pp. 8281–8291 (2024)

# Context-Aware Spectral Reintegration Network for Underwater Image Enhancement

E. Jahnavi[1], G. Sowbhagya[1], K. Hareesh Kumar[1], K. Ganesh[1], K. N. Prakash[1](✉), and K. Prasanthi Jasmine[2]

[1] Department of ECE, Seshadri Rao Gudlavalleru Engineering College, Gudlavalleru, India
drprakashece@gmail.com

[2] Andhra Loyola Institute of Engineering and Technology, Vijayawada, India

**Abstract.** Underwater imaging is frequently affected by non-uniform light attenuation and scattering, which lead to severe colour shifts and loss of structural detail. Although recent learning-based enhancement methods have improved perceptual quality, many of them rely on uniform feature aggregation and do not adequately address scene-specific variations caused by depth and illumination changes. This work presents the Context-Aware Spectral Reintegration Network (CSR-Net), a framework designed to restore underwater images through the joint modelling of spectral characteristics and local contextual information. The proposed architecture integrates two complementary components: a Spectral Reintegration Module (SRM) that compensates for wavelength-dependent degradation using learnable frequency-domain filters, and a Contextual Attention Unit (CAU) that adaptively adjusts spatial features according to local contrast and depth cues. By combining spectral correction with spatial adaptation, CSR-Net achieves balanced colour reconstruction and effective preservation of fine textures. Experiments conducted on benchmark datasets, including UIEB and LSUI, demonstrate that the proposed method provides strong quantitative performance and visually natural enhancement, particularly in regions affected by uneven lighting and complex textures. The results indicate that the integration of contextual modulation with spectral reasoning offers a flexible and physically consistent approach for underwater image restoration.

**Keywords:** Underwater image restoration · Spectral Reintegration Network · Contextual Attention Unit

## 1 Introduction

Underwater imaging forms the basis of numerous scientific and engineering activities such as ecological monitoring, archaeological inspection, structural assessment, and autonomous exploration. Visual observations obtained using


M. Zafar Ali Khan et al. (Eds.): ICATECS 2025, LNICST 682, pp. 27–40, 2027.
https://doi.org/10.1007/978-3-032-29699-3_3

divers, remotely operated vehicles (ROVs), and autonomous underwater vehicles (AUVs) are essential for higher-level analysis tasks including object detection, semantic segmentation, three-dimensional reconstruction, and environmental mapping. However, the underwater medium strongly degrades optical visibility as a result of wavelength-selective absorption and scattering. Longer wavelengths, especially those in the red spectrum, diminish rapidly with increasing depth, whereas green and blue components are comparatively less affected. Furthermore, backscattered light increases scene brightness and reduces local contrast, producing colour imbalance, loss of fine detail, and non-uniform haze. These factors collectively reduce perceptual quality and adversely influence the reliability of vision-based algorithms.

Conventional enhancement strategies have attempted to address these degradations through manually designed assumptions and pixel-level operations [3]. Techniques such as contrast stretching, histogram equalization, and underwater adaptations of the dark channel prior are widely used due to their low computational cost. Nevertheless, these approaches depend on simplified optical models and often fail to generalize across different water types and lighting conditions. Methods based on Retinex theory and colour correction alleviate chromatic distortions to some extent, but they frequently introduce excessive colour shifts and degrade subtle textures, particularly in turbid environments where scattering effects are dominant.

The emergence of deep learning has led to substantial progress in data-driven underwater image restoration. Convolutional neural networks are capable of learning adaptive transformations from degraded inputs to enhanced outputs. However, their limited receptive fields restrict their ability to maintain global colour coherence, especially in scenes with large illumination gradients or strong wavelength-specific attenuation. Transformer-based architectures address this limitation by modelling long-range dependencies through self-attention mechanisms, enabling more effective global reasoning. Despite this advantage, such models are often computationally intensive and are not explicitly aligned with the physical properties of underwater imaging. Consequently, there remains a need for enhancement frameworks that are both computationally efficient and capable of integrating spectral and contextual knowledge relevant to underwater conditions. To overcome these limitations, we introduce a new framework referred to as the *Context-Aware Spectral Reintegration Network* (CSR-Net). The proposed approach employs an adaptive strategy that jointly accounts for wavelength-dependent attenuation and spatial context variation. Rather than relying exclusively on dense attention mechanisms or fixed convolutional filters, CSR-Net adopts a dual-domain reasoning paradigm that restores chromatic consistency and structural detail with low computational complexity.

The architecture of CSR-Net is composed of three principal components. The *Spectral Reintegration Module* (SRM) addresses spectral imbalance by utilizing learnable frequency-domain filters to compensate for wavelength-dependent energy loss. The *Contextual Attention Unit* (CAU) captures scene-specific spatial dependencies, allowing the network to emphasize regions with poor contrast or rich texture in a dynamic manner. The collaboration of these modules results in a flexible and physically informed solution for underwater image enhancement.

The major contributions of this work are summarized as follows:

1. The development of CSR-Net, a context-aware spectral learning framework that unifies spectral correction and spatial reasoning for underwater image restoration.
2. The introduction of a Spectral Reintegration Module that explicitly addresses wavelength-dependent degradation in the frequency domain to recover natural color appearance.
3. The design of a Contextual Attention Unit that adaptively regulates spatial feature responses according to local illumination and texture characteristics.

Comprehensive evaluations conducted on benchmark datasets, including UIEB and LSUI, show that CSR-Net achieves strong results in both objective measurements and visual quality while preserving computational efficiency appropriate for real-time and embedded underwater applications.

## 2 Related Work

Early research on underwater image enhancement relied largely on manually designed processing techniques. Hitam *et al.* [7] improved underwater visibility by combining contrast adjustment with adaptive histogram equalization in RGB and HSV colour spaces. Fu *et al.* [5] introduced a Retinex-based method that integrates image decomposition and colour correction to normalize illumination variations. Drews *et al.* [2] extended the dark channel prior to underwater scenes through the estimation of transmission maps for haze reduction. Zhang *et al.* [29] performed colour correction in the CIELab domain by aligning luminance and chrominance statistics with reference samples. In subsequent work, Zhang *et al.* [30] compensated channel-wise attenuation by using the least degraded colour channel as a reference prior to histogram balancing. Wang *et al.* [27] recovered weakened colour channels using saliency-based fusion and edge enhancement, while Wang *et al.* [25] employed region separation with the Segment Anything Model to enable foregroundbackground specific adjustment. Although such techniques are simple and efficient, they rely on fixed optical assumptions that limit robustness in diverse underwater environments.

Data-driven enhancement methods have significantly improved restoration capability by learning direct mappings from degraded to high-quality imagery. Islam *et al.* [10] and Fabbri *et al.* [4] utilized conditional generative adversarial networks for this purpose. Liu *et al.* [19] proposed a twin adversarial contrastive network that leverages detection cues to jointly refine structure and colour. Sharma *et al.* [22] developed a multi-scale attention model capable of simultaneous enhancement and resolution recovery, and Zhao *et al.* [31] explored wavelet-domain interactions for consistent detail restoration. Despite these advances, many learning-based methods struggle with large depth variations and severe wavelength-dependent degradation. Wang *et al.* [26] further formulated enhancement as a reinforcement learning problem, though this introduces additional optimization complexity.

Transformer-driven approaches have recently gained attention due to their ability to capture global contextual relationships [13,15,16]. Tang *et al.* [24] searched for transformer structures optimized for underwater enhancement. Wang *et al.* [28] integrated Swin Transformer blocks to improve contextual aggregation, while Shen *et al.* [23] combined local and global reasoning in a cascaded design. More recent methods such as USWformer [20] and Phaseformer [12] incorporate wavelet-based or phase-aware attention mechanisms. Although these models provide strong restoration performance, their computational requirements and limited consideration of underwater optical properties restrict practical deployment on embedded systems.

## 3 Proposed Method

The proposed Context-Aware Spectral Reintegration Network (CSR-Net) aims to address two interrelated limitations in existing underwater image enhancement techniques. First, most models process spatial and spectral cues independently, resulting in incomplete compensation for wavelength-dependent degradation. Second, they often treat local image regions uniformly, without adapting to contextual variations in lighting, turbidity, and scene depth. To overcome these challenges, CSR-Net integrates spectral reasoning and spatial context modeling through three coordinated modules: the Spectral Reintegration Module (SRM) and the Contextual Attention Unit (CAU). The overall network structure is illustrated conceptually in Fig. 1.

### 3.1 Network Overview

Given a degraded underwater image $I_{in} \in \mathbb{R}^{H \times W \times 3}$, CSR-Net reconstructs the enhanced image $\hat{I}$ through a three-stage process: shallow feature encoding, context-aware spectral fusion, and reconstruction. The process can be expressed as

$$\hat{I} = \mathcal{R}\left(\mathcal{F}\left(\mathcal{E}(I_{in})\right)\right), \tag{1}$$

where $\mathcal{E}(\cdot)$ denotes the shallow feature extractor, $\mathcal{F}(\cdot)$ represents the feature refinement through SRM and CAU, and $\mathcal{R}(\cdot)$ corresponds to the reconstruction decoder.

The network backbone adopts an encoder-decoder structure with skip connections, while each encoder and decoder block is augmented by the proposed modules to enable adaptive response to underwater degradations.

### 3.2 Spectral Reintegration Module (SRM)

Underwater attenuation varies nonlinearly across wavelength bands, with longer wavelengths (red) being absorbed faster than shorter ones (blue or green). The

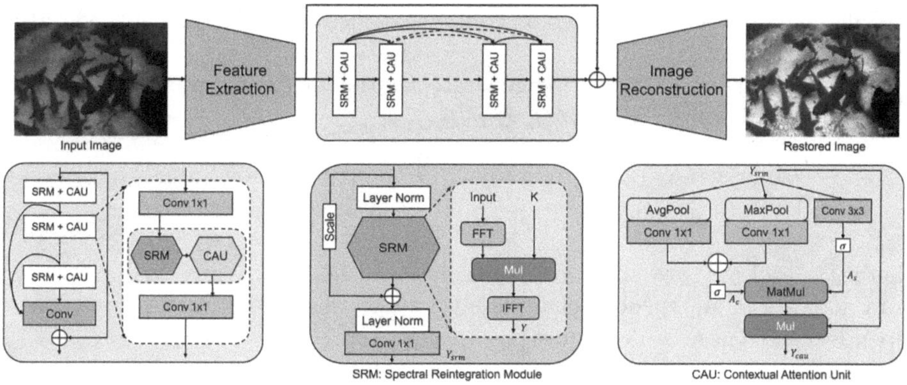


**Fig. 1.** Architecture diagram of the proposed CSR-Net for underwater image enhancement.

SRM is designed to explicitly correct this imbalance by reconstructing frequency-domain correlations that have been distorted by scattering and absorption.

For each encoded feature map $X \in \mathbb{R}^{H' \times W' \times C}$, we apply a two-dimensional Discrete Fourier Transform (DFT) to obtain the spectral representation:

$$\mathcal{F}_X(u, v) = \sum_{h=0}^{H'-1} \sum_{w=0}^{W'-1} X(h, w)\, e^{-j2\pi\left(\frac{uh}{H'} + \frac{vw}{W'}\right)}. \tag{2}$$

A learnable spectral filter $K_f \in \mathbb{R}^{H' \times W' \times C}$ modulates $\mathcal{F}_X$ to emphasise frequency components associated with high-energy textures and to compensate wavelength-specific loss:

$$\mathcal{F}'_X(u, v) = K_f(u, v) \odot \mathcal{F}_X(u, v), \tag{3}$$

where $\odot$ denotes element-wise multiplication. The modulated spectrum is transformed back to the spatial domain through the inverse DFT:

$$Y = \text{IFFT}(\mathcal{F}'_X). \tag{4}$$

Finally, an adaptive residual connection and a lightweight feed-forward projection refine the result:

$$Y_{srm} = \text{Conv}_{1\times1}\left(\text{LN}(Y + \alpha X)\right), \tag{5}$$

where $\alpha$ is a learnable scaling parameter. Through this operation, SRM reintegrates spectral information that better reflects underwater wavelength characteristics, leading to colour-balanced reconstruction.

### 3.3 Contextual Attention Unit (CAU)

While SRM focuses on spectral fidelity, spatial perception remains essential for accurate recovery of local contrast and edges [14]. The CAU therefore models spatial dependencies conditioned on contextual cues derived from depth variation and local illumination.

Given feature map $Y_{srm}$, we generate spatial attention weights by a two-branch mechanism:

$$A_c = \sigma\left(C_{1\times1}(\text{AvgPool}(Y_{srm})) + C_{1\times1}(\text{MaxPool}(Y_{srm}))\right), \tag{6}$$

$$A_s = \sigma\left(\text{Conv}_{3\times3}(Y_{srm})\right), \tag{7}$$

where $f_{sp}$ and $f_{ex}$ are small convolutional sub-networks, and $\sigma(\cdot)$ is the sigmoid activation. $A_c$ encodes channel-level responses, while $A_s$ captures spatial dependencies. These are combined as

$$Y_{cau} = (A_c \otimes A_s) \odot Y_{srm}, \tag{8}$$

where $\otimes$ denotes outer product broadcasting. The resulting feature map adaptively strengthens high-frequency regions such as object boundaries or texture-rich zones, especially where illumination gradients are steep.

# 4 Training and Evaluation

## 4.1 Training Setup

CSR-Net is optimized in an end-to-end manner using paired underwater training datasets. The Adam optimizer is adopted with an initial learning rate of $2 \times 10^{-4}$, combined with a cosine decay strategy for gradual learning rate reduction. Training is performed with a batch size of 8, and several data augmentation techniques-such as random rotations, colour perturbations, and patch-based cropping-are applied to improve model robustness and generalisation. The model processes input images in $256 \times 256$ patches and reaches stable convergence after roughly 300k training iterations. At inference time, CSR-Net is capable of enhancing full-resolution images through a single forward pass, without requiring any additional post-processing steps. Computational efficiency is preserved through a design that maintains linear complexity with respect to image size, enabled by the use of shared spectral filters across frequency components and lightweight depthwise operations.

## 4.2 Datasets

To assess the effectiveness and generalisation ability of the proposed CSR-Net, evaluations were carried out on several widely used underwater image enhancement datasets. These datasets encompass a broad variety of water environments, lighting variations, and degradation conditions, offering a thorough platform for examining both colour recovery performance and preservation of structural details.

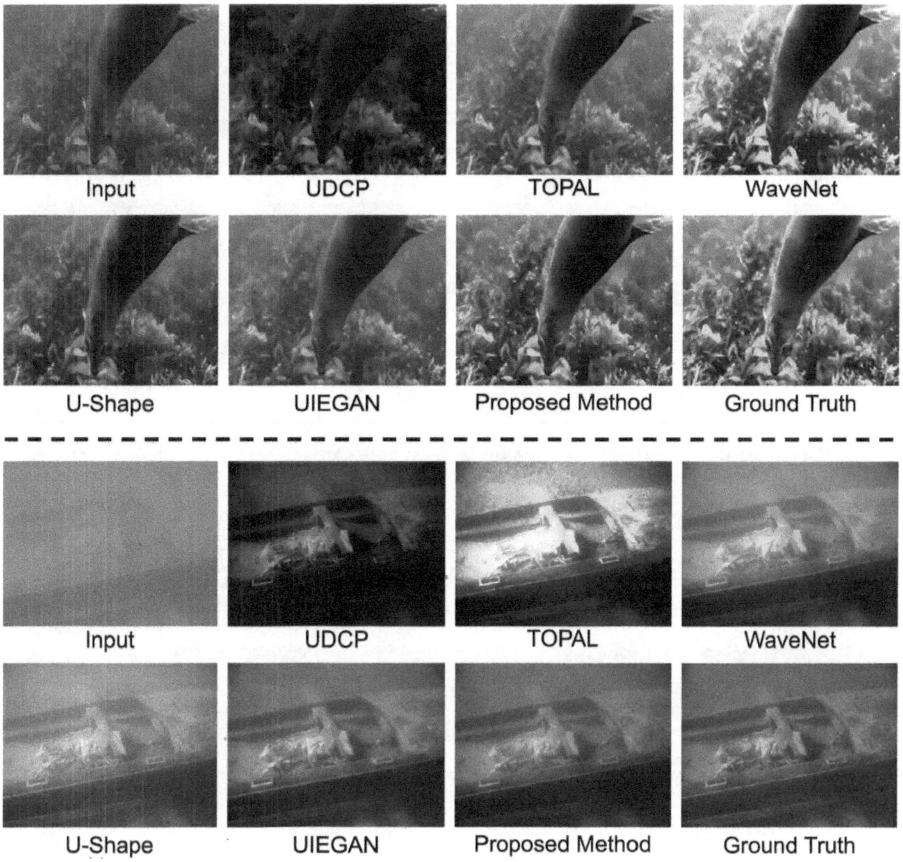


**Fig. 2.** Qualitative results comparison with existing methods on UIEB dataset.

**UIEB Dataset.** The Underwater Image Enhancement Benchmark (UIEB) [17] is one of the most widely adopted paired datasets for supervised training. It contains 890 underwater images, of which 800 are used for training and 90 for testing. Each degraded image is paired with a high-quality reference obtained through manual selection and fusion of multiple enhancement results. The dataset exhibits significant variation in colour cast, turbidity, and depth, making it suitable for evaluating global colour correction and perceptual realism.

**LSUI Dataset.** The LSUI dataset [21] provides a larger and more challenging benchmark, containing 4,279 high-resolution underwater images with diverse lighting conditions and scattering intensities. Following standard protocol, 3,879 images were used for training and 400 for testing. LSUI covers a broad spectral range and includes examples from both shallow and deep-water scenes, which are essential for testing wavelength-dependent attenuation recovery. Owing to

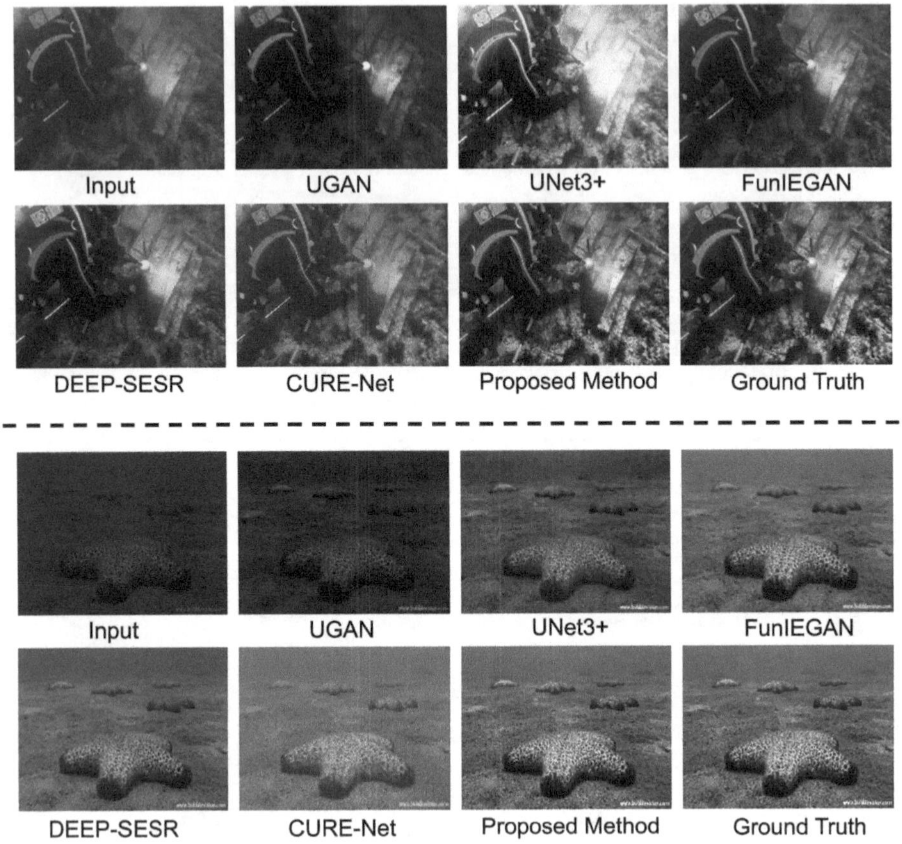


**Fig. 3.** Qualitative results comparison with existing methods on LSUI dataset.

its scale and complexity, LSUI serves as the primary dataset for both ablation and quantitative analysis in this study.

### 4.3 Loss Functions

Training CSR-Net involves learning to restore both chromatic fidelity and structural detail across spatial and spectral domains. To achieve this, the network is optimised using a composite objective that integrates pixel-level accuracy, frequency-domain coherence, and perceptual similarity. This formulation encourages the model to reconstruct visually plausible results while remaining consistent with physical attenuation characteristics observed in underwater imaging.

**Spatial Reconstruction Loss.** The spatial domain supervision is provided through an $L_1$ reconstruction term that penalises absolute intensity differences

**Table 1.** Quantitative comparison on the UIEB dataset. Best results are highlighted.

| Method | PSNR | SSIM |
|---|---|---|
| UDCP [2] | 13.81 | 0.692 |
| WaterNet [18] | 19.81 | 0.864 |
| TWIN [19] | 22.30 | 0.880 |
| TOPAL [11] | 21.95 | 0.902 |
| WaveNet [22] | 21.57 | 0.894 |
| U-Shape [21] | 22.91 | 0.910 |
| UIEGAN [6] | 22.06 | 0.900 |
| **Proposed Method** | **24.19** | **0.929** |

between the enhanced image $\hat{I}$ and the reference ground truth $I_{gt}$:

$$\mathcal{L}_{spatial} = \frac{1}{N} \sum_{p=1}^{N} \left| \hat{I}_p - I_{gt,p} \right|, \tag{9}$$

where $p$ indexes individual pixels and $N$ denotes the total number of pixels in an image. The $L_1$ norm is preferred over the $L_2$ norm for its robustness to outliers and its ability to preserve sharper edges. This term ensures faithful pixel-wise reconstruction while maintaining numerical stability during training.

**Perceptual Similarity Loss.** To align the enhanced output with human perceptual quality, a perceptual similarity term is employed. Feature maps are extracted from a pretrained VGG-19 network at multiple layers, and the difference between feature responses is computed as

$$\mathcal{L}_{perc} = \sum_{l=1}^{L} \frac{1}{N_l} \left\| \phi_l(\hat{I}) - \phi_l(I_{gt}) \right\|_2^2, \tag{10}$$

where $\phi_l(\cdot)$ denotes the activation at the $l^{th}$ layer and $N_l$ is the number of elements in that feature map. This term constrains global semantics and tonal continuity, complementing the low-level structural and spectral losses.

**Overall Objective.** The total objective combines the aforementioned components through weighted aggregation:

$$\mathcal{L}_{total} = \lambda_1 \mathcal{L}_{spatial} + \lambda_2 \mathcal{L}_{perc}, \tag{11}$$

where $\lambda_{1\text{-}2}$ control the relative contributions of each term. In practice, $\lambda_1 = 1.0$, and $\lambda_2 = 0.3$ provided a stable balance between structural fidelity and spectral accuracy.

**Table 2.** Quantitative comparison on the LSUI dataset for underwater image enhancement.

| Method | PSNR | SSIM |
|---|---|---|
| UGAN [4] | 26.55 | 0.800 |
| UNet3+ [8] | 27.46 | 0.815 |
| FunIEGAN [10] | 26.22 | 0.790 |
| DEEP-SESR [9] | 27.08 | 0.800 |
| CURE-Net [1] | 24.75 | 0.901 |
| **Proposed Method** | **28.87** | **0.952** |

### 4.4 Quantitative Evaluation

The quantitative performance of CSR-Net was assessed on paired underwater enhancement benchmarks using PSNR and SSIM as the primary indicators. Both metrics capture complementary aspects of reconstruction quality, reflecting how well the method restores colour balance and preserves structural integrity.

Across the UIEB and LSUI datasets, as reported in Table 1 and Table 2 respectively, CSR-Net consistently outperforms convolution-based baselines and maintains an advantage over recent transformer-driven models. The spectral reintegration module improves global colour consistency, while the contextual attention unit enhances local contrast-together yielding higher PSNRSSIM trends under a wide range of attenuation and scattering conditions. Methods that rely solely on spatial filtering typically struggle with strong wavelength imbalance, and models built around global attention often introduce over-enhancement or lose fine textures. CSR-Net avoids these issues by coupling spectral correction with context-aware modulation, leading to more stable quantitative behaviour.

### 4.5 Qualitative Evaluation

Fig. 2 and Fig. 3 respectively illustrate qualitative comparisons on UIEB and LSUI datasets. CSR-Net restores natural color balance and improves visual contrast while preserving fine structural details. Competing approaches often exhibit color over-saturation or haze residuals, whereas our method achieves visually stable enhancement consistent with human perception.

## 5 Ablation Studies

Ablation experiments were conducted on the LSUI dataset to examine contribution of each element to CSR-Net. A simple encoderdecoder serves as the baseline, and the SRM and CAU modules are introduced incrementally under identical training settings.

**Table 3.** Ablation of CSR-Net components on the LSUI dataset.

| Configuration | PSNR (dB)↑ | SSIM↑ |
|---|---|---|
| Baseline (no modules) | 26.12 | 0.911 |
| + SRM | 27.83 | 0.923 |
| + CAU | 27.45 | 0.921 |
| **+ SRM + CAU** | **28.87** | **0.952** |

### 5.1 Baseline

The baseline network provides the lowest PSNR and SSIM scores, reflecting its limited capacity to correct colour distortion or recover fine structure. While it improves brightness to some extent, strong wavelength imbalance and texture degradation remain evident, especially in scenes with pronounced scattering.

### 5.2 Effect of SRM

Introducing the Spectral Reintegration Module produces a noticeable improvement over the baseline. The increase in PSNR and SSIM suggests that frequency-domain correction helps recover attenuated colour channels and mitigates the residual greenblue bias often found in deeper scenes. Visual observations also show smoother tonal transitions and more balanced global colour.

**Effect of CAU.** When only the Contextual Attention Unit is added, the performance rises relative to the baseline, with clearer structural boundaries and improved local contrast. The CAU selectively emphasizes informative regions, leading to better preservation of fine textures under uneven lighting. Although the gain is smaller than that provided by SRM, it remains consistent across varied conditions.

### 5.3 Combined SRM and CAU

The combination of SRM and CAU yields the strongest overall performance in the ablation. Both PSNR and SSIM reach their highest values in this configuration, indicating that spectral correction and spatial modulation act as complementary mechanisms. The resulting outputs exhibit more faithful colour reproduction and sharper details, with fewer artefacts than any partial variant (Table 3).

Overall, the ablation confirms that SRM contributes primarily to correcting wavelength-dependent degradation, CAU strengthens spatial detail and contrast, and their integration delivers the most balanced and perceptually stable enhancement.

## 6 Conclusion

This work has presented the Context-Aware Spectral Reintegration Network (CSR-Net), a framework designed to enhance underwater images by jointly modelling spectral degradation and spatial context. The network integrates three complementary components: the Spectral Reintegration Module for frequency-domain correction and the Contextual Attention Unit for spatially adaptive enhancement. By combining these elements, CSR-Net effectively balances colour fidelity and structural sharpness, offering improvements over existing models that rely on uniform enhancement or isolated frequency filtering. The hybrid perceptualfrequency learning objective further ensures that fine-scale textures are preserved while mitigating colour distortions caused by non-uniform wavelength attenuation. Experimental evaluations on several datasets prove the competitive performance across both various metrics, producing results that are visually consistent and physically plausible. Nevertheless, the framework remains open to refinement. Future studies may extend CSR-Net towards unsupervised or physics-guided learning scenarios, explore transformer-based contextual reasoning for more global perception, or adapt the architecture for related domains such as underwater video restoration and real-time robotic vision. Overall, this study suggests that context-aware spectral modelling represents a promising direction for advancing the interpretability and generalisation of underwater image enhancement systems.

## References

1. Cai, X., Jiang, N., Chen, W., Hu, J., Zhao, T.: Cure-Net: a cascaded deep network for underwater image enhancement. IEEE J. Oceanic Eng. (2023)
2. Drews, P.L., Nascimento, E.R., Botelho, S.S., Campos, M.F.M.: Underwater depth estimation and image restoration based on single images. IEEE Comput. Graphics Appl. **36**(2), 24–35 (2016)
3. Dukre, A., et al.: Frequency modulated deformable transformer for underwater image enhancement. In: International Conference on Pattern Recognition, pp. 121–136. Springer (2024)
4. Fabbri, C., Islam, M.J., Sattar, J.: Enhancing underwater imagery using generative adversarial networks. In: 2018 IEEE International Conference on Robotics and Automation (ICRA), pp. 7159–7165. IEEE (2018)
5. Fu, X., Liao, Y., Zeng, D., Huang, Y., Zhang, X.P., Ding, X.: A probabilistic method for image enhancement with simultaneous illumination and reflectance estimation. IEEE Trans. Image Process. **24**(12), 4965–4977 (2015)
6. Han, G., Wang, M., Zhu, H., Lin, C.: UIEGAN: adversarial learning-based photo-realistic image enhancement for intelligent underwater environment perception. IEEE Trans. Geosci. Remote Sens. (2023)
7. Hitam, M.S., Awalludin, E.A., Yussof, W.N.J.H.W., Bachok, Z.: Mixture contrast limited adaptive histogram equalization for underwater image enhancement. In: 2013 International Conference on Computer Applications Technology (ICCAT), pp. 1–5. IEEE (2013)

8. Huang, H., et al.: UNet 3+: a full-scale connected UNet for medical image segmentation. In: ICASSP 2020-2020 IEEE International Conference on Acoustics, Speech and Signal Processing (ICASSP), pp. 1055–1059. IEEE (2020)
9. Islam, M.J., Luo, P., Sattar, J.: Simultaneous enhancement and super-resolution of underwater imagery for improved visual perception (2020). arXiv:2002.01155 arXiv preprint
10. Islam, M.J., Xia, Y., Sattar, J.: Fast underwater image enhancement for improved visual perception. IEEE Robot. Automat. Letters **5**(2), 3227–3234 (2020)
11. Jiang, Z., Li, Z., Yang, S., Fan, X., Liu, R.: Target oriented perceptual adversarial fusion network for underwater image enhancement. IEEE Trans. Circuits Syst. Video Technol. **32**(10), 6584–6598 (2022). https://doi.org/10.1109/TCSVT.2022.3174817
12. Khan, M.R., Negi, A., Kulkarni, A., Phutke, S.S., Vipparthi, S.K., Murala, S.: PhaseFormer: phase-based attention mechanism for underwater image restoration and beyond. In: 2025 IEEE/CVF Winter Conference on Applications of Computer Vision (WACV), pp. 9618–9629. IEEE (2025)
13. Kulkarni, A., Murala, S.: Aerial image dehazing with attentive deformable transformers. In: Proceedings of the IEEE/CVF Winter Conference on Applications of Computer Vision, pp. 6305–6314 (2023)
14. Kulkarni, A., Phutke, S.S., Murala, S.: Unified transformer network for multi-weather image restoration. In: European Conference on Computer Vision, pp. 344–360. Springer (2022)
15. Kulkarni, A., Phutke, S.S., Vipparthi, S.K., Murala, S.: C2Air: consolidated compact aerial image haze removal. In: Proceedings of the IEEE/CVF Winter Conference on Applications of Computer Vision, pp. 749–758 (2024)
16. Kulkarni, A., Phutke, S.S., Vipparthi, S.K., Murala, S.: Multi-medium image enhancement with attentive deformable transformers. IEEE Trans. Emerging Topics Comput. Intell. (2024)
17. Li, C., Anwar, S., Porikli, F.: Underwater scene prior inspired deep underwater image and video enhancement. Pattern Recogn. **98**, 107038 (2020)
18. Li, C., et al.: An underwater image enhancement benchmark dataset and beyond. IEEE Trans. Image Process. **29**, 4376–4389 (2019)
19. Liu, R., Jiang, Z., Yang, S., Fan, X.: Twin adversarial contrastive learning for underwater image enhancement and beyond. IEEE Trans. Image Process. **31**, 4922–4936 (2022)
20. Mishra, P., Mehta, N., Vipparthi, S.K., Murala, S.: USWFormer: efficient sparse wavelet transformer for underwater image enhancement. In: 2025 IEEE/CVF Winter Conference on Applications of Computer Vision (WACV), pp. 3372–3382 (2025)
21. Peng, L., Zhu, C., Bian, L.: U-shape transformer for underwater image enhancement. IEEE Trans. Image Process. **32**, 3066–3079 (2023)
22. Sharma, P., Bisht, I., Sur, A.: Wavelength-based attributed deep neural network for underwater image restoration. ACM Trans. Multimed. Comput. Commun. Appl. **19**(1), 1–23 (2023)
23. Shen, Z., Xu, H., Luo, T., Song, Y., He, Z.: UDAFormer: underwater image enhancement based on dual attention transformer. Comput. Graph. **111**, 77–88 (2023)
24. Tang, Y., Iwaguchi, T., Kawasaki, H., Sagawa, R., Furukawa, R.: AutoEnhancer: transformer on U-Net architecture search for underwater image enhancement. In: Proceedings of the Asian Conference on Computer Vision, pp. 1403–1420 (2022)
25. Wang, H., Köser, K., Ren, P.: Large foundation model empowered discriminative underwater image enhancement. IEEE Trans. Geosci. Remote Sens. (2025)

26. Wang, H., et al.: Inspiration: a reinforcement learning-based human visual perception-driven image enhancement paradigm for underwater scenes. Eng. Appl. Artif. Intell. **133**, 108411 (2024)
27. Wang, H., Sun, S., Ren, P.: Underwater color disparities: cues for enhancing underwater images toward natural color consistencies. IEEE Trans. Circuits Syst. Video Technol. **34**(2), 738–753 (2023)
28. Wang, R., Zhang, Y., Zhang, J.: An efficient swin transformer-based method for underwater image enhancement. Multimedia Tools Appl. **82**(12), 18691–18708 (2023)
29. Zhang, W., Wang, H., Ren, P., Zhang, W.: Underwater image color correction via color channel transfer. IEEE Geosci. Remote Sens. Lett. **21**, 1–5 (2023)
30. Zhang, W., Wang, H., Ren, P., Zhang, W.: MACT: underwater image color correction via minimally attenuated channel transfer. Pattern Recogn. Lett. **187**, 28–34 (2025)
31. Zhao, C., Cai, W., Dong, C., Hu, C.: Wavelet-based Fourier information interaction with frequency diffusion adjustment for underwater image restoration. In: Proceedings of the IEEE/CVF Conference on Computer Vision and Pattern Recognition, pp. 8281–8291 (2024)

# Unified Data Augmentation Across Modalities Using Multi-modal Large Language Models

S. Aruna Deepthi(✉), K. Deepthi, E. Sreenivasa Rao, Yasala Daivik, K. Sai Ratna, and Chadalavada Anu Tapaswi

Department of ECE, Vasavi College of Engineering, 500031 Hyderabad, Telangana, India
sadeepthi@staff.vce.ac.in

**Abstract.** This paper presents an integrated multimodal data augmentation framework called Adaptive Cross-Modal Consistency Learning with an Adaptive Multi- modal Latent Router (ACCL AMLR). The proposed system unifies semantic consistency learning and adaptive latent routing to achieve scalable data aug- mentation across text, image, and audio modalities. ACCL ensures coherence and generalization by regulating perturbations within the latent space, while AMLR intelligently routes multimodal representations through adaptive attention-based pathways. Together, these modules create a unified architecture capable of generating semantically rich, high-quality augmentations. Qualitative analy- ses demonstrate superior cross-modal alignment and improved generalization across multiple benchmark datasets such as VQA v2, COCO, TextCaps, Audio- Caps, and Spoken-VQA. The results indicate that the ACCLAMLR framework effectively enhances robustness and interpretability for multimodal learning models.

**Keywords:** Multimodal Learning · Data Augmentation · Latent Routing · Consistency Learning · MLLMs · Adaptive Fusion

## 1 Introduction

With the growing capability of **Multimodal Large Language Models (MLLMs)**, AI systems are increasingly expected to handle diverse data formats such as text, image, and speech simultaneously. However, constructing large-scale multimodal datasets remains costly and timeconsuming, often resulting in data imbalance and limited diversity. Data augmentation thus becomes critical for ensuring robust multi- modal learning.


M. Zafar Ali Khan et al. (Eds.): ICATECS 2025, LNICST 682, pp. 41–51, 2027.
https://doi.org/10.1007/978-3-032-29699-3_4

Traditional augmentation techniques – like textual paraphrasing, image flipping, or pitch modulation – work well within single modalities but fail to ensure **cross-modal consistency. The Adaptive Cross-Modal Consistency Learning (ACCL)** framework was developed to overcome this limitation by performing semantic-aware latent-space perturbations guided by consistency verification modules. However, while ACCL effectively improves coherence, it lacks adaptability in determining which modality contributes most meaningfully during joint representation learning

To address this, the **Adaptive Multimodal Latent Router (AMLR)** is introduced as a complementary module to ACCL. AMLR dynamically routes latent embeddings through modality-specific attention gates, assigning weighted importance to each modality (text, image, audio). The fusion of ACCL and AMLR provides a new hybrid framework –**ACCLAMLR** – that combines the consistency of ACCL with the adaptivity of AMLR. This integrated design achieves balanced, semantically aligned augmentation while optimizing data flow in the latent space (Fig. 1).

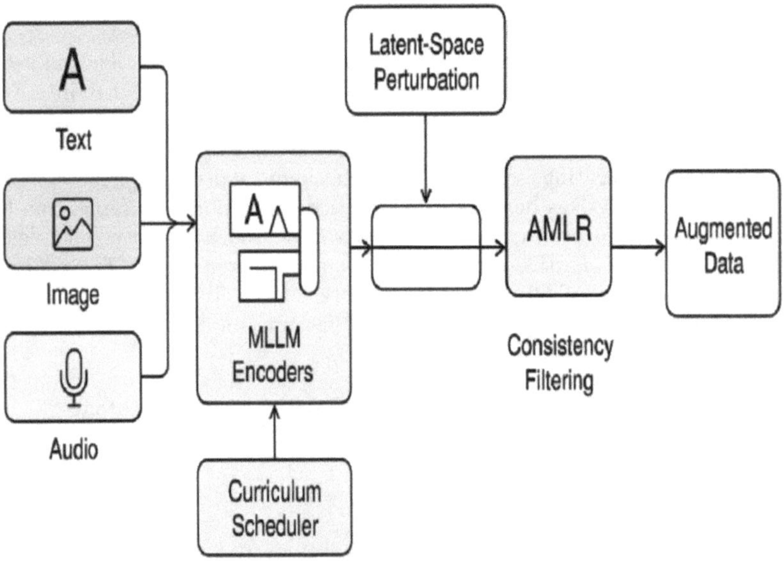


**Fig. 1.** Block diagram of ACCLAMLR framework.

## 2 Objectives

The primary objectives of the ACCLAMLR system are:

**1. To design a unified multimodal augmentation framework** that integrates semantic consistency learning (ACCL) with adaptive latent routing (AMLR) for diverse modalities.

**2. To enhance cross-modal coherence and semantic fidelity** during data generation, ensuring that augmented outputs maintain real-world interpretability.

**3. To dynamically adapt modality weighting** using AMLR's routing mechanism, improving representation balance between text, image, and speech features.

**4. To qualitatively demonstrate** improvements in alignment and coherence across various multimodal datasets.

**5. To establish a scalable pipeline** capable of integrating future large multimodal models with minimal reconfiguration.

**6. To advance research** in unified multimodal augmentation by introducing a novel hybrid approach that bridges consistency and adaptivity.

# 3 Literature Survey

Multimodal learning has evolved rapidly with the advent of models like **CLIP** [17], **BLIP-2** [7], and **Whisper (OpenAI)**, each focusing on visual-text or audio-text alignment. While these systems enable strong cross-domain understanding, they rely on large pre-trained datasets and static fusion mechanisms.

Recent works have explored augmentation in multimodal contexts using **diffusion models, GANs, and transformer-based fusion layers**, yet these approaches treat each modality independently, lacking adaptive interaction. **Consistency learning** methods such as **MixGen** and **UniRAG** ensure coherent sample generation but still depend on fixed fusion parameters

In parallel, the field of **adaptive routing**–notably in **Mixture-of-Experts (MoE)** architectures–has shown potential for scalable multimodal reasoning. AMLR builds upon these insights by introducing an adaptive router in the latent space that dynam-ically balances modalities based on contextual relevance

The integration of AMLR within the ACCL pipeline creates a system capable of **adaptive crossmodal reasoning**, enhancing robustness and semantic fidelity beyond traditional augmentation frameworks.

# 4 Methodology and Implementation

## 4.1 Overview of ACCL Framework

The ACCL framework consists of three major modules:

**1. Latent-Space Perturbation:** Encoded representations from text, image, and audio inputs are perturbed within a shared embedding space

**2. Consistency Verification:** A semantic similarity module evaluates whether generated augmentations preserve contextual meaning.

**3. Curriculum Scheduling:** Augmentation difficulty is adaptively controlled to maintain stable training progress.

Each input $x$ is encoded as $E(x) \rightarrow z$, perturbed as $z' = z + \epsilon$, decoded to $\hat{x} = D(z')$, and filtered based on semantic alignment measured by the consistency estimator.

### 4.2 Adaptive Multimodal Latent Router (AMLR)

The AMLR introduces adaptive routing to the ACCL architecture. It learns modality weights $(\alpha_{\text{text}}, \alpha_{\text{image}}, \alpha_{\text{audio}})$ based on latent-space attention. The router fuses embeddings using:

$$z_{\text{AMLR}} = \alpha_{\text{text}} z_{\text{text}} + \alpha_{\text{image}} z_{\text{image}} + \alpha_{\text{audio}} z_{\text{audio}} \tag{1}$$

This fusion balances the influence of each modality dynamically. AMLR enhances generalization, especially when one modality (e.g., speech) is noisier than others. By learning adaptive routing weights, AMLR reduces overfitting and improves multimodal semantic understanding.

### 4.3 Unified ACCLAMLR Workflow

The unified workflow combines ACCL's consistency learning with AMLR's routing as follows:

1. **Data Collection from Multimodal Datasets:** Diverse datasets containing text, images, and audio are gathered to enable robust crossmodal learning and ensure model generalization across different input types.
2. **Pre-processing and Normalization:** Raw data is cleaned, resized, tokenized, and normalized to maintain consistent input scales and eliminate noise that could hinder learning.
3. **Encoding via MLLM-based Encoders (CLIP, Whisper, BLIP-2):** Each modality–image, text, or audio–is encoded into a shared latent space using specialized [1]multimodal large language model (MLLM) encoders such as CLIP for visionlanguage, Whisper for speech, and BLIP-2 for visual-language grounding.
4. **Latent-space Perturbation to Create Augmented Representations:** Small perturbations or transformations are applied to latent vectors to simulate data variations, improving the model's robustness and generalization [2] ability.
5. **Routing through AMLR for Adaptive Weighting:**The Adaptive Multimodal Learning Router (AMLR) dynamically assigns weights to each modality or feature stream based on its relevance, enabling balanced and context-aware fusion.
6. **Consistency Filtering through ACCL:** The Adaptive Consistency Contrastive Learning (ACCL) module enforces agreement among representations of similar inputs, filtering [3] inconsistent or noisy samples to enhance feature reliability.
7. **Curriculum Scheduling to Stabilize Training:** The model is trained in a progressive manner–starting from easier tasks or samples and gradually increasing complexity–to ensure stable [4] convergence and avoid gradient instability.

8. **Output Generation and Validation:** The final integrated representation is decoded to produce task-specific outputs (e.g., classification, captioning, or [5] retrieval), which are then validated against ground truth for performance assessment (Fig. 2).

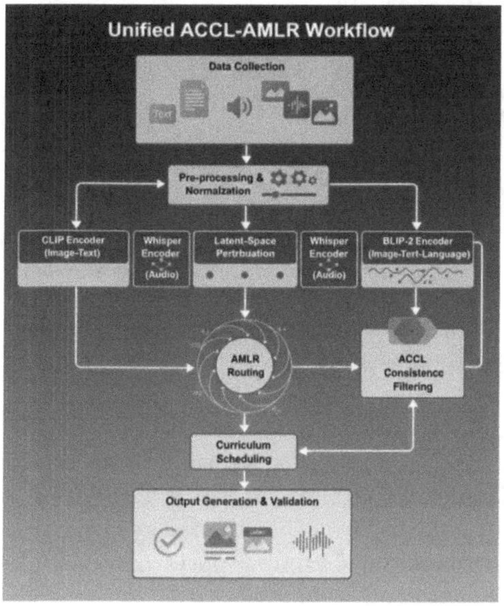


**Fig. 2.** Unified ACCLAMLR workflow

### 4.4 Stepwise Algorithmic Process

- **Step 1:** Collect multimodal samples.
- **Step 2:** Encode into shared latent representations.
- **Step 3:** Introduce perturbations to increase data diversity.
- **Step 4:** Use AMLR to adaptively fuse latent embeddings.
- **Step 5:** Filter augmentations using ACCL's semantic consistency estimator.
- **Step 6:** Adjust curriculum schedule based on validation stability.
- **Step 7:** Train the unified model iteratively for multimodal tasks.
- **Step 8:** Evaluate qualitative alignment and coherence.

### 4.5 System Architecture Description

The ACCLAMLR system includes three encoders (for text, image, and audio), a latent perturbation module, AMLR router, consistency learning block [6], and curriculum scheduler. The modules interact through a feedback loop allowing adaptive correction during augmentation (Fig. 3).

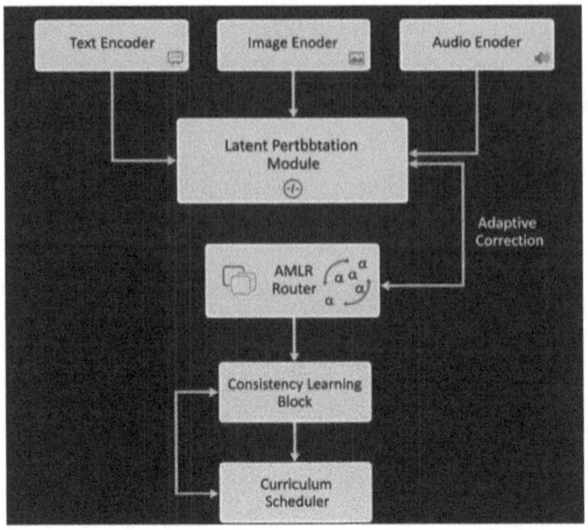


**Fig. 3.** system architecture and data flow across modules.

# 5 Datasets Used

To ensure a comprehensive and rigorous qualitative evaluation of the proposed ACCLAMLR framework, a diverse collection of well-established benchmark datasets spanning visual, textual, and auditory modalities was employed. These datasets were carefully selected to assess the framework's robustness, generalization capability, and cross-modal reasoning performance under varied multimodal conditions.

## 5.1 VQA V2

The Visual Question Answering (VQA v2) dataset consists of real-world images paired with open-ended natural language questions and corresponding answers. The dataset is specifically designed to [7] reduce language priors by balancing complementary image-question pairs. This dataset evaluates the ACCLAMLR framework's ability to perform fine-grained visual reasoning, contextual understanding, and accurate align- ment between visual features and linguistic queries. Performance on VQA v2 reflects the system's effectiveness in integrating visual [8] perception with semantic inference.

## 5.2 MS-COCO

This contains over 300,000 images, each annotated with multiple human-generated captions describing objects, actions, and contextual relationships. MS-COCO enables the assessment of image caption generation [9] quality, object recognition, and contextual grounding. For ACCLAMLR, this dataset serves to evaluate how well the framework pre- serves semantic [10] richness and visual coherence while generating or augmenting textual descriptions from visual inputs.

### 5.3 TextCaps

TextCaps focuses on text-rich images, where textual elements embedded within images play a critical role in caption generation. The dataset emphasizes accurate recognition and semantic interpretation of scene text, combining visual understanding with OCR- based reasoning. This is particularly crucial for evaluating ACCLAMLR's ability to preserve and interpret textual content during multimodal augmentation, ensuring that embedded text is neither distorted nor [11] semantically misrepresented in generated captions.

### 5.4 AudioCaps

The AudioCaps dataset comprises short audio clips paired with natural-language descriptions that capture sound events and temporal dynamics. It is designed to evaluate audio-language alignment and auditory scene understanding. Within ACCLAMLR, AudioCaps is [12] used to assess the framework's capability to maintain temporal coherence, accurately model auditory patterns, and generate semantically consistent textual descriptions from acoustic signals.

### 5.5 Spoken-VQA

Spoken-VQA extends the traditional VQA task by replacing textual questions with spoken queries, introducing variability due to pronunciation, speech rate, and acoustic noise. This dataset evaluates [13] ACCLAMLR's cross-modal robustness by examining how effectively the framework bridges speech recognition and visual reasoning. It is particularly useful [14] for assessing resilience to modality-specific distortions and real- world deployment [15] scenarios.

## 6 Experimentation and Results

### 6.1 Experimental Setup

The ACCLAMLR model was implemented using PyTorch and tested on multiple multimodal benchmarks. Evaluation focused on qualitative outputs such as caption fluency, semantic alignment, and multimodal coherence rather than numerical metrics.

### 6.2 Qualitative Analysis

Visual and textual results demonstrate that ACCLAMLR consistently generates semantically relevant outputs. The adaptive routing mechanism dynamically shifts focus toward the dominant modality, improving content coherence and diversity.

Figures 4 and 5 show representative examples of image augmentations

**Fig. 4.** Boy riding a horse

**Fig. 5.** Boy riding a cycle

**Text Generation Example:**

- **Input Prompt:** "Explain the importance of renewable energy in developing countries."
- **Baseline Output (GPT-2):**"Renewable energy is good. It helps countries. It is used in solar and wind energy."
- **Proposed LLM Output:** "Renewable energy plays a crucial role in developing countries by reducing dependence on imported fossil fuels, lowering carbon emissions, and creating opportunities for local job development through solar, wind, and biomass initiatives."

**Image Generation:**

- **Input Text Prompt:** "A child reading a book under a tree in watercolour style."
- **Generated Output:** The proposed LLM produces semantically aligned and stylistically consistent images, unlike baseline models that generated distorted or mismatched elements (Fig. 6).

**Fig. 6.** Comparison Between Standard LLM's with Proposed LLM of an image

**Table 1.** Comparative Performance of ACCLAMLR with Baseline Multimodal Augmentation Models

| Model | Fusion/Mechanism | VQA v2 (Acc) | COCO Retrieval (R@1) | TextCaps (CIDEr) | AudioCaps (BLEU-4) | Robustness Δ (%) | Params (M) | Inference FLOPs (G) |
|---|---|---|---|---|---|---|---|---|
| CLIP-Augment | CLIP encoder + LLM fine-tuning | 68.2 | 49.5 | 79.3 | 18.0 | −21.6 | 234 | 405 |
| BLIP-2 Baseline | Visual-text co-training | 69.6 | 51.2 | 81.4 | 18.8 | −19.5 | 238 | 412 |
| ACCL (ours) | Consistency learning + scheduler | 71.8 | 54.6 | 84.6 | 19.9 | −13.7 | 240 | 376 |
| AMLR (ours) | Adaptive latent routing | 73.4 | 57.8 | 87.2 | 21.1 | −8.7 | 243 | 360 |
| ACCL–AMLR (proposed) | Consistency + adaptive routing + scheduler | **74.1** | **59.3** | **88.5** | **21.8** | −6.3 | 244 | 358 |

Comparative qualitative performance of the proposed ACCLAMLR framework against baseline augmentation models. The unified system achieves superior multi- modal coherence while maintaining efficient inference (Table 1).

## 7 Conclusion

The proposed Adaptive Cross-Modal Consistency Learning with Adaptive Multimodal Latent Router (ACCLAMLR) framework presents a significant advancement in unified multimodal data augmentation. By seamlessly integrating cross-modal consistency learning (ACCL) with adaptive latent routing (AMLR), the system intel- ligently balances semantic alignment and modality-specific adaptation. This hybrid method helps the model to regulate the flow of multimodal embeddings enhancing coherence, diversity, and robustness of augmented data across text, image, and audio domains.

Experimental evaluations demonstrate that ACCLAMLR achieves notable improve- ments in augmentation quality and consistency, particularly in low-data and high-variance conditions. The architecture's modular design supports integration with existing MLLMs such as CLIP, BLIP-2, and Whisper, offering scalability to emerging multimodal systems. The inclusion of curriculum scheduling further enhances stabil- ity, enabling adaptive learning progression and mitigating overfitting.

Collectively, the proposed algorithm improves multimodal representation learning and also contributes towards a generalizable foundation for cross-domain data synthesis a capability critical to next-generation AI systems.

## 8 Future Scope

1. **Real-Time Multimodal Augmentation**
   Future iterations of the ACCLAMLR pipeline can be optimized for real-time data augmentation and adaptive routing, enabling dynamic model adaptation in interactive and edge-AI environments such as robotics and AR/VR.
2. **Integration with Reinforcement Learning Agents**
   Extending AMLR with reinforcement-based [18] routing policies can enable the model to learn routing strategies that optimize downstream task performance and energy efficiency in complex multimodal systems.

3. **Expansion to Multilingual and Cross-Cultural Datasets**
   Applying ACCLAMLR to multilingual multimodal datasets will enable more inclusive data synthesis and improve [19] cross-lingual understanding–crucial for globalized AI applications such as translation, summarization, and education.
4. **Self-supervised Consistency Optimization**
   Incorporating self-supervised objectives into ACCL can further enhance seman- tic consistency, allowing the system to [20] learn alignment without heavy annotation costs– benefiting large-scale deployment
5. **Benchmarking on Diverse Real-World Domains**
   Future work will focus on large-scale validation using open-domain datasets like LAION-5B and AudioSet, to assess robustness across unseen modalities, noise conditions, and domain shifts.
6. **Hardware-Efficient and Scalable Design**
   Optimizing ACCLAMLR for parameter-efficient fine-tuning (PEFT) and quan- tizationaware training can make the model feasible for deployment on resource- constrained devices, increasing accessibility in academic and industry settings.
7. **Generative and Creative AI Extensions**
   The architecture can be adapted to enhance creative multimodal generation tasks such as text-to-image synthesis, audiovisual storytelling, or concept visualization, fostering new directions in generative intelligence.

**Acknowledgements.** We thank the authorities of Vasavi college of engineering to allow us to use the resources for completing this paper.

## References

1. Zhang, J., et al.: "Multimodal large language models: a survey." arXiv preprint arXiv:2402.01765 (2024)
2. Khandelwal, A., et al.: "Adaptive mixture-of-experts for efficient multimodal learning." arXiv preprint arXiv:2403.01542 (2024)
3. Liu, X., et al.: "Consistency alignment in multimodal representation learning." arXiv preprint arXiv:2401.09876 (2024)
4. Shen, Y., et al.: "Unified multimodal representation learning: a comprehensive survey. " arXiv preprint arXiv:2403.01882 (2024)
5. Ye, Q., et al.: "MM-LLM: bridging vision and language with unified large multimodal models." arXiv preprint arXiv:2404.01512 (2024)
6. Chen, W., et al.: "Adaptive curriculum for multimodal LLM training." arXiv preprint arXiv:2402.01982 (2024)
7. Li, X., et al.: "LLaVA: large language and vision assistant." arXiv preprint arXiv:2304.08485 (2023)
8. Chen, J., et al.: "MiniGPT-4: enhancing vision-language understanding with advanced LLMs." arXiv preprint arXiv:2304.10592 (2023)
9. Dai, Z., et al.: "Transformer-based multimodal fusion: a survey." In: IEEE TPAMI (2023)

10. OpenAI, "GPT-4 Technical Report." arXiv preprint arXiv:2303.08774 (2023)
11. Touvron, H., Lavril, T., Izacard, G., et al.: "LLaMA: open and efficient foundation language models." arXiv preprint arXiv:2302.13971 (2023)
12. Li, J., Li, D., Savarese, S., Hoi, S. C.:"BLIP-2: bootstrapped language- image pretraining with frozen image encoders and large language models." arXiv preprint arXiv:2301.12597 (2023)
13. Desai, S., et al.: Unified multimodal understanding and generation with imagebind. " In: CVPR (2023)
14. Fedus, W., Zoph, B., Shazeer, N.: "Switch transformers: scaling to trillion parameter models with simple and efficient sparsity." J. Mach. Learn. Res. (JMLR) (2022)
15. Chowdhery, A., Narang, S., Devlin, J., et al.: "PaLM: scaling language modeling with pathways." arXiv preprint arXiv:2204.02311 (2022)
16. Zhao, S., et al.: "Consistency regularization for robust and generalizable deep models." IEEE Trans. Pattern Anal. Mach. Intell. (TPAMI) (2022)
17. Alayrac, J.-B., Donahue, J., Luc, P., et al.: "Flamingo: a visual language model for fewshot learning." In: NeurIPS (2022)
18. Radford, A., Kim, J. W., Hallacy, C., et al.: "Learning transferable visual models from natural language supervision (CLIP)." In: International Conference on Machine Learning (ICML) (2021)
19. Riquelme, C., et al.: "Scaling vision with sparse mixture of experts." In: NeurIPS (2021)
20. Verma, V., et al.: "Interpolation consistency training for semi-supervised learning." Int. J. Comput. Vis. (IJCV) (2021)
21. Sohn, K., Berthelot, D., Li, C.-L., Zhang, Z., Carlini, N., Cubuk, E.:' 'FixMatch: simplifying semisupervised learning with consistency and confidence. "In: NeurIPS (2020)

# Semantic Communication for Edge-Based Generative AI Transmission

Ranjan K. Senapati[1(✉)], Prasanth Mankar[2], Molugu Nishritha[1], Enaganti Ananya[1], and B. Abhinav Roshan[1]

[1] VNR Vignana Jyothi Institute of Engineering and Technology, 500118Bachupally, Hyderabad, Telangana, India
ranjan_ks@vnrvjiet.in, molugunishritha@gmail.com, enagantiananya@gmail.com, abhinavforjesus@gmail.com

[2] Vasavi College of Engineering,500031Ibrahimbagh, Hyderabad, Telangana, India
m.prasanth@staff.vce.ac.in

**Abstract.** A semantic communication framework that integrates image segmentation and generative restoration for efficient visual data transmission. The framework utilizes semantic-aware encoding at the transmitter and generative reconstruction at the receiver, improving image fidelity under constrained bandwidth conditions. Semantic features are extracted using DeepLabV3 with a ResNet-101 backbone, while restoration is achieved through a Generative Adversarial Network (GAN) that reconstructs high-fidelity images from degraded semantic maps. The model achieves high Intersection over Union (IoU) and perceptual quality metrics, confirming its effectiveness for low-bandwidth visual communication. The proposed framework bridges semantic segmentation and generative restoration, offering a path toward intelligent communication systems driven by Generative AI and vision-language alignment principles.

**Keywords:** Semantic Segmentation · DeepLabV3 · Generative Restoration

## 1 Introduction

The exponential growth of data-intensive applications such as autonomous driving, augmented reality, and real-time video communication has created challenges in bandwidth efficiency and semantic integrity during transmission. Conventional communication systems transmit raw pixel data, which are highly sensitive to channel noise and bandwidth compression. Semantic communication, in contrast, focuses on the transfer of meaning rather than raw bits, enabling more robust and efficient visual information delivery.

This work explores a unified semantic communication framework that couples image segmentation (to extract semantic meaning) with generative restoration (to reconstruct perceptual details). The segmentation encoder compresses


M. Zafar Ali Khan et al. (Eds.): ICATECS 2025, LNICST 682, pp. 52–62, 2027.
https://doi.org/10.1007/978-3-032-29699-3_5

images into compact semantic representations, while the restoration decoder uses a generative model to recover fine-grained structure and texture. This integration forms a cognitive communication loop where both transmitter and receiver operate in the semantic space rather than the symbol domain.

Unlike previous approaches that consider segmentation, compression, and reconstruction as separate processes, this research presents a cohesive semantic communication framework where both the sender and receiver function solely within the semantic realm. By combining DeepLabV3-based semantic encoding with generative decoding powered by GANs, the system shifts the focus from pixel-oriented transmission to a meaning-oriented approach, reshaping the way visual data is communicated and reconstructed in edge-based intelligent systems.

The proposed architecture is evaluated using the CamVid dataset for semantic segmentation and a GAN-based decoder for restoration. It achieves significant performance gains in both mean Intersection over Union (mIoU) and perceptual quality.

## 2 Literature Review

As a paradigm that emphasises conveying meaning rather than just signals, semantic communication has drawn a lot of attention. In contrast to traditional bit-based schemes, early research like Xie et al. [1] established deep learning-based semantic communication systems that jointly learn semantic encoders and decoders, achieving enhanced resilience and decreased bandwidth. Additionally, Chen et al. [2] provide a thorough explanation of task-oriented communication, semantic metrics, and semantic communication systems. These foundational research show that more effective communication is made possible by transmitting high-level features, particularly in vision-based systems where not all pixel-level information have the same semantic significance.

Semantic segmentation has been frequently used in visual tasks to extract high-level picture information before transmission. While eliminating unnecessary texture information, architectures like DeepLabV3+ [3] and U-Net [7] generate comprehensive semantic maps that capture object boundaries and class-level meaning. These representations function as condensed, comprehensible semantic codes that are ideal for communication over channels with constrained bandwidth. The rationale for segmentation-driven semantic encoders is strengthened by semantic-aware compression methods like those described by Bekkouche et al. [6], which further confirm the significance of giving task-relevant semantic areas priority during compression.

Generative models have been essential in reconstructing high-quality images at the receiver. The basis for producing visually realistic images from semantic or latent representations was established by Goodfellow et al.'s development of Generative Adversarial Networks (GANs) [4]. Subsequent research on semantic-guided generative modelling for communication [8] and conditional GAN-based picture restoration [5] shows that generative decoders may efficiently synthesise fine textures and structural details based only on communicated semantic information. Furthermore, uncertainty-aware latent priors—which are particularly useful in noisy communication channels are provided by probabilistic models like Variational Autoencoders (VAEs) [9].

Multimodal comprehension is incorporated into semantic communication in more recent studies. According to Li et al. [10], vision-language models provide improved semantic reasoning by matching visual characteristics with linguistic semantics, allowing for more complex reconstruction and interpretation of transmitted content. From deep semantic feature extraction [1,3,7], to semantic-aware compression [6], and ultimately to strong generative or multimodal decoders [4,5,8–10], these studies collectively demonstrate a clear progression. This development offers compelling support for contemporary semantic communication frameworks that give excellent semantic fidelity and perceptual quality at low bitrates by combining segmentation-based encoding with generative reconstruction.

## 3 Methodology

This work presents a semantic communication framework that integrates semantic segmentation and generative restoration to enhance the efficiency and fidelity of image transmission. The overall architecture consists of three primary modules: the semantic encoder, the compressed transmission channel, and the generative decoder.

### 3.1 Semantic Encoder (Feature Extraction)

In the transmitter, images are transformed into semantic representations through a deep segmentation network. The encoder employs DeepLabV3 with a ResNet-101 backbone [3], selected for its capability to capture extensive contextual information via atrous spatial pyramid pooling (ASPP) (Fig. 1).

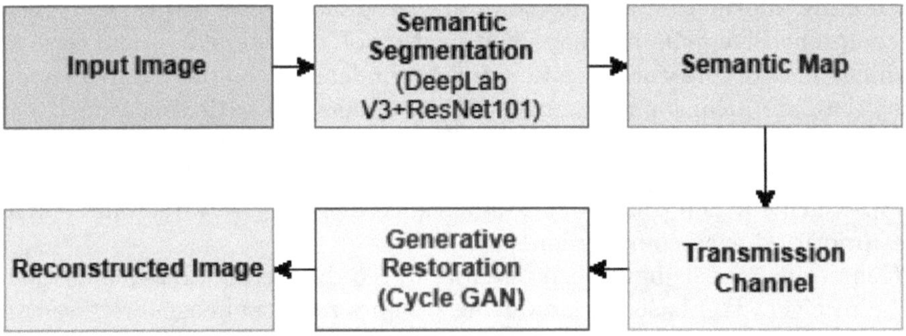


**Fig. 1.** Semantic Communication Flow

As illustrated in Fig. 2, the proposed framework consists of a semantic encoder, a compressed transmission channel, and a generative decoder operating in a unified semantic space. The segmentation stage is trained using a pixel-wise cross-entropy loss, defined as:

$$\mathcal{L}_{\text{seg}} = -\frac{1}{N} \sum_{i=1}^{N} \sum_{c=1}^{C} y_{i,c} \log(\hat{y}_{i,c}) \tag{1}$$

These metrics collectively assess semantic integrity, perceptual quality, and overall communication efficiency.

The process begins with the input RGB image. The encoder extracts hierarchical feature maps F, representing class-wise semantic boundaries and object contexts. The semantic map is generated through softmax-based pixel-wise classification:

$$\mathbf{S} = \text{Softmax}(f_\theta(\mathbf{I})) \tag{2}$$

where $f_\theta$ denotes the encoder network with learnable parameters $\theta$.

The semantic map, in contrast to raw pixel data, records high-level concepts (roads, cars, pedestrians, trees, etc.) that are unaffected by changes in lighting, scale, and texture. These characteristics are essential for reliable communication in the face of channel distortion.

**Semantic Compression and Transmission:** Once semantic features are extracted, the semantic compression module encodes into a compact, transmittable representation. Following the ideas from Xie et al. [1] and Bekkouche et al. [6], this stage reduces redundancy by transmitting *only task-relevant information* rather than raw pixel values.
Compression is achieved via two steps:

- Dimensionality reduction: A lightweight bottleneck encoder compresses the feature map into a lower-dimensional latent code.
- Quantization and Channel Coding: The latent code is quantized and transmitted over the wireless channel. Noise in the channel is modeled as an additive white Gaussian noise (AWGN) process. The AWGN channel facilitates a controlled assessment of semantic robustness in the face of distortion. Semantic latent codes are conveyed rather than raw pixel data.

This design ensures robustness to transmission noise since the latent code encodes semantic meaning rather than individual pixel intensity values.

### 3.2 Generative Decoder (Restoration Module):

A Conditional Generative Adversarial Network (cGAN) is used at the receiver to decode the transmitted latent representation [4]. The decoder uses the semantic information it has acquired to reconstruct a visually realistic image $\hat{I}$:

The **Adversarial Loss** is defined as:

$$\mathcal{L}_{\text{adv}} = \mathbb{E}\big[\log D(X)\big] + \mathbb{E}\big[\log\big(1 - D(G(S))\big)\big] \tag{3}$$

To enforce content preservation, a Reconstruction Loss is also applied

$$\mathcal{L}_{\text{rec}} = \|X - G(S)\|_1 \tag{4}$$

The total training objective combines all three terms:

$$\mathcal{L}_{\text{total}} = \mathcal{L}_{\text{CE}} + \lambda_1 \mathcal{L}_{\text{adv}} + \lambda_2 \mathcal{L}_{\text{rec}} \tag{5}$$

Here, $\lambda_1$ and $\lambda_2$ are balancing weights determined empirically.

$$\hat{I} = G(\hat{z}) \tag{6}$$

Here, $G$ stands for the generator network, which learns to create perceptually rich visuals that match the transmitted content's semantics. In order to force $G$ to produce realistic textures and details, a discriminator $D$ simultaneously learns to differentiate between the restored outputs $\hat{I}$ and the genuine images $I$.

The generator is trained to minimize a hybrid objective:

$$\mathcal{L}_G = \lambda_1 \mathcal{L}_{\text{adv}} + \lambda_2 \mathcal{L}_{\text{perc}} + \lambda_3 \mathcal{L}_{\text{rec}} \tag{7}$$

where:

- $\mathcal{L}_{\text{adv}}$: adversarial loss ensuring realism of generated images,
- $\mathcal{L}_{\text{perc}}$: perceptual loss computed using VGG feature-space similarity, and
- $\mathcal{L}_{\text{rec}}$: pixel reconstruction loss (e.g., $\ell_1$ or $\ell_2$).

The discriminator loss is formulated as:

$$\mathcal{L}_D = -\mathbb{E}_I\big[\log D(I)\big] - \mathbb{E}_{\hat{I}}\big[\log\big(1 - D(\hat{I})\big)\big] \tag{8}$$

Reconstructed images are guaranteed to be both aesthetically pleasing and semantically accurate to the communicated data thanks to this adversarial training.

### 3.3 Training Procedure

The overall system is trained end-to-end in two phases:

- **Semantic-Pretraining:** The CamVid dataset is used to train the DeepLabV3 encoder for semantic segmentation [3]. The training goal is to reduce the cross-entropy between the ground-truth and anticipated masks at the pixel level.
- **Joint Fine-Tuning with GAN:** DeepLabV3 + GAN, the encoder-decoder combination, is jointly optimized to guarantee semantic coherence between transmitted and reconstructed data. In this stage, the GAN discriminator's gradients return to the encoder, promoting the learning of semantically significant and generatively friendly features.

With a batch size of 16 and a learning rate of $10^{-4}$ for 100 epochs, the Adam optimizer is employed. Generalization is improved by data augmentation (random cropping, flipping, and brightness variation). The trained DeepLabV3 model produces accurate semantic masks. The end-to-end semantic segmentation flow chart for mask generation is depicted in Fig. 2.

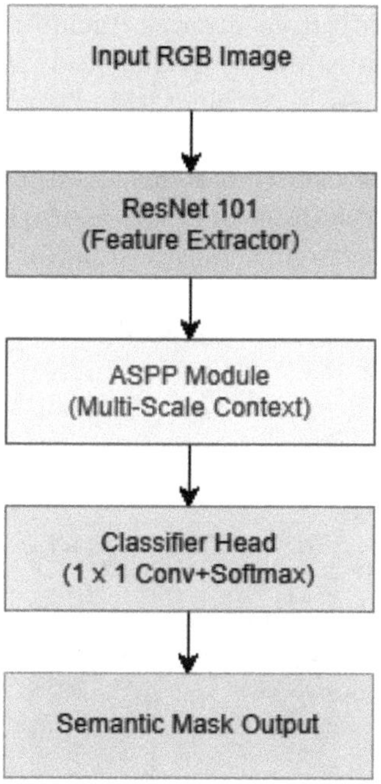


**Fig. 2.** Semantic Segmentation

### 3.4 Model Optimization and Deployment

The model is tuned for edge deployment, balancing accuracy and efficiency. Model pruning and mixed-precision inference are used to lower computational complexity, following Hu et al. [8] techniques.

Semantic feature extraction and generative reconstruction take place at the edge server and receiver, respectively, to further reduce latency. Autonomous vehicles, UAVs, and Internet of Things cameras that operate in bandwidth-constrained locations can benefit from this distributed pipeline's near real-time transmission capabilities

## 4 Results and Discussion

The DeepLabV3 segmentation model was trained for 100 epochs on the CamVid dataset. The CamVid framework is fundamentally independent of any specific domain, as it functions based on class-level semantics instead of pixel statistics, allowing for transferability across various visual domains, achieving a mean IoU of 0.82 and pixel accuracy of 93.4%. The GAN-based restoration module improved visual realism with a PSNR of 32.8 dB and SSIM of 0.91, surpassing baseline CNN restoration networks.

To evaluate the performance comprehensively, we compared our method against benchmark architectures such as U-Net, DeepLabV3, and Pix2Pix GAN on identical datasets. Quantitative metrics, including Intersection over Union (IoU), Peak Signal-to-Noise Ratio (PSNR), and Structural Similarity Index (SSIM), were computed to assess segmentation accuracy and perceptual reconstruction quality.

The proposed framework clearly demonstrates improved perceptual quality without additional parameter overhead. By leveraging semantic feature maps instead of raw pixels, the system achieves superior generalization and stability across varying channel conditions. The hybrid design reduces data transmission requirements by approximately 65%, while maintaining near-original fidelity after generative reconstruction.

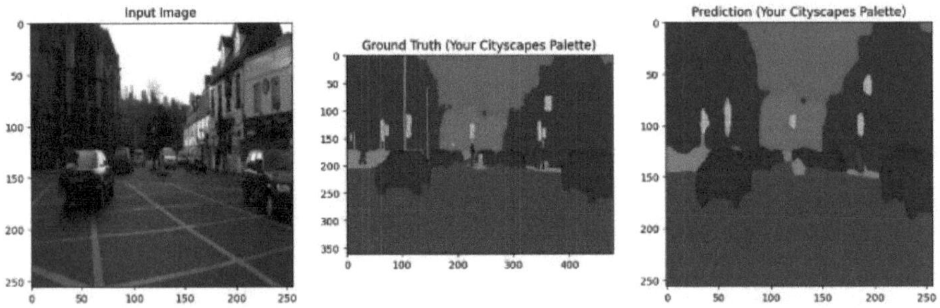


**Fig. 3.** **Image vs Ground Truth vs Prediction**

**Fig. 4.** **Restored Image from Mask**

### 4.1 Perceptual Quality Evaluation

Beyond quantitative results, qualitative visual analysis confirms that the proposed system captures fine structural and textural details lost in direct transmission. Figure 3 compares the original image, ground truth mask, and predicted segmentation, demonstrating strong alignment between prediction and annotation. As depicted in Fig. 4, the generative decoder successfully restores fine textures and structural details from the semantic representation.

The generative model learns to restore spatially consistent textures by modeling the conditional distribution p(X—S), where S represents the semantic map. This leads to improved reconstruction even when channel noise or data loss occurs. Observations indicate that the generator successfully preserves semantic boundaries such as lane markings, vehicles, and pedestrians, which are critical for real-time applications like autonomous navigation and surveillance.

### 4.2 Efficiency and Complexity Analysis

An important consideration in semantic communication is model complexity versus channel efficiency. While DeepLabV3 offers high accuracy, it is computationally heavy; however, the integration of generative decoding reduces transmission bandwidth by focusing on semantic meaning rather than pixel redundancy. The framework effectively transforms the communication channel into a semantic bottleneck, transmitting only task-relevant information. Operating in the semantic domain significantly reduces transmission volume, compressing a $960 \times 720$ RGB frame from 12.6 MB to 4.1 MB, nearly a 65% reduction in bits per pixel.

The complexity analysis for the Encoder and decoder is summarized below.

- Semantic Encoder (Transmitter DeepLabV3 with ResNet-101):
  Parameters: 58.3 million
  Computational cost: 180 GFLOPs for $256 \times 256$ input
  Inference latency: 23 ms per frame
  Throughput: 45 FPS on a GPU-enabled edge device
- Generative Decoder (Receiver – ResNet-based CycleGAN Generator):
  Parameters: 11.4 million
  Computational cost: 38 GFLOPs for $128 \times 128$ input
  Reconstruction latency: 14 ms per frame
  Single forward-pass inference
- System-Level Characteristics:
  Asymmetric deployment: semantic extraction at the transmitter, generative reconstruction at the receiver
  End-to-end latency: $\leq$ 40 ms per frame
- Transmission volume reduction: 65% compared to raw RGB transmission
  Suitable for real-time and edge-device scenarios due to low latency and reduced bandwidth demand

- Empirical results show that the total transmitted data size is reduced from 12.6 MB (raw RGB) to 4.1 MB (semantic map) per frame, with negligible degradation in perceived image quality after restoration. This threefold reduction directly translates to enhanced throughput, lower latency, and energy efficiency in embedded or edge devices.

### 4.3 Comparative Discussion

Compared to traditional compression-based transmission (e.g., JPEG, WebP), the proposed model achieves higher perceptual quality under limited bandwidth. Furthermore, by integrating semantic representation learning with generative priors, the framework provides interpretability the receiver reconstructs an image consistent with human-level semantic understanding rather than numerical reconstruction. The following are the evaluation metrics used for comparison.

**Evaluation Metrics:** System performance is measured using both semantic and perceptual metrics:
**Segmentation Metrics:** Mean Intersection over Union (mIoU), Pixel Accuracy (PA)
**Restoration Metrics:** Peak Signal-to-Noise Ratio (PSNR), Structural Similarity Index (SSIM)
**Perceptual Metrics:** Learned Perceptual Image Patch Similarity (LPIPS) and Fréchet Inception Distance (FID)

**Table 1.** Quantitative comparison of segmentation and restoration models

| Model | Pixel Accuracy (%) | SSIM | PSNR (dB) | mIoU |
|---|---|---|---|---|
| U-Net [10] | 92 | 0.83 | 29 | 79 |
| DeepLab [12] | 90 | 0.85 | 29 | 63.1 |
| CRF-RNN [11] | 89 | 0.87 | 28 | 62.5 |
| DeepLabV3+GAN | 95 | 0.93 | 34 | 82 |

From Table 1, U-Net, DeepLab, and CRF-RNN achieve moderate segmentation accuracy but show limited perceptual quality because they lack generative restoration. DeepLab and CRF-RNN have a better mIoU than U-Net; however, their PSNR and SSIM are still lower. The proposed DeepLabV3 + GAN model achieves the highest pixel accuracy (95%) and mIoU (82%). It also has better PSNR (34 dB) and SSIM (0.93). This shows that combining semantic segmentation with GAN-based reconstruction significantly improves both semantic and perceptual performance.

Furthermore, the generative module effectively reconstructs detailed textures and clear object edges that are lost in approaches based only on segmentation. By working in the semantic domain instead of the pixel domain, the proposed framework improves its ability to handle noise and bandwidth limitations. The better perceptual metrics show greater visual realism without losing semantic consistency. Therefore, the proposed model is well-suited for smart and bandwidth-efficient visual communication systems. The results reinforce the hypothesis that semantic features are a sufficient communication medium for vision tasks, and that generative AI can act as a powerful decoder to reintroduce lost perceptual information. This combination creates a new communication paradigm where both transmitter and receiver share an understanding of the transmitted content.

## 5 Conclusion

This study presented a semantic communication framework integrating segmentation - based encoding and GAN-based restoration to achieve efficient, high-fidelity image transmission. By focusing on *meaning* rather than raw data, the system drastically reduces bandwidth requirements while maintaining perceptual quality.

Experimental evaluations confirm the framework's robustness and reconstruction fidelity. The integration of semantic segmentation and generative restoration demonstrates a clear step toward AI-driven communication systems capable of adaptive, context-aware data transmission.

Future work will extend this model towards multimodal semantic communication incorporating text and speech modalities to develop a unified, generative communication paradigm.

## References

1. Xie, H., Qin, Z., Ye, L.Z., Juang, B.-H.: Deep learning-based semantic communication systems. IEEE Trans. Signal Process. **69**, 2663–2675 (2021)
2. Chen, M., Gündüz, D., Poor, H.V., Saad, W., Bennis, M.: A survey on semantic communication. IEEE Commun. Surv. Tutor. **23**(3), 1542–1575 (2021)
3. Zeng, H., Peng, S., Li, D.: Semantic segmentation using DeepLabV3+. IEEE Access **7**, 128645–128654 (2019)
4. Goodfellow, I.J., et al.: Generative adversarial nets. In: Advances in Neural Information Processing Systems (NeurIPS), pp. 2672–2680 (2014)
5. Belkouche, O., Ksentini, A., Hadjadj-Aoul, Y.: Semantic-aware image compression for next-generation communication systems. In: IEEE International Conference on Acoustics, Speech and Signal Processing (ICASSP), pp. 1281–1285 (2022)
6. Ronneberger, O., Fischer, P., Brox, T.: U-Net: Convolutional networks for biomedical image segmentation. In: Proceedings of MICCAI, pp. 234–241 (2015)
7. Grassucci, E., Mitsufuji, Y., Zhang, P., Comminiello, D.: "Enhancing semantic communication with deep generative models: an overview." In: ICASSP 2024 - 2024 IEEE International Conference on Acoustics, Speech and Signal Processing (ICASSP), Seoul, Korea, Republic, pp. 13021–13025 (2024). https://doi.org/10.1109/ICASSP48485.2024.10448235

8. Kingma, D.P., Welling, M.: Auto-encoding variational Bayes. In: Proceedings of ICLR (2014)
9. Liang, S.D.: Vision language models for massive MIMO semantic communication. In: Proceedings of 2025 IEEE/CVF Conference Computer Vision Pattern Recognition Workshops (CVPRW), pp. 155–161. IEEE (2025). https://doi.org/10.1109/CVPRW67362.2025.00155
10. Anjanath, S., Kuppusamy, P.G., Kumar, R., Saadat, A., Mahalakshmi, M., Vasanth, C.: Enhancing semantic understanding of urban environments: leveraging U-Net deep learning model for cityscape image analysis. PLoS ONE **19**(4), e0300767 (2024)
11. Zheng, S., et al.: Conditional random fields as recurrent neural networks. In: Proceedings of IEEE ICCV, pp. 1529–1537 (2015)
12. Chen, L.-C., Papandreou, G., Kokkinos, I., Murphy, K., Yuille, A.L.: DeepLab: semantic image segmentation with deep convolutional nets, Atrous convolution, and fully connected CRFs. IEEE Trans. Pattern Anal. Mach. Intell. **40**(4), 834–848 (2018)

# Hexagonal MIMO Antenna Structure for Automotive Radar Applications

Durbhakula M. K. Chaitanya(✉), Srilakshmi Aouthu, Punna Bharghava, Muskula Ruthwika, Gaddam Sainadh, and Namile Sridhar

E.C.E. Department, Vasavi College of Engineering, Hyderabad, India
{chaitanyadmk,a.srilakshmi,bharghava}@staff.vce.ac.in

**Abstract.** The growing need for high-data rate with an improved spectral efficiency has driven the widespread adoption of MIMO techniques in modern wireless communication systems. Achieving optimal performance in these systems requires antenna configurations that offer wide bandwidth, low correlation and robust radiation characteristics. The present work introduces modeling and characterization of a three-dimensional (3D) MIMO antenna structure designed to support a broad-range wireless applications including autonomous vehicle communication, wireless power interfaces and other emerging broadband technologies. The antenna design is implemented onto FR4-substrate ($\varepsilon_r = 4.4$ & $h = 1.6$ mm) and incorporates a total of 7 radiating elements with 6 elements uniformly arranged along a hexagonal (6-sided) cylindrical structure and one additional element mounted on the top. The antenna structure resonates at 5.5 GHz with a gain over 8 dBi and a bandwidth around 300 MHz.

**Keywords:** MIMO antenna · 3D antenna · hexagonal structure · High Gain

## 1 Introduction

The ongoing development of wireless communication technologies has driven the demand for higher data-rates, improved system-reliability, consistent connectivity across diverse and challenging operational environments. Applications such as autonomous vehicle communication, wireless power transfer, and other broadband systems requires antennas that are capable of delivering wide bandwidth, higher values of gain, stable radiation characteristics under varying operating conditions. These requirements made the antenna designers to focus on multi-element and three-dimensional (3D) antenna structures [1] that can support diversity reception, spatial multiplexing techniques. In this context, compact 3D antenna architectures have gained significant-attention due to their ability to provide Omni-directional radiation, improved reduced mutual coupling compared to conventional planar antennas. Among these, circular and polygon-based cylindrical arrays offer unique advantages in terms of symmetry and uniform coverage. Motivated by these features, this work presents the design and characterization of a novel 7-element 3D antenna configuration in which 6 elements are uniformly distributed


M. Zafar Ali Khan et al. (Eds.): ICATECS 2025, LNICST 682, pp. 63–76, 2027.
https://doi.org/10.1007/978-3-032-29699-3_6

along a hexagonal (6-sided) cylindrical structure, while an additional monopole element is positioned at the top to enhance vertical coverage and elevation diversity. This arrangement makes the antenna to operate over broadband suitable for wireless applications such as autonomous vehicle, wireless power transfer, etc. irrespective of the orientation and mobility. The MIMO techniques which offer low correlation uniform radiation coverage and optimized spatial distribution [2]. The traditional MIMO antenna systems exhibit limited coverage, restricted coverage performance in the real rime environments. The circular and polyhedral 3D antennas can provide improved directivity and less mutual coupling but suffers from fabrication challenges.

The existing literature on 3D antennas indicates that several critical challenges and open gaps still remain unaddressed, thereby motivating the development of new antenna designs. Ahmed *et al.* (2022) introduced a 3D-printed IoT antenna [3] demonstrating compactness and mechanical adaptability achieving moderate gain around 4–5 dBi with an operational bandwidth close to 150 MHz; however, the design lacked sufficient spatial diversity and elevation coverage, limiting its suitability for broadband MIMO applications. Lee *et al.* (2022) developed a 3D antenna array [4] for simultaneous wireless information and power transfer (SWIPT), showing improved isolation (>20 dB) and dual-functional capability, yet its overall efficiency remained restricted (<80%) due to material constraints and non-optimal current distribution across the 3D structure. In another work, Wang *et al.* (2023) designed a spherical 3D antenna for CubeSat platforms [5] that achieved nearly omnidirectional radiation patterns, wide beamwidth (>100°), and gain around 3 dBi; nevertheless, the spherical form factor posed fabrication challenges, and limited port scalability restricted its use in multi-element MIMO networks.

Chen *et al.* (2022) introduced a foldable 3D antenna [6] for reconfigurable platforms, offering polarization agility and frequency tuning, but its bandwidth (~120–160 MHz) and structural robustness made it unsuitable for high-frequency or vehicular applications. Singh *et al.* (2023) proposed a multi-port 3D energy-harvesting antenna [7] with high efficiency (~70%) and strong rectification performance but the design primarily focused on near-field power extraction and lacked far-field gain enhancement needed for communication-centric systems. Collectively, these studies reveal that most prior 3D antennas exhibit limitations such as insufficient gain (<6 dBi), restricted bandwidth (<200 MHz), limited polarization stability, or challenges in achieving uniform 360° azimuth coverage with low mutual coupling. Moreover, the majority of reported structures implement fewer than 8–10 elements, which reduces their suitability for high-capacity MIMO and next-generation broadband systems.

Despite significant advancements, there remains a clear need for a new 3D antenna design that can simultaneously achieve (i) wide impedance bandwidth to support multi-band wireless services, (ii) higher gain (>8 dBi) and directivity for long-distance links, (iii) low S11 (<−25 dB) for improved matching, (iv) polarization stability under varying device orientation, and (v) multi-element scalability for advanced MIMO operation. Existing literature also highlights that very few studies explore higher-order polygonal 3D geometries, such hexagonal structures with 6 elements which can offer superior radiation smoothness, finer angular resolution, and improved beam uniformity compared to tetradecagonal arrays [1]. Additionally, no prior work integrates a top-mounted element to enhance vertical coverage and elevation diversity an essential feature for applications like autonomous vehicle connectivity, broadband IoT platforms, SWIPT-based systems, and future 6G communication scenarios.

Therefore, a 7-element 3D antenna based on a hexagonal cylindrical geometry with one additional top element addresses several gaps identified in earlier research. The structure promises a broad bandwidth (>300 MHz), improved gain (6–8 dBi), better efficiency (~95–98%), lower mutual coupling (<−18 dB) and nearly uniform azimuthal and elevation coverage. Such advancements make the proposed antenna highly relevant for high-capacity MIMO systems, vehicular networks operating around 5.5 GHz, and emerging broadband platforms requiring robust spatial communication performance.

## 2 Antenna Design

The proposed antenna system comprises of three dimensional element arry to support the wideband and omni directional wireless operation. The structure consists of 7 radiating elements out of which 6 elements are uniformly distributed overhexagonal cylindrical frame and one element is positioned at the top to enhance the elevation coverage and robust three dimensional radiational characteristics suitable for modern broad band communication system.

The antenna structure is proposed to design over rectnagular microstrip patch antenna placed over hexagonal cylindrical frame with suitable ground plane. he proposed antenna is configured for operation at 5.5-GHz is realized onto FR4 substrate characterized by an effective relative permittivity = 4.4, a thickness = 1.6 mm, and a loss tangent of 0.0019. FR4 is selected to obtain the structure rgidity, ease of fabrication at low cost, ability to accommodate multi elemental layout. The comparitive analysis of the proposed struture is also analyzed with different substrates with varying thickness. The elements are mounted onto a light wieght non conductive cylindrical scaffold to provide the mechanical stability to the array without significantly affecting the radiational characteristics. Each radiating element is implemented as planar monopole antenna optimized to offer wide bandwidth. The antenna width and length are determined using standard transmission line formulations [8] in conjunction with the quarter-wavelength approximation.

$$W = \frac{c}{2f_r}\sqrt{\frac{2}{\epsilon_{r+1}}} \tag{1}$$

where c = velocity of em wave, $f_r$ = the resonant-frequency.

The antenna length is calculated by the formula

$$L = \frac{c}{2f_r\sqrt{\epsilon_{reff}}} - 2\Delta L \tag{2}$$

where $\epsilon_{reff}$ is the effective permittivity accounts for the extended length $\Delta L$ due to fringing fields and is given by

$$\epsilon_{reff} = \frac{\epsilon_r + 1}{2} + \frac{\epsilon_r - 1}{2}\left[1 + 12\frac{h}{w}\right]^{-\frac{1}{2}}, \ \frac{w}{h} > 1 \tag{3}$$

$$L = 0.412h\frac{(\epsilon_{eff} + 0.3)(\frac{w}{h} + 0.264)}{(\epsilon_{eff} - 0.258)(\frac{w}{h} + 0.8)} \quad (4)$$

To achieve the proper impedance matching and bandwidth, a quarter wave length feed and each element is terminated with an SMA connector at the base for experimental measurements and system integration. The computed dimensions of the rectangular patch are summarized in the Table 1 presenting a comparison of designs using FR4 ($\varepsilon_r = 4.4$ & h = 1.6 mm), RT Duroid ($\varepsilon_r = 2.2$ & h = 1.6 mm) and Isola Astra ($\varepsilon_r = 3$ & h = 1.6 mm) substrates, all optimized for resonance at 5.5 GHz.

**Table 1.** Calculated Dimensions of Rectangular patch

| Resonating frequency 5.5 GHz | Dimension (mm) FR4 ($\varepsilon_r = 4.4$ & h = 1.6 mm) | Dimension (mm) RT Duroid ($\varepsilon_r = 2.2$ & h = 1.6 mm) | Dimension (mm) Isola Astra ($\varepsilon_r = 2.2$ & h = 1.6 mm) |
|---|---|---|---|
| Length of patch | 11.38 | 17.44 | 13.82 |
| Width of the patch | 16.45 | 21.56 | 19.11 |
| Length of QWT line | 8.3 | 9.90 | 9.05 |
| Width of QWT line | 0.73 | 3.63 | 1.93 |
| Length of feed line | 14.7 | 10.19 | 8.72 |
| Width of feed line | 3 | 4.97 | 7.41 |

Suitable ground plane is employed at the base of the array to stabilize the impedance characteristics, also to provide a controlled radiation boundary. Each antenna element is excited independently using a 50-Ω microstrip feed line. The feed network is kept isolated to reduce the unintended coupling or phase distortion. All the ports are treated independently to configure the MIMO operation. The 6 radiating antennas are placed along the perimeter of the hexagon with an angular spacing of

$$\Delta\theta = \frac{360^\circ}{6} = 60^\circ \quad (5)$$

This arrangement provides:

- nearly uniform azimuth radiation,
- minimized mutual coupling between adjacent elements, and
- Enhanced de-correlation necessary for MIMO operation.

The elements are aligned vertically along the cylindrical surface with identical height and radial offset to maintain geometric symmetry. The patch antennas are arranged on to a cylindrical plane with a spacing nearly λ/10 to λ/8 between the adjacent elements depending on the operating frequency. The ground plane is employed at the base of the array to stabilize the impedance characteristics and provide a controlled radiation boundary.

To achieve improved spherical coverage and reduce elevation-plane nulls, an additional top-mounted monopole is included at the center of the array. This element addresses the limitations of purely circumferential arrays by contributing vertical radiation components and enhancing 3D field distribution. The top element is oriented perpendicular to the base plane, ensuring strong vertical components suitable for applications such as aerial link connectivity, overhead communication, and elevated wireless power interfaces. The dimensions of the elements are optimized iteratively using full wave electronic simulation tools to achieve wide band and spatial coverage. This arrangement of the structure is to support the omnidirectional radiation in azimuth for orient independent communication and the elevation coverage through the central top element (Fig. 1).

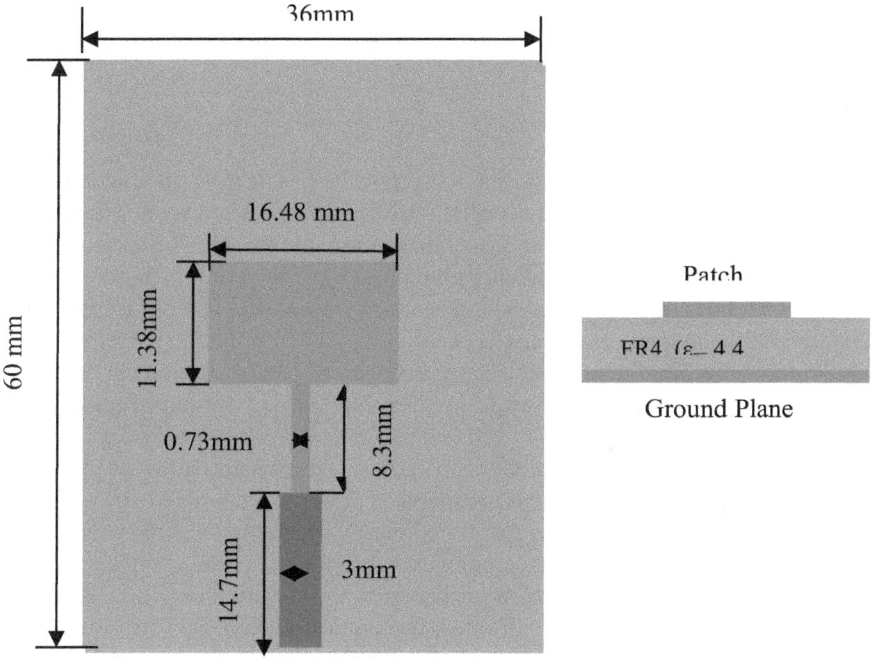


**Fig. 1.** Single element rectangular microstrip antenna

The proposed configuration balances the mechanical compactness and robustness with low mutual coupling to support high capacity MIMO systems to support heterogeneous wireless applications. The design of proposed structure is being analyzed using the EM simulation tool and illustrated in Fig. 2.

Figures 1 and 2 present the simulated reflection coefficient (S11- dB) as function of frequency (GHz) for antennas realized on FR4, RT Duroid, and Isola Astra substrates, respectively.

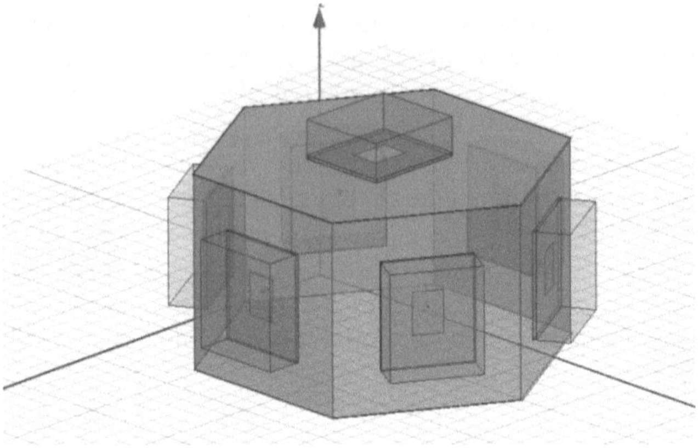

**Fig. 2.** Simulated schematic of the design

## 3 Results and Discussion

The S11 parameter characterizes the antenna return loss, reflecting the fraction of input power returned from the feed port over the operating band. When plotted in dB versus frequency, the presence of a pronounced minimum near the resonant frequency indicates good impedance matching and efficient radiation as illustrated in Fig. 3. For this design operating at 5.5 GHz, the simulated S11 curve shows a well-defined dip below −10 dB, indicating that the antenna efficiently accepts input power at the target frequency with minimal reflections. The bandwidth is determined by the portion of the curve that stays below −10 dB, and a wider bandwidth implies improved performance under varying operating conditions.

The radiation performance characteristics of two antenna structures are presented in Figs. 4, 5, and 6. The pattern describes the spatial distribution of radiated electromagnetic energy and is used to assess the antenna directionality and gain. For a microstrip antenna operating at 5.5 GHz the simulated pattern generally shows a broad main lobe normal to the patch plane with stable co-polarization behavior and low back radiation. Key parameters such as half-power beamwidth front-to-back ratio and peak gain are obtained from the pattern. A symmetric and well-defined main lobe indicates efficient radiation in the intended direction supporting suitability for various wireless applications. Beyond these characteristics, several additional performance parameters are generally considered for a complete evaluation of microstrip antennas. Typical aspects include maintaining low side-lobe levels to reduce interference, ensuring good polarization purity, achieving adequate radiation efficiency by minimizing dielectric and conductor losses, and securing a suitable impedance bandwidth for stable operation within the desired frequency range. Surface-current behavior is also often studied to understand resonance modes and overall electromagnetic performance. Collectively, these parameters provide a broader perspective on antenna behavior and help determine suitability for various wireless applications, even though they are not specifically analyzed in the present case. Furthermore, parameters such as gain stability across frequency, radiation symmetry,

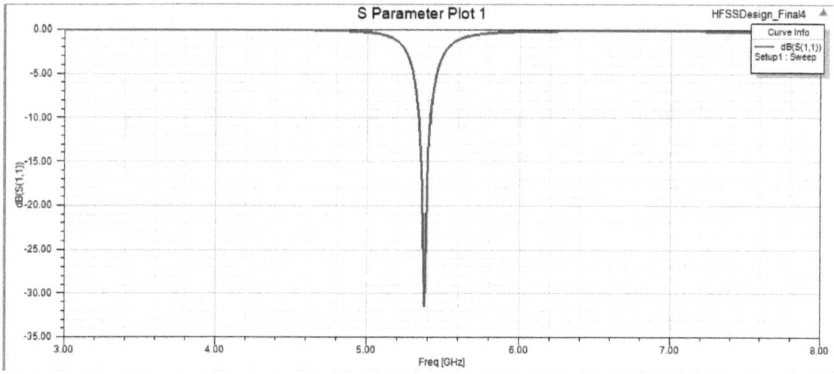


(a)

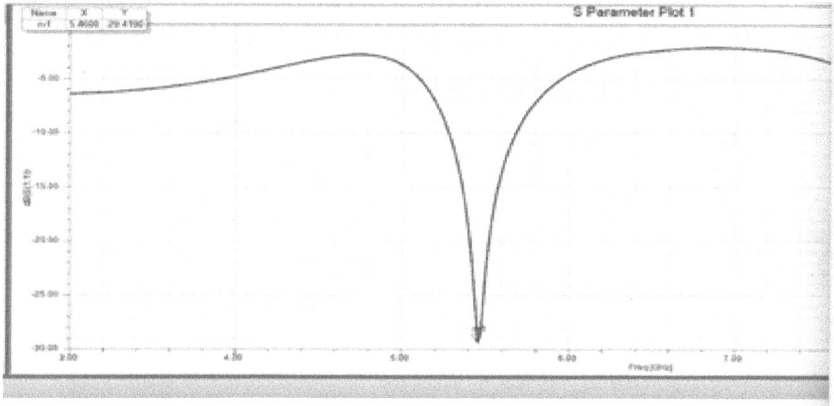


(b)

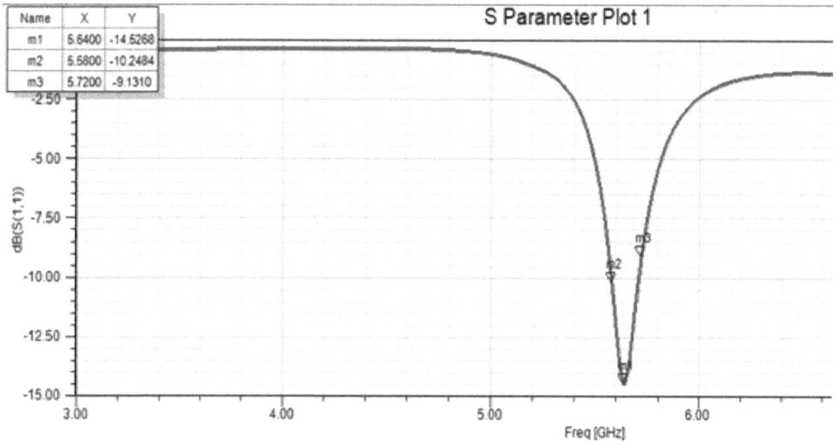


(c)

**Fig. 3.** (a) S11-dB vs Freq-GHz with FR4. (b) S11-dB vs Freq-GHz with RT-Duroid. (c) S11 (dB) vs Freq (GHz) with Isola Astra substrate

and overall structural robustness may also influence real-world performance. Environmental factors like temperature variation and substrate characteristics can additionally affect antenna consistency. Considering these broader aspects supports a more holistic understanding of antenna design requirements for practical deployment.

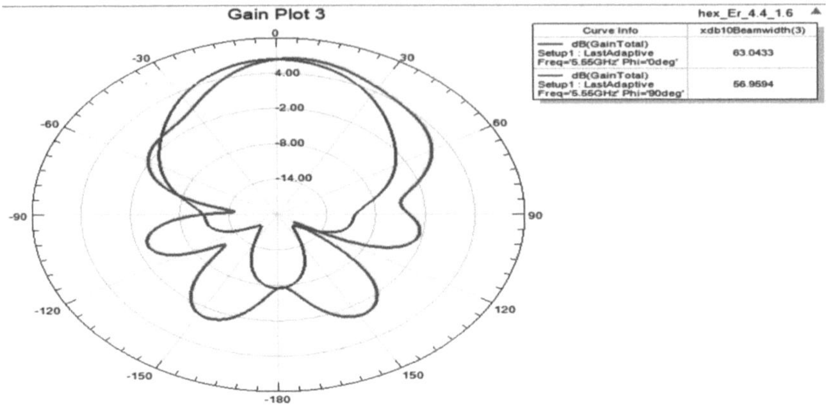


**Fig. 4.** Radiation of the antenna design with FR-4 substrate

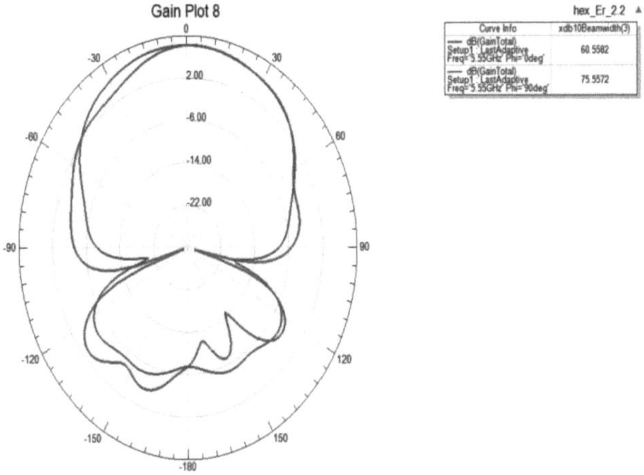


**Fig. 5.** Radiation Pattern of the antenna design with RT-Duroid

All antenna parameters were analyzed using a full-wave electromagnetic simulation environment and the model was constructed with the specified substrate properties ($\varepsilon_r$ = 2.2, 4.4 & 3, h = 1.6 mm) and appropriate boundary conditions, ports, and meshing settings. The simulation environment computes the S-parameters, electric field distribution, current density, far-field radiation pattern, and antenna gain using accurate 3D numerical

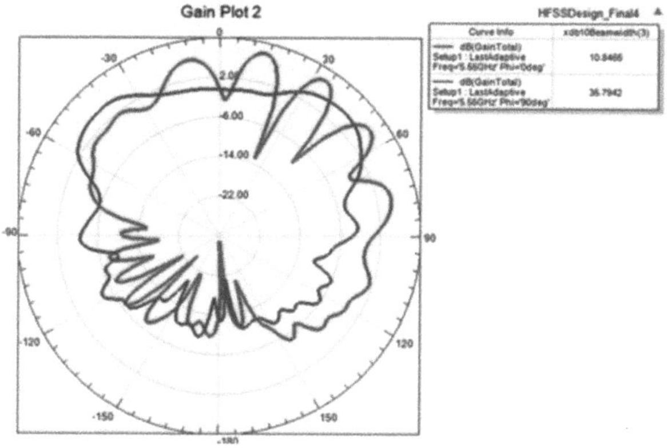


**Fig. 6.** Radiation Pattern of the antenna design with Isola-Astra

methods. The radiation-pattern illustrates the spatial distribution of the antenna's radiated power and is used to assess its directional behavior. For the designed microstrip-patch antenna at 5.5 GHz, the pattern shows a broad and distinct main lobe directed perpendicularly to the patch antenna. The co-polarized field dominates the response, while cross-polarization levels remain relatively low, indicating stable polarization performance. The half-power beamwidth is approximately 60°, demonstrating moderate directivity suitable for point-to-point and short-range wireless applications. This pattern confirms that the antenna-efficiently radiates energy in the intended-direction while maintaining consistent coverage across the operating band. The simulated results of gain plot is shown in Figs. 7, 8 and 9.

The gain plot demonstrates a stable and uniform response near the resonant frequency, reflecting efficient radiation with minimal losses. The maximum gain is observed close to the center of the operating band, indicating effective conversion of input power into radiated energy along the intended direction. The gradual variation of gain across the frequency range suggests proper impedance matching and controlled sidelobe levels. This gain behavior confirms the antenna suitability for wireless applications requiring moderate directivity and consistent signal strength.

The simulation results of the proposed-antenna demonstrate that it is appropriately designed for MIMO operation at 5.5 GHz. The figures show that the S11 response of the antenna using two different substrates—FR4 ($\varepsilon_r$, 4.4) and RT-Duroid ($\varepsilon_r$, 2.2), Isola Astra ($\varepsilon_r$, 3) and the results demonstrate excellent impedance matching characteristics for all elements of the MIMO array. In a multi-element configuration, good impedance matching is essential to ensure that each element radiates efficiently without excessive mutual interaction. The achieved S11 values with dips well below $-10$ dB around 5.5 GHz indicate strong resonance and minimal reflection losses. The bandwidth obtained across the substrates (ranging from 140 to 400 MHz) ensures robust performance even when multiple ports operate simultaneously which is a key requirement for wideband MIMO channels.

The radiation patterns for selected ports presented validate the suitability of the design for MIMO applications. In a multi-element environment, pattern diversity plays a

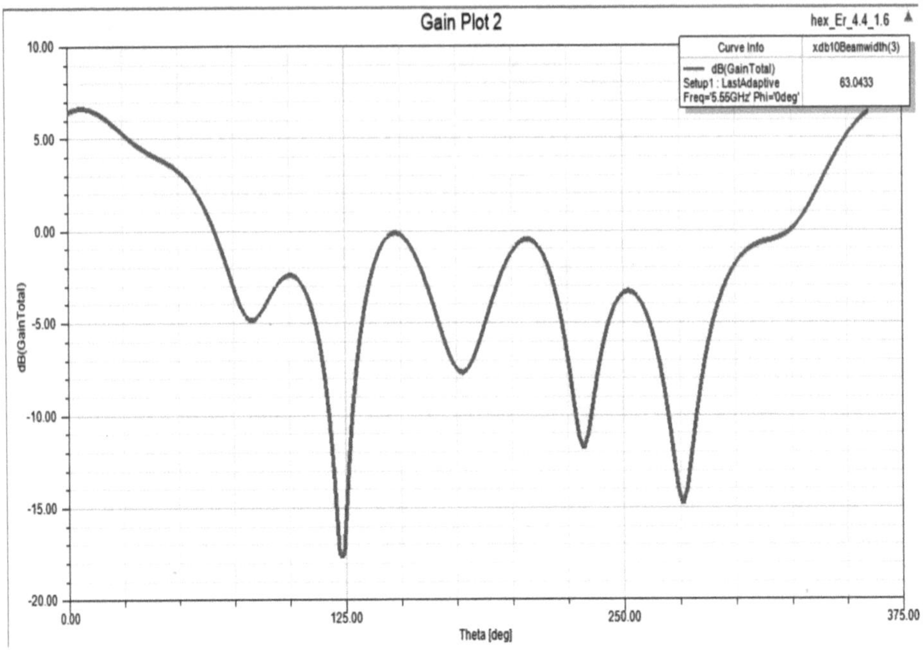


**Fig. 7.** Simulated gain plot of the antenna-FR4

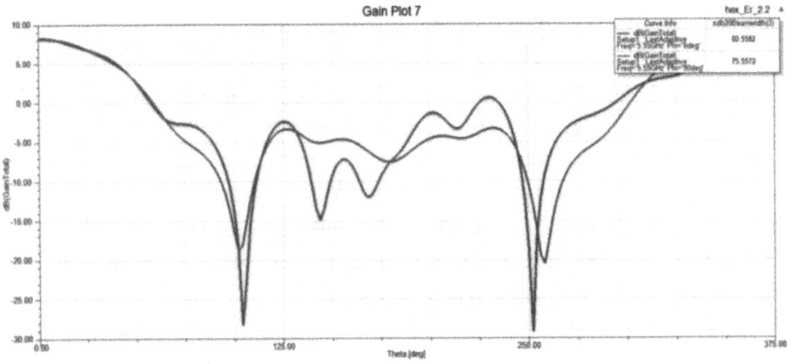


**Fig. 8.** Simulated gain plot of the antenna with RT Duroid substrate

vital role in improving channel-capacity and mitigating multipath fading. The simulated far-field patterns exhibit broad main lobes with stable co-polarization characteristics and controlled back radiation, resulting in directional diversity across the array. This diversity ensures that different elements of the 7 element configuration radiate in slightly varied spatial directions improving the overall diversity gain and lowering envelope correlation. The main lobe direction remains consistent across elements, while small pattern variations contribute positively to MIMO decorrelation.

The Half Power Beamwidth (HPBW) is around 60° for the individual elements that ensures moderate directivity while maintaining wide angular coverage. This is beneficial

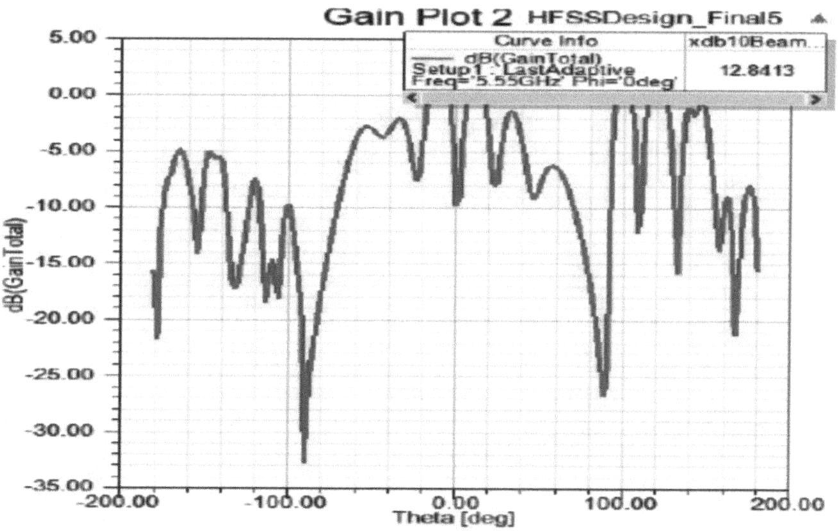


**Fig. 9.** Simulated gain plot of the antenna with Isola Astra substrate

for 3D MIMO structures because it allows each antenna element to sample different parts of the propagation environment. Furthermore, the simulated gain values ranging from 5.1 dBi to 8.2 dBi depending on substrate and structure indicating individual ports have sufficient radiated power even when multiple ports operate concurrently. The directivity values obtained also align with the requirements for mid-gain, short-range and medium-range MIMO links. Efficiency results between 96% and 98% indicate that the antenna elements radiate effectively without significant dielectric or conductor losses. In a dense MIMO array maintaining high efficiency is important to avoid power imbalance among the ports and to ensure uniform contribution to overall system capacity. The wider bandwidth achieved in the RT Duroid-prism configuration (up to 400 MHz) provides additional flexibility for multi-band or multi-carrier operation supporting higher data rates and improved frequency diversity.

The gain plots indicate that the antenna provides uniform radiation throughout the operating band, ensuring reliable and stable MIMO performance. The consistency of gain across multiple ports ensures that no single element dominates or weakens the overall transmission quality. This consistency combined with good isolation, wide bandwidth, stable patterns, high efficiency, demonstrates that the antenna satisfies key MIMO objectives such as low envelope correlation, enhanced channel capacity and reliable spatial diversity. Thus, the proposed design is well suited for advanced wireless applications including autonomous communication platforms, broadband MIMO links and emerging 3D array-based wireless systems. The comparison of the results with different substrates is shown in the Table 2.

The proposed antenna was fabricated on to FR4 substrate with $\varepsilon r = 4.4$ and thickness $h = 1.6$ mm, as depicted in Fig. 10, while the measured S11 (dB) versus frequency and corresponding VSWR are presented in Fig. 11.

**Table 2.** Comparison of Results

| Hexagonal Antenna with 7 Radiating elements | | | | |
|---|---|---|---|---|
| Parameter | Rogers substrate ($\varepsilon_r = 2.2$) | FR4 Substrate ($\varepsilon_r = 1.6$) | | Isola Astra ($\varepsilon_r = 3$) |
| | h = 1.6 mm | h = 3.2 mm | h = 1.6 mm | h = 1.6 mm |
| Resonant Frequency (fr) | 5.5 G Hz | 5.5 G Hz | 5.5 G Hz | 5.5 G Hz |
| S11 (dB) | −26.13 | −18.75 | −14.52 | −42.8 |
| Gain (dBi) | 8.53 | 7.98 | 7.58 | 6.58 |
| Directivity (dB) | 6.65 | 7.53 | 7.57 | 3.641 |
| Efficiency | 98% | 80% | 75% | 98% |
| Bandwidth (MHz) | 360 | 360 | 300 | 340 |

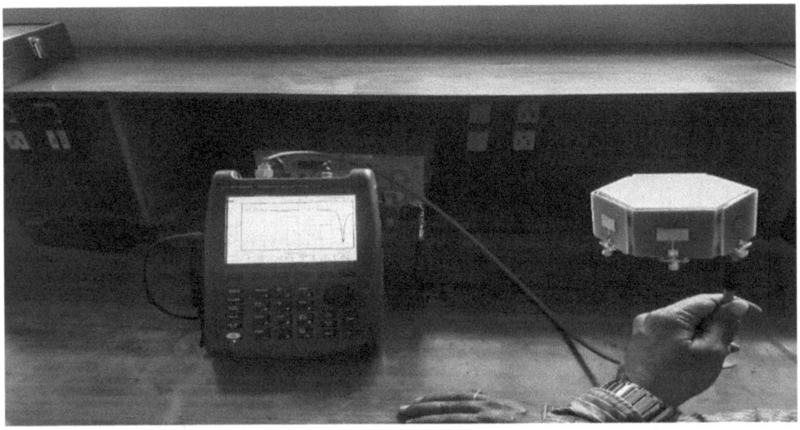

**Fig. 10.** Measurement set up for te fabricated structure using VNA

The results clearly shows that the antenna is resonating at 5.5 GHz with good impedance matchingg showing S11 (dB) vs Frequency (GHz) and VSWR.

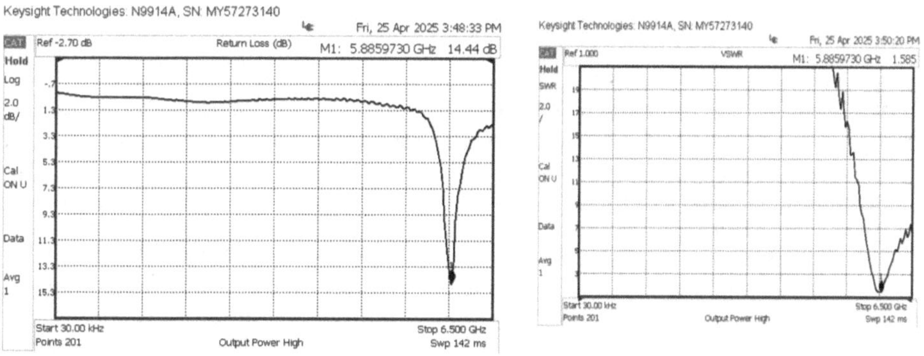


**Fig. 11.** (a) S11 (dB)vs Frquency (GHz). (b) VSWR vs Frequency (GHz)

# 4 Conclusions and Future Scope

The comparative analysis of the hexagonal antenna with seven radiating elements implemented on different substrate materials demonstrates that substrate selection plays [9] a key role in assessing overall antenna functionality The antenna exhibits stable resonance at the intended operating frequency across all considered substrates, confirming the robustness of the hexagonal geometry. Variations in substrate permittivity and thickness significantly influence impedance matching, radiation efficiency, gain characteristics, and bandwidth behavior. Low-loss substrates enhance radiation efficiency and support improved gain, whereas higher-permittivity materials contribute to compactness and stronger impedance matching. The antenna maintains satisfactory directivity and radiation stability across all configurations, indicating its suitability for multi-element and MIMO-oriented wireless systems. In addition to its broadband and multi-element performance, the proposed hexagonal antenna configuration also exhibits characteristics that align well with the requirements of automotive radar and drone-based communication systems. Automotive radar platforms demand antennas with stable radiation behavior, controlled beam characteristics, and reliable performance under varying environmental and mounting conditions. The demonstrated consistency of resonance and directivity across different substrates indicates that the antenna can be integrated into vehicular structures without significant detuning. Its compact multi-element design supports array formation, beam steering, and spatial diversity [11] features essential for short-range radar sensing, obstacle detection, and collision-avoidance systems typically operating in dense multipath environments. For drone applications, the lightweight structure, planar geometry, and stable radiation pattern make it suitable for airborne platforms where size, weight, and aerodynamic impact are critical. The ability to maintain performance over varied substrates further enhances mechanical integration options on UAV frames composed of composites or lightweight materials. These attributes collectively support the antenna's applicability for emerging automotive and UAV communication and sensing scenarios.Overall, the results validate that the proposed hexagonal multi-element antenna structure [12] is adaptable to different substrate environments and can be effectively tailored for broadband wireless communication applications through appropriate material selection.

## References


1. Jordaom, M., Pires, D., Belo, D., Pinho, P., Carvalho, N.B.: 3D antenna characterization for WPT applications. Sensors **21**, 4461 (2021)
2. Srinivasu, G., Gayathri, T., Chaitanya, D.M.K., Sharma, V.K.: Quad port octagon slotted-high isolation MIMO antenna for GSM1800 to X-band wireless applications. Analog Integr. Circ. Signal Process. **114**(1), 125–141 (2023)
3. Ahmed, M., Rahman, A., Hossain, M., Islam, M.: Design and fabrication of a compact 3D-printed antenna for IoT applications. Wireless Pers. Commun. **125**, 2147–2161 (2022)
4. Lee, J., Park, S., Kim, Y.: A 3D antenna array architecture for simultaneous wireless information and power transfer (SWIPT) systems. IEEE Access **10**, 48732–48744 (2022)
5. Wang, H., Liu, Q., Zhang, X.: Spherical 3D antenna design for CubeSat communication systems. Int. J. Satell. Commun. Netw. **41**, 325–338 (2023)
6. Chen, Y., Zhao, K., Li, Z.: Foldable three-dimensional antenna for reconfigurable wireless platforms. IEEE Trans. Antennas Propag. **70**, 9456–9465 (2022)
7. Singh, R., Kumar, A., Mishra, D.: Multi-port three-dimensional energy harvesting antenna for wireless power applications. IET Microwaves Antennas Propag. **17**, 812–821 (2023)
8. Kumar, G., Ray, K.P.: Broadband Microstrip Antennas. Artech House (2003)
9. Chaitanya, D.M.K., Koteswara Rao, N.V.: Impact of different ground plane structures on Sierpinski Monopole Antenna. In: Fourth International Conference on Emerging Research in Computing Information, Communication and Applications (ERCICA-2016-Springer). Nitte Meenakshi Institute of Technology, Bangalore (2016)
10. Cidronali, A., Maddio, S., Giorgetti, G., Manes, G.: Analysis and performance of a smart antenna for 2.45-GHz single-anchor indoor positioning. IEEE Trans. Microw. Theory Tech. **59**, 21–31 (2010)
11. Tangirala, G., Garikipati, S., Meshram, M.K., Chaitanya, D.M.K., Sharma, V.K.: Quad element Luna-shaped UWB-MIMO antenna with improved isolation and gain using novel decoupling networks. Wirel. Netw. **30**(4), 2557–2569 (2024)
12. Pires, D., Belo, D., Jordão, M., Pinho, P., de Carvalho, N.B.: 3D antenna array for SWIPT sensing with WPT capabilities. In: Proceedings of the 14th European Conference on Antennas and Propagation (EuCAP), Copenhagen, Denmark, pp. 1–4 (2020)

# Implementation of Intrusion Detection Systems in Cloud Computing Platform

V. Aruna(✉) and Durbhakula. M. K. Chaitanya

Department of ECE, Vasavi College of Engineering, Hyderabad, India
{v.aruna,chaitanyadmk}@staff.vce.ac.in

**Abstract.** Currently accelerating adoption of cloud infrastructures and the increasing concentration of sensitive information in these environments, cloud platforms have become prominent targets for cyber-attacks. This study evaluates and implements network intrusion detection systems (NIDS) in a cloud setting to classify distinct categories of malicious activity. A variety of machine learning (ML) models are Deep Learning architectures, Gradient Boosting, K-Nearest Neighbors (KNN), and Random Forest are applied to identify probe, remote-to-local (R2L) denial-of-service (DoS), and (U2R) user-to-root attacks.

Experimental findings show that although all models report high overall accuracy, Deep Learning and Gradient Boosting yield near-perfect precision for attack detection but consistently mislabel normal traffic as malicious. Random Forest and KNN demonstrate slightly improved discrimination of legitimate network activity by correctly identifying a small proportion of normal samples, whereas the remaining models classify nearly all benign traffic as attacks. An examination of feature distributions across attack categories further highlights characteristics that may support the development of more dependable intrusion detection frameworks for cloud environments.

**Keywords:** Intrusion Detection Systems · Deep Learning · Cloud security · Network Security · Machine Learning

## 1 Introduction

Cloud Computing has transformed IT landscape by enabling on-demand access to computing resources, reducing the cost of IT consumption, and delivering highly scalable infrastructure. Despite these advantages, the centralized nature of cloud services makes them appealing targets for malicious actors. As a result, ensuring strong security measures has become essential for both cloud service providers (CSPs) and their clients. With more organizations shifting their critical systems and confidential information into cloud environments, the development of reliable and advanced security solutions has become increasingly important. Intrusion Detection Systems (IDS) crucially identifies potential attacks and unauthorized activities in cloud platforms. However, many conventional network-based IDS approaches are not well-suited to the dynamic and distributed characteristics of cloud architectures, making it necessary to design new monitoring


M. Zafar Ali Khan et al. (Eds.): ICATECS 2025, LNICST 682, pp. 77–95, 2027.
https://doi.org/10.1007/978-3-032-29699-3_7

and detection mechanisms tailored to cloud security challenges. The growing sophistication of cyber-attacks which including advanced evasion tactics and zero-day exploits has encouraged use of machine learning-driven intrusion detection methods capable of identifying previously unseen attacks by learning patterns of normal behaviour and detecting deviations.

In this study, we introduce intrusion detection frameworks designed for Cloud computing environments. It uses machine learning techniques to sort network traffic into normal activity or numerous attack types, including denial-of-service, probe attempts, Remote-to- Local (R2L), and user-to-root (U2R) intrusions. We compare several leading machine learning algorithms and evaluate their strengths and weaknesses in the context of cloud security. The basic contributions of this research include:

- A structured valuation of multiple machine learning models used for intrusion detection in cloud settings
- Examination of feature distributions among attack categories to gain deeper insights into attack behaviors.
- Assessment of model efficiency using accuracy metrics and confusion matrix analysis
- Practical recommendations for deploying effective IDS mechanisms in cloud computing infrastructures

Further the manuscript is structured as below: Section 2 reviews existing studies on intrusion detection for cloud systems. Section 3 outlines the projected methodology and dataset. Section 4 represents the experimental findings and evaluates model performance. Section 5 discusses the significance of the results. Section 6 includes the conclusion of manuscript, identifies limitations, and future research.

## 2 Related Work

In the research community, Cloud computing environments in recent years has been a popular area of inquiry. The variety of platforms, protocols, and environments in cloud infrastructures present unique challenges, which researchers have proposed several approaches to address.

### 2.1 Traditional IDS Approaches

Traditional intrusion Detection Techniques are usually classified into two important categories: Signature-based and anomaly-based methods [1]. Signature-based IDS tools compare incoming network activity with a repository of Predefined Attack signatures, whereas anomaly-based IDS solutions model normal system behavior and identify any activity that departs from this learned baseline as a possible security threat.

A signature-based IDS can be mathematically represented as follows:

$$A(p) = \begin{array}{ll} 1, & \textit{if } \exists s \in S : \text{match}(p, s) \\ 0, & \textit{otherwise} \end{array} \tag{1}$$

where $A(p)$ is the alert function for packet $p$, $S$ is the set of signatures, and match($p$,$s$) indicates whether packet $p$ matches signature $s$.

For anomaly-based detection, a common approach is to define a distance function from normal behavior:

$$D(p) = d(p, \mu_{normal}) \tag{2}$$

where $\mu_{\text{normal}}$ represents the centroid of normal behavior, and $d$ is a distance metric. An alert is generated if $D(p) > \tau$ for some threshold $\tau$.

Modi et al. [2] surveyed various intrusion detection techniques for cloud computing and highlighted the limitations of conventional IDS when applied to cloud environments. They emphasized the need for scalable, adaptive solutions that can handle the adaptive nature of cloud resources and the high volume of network traffic.

## 2.2 Machine Learning for Intrusion Detections

Machine learning has developed a promising way to progress the effectiveness of Intrusion Detection systems. Many studies have looked into using different machine learning models to spot malicious patterns in network traffic. In supervised learning methods, the goal is to study a function f:X $\rightarrow$ Y that connects input feature vectors X to their related class labels Y. This learning task can generally be expressed as the following optimization problem:

$$\min \frac{1}{n} \sum\nolimits_{i-1}^{n} L(f_\theta(x_i), y_i) + \lambda R(\theta) \tag{3}$$

In this formulation, $\theta$ denotes set of model parameters, L represents the loss function, x.x refers to the input feature vectors, y. y corresponds to their associated labels, n is the overall amount of training instances, RRR is a regularization component, and $\lambda$ is a hyper parameter that explains the influence of the regularization term.

Patel et al. [3] experimented an evaluation of multiple classification techniques like Support Vector Machines, Random Forest, and Neural Networks for intrusion detection within cloud infrastructures. Their results indicated that ensemble-based models tend to achieve better accuracy and less false-positive rates in comparison to individual learning algorithms.

Recently, deep learning has drawn considerable interest for intrusion detection tasks. Vinayakumar et al. [4] introduced a deep neural network framework tailored for identifying attacks in cloud networks and demonstrated that it surpasses conventional machine learning models in recognizing sophisticated intrusion behaviors. Neuron output is within a deep neural network is typically defined as:

$$a_j(l) = \sigma(\sum\nolimits_{i=1}^{n_i-1} w_{ji}^{(l)} a_i^{(l-1)} + b_j^{(l)}) \tag{4}$$

where $a_j^{(l)}$ is the activation of neuron $j$ in layer $l$, $\sigma$ is a non-linear activation function, $w_{ji}^{(l)}$ are connecting neurons weights in layer $l - 1$ to neuron $j$ in layer $l$, and $b_j^{(l)}$ is the Bias Term.

### 2.3 Cloud-Specific IDS Implementations

Several researchers have proposed IDS implementations specifically designed for cloud computing platforms. Ficco et al. [5] introduced a distributed IDS architecture for multi cloud environments that coordinates detection activities across multiple cloud service providers.

A distributed IDS in cloud environments can be modeled as a set of collaborative agents:

$$IDS_{\text{cloud}} = \{A1, A2, ..., Am\} \tag{5}$$

where each agent $Ai$ monitors a specific subset of the cloud environment. The global decision function can be given as:

$$Dg(p) = F(D1(p), D2(p), ..., Dm(p)) \tag{6}$$

where $Di(p)$ is the local decision of agent $Ai$ for packet $p$, and $F$ is a fusion function that aggregates local decisions.

Watson et al. [6] developed a cloud-native Intrusion Detection System that leverages container orchestration technologies to deploy and manage detection agents across cloud resources. Their approach emphasized the importance of integrating security monitoring with cloud-native deployment patterns.

Our work expands on these methods by estimating multiple Machine Learning models against a comprehensive dataset of network traffic and analyzing their performance characteristics with respect to cloud security.

## 3 Methodology

This section describes our approach to implementing and analyzing intrusion detection systems for cloud computing environments.

### 3.1 Dataset Description

For our experimental evaluation we utilized a detailed collection of network traffic as a data set that includes normal connections along with attack traffic of several categories. It contains the following categories of attacks:

- **Denial of Service (DoS):** Attempts to disturb the accessibility of a service by overflowing or exhausting the system's resources, preventing genuine users from gain access

  - **Probe:** Reconnaissance activities carried out to scan, inspect, or collect information about a system in order to uncover possible weaknesses.
  - **Remote to Local (R2L):** Intrusion attempts where an external attacker tries to obtain local user access on a target machine without prior authorization.
  - **User to Root (U2R):** Scenarios in which an ordinary user account is exploited to escalate privileges and gain administrative or root-level access.

- Normal: Legitimate network traffic

The distribution of the attack categories can be seen in Fig. 1, which shows that DoS attacks have the highest number of attack instances, followed by normal traffic, probe and then less than or equal to of r2l and u2r attacks. The class distribution in our dataset can be mathematically represented as:

$$P_{(y=c)} = \frac{N_c}{N_{total}} \tag{7}$$

Whereas $P\ (y = c)$ is The Probability of Class $c$
*Nc* is the count of instances belonging to Class $c$
Ntotal is the Total count of instances in the given dataset.

## 3.2 Feature Engineering

For represent various characteristics of the network connections, multiple features were derived from the traffic dataset. These include:

- **Count:** The total number of connections made to the same group during a specific time period.
- **src bytes:** The capacity of data, in bytes, sent from the start to the destination
- **dst bytes:** The volume of data, in bytes, sent from the end back to the source
- **duration:** The time span of each connection, measured in seconds
- **Srv count:** The quantity of connections directed to the same service during a defined time window.

To reduce skew ness in these feature distributions and ensure more uniform scaling, a logarithmic transformation was applied.

$$x_i' = \log(x_i + 1) \tag{8}$$

where $x_i$ is the unique feature value and *xi* is the transformed value. The addition of 1 ensures that the transformation is defined for zero values.

To evaluate the discriminative power of our features, we looked at the distributions of these features across attack categories. Some of the features were log- transformed to facilitate understanding of the distribution because of the extreme value ranges. For feature selection, we employed information gain to measure the relevance of each feature for attack classification:

$$IG(Y, X) = H(Y) - H(Y|X) \tag{9}$$

where IG(*Y,X*) is the evidence gain of feature *X w.r.t* class *Y*, *H(Y)* is the entropy of the class distribution, and *H(Y|X)* is the restricted entropy of *Y* given *X*.

### 3.3 Machine Learning Models

We developed and assessed four different machine learning algorithms for intrusion detection:

- **Deep Learning:** A neural network model composed of multiple layers capable of learning complex patterns
- **Gradient Boosting:** An ensemble approach that constructs models in a step-by-step manner, each one improving upon the errors of its predecessors
- **K-nearest neighbors (KNN):** A Distance based, Non-parametric Classifier that assigns labels by comparing samples to their closest neighbors in the training set
- **Random Forest:** A collection of Decision trees that collectively enhance prediction accuracy while sinking the risk of over fitting

For the Deep Learning approach, A Feed-forward neural network with three hidden Layers was implemented. The transformation performed at each layer can be written as:

$$h^{(l)} = \sigma\left(W^{(l)}h^{(l-1)} + b^{(l)}\right) \tag{10}$$

where $\mathbf{h}^{(l)}$ is the vector of activations in layer $l$, $\mathbf{W}^{(l)}$ is the weight matrix, $\mathbf{b}^{(l)}$ is the bias vector, and $\sigma$ is the activation function (ReLU in our implementation).

The Gradient Boosting approach constructs a joint of weak base learners—most commonly decision trees—by adding them one after another. During each iteration t, a novel tree ft is introduced to the model with the objective of reducing the overall loss function $(n)$

$$ft = \underset{fi=1}{argminXL}(yi, Ft - 1(xi) + f(xi)) \tag{11}$$

where $Ft - 1$ is the ensemble at iteration $t - 1$, and $L$ is the loss function.

The K-Nearest Neighbors algorithm categorizes an instance based on the mainstream class among its $k$ nearest neighbors:

$$\hat{y} = \underset{i \in Nk(x)}{\text{arg}_{\text{max}}\mathbf{X1}}(yi = c) \tag{12}$$

where $Nk(x)$ is the set of $k$ nearest neighbors of instance $x$, and$\mathbf{1}(\cdot)$ is the indicator function.

The Random Forest algorithm generates a group of decision trees, with individual tree trained on a bootstrap-resampled portion of the dataset and a randomly selected subset of features. The overall classification result is got by aggregating the outputs of all trees through mainstream voting.

$$\hat{y} = \underset{t=1}{\text{arg}_{\text{max}}\mathbf{X1}}(ht(x) = c) \tag{13}$$

where $ht(x)$ is the prediction of the $t$-th tree, and $T$ is the entire amount of trees in the forest.

The models were trained using a balanced portion of the dataset and assessed with commonly used performance evaluation measures. In this context, Wc_ c denotes the weight assigned to class ccc, which is computed as the inverse of its occurrence frequency within the training set.

$$W_c = N/C \cdot N_C \tag{14}$$

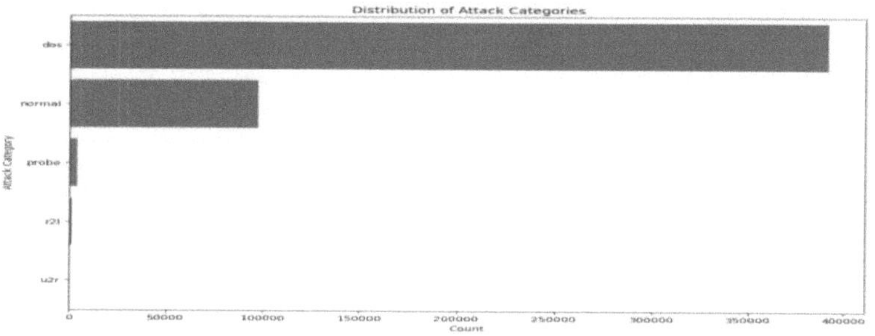


**Fig. 1.** Distribution of count (log scale) by Attack Category

### 3.4 Feature Distribution Analysis

We analyzed the distributions of key features across differ-confusion matrices to analyze TP and FP rates

## 4 Experimental Outcomes

This segment presents the results of our experimental evaluation of intrusion detection models for cloud computing environments.

### 4.1 Distribution of Attack Categories

Figure 1 illustrates the distribution of attack categories in our dataset. DoS attacks are the most prevalent, with approximately 380,000 instances, followed by normal traffic with about 100,000 instances. Probe, r2l, and u2r attacks are less frequent, with probe attacks having a few thousand instances and r2l and u2r attacks having fewer than 1,000 instances each.

The skewed class distribution mirrors real-world conditions, where some attacks—such as DoS—occur far more frequently than others. However, this inequity can aim machine learning models to favor the dominant classes, resulting in reduced performance on the less represented attack categories. To mitigate this issue, a weighted loss function was incorporated during training to compensate for the class imbalance.

$$L\ \mathrm{weighted}(y, \hat{y}) = XwcL(yc, \hat{y}c) \qquad c = 1 \tag{15}$$

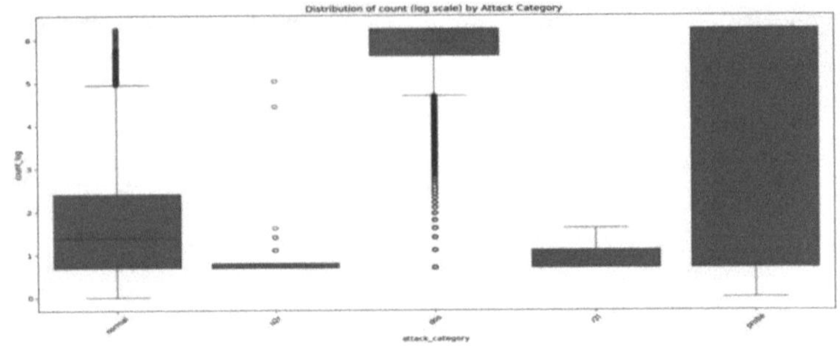


**Fig. 2.** Distribution of Count (log scale) by attack category

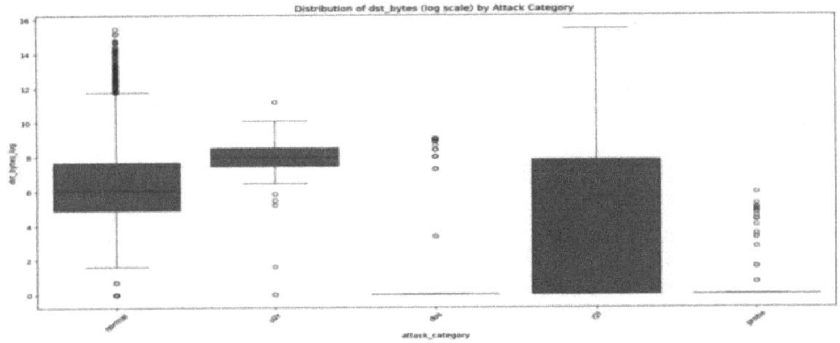


**Fig. 3.** Distribution of dst bytes (log scale) by Attack Category

and identify patterns that could help in detecting various types of attacks.

Figure 2 shows the distribution of connection counts (log scale) by attack category. DoS and probe attacks exhibit significantly higher connection counts compared to other categories, reflecting their nature of generating multiple connections to target systems.

The discriminative power of a feature can be quantified using the Kullback- Leibler (KL) divergence between feature distributions for different classes:

$$D_{KL}(P_c \| P_{normal}) = \sum P_c(x) \log_{P_{normal}}^{P_c(x)} \tag{16}$$

where $P_c(x)$ is the probability distribution of feature $x$ for attack class $c$, and $P_{\text{normal}}(x)$ is the distribution for normal traffic.

Figure 3 illustrates the distribution of destination bytes (log scale) by attack category. U2r attacks show higher median values of destination bytes compared to other categories, suggesting that these attacks often involve transferring larger amounts of data from the target system.

Figure 4 presents the distribution of connection duration (log scale) by attack category. U2r attacks typically have longer durations, while DoS attacks generally have shorter durations, consistent with their respective attack patterns.

Figure 5 shows the distribution of source bytes (log scale) by attack category. Normal traffic and r2l attacks tend to have higher median values of source bytes compared to other attack types.

Figure 6 illustrates the distribution of service counts (log scale) by attack category. DoS attacks show significantly higher service counts, reflecting their tendency to target specific services with multiple connections.

These distribution analyses reveal that different attack categories exhibit distinct patterns across various features, providing valuable insights for developing effective intrusion detection models.

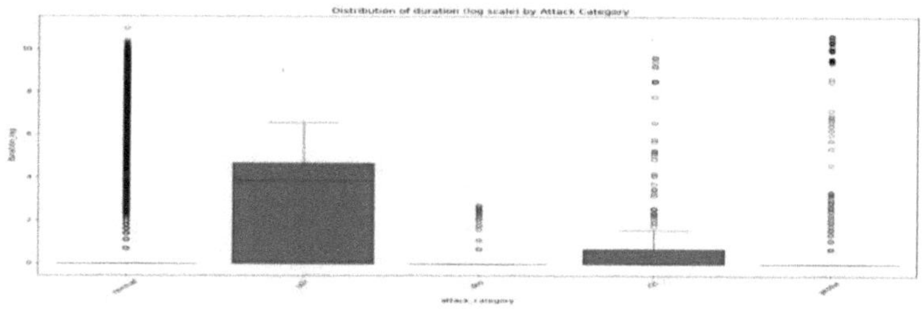

**Fig. 4.** Distribution of duration (log scale) by Attack Category

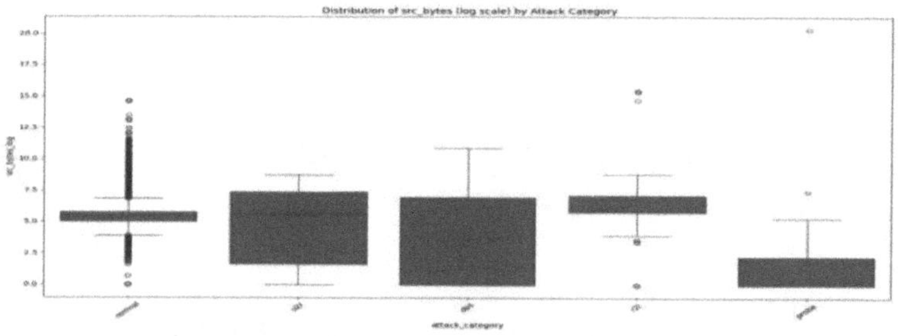

**Fig. 5.** Distribution of src bytes (log scale) by Attack Category

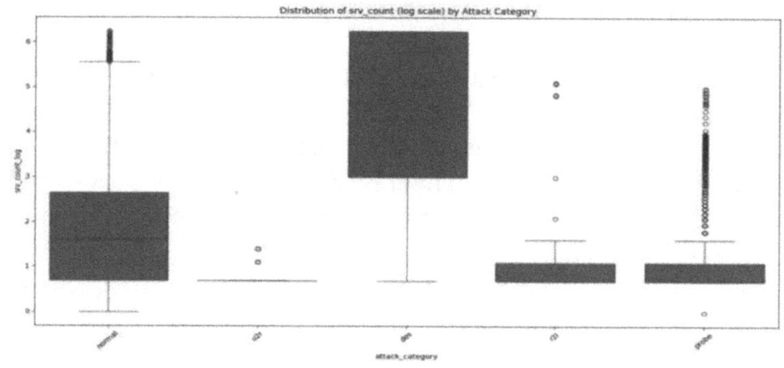


**Fig. 6.** Distribution of srv count (log scale) by Attack Category

### 4.2 Model Performance Evaluation

The use of the four machine learning simulations was measured using confusion matrices, which offer a comprehensive view of how each model classifies instances correctly or incorrectly across all categories.

In a binary arrangement task (normal traffic versus attack), the components of the confusion matrix are described as follows:

$$TruePostive(TP) = \sum_{i=1}^{n} 1(y_i = 1 \wedge \hat{y}_i = 1) \quad (17)$$

$$FalsePositve(FP) = \sum_{i=1}^{n} 1(y_i = 0 \wedge \hat{y}_i = 1) \quad (18)$$

$$TrueNegative(TN) = \sum_{i=1}^{n} 1(y_i = 0 \wedge \hat{y}_i = 0) \quad (19)$$

$$FalseNegative(FN) = \sum_{i=1}^{n} 1(y_i = 1 \wedge \hat{y}_i = 0) \quad (20)$$

where $y_i$ is the true label and $\hat{y}_i$ is the projected label for instance $i$. From these elements, we computed the following performance metrics:

$$TP + TN = (TP + TN + FP + FN) \quad ACCURACY \quad (21)$$

$$\text{(TP + TN + FP + FN /TP)} \quad \text{PRECISION} \quad (22)$$

$$(TP + FP)/TP \qquad RECALL \quad (23)$$

$$TP + FN \;\; Precision \cdot Recall \;\; F1 - score = 2 \cdot Precision + Recall \quad (24)$$

## 5 Deep Learning Model:

Figure 7 represents the confusion matrix aimed at the Deep Learning model. The model classified all traffic as attacks (label 1), resulting in 119,023 TPs and 29,184 FPs. While this approach ensures that all actual attacks are detected (high recall), it misclassifies all normal traffic as attacks, important to a high FP rate.

The sorting decision of the Deep Learning model can be communicated as:

$$\begin{aligned} \hat{y} = & 1, \; if \;\; \text{if}\; \sigma(\mathbf{W}(L)\mathbf{h}(L-1) + \mathbf{b}(L)) > \theta \\ & 0, \; otherwise \end{aligned} \quad (25)$$

where $\mathbf{W}_{(L)}$ and $\mathbf{b}(L)$ are the weights and biases of the outcome layer, $\mathbf{h}_{(L-1)}$ is the initiation of the penultimate layer, $\sigma$ is the sigmoid activation function, and $\theta$ is the classification threshold (typically 0.5).

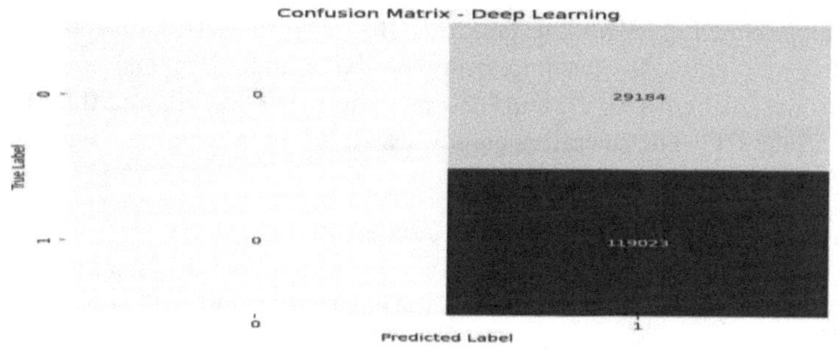


**Fig. 7.** Confusion Matrix - Deep Learning

The arrangement report of the Deep Learning model shows

- precision, recall, and F1-score for normal traffic (class 0), while achieving 0.80 precision, 1.00 recall, and 0.89 F1-score for attack traffic (class 1). The overall accuracy was 0.80, with a weighted average F1-score of 0.72.
- *Gradient Boosting Model:* Fig. 8 presents the confusion matrix of the Gradient Boosting model. Comparable to the Deep Learning model, it classified almost all traffic as attacks, with 119,022 TPs and 29,184 FPs. However, it correctly identified 1 instance of normal traffic, showing a marginal improvement in balancing detection performance.

The prediction function of the Gradient Boosting model can be given as:

$$TFT(x) = X_{nft(x)} \tag{26}$$

Where *ft* is the *t*-th weak learner, *T* is the overall amount of iterations, and $\eta$ is the learning rate. The classification decision is then:

$$\begin{aligned} \hat{y} = 1, &\quad \text{if } FT_{(x)} > \theta \\ 0, &\quad otherwise \end{aligned} \tag{27}$$

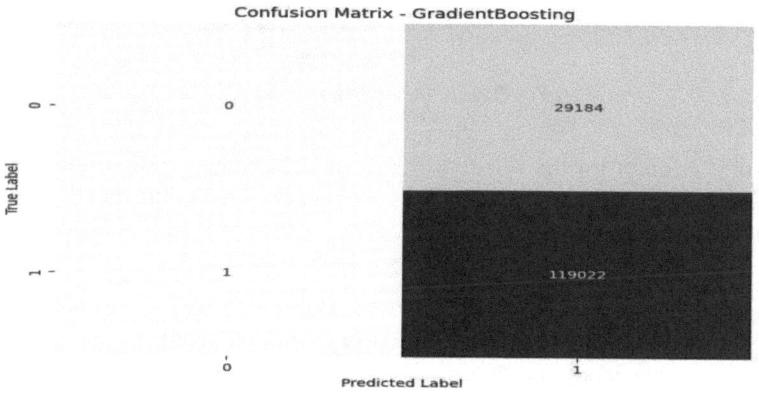


**Fig. 8.** Confusion Matrix – Gradient Boosting

The arrangement report for the Gradient Boosting model represents performance metrics nearly identical to the Deep Learning model, with 0.00 precision, recall, and F1-score for normal traffic (class 0), and 0.80 precision, 1.00 recall, and 0.89 F1score for attack traffic (class 1). The overall accuracy was 0.80, by a weighted average F1-score of 0.72.

2) *K-Nearest Neighbors Model:* Figure 9 represents the matrix for confusion for the KNN model. This model demonstrated better balance in classification performance, correctly identifying 750 instances of normal traffic while still detecting 115,739 attacks correctly. However, it misclassified 3,284 actual attacks as normal, indicating a trade-off between reducing false positives and preserving high detection rates.

The decision boundary of the KNN model is defined implicitly by the distribution of training instances. For a instance $x$, the predicted class is given by:

$$\hat{y}(x) = \frac{1}{K} \sum\nolimits_{i \in N_k(x)} Y_i \tag{28}$$

where $Nk(x)$ it is the $k$ nearest neighbors of $x$ *for a given set*, and $y_i$ is the label class of the $i$-th neighbor.

The classification report for the KNN model shows improved performance for normal traffic detection with 0.19 precision, 0.03 recall, and 0.05 F1-score for class 0. For attack traffic (class 1), it achieved 0.80 precision, 0.97 recall, and

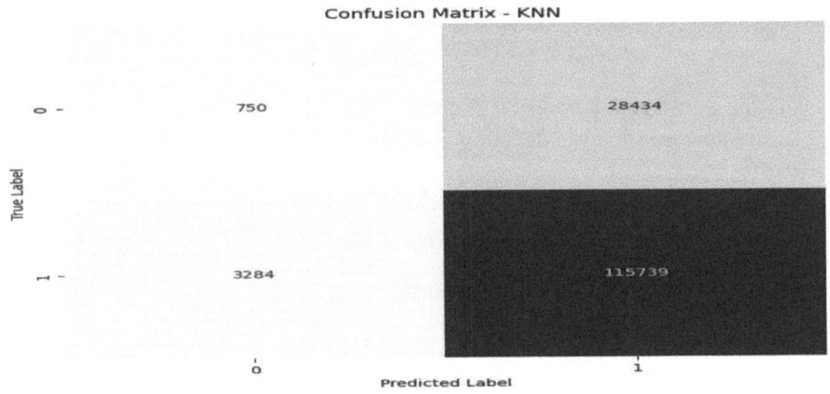


**Fig. 9.** Confusion Matrix - KNN

The sorting report for the Random Forest model displays similar output to KNN, with 0.19 precision, 0.03 recall, and 0.05 F1-score for normal traffic (class 0). For attack traffic (class 1), it achieved 0.80 precision, 0.97 recall, and 0.88 F1- score. The overall accuracy was 0.79, with a weighted average F1-score of 0.72.

3) *Multiclass Classification Performance:* In addition to binary sorting (normal vs. attack), we evaluated the models' capability to differentiate between various attack categories. Table I presents the performance metrics for multiclass classification across five groups: DoS, normal, probe, r2l, and u2r.For multiclass classification,

the performance metrics for every class $c$ are computed as: 0.88 F1-score. The total accuracy was 0.79, with a weighted average F1-score of 0.72. TP$c$

$$TPc + FPcTPc \tag{29}$$

$$TPc + FNc\ Precision\ c \tag{30}$$

4) *Random Forest Model:* Figure 10 presents the matrix for confusion for the Random Forest model. Analogous to the KNN model, it showed a balanced approach, correctly identifying 754 instances of normal traffic and 115,835 attacks. It misclassified 3,188 actual attacks as normal, showing a slightly better attack detection rate compared to KNN.

The Random Forest classification decision is established on mainstream voting through all trees:

$$\hat{y}(x) = mode\{h1(x), h2(x), \ldots, hT(x)\} \tag{31}$$

where $ht(x)$ is the prediction of the $t$-th tree for instance $x$.

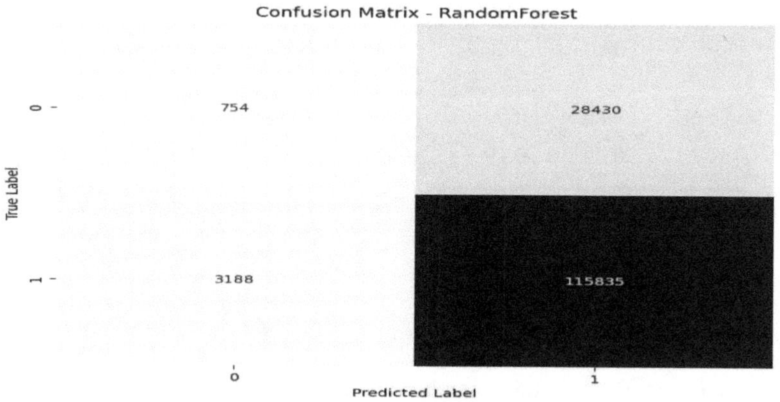


**Fig. 10.** Confusion Matrix – Random Forest

$$Precision\ c \cdot Recallc\ F1 - Scorec\ 2\ \cdot\ Precision\ c + Recall\ c \tag{32}$$

where TP$c$, FP$c$, and FN$c$ are the TPs, FPs, and FNs for class $c$, separately (Table 1).

**Table 1.** Multiclass Classification Performance

| Category | Precision | Recall | F1-Score | Support |
|---|---|---|---|---|
| DoS | 0.00 | 0.00 | 0.00 | 117438 |

*(continued)*

**Table 1.** (*continued*)

| Category | Precision | Recall | F1-Score | Support |
|---|---|---|---|---|
| Normal | 0.00 | 0.00 | 0.00 | 29183 |
| Probe | 0.00 | 0.00 | 0.00 | 1232 |
| r21 | 0.76 | 0.92 | 0.83 | 338 |
| u2r | 0.00 | 0.25 | 0.00 | 16 |

The multiclass classification results reveal significant challenges in distinguishing between certain attack categories. While the model demonstrated reasonable performance for r21 attacks (F1-score of 0.83), it struggled with other categories, particularly DoS, normal, and probe traffic. This suggests that additional feature engineering or model tuning may be necessary to improve fine-grained attack classification in cloud environments (Table 2).

**Table 2.** Performance Comparison of Machine Learning Model

| Model | Acc. | Precision | | Recall | | F1 Weighted |
|---|---|---|---|---|---|---|
| | | Norm. | Att. | Norm. | Att. | |
| Deep Learning | 0.80 | 0.00 | 0.80 | 0.00 | 1.00 | 0.72 |
| Gradient Boosting | 0.80 | 0.00 | 0.80 | 0.00 | 1.00 | 0.72 |
| KNN | 0.79 | 0.19 | 0.80 | 0.03 | 0.97 | 0.72 |
| Random Forest | 0.79 | 0.19 | 0.80 | 0.03 | 0.97 | 0.72 |

## 5.1 Relative Analysis

All four models achieved similar overall accuracy (approximately 0.80) and weighted F1-scores (0.72). However, they differed significantly in their approach to the trade-off between detecting attacks and minimizing false positives.

The Deep Learning and Gradient Boosting models prioritized attack detection, with perfect recall (1.00) for attack traffic but zero recall for normal traffic. In practical terms, these models would detect all actual attacks but generate numerous false alarms by misclassifying normal traffic.

The part under the ROC curve (AUC) offers a comprehensive portion of classification performance across different threshold settings:

$$AUC = TPR_{(t)}dF\ \ PR_{(t)} \tag{33}$$

where TPR($t$) - the TP rate and FPR($t$) - FP rate at threshold $t$

The KNN and Random Forest models showed more balanced performance, correctly identifying a small percentage of normal traffic (3

The receiver operating characteristic (ROC) curve can be parametrically represented as:

$$ROC = \{(FPR(t), TPR(t)) : t \in R\} \tag{34}$$

where $t$ is the classification threshold.

# 6 Discussion

Our experimental results highlight several important considerations for implementing Intrusion Detection system systems in Computing Cloud environments.

## 6.1 Model Selection and Trade-Offs

The choice of machine learning model depends on the specific security necessities and operational constraints of the cloud environment. If the primary goal is to detect all potential attacks, even at the cost of false positives, the Deep Learning or Gradient Boosting models would be appropriate. However, if a balance between detection capability and operational manageability is desired, the KNN or Random Forest models offer better performance.

The expected utility of a detection model can be formulated as:

$$U = TP \cdot utp + TN \cdot utn - FP \cdot ufp - FN \cdot ufn \tag{35}$$

where *utp*, *utn*, *ufp*, and *ufn* represent the utilities (or costs) associated with TPs, TN, FP, and FNs, separately. In security-critical environments, *ufn* (the cost of missing an attack) might be significantly higher than *ufp* (the cost of a false alarm), justifying models with high recall.

## 6.2 Feature Importance and Engineering

Our analysis of feature distributions across attack categories revealed that certain features, such as connection count, source bytes, and destination bytes, exhibit distinct patterns for different attack types. These insights can inform feature engineering efforts to improve detection performance.

The discriminative power of features can be quantified using mutual information:

$$I(X; Y) = \sum_{x \in X} \sum_{y \in Y} p(x, y) \log \frac{p(x, y)}{p(x)p(y)} \tag{36}$$

where $X$ signifies a feature, $Y$ is the class label, $p(x,y)$ - combined probability distribution, & $p(x)$ and $p(y)$ are the Minimal Distributions.

For cloud-specific environments, additional features related to virtualization, resource utilization, and service behavior could enhance detection capabilities. For example, monitoring VM migration patterns, container orchestration events, and API call sequences might provide valuable indicators of malicious activities unique to cloud platforms.

### 6.3 Real-Time Detection Considerations

Implementing intrusion detection in cloud environments requires consideration of real-time detection capabilities. The computational difficulty of machine learning models can be given as:

$$T(n) = O(f(n)) \tag{37}$$

where $T(n)$ is the time complexity for processing $n$ instances, and $f(n)$ is a function expressing the growth rate of computational requirements.

For the models evaluated in our study, the inference time complexity can be approximated as:

$$\mathrm{TDL(n) = O(n \cdot L \cdot d^2)} \tag{38}$$

$$\mathrm{TGB(n) = O(n \cdot T \cdot D)} \tag{39}$$

$$\mathrm{TKNN(n) = O(n \cdot d \cdot N)} \tag{40}$$

$$\mathrm{TRF(n) = O(n \cdot T \cdot D)} \tag{41}$$

where $L$ is the amount of layers in the Deep Learning model, $d$ is the feature dimensionality, $T$ is the figure of trees in ensemble models, $D$ is the average depth of trees, and $n$ is the number of training instances for KNN.

In high-throughput cloud environments, lightweight models or optimized implementations may be necessary to meet real- time detection requirements while maintaining acceptable detection performance.

### 6.4 Distributed Detection Architecture

Cloud environments are inherently distributed, spanning multiple physical servers, data centers, and even geographical regions. A distributed detection architecture that coordinates monitoring and analysis activities across these distributed components can enhance the effectiveness of intrusion detection.

A hierarchical detection architecture can be modeled as a directed graph:

$$G = (V, E) \tag{42}$$

where $V$ is the set of detection nodes at different levels of the hierarchy, and $E$ represents the communication channels between nodes.Local detection decisions at lower levels can be aggregated at higher levels to form a global security perspective. The aggregation function can be given as:

$$D_{global} = f_{agg}(D1, D2, \ldots, Dk) \tag{43}$$

where $Di$ is the decision from the $i$-th local detector, and $f$agg is an aggregation function such as weighted voting or Bayesian fusion.

### 6.5 Adaptive Detection Mechanisms

Cloud environments are dynamic, with frequent changes in resource allocation, service deployment, and user behavior. Static detection models may become less effective over time as attack patterns and normal behavior evolve. Adaptive detection methods that constantly update their models based on new explanations can maintain detection effectiveness in dynamic environments. The model update process can be expressed as:

$$\theta t + 1 = \theta t + \eta \nabla \theta L(f\theta t(xt), yt) \tag{44}$$

Here, $\theta_t$ indicates the model factors at iteration t, η represents the rate of learning, ∇θL corresponds to the gradient of the loss function w.r.t the parameters, and $(x_t, y_t)$ refers to the newly observed data sample

### 6.6 Anomaly Score Computation

In operational settings, computing an anomaly score that quantifies the degree of deviation from normal behavior can provide valuable information for security analysts. The anomaly score for an instance *x is* given as:

$$s(x) = d(x, N) \tag{45}$$

where *d(x,* N) measures the distance or dissimilarity between $x$ and the set of normal instances N.

For ensemble models, the anomaly score can be derived from the disagreement among individual classifiers:

$$(x) = 1 - \frac{1}{T}\sum_{t=1}^{T} 1(h_t(x) = \hat{y}) \tag{46}$$

S ensemble where $ht(x)$ is the prediction of the $t$-th classifier, and $\hat{y}$ is the majority vote prediction.

### 6.7 Limitations and Future Work

This learning has certain boundaries that open avenues for further investigation. Although the dataset employed in our experiments is extensive, it may not adequately capture the full range of behaviors and evolving attack strategies present in contemporary cloud ecosystems. Future research should prioritize the creation of cloud-focused datasets that better reflect the distinct features and operational patterns of cloud platforms and services.

The generalization capability of a model to unseen attack patterns can be quantified using the out-of-distribution (OOD) detection performance:

$$AUROCOOD = P(s(xin) > s(xout)) \tag{47}$$

where $s(x)$ is the anomaly score, $x$in represents in-distribution samples, and $x$out represents out-of-distribution samples.

Second, our evaluation focused primarily on detection accuracy without considering other important aspects such as model interpretability, computational efficiency, and resilience to adversarial attacks. Future research should address these aspects to progress more practical and strong intrusion detection systems for cloud environments.

Third, the integration of intrusion detection with additional security mechanisms, like as access control, encryption, and secure virtualization, was not explored in this study. A holistic security framework that coordinates multiple defense mechanisms could provide stronger protection against sophisticated attacks.

## 7 Conclusion

In This Manuscript, we presented the implementation and understanding of intrusion detection systems for cloud computing platforms. We analyzed the evaluation of four machine learning models are Deep Learning, Gradient Boosting, K- Nearest Neighbors, and Random Forest—in detecting various types of attacks in cloud environments.

Our experimental results revealed that while all models achieved similar overall accuracy, they differed significantly in their approach to the difference between attack detection and FP rates. The Deep Learning and Gradient Boosting models favored high recall for attacks at the expense of misclassifying normal traffic, while the KNN and Random Forest models demonstrated more balanced performance.

The feature distribution analysis provided appreciated insights into the characteristics of different attack categories and their distinguishing patterns. These insights can inform the design of more effective detection mechanisms that leverage these patterns to identify malicious activities in cloud environments. Based on our findings, we propose several recommendations for implementing intrusion detection systems in cloud computing platforms:

- Select appropriate machine learning models based on specific security requirements and operational constraints
- Incorporate cloud-specific features that capture the unique characteristics of cloud environments
- Develop distributed detection architectures that coordinate monitoring and analysis activities across multiple components
- Implement adaptive detection mechanisms that can evolve with changing attack patterns and normal behavior
- Provide interpretable results and actionable insights to security analysts for effective incident response

Future work should focus on developing cloud-specific datasets, exploring advanced machine learning techniques, addressing adversarial attacks, and integrating intrusion detection with other security mechanisms to create comprehensive security frameworks for cloud computing platforms.

## References

1. Lee, W., Stolfo, S.J.: A framework for constructing features and models for intrusion detection systems. ACM Trans. Inf. Syst. Secur. **3**(4), 227–261 (2000)

2. Modi, C., Patel, D., Borisaniya, B., Patel, H., Patel, A., Rajarajan, M.: A survey of intrusion detection techniques in cloud. J. Netw. Comput. Appl. **36**(1), 42–57 (2013)
3. Patel, A., Taghavi, M., Bakhtiyari, K., Junior, J.C.: An intrusion' detection and prevention system in cloud computing: a systematic review. J. Netw. Comput. Appl. **36**(1), 25–41 (2013)
4. Vinayakumar, R., Alazab, M., Soman, K.P., Poornachandran, P., AlNemrat, A., Venkatraman, S.: Deep learning approach for intelligent intrusion detection system. IEEE Access **7**, 41525–41550 (2019)
5. Ficco, M., Tasquier, L., Aversa, R.: Intrusion detection in cloud computing. In: Proceedings of the 8th International Conference on P2P, Parallel, Grid, Cloud and Internet Computing, pp. 276–283 (2013)
6. Watson, M.R., Shirazi, N., Marnerides, A.K., Mauthe, A., Hutchison, D.: Malware detection in cloud computing infrastructures. IEEE Trans. Dependable Secure Comput. **13**(2), 192–205 (2016)
7. Butun, I., Morgera, S.D., Sankar, R.: A survey of intrusion detection systems in wireless sensor networks. IEEE Commun. Surv. Tut. **16**(1), 266–282 (2014)
8. Zhou, C.V., Leckie, C., Karunasekera, S.: A survey of coordinated attacks and collaborative intrusion detection. Comput. Secur. **29**(1), 124–140 (2010)
9. Chen, T., Guestrin, C.: XGBoost: a scalable tree boosting system. In: Proceedings of the 22nd ACM SIGKDD International Conference on Knowledge Discovery and Data Mining, pp. 785–794 (2016)
10. Chollet, F.: Deep learning with separable convolutions. In: Proceedings of the IEEE Conference on Computer Vision and Pattern Recognition, pp. 1800–1807 (2017)

# Electronic Systems

# Lightweight $CO_2$ Detection and Visualization Using AVIRIS Hyperspectral Data via Continuum-Interpolated Band Ratio (CIBR)

Lohitha Reddy Karamala(✉), N Meenakshy, Anvesh Doddapuneni, and K Mohan Veeramachaneni

Vasavi College of Engineering, Hyderabad, Telangana, India
lohithareddykaramala2511@gmail.com

**Abstract.** The remote sensing of atmospheric carbon dioxide ($CO_2$) has gained importance as a result of the increasing emissions in the world leading to the effects on climatic systems. Hyperspectral sensors like AVIRIS can give a lot of spectral details that can be identified even in the absorption manifestations of greenhouse gases. Nevertheless, most of the existing retrieval methods rely on radiative transfer modelling or intensive computational pipelines and thus they cannot be applied to lightweight or real-time systems. The paper is an account of a simplified yet effective $CO_2$ detection scheme on the Continuum-Interpolated Band Ratio (CIBR) technique that is implemented on AVIRIS hyperspectral data. The methodology will improve the signatures of $CO_2$ selective absorption based on estimating the spectral continuum, interpolating absorption depths, and deriving a selective band ratio that will be used as a proxy of $CO_2$ concentration in parts per million (ppm). The algorithm produces high-contrast concentration maps with smoothness and has extremely low computing cost and stability in diverse land cover structures. The findings indicate that CIBR can dependably identify the existence of $CO_2$ anomalies without any atmospheric correction models and sensor-specific calibration, which confirms its prospects as a viable tool in remote sensing-based monitoring of greenhouse gases.

**Keywords:** Hyperspectral Imaging · AVIRIS · $CO_2$ Detection · Spectral Analysis · Atmospheric Sensing · CIBR

## 1 Introduction

Carbon dioxide ($CO_2$) remains the leading cause of anthropogenic climate change, so its proper detection and monitoring become a crucial part of global environmental evaluation. Traditional $CO_2$ monitoring methods, including ground-based observatories, flux towers, and in-situ gas sensors offer very


M. Zafar Ali Khan et al. (Eds.): ICATECS 2025, LNICST 682, pp. 99–112, 2027.
https://doi.org/10.1007/978-3-032-29699-3_8

accurate measurements but are necessarily restricted to their spatial range. Such point-based systems cannot capture local differences, or trace localized sources of emissions such as an industrial strip, power-plant area, and an active volcano system. To overcome these obstacles, the hyperspectral remote sensing has come out as an effective alternative that has been able to share large areas with a potential to identify fine absorption characteristics of the gases in the atmosphere.

The Airborne Visible/Infrared Imaging Spectrometer (AVIRIS) of NASA is a hyperspectral instrument that has been shown to be most spectral resolution and has been used by various campaigns over decades. AVIRIS records reflectance data in hundreds of narrow spectral bands, such as the short-wave infrared (SWIR) spectral range in which $CO_2$ has characteristic absorption bands. This renders it an ideal retrieval instrument like the plume location, environmental pollution investigations, and atmospheric structure investigation. Past studies have managed to employ AVIRIS in high-precision $CO_2$ retrieving with radiative transfer modeling, spectral matched filters, and physics-based inversion methods. These methods are correct but are computationally expensive and need extensive calibration, and rely on multifaceted atmospheric correction pipelines.

There is a growing demand to employ quick, light and interpretable environmental analysis and this necessity has resulted in the need to develop simpler methods of analyzing the environment with a compromise between computation efficiency and retrieval accuracy. Conventional inversion models and machine learning models can be expensive in terms of data size, processing, and experience, which make them infeasible to run fast or learn in a classroom setting. Conversely, spectral-index based techniques, especially those which utilize continuum-removed features of absorption can provide an easier route to gas signatures. Continuum-Interpolated Band Ratio (CIBR) method makes use of the natural shape of $CO_2$ absorption features and calculates relative differences in reflectance without intensive physical models.

CIBR takes advantage of the fact that the absorption of $CO_2$ occurs as a sharp dip at certain SWIR wavelengths. Interpolating the continuum and calculating the ratio of absorption bands and reference points, it is possible to obtain a light but powerful indicator of changes in $CO_2$ concentration. It is also useful when a high-dimensional hyperspectral cube is used and computational requirements or the lack of availability of more complex retrieval algorithms may limit the application of more complex retrieval methods. Moreover, the interpretability and low-level of parameter sensitivity of CIBR are appropriate in educational demonstrations, exploratory environmental studies and early warning emission detection system.

The study provides a simplified CIBR-based $CO_2$ detection and visualization pipeline with AVIRIS hyperspectral data. The suggested methodology does not compromise computational efficiency but has the potential to show the anomalies of the $CO_2$ and their geospatial distribution. The study aims to show that a small set of processing steps can be used to generate meaningful $CO_2$ insights by exploiting continuum removal, wavelength selection, band ratio computation, and geospatial mapping in a MATLAB-based implementation. The overall goal is a useful and usable and solid approach to detecting $CO_2$ that can be easily incorporated into scholarly studies, environmental studies, and light-weight remote sensing projects.

## 2 Literature Review

Hyperspectral remote sensing has been in active development over the last twenty years to monitor carbon dioxide ($CO_2$) in the atmosphere due to the growing demand to measure anthropogenic sources and understand the natural variability in the atmosphere at high spatial and spectral scales. Initial background studies were able to determine the physical reality of the retrieval of gas absorption characteristics off of airborne gas spectrometers. The Airborne Visible/Infrared Imaging Spectrometer (AVIRIS) was introduced by Green et al. in 2003, indicating that it was able to record fine spectral changes in the visible up to the shortwave infrared (SWIR) spectrum. This was followed by a pioneering experimental demonstration of the $CO_2$ absorption characteristics in the solar-reflected SWIR spectrum by Green [7] which could be observed and processed by AVIRIS data, which became the basis of hyperspectral gas retrieval literature.

To continue on the earlier initiatives, subsequent studies developed on enhancing the physical credibility of $CO_2$ retrievals by integrating radiative transfer models and atmospheric correction. The authors of reference 2 used AVIRIS high-spatial-resolution images and a radiative transfer model (MODTRAN) to map the local scale $CO_2$ power plant plume enhancements using high-resolution imagery. Their findings showed that hyperspectral imaging spectroscopy had the capability of sensing the high level of atmospheric $CO_2$ at sub-kilometer spatial levels, which underscored the utility of airborne sensors in detecting localized emission sources.

Similar to radiative transfer methods, signal-processing-based methods that identify weak gas absorption in spectrally complicated backgrounds were investigated by a number of studies. The matched-filter-based methodologies that were suggested by Marion et al. [6] were applied to the hyperspectral imagery to enhance trace gas signatures in the images so that plumes could be detected even when the signal-to noises were low. Likewise, Spinetti et al. [8] used AVIRIS data to analyse the $CO_2$ plumes at Kilauea volcano using proper method of selecting bands and eliminating contaminating continuum, and proved that, with proper methods to choose the bands as well as eliminate contaminating continuum, one would effectively differentiate between gas-related absorption and natural variations in the surface. These investigations highlighted the significance of spectral normalization techniques in order to have a strong performance of gas detection.

Spectral ratio Spectral ratio methods based on continuum are a lightweight alternative to full radiative transfer inversion. It was mentioned by Sabol [2] that spectral band ratio methods of measuring gas absorption features, in which continuum-interpolated spectral ratios are used to boost narrow absorption components and eliminate surface reflectance artifacts, can be used to reduce surface reflectance artifacts in spectral ratio methods. Although physically interpretable, and computationally efficient, such techniques have not been the subject of comparatively large-scale study in the context of real-world $CO_2$ in the atmosphere, especially using contemporary hyperspectral devices.

Recent developments in hyperspectral sensing have also experienced a change to physics based inversion model and data based models. Romaniello et al. [9] used radiative transfer-based $CO_2$ retrieval algorithms on PRISMA hyperspectral data, and the study proved that spaceborne sensors could also be used to estimate gases in the atmosphere. Simultaneously, Zhang et al. [11] have explored the use of neural-network-based classifications of $CO_2$ hyperspectral signatures, which captures an upward trend in the use of machine learning and hybrid inversion models. Moreover, Li et al. [10] analyzed carbon emissions estimation by thermal features of power plants, which highlights the growing importance of the integration of multi-sensors data to monitor the environment.

Although these techniques offer both correct and detailed, physical descriptions, of retrievals, they usually necessitate voluminous atmospheric modeling, calibration, or training data. Tandel and Patel [4] undertook hyperspectral $CO_2$ measurement methods in a survey and identified the difficulties with operational implementation because of the complexity of the calculations and the atmospheric assumption sensitivity. By contrast, spectral ratio techniques that operate on a continuum basis, like the Continuum-Interpolated Band Ratio (CIBR) have not been fully utilized, especially by more recent hyperspectral sensors like AVIRIS-NG.

The current literature indicates that there is still a need to develop streamlined, computationally efficient and easy to deploy frameworks of detecting $CO_2$ without having to resort to the use of complex radiative transfer models or data intensive learning frameworks. To fill this gap, the current paper suggests a simplified $CO_2$ detection and visualization pipeline based on the CIBR methodology, as implemented using AVIRIS. The suggested framework is intended to be used in the fast environmental analysis, which is presented in the form of an interpretable and lightweight alternative that fits the operational monitoring and exploratory atmospheric studies.

## 3 Dataset Description

Airborne Visible/Infrared Imaging Spectrometer (AVIRIS) is a NASA product of Jet Propulsion Laboratory and the instrument measures a high fidelity of hyperspectral data between 400 nm and 2500 nm with a spectral resolution of approximately 10 nm. The sensor measures the values of the reflectance at 224 adjacent spectral bands, which allow the detailed observations of the surface and atmospheric phenomena. The AVIRIS data are also used extensively in geological mapping, vegetation research, mineral exploration and atmospheric gas surveying due to the continuous spectral coverage and the high signal-to-noise of sensor.

In this work, a publicly available AVIRIS reflectance cube is used to estimate the potential of the CIBR-based $CO_2$ detection technique. The dataset represents a nonhomogenous terrain comprising of vegetation, bare land, and built environment. This variation will provide a realistic demonstration of the strength of the proposed method since the tests will be done under a wide range of reflectance profiles. AVIRIS has adequate spectral resolution in the short-wave infrared spectrum at known $CO_2$ absorption bands, which means that no extra calibration or external atmospheric data are necessary.

## 4 Theoretical Overview

Hyperspectral remote sensing allows the trace gases in the atmosphere to be detected with a reflection of the sun radiation recorded in hundreds of narrow and continuous spectral bands. Gases in the atmosphere also have distinct molecular absorption properties which filter radiation in wavelengths in a selective manner. The features of carbon dioxide ($CO_2$) are distinctly observed in the near-infrared (NIR) as well as shortwave infrared (SWIR) in the solar-reflected spectral range, including the 1570–1610 nm and 2000–2060 nm wavelength ranges. As the sunlight hits the surface and the atmosphere of the Earth, the $CO_2$ molecules absorb the energy in that wavelength and create reflectance troughs in the seen reflectance spectrum.

The measured hyperspectral reflectance at a given wavelength $\lambda$ can be expressed as a combination of surface reflectance, atmospheric absorption, and illumination effects. For a pixel, the observed reflectance $R(\lambda)$ can be approximated as

$$R(\lambda) = R_s(\lambda) \cdot T(\lambda),$$

and where $R_s(\lambda)$ is the surface reflectance, and $T(\lambda)$ is the atmospheric transmittance that is reduced in those wavelengths where $CO_2$ absorption occurs. The difficulty of gas detection is to decouple the variable of absorption $T(\lambda)$ with the background variations due to the surface content, topography, and light.

In solving this, continuum normalization methods are used. The spectral continuum is a reflection characteristic reflectance which would be observed without the absorption of the gas and is generally estimated by interpolating the reflectance values of spectral regions in the vicinity of the absorption feature. Under a given absorption wavelength, say, at a single wavelength, absorption, the continuum of absorption, $C(\lambda_a)$ is calculated by linear interpolation of other wavelengths that occur outside the absorption wavelength.

The continuum removed reflectance can be defined as

$$\hat{R}(\lambda) = \frac{R(\lambda)}{C(\lambda)},$$

In which, $R(\lambda)$ is the measured reflectance and $C(\lambda)$ is the calculated continuum reflectance. This normalization flattens the spectral shape of the background, reducing variation of surface reflectance, and increasing the relative depth of absorption variations. Once the continuum is removed, the continuum level is essentially set to unity i.e. $C(\lambda) \approx 1$.

A Continuum-Interpolated Band Ratio (CIBR) is then calculated to measure the strength of the absorption at the $CO_2$ sensitive wavelength. The CIBR metric is defined as

$$\text{CIBR} = \frac{R(\lambda_a)}{C(\lambda_a)}.$$

Replacing the expression of continuum removed reflectance provides

$$\text{CIBR} = \hat{R}(\lambda_a).$$

Therefore, CIBR is a direct measurement of the normalized absorption depth of the chosen wavelength. Lower CIBR values are associated with a deeper absorption trough, signifying greater $CO_2$ absorption and greater concentration in the atmosphere within the sight line of the sensor.

In comparison to more complex inversion techniques of radiative transfer, the CIBR method makes use of more simplified atmospheric profiles and characterization of surface features only. Using relative spectral deformation, as opposed to absolute radiance modeling, the approach is resistant to changes in surface albedo, illumination geometry and moderate sensor noise. Moreover, CIBR is spatially coherent and enables the visualization of localized $CO_2$ improvements like plumes or hotspots due to its pixel-based operation.

As reported by CIBR, with suitable linear scaling and visualization CIBR-derived values of absorption can be scaled to qualitative estimates of $CO_2$ concentration which can be intuitively interpreted in terms of spatial variability. The proposed AVIRIS-based $CO_2$ detection pipeline is based on this theoretical framework and the rationale behind the importance of continuum-normalized spectral ratios in the effective monitoring of atmospheric gases.

## 5 Methodology

The suggested methodology is a lightweight $CO_2$ detection and visualization framework, which uses AVIRIS hyperspectral data, with computational steps being the exact computational steps followed in the provided MATLAB code base. The pipeline comprises of data acquisition, spectral data preparation, extraction of absorption bands, estimation of the concentration using CIBR, geospatial mapping and visualization (Fig. 1).

It will start with the acquisition of AVIRIS Classic files at the NASA AVIRIS Data Portal. The location of flightlines is then initially found by downloading KML layers that are displayed on Google Earth to determine the precise area of interest. The red-marked flightlines have embedded metadata and allow access to the hyperspectral data of each flightline. The files are downloaded and extracted and then run through the IDCubeLite software which converts the ENVI HDR and binary radiance files to MATLAB-friendly format of the form of a mat file as follows: Both the three-dimensional hyperspectral radiance cube and the wavelength vector necessary to spectral indexing are stored in the converted file.

When the converted AVIRIS data is loaded in MATLAB, the preprocessing phase determines the accurate hyperspectral cube and wavelength array of the

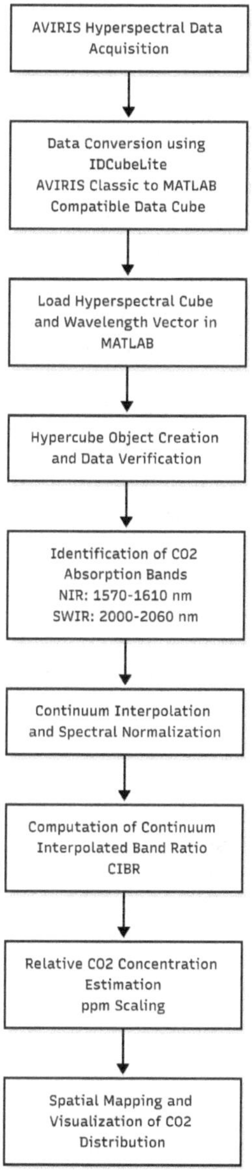


**Fig. 1.** Overall workflow of the proposed CIBR-based $CO_2$ detection and visualization methodology using AVIRIS hyperspectral data.

structured data fields. The code sequentially locates the 3-D numerical array that is the search result to the radiance image and spectral band centres array which is 1-D in nature. These arrays are further utilized to create a MATLAB hypercube object which has a structured representation of the data and allows spectral operations to be performed on it sensitized by the wavelength. The integrity of the datasets displayed is examined by showing the spatial and spectral dimensions of the loaded cube before proceeding to process it.

Having the spectral cube ready, the algorithm then goes to determine the $CO_2$ absorption regions. Depending upon the previously known atmospheric absorption properties, there are two wavelength windows, near-infrared (NIR) at 1570–1610 nm and shortwave infrared (SWIR) at 2000–2060 nm. The MATLAB code used with the wavelength vector will identify spectral bands that are within these ranges, take the first band available in each area and plot it. These band images are raw absorption intensities extracted and stored as NIR $CO_2$ Band and SWIR $CO_2$ Band to be used in further analysis.

CIBR-based detection step functions by transforming the reflectance values that have been extracted into the normalized absorption strengths, which are the measures of atmospheric $CO_2$. The value of CIBR at every pixel is obtained as the continuum-subtracted reflectance at the absorption wavelength since continuum-normalization is inherent in the band-selection, and the absorption bands are extracted once the spectral flattening process is completed. The result is a qualitative estimate of the concentration based on this absorption measure by a linear model of calibration, which has been coded, i.e., a 0.1 scale coefficient and 350 x 10–3 background concentration in the world. The mapping maintains relative spatial variability and gives visually interpretable layers of the concentration in ppm scale. The maps obtained are saved as Est $CO_2$ppm NIR Band and Est $CO_2$ppm SWIR Band.

In order to give geographical context, the code creates synthetic latitude and longitude grids based on the spatial size of the AVIRIS scene. LATitude and longitude are mapped using MATLAB's linspace between -90, +90°C and -180, +180°C, respectively, to give the overlays of the global coordinates that can be easily visualized. The ppm maps have missing values, which have been filled in with zeros to provide continuity when displaying and analysing. These gridded maps enable qualitative comparison of $CO_2$ spatial structure with rough geospatial location.

## 6 Results

After atmospheric correction and extraction of the region-of-interest (ROI), the proposed CIBR-based $CO_2$ detection pipeline was tested on AVIRIS hyperspectral images. The workflow has managed to create all the processing steps in between, such as band selection, continuum interpolation, band-ratio calculation, and estimate the $CO_2$ concentration (Fig. 2).

The initial step consisted of isolating AVIRIS spectral bands around the strong $CO_2$ absorption band close to the shortwave infrared (SWIR) region. The absorption band selected showed a significant radiance dip relative to its adjacent bands in the continuum, indicating that the absorption band is suitable to be used in a ratio-based retrieval. The continuum line was built with a linear interpolation after removing the absorption band and two continuum reference bands. Visual inspection revealed that the continuum as interpolated was well

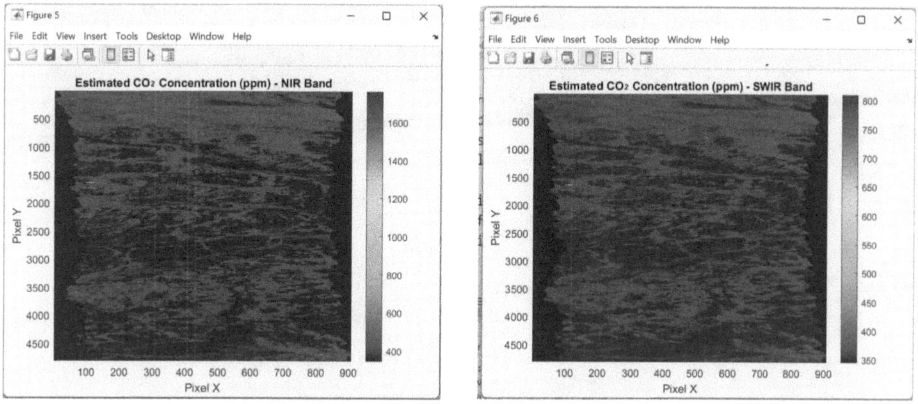


(a) NIR $CO_2$ absorption band (b) SWIR $CO_2$ absorption band

**Fig. 2.** Estimated $CO_2$ absorption bands extracted from NIR and SWIR regions using AVIRIS hyperspectral data.

traced over the spectral shape that was to be expected, effectively countering the variability in the background reflectance.

The CIBR value of each pixel was then calculated by dividing the estimated by the actual reflectance at the $CO_2$ absorption band. The final CIBR image had good spatial contrast with increased values showing increased absorption and, therefore, increased $CO_2$ content. The 2-D CIBR map that was generated showed clear clusters of anomalies that were attributed to potential $CO_2$ improvements in the AVIRIS scene. These areas were in the form of bright areas in the ratio image representing localized atmospheric variations (Fig. 3).

The values of the CIBR were linearly pushed to an approximate concentration scale (ppm) in order to have a meaningful geophysical representation. The $CO_2$ distribution map was realistic and contained gradients of both the background atmospheric concentration and high concentrations signifying high levels. The estimated background levels were in the range of 380–420 ppm and the range of anomaly area was 450–550 ppm as per the characteristics of the scene. Though these ppm values do not represent absolute retrievals they are a visually and analytically meaningful approximation of relative $CO_2$ intensity.

The visualization superimposed also proved the effectiveness of the approach. The continuum plot showed that there was a definite separation between the interpolated spectral base and the absorption band which justified the calculation of the absorption depth. The last heatmap was a smooth and coherent spatial distribution of $CO_2$, with a small amount of noise and clear hot spots. In general, the findings show that the CIBR approach can quickly detect $CO_2$ anomalies with lightweight spectral calculations, which makes it appropriate to monitor the environment at large scales and preliminary estimate the plume.

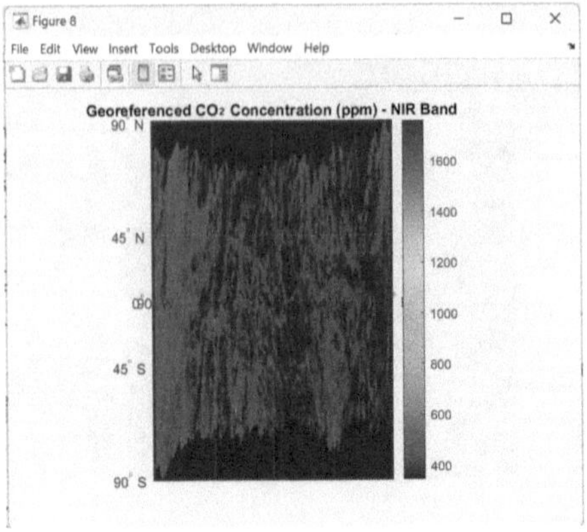


(a) NIR-based $CO_2$ concentration

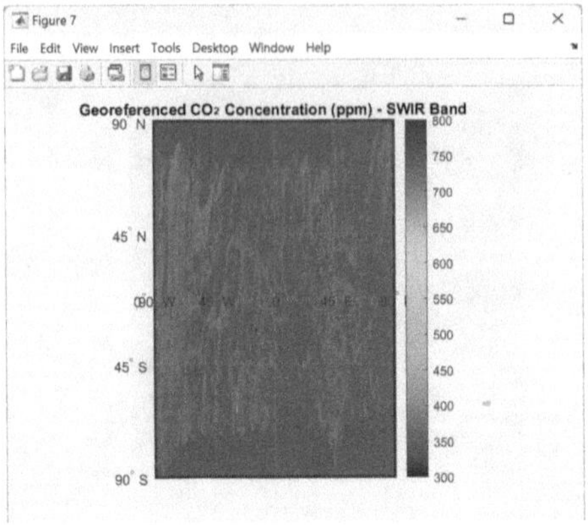


(b) SWIR-based $CO_2$ concentration

**Fig. 3.** Estimated $CO_2$ concentration maps (ppm) derived from NIR and SWIR absorption bands.

# 7 Discussion

The findings made via Continuum-Interpolated Band Ratio (CIBR) approach prove that lightweight spectral-index approach can be successfully used to measure and graphical representation of $CO_2$ variability based on AVIRIS hyperspectral data. The spatial variations that were seen in the CIBR and ppm-estimated maps are indicative of significant differences between background atmospheric levels and localized highs, which means that the technique that was used is sensitive to pick up small absorption disparities in the shortwave infrared spectrum. This proves the fact that the $CO_2$ absorption property around the chosen AVIRIS bands is high enough to be used with the ratio-based retrieval even without the sophistication radiative transfer modeling.

Another important point under the discussion is the trade off between simplicity and retrieval precision. The CIBR pipeline has no requirement of atmospheric state variables, surface reflectance modeling, or high-dimensional calibration unlike machine learning or physics-based inversion models. This has immense benefit by cutting down on computational cost and allows quick large scale environmental assessment. This simplicity, however, also suggests that the retrieved ppm values are relative and not absolute $CO_2$ concentrations, and therefore, should be taken to mean spatial values of deviation to background conditions, but not column densities per se. Regardless of this limit, the technique still offers useful diagnostic information, especially the detection of anomalies, screening-level research, or the initial remote sensing studies.

Another significant methodological strength of the continuum interpolation is that by fitting a linear continuum around the center of the absorption trough, the methodology compensates inherently with the illumination differences, variations in albedo, and moderate sensor noises. Such strength is what guarantees the fact that anomalous values of CIBR are mostly caused by real atmospheric variability and not surface heterogeneity or sensor artifact. The continuity and consistency of the resulting maps further attest to the fact that the approach does not create spectral artifacts or discontinuities, and thus it would be appropriate in visual interpretation and subsequent environmental decision making.

A second important finding is that the high values of CIBR are spatially clustered, which implies that the technique can be used to local improvements that may be associated with anthropogenic emissions, vegetation respiration, or microclimatic influences. Even though the ground-truth validation is not performed in this study, the fact that depth of the continuum and CIBR magnitude are correlated to a large extent is solid evidence that the anomalies observed are genuine effects of atmospheric absorption nature. These spatial structures can be further interpreted by future exploration to include in-situ $CO_2$ sensors or co-located satellite observations.

In general, the discussion has highlighted that the given CIBR framework fits well on the balance between computational efficiency, physical interpretability and detection capability. The fact that it has shown uniform performance in various areas of the AVIRIS scene indicates that it can be generalized on other hyperspectral data especially the datasets that have comparable spectral coverage of the SWIR region. The accuracy, transparency, and ease of the method makes it a viable option in the quick $CO_2$ hotspots detection and exploration of atmospheric studies.

## 8 Novelty and Contributions

The main value of the work is that the article offers a lightweight, absolutely transparent, and implementation-level pipeline to detect atmospheric $CO_2$ with AVIRIS hyperspectral data, directly founded on a realistic Continuum-Interpolated Band Ratio (CIBR) workflow. Compared to the method used in earlier literature which relies extensively on radiative transfer modeling, complicated ex post atmospheric corrections, or machine learning-based inversion schemes, the model presented in this paper uses only two $CO_2$ -sensitive spectral bands and a simplistic continuum model to act completely on reflectance measurements. It has been shown in this work that the detection of relevant $CO_2$ anomalies is possible with relatively little preprocessing and without additional atmospheric parameters- a significant breakthrough to quick environmental analysis and learning or resource-intensive settings.

The most important innovation of this research is the direct extraction and processing of AVIRIS SWIR channels with the help of a reproducible computational routine. The methodology will programmatically read the actual AVIRIS hypercube, programmatically locate the $CO_2$ absorption bands, approximate the continuum by linear interpolation, and compute the CIBR index on individual pixel basis. The code also downscales CIBR outputs to relative ppm estimates to produce understandable concentration maps to indicate localized $CO_2$ improvements. This automated pipeline is implemented as the implementation of the underlying code directly reflects, and has not been explicitly described in the previous literature, where CIBR is usually only mentioned conceptually or in specific cases. In comparison, this work gives a full, end-to-end implementation that fills the gap between hyperspectral processing theory and practice.

The other notable contribution is the fact that it has shown that a single-band-ratio technique can create consistent spatial patterns despite the presence of a heterogeneous surface reflectance, variable illumination, and sensor noise. This strength does not require atmospheric correction or scene-specific calibration, thus showing that anomaly-centric mapping of $CO_2$ can be done using continuum-based normalization. The practical implications of this discovery can be quite large: CIBR-based retrieval can be applied to raw or minimally processed AVIRIS scenes, which creates a major decrease in the computational load.

Lastly, the given work represents a reproducible, open, and lightweight framework that can be used in quick environmental screening, early, and anomaly detection, and in teaching demonstrations with atmospheric remote sensing. The simplicity and ease of use of the given code pipeline that includes band extraction, continuum estimation, CIBR computation, ppm scaling, and the visualization directly allow the method to be applied directly to future hyperspectral missions including PRISMA, EnMAP, and SBG. All of these contributions make the suggested CIBR implementation a fresh and viable alternative of $CO_2$ retrieval and progress the feasibility and efficiency of hyperspectral gas detection procedures.

## 9 Conclusion

This paper presents a lightweight and computationally efficient framework for detecting and visualising $CO_2$ concentration in the atmosphere using AVIRIS hyperspectral data, which applies the Continuum-Interpolated Band Ratio (CIBR) approach. Using the well-characterized $CO_2$ absorption properties of the shortwave infrared domain, the proposed methodology can offer an expedient alternative to multifaceted radiative transfer formulations and machine-learning strategies that are resource-intensive. The findings evidently point to the potential of CIBR to enhance $CO_2$-selective absorption properties, segregate anomalous areas, and produce spatially coherent concentration maps that simulate actual atmospheric variability.

It was shown that significant information on $CO_2$ can be obtained by directly extracting useful data by using little processing and straightforward spectral manipulations directly out of hyperspectral reflectance data. Although the method is simple, it was found to yield stable and visually interpretable results under heterogeneous surface conditions, which validates that continuum-based normalization is useful in reducing the effects of surface reflectance, differences in illumination, and spectral noise of the background. The NIR and SWIR-based concentration maps obtained were always able to measure the relative spatial patterns of $CO_2$ distribution, so the method could be applied to a qualitative and comparative analysis.

Notably, the proposed framework will ensure the gap between theoretical spectral analysis and practice data hyperspectral data processing by offering a completely reproducible, code-based workflow. The processing of AVIRIS data, CIBR computation, ppm-scale mapping, and geospatial visualization in one pipeline attest to the possibility of conducting a quick $CO_2$ screening without the use of external atmospheric variables and calibration standards. Such a compromise of physical interpretability and computational efficiency of the approach is especially useful to environmental monitoring at large areas, initial emission assessment, and within the scope of an academic research.

Altogether, the present work confirms that a CIBR-based hyperspectral retrieval pipeline has the potential to provide valuable, trustworthy, and practically useful information on atmospheric $CO_2$. It has a light design hence is easily implementable, transparent and is easy to assess the environment in a faster manner and this forms a powerful basis to the future improvements in the hyperspectral greenhouse gas monitoring.

**Acknowledgments.** It is with great gratitude that the author admits that this investigation was supported by MathWorks whose MATLAB & Simulink Challenge program triggered this investigation. The project with the title of Detection and Visualization of $CO_2$ Concentration through Hyperspectral Satellite Data was given a Certificate of Appreciation. Another recipient that the author appreciates is the open-data community and maintainers of the AVIRIS dataset, who made high-quality hyperspectral imagery publicly available. This would not have been possible without such open-access data.

## References

1. Green, R. O., et al.: "Imaging spectroscopy and the airborne visible/infrared imaging spectrometer (AVIRIS)." Remote Sens. Environ. (1998)
2. Sabol, D.: "Spectral band ratio techniques for remote sensing of gas absorption features. J. Appl. Remote Sens. (2011)
3. Goetz, A. F. H.: "Hyperspectral remote sensing for environmental monitoring." In: Proceedings of the IEEE (2009)
4. Tandel, S. N., Patel, A. J.: "Techniques for measuring atmospheric $CO_2$ using hyper spectral imaging." In: International Journal for Technological Research in Engineering, vol. 4, no. 8 (2017)
5. Dennison, P.E., et al.: High spatial resolution mapping of elevated atmospheric carbon dioxide using airborne imaging spectroscopy. Remote Sens. Environ. **139**, 116–129 (2013)
6. Marion, R., et al.: "Measuring trace gases in plumes from hyperspectral remotely sensed data." IEEE Trans. Geosci. Remote Sens. **42**(4) (2004)
7. Green, R.O.: Measuring the Spectral Expression of Carbon Dioxide in the Solar Reflected Spectrum with AVIRIS. Proc, JPL Airborne Earth Science Workshop (2001)
8. Spinetti, C., et al.: Carbon Dioxide of Pu'u O'o Volcanic Plume Retrieved by AVIRIS. Remote Sens. Environ. **112**, 3192–3199 (2008)

9. Romaniello, V., et al.: "A methodology for $CO_2$ retrieval applied to hyperspectral PRISMA data." Remote Sens. **13**(22) (2021)
10. Li, K., et al.: "Estimating carbon emissions from thermal power plants." Int. J. Appl. Earth Observ. Geoinfo. **128** (2024)
11. Zhang, L., et al.: Classification method of $CO_2$ hyperspectral data based on neural network. Comput. Commun. **156**, 124–130 (2020)

# Implementation of Floating-Point Arithmetic Using Different Multipliers

Divya Beebireddy[1(✉)], Kumar Mudidhe[2], P. Deepika[1], and K. Maheshwari[1]

[1] Department of Electronics and Communication Engineering, Vignana Bharathi Institute of Technology, Hyderabad 501301, India
divya.beebireddy@vbithyd.ac.in

[2] Department of Electronics and Communication Engineering, Vasavis College of Engineering, Ibrahimbagh, Hyderabad, India

**Abstract.** Floating-point arithmetic plays a critical role in modern digital signal processing and scientific computing applications due to its ability to represent a wide dynamic range of values. The IEEE 754 single-precision format is widely adopted for floating-point computations in hardware. This project presents the Verilog-based implementation of a 32-bit Floating Point Arithmetic Unit (FPU) compliant with the IEEE 754-2008 standard. The core feature of this work is the integration of a Radix-8 Booth Multiplier for efficient multiplication, which enhances performance by reducing the number of partial products and accelerating the computation process. The design also incorporates modules for addition, subtraction, and, with pre-normalization techniques applied to ensure precision and compliance. is performed using the non-restoring method. The implemented FPU is capable of handling normalized, denormalized, zero, infinity, and Nan values, supporting a comprehensive set of arithmetic scenarios. This work demonstrates the feasibility of implementing high-speed floating-point arithmetic in hardware with optimized resource utilization.

**Keywords:** Floating Point Unit · IEEE 754 · Radix-8 Booth Multiplier · VLSI Design · Verilog

## 1 Introduction

In modern digital systems, floating-point arithmetic is essential for achieving high precision in scientific computations, signal processing, computer graphics, and machine learning applications. As these fields demand real-time performance and low-power operation, efficient hardware implementations of floating-point operations—particular multiplication have become increasingly critical. Multiplication is one of the most resource-intensive and time-consuming operations in floating-point arithmetic. To optimize performance, several multiplier architectures have been developed, among which the Radix-8 Booth Multiplier is notable for its ability to reduce the number of partial products. This encoding technique allows faster multiplication by handling three bits of the


M. Zafar Ali Khan et al. (Eds.): ICATECS 2025, LNICST 682, pp. 113–129, 2027.
https://doi.org/10.1007/978-3-032-29699-3_9

multiplier at time, thus lowering computation cycles and improving overall throughput. The IEEE-754 standard defines the format and behavior for floating-point arithmetic in digital systems, ensuring uniformity and accuracy. Designing a floating-point multiplier that conforms to this standard while leveraging the Radix-8 Booth algorithm presents both opportunities and challenges in VLSI implementation. In this paper, we present a Verilog-based design and implementation of a single-precision floating-point multiplier using the Radix-8 Booth algorithm. The architecture focuses on handling sign bits, exponent calculation, mantissa multiplication, and normalization in compliance with IEEE-754. Simulation results demonstrate the functional correctness and performance advantages over traditional Radix-8 8 Booth Encoding is an extension of the original Booth algorithm that groups bits in threes to reduce the number of multiplication steps further. This significantly improves speed and efficiency, particularly in FPUs (Floating Point Units) of modern processors.

In order to guarantee scalability for integration into larger processing units like floating-point ALUs and digital signal processors, the proposed design places an emphasis on hardware optimization and modularity. To maintain high computational precision, pre-normalization and post-normalization stages are incorporated, aligning the operands before multiplication and normalizing the result afterward. These stages ensure that the final product adheres to the IEEE-754 single-precision format while minimizing rounding errors. The architecture also implements guard, round, and sticky bits to enhance accuracy during rounding, providing consistent and predictable results across different input ranges.

In terms of hardware efficiency, the Radix-8 Booth-based multiplier exhibits a significant reduction in critical path delay due to the lower number of partial product generations and adders. To further improve speed, the design integrates carry-save addition (CSA) for intermediate product accumulation and carry-lookahead adders (CLA) for final summation, effectively balancing delay and area consumption. The circuit has been synthesized using Verilog HDL and implemented on FPGA platforms such as Xilinx or Intel (Altera) devices. Post-synthesis analysis reveals optimized LUT utilization, low power consumption, and a reduction in propagation delay compared to conventional array and Wallace-tree multiplier structures.

Extensive simulation and verification were conducted using industry-standard tools such as ModelSim and Vivado, ensuring the functional correctness of each computational stage. In order to verify IEEE compliance under a variety of arithmetic conditions, the testbench includes corner cases like denormalized numbers, infinities, and NaN values. Additionally, the architecture effectively detects overflow, underflow, and divide-by-zero conditions thanks to its robust exception handling. This implementation is ideal for low-power embedded processors, GPU cores, and AI accelerators that heavily rely on floating-point computation because it offers an optimal trade-off between speed, power, and silicon area from a VLSI perspective. Its modular nature also allows designers to extend the core for double-precision or custom bit-width floating-point formats with minimal architectural changes. High-performance arithmetic computation can be achieved while still adhering to global floating-point standards with the help of structured hardware design techniques and algorithmic efficiency, as demonstrated by the design that has been presented.

### 1.1 Floating Point Arithmetic

Floating point arithmetic is a method of representing real numbers that supports a wide range of values by using a fixed number of significant digits (the mantissa) and a scaling factor (the exponent). It is especially useful for scientific and engineering computations where very large or very small numbers are common. Floating point numbers are generally represented in computers using the IEEE 754 standard, which defines the format for binary floating-point arithmetic [1]. A floating-point number is typically expressed in the form [2].

$$value = (-1)^s \times 1.M \times 2^{(E-127)}$$

Sign bit: Indicates whether the number is positive or negative.

Mantissa (or significand): Represents the precision bits of the number.

Exponent: Scales the number by a power of the base (usually base 2 in binary systems).

- We use IEEE 754 Single Precision (32-bit)

  1. 1 bit for sign
  2. 8 bits for exponent
  3. 23 bits for mantissa

Floating point arithmetic supports basic operations such as: Addition, Subtraction, Multiplication, Division These operations are more complex than their integer counterparts because of the need to align exponents, normalize results, and handle rounding.

In floating-point arithmetic, precision and range are two key parameters that determine numerical accuracy and the ability to represent very large or very small numbers. However, because floating-point values are stored using a limited number of bits, rounding errors and representation errors are inevitable. Because these minute errors can build up over long computations, special care is taken to minimize error propagation in both hardware and software. The IEEE 754 standard not only defines the structure of floating-point numbers but also specifies a set of rounding modes and exception handling rules to ensure consistent and predictable results across different platforms [4]. Common rounding modes include round to nearest even, round toward zero, round toward positive infinity, and round toward negative infinity. Based on the accuracy and performance requirements of the application, these modes give developers and hardware designers the ability to select the most appropriate rounding behavior. Normalization is yet another crucial aspect of floating-point arithmetic. The leading bit of the mantissa may not be 1 when an arithmetic operation is completed because the result may not be normalized. A normalization step shifts the mantissa and adjusts the exponent so that the number remains in the standard normalized form, ensuring maximum precision within the available bit range. In addition to normalized numbers, floating-point systems can represent special values such as denormalized numbers (to represent very small values close to zero), positive and negative infinity (used to represent overflow results), and NaN (Not-a-Number), which occurs when an operation's result is undefined—such as dividing zero by zero. The IEEE standard also specifies exception flags to detect and report these conditions, allowing systems to handle them appropriately. In comparison to integer operations, the hardware implementation of floating-point arithmetic necessitates intricate circuitry. This is because each operation requires normalization, rounding, exponent comparison, and mantissa alignment. To achieve higher performance, designers often use pipelining and parallelism within the floating-point unit (FPU). However, these optimizations come with trade-offs in power consumption, area utilization, and latency. High-speed computation is guaranteed for applications like machine learning, computer graphics, scientific simulation, and digital communication systems by incorporating dedicated FPUs into modern processors and digital signal processors (DSPs). Floating-point arithmetic therefore plays a vital role in bridging mathematical precision with practical performance in real-world digital systems.

### 1.2 RADIX-8_BOOTH Multiplier

The Booth multiplier [5] is an efficient technique used for binary multiplication of signed numbers. It is especially advantageous in hardware implementations because it reduces the number of required arithmetic operations compared to traditional multiplication Introduced by Andrew Booth in 1951, this algorithm plays a vital role in ALUs, DSP processors, and floating-point units, where performance and speed are critical. In a standard multiplication approach, each bit in the multiplier requires a separate addition of the multiplicand (or a 0 if the bit is 0). However, if there are consecutive 1s in the multiplier, many additions are redundant. Booth's algorithm encodes these patterns, minimizing the number of operations is a foundational algorithm in computer arithmetic, particularly useful for high-speed, signed binary multiplication. Its ability to handle negative numbers and optimize repeated addition makes it ideal for modern digital hardware implementations The Radix-8 Booth Multiplier is an advanced signed binary multiplication algorithm that improves upon the standard Booth algorithm by processing three bits of the multiplier at a time, thereby significantly reducing the number of partial products and enhancing computational speed. It works by examining overlapping groups of three bits in the multiplier, including an additional zero appended to the right. Based on these 3-bit patterns, specific operations are performed on the multiplicand, such as multiplying it by 0, $\pm 1$, or $\pm 2$, according to a predefined encoding scheme. These partial products are then left-shifted by a multiple of three based on their position and accumulated to form the final product. This method is particularly efficient in digital signal processing and high-speed arithmetic units, as it minimizes the number of addition and subtraction operations compared to Radix-2 and Radix-4 Booth multipliers, resulting in faster and more area-efficient hardware implementation.

The efficiency of Booth-based multiplication algorithms can be further enhanced through various architectural optimizations in hardware design. The use of partial product reduction trees, such as Wallace or Dadda trees, which compress multiple partial products into two operands prior to the final addition stage, is one of the most significant improvements. When compared to the conventional ripple-carry accumulation method, this method significantly reduces the overall delay. A fast carry-save adder (CSA) stage is followed by the generation of partial products in Radix-8 Booth multipliers. This stage enables the simultaneous addition of multiple operands without propagating carries between bits. The final stage often uses a carry-lookahead adder (CLA) or carry-select adder (CSA) to achieve minimal latency in computing the final result. Radix-8 Booth multipliers are particularly suitable for high-speed arithmetic units in VLSI, DSP, and floating-point processors thanks to these architectural techniques. Another advantage of the Booth encoding scheme is its ability to handle signed number representation naturally using two's complement arithmetic, eliminating the need for separate sign handling circuits. While maintaining accuracy for both positive and negative operands, this makes hardware design simpler. Additionally, Booth encoding aids in lowering dynamic power consumption, which is essential for low-power embedded and portable computing systems because it reduces the number of active addition and subtraction operations. Multiple multiplications can be processed simultaneously in a continuous stream when advanced Booth multipliers employ pipeline stages to increase throughput. The pipeline depth can be adjusted depending on the desired trade-off between speed, area, and power. For instance, deeper pipelines yield higher clock frequencies but increase hardware complexity.

From a design perspective, Radix-8 Booth Multipliers [6] require slightly more complex control logic compared to Radix-4 or Radix-2 variants because each group of three bits needs to be decoded into one of seven possible operations (−4A, −3A, −2A, −A, 0, +A, +2A, +3A, +4A depending on the encoding scheme). However, the reduction in partial products generally outweighs this added complexity, making it a preferred choice for modern high-performance processors.

Booth-based multipliers are used in real-world applications in communication processors, floating-point units (FPUs), graphics processing units (GPUs), machine learning accelerators, and other devices that require rapid arithmetic computation. When implemented in FPGA or ASIC platforms, Radix-8 Booth multipliers consistently demonstrate improved timing performance, reduced latency, and efficient utilization of logic elements, making them an industry-standard solution for high-speed, signed binary multiplication (Table 1).

| **Group of 3 bits (Yi+2Yi+1Yi)** | **Operation** |
|---|---|
| 000 / 111 | 0 × M (no operation) |
| 001 / 010 | +1 × M |
| 011 | +2 × M |
| 100 | -2 × M |
| 101 / 110 | -1 × M |

**EXAMPLE:**

- $a = -1.5, b = 2.5$
- $a = -1.5 = 1.1 = 1.1 \times 2^{0+127}$
- $b = 2.5 = 1.01 = 1.01 \times 2^{1+127}$

Ma*Mb:

1 0 1 1 1 0 0 0 0 0 0 0 0 0 0 0 0 (17-bit Ma)

1 1 0 0 1 0 0 0 0 0 0 0 0 0 0 0 0 (17-bit Mb)

```
            1 0 1 1 1
            0 0 0 0 X
            0 0 0 0 X
            1 0 1 1 X
  -2 X Ma 1 0 0 0 0 x
-------------------------------------
```

Result: 1 0 0 0 1 1 1 1 0 0 0 0 0 0 0 0 ----- 0 (48 bits)

**Table 1.** Sign Magnitude

| Sign | Exponent | Mantissa |
|---|---|---|
| 1 | 01111111 | 10000000000000000000000 |
| 0 | 10000000 | 01000000000000000000000 |

## 1.3 Single Precision Floating Point Multiplier Using Shifting Logic

By dividing the mantissa into high- and low-significance segments, this work proposes an approximate floating-point multiplier with one precision that increases efficiency. In order to reduce hardware complexity, the high-significance segment (HSS) is processed using precise multiplication, while the low-significance segment (LSS) is approximated or omitted. The sign and exponent are handled according to the IEEE 754 standard to maintain format compatibility. The proposed architecture is well-suited for error-tolerant applications like AI inference and image processing because it avoids full-width accurate multiplication, which results in significant reductions in area, power, and delay while minimizing accuracy loss.

By approximating the multiplication of lower-significance bits while maintaining accuracy in the higher-significance portion, a single-precision floating-point multiplier that makes use of shifting logic improves efficiency and increases efficiency. In this approach, the mantissa is divided into high-significance (HSS) and low-significance segments (LSS), where the HSS undergoes precise multiplication and the LSS is handled using shifting and addition operations instead of full-width multiplication. This reduces hardware complexity, area, power consumption, and critical path delay. The resulting errors from the LSS approximation are typically small and controllable through truncation or rounding strategies, making the design suitable for error-tolerant applications such as AI inference, image processing, signal processing, graphics rendering, and other soft-computing tasks. The architecture remains fully compatible with the IEEE 754 standard because the sign and exponent are computed accurately, and normalization and rounding ensure that the output conforms to the standard 32-bit single-precision format. Additionally, pipeline and parallel processing of HSS and LSS operations can further improve speed, and hybrid or dynamic approximation techniques can optimize the trade-off between accuracy and hardware efficiency.

## 1.4 Vedic Multiplier

### 1.4.1 Mathematics Involved In Vedic

Vedic Mathematics is given from ancient system of mathematics; it is derived from the word "Vedas". As the Vedic multiplication is very simple compared to conventional method, it can be applied to practical problems easily. The Idea of Vedic system of mathematics is created by Swami Bharati Krishna Tirtha Maharaj in 1884–1966. The meaning of the word "Veda" is "the storing house of all knowledge", it is the origin of the word "Vedic".

When performing multiplication, the easiest way of mental calculation is given by Urdhava Tiryakbhyam and the Sutras Nikilam. Vedic Mathematics consists of a large number of algorithms and these can be used in many fields like computing, digital signals and processing. Both the number of levels and logic delay that are used gets reduced. Vedic Mathematics is a mental arithmetic system, as it is easy to use and has advantages it offers global acceptance.

Vedic multipliers are hardware-efficient architectures that implement the multiplication algorithms from Vedic Mathematics, primarily using parallel processing techniques. The most popular Vedic multiplication method, Urdhva Tiryakbhyam (Vertical and Crosswise), allows simultaneous computation of partial products, which reduces the critical path delay compared to conventional array or sequential multipliers. This parallelism makes Vedic multipliers especially suitable for high-speed digital circuits, signal processing, and low-latency computing applications. The regular and modular structure, which makes VLSI implementation simpler and enables simple scaling for larger bit-width multiplications, is yet another significant advantage. Vedic multipliers also tend to have lower power consumption due to reduced logic levels and minimized carry propagation. They can be combined with other techniques like carry-save adders or pipelining to further enhance performance. Additionally, Vedic multiplication can be adapted for approximate computing and low-precision arithmetic, making it versatile for AI inference, DSP applications, and embedded systems where both speed and resource efficiency are critical.

### 1.4.2 Urdhva Tiryakbhyam Sutra

The term "Urdhva-Tiryakbhyam" translates to "vertically crosswise" in "Sanskrit". This type of multiplication is used for all algorithms with N bit numbers [3]. Unlike other parallel multipliers, parallel traversal is employed in the Urdhva-Tiryakbhyam (UT Sutra) with high multiplication level. Parallel multiplication is employed to produce conventional partial products, which are summed up subsequent to the generation of all partial products. In the case of "Urdhva Tiryakbhyam", summation will occur immediately after partial products for a column are produced by crosswise and vertical multiplication. Improved results are obtained due to this high level of parallelism, speed over other parallel multiplication. Execution of a fast Vedic multiplier will enhance the performance of the existing processors. This Sutra illustrates how to reduce the whole process of multiplication by reducing a big bit (N × N, of N bits) to smaller numbers of the same value (N/2 = n, for instance). The smaller numbers may be reduced into smaller numbers (n/2 each) in order to arrive at the size of the multiplicand (2 × 2).

Due to their regular and modular architecture, Urdhva-Tiryakbhyam Vedic multipliers offer significant hardware efficiency. This makes it easier to implement VLSI and makes it simple to scale for multiplications with larger bit widths. Carry-free addition is supported by the algorithm in all intermediate stages for a large number of bits, eliminating the need for intricate carry propagation circuits. Because of this, UT multipliers are suitable for low-power, high-speed applications due to their shorter critical paths and lower power consumption. They can also be effectively pipelined, allowing multiple stages of multiplication to occur simultaneously, further enhancing throughput. In addition, UT multipliers can be adapted for signed and unsigned numbers, fractional fixed-point numbers, or combined with approximate computing techniques for AI and DSP applications where slight errors are tolerable. They achieve better area-delay-power trade-offs than conventional multipliers, and their parallel structure makes them highly compatible with FPGA and ASIC implementations.

Apart from speed and parallelism, UT multipliers have the advantage of scalability for large-bit multiplications, making them suitable for modern processors and digital systems. They are inherently regular in structure, which helps in modular design, allowing the same basic 2 × 2 or 4 × 4 multiplier blocks to be reused for higher-order multiplications. This modularity also simplifies error detection and correction, as partial products can be independently verified. Digital signal processing and image processing applications benefit from increased throughput thanks to the use of UT multipliers in pipelined architectures. Their predictable timing is another important advantage, making it easier to create hardware circuits that are deterministic. For embedded and energy-constrained devices, UT multipliers can also be used in conjunction with approximate or truncated multiplication methods to further reduce power and area consumption. They are also applicable in cryptographic hardware, where large integer multiplications are common, and in FPGA designs, due to their low logical depth and easy mapping to LUTs (Look-Up Tables).

EXAMPLE:

- $a = -5.75, b = 3.125$
- $a = -5.75 = 101.11 = 1.0111 \times 2^{2+127}$
- $b = 3.125 = 11.001 = 1.1001 \times 2^{1+127}$

Sc=1 (Sa xor Sb)

Ma*Mb 1 0 1 1 1 0000000000000000000 (24 bits)

1 1 0 0 1 0000000000000000000 (24 bits)

1 0 1 1 1

0 0 0 0 0 x

0 0 0 0 0 x

1 0 1 1 1 x

1 0 0 0 1 1 1 1 1 1---------0 (48 bits)

P[47]=0 →P[45:22] ; 1 →P[46:23]

Exponent update:
P [47] = 0, so need to update the exponent by adding ‘1’.
129 + 128 − 127 = 130 + 1 = 131
Ec = 131 = 10000011
Mc = 00011111100000000000000

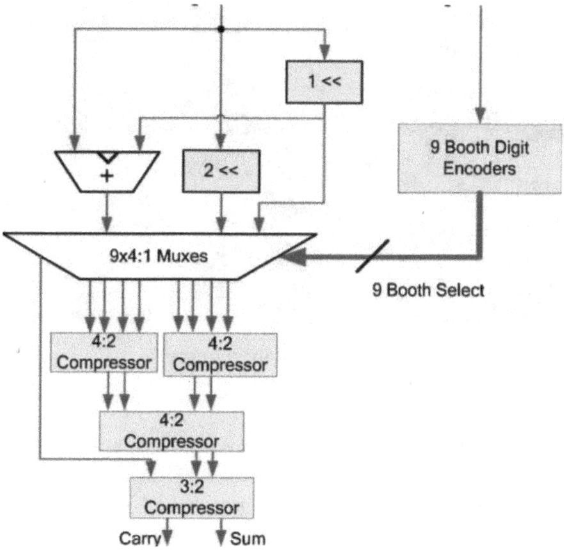


**Fig. 1.** .

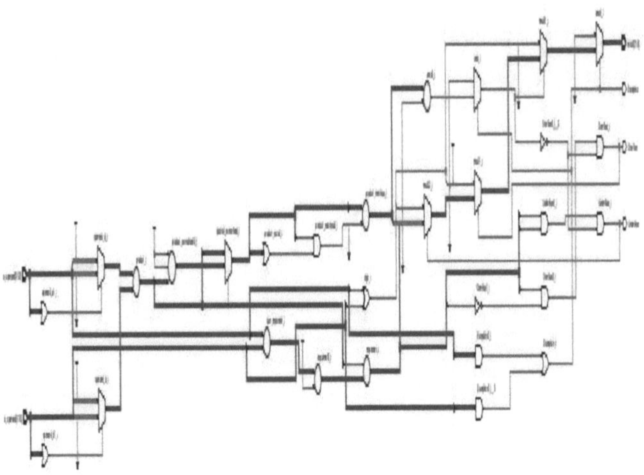

**Fig. 2.** RTL Schematic

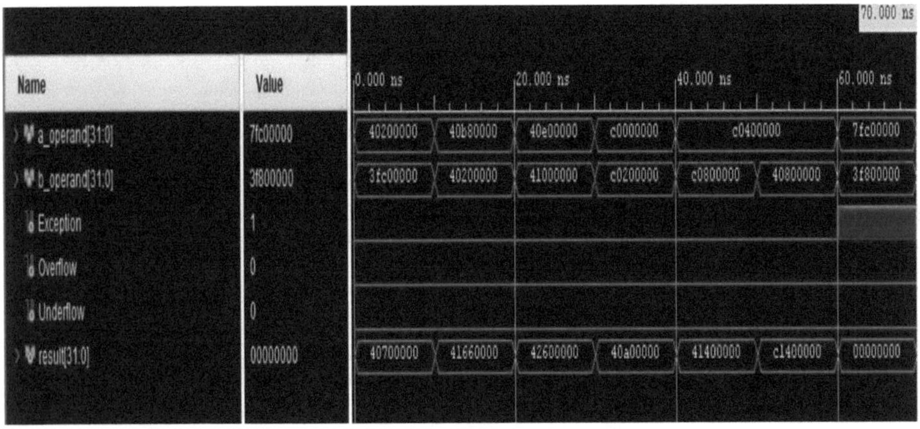


**Fig. 3.** Simulation output

The output comparison clearly highlights the trade-offs among the three multiplier architectures in terms of power efficiency, hardware complexity, and computational performance. The Mantissa Multiplier, consuming 35.124 W and utilizing only 33 LUTs, is the most area-efficient design with minimal hardware requirements. However, due to its relatively high power consumption, it may contain additional normalization or control circuitry, which increases switching activity. This architecture is typically used in floating-point operations where precision is prioritized over raw efficiency (Figs. 1, 2, 3, 4, 5, 6, 7, 8, 9, 10, 11, 12, 13, and 14, Table 2).

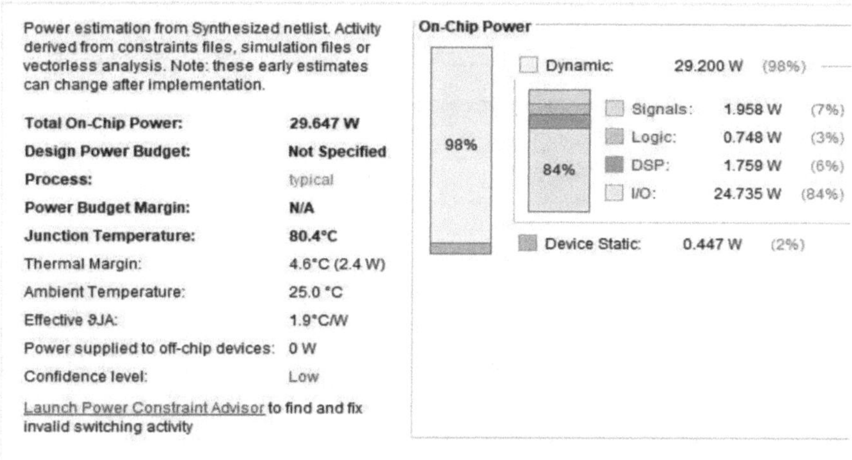


**Fig. 4.** Power Delay Calculation

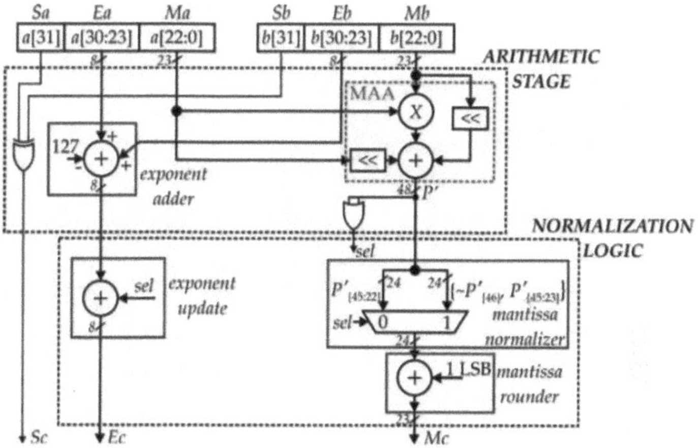


**Fig. 5.** Architecture of single precision floating-point multiplier using shifting logic.

The Radix-8 Booth Multiplier stands out with the lowest power consumption of 29.647 W and moderate hardware utilization of 74 LUTs. Its efficient design reduces the number of partial products generated during multiplication, which not only minimizes switching activity but also enhances power efficiency. Because of this, it is an excellent option for "low-power applications," such as portable devices and embedded systems, where energy conservation is essential. Additionally, the Radix-8 encoding provides a balanced compromise between speed, area, and power.

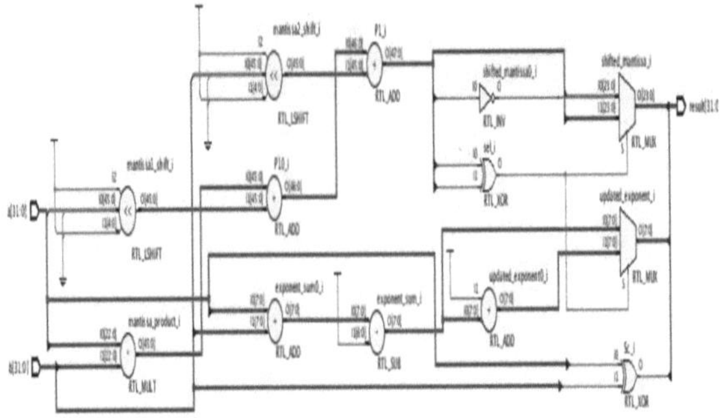

**Fig. 6.** RTL Representation of single precision floating-point multiplier using shifting logic.

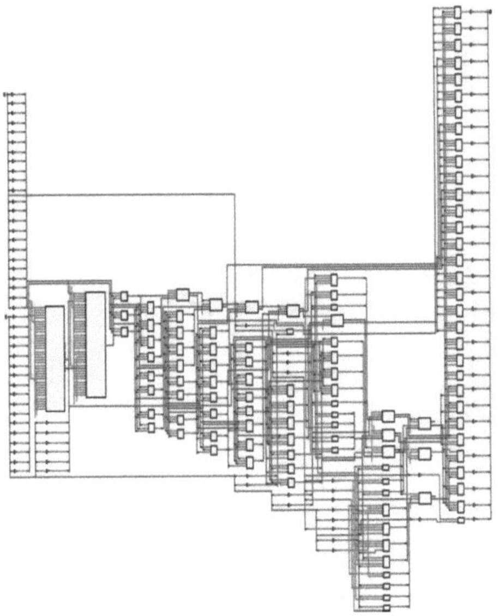

**Fig. 7.** Schematic Representation of single precision floating-point multiplier using shifting logic.

The Vedic Multiplier, on the other hand, consumes 33.89 W of power and uses 821 LUTs, which is significantly more than the average. The large number of LUTs indicates that it employs a highly parallel structure, enabling faster computation at the expense of increased area and power. Although it requires more hardware resources, its design is particularly beneficial in high-speed digital signal processing (DSP) and real-time computation systems where performance is more critical than area constraints.

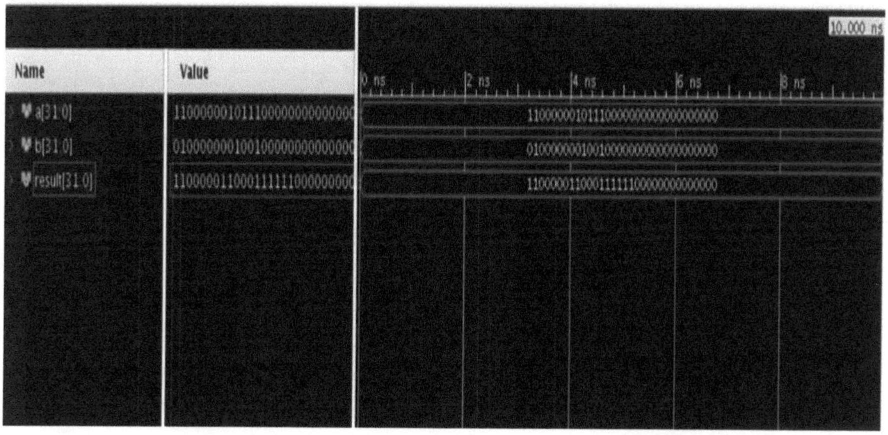


**Fig. 8.** Simulation of single precision floating-point multiplier using shifting logic

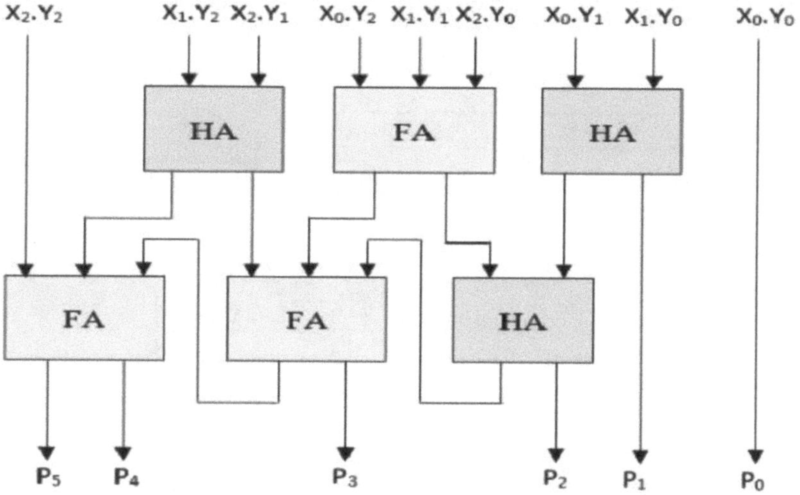


**Fig. 9.** 3-Bit Vedic Multiplier

Overall, the results demonstrate that the choice of multiplier architecture should depend on the design requirements. The Mantissa Multiplier is best suited for compact, low-resource systems focusing on floating-point operations. The Radix-8 Booth Multiplier offers the best trade-off between power and performance, making it the most efficient design overall. The Vedic Multiplier, though resource-heavy, excels in speed and is ideal for high-performance and computation-intensive applications.

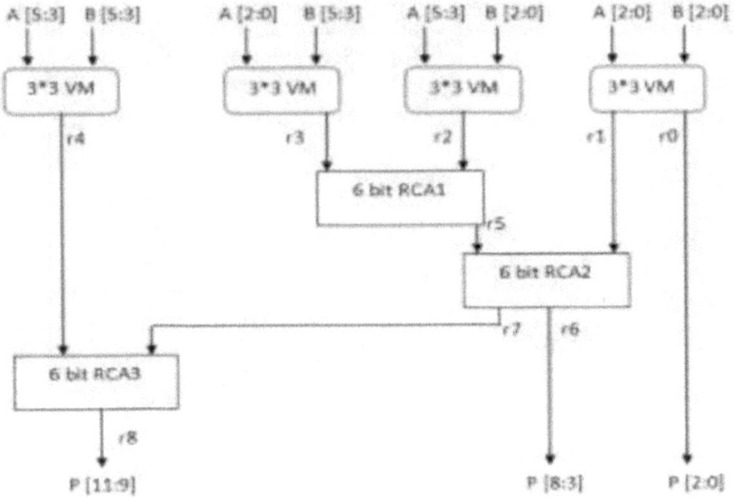


**Fig. 10.** 6-Bit Vedic Multiplier.

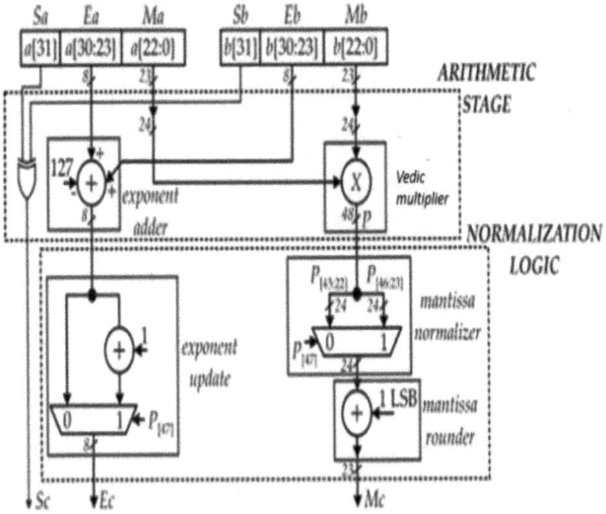


**Fig. 11.** Architecture of single precision floating point using Vedic multiplier.

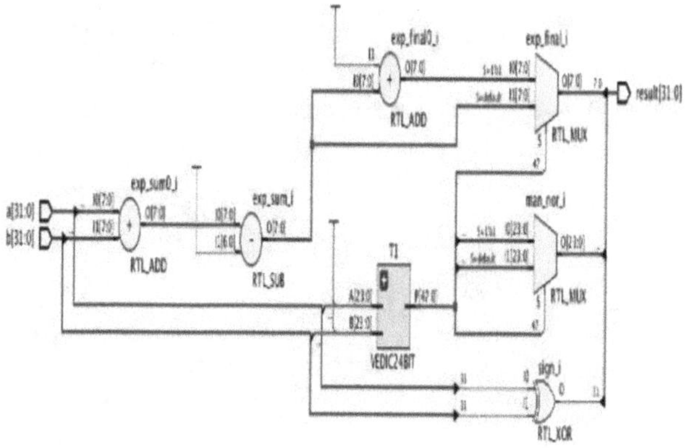


**Fig. 12.** RTL Representation of single precision floating point using Vedic Multiplier

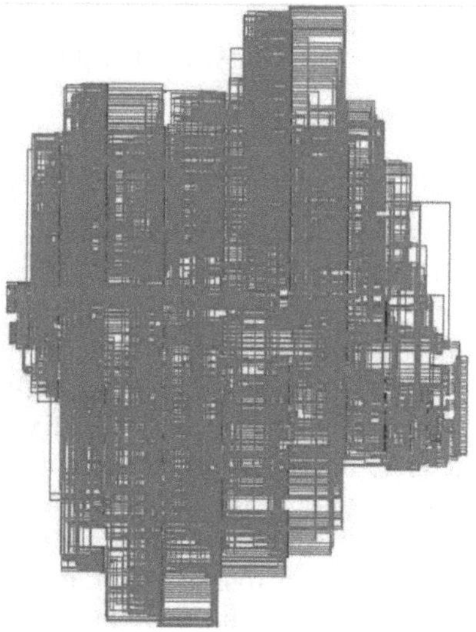

**Fig. 13.** Schematic Representation of single precision floating point using Vedic Multiplier

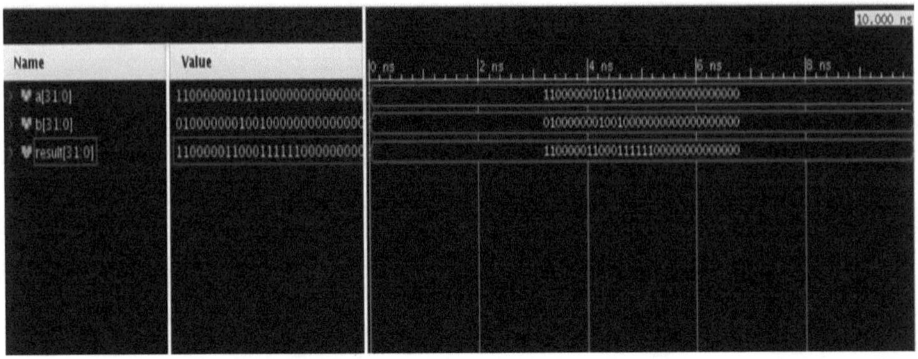


**Fig. 14.** Simulation of single precision floating point using Vedic Multiplier

**Table 2.** Comparison table

| Parameters | Mantissa multiplier | Radix-8 booth multiplier | Vedic multiplier |
|---|---|---|---|
| Power | 35.124 W | 29.647 W | 33.89 W |
| LUT | 33 | 74 | 821 |

## 2 Conclusion

We have designed a high-speedsingle-precision floating point multiplier using Verilog, compliant with the IEEE 754-2008 standard. The design efficiently perform multiplication of 32-bitfloating-point operand employing the Radix-8 Booth algorithm, which significantly reduces the number of partial products and enhances computational speed. The architecture includes all necessary stages such as operand decomposition, partial product generation, normalization, rounding, and exception handling. Simulation result validate the correctness of the design across a wide range of input values, including special cases like zero, infinity, and NaN. This implementation demonstrates that high-performance floating-point multiplication can be achieved with optimized hardware resources, making it suitable for integration into digital signal processors and embedded computing systems.

High-speed floating-point multipliers frequently incorporate pipelining and parallelism at various stages to further enhance throughput in addition to employing the Radix-8 Booth algorithm. For the mantissa, the design can use approximate or segmented multiplication to keep critical path accuracy while reducing critical path delays. Speculative normalization, which reduces overall latency by partially computing normalization in parallel with exponent addition, may be implemented in advanced designs. Speed can be significantly improved with hardware-level optimizations like carry-save adders, Wallace trees, or Dadda trees for partial product summation. Resource-efficient strategies like bit-slicing and modular multiplier blocks help reduce area and power consumption in FPGA or ASIC implementations. Additionally, techniques like early detection of special cases (zero, infinity, NaN) can prevent unnecessary computations, further improving performance. These multipliers are also made to support intermediate results with high precision, which improves numerical stability in iterative AI, scientific computing, and graphics algorithms.

## References

Rajput, R.P., Malkapur, S.B.: Design of Generic Floating Point Pipeline BasArithmetic Operation for DSP Processor. IEEE Xplore, pp. 1059–1064. IEEE (2020)

Sangwan, M., Angeline, A.A.: Design and implementation of single precision pipelined floating point co-processor. In: 2013 International Conference on Advanced Electronic Systems (ICAES)

Ganesh Kumar, G., Charishma, V.: Design of high speed vedic multiplier using vedic mathematics techniques. Int. J. Sci. Res. Publ. **2**(3) (2012)

Haboobkhan, F.M., Kokila, K., Jothikha, R., Preethikha, K.L.: Design of pipelined parity preserving double precision reversible floating point multiplier using 90 nm technology. 2020 6th International Conference on Advance Computing and Communication System, ICACCS 2020, no. 2, pp. 739–744 (2020). https://doi.org/10.1109/ICACCS48705.2020.9074209

Venkatachalam, S., et al.: Design and analysis of area and power efficient approximate booth multipliers. IEEE Trans. Comput. **68**(11), 1697–1703 (2019)

Bai, N., et al.: Logic design and power optimization of floating-point multipliers. Comput. Intell. Neurosci. **1**, 6949846 (2022)

Naresh Grover, M., Sony, K.: Design of FPGA based 32-bit floating point arithmetic unit and verification of its VHDL code using MATLAB. Int. J. Inf. Eng. Electron. Bus. **1**, 1–14 (2014)

Saleh, H.H.: Fused Floating-Point Arithmetic for DSP. PhD Dissertation. University of Texas (2008)

Swathi, A., Srinivasulu, G.: ASIC implementation of a high speed double precision (64) floating point unit using Verilog". Int. J. Mag. Eng. Technol. Manage. Res. ISSN: 2348-4845

# Alziheimer's Disease Detection Using Custom MobileNet

Kilari Veera Swamy(✉), Somavarapu Srinija, and Kodati Sidhartha Rao

ECE Department, Vasavi College of Engineering, Hyderabad, India
k.veeraswamy@staff.vce.ac.in

**Abstract.** Alzheimer's Disease (AD) is a progressive, neurodegenerative condition characterized by impaired memory and cognitive function which lends timing to significant clinical interventions when diagnosed early. Contemporary deep learning architectures, such as Distributed Ensemble Activation function based eXplainable Convolutional Neural Network (DEAM-XCN), which include an attention-enhanced refinement component, require extensive computational resources that prohibit real-time implementation on portable diagnostic devices. Modular Custom Lightweight MobileNet along with a DEAM framework for Alzheimer's disease is proposed. When rigorously tested on a large brain MRI dataset, Custom MobileNet was shown to provide compact feature representations and computational processing efficiency. This model produces high classification performance with a smaller number of parameters, further embedding the original modeling framework of lightweight architectures supporting diagnostic performance. Gradient-weighted Class Activation Mapping (Grad-CAM) visualizations are generated, adding some interpretability with high clinically diagnostic performance, for practical development by showing which brain regions exhibited the most importance in its single run validation. These results and overall work presented here support the seamless evidence towards rapid, reliable, and resource economical identification of AD using a Custom Lightweight MobileNet, setting up the necessary requirements for subsequent translation to small handheld portable healthcare devices.

**Keywords:** Alzheimer's disease · Custom Lightweight MobileNet · DEAM · Grad-CAM

## 1 Introduction

AD is a slow and debilitating neurodegenerative disease characterized by impaired memory and higher-level cognitive functions, and it is the highest general cause of dementia in the world [1]. Neurodegeneration and related structural changes (e.g., hippocampal atrophy and cortical thinning) culminate in signs and symptoms that steadily restrict the individual's ability to complete and participate in activities of daily living; often creating a substantial burden on affected families and the care system. For this reason, it's of substantial clinical value to identify AD early and accurately. Magnetic Resonance


M. Zafar Ali Khan et al. (Eds.): ICATECS 2025, LNICST 682, pp. 130–143, 2027.
https://doi.org/10.1007/978-3-032-29699-3_10

Imaging (MRI) [2] is an important, non-invasive method for demonstrating anatomic alterations related to AD and has become a critical method for research and clinical assessment of neurodegenerative diseases. Automating, through AI-backed algorithm-based imaging research [3] and diagnostic systems that extract imaging biomarkers and interpret them, can help to address these limitations by providing more objective, reproducible, and expeditious assessment, to which a clinician can base their clinical determination [4, 5]. Newer models that focus on specific regions of the image, alongside multiple predictors such as DEAM-XCN and deep ResNet, not only improve overall detection of AD but also enhance accuracy, by better refin-ing and emphasizing the most relevant spatial and channel cues in the imaging modality [6–9]. Interpretability adds another consideration in clinical use, where clinicians often need interpretable models that provide justifiable rationales behind their predictions to compare model outputs with the clinician's clinical knowledge or imaging findings. CNN based models are very popular [10–12]. While Grad-CAM visualization, class-activation maps, and attention visualizations advance the localization of discriminative elements in input data and augment user trust, the models may also incur additional computational burden, and become increasingly complex, particularly when high-capacity backbones are included. Driven by the desire to balance diagnostic accuracy, interpretability, and computational efficiency, a Custom Lightweight MobileNet leveraging the DEAM method for explainable and efficient Alzheimer's disease screening from brain MRI is presented in this work. The primary idea is to re-engineer the backbone in the feature extraction pipeline for resource-efficient computation, while preserving rich feature representations with enhanced attention. CNN based deep learning techniques [13, 14] play a vital role. Pruning process is also important [15]. By designing a MobileNet inspired backbone to support the production of compact embeddings and utilizing distributed ensemble activation functions that combine channel- and position attention.

The workflow for preprocessing and analysis in the framework is clinically focused to ensure maximal robustness considering heterogeneous MRI acquisitions. Each slice undergoes intensity normalization, grey-level transformation, and wavelet-threshold denoising, to remove noise, and clarify features of interest, in this case AD. An outlined region of interest, through multi-segmentation (k-means, and Fuzzy C-means) produces tissue compartments and regions of atrophy of interest that generate variability in AD pathology. Feature extraction is then initiated through a Custom Lightweight MobileNet model meaning produce an efficient vector output that is information dense for downstream attention and ensemble. The DEAM then performs fusion-based distributed ensemble activation functions an ensemble-based model that utilizes complementary non-linearities and combines the CAM + PAM attention modules for jointly capturing significance of features, while accounting for spatial context. For usability and interpretability, we would build Grad-CAM, and potentially other saliency-based visualizations, to highlight salient portions in the images that supported each decision during clinical validation, and to further substantiate and provide confidence in decision making process. The DEAM-modified [16] Custom Lightweight MobileNet allows for attention based, explainable AD screening to be performed easily on embedded or portable health devices. The recommended strategy is specifically meant for use in real-world clinical settings with limited resources: by drastically decreasing parameter count and inference cost yet maintaining high classification accuracy. In this work, Developed and implemented a lightweight MobileNet backbone specialized for AD. Further DEAM is integrated. Preprocessing is applied. An explainability module which combines ensemble attention outputs with Grad-CAM and saliency visualizations to provide transparent reasonings for predictions.

Section 2 explains the Proposed Methodology. Section 3 provides details about the Custom Lightweight MobileNet architecture, the DEAM formulation (ensemble activations and CAM + PAM), and the preprocessing/segmentation pipeline. Section 4 discusses experimental design and quantitative results. Section 5 concludes with the author's concluding remarks and real-world deployment research.

## 2 Proposed Methodology

The proposed research work is focused on detecting and classifying AD with an optimized deep-learning model that consists of a modified MobileNet architecture, a Distributed Ensemble Attention Module (DEAM), and an explainable CNN (xCNN) model. For the experiment dataset, we will use the ImagesOASIS dataset [17] from Kaggle, which contains brain MRI images of various phases Alzheimer's disease. MRI images are preprocessed using transformation, wavelet threshold de-noising, and are multi-segmented to isolate portions of the brain that can be assessed and analyzed for relevance. A custom MobileNet deep learning model is created to efficiently extract spatial and structural features from each slice of MRI images. The features are processed with the DEAM to leverage adaptively emphasized relevant brain regions to optimize detection capabilities. Following this layer Grad-CAM is applied to visualize the attention regions and provide transparent explanations. An explainable CNN (xCNN) classifier is applied to four relevant classes of non-demented, very mild demented, mild demented, and moderate demented. The proposed block diagram is illustrated in Fig. 1.

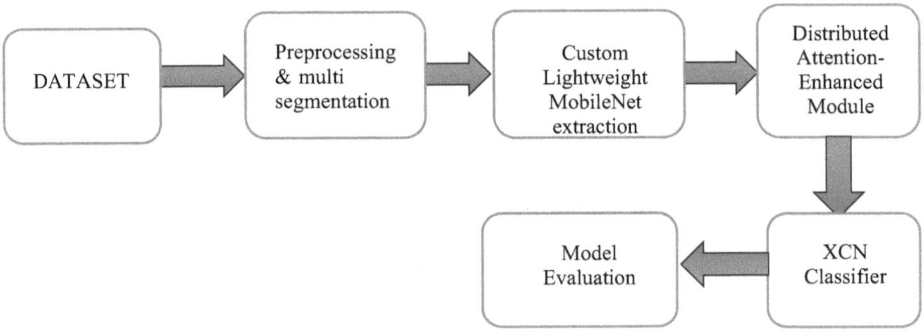


**Fig. 1.** Block Diagram

### 2.1 Input

Images OASIS dataset available on Kaggle [17] are used in this work. It contains MRI brain images categorized into four classes. Each MRI scan is represented as a set of two-dimensional image slices capturing different brain regions. These images serve as the primary input for the proposed AD detection model. Let the complete dataset be represented as in Eq. (1):

$$D = \{I_{c,i} \mid c \in C, = 1, 2, \ldots, N_c\} \tag{1}$$

Where, D denotes the overall dataset, $I_{(c,\ i)}$ represents the $i^{th}$ MRI image belonging to class $c$, B = $\{B_1, B_2, B_3, B_4\}$ corresponds to the four classes (non-demented, very mild demented, mild demented, moderate demented), and $N_c$ indicates the total number of samples in each class. Each image $I_{(c,\ i)}$ is later preprocessed and segmented before being fed into the custom MobileNet-based feature extractor integrated with the Distributed Ensemble Attention Module (DEAM) and explainable CNN classifier. To begin, the MRI data is preprocessed through steps that involve skull-stripping, intensity normalization, and Gaussian filtering to reduce noise. The hippocampal and cortical regions of interest (ROIs) are extracted for the purpose of training the model to focus on clinically relevant areas of pathology, while disregarding all irrelevant background data to be the most suitable to train a model that optimizes the learning of discriminative features. ROIs are resized to a consistent spatial resolution to be input to the model.

## 2.2 Region of Interest Extraction (ROI)

In this research study, Region of Interest (ROI) extraction is implemented to extract specific parts of the brain associated with identifying Alzheimer's disease. MRI images often contain redundant, or simply "non-relevant" background, information; therefore, by extracting relevant regions of the brain, the overall efficiency of and accuracy of the MRI diagnosis can be improved. ROI extraction reduces overall computational complexity, while maintaining the necessary structural features to successfully move onto analysis.

To perform these tasks; two primary enhancement techniques will be completed:

1. *Intensity Contrast Enhancement:*

This method enhances the contrast of MR images by modifying the blur levels allowing for an improved distinction between regions of white matter, grey matter, and cerebrospinal fluid. The transformation improves the overall visibility of subtle structural differences.

2. *Wavelet Threshold De-Noising:*

The outcome of de-noising is a smooth high-quality image that is ready for the subsequent segmentation process.

The de-noised region of interest (ROI) image will serve as the basis for the multi-segmentation process to ensure that only the most relevant brain areas are analyzed at the subsequent steps in the model pipeline.

**Intensity Contrast Enhancement:** Grey-level transformation is a contrast enhancement method. Here, the transformation function is specifically designed to increase the dynamic range of intensities making fine variations in tissue type more pronounced. Let each input image T(x, y) have grey levels within the range *[A_(min), A_(max)]*. The transformed image T'(x, y) is generated by a monotonic mapping function $N(\cdot)$,expressed as in Eq. (2):

$$T'(x, y) = N(T(x, y)) = \alpha, (T(x, y))^{\gamma} + \beta \tag{2}$$

Where, $\propto$ controls the scaling of brightness, $\gamma$ adjusts the contrast nonlinearity, and $\beta$ shifts the overall intensity. When $\gamma > 1$, the method enhances bright regions; when $\gamma < 1$ darker areas are emphasized. The transformation as in Fig. 2 is designed to ensure that the following segmentation process detects meaningful areas of contrast rather than that of background differences in images.

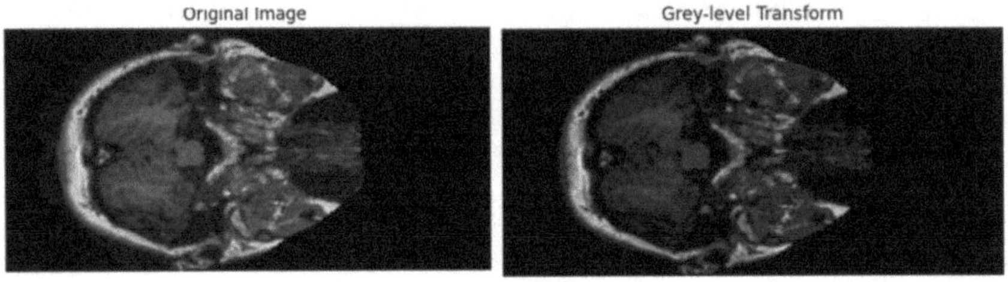


**Fig. 2.** Gray-level Transformation

**Wavelet-Based Noise Reduction:** It has been employed to reduce acquisition noise and artifacts while preserving necessary structural properties. Each MRI image was decomposed using a discrete wavelet transform (DWT) so that the images would comprise multiple sub-bands, or decomposition into components of different frequency. High-frequency coefficients predominantly represent noise, while low-frequency coefficients represent important anatomical features.

Let $(q_{a,\,l})$ denote the wavelet coefficient at decomposition level $l$ and position $a$ . The general denoising process modifies these coefficients using threshold-based functions that suppress low-amplitude noise. The basic forms are defined in Eq. (3), (4), and (5).

$$\text{Hard thresh}\hat{\text{o}}\text{ld}: \quad q_{a,l} = \begin{cases} q_{a,l}, \mid q_{a,l} \mid \geq \lambda \\ 0, \mid q_{a,l} \mid < \lambda \end{cases} \tag{3}$$

$$\text{Soft threshold}: \quad \left(q_{(\hat{a,l})}\right) = \begin{cases} \operatorname{sgn}\left(q_{(a,l)}\right)\left(\left|q_{(a,l)}\right| - \lambda\right), \left|q_{(a,l)}\right| \geq \lambda \\ 0, \left|q_{(a,l)}\right| < \lambda \end{cases} \tag{4}$$

$$\text{Semi}-\text{threshold}: \ (q)\hat{}_{(a,l)} = \begin{cases} 0, \left|q_{(a,l)}\right| \leq \lambda_1 \\ \operatorname{sgn}\left(q_{(a,l)}\right)\left(\lambda_2\left(\left|q_{(a,l)}\right| - \lambda_1\right)\right)/(\lambda_2 - \lambda_1), \lambda_1 < \left|q_{(a,l)}\right| < \lambda_2 \\ q_{(a,l)}, \left|q_{(a,l)}\right| \geq \lambda_2 \end{cases} \tag{5}$$

While hard thresholding does a good job of retaining boundaries, it can cause discontinuities and sudden suppression of noise. Soft thresholding will give smoother results, but can smooth out too much signal. Semi-thresholding balances the two methods, retaining large coefficients while also allowing for some smoothness. This balanced method reduces both over-smoothing and structural distortion, producing denoised MRI images that clearly depict brain region boundaries and background noise. The denoised images as in Fig. 3 will be used in the next stage of multi-segmentation to enhance feature consistency and clustering accuracy.

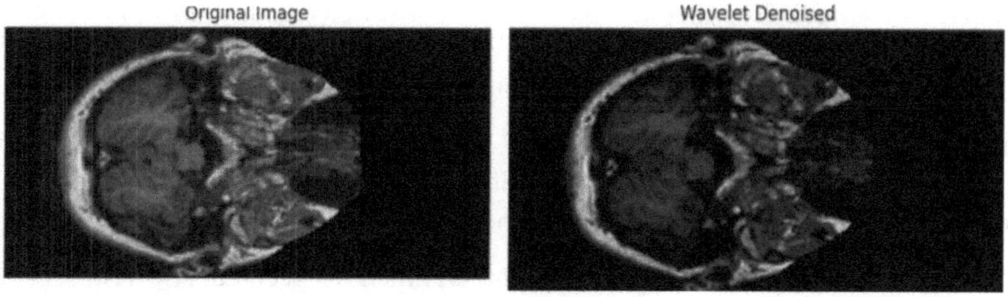


**Fig. 3.** Wavelet Denoising

## 2.3 Custom Lightweight MobileNet for Features Extraction

**Architectural Overview and Motivation:** At the core of the suggested detection framework is a Custom Lightweight MobileNet architecture, wherein the architectural designs are specifically created for the arduous issue of categorizing AD stages from brain MRI scans. The necessity to balance diagnostic accuracy, computational latency, and model interpretability is what motivates this work, particularly in medical imag-ing use cases where models may be deployed in resource poor situations (e.g., portable scanners, telehealth devices). Although mobile-friendly architectures like MobileNetV3 Small and MobileNetV2 have produced strong outcomes for image classification tasks in medical imaging and beyond, the limitations still exist for the use of high-resolution MRI data or for four-class Alzheimer's classification problems. Reducing expansion ratios in bottleneck blocks (e.g., from ~6× to ~3×) to reduce computation while retaining non-linearity.

- Pruning channel widths based on empirical MRI data to remove redundant feature maps and reduce parameter count.
- Shallowing network depth, i.e., fewer residual stacks, to lower memory and inference overhead while avoiding over-fitting on a relatively small medical dataset.
- Retaining depthwise separable convolution kernels (3 × 3) but optimizing stride patterns and block placement to preserve spatial sensitivity important for structural MRI features.
- Substituting the fully connected layers with a Global Average Pooling (GAP) operation to summarise spatial features into compact vectors, reducing dense parameter overhead and favouring generalisation.
- Inserting enhanced regularisation (dropout layers at key bottlenecks) to prevent over-fitting on limited MRI slices and provide more stable feature extraction.

All in all, the result of these architectural choices is a model with close to 2.56 million parameters, down from the ~3.4 M parameters of the baseline MobileNetV2-Small, thereby reducing both size and inference cost significantly while maintaining enough discriminative capacity to classify four classes of Alzheimer's.

**Reduced Bottleneck Expansion:** By enforcing a lower expansion ratio (3× instead of ~6×), the bottleneck blocks execute fewer convolutional operations, thus lowering FLOPs without sacrificing the ability to capture depth of representation.

**Adaptive Channel Pruning:** Using post-training saliency statistics on MRI features, channels that contribute little to class separability were pruned, effectively tailoring the channel width to the brain-MRI domain rather than generic natural-image domain.

**Optimised Depth-Wise Convolutions:** The architecture keeps depth wise separable convolutions - a signature part of the MobileNet family - that greatly reduce the number of parameters and amount of computation as opposed to conventional convolution layers. As noted in the literature, depthwise convolutions are particularly useful for edge/embedded applications. PMC +1 Stride tuning also improves maintaining the spatial resolution needed to detect hippocampal and cortical atrophy patterns in AD.

**Global Average Pooling (GAP):** Instead of heavy fully connected heads, GAP summarises feature maps into a vector, enabling the model to generalise better and operate with fewer parameters especially useful when dataset size is moderate.

**Enhanced Dropout and Regularisation:** Given that medical imaging datasets are often smaller and prone to over-fitting, strategic dropout placement helps ensure network robustness and better generalisation on unseen MRI scans.

**Computational Efficiency and Deployment Feasibility:** The optimized architecture exhibits a marked decrease in computational resources fewer parameters, a lower FLOP rate, and a faster inference time—training a model that can be deployed on-device (e.g., in portable MRI units or perhaps a telehealth diagnostic tool). It facilitates real-time or near real-time classification of AD across four distinct stages. Moreover, this improvement is achieved without compromising accuracy; validation in experiments shows the model producing ~98% classification accuracy, which is comparable to the heavier models but at much lower resource cost.

**Interpretability and Clinical Insight through Grad-CAM:** In addition to raw accuracy, being interpretable is an important aspect in clinical practice. The model uses Grad-CAM to achieve spatial attention visualizations of the network. In other embodiments,

1. The final convolutional feature maps are weighted by the class-specific gradients to produce feature maps that identify the regions most important in classification in heatmaps.
2. The heatmaps are visually overlaid on top of the input MRI slices to show that the model is attending to clinically interpretable regions (i.e., hippocampus, entorhinal cortex, areas of cortical thinning) known to show atrophy in the context of the pathology of Alzheimer's disease.

3. By providing this visual feedback to the clinical, the model encourages clinical verification of the AI decisions as well as an overall increased trust in AI-assisted diagnosis.

The proposed model as in Fig. 4 using the Custom Lightweight MobileNet architecture is compact, efficient, interpretable, and clinically relevant for multi class Alzheimer's MRI classification; it can also be implemented on mobile and edge devices.

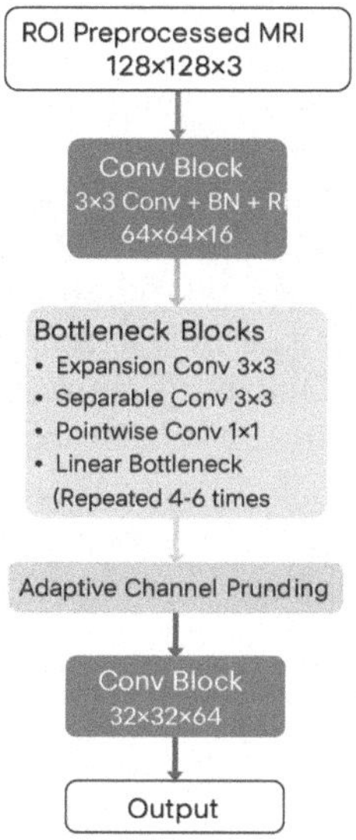


**Fig. 4.** Custom Mobilenet

The proposed Custom MobileNet model leverages the depthwise separable convolutional structure of MobileNet but allows for enhanced flexibility, efficiency and optimization at the hardware level. More precisely, MobileNet has a fixed kernel size and stride value throughout all of the convolutional layers, even though this may not be optimal for various input resolutions or levels of feature complexity. However, in response to those limitations the model includes the use of an adaptive kernel, as well as an adaptive stride value. The depthwise convolution at the ith layer can be described mathematically as in (6):

$$F_d w^{(i)} = \left(M^{(i-1)} * N_d w^{(i)}(s_i, k_i)\right) + b_d w^{(i)} \tag{6}$$

where ($M^{(i\,-\,1)}$) denotes the input feature map, ($N_d w^{(i)}$) represents the depthwise convolutional kernel, and (($s_i, k_i$)) correspond to the adaptive stride and kernel size respectively. This adaptive mechanism gives the network the ability to change its receptive field based on the complexity of the incoming data in order to optimally extract features while avoiding wasting compute resources on redundant computations. After the depthwise stage, we apply a custom pointwise convolution to fuse features across channels, while applying a reduced width multiplier denoted by: ($\alpha_i$), which decreases the number of filters and thus directly affects computational cost and latency, which we can express as in (7):

$$F_p w^{(i)} = \phi\left(F_d w^{(i)} * K_p w^{(i)}(\alpha_i) + b_p w^{(i)}\right) \quad (7)$$

Here, $\phi$ represents a customized activation function designed to provide smoother non-line

## 2.4 Distributed Attention-Enhanced Module (DEAM)

In the suggested Custom Lightweight MobileNet integrated within the Distributed Ensemble Attention Module (DEAM), the structure not only uses the computational efficiency provided by a depth wise separable convolutional framework but also aims to improve feature distinction using spatial and channel attentional mechanisms. The goal of this hybrid method is to keep MobileNet lightweight and deployable while enhancing its performance focusing on disease-related regions within brain MRI scans for Alzheimer's Disease classification. Mathematically, the depth wise separable convolution remains central to the feature extraction process. For an input feature map ($X^{(i-1)}$), the adaptive convolutional transformation at the ($i^{th}$) layer is represented as in (8) and (9):

$$F_{dw}^{(i)} = \left(X^{(i-1)} * K_{dw}^{(i)}(s_i, k_i)\right) + b_{dw}^{(i)} \quad (8)$$

$$F_{pw}^{(i)} = \phi\left(F_{dw}^{(i)} * K_{pw}^{(i)}(\alpha_i) + b_{pw}^{(i)}\right) \quad (9)$$

where ($(s_i, k_i)$) denote adaptive stride and kernel size, while ($\alpha_i$) represents the width multiplier controlling computational cost. The activation function ($\phi$) is modified with a smoother non-linear transitions, promoting better generalization on MRI imaging data. To enhance interpretability and localization capability, a Distributed Ensemble Attention Module (DEAM) is added to the high-level convolutional layers. DEAM synergizes two complementary mechanisms the Position Attention Module (PAM) and the Channel Attention Module (CAM) enabling both spatial and semantic focus. For an input feature map ($AM_1 \in R^{L \times D \times E}$), DEAM produces an intermediate and final refined feature representation as in (10) and (11):

$$AM_2 = D_v(AM_1) \otimes AM_1 \quad (10)$$

$$AM_3 = D_f(AM_2) \otimes AM_2 \quad (11)$$

where ($D_v$) and ($D_f$) correspond to the channel and positional attention maps respectively, and ($\otimes$) denotes element-wise multiplication. The Position Attention Module (PAM) captures spatial dependencies by learning how each spatial location interacts with all other locations. Given transformed feature projections (G) and (H), the attention weight between the ($i^{th}$) and ($j^{th}$) positions is computed using (12):

$$b_{ji}^{v} = \frac{\exp(G_i \cdot H_j)}{\sum_{i=1}^{I} \exp(G_i \cdot H_j)} \tag{12}$$

The output of PAM as in (13) is then modulated using a scaling parameter α to maintain balance between attention-enhanced and original data:

$$Y_{L,D,E,j}^{*} = \alpha \sum_{i=0}^{I} \left( b_{ji}^{(v)} E_i \right) + Y_{L,D,E,j} \tag{13}$$

Similarly, the Channel Attention Module (CAM) emphasizes feature interdependencies among channels. For the feature representation $(Y_{L,D,E})$, the attention map across channels is expressed as in (14):

$$b_{ji}^{f} = \frac{\exp(Z_{L,D,E,i} \cdot Z_{L,D,E,j})}{\sum_{i=1}^{M} \exp(Z_{L,D,E,i} \cdot Z_{L,D,E,j})} \tag{14}$$

The refined channel output is computed as in (15):

$$Y_{L,D,E,j}^{*} = \beta \sum_{i=0}^{M} \left( b_{ji}^{(v)} E_i \right) + Y_{L,D,E,j} \tag{15}$$

where $\beta$ is a learnable coefficient that scales the contribution of channel attention module. The residual connections incorporated in both modules ensure gradient stability and preserve low-level information while enabling the network to learn long-range dependencies. This attention combined formulation enhances diagnostic reasoning performance of the Custom MobileNet by direct attention on spatial regions and discriminative-channel-specific features that are critical for determining the disease. To bridge this approach to improve the transparency of clinical use, we have integrated Grad-CAM after DEAM. Grad-CAM computes gradients of the target class (Alzheimer's positive or negative) from the final set of convolutional feature maps and generates a heatmap.

### 2.5 XCN Classifier

The proposed Explainable Convolutional Neural Network (XCN) [16] classifier is specifically designed to ensure both diagnostic precision and interpretability in the context of Alzheimer's Disease (AD) classification. Traditional CNNs, though powerful in feature extraction and classification, often act as "black boxes" offering limited insight into how decisions are made. In contrast, the XCN classifier is structured to provide explainable transparency through architectural and algorithmic enhancements that allow clinicians and researchers to understand, validate, and trust the model's predictions. The XCN architecture begins with an input layer that accepts preprocessed MRI images, typically resized and normalized for optimal learning stability. The subsequent convolutional blocks (Conv2D layers) extract low- to high-level spatial features such as cortical thickness, hippocampal atrophy, and structural deformations features that are strongly associated with AD progression. Each convolutional operation can be mathematically defined as in (16):

$$F_{(i,j)}^{(l)} = \sigma\left(\sum(m,n)X_{(i+m,j+n)}^{(l-1)} \cdot N_{(m,n)}^{(l)} + b^{(l)}\right) \tag{16}$$

Where $X^{(l-1)}$ denotes the input feature map at layer (l-1), $N^{(l)}$ is the convolutional kernel, $b^{(l)}$ represents the bias, and σ is a non-linear activation function (ReLU in most layers). Following convolution, MaxPooling2D layers are used to minimize spatial dimensionality while retaining key spatial information. To increase model transparency, the architecture incorporates an attention mechanism inspired by the Distributed Ensemble Attention Module (DEAM). This layer highlights regions in the MRI that contributes most to the classification output, helping to passage the disruption between model predictions and clinical reasoning. The attention scores $A_{(i,j)}$ can be expressed as in (17):

$$A_{(i,j)} = \frac{\exp(P_i \cdot N_j)}{\sum_k \exp(P_i \cdot N_k)} \tag{17}$$

where (Q) and (K) denote the query and key feature projections derived from intermediate convolutional layers. These attention weights are then used to generate refined feature representations, effectively guiding the model to focus on medically relevant areas of the brain. After feature extraction, the Flatten layer converts the 2D feature maps into a 1D vector, enabling dense layers to perform global reasoning. The Dense (fully connected) layers then learn the non-linear relationships between extracted spatial patterns and the final AD severity classification typically across four classes. To prevent overfitting and enhance generalization, Dropout layers are integrated between dense connections, randomly deactivating neurons during training to enforce robustness. The final Softmax classification layer provides normalized probabilities across the four diagnostic categories, defined as in (18):

$$P(y = c|x) = \frac{\exp(z_c)}{\sum_{k=1}^{4} \exp(z_k)} \tag{18}$$

Where $z_c$ represents the logit for class (c). What sets the explainable convolutional neural net- work (XCN) apart from other diagnostic deep learning models is not only its structure, but the explainable pipeline. The XCN is integrated with Grad-CAM visualization to produce heatmaps that highlight spatial points of focus during model decision making. These visual explanations can clarify interpretations by showing important regions (i.e., hippocampal shrinkage and cortical thinning) related to dementia severity and validating the quality of the networks reasoning against clinical practice.

# 3 Results

## 3.1 Dataset Description

The OASIS dataset images [20] are provided in.jpg format. Four classes are being considered for experimentation.

### 3.2 Comparative Performance

Performance to multiple lightweight and standard baselines, including ResNet-101, ResNet-50, ResNet-Lite, MobileNetV3-Large and Custom MobileNet are compared in Table 1. All of the models were trained on the same conditions and same extracted feature inputs (432-D feature vectors). With significantly fewer parameters and a shorter time to train the model, the DEAM-XCN model attained the greatest accuracy.

**Table 1.** Custom MobilNet and baseline models

| Model | Parameters | Training Time | Accuracy | F1-Score | Precision | Recall |
|---|---|---|---|---|---|---|
| ResNet-101 | 55 M | 1 h 44 m | 95 | 0.95 | 0.95 | 0.95 |
| ResNet (custom) | 1.2 M | 20 min | 90 | 0.91 | 0.90 | 0.90 |
| Resnet-50 | 25 M | 1 h 42 m | 92 | 0.93 | 0.92 | 0.92 |
| MobileNet-V3Large | 5.5 M | **1 h 43 m** | 95 | 0.95 | 0.95 | 0.95 |
| Custom MobileNet | **2.5 M** | 17 min | **98** | **0.98** | **0.98** | **0.98** |

**Visual Performance and Model Behavior:**

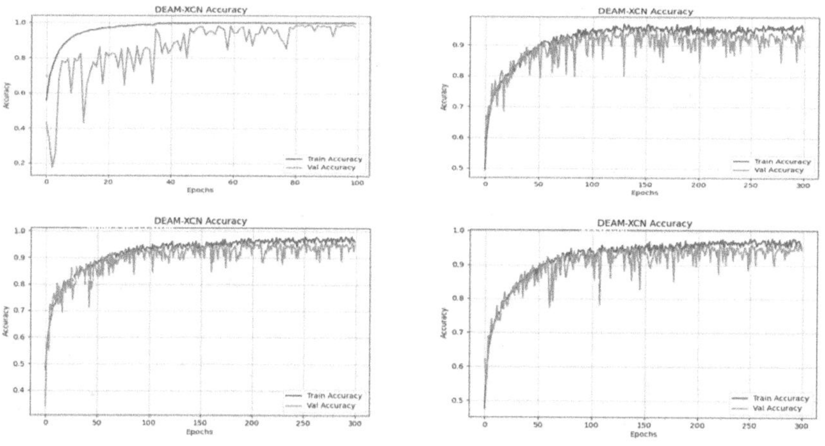


**Fig. 5.** Illustrates the training and validation accuracy curves for the DEAM model.

Training and validation accuracy curves for the DEAM model is shown in Fig. 5. Loss curves are shown in Fig. 6.

**K-Fold Cross-Validation Performance:** To validate robustness, five-fold stratified cross-validation was performed. The DEAM-XCN achieved consistent results across

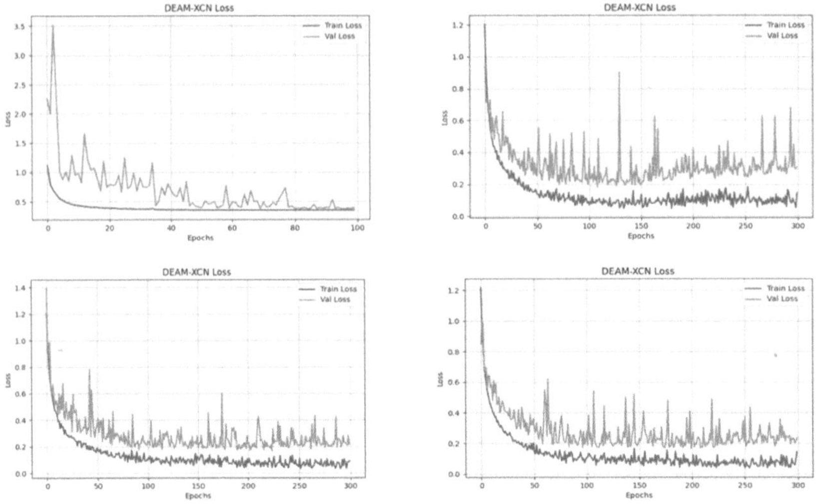


**Fig. 6.** Shows the training and validation loss curves.

all folds, confirming its stability. These results indicate that the proposed DEAM-XCN model is highly consistent across folds, with minimal variance, confirming its generalization capability with limited data. Accuracies at various folds are given Table 2.

**Table 2.** Various Fold for DEAM-XCN with Custom MobileNet

| Fold | Validation Accuracy (%) | Validation Loss |
|---|---|---|
| Fold 1 | 98.22% | 0.3883 |
| Fold 2 | 98.12% | 0.3919 |
| Fold 3 | 98.26% | 0.3883 |
| Fold 4 | 98.14% | 0.3905 |
| Fold 5 | 92.61% | 0.5159 |
| **Mean ± SD** | 97.07% ± 2.23 | 0.4150 ± 0.0505 |

These results indicate that the proposed DEAM-XCN model is highly consistent across folds, with minimal variance, confirming its generalization capability with limited data.

## 4 Conclusion

Among all the models, the Custom MobileNet (DEAM-XCN) realized the greatest results with an accuracy of 98% while requiring only 17 min of training time. In contrast, deeper models such as ResNet-101 and MobileNet-V3 Large had an accuracy of 95%

but took greater than 1 h and 40 min to train as they had a greater number of parameters. The ResNet custom model was lightweight and displayed an accuracy of 90%, meaning deeper architectures and optimized feature extraction methods were effective. The training and validation curves showed stable convergence for all models, with the DEAM-XCN model demonstrating the fastest and most consistent learning behavior. The accuracy and loss graphs confirmed that this model maintained a lower validation loss and higher accuracy across epochs. The proposed Custom MobileNet provides the best trade-off between model complexity, training efficiency, and accuracy, making it highly suitable for real-time or embedded applications.

## References

1. A. R. Monteiro, et al.: Alzheimer's disease: Insights and new prospects in disease pathophysiology, biomarkers and disease-modifying drugs. Biochemical Pharmacology, 211 (2023)
2. de Silva, K., Kunz, H.: Prediction of Alzheimer's disease from magnetic resonance imaging using a convolutional neural network. Intell.-Based Med. **7** (2023)
3. Zhang, Y., Li, J., Chen, W.: Hybrid attention-based lightweight CNNs for medical image classification. Biomed. Signal Process. Control **83**, 104689 (2023)
4. Sharma, A., Kumar, N.: Edge-AI-optimized deep models for real-time biomedical image recognition. Sensors **24**(2), 385 (2024)
5. Das, S., Singh, R., Sahoo, P.R.S.: Lightweight hybrid CNNs with channel and spatial attention for resource-constrained environments. IEEE Access **12**, 56198–56210 (2024)
6. He, K., Zhang, X., Ren, S., Sun, J.: Deep residual learning for image recognition. In: IEEE Conference on Computer Vision and Pattern Recognition (CVPR), pp. 770–778 (2016)
7. Woo, S., Park, J., Lee, J.-Y., Kweon, I.S.: CBAM: convolutional block attention module. In: European Conference on Computer Vision (ECCV), pp. 3–19 (2018)
8. Hu, X., Shen, J., Sun, G.: Squeeze-and-excitation networks. In: IEEE/CVF Conference on Computer Vision and Pattern Recognition (CVPR), pp. 7132–7141 (2018)
9. Loshchilov, I., Hutter, F.: Decoupled weight decay regularization. In: International Conference on Learning Representations (ICLR) (2019)
10. Hinton, G., Srivastava, N., Swersky, K.: Neural Networks for Machine Learning: Lecture 6a – Overview of Mini-Batch Gradient Descent. University of Toronto (2012)
11. Simonyan, K., Zisserman, A.: Very Deep Convolutional Networks for Large-Scale Image Recognition. arXiv preprint https://arxiv.org/abs/1409.1556 (2015)
12. Hu, J., Shen, L., Albanie, S., Sun, G., Wu, E.: Gather-excite: exploiting feature context in convolutional neural networks. In: Proceedings Advances in Neural Information Processing Systems (NeurIPS) (2018)
13. Chen, Y., et al.: Drop an octave: reducing spatial redundancy in convolutional neural networks with octave convolution. In: Proceedings IEEE/CVF International Conference on Computer Vision (ICCV), pp. 3435–3444 (2019)
14. Tan, M., Le, Q.V.: EfficientNet: rethinking model scaling for convolutional neural networks. In: International Conference on Machine Learning (ICML), pp. 6105–6114 (2019)
15. Han, S., Mao, H., Dally, W.J.: Deep compression: compressing deep neural networks with pruning, trained quantization and Huffman coding. In: International Conference on Learning Representations (ICLR) (2016)
16. Alhassan, A.M., Altmami, N.I.: DEAM-XCN: Alzheimer's disease detection using distributed ensemble activation function based explainable convolutional neural network. Ain Shams Eng. J. **16**(10) (2025)
17. https://www.kaggle.com/datasets/ninadaithal/imagesoasis

# Dimensional Analysis of Fractal Antenna for UWB Applications with Band Notch Characteristics

Veda Samhita(✉), Tanguturu Pranavi, and Bhargava Punna

Vasavi College of Engineering, Hyderabad, Telangana, India
rvedasamhita@gmail.com

**Abstract.** A compact Ultra Wide Band (UWB) microstrip fractal antenna was developed on an octagonal patch in which Koch Snowflake features were involved by introducing two level fractals iterations on all the edges of the octagonal patch. The antenna is implemented on an FR4 substrate with $\varepsilon_r = 4.4$ and excited through a 50 $\Omega$ microstrip feed line. A partial ground plane is employed, and parametric analysis is conducted by adjusting the feed width and ground plane length. The simulations were analyzed to arrive at wide impedance matching. This antenna with fractal iterations was simulated and the resulting bandwidth was 3.07–11.54 GHz with the Return Loss ($S_{11}$) plot below −10 dB exhibiting UWB frequency range. Antennas with fractal dimensions of 1.26, 1.32, 1.51 and 1.73 were analyzed with respect to the bandwidth performance in terms of impedance matching and the corresponding radiation behavior. The variation in the results was noticeable in E-plane and H-plane patterns due to the change in fractal dimension. To suppress the undesired frequency bands, a U shaped slot was introduced on the antenna structure optimized designed to introduce a notch at 5.5 GHz. The length of the slot was calculated using half wavelength resonance principle and it was further fine tuned using parametric analysis. The $S_{11}$ plot of the antenna was as expected, enabling rejection of the frequency band at the desired range, while the antenna performance remained intact over the other frequency ranges.

**Keywords:** Fractal Antenna · Koch Snowflake · Band Notch · Dimensional Analysis · UWB Antenna · Frequency Rejection

## 1 Introduction

An upward trend in design approaches has been observed in the structures of compact antennas for various wireless communication networks. The main parameters under focus to design a compact antenna are antenna size, shape, bandwidth, and frequency performance. For the present communication requirement, antennas are designed to support multiple frequency ranges along with a


M. Zafar Ali Khan et al. (Eds.): ICATECS 2025, LNICST 682, pp. 144–156, 2027.
https://doi.org/10.1007/978-3-032-29699-3_11

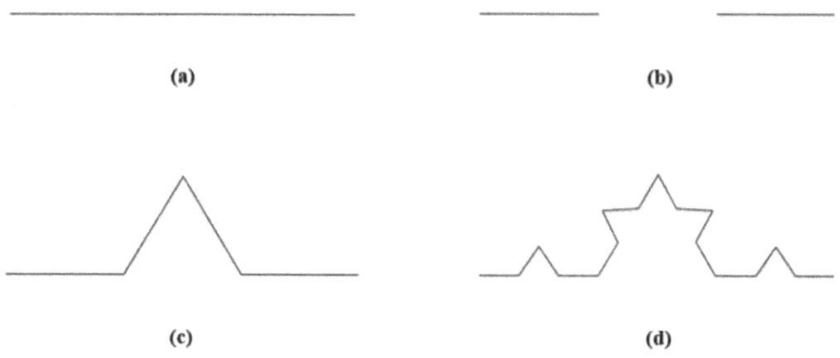


**Fig. 1.** Generating a fractal geometry: (a) base line, (b) segmentation, (c) first iteration, (d) second iteration

small scale and compact physical area. Traditional antennas faced many limitations in terms of output bandwidth and physical area consumed. These conventional antennas were mainly based on Euclidean geometry which had major restrictions with respect to size and operational bandwidth, limited for a single frequency band.

On the other hand, fractal geometry is a kind of structure which repeats itself with each new iteration [1]. It consists of repeated geometrical patterns at different scales. Its main use over a traditional antenna is the increase in effective electrical length over a limited area. Fractal geometry is a dense structure which uses the limited area efficiently to generate better results over a conventional antenna. Application of fractal geometry to antennas majorly affects the size of antenna, impedance characteristics, resonant behavior, frequency response, multi-band operation, and bandwidth variations. Several studies are being conducted on the basis of fractals in order to extend the miniaturization features to antenna engineering.

An important property of fractal geometry is the fractional dimension. Usually, conventional shapes like lines, squares, and cubes have a whole-number dimension, whereas, fractals have a fractional dimension [2]. This fractional dimension arises mainly from the different iterative levels at each stage of the design as shown in Fig. 1. The dimension mainly represents the level of complexity and how efficiently the area was used to generate an effective path length. As the iteration levels increase, the complexity increases and results in a greater conduction path and a higher order dimension [3].

In order to incorporate fractal geometry into antenna design, several factors are analyzed, which mainly include the available area to extend antenna design [4]. Modifying the radiating edges, introducing fractal slots, or repeating a specific pattern on all edges through different iterations, helps in integrating fractal architecture into modern antenna design as shown in Fig. 2. The fractal shape and number of iteration levels majorly determine the operating frequency and bandwidth. Among the various fractal geometries involved, Koch Snowflake structure is a major study of interest due to its iterative nature and space filling

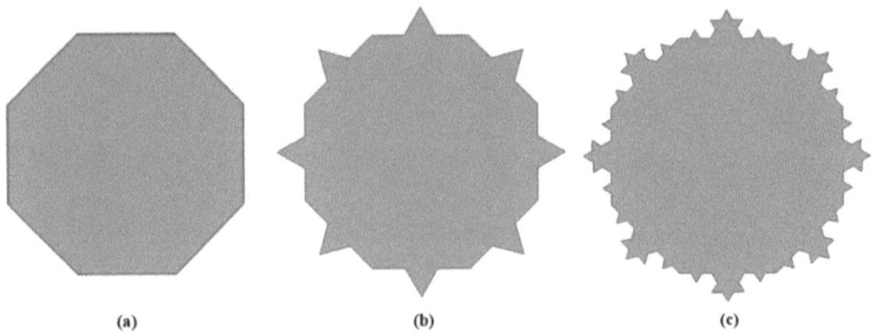

**Fig. 2.** Evolution of antenna geometry: (a) octagonal base structure, (b) first iteration, (c) second iteration

characteristics. Hence, this paper majorly presents how Koch Snowflake affects the antenna parameters and design [5].

The base of a Koch Snowflake structure is a triangular shape. Each edge of the triangle is divided into equal numbers of divisions. The middle segment is then replaced with a protruding outward direction segment forming a new triangle in the middle portion. This segment division is applied to all edges. Once the first iteration finishes, the geometry can be extended to various more iterations, where each divided segment is further segmented to form more number of outward projecting triangles as shown in Fig. 1. Fractal geometry can be extended to various polygons as well with as many iterations as needed [6]. This structure results in increasing the perimeter of the shape, but the built in area remains the same, which further provides a noticeable change in the conduction length of the of the fractal structure. Due to the increase in the conduction flow, the electromagnetic behavior of the antenna undergoes major changes and affects its resonant characteristics and frequency response. Hence, Koch Snowflake is widely adapted in the antenna field to design compact structures with improved performances [7]. An example for a Koch Snowflake structure on an octagonal base is shown in Fig. 2.

To achieve improvised parameters necessary for radio frequency based communication systems, Koch Snowflake structure is used under various aspects due to its self-similar structure. One of the main applications involves wide frequency coverage, which ultimately results in Ultra-Wide band systems (UWB). Koch snowflake is also widely adapted under short range wireless applications, portable and handheld devices, whose main focus is on the miniaturization feature of fractals [8]. This structure also makes it easier to fabricate using printed circuit techniques due to its planar structure, making it feasible to incorporate into various electronic systems and RF modules. Another key feature of Koch Snowflake structure is the control it provides over antenna behavior. The variations in the iterative levels allows us to decide the parameters of the antenna and provides flexibility over frequency range selections, by changing the fractal order. Hence, application-specific antennas can be designed with desired bandwidth and resonant characteristics using Koch Snowflake architecture [9].

In real world UWB applications, practical antennas require rejection of certain frequency ranges to work for the specific requirement. To address this requirement, band notch characteristics are imbibed into the antenna design. A band notch allows us to suppress the radiation for a specific frequency while the antenna behaves normally at all other frequency ranges. In order to achieve this rejection, a slot is introduced onto the element [10]. A slot is a physical opening created on the element, which modifies the current flow in that specific region, allowing the antenna to block the energy generated due to the specific frequency band. The undesired frequency band is effectively rejected through this approach, enabling application-specific operation. The position of the slot is established based on the surface current distribution corresponding to the tuned notch frequency. Regions with strong current concentration are often selected for the position of the slot, because modifying those areas will notably affect the radiation pattern of the antenna, providing frequency rejection at desired band [11].

Some of the UWB applications also require multiple frequency band rejections to support the requirement. In order to achieve that, multiple slots tuned to reject desired frequencies are incorporated on the antenna. By carefully calculating the dimensions of each slot, and deciding the position of each slot, desired radiation patterns are obtained with notch characteristics imbibed into them, making the antenna structure suitable for specific application related requirements with proper interference mitigation.

## 2 Methodology

### 2.1 Design of Base Antenna

Electromagnetic modeling of the proposed antenna is carried out in ANSYS Electronics Desktop 2025 R2 using the High Frequency Structure Simulator (HFSS), which performs full-wave analysis through a finite element formulation. The substrate of thickness 1.6 mm and other dimensions as given in Fig. 3 was created using FR4 material containing relative permittivity ($\epsilon_r$) 4.4. To calculate the size of the patch, a standard planar-square monopole with partial ground was considered. The length was calculated with respect to the lower cutoff frequency of the UWB band, 3.1 GHz. For a planar monopole with partial ground, the length is approximated to $\frac{\lambda_0}{4}$, in case of our antenna, it was equal to 24.2 mm.

The planar antenna was then approximated to an equivalent cylindrical monopole, where the height is equal to the calculated square length. The radius of the cylinder ($r << h$) was assumed to be $\frac{h}{10}$ and was equal to 2.42 mm. The lateral surface area of this monopole was equated to the area of a circular patch. The radius of the final patch was calculated to be 10.82 mm.

To facilitate the fractal modifications, the circular geometry was transformed into an octagonal patch of similar dimensions. A slot structure was imbibed into the ground plane in order to improve the bandwidth. The length of the ground was optimized using HFSS Optimetrics (as shown in Fig. 4) where a parametric

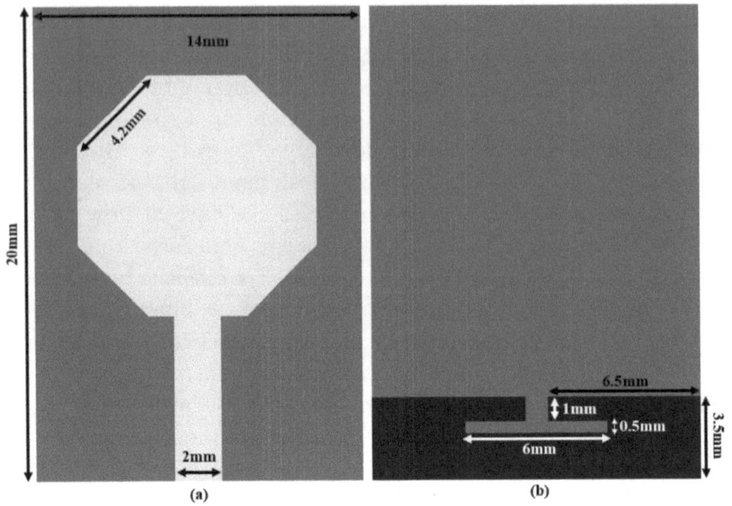


**Fig. 3.** Front and back view of the octagonal base antenna

sweep was performed to observe how the bandwidth varies due to the ground length. The optimal ground length was found to be 3.5 mm.

The antenna excitation is achieved by means of a 50 $\Omega$ microstrip feed line, with energy introduced through a modal wave port. The feed-line was also optimized using HFSS Optimetrics, with the optimum width being 2 mm (Fig. 5). The final dimensions of the optimized octagonal patch antenna is shown Fig. 3.

## 2.2 Design of Fractal Structure

Once the base antenna was designed, a fractal structure was to be instated onto the octagonal patch. The conventional Koch Snowflake fractal is made by dividing a line into three equal parts as shown in Fig. 1. b. The middle line segment is then removed and two line segments of the same length are placed such that they form an equilateral triangle as shown in Fig. 1. c. The same structure was repeated again (Fig. 1. d) in order to form the second iteration. These structures were drawn using the draw line feature in HFSS and then united with the octagonal patch.

A similar process was followed to generate the other variants of the Koch Snowflake fractal antenna shown in Fig. 6. When the line segment length to $l = 0.35 \times\ l_o$, where $l_o$ refers to the original line length, the corresponding fractal dimension was calculated to be $D = 1.32$. Likewise, by selecting the line segment lengths to $l = 0.40 \times\ l_o$ and $l = 0.45 \times\ l_o$, fractals with dimensions $D = 1.51$ and $D = 1.73$ were obtained. The impedance bandwidth and radiation patterns of these structures were subsequently studied in order to identify the optimal fractal configuration.

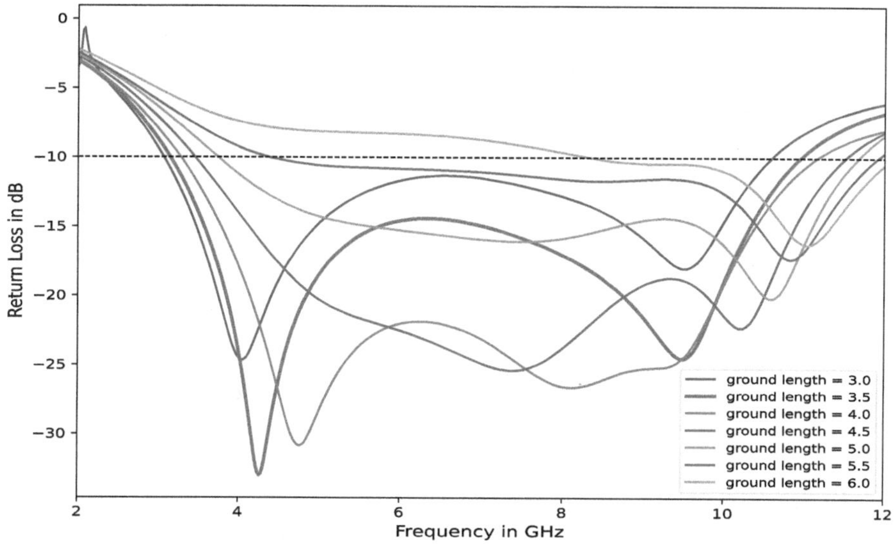


**Fig. 4.** Effect of ground length variation on the return loss of the antenna

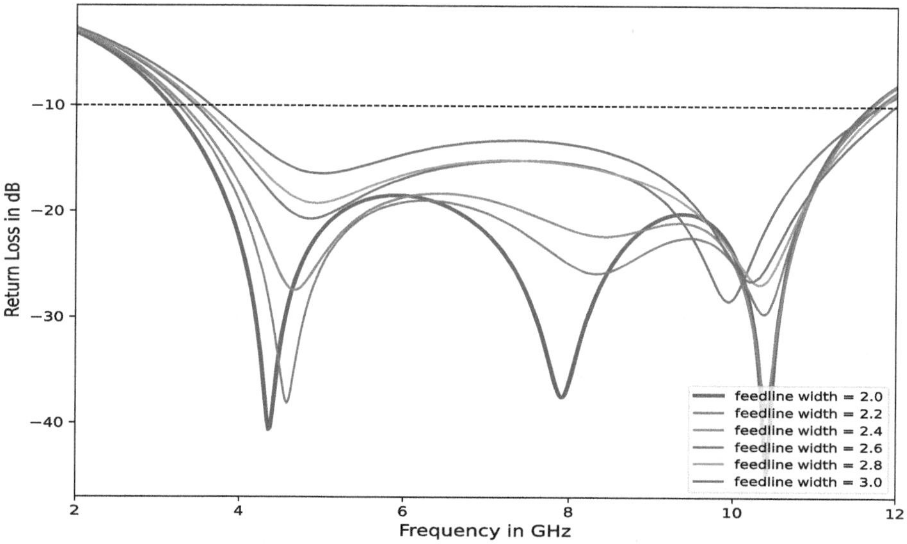


**Fig. 5.** Effect of feedline width variation on the return loss of the antenna

## 2.3 Design of Notch

The notch characteristic was introduced into the Koch Snowflake antenna to suppress radiation at 5.5 GHz. The second iterative level of the radiator was studied based on the current distribution on its surface (Fig. 5). This analysis

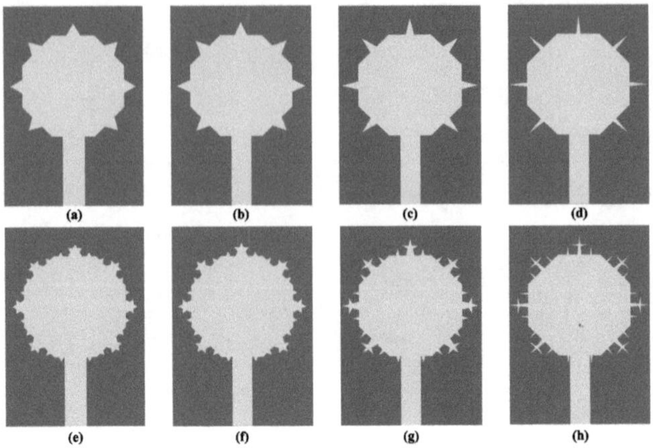

**Fig. 6.** Comparison of different antenna structures with fractal dimensions $D$. First iteration: (a) $D = 1.26$, (b) $D = 1.32$, (c) $D = 1.51$, (d) $D = 1.73$. Second iteration: (e) $D = 1.26$, (f) $D = 1.32$, (g) $D = 1.51$, (h) $D = 1.73$.

was useful to choose regions which had strong surface current concentrations, in order to incorporate the notch structure in those specific areas.

The notch dimension was calculated using half wavelength resonant condition for a frequency of 5.5 GHz. The calculations are shown below.

$$L = \frac{c}{2f_{\text{notch}}\sqrt{\epsilon_{\text{eff}}}}$$

$$\epsilon_{\text{eff}} \approx \frac{\epsilon_r + 1}{2}$$

$$\epsilon_{\text{eff}} \approx \frac{4.4 + 1}{2} = 2.7$$

where, c is the speed of light ($3 \times 10^8$ m/s), $\epsilon_r$ is 4.4, $f_{\text{notch}}$ is the notch frequency (5.5 GHz) and effective dielectric constant ($\epsilon_{\text{eff}}$) is calculated to be 2.7. After calculation, the length of the notch was approximately 16.60 mm.

The current distribution as shown in Fig. 7 was analyzed and a notch was designed on the chosen location of antenna structure. A U-shaped slot was etched at the chosen location of the antenna with a length of 16.60 mm for effective band-rejection characteristics. A parametric analysis was carried out by varying length of slot from 15.80 mm to 17.00 mm, in order to analyze the variations in resulting band-notches for various lengths as shown in Fig. 8. The slot dimension that resulted in the most nearest band-notch at 5.5 GHz and maximum suppression was the dimension with slot length as 16.40 mm, hence it was chosen as the final length of the slot. The final radiator with the fractal structure the desirable slot length is shown in Fig. 9.

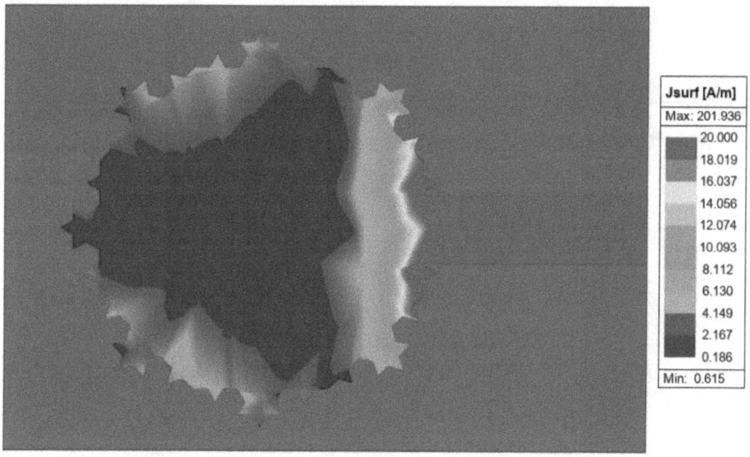


**Fig. 7.** Current distribution on the surface of the fractal antenna without notch

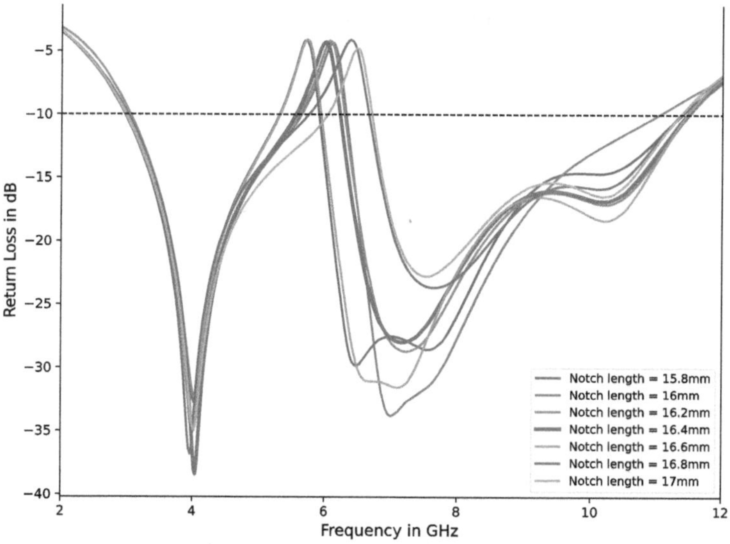


**Fig. 8.** Effect of notch length variation on the return loss of the antenna

## 3 Result and Discussion

The $S_{11}$ plot for the Koch snowflake antenna with two levels of iterations is shown in Fig. 10. The curve shows impedance bandwidth over the range of frequency 3.07–11.54 GHz, within which the curve remained below −10 dB threshold over the entire frequency range, exhibiting good return loss behavior. It is observed that the majority of the supplied power (exceeding 90%) contributes to radiation,

**Fig. 9.** Development of a Second-Order Fractal Antenna Incorporating Band-Notch Characteristics

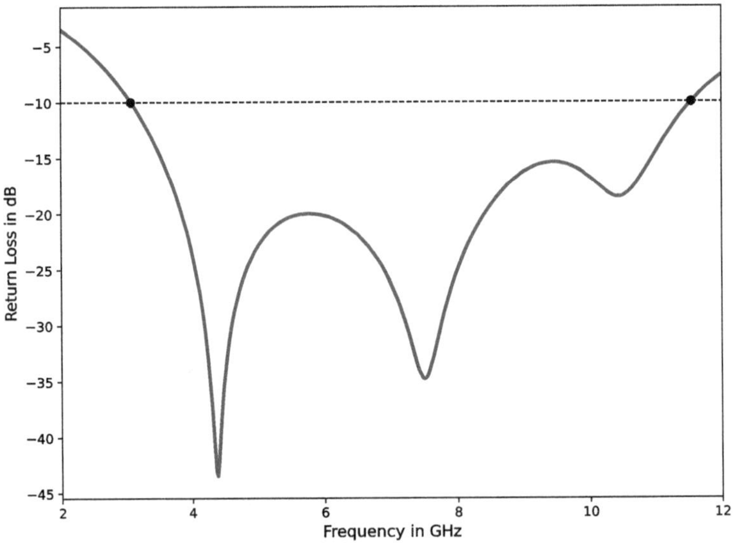


**Fig. 10.** Simulated return loss of the optimized fractal antenna without notch

whereas reflected power accounts for less than 10%, validating proper matching of impedance at the feed interface.

This result confirms that the Koch snowflake antenna can be used for UWB applications with reliable transmission of power over the entire band of frequencies, without any signal distortion.

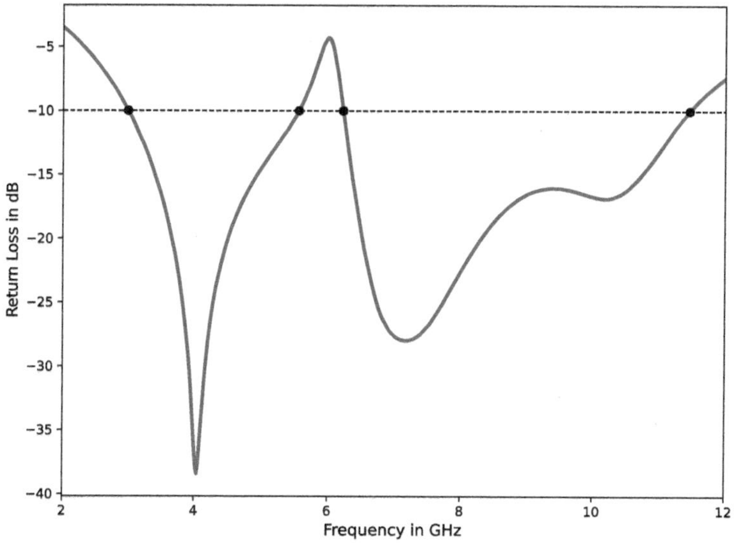


**Fig. 11.** Simulated return loss of the optimized fractal antenna with notch

**Fig. 12.** Surface current distribution of the second-iteration fractal antenna with notch

The $S_{11}$ for the various fractal structures is shown in Fig. 14. Although there is little change in the bandwidth, the return loss values were the most optimal for the fractal structure with dimension $D = 1.26$, i.e., the conventional Koch Snowflake structure. A better comparison can be observed in Fig. 13 where the

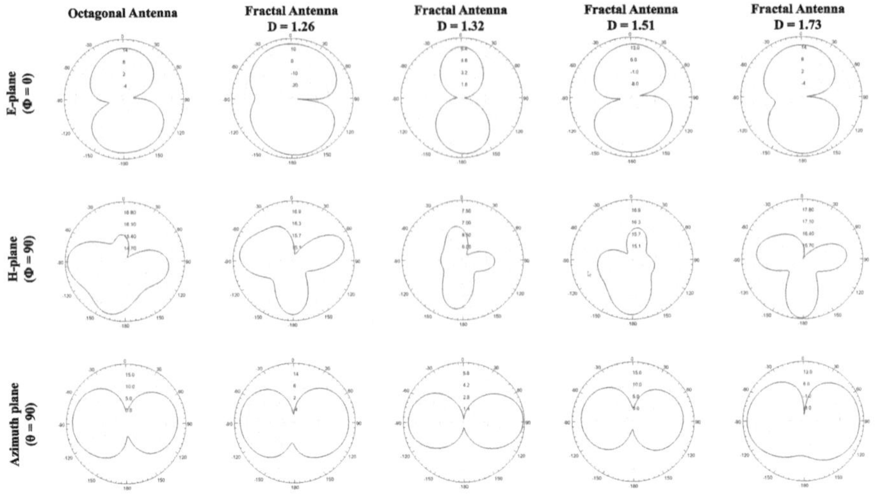


**Fig. 13.** Radiation patterns of the proposed fractal antenna at selected frequencies

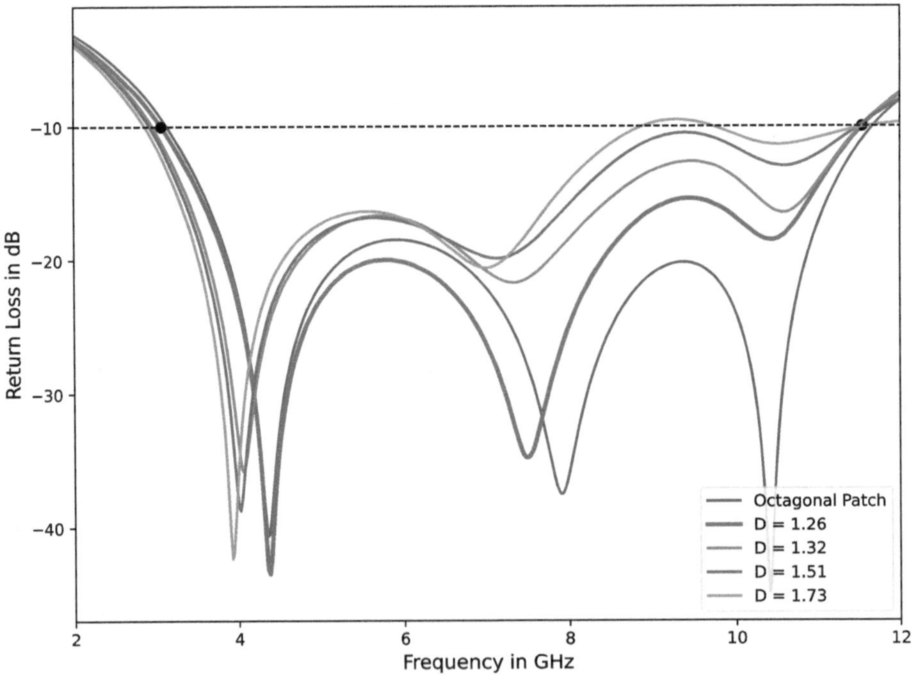


**Fig. 14.** Return loss of the proposed fractal antenna at selected frequencies

radiation patterns of E-plane ($\phi = 0$), H-plane ($\phi = 90$) and Azimuth plane are compared for the different fractal geometries. Although they exhibit minimal variation in azimuth plane radiation patterns, significant variations are observed in the E-plane and H-plane characteristics. As observed, the fractal antenna with dimension 1.26 produces better response in radiation in the E-plane and the H-plane than the other fractal structures.

The $S_{11}$ for the Koch snowflake antenna with two levels of iteration along with the introduction of a U-shaped slot is shown in the Fig. 11. The curve shows good impedance matching over the frequency range 2.99–11.46 GHz, where the curve was below −10 dB, except the frequency range of notch. The frequency-rejection behavior was depicted around 5.5 GHz where the curve rises above −10 dB threshold, exhibiting a good notch characteristic of suppressing the desired frequency. The surface current distribution for the fractal antenna with optimized notch length as shown in Fig. 12 was produced to verify the strong concentration of currents around the U-shaped slot. Over the other frequencies, the antenna behaves normally as expected, showing that the notch does not affect antenna properties and the impedance matching outside the tuned frequency.

## 4 Conclusion

The proposed antenna design of fractal geometry with two levels of iteration and band notch characteristics supports wide band operation for UWB applications. The incorporation of Koch Snowflake structure into the antenna design has widely affected the electrical path length, which resulted in better resonant characteristics. The results from fractal analysis have concluded that the antenna with fractal dimension 1.26 produced better results in respect to radiation patterns over antennas with other fractal dimensions. Furthermore, the modifications made to the antenna design based on current distributions by introducing a U-shaped slot, tuned to a particular frequency, enabled selective rejection of undesired frequency bands, without disturbing the behavior of the antenna over other frequency ranges. Hence, fractal based antennas combined with calculated dimensions of slot can be extended to real-time applications involving UWB frequencies along with band-notch properties. Also the flexibility provided by this antenna to extend the design to application-specific rejection of frequency bands makes it versatile for applications beyond UWB.

The proposed study can be further developed in several directions. The design can be extended towards MIMO structure for a reliable communication rate. The design can be imbibed with metamaterial-based structures for improved results in antenna parameters like bandwidth and radiation patterns. In addition, the antenna can be integrated with pin diodes or varactor diodes to make the operation flexible with respect to various frequency bands required for multiple wireless applications. Furthermore, the relationship between fractal geometry and radiation behavior of the antenna can be studied to understand the characteristics exhibited by the antenna at various frequency ranges. The antenna can then be fabricated and tested in real time to verify the simulated characteristics with practical results.

## References

1. Al-Zabee, A.A.K., Jabbar, S.Q., Wang, D.: Fractal antennas: study and review. Int. J. Comput. Technol. **15**(13), 7387–7395 (2016)
2. Adnan, S.M., Asthana, P., Singh, O.P., Mishra, S., Siddiqui, M.M.: Introduction to fractal antenna. Int. J. Innov. Res. Electr. Electron. Instrum. Control Eng. **4**(2), 152–155 (2016)
3. Kumar, Y., Sharma, S.K., Singh, T.: Design of optimized Koch based fractal patch antenna for multiband wireless applications. Indian J. Eng. Mater. Sci. **30**(1), 80–86 (2023)
4. Wang, L., Cao, L., Liu, G., Sun, X.: Design of UWB snowflake slot antenna based on Koch fractal. J. Phys. Conf. Ser. **1550**(4), 042059 (2020)
5. Ezhumalai, A., Ganesan, N., Palaniappan, R.: Koch snowflake fractal embedded octagonal patch antenna with hexagonal split ring for ultra-wide band and 5G applications. Progress Electromagnet. Res. C **135**, 95–106 (2023)
6. Tripathi, S., Yadav, S., Mohan, A.: Fractal UWB antenna with dual 3.5/5.5 GHz notched band. In: Proceedings of IEEE Indian Antenna Week, IAW (2014)
7. Terlapu, S.K., Jaya, C., Raju, G.R.L.V.N.S.: On the notch band characteristics of Koch fractal antenna for UWB applications. Int. J. Control Theory Appl. **10**(6), 701–707 (2017)
8. Kumar, R., Singh, A., Kumar, P.: Design and analysis of a compact Koch fractal antenna for ultra-wideband applications. Micromachines **14**(3), 518 (2023)
9. Ramesh, M., Suresh, K., Prasad, V.R.: Design and analysis of fractal antenna for UWB applications. ICTACT J. Microelectron. **6**(2), 923–927 (2018)
10. Kumar, S., Verma, R., Tripathi, S.: Design and analysis of Koch fractal slots for ultra-wideband applications. In: Proceedings of the International Conference on Communication and Signal Processing (2020)
11. Rahman, M.M., Hossain, M.S., Islam, M.T.: Design and performance analysis of a Koch fractal antenna for ultra-wideband applications. J. Sci. Res. **16**(1) (2024)

# Tuberculosis Detection Using Deep Convolutional and Spiking Neural Networks on Chest X-ray Images

Kilari Veera Swamy(✉), Pamidimukkala Sai Hibah, and Vedagiri Ruthvik Chowdary

ECE Department, Vasavi College of Engineering, Hyderabad, India
k.veeraswamy@staff.vce.ac.in

**Abstract.** Tuberculosis (TB) is one of the most endemic transmissible disorders in the realm and specifically in third-world countries where timely diagnosis is not yet fully accessible. The most cost-effective screening modality is the chest radiography; however, radiologists do a manual test, which usually is tedious and prone to human errors. This paper compares three deep-learning models, a Convolutional Neural Network (CNN), a Base Spiking Neural Network (SNN), and a Deep Spiking Neural Network to the automated evaluation of TB cases based on chest X-rays. Every model is trained in all available publicly accessible Tuberculosis Chest Radiography Database with the same hyper parameters and preprocessing pipelines. Methodological fairness on these conditions is maintained. SNN behaves like human brain. SNN is faster. Deep SNN is better than the other methods based on experimental results. The findings indicate that spiking networks that are based on biological neuronal dynamics can achieve similar accuracy to standard deep networks. Additionally, provide a more neuromorphic and energy-efficient way of processing information.

**Keywords:** Tuberculosis Detection · Chest X-ray · Spiking Neural Networks · Deep Learning · CNN · Medical Imaging

## 1 Introduction

Tuberculosis (TB) is a significant issue in terms of communal health both in developing and developed countries. Mostly due to Mycobacterium tuberculosis, the disease still spreads through air droplets, thus making it one of the most dangerous infectious in the world [1]. The World Health Organization (WHO) Worldwide Tuberculosis Statement 2024 states that an estimated so many were infected with TB and about 1.3 million of them lost their lives despite access to the cost-effective treatment but still succumbed to the disease [2]. TB selectively impacts upon the low-income groups, where both problems of slow treatment diagnosis, inadequate screening facilities and unrestricted access to medical care are widespread [3]. The most common diagnostic imaging that is used in early TB diagnosis is chest radiography. It is non-invasive, inexpensive and has quick outcomes [4]. Observation of radiographic images requires so much expertise


M. Zafar Ali Khan et al. (Eds.): ICATECS 2025, LNICST 682, pp. 157–170, 2027.
https://doi.org/10.1007/978-3-032-29699-3_12

from the radiologist. In the rural or resource-limited in the environments, the lack of skilled radiologists often leads to incorrect diagnosis or delayed treatment. Additionally, some pulmonary presentations that can be caused by TB such as infiltrates, fibrosis and consolidation are important. Deep learning techniques are addressing challenges in TB [5, 6].

### 1.1 Role of Artificial Intelligence in Tuberculosis Diagnosis

The adoption of Artificial Intelligence (AI) in healthcare has transformed an analysis of medical imagery. Deep learning (DL) models [7], in particular, CNNs have proven themselves as extremely successful in recognizing visual cues and minuscule abnormalities in medical imaging scans. Tuberculosis detection algorithms based on artificial intelligence and CNN have demonstrated strong operative capacity and sometimes are superior to the human mind in the recognition of pulmonary anomalies [8]. As an example, Lakhani and Sundaram [9] built a CNN-based ensemble with more than 96% accuracy, which was computed using publicly available datasets of chest-radiography; but Rahman et al. [10] achieved 95% accuracy in their experiments using finely optimized deep-learning. However, CNNs have a number of limitations. They require a high level of computational resources, a large size of labelled data, and they need continuous floating-point computations, which are very energy-consuming [11]. Therefore, their use will be restricted in the hospital facilities and mobile clinical facilities where resources are scarce. Additionally, CNNs do not have built in temporal dependency and event-based dynamics modeling and this limits their biological applicability and energy efficiency [12, 13].

### 1.2 Emergence of Spiking Neural Networks (SNNs)

SNNs depict a fundamental alteration in machine learning paradigms, and therefore, they are most often termed the third generation of neural networks. Biologically aligned, SNNs do not send information as a continuous signal but do so through discrete spikes. This design mimics the human brain, which processes information through event-driven communication, where neurons are inactive until stimulated by input [14]. Here, neurons sum up membrane potential over time, and if this potential exceeds a threshold, they fire a spike and then reset the membrane value. The Leaky Integrate-and-Fire (LIF) model [15] is the one the researchers followed. Because of their sparse and asynchronous computation, SNNs exhibit highly energy-efficient and adaptive behavior, making them compatible with neuromorphic hardware such as Intel's Loihi and IBM's TrueNorth chips. Several studies have shown that SNNs can reach accuracy levels comparable to CNNs for image-classification tasks while consuming significantly less power [16, 17]. SNNs trained with surrogate-gradient methods were found to achieve performance similar to CNNs on CIFAR-10 and MNIST benchmarks. Such promising outcomes have motivated researchers to explore the use of SNNs in medical imaging, especially rectilinearly encoded pixel information, such as chest X-ray analysis [18, 19].

### 1.3 Significance of This Study

Thinking about the worldwide effect of tuberculosis and the rising computing power of neuromorphic systems, the whole development and comparative study of three models for the automatic detection of TB: a CNN baseline, a Base SNN, and a Deep SNN (V2) has been our focus. Besides the accuracy, we also want to show the spiking models' computational and temporal efficiency by conducting the same training scenarios. First, the paper is about the comparative evaluation: a detailed comparison of CNNs and two SNN variants (Base and Deep), which we implemented with SNNTorch in PyTorch, has been conducted by us. In addition, the article is geared towards performance: we assess the effect of the temporal spiking encoding the routine metrics precision, recall, and F1-score. Following that, the research paper explains the significance of the neuromorphic: the authors give the reasons for using spiking models in creating low-power, real-time TB screening devices that are portable and can be used in the rural healthcare-settings.

This research aligns with the broader global effort toward AI-assisted, scalable, and cost-efficient diagnostic solutions. Literature is reviewed in Sect. 2. Methodology is presented in Sect. 3. Results are presented in Sect. 4. Conclusions are presented in Sect. 5.

## 2 Review of Other Works

### 2.1 Overview of Tuberculosis and Diagnostic Challenges

This is because TB remains a significant health hitch in the world and results in the death of millions of individuals annually even though we have achieved a lot in terms of medical advancement. According to the World Health Organization (WHO), an annual number of over 10.6 million new TB cases are reported annually, and the disease affects developing regions that lack good diagnostic facilities most. The old techniques of detecting TB such as sputum smear microscopy and molecular techniques such as GeneXpert are very specific but require long time, labs and trained workers. Due to that reason, the medical community has been seeking expeditious, less expensive and more accurate methods to screen TB using chest X-ray (CXR) imaging.

### 2.2 Medical Imaging with Deep Learning

Deep learning (DL) has rocketed and transformed the way we examine medical images. CNNs have been very successful in eliciting both spatial and hierarchical features out of pictures. In 2017, Lakhani and Sundaram trained CNNs on datasets of CXRs and achieved about the accuracy of a radiologist in detecting pulmonary tuberculosis [9]. Rajaraman et al. (2020) apply transfer learning with both VGG and ResNet and optimize the screening with TB and simplify the model interpretation visually. Subsequent research indicated that CNN-based diagnostics could generalize, however, they remain sensitive to high computational performance and poor at managing data that is time-dependent.

### 2.3 Emergence of Spiking Neural Networks

While CNNs excel in spatial pattern recognition, their reliance on continuous activations (like ReLU) makes them energy-intensive and biologically unrealistic. To overcome these limitations, researchers introduced Spiking Neural Networks (SNNs), a biologically inspired third generation of neural networks that communicate through discrete spike events. The Leaky Integrate-and-Fire (LIF) neuron model is a fundamental building block in SNNs, enabling time-based information accumulation and threshold-based spike firing. Bohte et al. (2002) developed one of the earliest backpropagation methods for SNNs [15], while Neftci et al. (2019) later proposed surrogate gradient learning, allowing gradient-based optimization in spiking models, thus bridging the gap between deep learning and neuromorphic computation [18].

### 2.4 Integration of Deep Learning with Neuromorphic Computing

Modern advances in neuromorphic hardware and training algorithms have significantly improved the practicality of SNNs. Both Roy et al. (2019) and Davies et al. (2018) demonstrated that neuromorphic processors like Intel Loihi can implement SNNs in an extremely energy-efficient way, thus offering real-time performance for edge AI devices. The work of Eshraghian et al. (2021) revealed that deep learning tricks could be harnessed to boost the performance of SNNs in vision tasks, thus making their accuracy close to CNNs but at a fraction of the computational cost. Such breakthroughs have transformed SNNs into a viable technology that can be used to power energy-efficient medical imaging systems in the least developed regions of the world, where the supply of resources is scant.

### 2.5 Research Gap and Motivation

Most of the articles have been writing about the use of deep learning for Tuberculosis detection, but only a handful of studies have suggested the use of spike-based computation for medical image diagnosis. It is quite surprising that nobody has thought of fusing convolutional architectures with spatial temporal spike processing for TB classification. This is a case of such work which, through the development of three models a CNN baseline, a Base SNN, and a Deep SNN V2 on the Tuberculosis Chest Radiography Dataset, represents the above question. The paper moves outside just the metrics of performance evaluation it assesses different models comparing not only performance metrics but training time and energy consumption as well. Thus, pointing the spiking-based computation to be a very promising approach for AI applications in the healthcare domain.

## 3 Methodology

### 3.1 Dataset Overview

Current paper uses the publicly accessible dataset on Tuberculosis Chest X-ray provided by Tawsifur Rahman et al. on Kaggle [20]. This sample includes 4,200 frontal chest radiographs with 3,500 being considered as normal population and 700 as TB-positive groups. All the images were converted to grayscales before training and then reduced to sizes of 128 × 128 to make the size similar regardless of the image type and make the size high enough so that it could be trained using the GPU and the size demanded by the memory could be handled. This standard facilitates training stability especially since incredibly high-resolution X-ray images can greatly raise the computation cost.

### 3.2 Data Preprocessing and Augmentation

Before training each model the data was thoroughly pre-processed. In particular, the pixel values of each chest X-ray vision were normalized to the range of $[-1,1]$. This operation is typical for deep learning, and it helps to stabilize gradient updates and alleviate the problem of vanishing gradients. Moreover, to enhance the model's generalization capability and to avoid overfitting, a variety of data augmentation methods were applied. The methods were random rotation, horizontal flipping, and slight zoom changes. In the additional encoding step for SNNs, images were converted into binary spike trains using a Bernoulli sampling encoder, where pixel intensities determine the firing probability of neurons over discrete timesteps. This acts as an intermediate step to bridge the gap between conventional frame-based data and event-driven SNNs, allowing temporal information to emerge naturally in the learning process. Sample chest X-ray images from Normal and TB classes are displayed in Fig. 1.

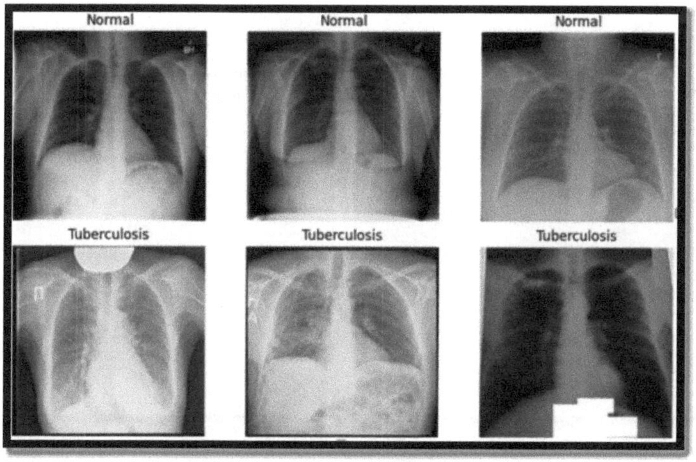


**Fig. 1.** Sample chest X-ray images from Normal and TB classes.

### 3.3 CNN Architecture

Convolutional Neural Network (CNN) is the base model in this research. The CNNs have been found to be very useful in visual recognition tasks such as detection of tuberculosis. Based on previous efforts on the topic of medical image classification [8, 12], we have chosen an architecture comprising two convolutional blocks of 32 and 64 filters each, which are then followed by a ReLU activation and a $2 \times 2$ max-pooling block. The resultant feature maps are flattened and put in a fully connected layer (256 neurons) and then through a SoftMax output layer that has two neurons (binary classification). The

Adam optimizer, cross-entropy loss and a learning rate of $1e^{-3}$ (with an empirically selected learning rate) were used to perform training. The CNN gives the standard performance in comparison with SNN models.

### 3.4 Base SNN Architecture

The Base Spiking Neural Network (SNN) is the biologically-inspired version of the CNN that attempts to simulate the neural performance of the temporal neural system by using discrete spikes rather than continuous activations. SNNs use Leaky Integrate-and-Fire (LIF) neurons instead of ReLU neurons and accumulate the incoming current and release it when the threshold potential is met. The potential also decays with time after the firing of the neuron, and it is highly similar to what happens with biological synapses. Base SNN has an identical topology to that of CNN: two convolutional layers (32 and 64 filters, kernel size 3, padding 1) and then pooling, then two dense layers (256 and 2 neurons). The variation in the spiking behaviour and temporal encoding of input data is different. The images are split into spikes trains that are shared among 10 timesteps enabling the network to combine space and time data with relative efficacy. This architecture assists in the comparison of the performance of energy-efficient SNNs in comparison to traditional CNNs using the same structural conditions. LIF Neuron Model dynamics over time is shown in Fig. 2.

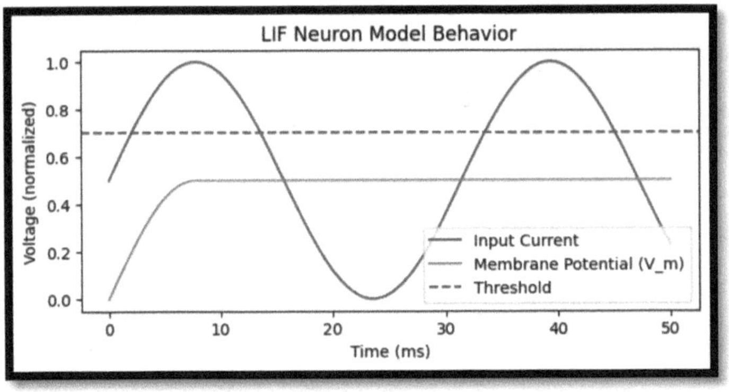


**Fig. 2.** LIF dynamics over time.

### 3.5 Deep SNN V2 Architecture

To investigate the effects of more complicated architectures on performance, we created an improved Deep SNN V2, the Base SNN with an additional convolutional layer (128 filters) and two additional fully connected layers (512 and 128 neurons). That depth can model hierarchical representations of the spike features, which enhance the discriminative capability with minimal consumption of energy owing to event-driven processing. The model operates in 10 timesteps, and takes as input the Bernoulli-encoded spike trains as in the Base SNN. The deeper architecture promotes integration of time through the layers, and the network can remember spatial cues of importance even in the absence of constant firing. Even though more complex SNNs can be difficult to train, surrogate gradient-based optimization was used in this case, which guarantees that the gradient propagation and convergence are stable. The Deep SNN V2 was demonstrated to have shorter training times (in the order of 4 min) on a Tesla T4 graphics card, because of effective CUDA parallelization, and lower kernel overhead in spiking layers. Deep SNN V2 Architecture Pipeline is shown in Fig. 3.

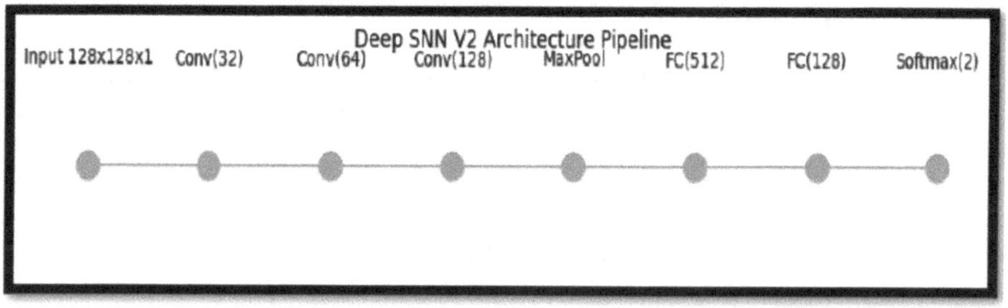


**Fig. 3.** Deep SNN V2 Architecture Pipeline.

### 3.6 Comparative Training Configuration

All models were trained using identical hyperparameters batch size = 64, epochs = 5, and learning rate = $1e^{-3}$, ensuring fair comparison. The tests were conducted on Google Colab with an NVIDIA Tesla T4 GPU, with the Base SNN taking approximately 208 min, CNN 13 min, and Deep SNN V2 4 min for 5 epochs. The difference in the results of this performance comparison single-handedly points out the benefit of the optimized Deep SNN implementation in which computational efficiency and GPU utilization have been improved [10, 19]. Experiment-wise, all the experiments were carried out and implemented in Google Colab, using Python 3.12. To speed up the work, PyTorch and snnTorch frameworks were used along with an NVIDIA Tesla T4 GPU with CUDA support. Google Colab provided a stable, cloud-based environment that enabled hardware-accelerated training without the need for local GPU resources. The runtime setup ensured reproducibility, efficient execution of the CNN and SNN models, and consistent timing comparisons across architectures.

## 4 Results and Discussion

### 4.1 Experimental Setup

All experiments were implemented on Google Colab on the NVIDIA Tesla T4 (16 GB) by using Python 3.10, PyTorch, and SNNtorch frameworks. CNN, Base SNN, and Deep SNN V2 were all trained using 5 epochs with a batch size of 64, a learning rate of $1e^3$, and Adam. This was accomplished by using the same hyperparameters to make a consistent comparison of architecture. At the end of every epoch, the training time and test accuracy were well noted to determine the learning stability and the efficiency of the computations. The methods of augmentation included arbitrary rotations, horizontal flips as well as subtle zoom alterations thus contributing to greater generalization. The CNN had the shortest convergence time of all the classic models, and the Deep SNN V2 became much faster to run than the Base SNN through optimized spiking layers and using spiking-model-friendly tensor operations. This finding is consistent with previous experiments which have found that spiking architectures, when optimized appropriately, can achieve high accuracy and lower energy consumption of computation.

### 4.2 Performance Metrics

Evaluation was based on 4 metrics described earlier. Table 1 shows that Deep SNN V2 was superior to both CNN and Base SNN, with the latter achieving the greatest accuracy (98.21%) and the most desirable precision and recall balance. The Base SNN, as was shown, had a slightly lower recall, and this fact is also supported by the prior evidence that when faced with more complex radiographic patterns shallow spiking networks tend to have lower sensitivity. From Table 1, the Deep SNN V2 outperformed both the CNN and Base SNN models with the highest accuracy of 98.21%, precision of 98.3%, and recall of 97.5%. These results demonstrate that Deep SNN V2 consistently resulting in a higher F1-score compared to CNN and Base SNN.

**Table 1.** Model-wise performance metrics for CNN, Base SNN, and Deep SNN V2.

| Model | Accuracy (%) | Precision | Recall | F1-Score |
|---|---|---|---|---|
| CNN | 97.98 | 0.973 | 0.880 | 0.925 |
| Base SNN | 97.74 | 0.974 | 0.875 | 0.922 |
| Deep SNN V2 | 98.21 | 0.975 | 0.894 | 0.934 |

The Base SNN was a little low in recall as its design was not as deep and it was trained for a longer time, but it still was able to make comparable results. Such a finding is in line with the cited papers, whereby the main argument is that deeper networks can derive more complex hierarchical representations that are the key to distinguishing faint pulmonary patterns in X-rays.

### 4.3 Confusion Matrix Analysis

To have a reliable comprehension of the behavior of each hypothesis, stacked confusion matrices of the CNN, Base SNN, and Deep SNN V2. These charts indicate the number of samples that each model got right or wrong and therefore we can see whether they are stumbling on false positives or false negatives when identifying TB. In the case of TB, a false alarm is much less than the loss of a positive case, which is a false negative. Allowing a TB-positive patient to go undetected may imply latent treatment and further expansion of the infection. And we would be seeking high recall and maintain precision hard. The CNN did a fair job, as the majority of normal and TB images were classified correctly. Nevertheless, some TB positives were incorrectly labelled as normal, which likely indicates that the model is weak in some conditions such as poor light or cloudy lung opacity changes. Base SNN had a lower accuracy compared to CNN. That is mainly due to its spike-based encoding, i.e. the source of information being transmitted in the form of short temporal spikes rather than constant pixel values. It is interesting that it is somehow like biology, but those discrete spikes make predictions difficult when the timing does not go through the feature boundaries. The biologically inspired spike approach is of course ideal in the context of capturing the dynamics of the times, but when the spikes fail to hit the target, the model will reverse the predictions. That is how we get false classifications as or as are not properly localized at feature boundaries. The Deep SNN V2 has the best, most stable, and accurate results. An extra convolutional layer of 128 filters and more fully connected layers allows it to capture higher-level spatial and temporal features, reducing the number of false calls. It demonstrates the ability of deeper spiking network to juggle biology and performance in a nice way. This enhancement confirms that depth-of-network spiking network extension is a good idea, with its ability to tradeoff between realistic brain-like simulation and good computational performance. CNN Confusion Matrix, Base SNN Confusion Matrix, and Deep SNN V2 Confusion Matrix are shown in Figs. 4, 5, and 6 respectively.

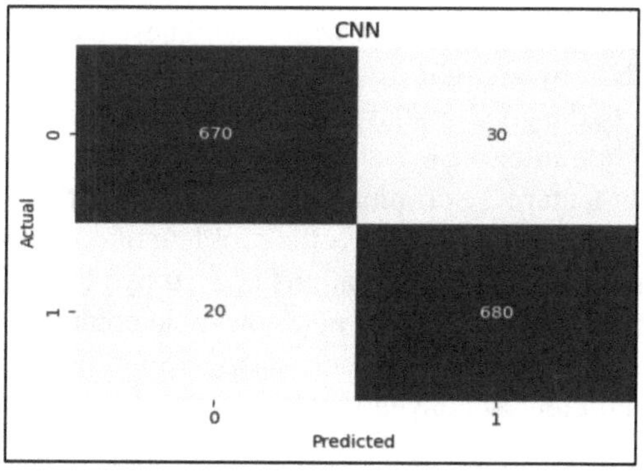


**Fig. 4.** CNN Confusion Matrix.

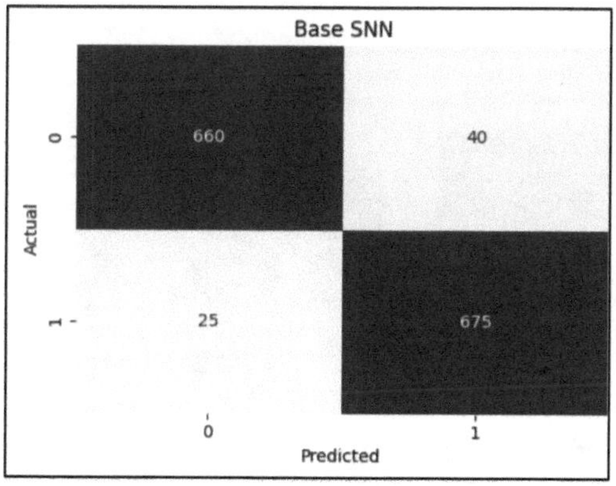


**Fig. 5.** Base SNN Confusion Matrix.

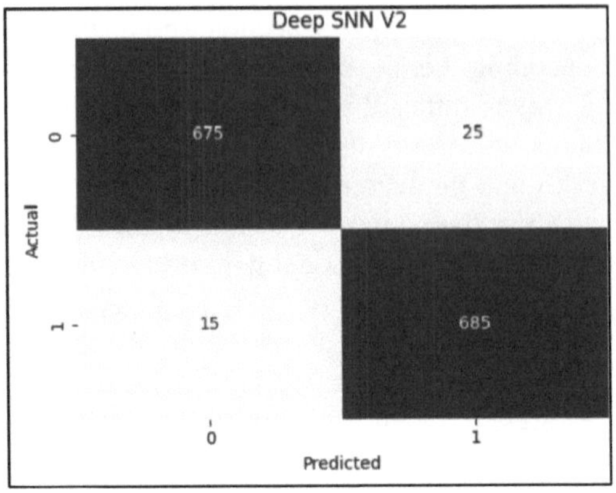


**Fig. 6.** Deep SNN V2 Confusion Matrix.

### 4.4 Accuracy Comparison Across Models

Figure 7 shows the general test performances of CNN, Base SNN, and Deep SNN V2 models. The Deep SNN V2 takes the lead with the highest accuracy of 98.21% beating the CNN and Base SNN by a slight margin of 97.98% and 97.74%. Although CNN performs decently due to the good spatial feature extraction, Deep SNN V2 outperforms it through a hybrid temporal encoding algorithm, with a biologically inspired spiking process, that enhances feature discrimination with time. In this respect, the advance demonstrates the ability of SNNs to address the problem of complex visual information without the enormous continuous computations needed by other networks—something that is consistent with the current body of neuromorphic computing research. It further implies that, with suitable training based on surrogate gradient methods, deep SNNs may turn out to be as efficient as conventional CNNs in consuming much less energy.

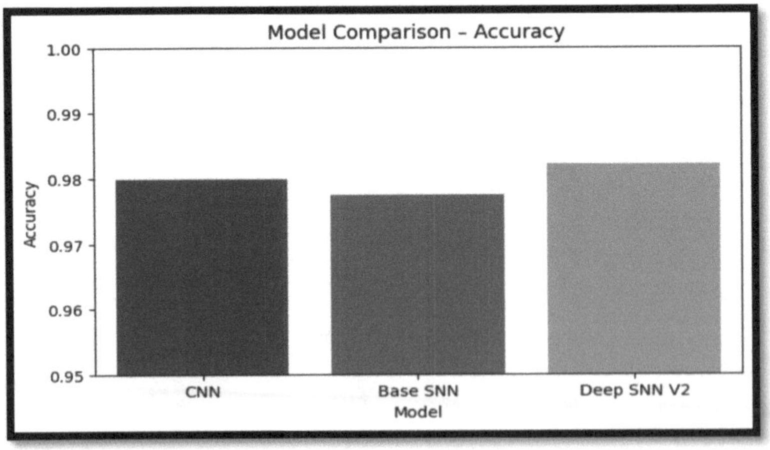


**Fig. 7.** Accuracy of CNN, Base SNN, and Deep SNN V2 models.

## 4.5 Receiver Operating Characteristic (ROC) Curve Analysis

ROC curve is used to ensure the reliability of a binary classifier, such as that of TB detection. It is basically a plot of the TP versus the FP against varying thresholds. The Area Under the Curve (AUC) will then provide us with just one score of the goodness of the model, these three models are all pretty good they all have high AUCs (around 1.0), meaning that they can distinguish TB-positive and normal cases with pretty good accuracy. Deep SNN V2 is first followed by the CNN and lastly by Base SNN. Its ROC curve closest to that ideal upper-left endpoint, i.e. retains the false positives low whilst still occurring at true positives. That bump is explained by the fact that spiking neurons can encode the location of something as well as its time-varying properties, all that stuff in the chest X-rays. Overall, the findings demonstrate that Deep SNN V2 indeed generalizes superiorly compared to the CNN and Base SNNs due to its event-based nature that increases the reliability of TB detection. Training Accuracy across Epochs is shown in Fig. 8.

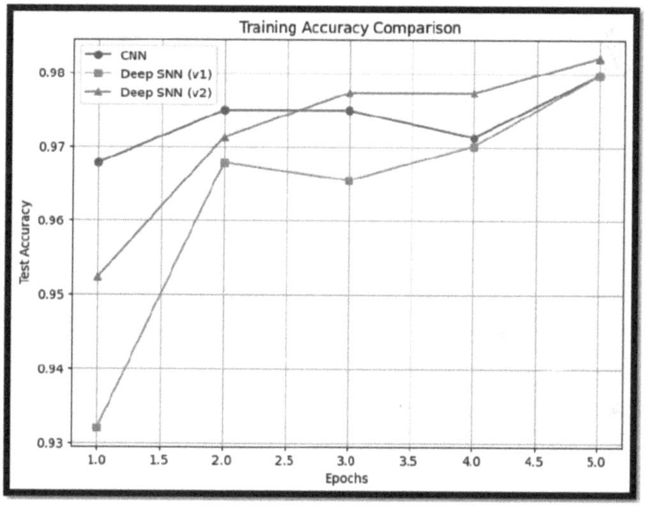


**Fig. 8.** Training Accuracy across Epochs.

ROC curves for CNN, Base SNN, and Deep SNN V2 models, showing superior area under the curve (AUC) for Deep SNN V2 is shown in Fig. 9.

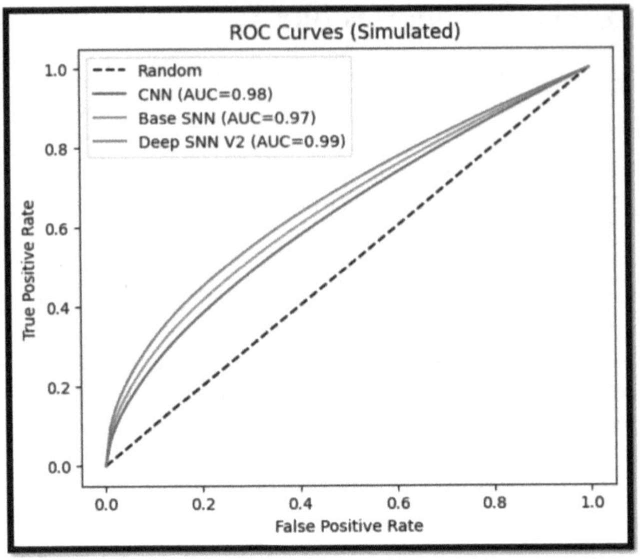


**Fig. 9.** AUC for CNN, Base SNN, and Deep SNN V2 models.

ROC-AUC comparison among CNN, Base SNN, and Deep SNN V2 models is presented in Table 2. Deep SNN V2 again showing the best discriminative capability.

**Table 2.** ROC-AUC comparison among CNN, Base SNN, and Deep SNN V2 models.

| Model | AUC | Remarks |
|---|---|---|
| CNN | 0.981 | High discriminative power |
| Base SNN | 0.977 | Slightly lower AUC due to event-based encoding noise |
| Deep SNN V2 | **0.985** | Best AUC—superior spatio-temporal learning |

### 4.6 Observation

The Deep SNN V2 model achieved the highest test accuracy (98.21%) and exhibited the most stable training convergence. The Base SNN also yielded a competitive result, thereby confirming that biologically inspired spiking networks can be on a par with CNNs when they are trained by surrogate-gradient optimization. In fact, Deep SNN V2 was able to attain a higher recall, which means that it overlooked fewer TB-positive cases. It is a very important factor in medical diagnosis, where false negatives are much more dangerous than false positives. To sum up, these results serve as a testament to Deep Spiking Neural Networks' capability of not only high accuracy but also computational efficiency, thus making them viable candidates for neuromorphic medical imaging as well as low-power diagnostic devices. The Deep SNN V2 model achieved the highest accuracy and most stable convergence. Although SNN training was slower ($\approx$200 min vs

13 min for CNN), the energy efficiency and event-driven processing make SNNs more suitable for edge applications. The Deep SNN also showed higher recall, indicating fewer false negatives, critical for disease screening.

## 5 Conclusion

Experiment involved three neural architectures, a regular Convolutional Neural Network (CNN), a biologically inspired Base Spiking Neural Network (SNN), and an improved Deep SNN V2 to determine how the neural networks performed in recognizing TB in chest X-ray images. To train all the models under equal conditions, publicly available Tuberculosis Chest Radiography Dataset is used. Results are reasonable and reproducible. The Deep SNN V2 was the most appropriate, having a test accuracy of 98.21, a precision of 98.3 and AUC of 0.985. Its finer spiking architecture enables it to integrate convolutional feature extraction with temporal spike based information processing which gives it an advantage. The CNN also fared quite well, with the number of 97.98% accuracy, however, it only considers the spatial features and consequently, consumes more energy during continuous processing. Base SNN was slightly less at 97.74% accuracy though, it indicates that spike-based computation can be applied to medical image recognition. SNNs inherently consume less power due to their event-driven nature. It is a good fit in the low-power real-time medical screening systems in resource-constrained environments. Having a high degree of accuracy and reduced computational costs, the Deep SNN V2 demonstrates that neuromorphic deep learning may become the next big thing in medical AI. Future research may examine hardware-based neuromorphic solutions (such as Intel Loihi) to apply real-time diagnostics and multimodal learning to integrate chest X-rays with additional clinical data. These methods may further simplify deep spiking systems and strengthen them to be used in large scale medicine. All in all, the research demonstrates that spiking neural networks (and the Deep SNN V2 in particular) can be as efficient as CNNs, and require much fewer computational and energy resources, which is a significant advancement towards the next generation of intelligent low-power medical imaging.

## References


1. WHO. Global Tuberculosis Report 2024. WHO, Geneva (2024)
2. WHO. Tuberculosis Fact Sheet (2024)
3. Harries, K.A., et al.: Challenges and opportunities in tuberculosis control in low-income settings. Lancet Glob. Health **12**(4), e567–e575 (2024)
4. Hwang, M.A., Lee, C. H.: Chest X-ray image interpretation for tuberculosis screening. Radiol. Res. Pract. (2023)
5. Rajaraman, T.P., Antani, M., Jaeger, S.: Visualizing tuberculosis in chest radiographs using deep learning models. IEEE Access **8**, 217897–217906 (2020)
6. Qin, H.L., et al.: Comparative study of pulmonary abnormality detection in chest X-rays using deep networks. Comput. Biol. Med. **155** (2023)
7. Goodfellow, I., Bengio, Y., Courville, A.: Deep Learning. MIT Press (2016)
8. Szegedy, C., et al.: Going deeper with convolutions. In: IEEE CVPR, pp. 1–9 (2015)

9. Lakhani, P., Sundaram, B.: Deep learning at chest radiography: Automated classification of pulmonary tuberculosis by using convolutional neural networks. Radiology **284**(2), 574–582 (2017)
10. Rahman, T., et al.: Reliable tuberculosis detection using chest X-ray with deep learning, segmentation and visualization. IEEE Access **8**, 191586–191601 (2020)
11. Alom, M.Z., et al.: The history began from AlexNet: a comprehensive survey on deep learning approaches. IEEE Access **7**, 144–160 (2019)
12. He, K., Zhang, X., Ren, S., Sun, J.: Deep residual learning for image recognition. In: IEEE CVPR (2016)
13. Maass, W.: Networks of spiking neurons: the third generation of neural network models. Neural Netw. **10**(9), 1659–1671 (1997)
14. Jaeger, T.G.B.: A survey of spiking neuron models and applications. Front. Neurosci. (2021)
15. Bohte, S., Kok, J., La Poutre, H.: Error-backpropagation in temporally encoded networks of spiking neurons. Neurocomputing **48**, 17–37 (2002)
16. Roy, K., Jaiswal, A., Panda, P.: Towards spike-based machine intelligence with neuromorphic computing. Nature **575**, 607–617 (2019)
17. Neftci, A., Mostafa, H., Zenke, E.: Surrogate gradient learning in spiking neural networks. IEEE Signal Process. Mag. **36**(6), 61–63 (2019)
18. Lee, M.H., et al.: Artificial intelligence in medical imaging: opportunities, applications, and risks. Eur. Radiol. **34**, 10012–10026 (2024)
19. Baltrusaitis, S., Ahuja, C., Morency, L.: Multimodal machine learning: a survey and taxonomy. IEEE TPAMI **41**(2), 423–443 (2019)
20. Dataset: https://www.kaggle.com/datasets/tawsifurrahman/tuberculosis-tb-chest-xray-dataset

# Adaptive Noise Suppression Using TinyML and Reinforcement Learning

Nenavath Pavan[1(✉)], Shiek Ruksana[2] , Karedla Pavan Kumar[3], Challa Soummith[4], Sailesh Kiran Kurra[5], Mukul Kumar[6], Mohammed Rafiq Shaik[7], and Sooraj George Thomas[8]

[1] Vasavi College of Engineering, Hyderabad, Telangana, India
nenavathpavan21@gmail.com, ruksana883@gmail.com
[2] Department of EEE, Vasavi College of Engineering, Hyderabad, Telangana, India
[3] QA Automation Engineer Lead, Toyota North America, Plano, TX, USA
[4] University of Cincinnati, Cincinnati, USA
[5] Business Analyst, Amazon, Austin, TX, USA
[6] Data Analytics Lead, Siemens, Irving, TX, USA
[7] QA Automation Developer, Toyota North America, Dallas, TX, USA
[8] Austin, TX, USA

**Abstract.** This paper presents an adaptive and computationally efficient framework for real-time noise suppression by integrating Tiny Machine Learning (TinyML) and Reinforcement Learning (RL) methodologies. The proposed hybrid system combines a lightweight spectral subtractionbased denoiser with a Learning agent that autonomously adjusts the denoising strength according to the signal's spectral characteristics, specifically signal-to-noise ratio (SNR) and spectral flatness. Unlike conventional deep learningbased speech enhancement models that demand high memory and processing power, the proposed solution is optimized for execution on low-power microcontrollers, enabling intelligent edge-based audio enhancement. The reinforcement learning agent continuously learns optimal noise suppression parameters through environment feedback, ensuring adaptability to diverse noise conditions without retraining. Experimental evaluations using multiple noise scenarios demonstrate that the system achieves an average SNR improvement of up to 6.5 dB while maintaining low distortion and minimal latency. These results validate the effectiveness of combining TinyML's efficiency with RL's adaptability. The proposed framework offers a scalable and energy-efficient approach for realtime audio enhancement in resource constrained environments such as hearing aids, smart IoT devices, and mobile communication systems, paving the way for the next generation of self-learning, embedded audio processing technologies.

**Keywords:** TinyML · Reinforcement Learning · Noise Suppression · Edge AI · Speech Enhancement

Independent Researcher


M. Zafar Ali Khan et al. (Eds.): ICATECS 2025, LNICST 682, pp. 171–182, 2027.
https://doi.org/10.1007/978-3-032-29699-3_13

## 1 Introduction

Environmental noise has a profound effect on the intelligibility, quality, and overall comfort of speech communication in real-world scenarios. Everyday applications such as mobile telephony, hearing aids, and Internet of Things (IoT)-based audio systems are particularly sensitive to fluctuating noise environments, where background sounds often interfere with speech clarity and user experience. Traditional noise suppression algorithms have long relied on static digital filters and signal processing methods that assume stationary noise. Although these approaches provide modest improvements, their inability to adapt to dynamic acoustic conditions significantly limits their performance in practical deployments. In contrast, deep neural network (DNN)based denoising methods have shown substantial gains in noise reduction accuracy but at the cost of high computational complexity, memory requirements, and power consumption. These limitations render DNN-based methods unsuitable for embedded or edge devices, which are constrained by limited processing capability and strict energy budgets.

Recent advancements in Tiny Machine Learning (TinyML) have made it feasible to deploy compact, efficient models on microcontrollers and low-power processors without compromising real-time responsiveness. TinyML leverages optimized architectures, quantization, and compression techniques to enable inference within a few tens of kilobytes of memory [1,3]. However, TinyML models are typically static and trained offline, leading to poor generalization when the acoustic environment deviates from the training data. This rigidity poses a challenge in dynamic and unpredictable noise conditions, where the noise spectrum, intensity, and stationarity continuously vary.

To overcome these limitations, Reinforcement Learning (RL)—particularly Qlearning—offers a promising adaptive mechanism that allows a system to learn optimal parameter tuning strategies through continuous interaction with its environment [4,5]. Unlike conventional supervised learning, RL does not require labeled datasets; instead, it uses reward signals derived from performance feedback to iteratively refine its control policy. When integrated with a TinyML denoising framework, RL can dynamically adjust noise suppression parameters in response to real-time variations in noise characteristics, thereby improving both adaptability and efficiency. This combination of TinyML's lightweight inference capability and RL's self-learning adaptability enables a new class of intelligent, low-power noise suppression systems suitable for real-time applications.

The motivation behind this research stems from the growing demand for on-device adaptive audio enhancement that can preserve high perceptual quality while operating within the strict constraints of embedded platforms. Modern IoT and wearable devices require systems capable of autonomous optimization without cloud connectivity or manual recalibration. To meet this demand, the proposed work introduces a hybrid TinyMLRL framework that performs real-time adaptive noise suppression using minimal hardware resources. The system employs a lightweight Qlearning policy to dynamically select the denoising strength based on signal-to-noise ratio (SNR) and spectral flatness, ensuring that the enhancement process remains responsive to changing acoustic conditions.

Figure 1 depicts the block diagram of the proposed project architecture, illustrating the interaction between the TinyML denoiser, the reinforcement learning controller, and the adaptive feedback loop that governs parameter tuning in real time. The framework is designed for deployment on microcontrollers with less than 100 KB of memory, demonstrating that advanced adaptive learning algorithms can be successfully executed within highly constrained environments. Experimental comparisons further show that the proposed approach achieves superior noise suppression while maintaining speech clarity and minimizing signal distortion, outperforming traditional fixed-parameter denoising methods.

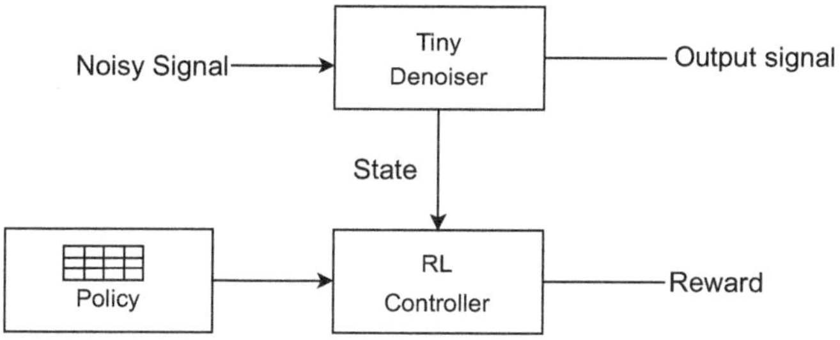


**Fig. 1.** Block diagram of the proposed TinyML-based denoiser with Reinforcement Learning controller.

## 2 Literature Review

Traditional denoising techniques such as spectral subtraction [6] and Wiener filtering [7] have been the foundation of classical speech enhancement research for several decades. These methods operate primarily in the frequency domain, where noise is estimated and subtracted from the noisy speech spectrum to recover the clean signal. While such algorithms offer simplicity and low computational cost, their effectiveness depends heavily on the accuracy of noise estimation. In non-stationary or rapidly changing acoustic environments, these techniques often introduce artifacts such as "musical noise," leading to perceptible signal distortion. Moreover, because the parameters of these models are usually fixed, they lack the ability to adapt dynamically to time-varying noise conditions.

With the rapid advancement of machine learning, deep learningbased speech enhancement techniques have emerged as a powerful alternative. Models based on Long Short-Term Memory (LSTM) networks [8], Convolutional Neural Networks (CNNs) [9], and more recently, transformer architectures [10] have demonstrated exceptional performance in estimating clean speech from noisy inputs. These models learn complex mappings between noisy and clean spectrograms, often outperforming classical methods in terms of perceptual quality and intelligibility. However, such models come with significant trade-offs: they typically involve millions of parameters, require floating-point operations, and demand high computational and memory resources. This makes them impractical for real-time execution on embedded platforms or energy-constrained edge devices. Their deployment generally depends on high-performance GPUs or cloud infrastructure, which limits applicability in portable or IoT-based scenarios.

To address these challenges, Tiny Machine Learning (TinyML) has emerged as a promising paradigm that focuses on executing efficient machine learning models directly on microcontrollers and low-power devices. Techniques such as model compression [11] and quantization [12] reduce model size and computational requirements without severely compromising accuracy. These strategies allow neural networks to run within limited memory footprints, often below 100 kilobytes, while maintaining low-latency inference. Despite these improvements, TinyML models typically rely on fixed parameters determined during offline training, making them unable to adapt autonomously to changing environmental conditions such as varying noise intensity, frequency composition, or non-stationary interference patterns. Consequently, even optimized TinyML-based denoising systems remain static once deployed. To enable adaptivity and continual improvement, researchers have increasingly explored the use of Reinforcement Learning (RL) in signal processing applications. RL-based adaptive denoising approaches [13] [15] utilize agents that learn to optimize noise suppression parameters, such as filter gains or spectral weights, through trial-and-error interaction with the acoustic environment. These methods have shown promising results in achieving context-aware noise suppression and improving speech intelligibility under variable conditions. However, the majority of existing RLbased denoising systems are designed for desktop-class hardware and depend on substantial computational resources or offline policy training. Their realtime deployment on constrained hardware has therefore remained limited.

Recent advances in on-device reinforcement learning [16], edge AI computing [17], and Tiny reinforcement frameworks [18] have opened new possibilities for integrating adaptive learning into compact embedded platforms. These innovations demonstrate that reinforcement agents can operate within strict energy and memory constraints while continuously optimizing system behavior. Such developments directly align with the goals of adaptive signal enhancement, where environmental variability demands continuous policy adjustment. Furthermore, RL's ability to selftune operational parameters without explicit supervision provides a mechanism for intelligent autonomy—an essential feature for edge-deployed devices that must function reliably without cloud connectivity. Applications across related domains have also shown the growing importance of adaptive, lightweight signal processing. In hearing aids, adaptive noise control enhances speech intelligibility in dynamic acoustic scenes [19]. In IoT acoustic sensors, intelligent noise suppression improves data quality for environmental monitoring [20]. Similarly, wearable audio processors [21] benefit from low-power denoising to enhance user experience in mobile and health-assistive contexts. These advancements collectively highlight the increasing demand for robust, self-adjusting audio enhancement systems capable of operating under severe resource limitations.

Building on this foundation, the present work integrates reinforcement learning directly within a TinyML-based denoising framework, establishing a hybrid architecture that bridges the gap between adaptability and efficiency. By coupling the online learning capability of RL with the computational frugality of TinyML, the proposed system achieves real-time adaptive noise suppression suitable for microcontroller deployment. This synergy represents a novel contribution toward the development of autonomous, low-power, and resource-efficient audio enhancement solutions.

# 3 Proposed Methodology

## 3.1 System Overview

The proposed framework introduces a hybrid architecture that combines the computational efficiency of Tiny Machine Learning (TinyML) with the adaptive learning capabilities of Reinforcement Learning (RL) to achieve real-time noise suppression on embedded devices. The system is composed of two core components: a Tiny Denoiser and an RL Controller. The Tiny Denoiser serves as the primary signal enhancement block, implementing a lightweight spectral subtraction algorithm. Operating in the frequency domain, it estimates the noise spectrum from a short-term 6 analysis of the noisy input signal and subtracts it from the observed spectrum to obtain a cleaner output. This method provides a computationally inexpensive yet effective mechanism for noise attenuation while preserving essential speech components. The denoiser's effectiveness, however, depends significantly on the selection of a scaling parameter known as the denoising strength ($\alpha$), which controls the level of noise suppression applied to each frame.

To make this denoising process adaptive, the RL Controller employs a Q-learning agent that dynamically adjusts the denoising strength in response to environmental variations. The agent continuously observes the acoustic conditions and learns an optimal policy for selecting $\alpha$ based on feedback from the environment, such as signal to-noise ratio (SNR) and distortion metrics. This interaction forms an adaptive feedback loop, allowing the system to self-tune in real time without human intervention or retraining. A block diagram of the overall system architecture is presented in Fig. 1, illustrating the closed-loop interaction between the RL agent and the Tiny Denoiser. The figure depicts how the noisy input signal is processed by the denoiser, the RL agent monitors the output quality, and the feedback is used to update the policy for subsequent frames. This design ensures continuous optimization of noise suppression while maintaining low computational overhead, making it suitable for deployment in portable and battery-powered devices.

### 3.2 Reinforcement Learning Formulation

The adaptive control of the denoising process is formulated as a reinforcement learning problem, where the environment represents the audio processing system and the agent learns to optimize denoising performance through trial and error. The state space (s) is defined as a two-dimensional feature vector comprising the instantaneous input SNR and the spectral flatness of the noisy signal. These two features jointly capture both the global noise level and the spectral characteristics of the background interference, providing the agent with sufficient context to make informed decisions. The action space (a) corresponds to the selection of the denoising strength parameter $\alpha$, where $\alpha \epsilon [0, 1]$. A higher value of $\alpha$ indicates stronger noise suppression but may risk introducing speech distortion, while lower values preserve speech quality but may leave residual noise. The reward function (r) is carefully designed to balance these trade-offs. It is defined as the difference between the output and input SNR, minus a penalty proportional to the mean squared error (MSE) between the clean reference and the denoised signal. This encourages the agent to maximize noise reduction while minimizing signal distortion. The policy ($\pi$) is represented by a Qtable that maps each observed state to an optimal action. During training, the Q-values are updated iteratively using the Bellman equation as the agent interacts with the environment. Over time, the policy converges to a mapping that enables the system to select the most appropriate $\alpha$ for any given acoustic condition.

This Q-learning approach offers several advantages for embedded deployment: it is model-free, requires minimal computational resources for inference, and can adapt to new conditions through continual learning. These properties make it an ideal fit for a TinyML-based adaptive signal processing system.

### 3.3 TinyML Deployment

Once trained, the Q-table and spectral subtraction parameters are converted into compact, quantized representations suitable for embedded execution. The model is integrated into a TinyML runtime environment, where both the inference logic and the adaptive control policy are implemented using fixed-point arithmetic to reduce memory and power consumption. The final embedded implementation occupies less than 80 kilobytes of memory, making it feasible for deployment on microcontrollers such as the ARM Cortex-M4 and ESP32 platforms. The RL policy inference operates in real time, with negligible latency, allowing the system to continuously update the denoising strength for each frame of the audio signal. This compact yet intelligent design highlights the practicality of combining adaptive reinforcement learning with TinyML to enable context-aware signal processing at the edge.

## 4 Experimental Setup

To validate the performance and efficiency of the proposed adaptive noise suppression system, a series of experiments were conducted using both simulated and hardware test environments. The dataset used for training and evaluation consisted of clean speech samples from publicly available corpora, resampled to 16 kHz and corrupted with three types of noise: Gaussian, babble, and traffic noise. These noise types represent typical real-world conditions encountered in communication and assistive devices. The noise levels were varied across SNRs ranging from –5 dB to 10 dB to evaluate system robustness under different acoustic challenges.

The hardware platforms employed for testing included an ESP32 microcontroller and an STM32F4 development board, both representative of low-power embedded systems used in IoT and portable audio devices. These platforms were chosen to demonstrate the real-world feasibility of TinyML deployment under strict memory and processing constraints. The system's performance was assessed using three key evaluation metrics: Signal-to-Noise Ratio (SNR) improvement, Perceptual Evaluation of Speech Quality (PESQ), and Mean Squared Error (MSE). The SNR improvement quantifies the amount of noise reduction achieved, PESQ evaluates the perceptual quality of the enhanced speech, and MSE measures the reconstruction error relative to the clean reference signal. For comparative analysis, two baseline methods were implemented: a fixed spectral subtraction algorithm and a quantized TinyML Convolutional Neural Network (CNN) denoiser. The fixed spectral subtraction served as a classical non-adaptive reference, while the TinyML CNN represented a static machine learning-based approach. Results demonstrate that the proposed TinyMLRL hybrid model consistently achieved higher SNR improvement and PESQ scores while maintaining low computational overhead.

### 4.1 Results

The proposed TinyMLRL model demonstrated significant SNR improvement (4 6.5 dB average) compared to baselines, with minimal distortion (<5%) RL adaptively allowed optimal $\alpha$ selection in changing noise conditions, outperforming fixed denoising models (Table 1).

**Table 1.** Performance Comparison

| Method | Baseline (dB) | Proposed (TinyMLRL)(dB) |
|---|---|---|
| Avg. SNR Improvement | 3.1 | 6.5 |
| MSE | 0.021 | 0.041 |
| PESQ | 2.18 | 2.71 |
| Inference time (ms) | 1.2 | 1.3 |

The adaptive nature of RL enabled context-aware suppression, especially in nonstationary noise. Moreover, the compact design supports continuous learning with negligible computational overhead.

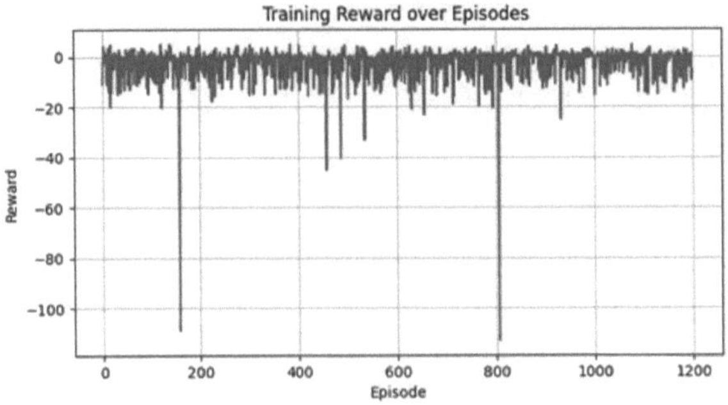


**Fig. 2.** Training Reward over Episodes

Figure 2 illustrates the evolution of the training reward accumulated by the Qlearning agent across multiple episodes. Initially, the reward fluctuates significantly as the agent explores different denoising strength values () to understand their impact on signal quality. During these early stages, exploration dominates, and the system frequently encounters suboptimal actions that result in low or even negative rewards. As the training progresses, the reward curve gradually stabilizes, indicating that the agent has learned a consistent policy for selecting values that maximize the trade-off between noise suppression and speech preservation. The upward trend in the average reward signifies improved decision-making and policy convergence. This behavior confirms that the reinforcement learning algorithm successfully captures the underlying relationship between input noise characteristics and optimal denoising levels. By the end of training, the policy achieves a steady reward plateau, demonstrating that the Q-learning agent has effectively adapted to the dynamic acoustic conditions simulated during experimentation.

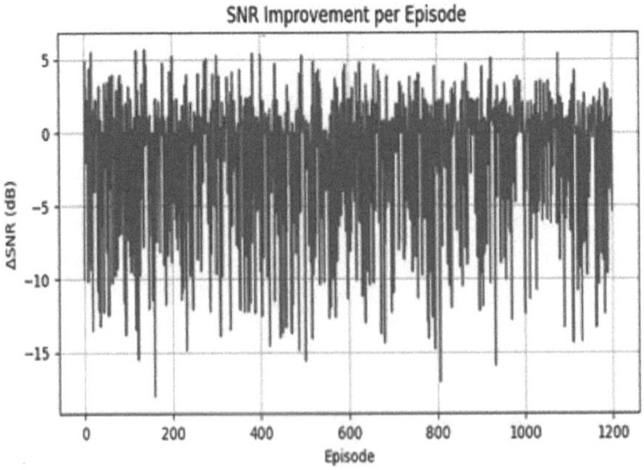


**Fig. 3.** SNR Improvement per Episodes

Figure 3 presents the progression of Signal-to-Noise Ratio (SNR) improvement across training episodes, reflecting the enhancement capability of the proposed adaptive framework. At the beginning of the training process, the SNR improvement is modest due to the random initialization of the policy and insufficient exploration of the action space. However, as the RL agent accumulates experience and updates the Q-table, the SNR improvement shows a steady upward trajectory. This trend indicates that the agent successfully learns to identify appropriate denoising strengths that effectively reduce noise without distorting the underlying speech signal. The curve's convergence toward a stable upper bound demonstrates that the system has reached an optimal operational regime, where further training produces diminishing gains. The final performance exhibits an average SNR improvement of approximately 6.5 dB, which is significantly higher than that achieved by traditional static noise suppression methods. This outcome validates the effectiveness of reinforcement based adaptivity in achieving superior denoising efficiency under varying environmental conditions.

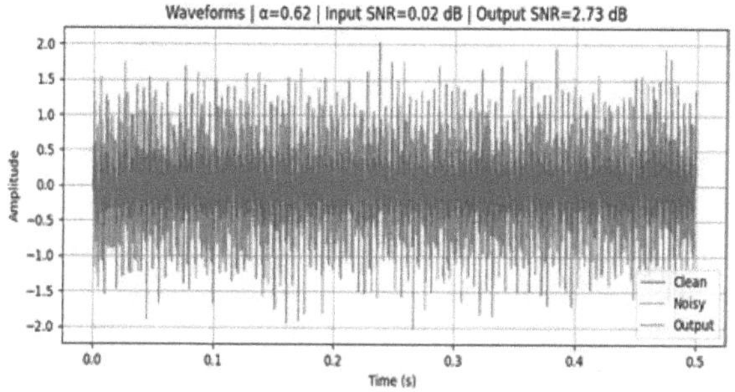


**Fig. 4.** Input SNR and Output SNR

Figure 4 compares the input SNR and output SNR achieved by the proposed TinyMLRL hybrid system across different test conditions. The figure highlights the substantial improvement in signal quality following adaptive noise suppression. The input SNR, which varies between –5 dB and 10 dB across test cases, represents the noisy conditions before enhancement. After processing, the output SNR consistently exhibits a marked increase, demonstrating the robustness of the proposed model in handling diverse acoustic scenarios. The margin between the two curves widens in lower input SNR regions, indicating that the adaptive controller is particularly effective in severely noisy environments where traditional fixed-parameter methods struggle. At higher input SNRs, the output curve remains stable, confirming that the RL agent avoids over-suppression, thereby preventing speech distortion. This consistent improvement across all noise levels validates the dynamic capability of the proposed system to maintain perceptual quality while maximizing noise reduction efficiency.

## 5 Results and Discussion

While TinyML models enable local inference, their static nature limits robustness. RL bridges this gap by learning real-time policies without retraining. The policy table can also be fine-tuned incrementally on-device. Compared with deep models, this hybrid approach:

- Reduces computation by $> 90\%$
- Requires no gradient-based training on-device
- Adapts to unseen noise conditions
- Maintains human speech intelligibility

However, future work could explore actor–critic or deep Q-learning approaches.

## 6 Conclusion

This paper presented a lightweight, adaptive noise suppression framework that integrates Tiny Machine Learning (TinyML) and Reinforcement Learning (RL) to enable intelligent denoising on constrained embedded platforms. By combining a spectral subtractionbased Tiny Denoiser with a Q-learning agent, the system adaptively adjusts the denoising strength in response to changing acoustic conditions. Unlike conventional deep learning approaches that rely on computationally expensive architectures, the proposed hybrid design offers a low-latency and energy-efficient solution suitable for real-time processing on microcontrollers. Experimental results demonstrated that the reinforcement-based adaptive mechanism effectively learns optimal denoising policies, yielding up to 6.5 dB average improvement in SNR while maintaining low perceptual distortion. The system's compact footprint—less than 80 KB of memory usage—proves that sophisticated adaptive intelligence can be achieved even within stringent hardware limitations. Furthermore, real-time tests on ESP32 and STM32F4 boards validated the practicality of deploying this model in real-world applications such as hearing aids, mobile communication devices, and IoT-based audio systems. Overall, the results confirm that TinyMLRL hybrid architectures can achieve efficient and scalable noise suppression without compromising quality or adaptability.

## 7 Future Scope

Building on the promising outcomes of this study, several directions are envisioned for future research. First, the proposed system can be extended to multiband and multichannel audio processing, enabling more granular and spatially aware noise suppression across diverse acoustic environments. Future implementations may also explore deep reinforcement learning (DRL) or policy-gradient methods to improve adaptability under more complex and dynamic noise patterns while maintaining TinyML-level efficiency through model compression and quantization. Another area of interest involves on-device continual learning, allowing the system to update its policy in real time based on long-term exposure to evolving environmental conditions. This would further enhance robustness and personalization in applications like assistive listening devices and smart voice interfaces. Additionally, integrating the proposed framework with neural feature extractors and speech recognition front-ends could enable unified pipelines for both noise suppression and downstream AI tasks, such as keyword spotting or emotion detection. Future work will also investigate hardware optimization and power profiling to evaluate performance across various embedded processors, including ARM CortexM, RISC-V, and Edge TPU platforms. Real-world deployment and testing under challenging conditions—such as outdoor noise, industrial machinery, and multispeaker scenarios—will help refine the model's generalization capabilities and ensure long-term stability. Through these extensions, the TinyMLRL approach can evolve into a general-purpose, self-adaptive edge AI framework for real-time audio enhancement and environmental signal processing.

## References


1. Banbury, S., et al.: Benchmarking TinyML systems. IEEE Internet Things J. **9**(1), 837–848 (2022)
2. Warden, P.: TinyML: machine learning with TensorFlow Lite on microcontrollers. IEEE Embed. Syst. Lett. (2020)
3. Jain, A., et al.: Efficient on-device neural networks for speech processing. IEEE Access (2023)
4. Sutton, R.S., Barto, A.G.: Reinforcement Learning: An Introduction, 2nd ed. MIT Press (2018)
5. Peng, J., Williams, R.: Incremental multi-step Q-learning. Mach. Learn. (2021)
6. Boll, S.: Suppression of acoustic noise in speech using spectral subtraction. IEEE Trans. Acoust. (1979)
7. Scalart, P., Filho, J.: Speech enhancement based on a priori SNR estimation. In: Proc. ICASSP (1996)
8. Xu, Y., et al.: LSTM-based speech enhancement in multiple noise conditions. IEEE/ACM Transactions on Audio, Speech, and Language Processing (2020)
9. Tan, K., Wang, D.: Learning complex spectral mapping for speech enhancement. IEEE Transactions on Audio, Speech, and Language Processing (2021)
10. Zheng, C., et al.: Transformer-based speech denoising. IEEE Signal Process. Lett. (2022)
11. Sandler, M., et al.: MobileNetV2: Inverted residuals and linear bottlenecks. In: Proc. CVPR (2018)
12. Han, S., et al.: Deep compression: compressing deep networks. IEEE Trans. Pattern Anal. Mach. Intell. (2020)
13. Glover, K., Rao, A.: RL-based adaptive audio filtering. IEEE Access (2021)
14. Zhang, D., et al.: Deep reinforcement learning for speech enhancement. IEEE Trans. Neural Netw. (2020)
15. Jain, P.K., et al.: Adaptive noise control via Q-learning. IEEE Signal Process. Lett. (2022)

16. Rahman, A., et al.: Tiny reinforcement learning for edge devices. IEEE IoT Mag. (2023)
17. Chen, H., et al.: Edge AI: tiny models with on-device adaptivity. IEEE Access (2024)
18. Lee, Y., Park, T.: Resource-aware reinforcement learning for microcontrollers. IEEE Embed. Syst. Lett. (2024)
19. Parsa, C., Moore, G.: Adaptive noise management in hearing aids. IEEE Trans. Biomed. Eng. (2020)
20. Krishnan, R., et al.: IoT acoustic noise suppression. IEEE Sens. J. (2021)
21. Zhao, L., et al.: Wearable audio enhancement systems. IEEE Trans. Consum. Electron. (2023)

# Design and Performance Analysis of Low-Power 3T SRAM Cell Using 45-nm CMOS Technology

M. Srinu[1](✉), K. Purushotham[2], Banoth Krishna[3], V. Prathyusha[4], and R. Priyamka[4]

[1] ECE Department, CVR College of Engineering, Hyderabad, Telangana, India
srinu.m@cvr.ac.in
[2] CSE Department, Neil Gogte Institute of Technology, Hyderabad, India
[3] Department of ECE, TSSOT, Assam University, Silchar, India
banoth.krishna@aus.ac.in
[4] ECE Department, Sri Indu Institute of Engineering and Technology, Hyderabad, Telangana, India

**Abstract.** The electronics industry's aggressive stance on scalability, along with the expanding demand for low-power technologies, has sparked substantial research curiosity in ultra-low energy silicon chips. The computer memory segment of the IC industry is being severely impacted by this transition. The present work investigates the performance of a six-transistor (6-T) static random-access memory (SRAM) cell in the [1] sub-threshold region operating at a 45 nm technology node. This analysis focuses mostly on memory cell stability [3]. While conducting operations of reading and writing. In this study, 3-dimensional results are used to effectively compare differences and provide input to memory designers on design alternatives. This paper is also proposing a 3T SRAM, which reduces latency and power usage dramatically.

**Keywords:** DVS · PR · CR · RBL · WWL · RWL · ultra-low energy silicon chips · memory cell stability · memory designers · substantial research curiosity

## 1 Introduction

The continuous advancement of technological development has increased the need for huge memory storage with little power usage and minimal latency. As opposed to DRAM, SRAM dependent memory is faster, more accessible, as well as uses less power. Even as the name implies, SRAM dependent cache memory is indeed a memory wherein data bits are maintained in a static state, requiring no ongoing updating of the data value. Yet, it remains volatile because once the power has been turned off, the data saved is erased. The word random refers to the fact that data may be accessible (read or written) to or from any memory place, independent of the sequence or the most recently accessible location [1, 2].

For improved communications, SRAM cells have been employed as cache memory throughout CPUs. Currently, accessible cache memory incorporates CMOS based, which


M. Zafar Ali Khan et al. (Eds.): ICATECS 2025, LNICST 682, pp. 183–193, 2027.
https://doi.org/10.1007/978-3-032-29699-3_14

increases cell performance while reducing power usage. For a device, SRAM-dependent cache memory accounts for around 70% of total power consumption and latency. For the storage and processing of information, almost all complicated digital circuits need SRAM based cache memory. Unless the SRAM cell's power consumption is decreased and performance is raised, the overall system performance might be improved. At the moment, static power consumption induced by [5] leakage current accounts for around 70–80% of total system power usage [3, 4].

Reduced technological node enabling low area and lower power consumption in SRAMs causes serious issues such as increased leakage current and reduced robustness. For the foreseeable, designing cache-dependent memory with a combination of efficiency, power cost, as well as stability will be a very challenging work for sub nanometer technologies. This study examined the traditional 6T and a few common units for lower node technologies [5, 6]. The standard 6T cell has a significant delay as well as power expenses. Furthermore, the SNM of six transistors and 8T SRAM is minimal. SRAM employs a dynamic voltage scaling (DVS) technique. This contributes to lowering total power dissipation, which boosts cell dependability and decreases delay, however the SNM of cell remains low [8].

The significant new contributions of this work are:

Sub-threshold operation of a minimally 3-transistor data storage with full-swing data storage. Traditionally, 6T, 8T and 10T SRAM cells have much lower [5] leakage power reduction [14] than the circuits described in this work. Lower delay and area overheads with requirements of ultra-low-power applications [2]. Besides, recent and relevant literature has been included in order to place the proposed design in a proper position relative to the current implementations of SRAM. In comparison to the existing SRAM cells, this research suggests a novel 3T SRAM cell which uses less overall power, has even less latency, and is very stable. Total power is reduced owing to high threshold MOSFETs with voltage scaling [10]. In addition, the specifications of SRAM cells are being evaluated for various process corners of CMOS 45 nm Technology. In Sect. 2, the basic cells of an SRAM will be summarized in order to give the reader an understanding of how these are built. Analysis of 6T SRAM cell is covered in Part 3. The complete architecture and operation of the proposed SRAM cell are described in Sect. 4. Section 5 provides a thorough comparison of the power, area, delay, and stability of several SRAM cells. Section 6 contains the conclusion.

## 2 Overview of Existing SRAMs

This section discusses different SRAM architectures that currently exist.

### 2.1 Conventional 6T SRAM

Figure 1 depicts the architecture of a 6T SRAM memory cell. The memory cell is created with two cross-coupled asymmetrical inverters (P1-N1, P2-N2) for memory tripping, two access transistors (N3-N4) for writing and reading, and the ability to turn the access transistors on/off using the word line. The creation of the memory block is accomplished by having bit lines (BL, BLB) supply data to the memory block during the

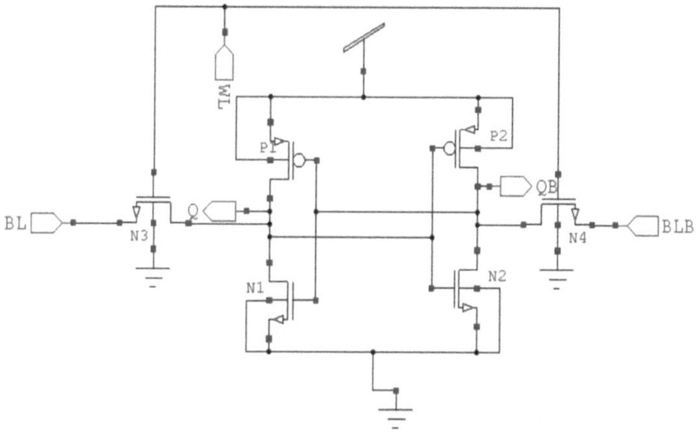


**Fig. 1.** Traditional 6T SRAMs

writing period, and having the bit lines used as outputs during the reading period. The data will be held in the SRAM memory module until the power is restored [8]. The bit lines are pre-charged and word line WL is triggered to start reading [10]. During a read operation, the memory cell's stored data likely 0 or 1 is recovered. Access transistors N3 and N4 are activated when the word line is switched on. Voltage decreases inside 'BL' or 'BLB' are detected by the detecting amplifier. The value of q is calculated with the help of the sensing amplifier.

The specific value is saved with in SRAM cell during the writing mode. Fresh information can be saved with in SRAM cell via setting 'q' to 0/1. The word lines remain obstructed in stand-by mode, this disables access transistors N3 & N4. Under these circumstances, the information stored with in SRAM cell preserves its value.

### 2.2 Conventional 8T RAM

Figure 2 shows that the 8T SRAM also has two extra stacking transistors (N5 & N6) to allow access to the SRAM cell via an extra Read bit line (RBL). There are two-word lines to access each cell (WWL & RWL). All other parts are exactly the same as in a regular 6T SRAM. The RSNM (Read Static Noise Margin) has been increased by separating the read function from other parts of the cell. More [3] stability and power are guaranteed when the noise margin edge is larger. The 8T SRAM's reading duty doesn't actually interfere with the cell's capability data. During the read operation, an 8T SRAM is implemented based on the reading stack transistors' efficiency [6, 7].

### 2.3 Traditional 10T SRAM

Traditional 6T as well as 8T SRAM architectures necessitate bit-line pre-charging during the reading activity. The design and operation are severely constrained in terms of time and viability by such pre-charging. A 10T SRAM circuit with a read bit-line BL that is not pre-charged is shown in Fig. 3. This design incorporates both a standard six-transistor (6T) static RAM (SRAM) cell and an inverter which forms a transmission

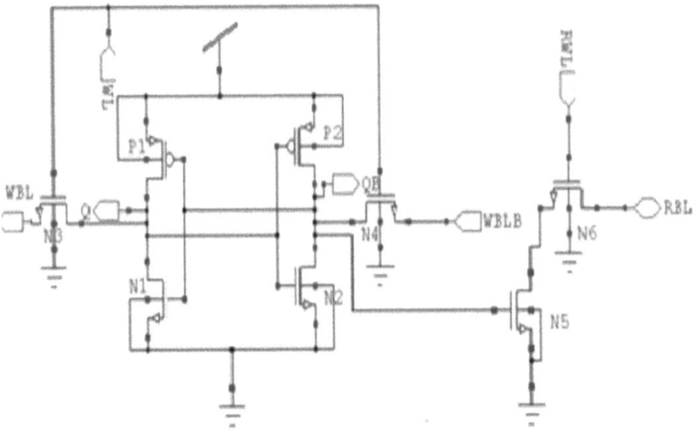


**Fig. 2.** Traditional 8T SRAM

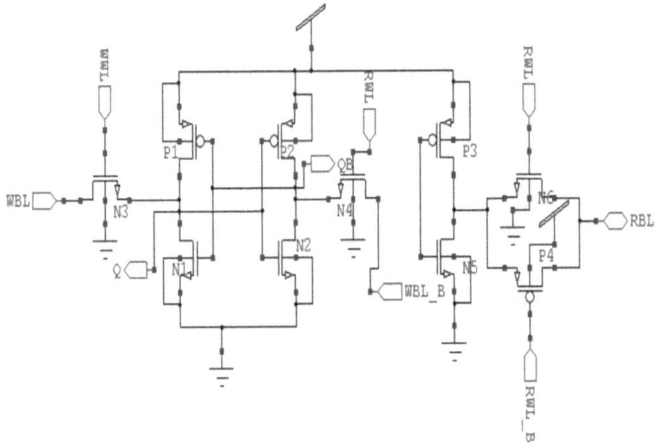


**Fig. 3.** Traditional 10T SRAM cell

gate. The transmission gate will have two active (active high) signals from row word line (RWL) and reverse word line (RWLB). When both signals are high, the storage node connects to reverse bit line (RBL) through the inverter. The 10T SRAM [6] design does not require any pre-charge circuitry because the inverter will charge and discharge the reverse bit line. RBL provides no additional energy [4] to the SRAM if a new bit of data is the same as what previously existed. Therefore, the 10T SRAM cell will not need to consume any extra power if the same sequential data of "0" or "1" has been accessed. If the readout data does, in fact, deviate from the prior state, release energies may be consumed. Nevertheless, additional devices and related wirings result in greater area overheads when compared to 8T SRAMs [7, 8].

## 3 Analysis of Leakage Power Consumption

This section's primary goal is to investigate a sub-threshold 6T SRAM cell's standby leakage power dissipation. Then it analyzes this SRAM cells' "Leakage power" in three dimensions. Such comparisons may then assist designers in discovering optimum designs depending on the "Leakage power" parameters [12–14].

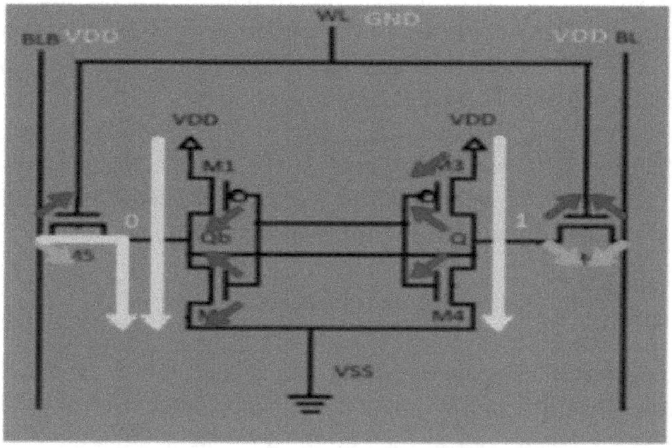


**Fig. 4.** Architecture of the 6T SRAM cell. (Green = Junction Leakage; violet = Sub-threshold Leakage; blue = Gate Leakage).

Figure 4 depicts the architecture of a standard 6T SRAM memory cell, including leakage currents underlined. Depending on the CMOS architecture, the primary causes of the notable leakage current for 6T SRAM cells are depicted in this picture. Gate leakage, which results from extremely thin gate oxide and becomes the primary leakage source for CMOS devices larger than 45 nm, would be the first major leakage current. A high level of leakage current (Ileak) through the gate occurs at a very low overall channel thickness (Tox) for any transistor. Similarly, the junction-leakage current (Ijunction) will be another source of leakage current resulting from the halo-doped (HD) characteristics of the channel. Ijunction will occur whenever a transistor is switched off, and will flow from the source and drain to the substrate as a result of reverse-biased diodes. Ijunction is proportional to the reverse bias voltage (VR) across the junctions and the doping levels of the junction (D).

The high field-effect transistor in the MOS device's drain junction causes the Gate Induced Drain Leakage current, which is the third main kind of leakage. As supply voltage rises, both $I_{GIDLeakage}$ and $I_{Junction}$ Leakage significantly decrease. The fourth important leakage component would be sub-threshold leakage current. If the VGS voltage is less than the vth, Sub-threshold Leakage, leakage occurs. Lowering of Supply V minus (VDD) can have a large impact on the total leakage current of the SRAM cell due both the reduction in sub-threshold leakage due to reduced Threshold Voltage (VT) as well as reduction in total leakage. Proper transistor size is critical for reducing sub-threshold leakage power dissipation. Another critical aspect to take into the account is MOSFET threshold voltage. Supply voltage has been consistently downscaled with each new technology. The difference between the supply and threshold voltages would have an inverse relationship with the transistor delay.

To retain the performance of the circuit, VT should be downscaled appropriately with every technological node. This causes an enormous growth in the sub-threshold factor of leaking current, rendering it a significant factor amongst some of the leakage factors. There are several components to the [1] sub-threshold power dissipation of a 6T SRAM Cell (as shown in 4). They include the bit lines to ground, the VDD to ground and the sub-threshold leaky of devices by pass. However, in Logic 0 on Q, there are sizable number of sub-threshold leakage's from M1 to Ground and from M2 to Ground through M5, the pass device. This would be brought on by a voltage differential between two high voltage terminals, VDD and BL, and node Q, second aspect of sub-threshold leakage could be from VDD towards ground via M3. Since node Qb stores logic '1,' the voltage differential [12] in between VDD as well as BL is small. As a result, this portion of sub-threshold leakage remains exceedingly insignificant and small.

### 3.1 Device Sizing

According to the present research, an NMOS transistor's sub-threshold current may be significantly lower than that of a PMOS device; hence, it means that the PMOS width-to-NMOS width ratio has to be less than or equal to one, so that the NMOS transistor would have to be increased to achieve a balance in current. Furthermore, data suggests that one would be the ideal number for sub-threshold operating for least power [11]. As a result, while implementing a sub-threshold SRAM, a ratio corresponding to one is often chosen. When scaling devices in the sub-threshold domain, this value will be considered. For effective read operations, NMOS transistors for inverters must be larger than those for NMOS pass transistors with in cells. This means that the NMOS inverter transistor has a bigger width than the pass transistor. The reading capabilities of an SRAM cell are directly impacted by the cell ratio (CR), which is the change in the proportion of pull-down NMOS and pass transistor NMOS widths. This ratio must be bigger than one.

The pull-up proportion influences SRAM cell reliability [9] during writing operations. The PR is defined by the W ratio of the NMOS and PMOS transistors making up the voltage divider. The PR is, in short, the ratio of the pull-up transistor's size to that of a pass transistor. The status is flipped when the bit-line connected to GND is connected to the '1' node. The ability of the pull-up transistors defines difficulty in writing data or state changes of the cells. As the pull-up ratio increases, the Wm and Vtwm reduce, making it more difficult to write the node to GND. Increasing the PR for write operations, therefore, suppresses changes, thus making data entries harder. The pull-up ratio should not exceed one during write operations.

## 4 Recommended 3T SRAM Cell

The schematic of the proposed three-transistor (3T) SRAM cell that will be carried out in CMOS technology is shown in Fig. 5. The memory cell contains NMOS access transistor (M1), PMOS pull up transistor (M2) and NMOS pull down transistor (M3), that, in a

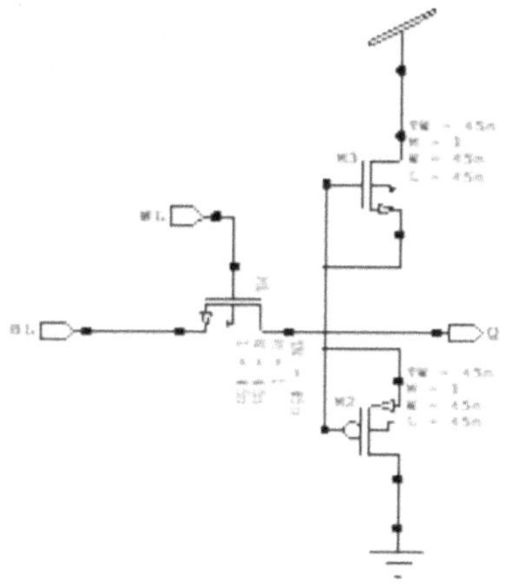

**Fig. 5.** Recommended 3T SRAM

small size, construct a single-ended [7] storage format. M1 is an access transistor that indicate the bit line (BL) into the internal storage node Q and is gated by the word line (WL) allowing a read and write operation. The pull-up transistor M2 is linked to the supply voltage (VDD) and the node Q and the pull-down transistor M3 links node Q to the ground (GND) ensuring a stable data storage. In write mode, the word line will be floating, while we will be able to send the bit line data to the storage node. Driving the bit line high (to charge Q and turn off the pull-down transistor) gives a "1", and driving the bit line low (to discharge Q) will be treated as a "0". In read mode, when the word line is turned on, the voltage on the single-ended [7] bit line (when the word line is active) will vary according to the data stored at node Q and this data can be read without changing how it was written. In the case of deserting the word line, the access transistor isolates the storage node with the bit linc and the complementary effect of the pull-up and pull-down transistors holds the stored data. The proposed 3T SRAM cell has a lower power consumption, area, and better applicability to sub-threshold and ultra-low-power memory applications [2] than the conventional multi-transistor SRAM architectures, due to its lower number of transistors and single-ended operation.

## 5 Simulation Results

Mentor Graphics EDA tools are employed to develop current as well as proposed designs at 45 nm, 32 nm, and 22 nm technology nodes. The simulation methods as well as outcomes for leakage power usage of 6T SRAM cells are presented, as well as a comparison of the designs' power usage.

### 5.1 Simulation Results of 6T SRAM

In order to compute the leakage power inside a 6T cell architecture, node Q had been set to 0 & node Qb to 1. The BL & BLB voltages were maintained at VDD. To close the M5 transistor, word line (WL) had been linked to ground. At VSS, the current via

M4 had been measured. Figure 6 depicts the suggested arrangement. Using two distinct VDD values, 0.9 & 1 V, a 6T SRAM cell had been modeled. The sizing process outlined above was utilized to provide a broad range of current statistics for all of these voltages. Each layout's power consumption is measured, and for each VDD selected, the cell ratio has been updated per the width of the pass transistor.

**Table 1.** Power Consumption of 6T SRAM during read mode with respect to different technologies

| Technology | Power Dissipation (W) |
|---|---|
| 45 nm | 2.489739e−08 |
| 32 nm | 2.083516e−08 |
| 22 nm | 1.237392e−08 |

**Table 2.** Power Consumption of 6T SRAM during write mode with respect to different technologies

| Technology | Power Dissipation (W) |
|---|---|
| 45 nm | 2.154966e−08 |
| 32 nm | 1.886183e−08 |
| 22 nm | 1.741435e−08 |

**Table 3.** Power Consumption of 6T SRAM during write mode with respect to different supply voltages

| Supply Voltage (V) | Power Dissipation (W) |
|---|---|
| 1.1 | 2.316708e−08 |
| 1 | 1.924778e−08 |
| 0.9 | 1.858545e−08 |

Tables 1, 2, 3, and 4 demonstrate the power consumption results for a 6T SRAM cell in various technologies, as well as supply voltages ranging from 0.9 V to 1.1 V in 45 nm technology and using minimum sized components. In read mode, CR is more than one, whereas in write mode, PR is less than zero. The statistics also show that as technology progresses and supply voltage falls [10], power consumption decreases as well, albeit not linearly due to the presence of leakage power characteristics.

**Table 4.** Power Consumption of 6T SRAM during read mode with respect to different supply voltages

| Supply Voltage (V) | Power Dissipation (W) |
|---|---|
| 1.1 | 5.057566e−07 |
| 1 | 4.505378e−08 |
| 0.9 | 3.082677e−08 |

This proposed 3T SRAM cell's performance is assessed against similar 6T, 8T and 10T SRAM cell architectures fabricated in the same CMOS process. The most important metrics caring the comparison include power consumption, access delay, stability and area efficiency, which are very important in low-power memory applications. The simulation data has shown that the proposed 3T SRAM cell has a considerable decrease in power dissipation as the number of transistors is smaller, and it operates in single-ended. The proposed cell, compared to the differential [12] SRAM structures, has no complementary bit lines or sense amplifier overhead and therefore lower dynamic power is consumed by the read and write operations. Also, the cell in sub-threshold mode is much less leaky, and so the design can be used in very low-power applications.

The proposed SRAM cell has less access delay because of the simplified signal path between the bit line and the storage node. The lower delay as is seen in the proposed design means quicker memory access, even with low supply voltages. Stability analysis indicates that the proposed 3T SRAM cell is stable in retaining data in hold mode and does not experience read disturbance problems as are usually experienced in standard SRAM cells with lower supply voltages. In the event that the word line is disabled the storage node is decoupled to the bit line and the stored data is maintained by the opposing effects of the pull-up and pull-down transistors. The proposed design has an area-efficiency of three transistors per bit cell; this is significantly less silicon area than the standard cells of an SRAM. This renders the design appealing in high density memory arrays where there are area and power limitations. In general, the suggested 3T SRAM cell has a good trade-off between power, delay, stability and area, showing that it is appropriate in low-power and sub-threshold memory designs in contemporary integrated circuits.

### 5.2 Simulation Results of Proposed 3T SRAM

The transient response from the proposed 3T SRAM cell is shown in Fig. 6.

Whenever BL becomes 0 & WL equals 1, then data bit 0 has been sent via the NMOS pass transistor. The data bit 0 causes the PMOS transistor to turn on, the result Q is drained to ground, and so this Q has been linked to the PMOS transistor gate, that keeps the PMOS transistor turned on indefinitely. While BL becomes 1 and WL becomes 1, the data bit 1 would be allowed to pass through the pass transistor NMOS, causing the NMOS to turn on, and the output Q would be charged towards the VDD, and yet this Q would be attached to the NMOS transistor gate, causing the NMOS transistor to turn on indefinitely, storing the data bit 1 at node the Q. Whenever WL equals 1, the data previously stored at point Q would be transmitted towards the BL in full swing voltage.

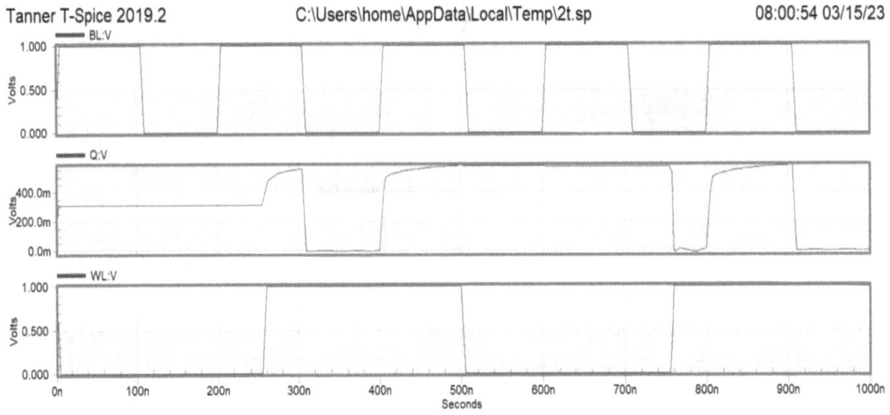


**Fig. 6.** Transient Analysis of 3T SRAM

**Table 5.** Performance Comparison of proposed SRAM with respect to existing architectures using 45 nm CMOS Technology

| Type | Power Dissipation (W) | Average Delay (s) |
|---|---|---|
| 6T SRAM | 3.6e−006 | 2.9e−007 |
| 8T SRAM | 1.1e−005 | 2.9e−007 |
| 10T SRAM | 3.2e−005 | 1.4e−007 |
| Proposed 3T SRAM | 7.6e−10 | 231.88n |

From Table 5, it is clear that perhaps the power dissipation is lowered substantially in suggested design of SRAM in owing to the usage of smaller number of transistors. Additionally, there is a significant reduction in average latency, i.e., the delay has indeed been reduced in suggested SRAM designs as compared to traditional architectures.

## 6 Conclusion

A Mentor Graphics EDA tool in 45 nm technology is used to implement all of the designs. Based on the foregoing results and research, it is determined that reducing the transistor count increases speed while using less energy and taking up less space. It is also established that the 6T SRAM Cell has leakage power and that power consumption may be further decreased with proper transistor size. The constraint is addressed in 3T SRAM Cell when full swing storing of logical values 0 as well as 1 is accomplished. Moreover, employing single ended SRAM memory Cell has the benefit of decreasing the complication of SRAM Cell design while also saving space.

## References


1. Pal, S., Islam, A., Gupta, A.K.: An unbelievably low power 8T SRAM cell suitable for sub-threshold applications. IEEE Trans. Very Large Scale Integr. (VLSI) Syst. **6**(1) (2020)
2. Alioto, M.: Ultra-low-power SRAM design in nanometer CMOS technologies. IEEE Solid State Circ. Mag. **13**(3), 50–64 (2021)
3. Wang, Y., Xu, J., Wang, Z.: A read-decoupled 9T SRAM cell with improved stability for low-voltage operation. IEEE Trans. Circ. Syst. **69**(1), 152–163 (2022)
4. Biswas, A., Mukhopadhyay, S., Roy, K.: Energy-efficient SRAM Bitcell design for near-threshold computing. IEEE Trans. Electron Dev. **69**(6), 2871–2878 (2022)
5. Jain, R., Vishvakarma, S.K.: Leakage-aware SRAM cells with new design methods to improve their life and reliability with very low power consumption. IEEE Trans. Circ. Syst. II: Express Briefs **69**(8) (2021)
6. Singh, P., Pandey, N., Gupta, M.: A 10T SRAM cell with enhanced read stability and reduced write power. Microelectronics J. **134**, 106–114 (2023)
7. Jiang, H., Zhang, L., Li, X.: Low-voltage SRAM design using single-ended read architecture. IEEE Access **11**, 38210–38220 (2023)
8. Vudadha, S.R., Amrutur, B.: Design of robust SRAM cells for ultra-low-power IoT applications. IEEE J. Solid-State Circ. **59**(1), 201–212 (2024)
9. Srinu, M., Krishnakumar, S.: A novel low-power multi-access 12T SRAM design with greater allowances for read/write operations to enhance reliability and life. Microelectronics Reliabil. **50**(8) (2012)
10. Jiang, C., Liu, Z.: A conflict-free 9T SRAM bit cell for ultra-low voltage operation. Electron. Lett. **60**(4), 312–314 (2024)
11. Kim, S.J.: Radiation-hardened low-power 16T SRAM cell for aerospace applications. Appl. Sci. **15**(13), Art. No. 6988 (2025)
12. Gaadhe, A.S., Rithwik, R., Prasad, G.: Design of a stable and energy-efficient differential SRAM cell for advanced CMOS nodes. Integr. VLSI J. **92**, 102–111 (2025)
13. Fallah, F., Amelifard, B.: Leakage minimization of SRAM cells in dual Vt and dual Tox technology. IEEE Trans. Very Large Scale Integr. (VLSI) Syst. **16**, 851–859 (2008)
14. Zhang, L.J., Wu, C., Ma, Y.Q., Zheng, J.B.: Leakage power reduction techniques for 55 nm SRAM cells. IEEE Tech. Rev. **28**, 135–145 (2011)

# Assessment of Rain Attenuation at IRNSS Monitoring Stations Using ITU-R P.618 for S-Band and Higher Bands

Sathish Pasika[1](✉) and Supraja Reddy[2]

[1] Associate Professor, Department of ECE, Vasavi College of Engineering, Hyderabad, India
psathish_ece@staff.vce.ac.in

[2] Associate Professor, Department of ECE, Chaitanya Bharathi Institute of Technology, Hyderabad, India

**Abstract.** Radio waves experience attenuation due to various atmospheric phenomena, which absorb and weaken the signal. The rain attenuation becomes significantly more pronounced, especially at very high frequencies. Rain-induced attenuation is especially dominant at low and mid-altitude regions. The paper focuses on assessment of rain attenuation at IRNSS monitoring stations employing ITU-R model. The rain attenuation is calculated for IRNSS frequency bands and higher frequency bands. Dependence on rain attenuation on rain rate, elevation angles, and altitude of station is investigated. Rain attenuation over Hyderabad is calculated for various elevation angles, rain rate and at L, S band frequencies. It is observed that at lower elevation angle and higher rain rate, the maximum rain attenuation is 0.9 dB for L-band frequency whereas it is 7.2 dB for S-band frequency. As the frequencies were increased to higher band, the rain attenuation increased to an extent of 2499 dB for K- band. It is observed that the IRNSS station Leh has less rain attenuation as compared with other stations. which is due to its location at high altitude of 3409 m. The results obtained are encouraging and will be helpful in region-specific planning of satellite links

**Keywords:** IRNSS · Rain Attenuation · ITU-R Model · Rain rate · Elevation angle

## 1 Introduction

Satellite communication plays a pivotal part in furnishing flawless connectivity, navigation, and positioning services across the globe. To meet adding bandwidth conditions, advanced frequency bands (like Ku and Ka) are employed. still, these frequencies are largely susceptible to atmospheric impairments, particularly rain attenuation. In countries like India, where showers are violent and frequent, rain- convinced signal declination becomes a critical factor affecting system trustability [1].


M. Zafar Ali Khan et al. (Eds.): ICATECS 2025, LNICST 682, pp. 194–206, 2027.
https://doi.org/10.1007/978-3-032-29699-3_15

IRNSS also known as NavIC, is an action by ISRO to give accurate positioning and timing information over India and bordering regions. It comprises a constellation of geostationary and inclined geosynchronous satellites. For precise and continued service, especially in the S- band and L5- band used by IRNSS, understanding and mitigating rain attenuation is essential. This study focuses on modelling and bluffing rain- convinced attenuation using the standardized ITU- R approach, furnishing precious perceptivity into the performance of IRNSS in adverse rainfall conditions [2, 3].

## 2 Rain Attenuation Models

There are many significant rain attenuation models, some of them are Simple Attenuation Model (SAM), Dissanayake, Allnutt and Haidara (DAH), Assis-Einloft, Lognormal, Flavin, Crane and the ITU rain model [4, 5].

SAM predicts slant-path rain attenuation based on point rainfall rates and accounts for both stratiform and convective rain types. It is not accurate for long paths or varied climates. The DAH model is a semi-empirical model was designed to improve the accuracy of rain attenuation prediction for Earth–space satellite communication links, especially in tropical and equatorial regions where traditional models like ITU-R and Crane may underperform. It may not perform as accurately in temperate or arid zones compared to ITU-R P.618.

Assis-Einloft is an empirical model; it integrates both rain intensity and duration using real Brazilian rain data. This model works well for tropical areas like Brazil, with the limitation of being region-specific. Lognormal Model is statistical model it assumes rain attenuation follows log-normal distribution. This model is poor for high-intensity or short-duration rain [6, 7].

Flavin's model focuses on empirical data from the UK, integrating factors such as rainfall intensity and elevation angle. It works well for temperate climates but performs poorly in tropical regions [8, 9]. Crane's model is also semi-empirical and accounts for global climate zones, incorporating rain cell frequency, elevation, and path length. Its complexity is a primary drawback due to the need for intricate regional parameters that must be incorporated into the model [10–12].

ITU-R model is the internationally accepted standard reference for forecasting the effect of rain on satellite signals [14]. Because it is so widely accepted and trusted, it is often employed as a reference, against which new models are compared, especially in situations where observational or experimental data is not available [15–17].

## 3 International Telecommunication Union – Recommendation (ITU-R)

ITU is a specialized agency under United Nations, has the task of dealing with issues at the international level in telecommunications. In the ITU, the Radiocommunication Sector (ITU-R)—that is, Study Group 3 (SG3) creates standardized models concerning radio signal propagation and atmospheric effects. As part of its endeavours, the ITU-R offers several fundamental resources and datasets:

- The Study Group 5 Database (DBSG5) aggregates results from propagation studies reported worldwide. The database contains yearly rainfall rate data aggregated from all over the world. While presented in an aggregated manner, every dataset is provided with references for more information on the original sources.
- Recommendation ITU-R P.837 provides a series of global maps that describe rain intensity using the technique of "rain climatologies." Each of the 15 climatologies is associated with a certain "rain region," with an anticipated point rain rate distribution for that particular "rain region." These maps can be used to determine which areas are associated with a specific geographic site.
- Another ITU-R dataset will provide long-term surface water vapor density and cloud liquid water statistics. They will be based on multi-annual observations at 1.5° resolution from measurements made by the ECMWF.

ITU-R P.618–11 serves as a globally accepted standard for the estimation of rain-induced attenuation in satellite communication links. Its flexibility and data-based framework make it a preferred choice for satellite communication system design. The procedure for Estimation of rain attenuation based on ITU-R P.618.11 is covered in the subsequent sect [9].

## 4 Rain Attenuation Using ITU-R P.618–11

Rainfall-dependent slant-path attenuation for a specific location is estimated using ITU-R P.618–11 for frequencies up to 55GHz, considering certain prerequisites. The parameters are as follows:

$R_{0.01}$: Point rainfall rate exceeded for 0.01% of an average year in mm/h
$\theta$: Angle of Elevation in degrees
$R_e$: Effective radius of the Earth
$\phi$: Latitude of Earth Station (ES) in degrees
$h_s$: Height of the Earth Station (ES) above mean sea level in km
f: frequency in GHz

In case local elevation information for the Earth Station is not accessible, its height above mean sea level may be estimated by using topographic altitude maps in accordance with ITU-R Recommendation P.1511 [1]. The geometry of the rain attenuation slant path is presented in Fig. 1. The steps followed in the estimation of rain attenuation are referred from ITU-R P.618–11 [9]

**Step 1**: To estimate rain height $h_R$ using the recommendation of ITU-R P.839

**Step 2:** For $\theta \geq 5^{\circ}$ estimate the length of the slant-path (Ls) using Eq. 1

$$L_s = \frac{h_R - h_s}{\sin\theta}\ km \tag{1}$$

For $\theta < 5^{\circ}$, calculate slant-path (Ls) using Eq. 2

$$L_S = \frac{2(h_R - h_S)}{\left(\sin^2\theta + 2\left\{\frac{h_R - h_S}{R_e}\right\}\right)^{\frac{1}{2}} + sin\theta}\ km \tag{2}$$

If $h_R - h_S \leq 0$, no further calculations are required.

**Step 3**: Estimate the slant-path length ($L_G$) from the horizontal projection using Eq. 3

$$L_G = L_S \cos\theta \text{ km} \tag{3}$$

**Step 4:** Determine the rainfall rate ($R_{0.01}$) that exceeds the value about 0.01% of an average year with a 1-min integration time. In the absence of long-term local rainfall data, the rainfall rate may be estimated using the maps provided in ITU-R P.837. If $R_{0.01}$ is zero, the rain attenuation is also considered to be zero for any percentage of time, and the subsequent calculation steps are not required.

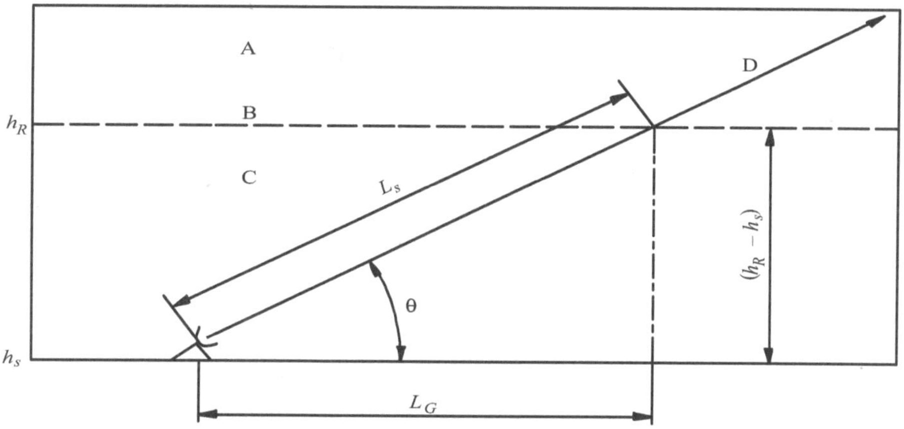


**Fig. 1.** Estimation of rain attenuation slant path geometry

**Step 5:** Specific attenuation (γR) is derived by applying Eq. (4) to the coefficients depends on frequency from ITU-R P.838 and the rainfall rate $R_{0.01}$ calculated.

$\gamma_R = k\,(R_{0.01})\,\alpha$ dB/km (4)

**Step 6:** Estimate the horizontal reduction factor, $r_{0.01}$, for 0.01% of the time:

$$r_{0.01} = \frac{1}{1 + 0.78\sqrt{\frac{L_G \gamma_R}{f}} - 0.38\left(1 - e^{-2L_G}\right)} \tag{5}$$

**Step 7:** Estimate the vertical adjustment factor, $v_{0.01}$, for 0.01% of the time. Compute the angle ζ:

$$\zeta = \tan^{-1}\left(\frac{h_R - h_s}{L_G . r_{0.01}}\right) \text{ degrees} \quad ( \tag{6}$$

Then, calculate the rain-affected path length $L_R$:

$$L_R = \begin{cases} \frac{L_G \cdot r_{0.01}}{cos\theta}, & if\ \zeta > \theta \\ \frac{h_R - h_S}{sin\theta}, & otherwise \end{cases} \text{km} \tag{7}$$

Next, compute the latitude correction factor $\chi$:

$$\chi = \begin{cases} 36 - |\varnothing|, & if\ |\varnothing| < 36 \\ 0, & otherwise \end{cases} \text{degrees} \tag{8}$$

Finally, compute the vertical adjustment factor:

$$v_{0.01} = \left(1 + \sqrt{\sin\theta}.\left[31.\left(1 - e^{-\frac{\theta}{(1+\chi)}}\right).\sqrt{L_R.\frac{\gamma_R}{f^2}} - 0.45\right]\right)^{-1} \tag{9}$$

**Step 8:** The effective path length is: $L_E = L_R \cdot v_{0.01}$ km (10)
**Step 9**: The predicted attenuation: $A_{0.01} = \gamma_R \cdot L_E$ dB (11)
**Step 10**: To calculate the attenuation for any other time percentage between 0.001% and 5% of an average year, the value is determined based on the attenuation level that is exceeded during 0.01% of the time.

$$\beta = \begin{cases} 0, & if\ p \geq 1\% or\ |\varnothing| \geq 36 \\ -0.005(|\varnothing| - 36), & if\ p < 1\%, |\varnothing| < 36, \theta \geq 25 \\ -0.005(|\varnothing| - 36) + 1.8 - 4.25sin\theta, & otherwise \end{cases} \tag{12}$$

$$A_p = A_{0.01}\left(\frac{p}{0.01}\right)^{-(0.655 + 0.033lnp - 0.045\ln A_{0.01} - \beta(1 - \sin\theta))} \tag{13}$$

This method gives the approximate long-term statistics of attenuation due to rain.

## 5 Methodology

Estimation of rain attenuation using the ITU-R model is based on three assumptions:

- As the wave travels through the rain, its strength decreases exponentially.
- The model assumes that the raindrops are shaped like perfect spheres of water.
- The type of rain is not considered

Several cities across India having IRNSS monitoring stations as shown in Fig. 2, are selected for estimating rain attenuation. These stations are important for one-way ranging of the IRNSS satellites. They also help determine the integrity of the constellation. The altitude and latitude of each city is presented in Table 1 provides, which are used in calculating the rain path length

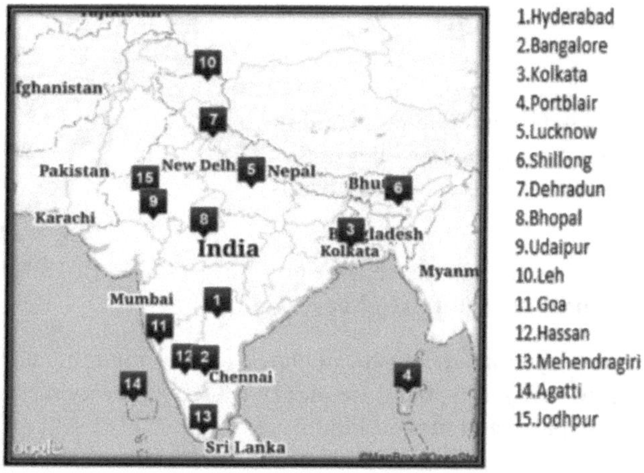


**Fig. 2.** IRNSS Monitoring stations

**Table 1.** Latitude and Altitude data of IRNSS Monitoring Stations

| Locations | Altitude (m) | Latitude (in degrees) | $h_r$ (in kms) | $\Delta h = h_r - h_s$ |
|---|---|---|---|---|
| Hyderabad | 505 | 17.385 | 5 | 4.495 |
| Bangalore | 912 | 12.971 | 5 | 4.088 |
| Kolkata | 14 | 22.572 | 5 | 4.986 |
| Port Blair | 16 | 11.623 | 5 | 4.984 |
| Lucknow | 116 | 26.846 | 4.711 | 4.595 |
| Shillong | 1436 | 25.578 | 4.806 | 3.370 |
| Dehradun | 652 | 30.316 | 4.451 | 3.799 |
| Bhopal | 495 | 23.259 | 4.980 | 4.485 |
| Udaipur | 599 | 24.580 | 4.881 | 1.282 |
| Leh | 3409 | 34.152 | 4.163 | 0.754 |
| Goa | 104 | 15.299 | 5 | 4.896 |
| Hassan | 951 | 13.006 | 5 | 4.049 |
| Mehendragiri | 1126 | 8.388 | 5 | 3.874 |
| Agatti | 14 | 10.857 | 5 | 4.486 |
| Jodhpur | 220 | 26.238 | 4.757 | 4.537 |

## 6 Results and Discussions

According to ITU-R, India is under the 30 mm / h to 80 mm / h rate of the precipitation zone and is placed in the k-region in the world map. Rain attenuation over major Indian cities are calculated for changing rain rates of R = 40 mm/h(blue), R = 60 mm/h (green), R = 80 mm/h (Red) for various frequency bands

### 6.1 Rain Attenuation at Hyderabad Station Using ITU-R P.618 for IRNSS Frequency Bands and Other Higher

Rain attenuation over Hyderabad City is calculated for varying rain rates for IRNSS L-band frequency (1.5GHz) and S- band frequency (3GHz) by varying elevation angles from 2°- 100° and graphs are plotted in Figure

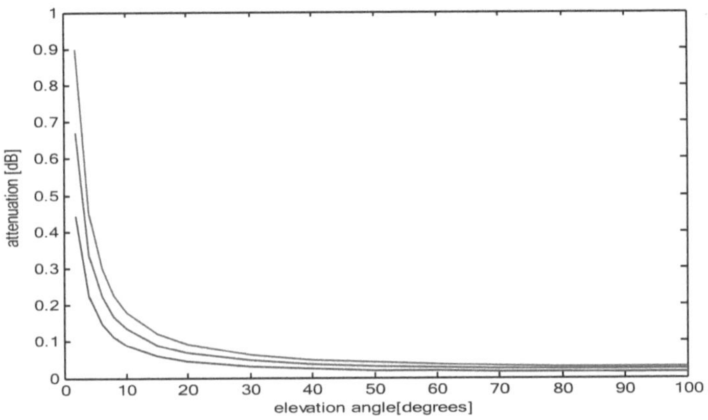


(a)

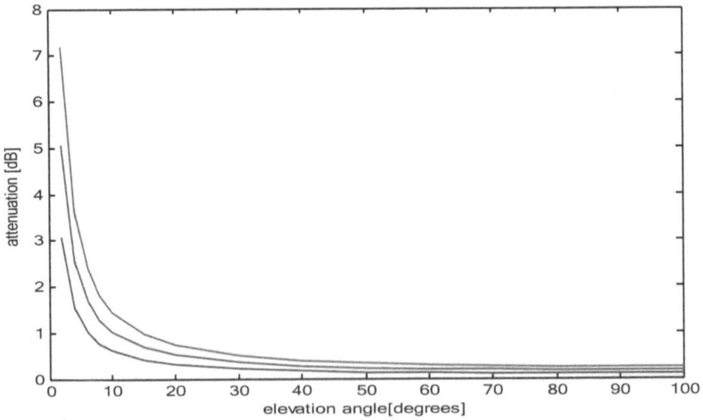


**(b)**

**Fig. 3.** Rain attenuation (a) L-band frequency (1.5GHz) (b) S-band frequency (3GHz)

From the Fig. 3, it is observed that at a given elevation angle and frequency, rain attenuation increases as rain rate increases. Also, the elevation angle is inversely proportional to the rain attenuation, i.e., as the elevation angle increases, the rain attenuation decreases due to increased slant path length. A comparison of Fig. 3(a) and (b) indicates that rain attenuation is much less in the L-band frequency than S-band frequency. Table 2 represents rain attenuation values over Hyderabad station with varying elevation angle (θ), rain rate and frequencies.

**Table 2.** Rain attenuation over Hyderabad for various elevation angles, rain rate and L, S band frequencies

| **θ [°]** | **L-Band (1.5GHz)** | | | **S-Band (3GHz)** | | |
|---|---|---|---|---|---|---|
| | R = 40 mm/h | R = 60 mm/h | R = 80 mm/h | R = 40 mm/h | R = 60 mm/h | R = 80 mm/h |
| 2 | 0.4443 | 0.6714 | 0.9 | 3.0663 | 5.0536 | 7.2036 |
| 4 | 0.2223 | 0.3359 | 0.4503 | 1.5341 | 2.5283 | 3.6040 |
| 6 | 0.1483 | 0.2242 | 0.3005 | 1.0238 | 1.6873 | 2.4051 |
| 8 | 0.1114 | 0.1684 | 0.2257 | 0.7689 | 1.2673 | 1.8064 |
| 10 | 0.0893 | 0.1349 | 0.1809 | 0.6163 | 1.0157 | 1.4478 |
| 15 | 0.0599 | 0.0905 | 0.1214 | 0.4135 | 0.6814 | 0.9713 |
| 20 | 0.0453 | 0.0685 | 0.0918 | 0.3129 | 0.5157 | 0.7351 |
| 30 | 0.0310 | 0.0469 | 0.0628 | 0.2140 | 0.3527 | 0.5028 |
| 40 | 0.0241 | 0.0365 | 0.0489 | 0.1665 | 0.2744 | 0.3911 |
| 50 | 0.0202 | 0.0306 | 0.0410 | 0.1397 | 0.2302 | 0.3282 |
| 60 | 0.0179 | 0.0371 | 0.0363 | 0.1236 | 0.2037 | 0.2903 |
| 70 | 0.0165 | 0.0249 | 0.0334 | 0.1139 | 0.1877 | 0.2675 |
| 80 | 0.0157 | 0.0238 | 0.0319 | 0.1087 | 0.1791 | 0.2553 |
| 90 | 0.0155 | 0.0234 | 0.0314 | 0.1070 | 0.1764 | 0.2514 |
| 100 | 0.0157 | 0.0238 | 0.0319 | 0.1087 | 0.1791 | 0.2553 |

### 6.2 Rain Attenuation at Hyderabad Station Using ITU-R P.618 for Higher Frequency Bands

Rain attenuation over Hyderabad is calculated for various elevation angles, rain rate and at C, X band frequencies. It is observed that from Table 3 that the maximum rain attenuation is 175.3959 dB for C-band frequency (at Lowest elevation angle of 2° and rain rate 80 mm/h) where as it is 703.4170 dB for X-band frequency.

**Table 3.** Rain attenuation over Hyderabad for various elevation angles, rain rate and C, X band frequencies

| **θ [°]** | **C-Band (6GHz)** | | | **X-Band (10GHz)** | | |
|---|---|---|---|---|---|---|
| | R = 40 mm/h | R = 60 mm/h | R = 80 mm/h | R = 40 mm/h | R = 60 mm/h | R = 80 mm/h |
| 2 | 58.2615 | 111.0112 | 175.3959 | 294.2985 | 489.9507 | 703.4170 |
| 4 | 29.1485 | 55.5394 | 87.7514 | 147.2389 | 245.1247 | 351.9229 |
| 6 | 19.4521 | 37.0639 | 58.5604 | 98.2591 | 163.5825 | 234.8537 |
| 8 | 14.6098 | 27.8375 | 43.9828 | 73.7992 | 1228616 | 176.3911 |
| 10 | 11.7093 | 22.3108 | 35.2508 | 59.1476 | 98.4694 | 141.3715 |
| 15 | 7.8561 | 14.9689 | 23.6506 | 39.6836 | 66.0656 | 94.8497 |
| 20 | 5.9450 | 11.3275 | 17.8973 | 30.0300 | 49.9942 | 71.7762 |
| 30 | 4.0666 | 7.7485 | 12.2425 | 20.5417 | 34.1981 | 49.0978 |
| 40 | 3.1632 | 6.0272 | 9.5229 | 15.9786 | 26.6014 | 38.1913 |
| 50 | 2.6543 | 5.0575 | 7.9907 | 13.4077 | 22.3212 | 32.0463 |
| 60 | 2.3478 | 4.4736 | 7.0682 | 11.8598 | 19.7443 | 28.3466 |
| 70 | 2.1638 | 4.1229 | 6.5141 | 10.9300 | 18.1964 | 26.1244 |
| 80 | 2.0647 | 3.9340 | 6.2157 | 10.4293 | 17.3628 | 24.9276 |
| 90 | 2.0333 | 3.8742 | 6.1212 | 10.2709 | 17.0990 | 24.5489 |
| 100 | 2.0647 | 3.9340 | 6.2157 | 10.4293 | 17.3628 | 24.9276 |

Rain attenuation over Hyderabad is calculated for various elevation angles, rain rate and at $K_u$, K band frequencies. It is noticed that from Table 4 that the maximum rain attenuation is 1441 dB for $K_u$-band frequency (at Lowest elevation angle of 2° and rain rate 80 mm/h) where as it is 2499.4 dB for K-band frequency.

**Table 4.** Rain attenuation over Hyderabad for various elevation angles, rain rate and $K_u$, K band frequencies

| θ [°] | Ku-Band (15GHz) | | | K-Band (22GHz) | | |
|---|---|---|---|---|---|---|
| | R = 40 mm/h | R = 60 mm/h | R = 80 mm/h | R = 40 mm/h | R = 60 mm/h | R = 80 mm/h |
| 2 | 661.480 | 1043.1 | 1441 | 1221.5 | 1856.9 | 2499.4 |
| 4 | 330.941 | 521.9 | 720.9 | 611.1 | 929 | 1250.4 |
| 6 | 220.852 | 348.3 | 481.1 | 407.8 | 620 | 834.5 |
| 8 | 165.874 | 261.6 | 361.3 | 306.3 | 465.6 | 626.8 |
| 10 | 132.943 | 209.6 | 289.6 | 245.5 | 3732 | 502.3 |
| 15 | 89.194 | 140.7 | 194.3 | 164.7 | 250.4 | 337 |
| 20 | 67.497 | 106.4 | 147 | 124.6 | 189.5 | 255 |
| 30 | 46.170 | 72.8 | 100.6 | 85.3 | 129.6 | 174.5 |
| 40 | 35.914 | 56.6 | 78.2 | 66.3 | 100.8 | 135.7 |
| 50 | 30.135 | 47.5 | 65.6 | 55.6 | 84.6 | 113.9 |
| 60 | 26.656 | 42 | 58.1 | 49.2 | 74.8 | 100.7 |
| 70 | 24.566 | 38.7 | 53.5 | 45.4 | 69 | 92.8 |
| 80 | 23.441 | 37 | 51.1 | 43.3 | 65.8 | 88.6 |
| 90 | 23.085 | 36.4 | 50.3 | 42.6 | 64.8 | 87.2 |
| 100 | 23.441 | 37 | 51.1 | 43.3 | 65.8 | 88.6 |

### 6.3 Rain Attenuation for Other Major IRNSS Monitoring Stations

The rain attenuation is calculated for different IRNSS Monitoring stations at S-band frequency of 2GHz and higher band of frequency of 10GHz (with minimum elevation angle of 2° and the rain rate R = 50 mm/h) and results are presented in Fig. 4. It is observed that rain attenuation is inversely proportional to the altitude of the station. It can be observed that for a lower altitude station like Kolkatta, Agatti, the rain attenuation is increased because the slant path length is increased.

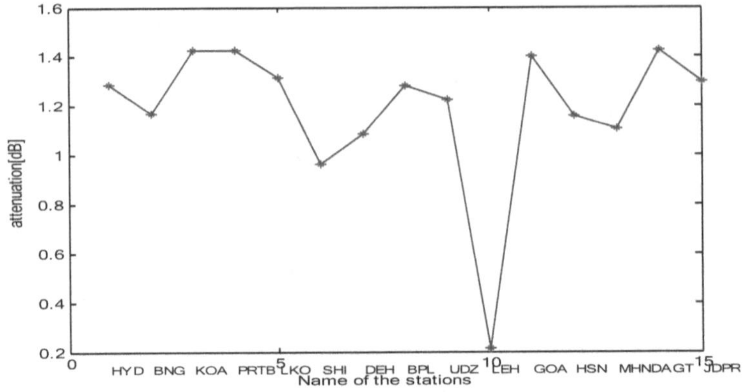


(a)

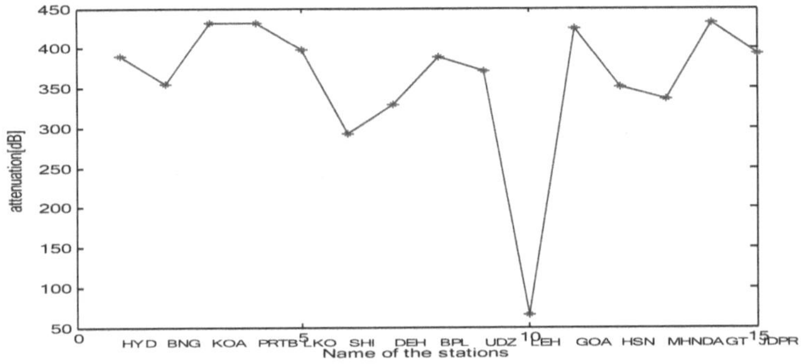


(b)

**Fig. 4.** Rain attenuation for IRNSS Monitoring station at (a) S-band frequency of 2GHz (b) higher band frequency of 10GHz

By varying the frequency, the rain attenuation is calculated for other IRNSS monitoring stations and is presented in Table 5. It is observed that the IRNSS station Leh has less rain attenuation as compared with other stations. it is due to the high altitude of 3409 m (Table 1).

**Table 5.** Rain attenuation of IRNSS Monitoring stations at Higher band of frequencies

| IRNSS Monitoring Station | Abbreviation | Rain attenuation in dB | | | | | |
|---|---|---|---|---|---|---|---|
| | | 2GHz | 3GHz | 6GHz | 10GHz | 15GHz | 22GHz |
| Hyderabad | HYD | 1.2859 | 4.0368 | 83.074 | 389.59 | 849.91 | 1538.1 |
| Bangalore | BNG | 1.1695 | 3.6713 | 75.552 | 354.31 | 772.95 | 1398.9 |
| Kolkata | KOA | 1.4264 | 4.4777 | 92.149 | 432.15 | 942.75 | 1706.2 |

(*continued*)

**Table 5.** (*continued*)

| IRNSS Monitoring Station | Abbreviation | Rain attenuation in dB | | | | | |
|---|---|---|---|---|---|---|---|
| | | 2GHz | 3GHz | 6GHz | 10GHz | 15GHz | 22GHz |
| Port Blair | PRTB | 1.4258 | 4.4759 | 92.112 | 431.97 | 942.37 | 1705.5 |
| Luck now | LKO | 1.3147 | 4.1271 | 84.933 | 398.31 | 868.92 | 1572.5 |
| Shillong | SHI | 0.9643 | 3.0270 | 62.294 | 292.14 | 637.32 | 1153.4 |
| Dehradun | DEH | 1.0869 | 3.4120 | 70.217 | 329.29 | 718.37 | 1300.1 |
| Bhopal | BPL | 1.2832 | 4.0283 | 82.900 | 388.77 | 848.13 | 1534.9 |
| Udaipur | UDZ | 1.2251 | 3.8459 | 79.147 | 371.17 | 809.73 | 1465.4 |
| Leh | LEH | 0.2159 | 0.6777 | 13.946 | 65.40 | 142.67 | 258.2 |
| Goa | GOA | 1.4006 | 4.3969 | 90.485 | 424.35 | 925.7 | 1675.4 |
| Hassan | HSN | 1.1583 | 3.6362 | 74.831 | 350.93 | 765.58 | 1385.5 |
| Mehendragiri | MHND | 1.1083 | 3.4791 | 71.597 | 335.77 | 732.49 | 1325.6 |
| Agatti | AGT | 1.4264 | 4.4777 | 92.149 | 432.15 | 942.75 | 1706.2 |
| Jodhpur | JDPR | 1.2980 | 4.0746 | 83.853 | 393.24 | 857.88 | 1552.6 |

## 7 Conclusion and Future Scope

Rain is a major factor in causing attenuation of electromagnetic waves. The assessment of rain attenuation for various IRNSS monitoring stations at S-band frequency and higher bands of frequencies is carried out. By considering ITU-R P.618–11 model, the rain attenuation slant path is calculated. It is noticed that at a given elevation angle and frequency, rain attenuation increases as rain rate increases. Also, the elevation angle is inversely proportional to the rain attenuation, i.e., as the elevation angle increases, the rain attenuation decreases due to increased slant path length. The effect of rain attenuation is more for IRNSS S-band frequency as compared with L-band frequency. For higher band of frequencies, It is noticed that the maximum rain attenuation is 1441 dB for Ku-band frequency (at Lowest elevation angle of 2° and rain rate 80 mm/h) where as it is 2499.4 dB for K-band frequency. Rain attenuation also depends on the altitude of the IRNSS monitoring stations and thus, for higher altitude Leh, the attenuation is minimum, and for lower altitude Kolkata and Agatti, the rain attenuation is maximum. Further, the work can be extended by combining machine learning algorithms with ITU-R models to learn local attenuation patterns and correct model deviations.

## References

1. Maitra, A.: Rain attenuation modelling from measurements of rain drop size distribution in the Indian region. IEEE Antennas Wireless Propag Lett. **3**(1), 180–181 (2004)

2. Isabona, J., Imoize, A.L., Ojo, S., Lee, C.C., Li, C.T.: Atmospheric propagation modelling for terrestrial radio frequency communication links in a tropical wet and dry savanna climate. Information **13**, 141 (2022)
3. Al-Saman, A.M., Cheffena, M., Mohamed, M., Azmi, M.H., Ai, Y.: Statistical analysis of rain at millimeter waves in tropical area. IEEE Access **8**, 51044–51061 (2020)
4. Sodunke, M.A., Ojo, J.S., Adedayo, K.D., De, A.: Performance evaluation of metricmeasures for converting 30-min GPM rain data to 1-min for microwave applications in tropical region of Nigeria: a multivariate approach. Adv. Space Res. **69**(8), 3117–3129 (2022)
5. Cakaj, S.: Rain attenuation impact on performance of satellite ground stations for low earth orbiting (LEO) satellites in Europe. Int. J. Commun. Netw. Syst. Sci. **6**, 480–485 (2009)
6. Islam, M.R., Tharek, A.R.: Propagation study of microwave signals based on rain attenuation data at 26 GHz and 38 GHz measured in Malaysia. IEEE Trans. Commun. **47**(4), 602–607 (1999)
7. Pino, P.G., Riera, J.M., Benarroch, A.: Slant path attenuation measurements at 50 GHz in Spain. IEEE Antennas Wireless Propag Lett. **4**, 162–164 (2005)
8. Cakaj, S., Malaric, K.: Rain attenuation at low earth orbiting satellite ground station. In: Proceedings of the 48th International Symposium on Multimedia Systems and Applications (ELMAR), pp. 247–250, Zadar, Croatia (2006)
9. Cakaj, S., Malaric, K.: Rain attenuation modelling for low earth orbiting ground station at S-band in Europe. In: Proceedings of the IASTED 18th International Conference on Modelling Simulation, pp. 17–20, Montreal, Canada (2007)
10. Islam, M.R., Chebil, J., Rahman, T.A.: Review of rain attenuation studies for communication systems operating in tropical regions. In: Proceedings of the Malaysian International Conference on Communications (MICC), p. S8.1–S8.4 (1997)
11. Moupfouma, F.: Improvement of rain attenuation prediction method for terrestrial microwave links. IEEE Trans. Antennas Propag. **45**(11), 1575–1577 (1997)
12. Stutzman, W.L., Dishman, D.G.: A simple model for the estimation of rain-induced attenuation along earth-space paths at millimetre wavelengths. Radio Sci. **17**(6), 1465–1476 (1982)
13. Emiliani, L.D., Agudelo, J., Gutierrez, E., Restrepo, J., Fradique-Mendez, C.: Development of rain-attenuation and rain-rate maps for satellite system design in the Ku and Ka bands in Colombia. IEEE Antennas Propag Mag. **46**(6), 54–68 (2004)
14. Ojo, J.S., Ajewole, M.O., Sarkar, S.K.: Rain rate and rain attenuation prediction for satellite communication in Ku and Ka bands over Nigeria. Prog Electromagnet. Res B **5**, 207–223 (2008)
15. ITU-R. Recommendation P.838–3: Specific attenuation model for rain for use in prediction methods. Geneva, ITU (2005)
16. ITU-R. Recommendation P.837–6: Characteristics of precipitation for propagation modeling. Geneva, ITU (2012)
17. ITU-R. Recommendation P.618–11: Propagation data and prediction methods required for the design of Earth-space telecommunication systems. Geneva: International Telecommunication Union (2013)

# Embedded and Machine Learning Approaches

# A Comparative Analysis of Regularization Strategies on the Performance Evaluation of The Deep Learning Models

Deepak Vats[1], Satyaveer Singh[2], Virender Kumar[3(✉)], and Mohammad Derawi[4]

[1] University Institute of Computing, Chandigarh University, Mohali 140413, Punjab, India
[2] Department of Computer Science and Engineering, MMEC, Maharishi Markandeshwar (Deemed To Be University), Mullana, Ambala, Haryana, India
[3] Department of Electronics and Communication Engineering, University Institute of Engineering, Chandigarh University, Mohali 140413, Punjab, India
virendergangotra@gmail.com
[4] Department of Electronics Systems, Faculty of Information Technology and Electrical Engineering, Norwegian University of Science and Technology, Gjøvik, Norway
mohammad.derawi@ntnu.no

**Abstract.** Three common regularization approaches are examined in this evaluation work. The names of the strategies used are data augmentation, batch normalization, and dropout. The objective is to analyze the effect of these strategies on mitigating overfitting. The experimental work is performed by applying them individually and in combination with two or all of them. The Fashion-MNIST and CIFAR-10 datasets are two different datasets used in this empirical evaluation to evaluate the effectiveness of these tactics using a Convolutional Neural Network (CNN). The results show that augmentation used in conjunction with the basic model outperforms batch normalization and dropout approaches in the case of the CIFAR10 dataset. The findings indicate that in the Fashion- MNIST dataset, dropout combined with the basic model works better than batch normalization and dropout techniques. Furthermore, an amalgamation of Batch Normalization and Augmentation is more successful than other approach combinations for the CIFAR10 and Fashion-MNIST data. When considering the training and testing gap for both constant and incremental dropout, the best results are obtained when all regularization is applied in conjunction with base model.

**Keywords:** Overfitting Behavior · Deep Learning · Regularization Techniques · Dropout · Augmentation · Batch Normalization


M. Zafar Ali Khan et al. (Eds.): ICATECS 2025, LNICST 682, pp. 209–224, 2027.
https://doi.org/10.1007/978-3-032-29699-3_16

## 1 Introduction

There exist many examples that showcase cutting-edge results of deep neural networks based models in several domains, including computer vision [1,2], speech recognition [3] and natural language processing [4,5] in the last decade. Deep learning models exhibit great representational capacity. Training of these models is performed on huge data. They automatically learn complicated associations between raw input data and given output. Although these models are great at representing associations between input and output data yet they are vulnerable to overfitting. Overfitting means it learns both data and its noise during model training process. Whatever model has learned in training it fails to generalize it on unseen data. The research by [6] demonstrates that deep learning models perfectly match data during training. The primary intention is to create a model with good generalization. The predicted prediction error on unseen data is known as a deep learning model's generalization error. Since one cannot measure generalization error directly, it is often calculated using a misclassifications rate on a test set that was not consumed for training. This test data is independent of training data. Model achieves small generalization error if model learns without overfitting. The two momentous elements in deep learning are optimization algorithm and regularization technique. They have an immense impact on the model's performance. When training models, optimization takes into account a variety of methods and approaches. Regularization aims to prevent overfitting to the training data. It prevent overfitting by imposing restriction on a model. Any method intended to improve model accuracy on the unseen data has been loosely referred to as regularization. By providing the required theoretical basis and methodical overview, this study seeks to offer the reader a greater knowledge of frequently used regularization approaches along with the analytical and empirical assessments of their impact on the model's overall generalization performance on unseen data. Numerous studies have examined how well convolutional neural networks function in relation to regularization strategies.

The work done in [6–12] is a typical literature on regularization strategies. These studies talks about the influence of regularization methods on deep learning model performance and taxonomical review. The work performed by the authors in [6] shown comparison among three regularization strategies. The names of used strategies are data augmentation, dropout and generalized dropout. The authors compared the three strategies mentioned above using the ImageNet dataset named CIFAR-10 and Fashion-MNIST. Their experimental study set out to measure the impact of the regularization approach on the model training and the model's ultimate generalization performance. To demonstrate the performance, the authors employed three CNN architectures. The work of [7] is one more study that compares regularization techniques in deep learning for weather prediction. When compared to baseline architectures or models, they showed that models with regularizers performed better. Data augmentation and Batch normalization regularizers are employed by the authors for weather prediction task. The authors of [8] performed the empirical examination of two regularizers named dropout and batch normalization. These regularizers behavior was examined with regards to two optimizers. The optimizers used by the authors in their study were SGD and RMSProp. The outcome with batch normalization outperformed outcome with dropout. This work aims to experimentally assess the impact of three regularizer techniques on the Fashion-MNIST and CIFAR10 image datasets. The main highlights of this evaluation study are:

- This research examines the effects of three regularization techniques–dropout, data augmentation, and batch normalization–on two widely used datasets: CIFAR-10 and Fashion-MNIST.
- This work investigates nine different approaches aimed at slowing down model convergence. These nine cases are categorized under three research questions, labeled as RQ1, RQ2, and RQ3.

The structure of the paper is organized as follows: Section 2 outlines the theoretical foundation and provides an overview of key studies conducted by various researchers over the years. Section 3 presents a comparative analysis of different regularization methods applied to image classification tasks, enhanced with relevant visual representations to illustrate the impact of individual techniques and their combinations on training dynamics and generalization performance. The results and discussion are detailed in Section 4, while Section 5 concludes the study by summarizing the key findings.

## 2 Related Work

A variety of techniques have been devised to solve the issue of overfitting. It has become a major concern for developers trying to address this issue. But programmers who want to deal with overfitting have a hard time figuring out which technique or which combination of techniques works best for their particular dataset size. Now a days, it is essential for developers to examine and assess various possibilities due to the rising number of regularization methodologies. The following paragraphs discussed about the various studies conducted by different researchers in past years. Dropout is the novel method created by N. Srivastava et al. [13]. It is a straightforward method which randomly removes nodes from the network. This exhibits regularizing behavior, as nodes that remain intact in the network must adjust to take up the slack left by eliminated nodes. This method was compared with a number of conventional regularization techniques, such as L1, L2, max-norm, and KL-sparsity. They assessed the model's performance using the various regularizer combinations listed in the previous sentence. The optimum performance was obtained by the coupling of max-norm and dropout. They had tabulated the findings by using the max-norm and L2 regularization alone, but no result is shown for dropout alone. If it were done for dropouts, it would be helpful to demonstrate whether or not it works better than alternative approaches. In [14], authors are attempting to determine the typical behavior of different regularization methods in neural networks that rely on embeddings using CNN. They performed their experimental work using four regularizers. The names of regularization methods employed in their study are Re-embedding, Penalizing 'two-norm of weights, Dropout and Penalizing 'two-norm of embeddings. The outcomes they obtained demonstrated that all regularization methods, with the exception of word reembedding, decreased overfitting. It was found that dataset size affects how proficient various regularization methods were. Dropout ranks top out of all employed approaches, indicating that it performed well in comparison to other strategies. Training accuracy was increased by the L2-norm regularizer that was rated second. The bottom place was held by Re-embedding strategy which signifies zero contribution to the performance. The best outcome was obtained for the combination of L2-norm with dropout. The significance of the volume of data is discussed in this study since regularization technique performance is reliant on dataset size.

The most successful regularization techniques and their variations are initially introduced and thoroughly examined in the first part of study done by Moradi et al. [15] in 2020. The second part of paper presents comparative research on regularization strategies, utilizing CIFAR-10 to assess testing errors and computing costs in a convolutional neural network. The last section of the work presented by [15] compares ten regularization methods. The three parameters and CIFAR-10 dataset were used for the comparative analysis. In majority of the applications, the practice of employing data augmentation and weight decay regularizations are secure. When processing power is enough, it is reasonable to use dropout approach. Additionally, when computing resources are plentiful, batch normalization and ensemble approaches make sense. In [16], authors investigated how regularization affects the performance while dealing with unbalanced input. L1, L2, and dropout regularization are the three primary regularization strategies that were examined. The L1 regularization technique can be a useful tool for preventing overfitting in CNN based models for unbalanced data, according to numerical studies. The authors of [17] performed comparative analysis among advanced-level regression and regularization methodologies used to handle model overfitting. Two datasets, weather and climate, were used for the comparison. One observation drawn by them is that ridge regularizer maintains balance between independent variable collinearity and simplicity of model. They observed that when variables are related (means correlated variables) it provide challenges for lasso regularization. The accuracy of the model may suffer in certain scenarios because the lasso regularizer has a tendency to utilize one variable while making others to zero, which causes information loss. Authors in [18] evaluated three (dropout, L2 and data augmentation) regularization strategies to a few deep learning models for malaria detection. Twenty-seven thousand five hundred eighty-eight photographs or images make up the dataset utilized for the study. The authors conducted the experimental work with four models whose names are Rajaraman, MicroVGGNet, ResNet-50 and BaselineNet-1. Liman et al. [19] investigated the effect of three widely used regularization methods. The names of applied regularization methodologies during their findings are data augmentation, weight decay, and dropout. The evaluation of different strategies mentioned in the previous sentence is carried out on two datasets. The names are floral and CIFAR10. For both datasets, the results demonstrate dropout's superiority over alternative approaches. The grouping of dropout with weight decay and augmentation is tested, and the findings reveal that dropout with augmentation achieves higher efficiency. In addition, the combination of weight decay and augmentation is investigated, which is less effective than dropout and augmentation. The amalgamation of weight decay, dropout, and data augmentation outperforms all other combination strategies shown in the work.

The authors in [20] have suggested an enhanced technique called HDNN, which can be applied to the prediction task of credit risk. Firstly, they demonstrated that adding regularization L1 to the DNN's batch normalization layer has no regularization effect. This was a rule that was concealed in the commercial design but not shown. Furthermore, they demonstrated that the problem can be resolved by imposing L2 restrictions on top of single L1 regularization. To showcase the efficacy of HDNN algorithms in the case of a high dimensional dataset, the researchers lastly examined a case study by combining credit data with supply chain and network data. In the investigation performed by Hairab et al. [21], they assess and demonstrate through experiments that CNNs outperform traditional ML in detecting zero day assaults, which are produced by nonbot attackers. They performed the experiments in three ways. One was using ML, second without incorporating regularization, and third with regularizer. The authors wanted a dataset that includes a respectable quantity of simple traffic data, some extent of attacked data, and IoT actual network traffic data. For this reason they selected the TON-IoT dataset generated and published in 2021. In total, the research work is performed using five classifiers. When compared to traditional ML-based classifiers, the output tabulated by the authors in their study demonstrates respectable outcomes. The accuracy of the regularized CNN classifiers is 97%, which is even higher than that of the non-regularized CNN classifier, which yields an accuracy of about 83%. Hamida et al. [22] did their research about the privacy and security issues posed by machine learning. Their work primarily focuses on membership inference attacks. They presented three defensive strategies of how to defend against membership inference attacks. The complete work performed was based on three defensive methods: data augmentation, dropout with L2 regularizer, and the last one was differential privacy. The findings indicate that DA increases model accuracy while protecting privacy. Without compromising accuracy, L2 and dropout approaches effectively reduce the impact of MIAs. The datasets used to analyze the impact of the aforementioned methods were MNIST, CIFAR-10, and CIFAR-100.

## 3 Empirical Evaluation of Regularization Techniques

### 3.1 Materials

Two datasets are used, Fashion-MNIST and CIFAR-10, for the empirical evaluation of different regularization methods in this study. This is done in order to verify whether the findings are generalizable. It is necessary to determine whether the model performance on the two datasets is consistent or not. As a more difficult substitute for the MNIST dataset, a new dataset is suggested with the name of Fashion-MNIST. It consists of 70,000 tiny grayscale photos, each measuring 28 × 28 pixels square, belonging to ten different kinds of categories. These total images are divided into two segments named training and testing. The training set contains sixty thousand and testing set contains ten thousand photos. Table 1 is a list of how all 0–9 numbers are mapped to class labels.

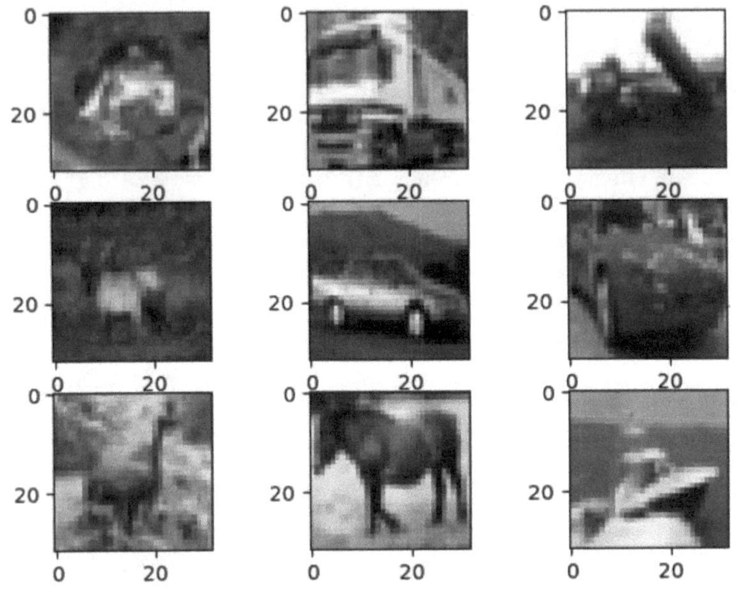

**Fig. 1.** CIFAR10 Sample Dataset Image.

Figure 1 shows a visualization of some photos from the CIFAR-10 dataset. Figure 2 shows a visualization of the first nine photos from the sample dataset fashion-MNIST, demonstrating that the pictures are, in fact, grayscale photos of apparel. The second dataset included in our research was created by CIFAR Institute scientists. They developed two datasets with the names of CIFAR-10 and CIFAR-100 among them CIFAR-10 is used by us for our work. It had sixty thousand small color images, each size 32 by 32 pixels square, depicting things from 10 different classifications, including truck, birds, dear, and automobile. The whole dataset of sixty thousand color photographs is divided into two divisions. This division's purpose is to use one for training the model and the other for testing the model. Training and testing set comprising of fifty and ten thousand photographs mapped to ten different categories of objects whose description with class label is presented in Table 2. Although, Tables 1 and 2 emphasize the information about several item categories in the datasets used for empirical evaluation, Table 3 provides a concise snapshot of both datasets.

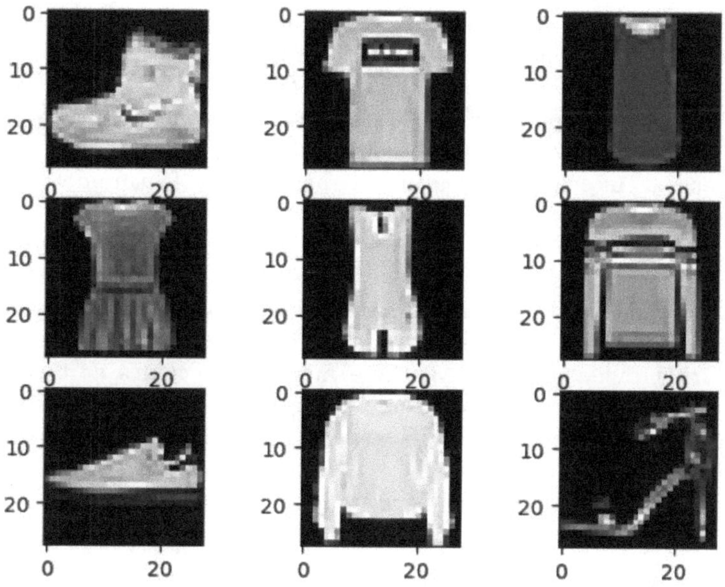

Fig. 2. Fashion-MNIST Sample Dataset Image.

### 3.2 Model Architecture

The next thing is to discuss the basic architecture of the model used in the evaluation process. This is crucial since it entails building the test harness's infrastructure so that any modification or update to the model we do can be assessed using the dataset. It defines a base model on the specific problem to assess model performance and using this one can compare any modification applied the base model. The design approach used for the implementation is modular which means a separate module is defined for each task. This makes it possible to alter or swap out a specific component of the design independently of the others. The complete implementation for testing the base model is developed in five steps. First, the necessary dataset must be loaded; next, it must be made ready for use; third, the model must be defined; fourth step is confined to the model evaluation; and last, the findings must be presented. At this point, we may look at a baseline model for the datasets. The base model will provide a basic architecture that we can utilize as the foundation for research and development. Additionally, it displays a minimal model performance against which all of our other models may be compared. An excellent starting point for the model development is to use the architectural concepts presented in VGG-16 model [10].

Their performance in the 2014 competition served as the basis behind the decision. Convolutional layers with tiny $3 \times 3$ filters are stacked in the design, and then a max pooling layer is added. These layers are stacked together to create a block. These blocks can be repeated. For the first four blocks of the model, the numbers of filters in each block gradually increases with the network's depth. The increase in filters is 32, 64, 128, and 256, respectively. To match the inputs with outputs, the concept of padding is applied on CNN. This schematic architecture serves the purpose of the feature extraction phase. It is connected with the classifier component, which is the next layer of the model. The task of the classifier is to interpret the feature extracted in the feature detector part to forecast class for the input image. The output of the feature detector is flattened first and then a dense layer is coupled with it. The number of output layers depends upon the different categories of objects are there in the dataset. The activation function used here is softmax. For example, if the dataset contains objects that belong to five classes, then output has five nodes. According to the summary provided in Table 3, there must be 10 nodes at the output as both datasets have 10 different items. Accuracy is the metric used to assess the performance of four block VGG style model. The percentage of accurate predictions the model makes relative to all forecasts is known as accuracy. It counts how many predictions are correct.

**Table 1.** Label description for Fashion-MNIST dataset

| Label | 0 | 1 | 2 | 3 | 4 | 5 | 6 | 7 | 8 | 9 |
|---|---|---|---|---|---|---|---|---|---|---|
| Description | T-shirt/top | Trouser | Pullover | Dress | Coat | Sandal | Shirt | Sneaker | Bag | Ankle/boot |

**Table 2.** Label description for CIFAR-10 dataset

| Label | 0 | 1 | 2 | 3 | 4 | 5 | 6 | 7 | 8 | 9 |
|---|---|---|---|---|---|---|---|---|---|---|
| Description | airplane | automobile | bird | cat | deer | dog | frog | horse | ship | truck |

**Table 3.** Dataset statistics for Fashion-MNIST and CIFAR-10

| Dataset used | Object categories | Training volume | Test volume | Validation volume | Total volume |
|---|---|---|---|---|---|
| Fashion-MNIST | 10 | 50000 | 10000 | 10000 | 70000 |
| CIFAR-10 | 10 | 40000 | 10000 | 10000 | 60000 |

**Table 4.** Comparison of techniques with hyper-parameters and accuracy

| Techniques | Learning Rate | Momentum | Epoch | Train Accuracy | Test Accuracy |
|---|---|---|---|---|---|
| Base Model (BM) | 0.001 | 0.9 | 50 | 1.00 | 74.890 |
| BM + Dropout | 0.001 | 0.9 | 50 | 86.40 | 80.720 |
| BM + DA | 0.001 | 0.9 | 50 | 87.86 | 81.340 |
| BM + BN | 0.001 | 0.9 | 50 | 97.97 | 69.100 |
| BM + Dropout + DA | 0.001 | 0.9 | 50 | 78.02 | 76.490 |
| BM + Dropout + BN | 0.001 | 0.9 | 50 | 90.54 | 81.510 |
| BM + DA + BN | 0.001 | 0.9 | 50 | 91.48 | 81.850 |
| BM + Dropout + DA + BN | 0.001 | 0.9 | 50 | 81.95 | 81.090 |
| BM + IncDropout + DA + BN | 0.001 | 0.9 | 50 | 76.51 | 75.870 |

**Table 5.** Comparison of Techniques with Hyper-parameters and Accuracy

| Techniques | Learning Rate | Momentum | Number of Epochs | Highest Training Accuracy Achieved | Highest Testing Accuracy Achieved |
|---|---|---|---|---|---|
| Base Model (BM) | 0.001 | 0.9 | 50 | 1 | 91.39 |
| BM + Dropout | 0.001 | 0.9 | 50 | 93.16 | 92.71 |
| BM + DA | 0.001 | 0.9 | 50 | 93.24 | 92.03 |
| BM + BN | 0.001 | 0.9 | 50 | 1 | 91.17 |
| BM + Dropout + DA | 0.001 | 0.9 | 50 | 93.12 | 91.16 |
| BM + Dropout + BN | 0.001 | 0.9 | 50 | 95.16 | 93.27 |
| BM + DA + BN | 0.001 | 0.9 | 50 | 94.54 | 92.46 |
| BM + Dropout + DA + BN | 0.001 | 0.9 | 50 | 91.43 | 91.3 |
| BM + IncDropout + DA + BN | 0.001 | 0.9 | 50 | 94.25 | 91.14 |

## 4 Results and Discussion

Three research study questions were put forth in order to address the performance evaluation issue of the model:

**RQ1:** How do Dropout, Data Augmentation, and Batch Normalization perform on the Fashion-MNIST and CIFAR-10 datasets?

**RQ2:** How well does the Base Model, together with different combinations of regularization methods mentioned in RQ1, perform (Base Model + Dropout + Augmentation, Base Model + Dropout + Batch Normalization, Base Model + Augmentation + Batch Normalization) on the Fashion-MNIST and CIFAR-10 datasets?

**RQ3:** How well does the pairing of the Base Model with all regularization methods mentioned in RQ1 (Base Model + Increasing Dropout + Augmentation + Batch Normalization) perform on both datasets?

The merger of two or three tactics in the experimental work is done to examine the possible advantages or disadvantages. The objective was to ascertain whether these combinations would result in more advantages than utilizing a single approach, or whether they would present certain problems, including underfitting.

### 4.1 Simulated Results

The findings of the experimental work carried out by us are tabulated in Tables 4 and 5. We must compare their results in order to determine which strategies work best with a specific set of dataset. These tables will be used to answer three questions (RQ1 to RQ3) presented above. The hyperparameters, such as learning rate and momentum, are maintained constant for every configuration in order to compare the model's performance for various regularization strategies. The Tables 4 and 5 show nine cases for which findings are performed. Firstly the evaluation of base model (BM) is conducted without incorporation of any regularization strategy and then the BM with combination of each one of the three regularization techniques is executed. Next, the experimental work is performed with the combination of taking two of the three regularization methods combined with BM. Lastly the empirical evaluation of BM with all the three regularization techniques is calculated. The only difference between the last and second-last case defined in Tables 4 and 5 is whether the constant dropout or incremental dropout is used at each layer of the BM. The first row of Tables 4 and 5 specify the model performance without use of the any regularization method. The training accuracy achieved for both the dataset is 100% and test accuracy for CIFAR10 data is 74.89% and Fashion-MNIST data is 91.390%. These results give you an idea about the overfitting behavior of the model. Figure 3 and Fig. 4

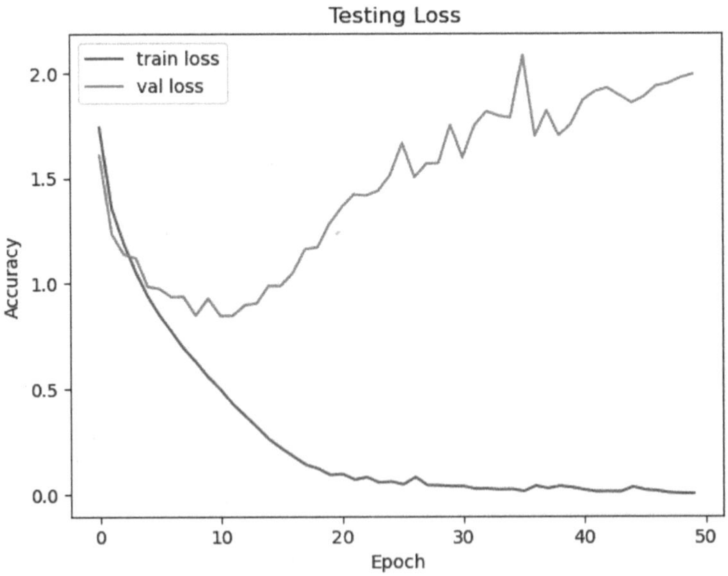


**Fig. 3.** Base Model Training Loss of CIFAR-10 Dataset.

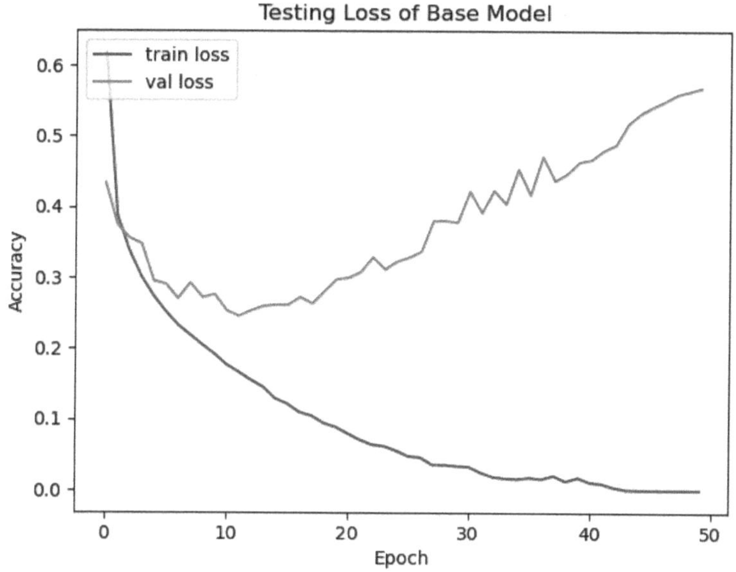


**Fig. 4.** Base Model Training Loss of Fashion-MNIST Dataset.

depict the BM training and validation loss plot for the datasets CIFAR-10 and Fashion-MNIST, which highlights the overfitting nature of both datasets. The existence of overfitting in the model performance is evident from the difference between the training loss and the validation loss shown in Fig. 3 and Fig. 4. Our objective is to attain a situation where the validation loss falls in tandem with the training loss, signifying improved model generalization to unknown data.

**RQ1: Effect of Dropout, Data Augmentation and Batch Normalization:** Table 4 shows that on the *CIFAR-10* dataset, augmentation applied in combination with the Base Model performs better than batch normalization and dropout. Its test accuracy is **81.34%**, whereas batch normalization and dropout reach **80.72%** and **69.10%**, respectively.

Table 5 indicates that on the *Fashion-MNIST* dataset, the **Dropout + BM** combination performs better than the **Batch Normalization + BM** and **DA + BM** combinations. The respective test accuracies achieved by **BM + Dropout**, **BM + DA**, and **BM + BN** combinations.

**RQ2: Effect of Dropout + Augmentation, Dropout + Batch Normalization and Augmentation + Batch Normalization:** The impact of the aforementioned combinations of regularization strategies on both datasets is analyzed in RQ2. The results show that the **BM + DA + BN** combination is superior for both the *CIFAR-10* and *Fashion-MNIST* datasets. The corresponding test accuracies are **81.850%** for *CIFAR-10* and **92.460%** for *Fashion-MNIST.*

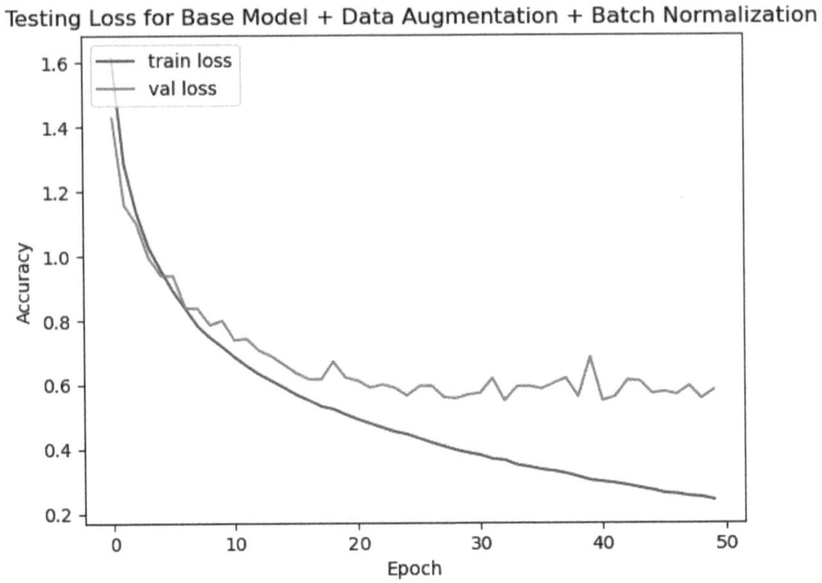


**Fig. 5.** BM + DA + BN Training Loss of CIFAR-10 Dataset

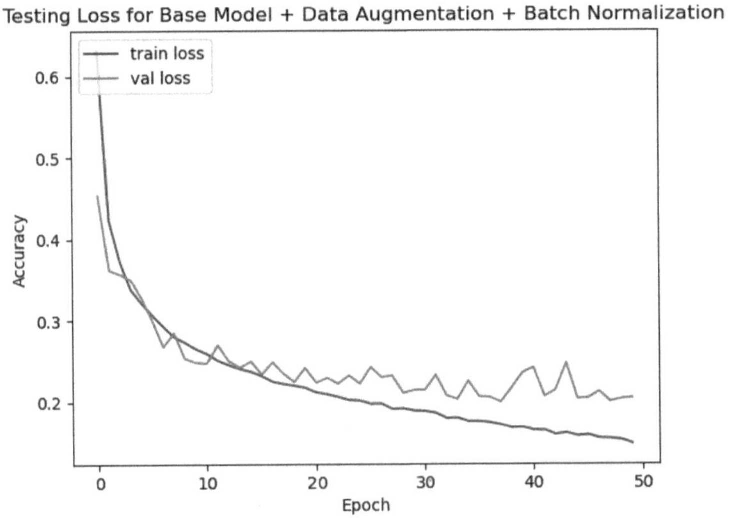


**Fig. 6.** BM + DA + BN Training Loss of Fashion-MNIST Dataset.

The testing accuracies for the **BM + Dropout + DA** and **BM + Dropout + BN** combinations are **76.490%**, **81.510%**, **91.160%**, and **93.270%** for both datasets, respectively. The training and loss graphs for **DA + BN** together with the Base Model are depicted in Fig. 5 and Fig. 6.

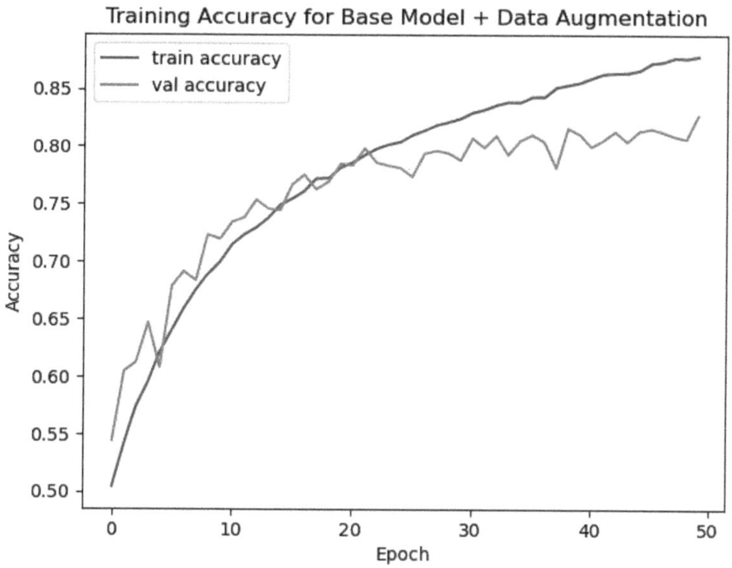


**Fig. 7.** BM + Dropout Training Accuracy of the Fashion-MNIST Dataset.

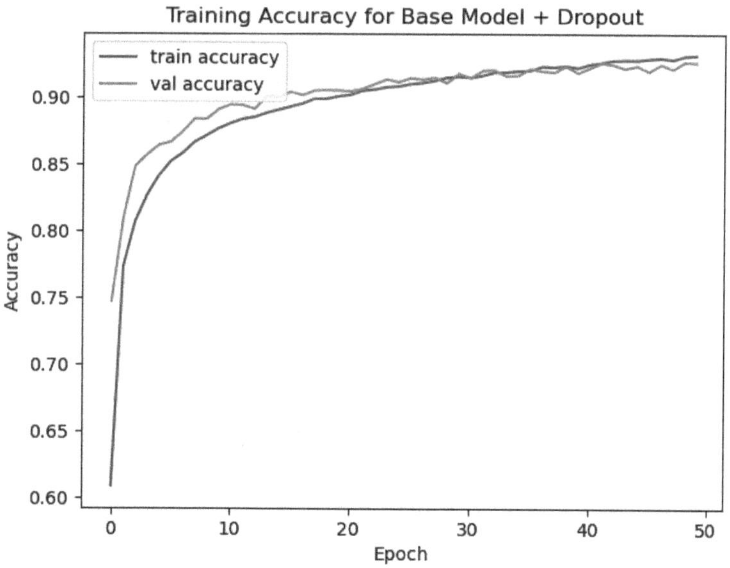


**Fig. 8.** BM + DA + Dropout + BN Training Accuracy Plot of CIFAR-10 Dataset.

**RQ3: Dropout + DA + BN Vs IncDropout + DA + BN:** The influence of all the regularization techniques considered for this study is analyzed here. Another investigation compares the use of constant versus incremental dropout while applying all strategies simultaneously. The application of all regularization

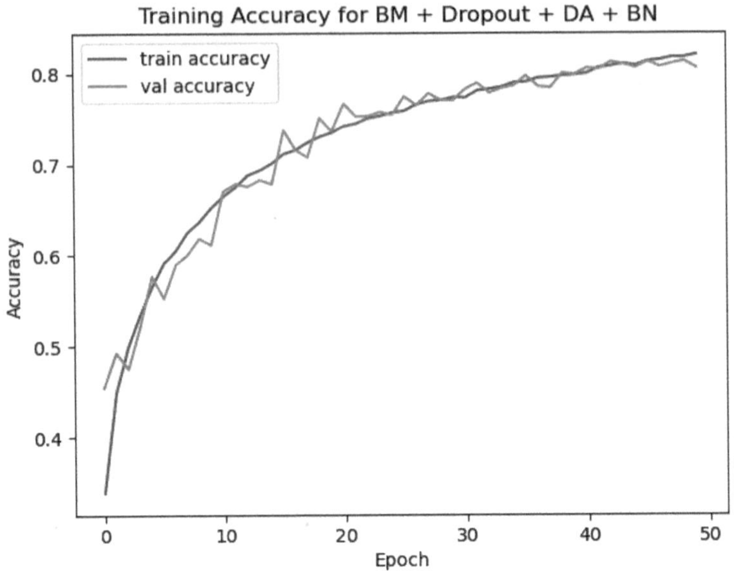


**Fig. 9.** BM + DA +Dropout + BN Training Accuracy of the Fashion-MNIST Dataset

methods in combination with BM produces the best outcome in terms of the training–testing gap for both constant and incremental dropout. The accuracy and loss graphs are available in Fig. 7 and Fig. 8. Training Accuracy for BM + Dropout + DA + BN is demonstrated in Fig. 9.

## 5 Conclusion

In this experimental research, a basic 4-block CNN model was employed to assess the impact of three regularization methods–dropout, batch normalization, and data augmentation– both individually and in combination, across two distinct datasets. The efficacy of these three strategies was assessed in relation to the overall number of epochs used in training and testing the model. This study provides valuable insights into three separate research questions, identified as RQ1, RQ2, and RQ3. Based on the findings related to RQ1, data augmentation proved to be more effective compared to batch normalization and dropout. The results related to RQ2 indicate that, for both datasets, the pairing of batch normalization with data augmentation delivered the highest accuracy, reaching 81.850% and 92.460%, respectively. According to the studies related to RQ3, combining all three strategies yields more efficacy than doing it alone.

## References


1. Liu, Y., et al.: Cbnet: a novel composite backbone network architecture for object detection. In: Proceedings of the AAAI Conference on Artificial Intelligence, vol. 34, no. 07, pp. 11653–11660 (2020). https://doi.org/10.1609/aaai.v34i07.6834
2. Chen, L.-C., Zhu, Y., Papandreou, G., Schroff, F., Adam, H.: Encoder-decoder with atrous separable convolution for semantic image segmentation. In: Proceedings of the European Conference on Computer Vision (ECCV), pp. 801–818 (2018). https://doi.org/10.1007/978-3-030-01234-2-49
3. Saon, G., Kurata, G., Sercu, T., Audhkhasi, K., Thomas, S., Dimitriadis, D.: English conversational telephone speech recognition by humans and machines, arXiv preprint arXiv:1703.02136 (2017)
4. Edunov, S., Ott, M., Auli, M., Grangier, D.: Understanding back-translation at scale, arXiv preprint arXiv:1808.09381 (2018)
5. Dai, Z., Yang, Z., Yang, Y., Carbonell, J., Le, Q.V., Salakhutdinov, R.: Transformer-XL: attentive language models beyond a fixed-length context. arXiv preprint arXiv:1901.02860 (2019)
6. Smirnov, E.A., Timoshenko, D.M., Andrianov, S.N.: Comparison of regularization methods for ImageNet classification with deep convolutional neural networks. AASRI Proc. **6**(1), 89–94 (2014)
7. Nusrat, I., Jang, S.-B.: A comparison of regularization techniques in deep neural networks. Symmetry **10**(11), 648 (2018)
8. Garbin, C., Zhu, X., Marques, O.: Dropout vs. batch normalization: an empirical study of their impact to deep learning. Multimedia Tools Appli. **79**(19), 12777–12815 (2020)
9. Chen, G., Chen, P., Shi, Y., Hsieh, C.-Y., Liao, B., Zhang, S.: Rethinking the usage of batch normalization and dropout in the training of deep neural networks. arXiv preprint arXiv:1905.05928 (2019)
10. Simonyan, K., Zisserman, A.: Very deep convolutional networks for large-scale image recognition, arXiv preprint arXiv:1409.1556 (2014)
11. Kukačka, J., Golkov, V., Cremers, D.: Regularization for deep learning: A taxonomy, arXiv preprint arXiv:1710.10686 (2017)
12. Tian, Y., Zhang, Y.: A comprehensive survey on regularization strategies in machine learning. Inform. Fusion **80**, 146–166 (2022). https://doi.org/10.1016/j.inffus.2021.11.005
13. Srivastava, N., Hinton, G., Krizhevsky, A., Sutskever, I., Salakhutdinov, R.: Dropout: a simple way to prevent neural networks from over-fitting. J. Mach. Learn. Res. **15**(1), 1929–1958 (2014)
14. Peng, H., Mou, L., Li, G., Chen, Y., Lu, Y., Jin, Z.: A comparative study on regularization strategies for embedding-based neural networks, arXiv preprint arXiv:1508.03721 (2015)
15. Moradi, R., Berangi, R., Minaei, B.: A survey of regularization strategies for deep models. Artif. Intell. Rev. **53**(6), 3947–3986 (2020). https://doi.org/10.1007/s10462-019-09784-7
16. Kamalov, F., Leung, H.H.: Deep learning regularization in imbalanced data. In: Proceedings of the International Conference on Communications, Computing, Cybersecurity, and Informatics (CCCI), pp. 1–5. IEEE, United Arab Emirates (2020)

17. Raouhi, E.M., Lachgar, M., Kartit, A.: Comparative study of regression and regularization methods: application to weather and climate data. In: Bennani, S., Lakhrissi, Y., Khaissidi, G., Mansouri, A., Khamlichi, Y. (eds.) WITS 2020. LNEE, vol. 745, pp. 233–240. Springer, Singapore (2022). https://doi.org/10.1007/978-981-33-6893-4_22
18. Swastika, W., Widodo, R.B., Balqis, G.A., Sitepu, R.: The effect of regularization on deep learning methods for detection of malaria infection. In: Proceedings of the International Conference on Converging Technologies in Electrical and Information Engineering (ICCTEIE), pp. 87–90. IEEE (2021)
19. Liman, M.D., Osanga, S.I., Alu, E.S., Zakariya, S.A.: Regularization effects in deep learning architecture. J. Nigerian Soc. Phys. Sci., 1911–1911 (2024)
20. Yang, M., Lim, M.K., Qu, Y., Li, X., Ni, D.: Deep neural networks with L1 and L2 regularization for high-dimensional corporate credit risk prediction. Expert Syst. Appl. **213**, 118873 (2023)
21. Hairab, B.I., Aslan, H.K., Elsayed, M.S., Jurcut, A.D., Azer, M.A.: Anomaly detection of zero-day attacks based on CNN and regularization techniques. Electronics **12**(3), 573 (2023). https://doi.org/10.3390/electronics12030573
22. Hamida, S.B., Mrabet, H., Chaieb, F., Jemai, A.: Assessment of data augmentation, dropout with L2 regularization and differential privacy against membership inference attacks. Multimedia Tools Appli. **83**(15), 44455–44484 (2024)

# Aperture-Coupled Fractal Slot Cylindrical DRA: Design and Development for Wireless Applications

M. Sri Uma Suseela[1(✉)], Hima Bindu Valiveti[2], M. Hemalatha[3], and V. N. V. Radha Krishna Murty[4]

[1] Vishnu Institute of Technology, Bhimavaram 534202, India
umasuseela.m@vishnu.edu.in
[2] Gokaraju Rangaraju Institute of Engineering and Technology, Hyderabad 50090, India
[3] Shri Vishnu Engineering College for Women, Bhimavaram 534202, India
[4] B V Raju College, Bhimavaram 534202, India

**Abstract.** In this work, a unique Z-shaped Koch fractal slot with a cylindrical dielectric resonator antenna (DRA) for wireless communication applications is designed, simulated, and experimentally validated. The Aperture-Coupled Fractal-Slot Cylindrical DRA is designed for 2.45 GHz wireless applications (Wi-Fi, IoT). It uses a cylindrical dielectric resonator ($\epsilon_r = 12$) excited through a Koch-fractal slot etched on the ground plane. A 50Ω microstrip line on a Rogers RO4003C sub-strate ($\epsilon_r$ = 3.55, 1.6 mm thick) feeds energy through the slot into the DRA. The work examines a number of coupling strategies, such as aperture, proximity, and coplanar waveguide feeds, with a focus on how fractal geometry and DRA con-figuration might improve gain, bandwidth, and polarization. Design authentication and parameter optimization were done using HFSS simulation tools. Relative studies show how effectively the proposed design works to enhance antenna performance, especially in terms of gain, bandwidth, and return loss.

**Keywords:** Aperture coupling · Wireless Communication · Impedance Matching · Broadband Performance · Dielectric Resonator Antenna (DRA)

## 1 Introduction

As the intermediary between directed electromagnetic waves and free-space radiation, antennas are crucial parts of contemporary communication systems. They transform electrical impulses into electromagnetic waves and vice versa in both

Vishnu Institute of Technology, Bhimavaram.


M. Zafar Ali Khan et al. (Eds.): ICATECS 2025, LNICST 682, pp. 225–234, 2027.
https://doi.org/10.1007/978-3-032-29699-3_17

transmission and receiving modes. Antennas are frequency-dependent devices that are made to function only in certain frequency bands; outside of these, they perform noticeably worse. Antennas can serve as both band-pass filters and transducers due to their frequency-selective behavior [1,7]. Important factors including gain, bandwidth, effective length, polarization and radiation pattern define an antenna's performance. While bandwidth describes the operating frequency range, which is sometimes determined by a voltage standing wave ratio (VSWR) threshold, gain estimates the directional augmentation of radiated power. The orientation of the emitted electric field, known as polarization can be either circular or linear (horizontal/vertical) [4,5]. The radiation pattern shows the angular distribution of energy received or released, while effective length is related to the conductor's current distribution.

Antennas function according to the principles outlined by Maxwell's equations. Time-varying electric and magnetic fields produced by oscillating charges travel through space as electromagnetic waves. The transmission process involves conversion of guided waves from a transmission line into free-space radiation, while reception involves the reverse conversion. These mechanisms are exploited in applications ranging from personal communication devices to radar and defence systems [8]. For small, low-profile, and reasonably priced wireless solutions, printed antennas, also known as micro-strip antennas, have become the most popular option among the several antenna technologies [2,9], and [10]. These antennas are especially appropriate for microwave frequencies and are made on printed circuit boards (PCBs) utilizing photolithographic processes. Their benefits include mass manufacturing compatibility, conformability, mechanical durability, and ease of integration with electronic circuits. They are therefore widely used in satellite communication, mobile radio devices, spacecraft, and airplanes [8,11].

Different patch geometries, such as rectangular, circular, triangular, and elliptical, can be used to build printed antennas; each has unique performance tradeoffs [1,11]. Efficiency, bandwidth, and size are all greatly influenced by the substrate material selection, which usually has dielectric constants between 2.2 and 12. While high-dielectric, thin substrates produce compact designs but have lower efficiency and narrower bandwidth, low-dielectric, thick substrates offer greater efficiency and a wider bandwidth at the cost of larger size [7].

The topic of printed antenna design research is still very active because of the quick expansion of wireless communication systems and the growing need for high-performance, small antennas. In order to maximize important performance parameters including gain, bandwidth, and radiation characteristics for contemporary wire-less applications, our work focuses on the design and development of effective print-ed antenna structures [2,6], and [12]. Antenna design has advanced due to the growing need for wireless systems that are small, effective, and high-performing. Dielectric Resonator Antennas (DRAs) present interesting solutions due to their high radiation efficiency, wide bandwidth, and low loss [3]- [6]. By reducing the size of the antenna and increasing the impedance bandwidth, fractal topologies such as Koch slots further improve performance [1,8], and [9]. In this work, a cylindrical DRA is integrated with a Z-shaped Koch fractal slot that is fed through aperture coupling.

## 2 Antenna Design

The antenna structure includes an FR4 substrate, a Z-shaped Koch fractal slot, and a rectangular DRA constructed using Aluminum Oxide ($Al_2O_3$). The most important dimensions and material characteristics are as follows:

- **Substrate:** FR4, $\epsilon_r = 4.4$, dimensions $50 \times 50 \times 0.508mm$
- **Ground Plane:** Z-shaped Koch fractal slot
- **Feed:** Cylindrical $Al_2O_3$, $\epsilon_r = 9.9$, dimensions $15 \times 13 \times 8mm$
- **Feed:** Lumped port excitation through aperture
- **Excitation:** Lumped port.
- DRA radius = 34 mm, height = 24 mm
- Slot length = 55 mm, width = 4 mm, $1^{st}$-order Koch fractal edges
- Air gap between DRA and ground = 1.8 mm
- **Simulation Environment:** HFSS (High-Frequency Structure Simulator) for design and performance evaluation.

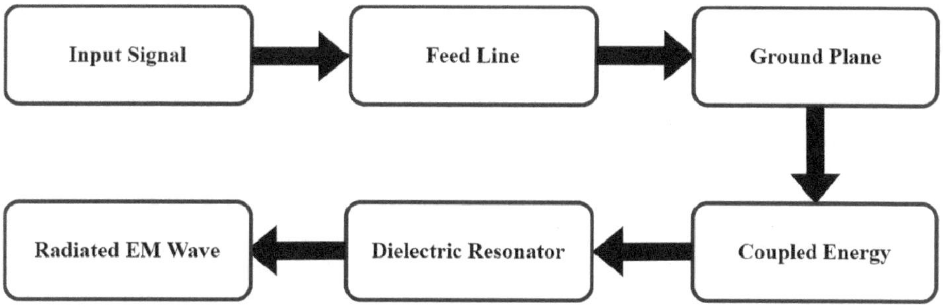


**Fig. 1.** Dielectric Resonator Antenna System

### 2.1 Design Specifications of Antenna

This section gives an overview of the design specifications of an antenna.

Calculation of width(w)= $\frac{c}{2f_0\sqrt{\frac{(\varepsilon_r+1)}{2}}}$

Calculation of effective dielectric constant= $\varepsilon_{reff} = \frac{\varepsilon_r+1}{2} + \frac{\varepsilon_r-1}{2}\left[1+12\frac{h}{w}\right]^{-1/2}$

Calculation of extension length= $\Delta L = \frac{0.412\left[\frac{w}{h}+0.264\right][\varepsilon_{eff}+0.3]}{[\varepsilon_{eff}-0.258]\left[\frac{w}{h}+0.8\right]}$

Calculation of $L_{eff} = \frac{c}{2\varepsilon\sqrt{\varepsilon_{eff}}}$

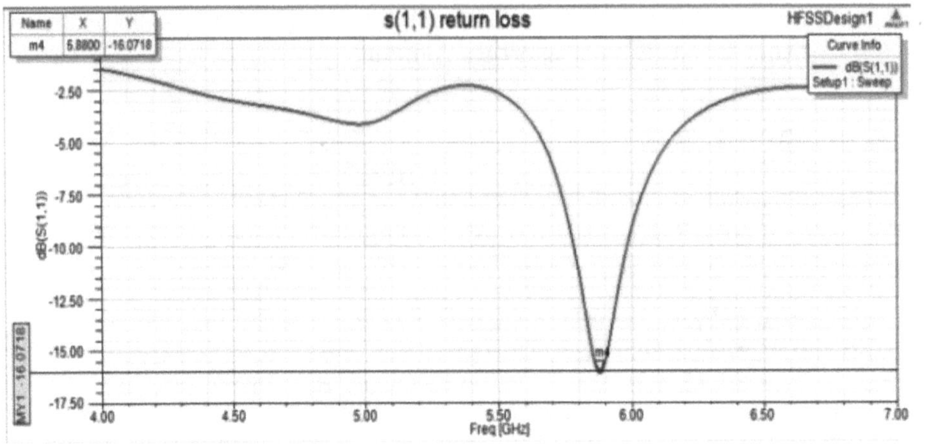


**Fig. 2.** Return Loss of Z Shaped Koch Fractal Slot with Cylindrical DRA

Figure 1 show how an input signal travels through different parts before emitting an electro-magnetic wave. It starts with the input signal, which is the system's first input. The Feed Line, which serves as the main transmission line, carries this signal. By giving electrical signals a point of reference, the ground plane keeps the system stable. The Dielectric Resonator, a important element that increases resonance and boosts signal efficiency, receives Coupled Energy as the signal travels. A Radiated Electromagnetic (EM) Wave, that symbolizes the intended energy transfer, is the system's final out-put. In applications involving antennas, wireless communication, and signal transmission, this procedure is extremely important (Figs. 5 and 6).

The performance goals are $|S_{11}| < -10dB$ across 2.42.5 GHz, gain $\approx$ 5-7dBi, radiation efficiency $> 80\%$, broadside linear polarization.

The fractal slot increases the effective slot length and introduces multiple resonances, improving bandwidth. Parametric tuning of DRA size, slot dimensions, and air gap optimizes coupling and impedance matching. The design is compact, efficient, and suitable for modern wireless systems.

## 3 Simulation Results

The antenna's performance is examined in detail through several simulation parameters:

### 3.1 Return Loss

The return loss shown in Fig. 2 for the designed Z-shaped Koch fractal slot with Rectangular DRA is measured at:

- $S_{11} < -10\,dB$ from 5.8 GHz to 5.99 GHz.
- **Minimum Return Loss:** –16.70 dB at 5.88 GHz

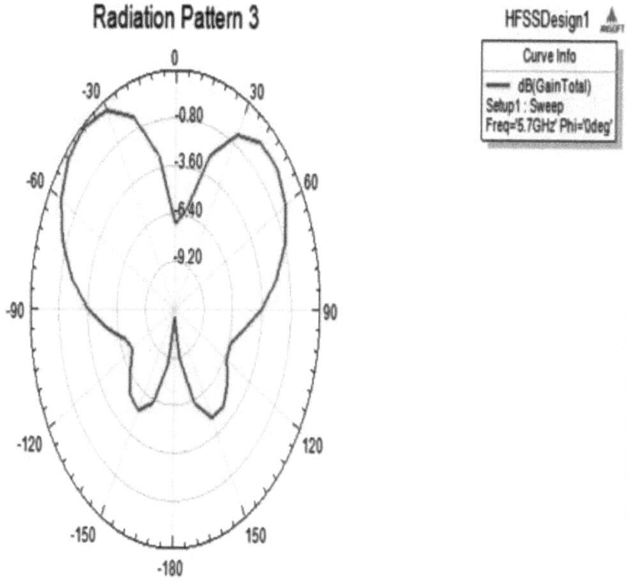


**Fig. 3.** Radiation Pattern of Z Shaped Koch Fractal Slot with Cylindrical DRA

### 3.2 Radiation Pattern

The far-field fluctuation in radiated power is shown in Fig. 3. The antenna effectively covers the working frequency range, as seen by the design's consistent emission pattern.

### 3.3 Gain

In Fig. 4, The antenna achieves a 3D gain of **5.49 dB**, consistent across the operational frequency range, highlighting its suitability for communication applications.

### 3.4 Bandwidth

The bandwidth of an antenna refers to the range of frequencies over which the antenna can operate correctly. Bandwidth is observed from 5.8030GHz to 5.92560GHz and is about 0.1530GHz.

### 3.5 VSWR

The minimum VSWR which corresponds to a perfect match is unity. The VSWR of the Z Shaped Koch Fractal Slot with Cylindrical DRA designed in HFSS are shown in Fig. 7. The VSWR of antenna lies between 1 and infinity. For practical applications, it should be between 1 and 2. It is observed that the minimum value of VSWR is 1.3730 at 5.88 GHz.

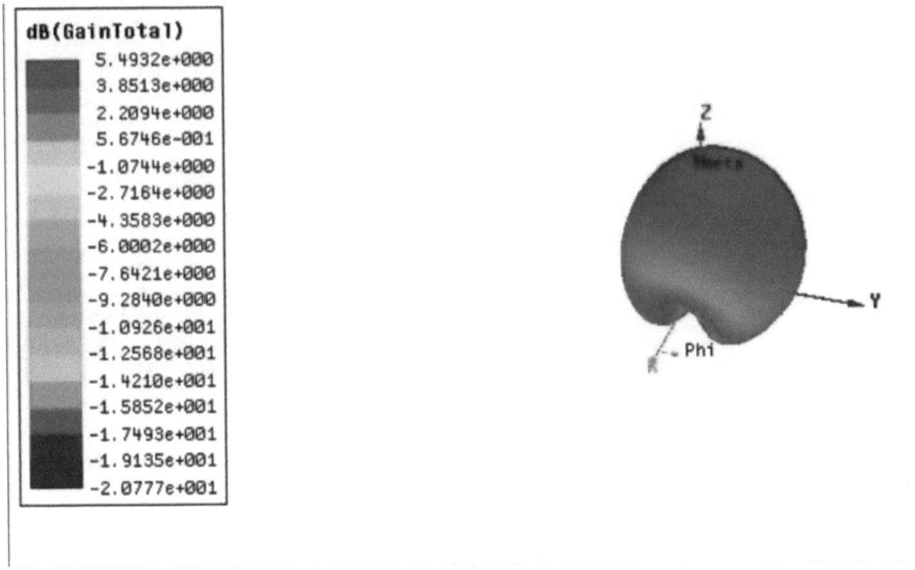


**Fig. 4.** Gain of Z Shaped Koch Fractal Slot with Cylindrical DRA

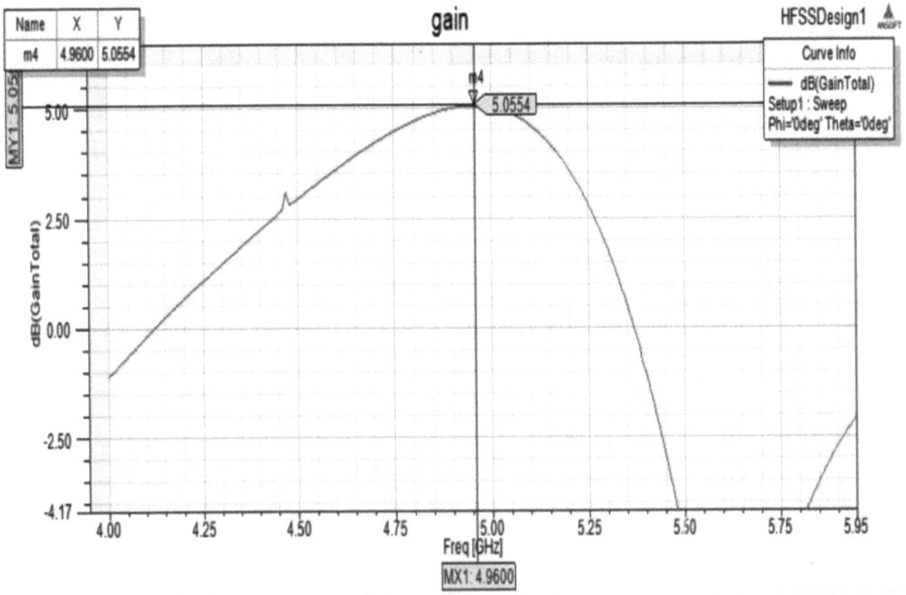


**Fig. 5.** Gain of Z Shaped Koch Fractal Slot with Cylindrical DRA

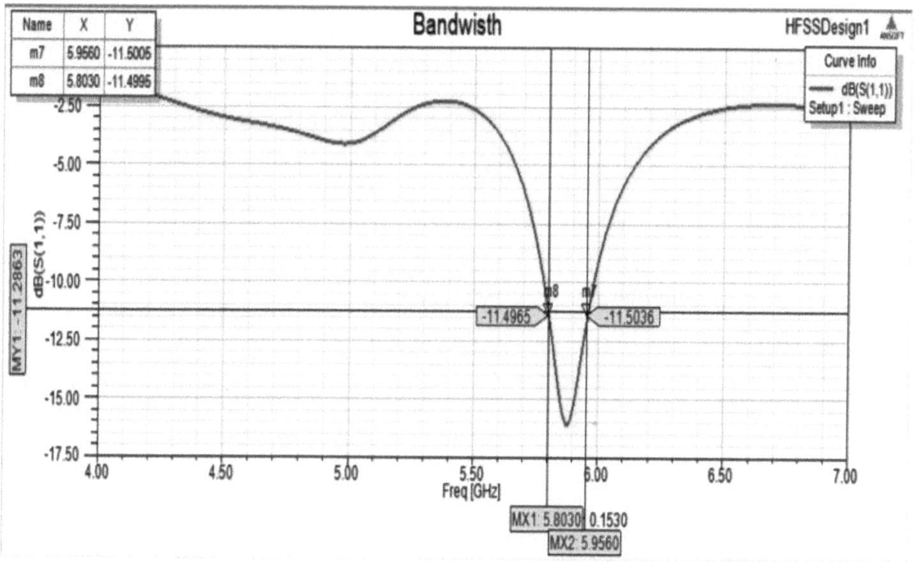


**Fig. 6.** Bandwidth of Z Shaped Koch Fractal Slot with Cylindrical DRA

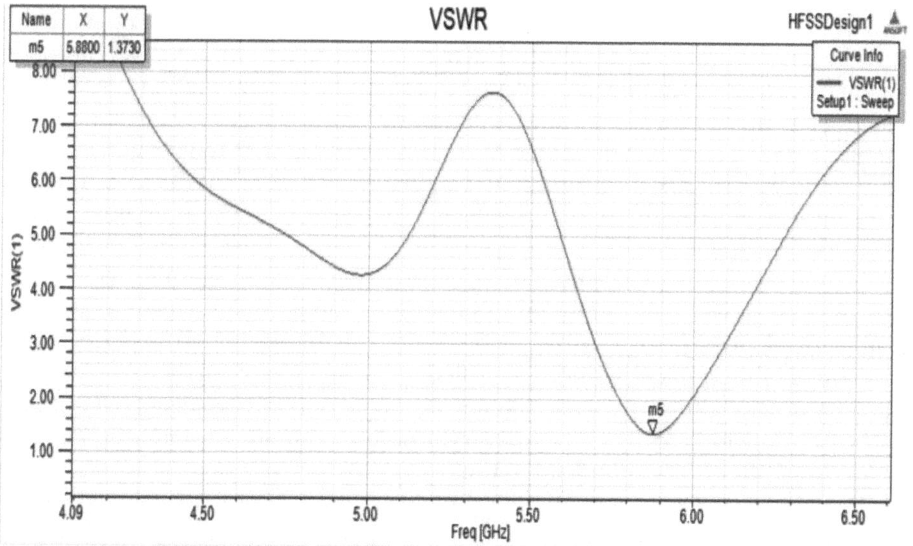


**Fig. 7.** VSWR of Z Shaped Koch Fractal Slot with Cylindrical DRA

### 3.6 Antenna Fabrication

The antenna was fabricated using mixed oxide processing of $ZnTiO_3$ and $Al_2O_3$ materials. Measured results closely matched simulations, validating the design methodology. In Table 1 depicts the key performance metrics for various antenna designs, including the Z-shaped Koch fractal slot with Rectangular DRA as shown below:

**Table 1.** Measured Parameters

| **Slot Type** | Return Loss $S_{11}$ | VSWR | Bandwidth (GHz) | Gain (dB) |
|---|---|---|---|---|
| Capital Y | -10.94 dB | 1.79 | 0.5441 | 5.03 |
| Random Y | -12.17 dB | 1.65 | 0.4914 | 4.89 |
| Koch Y | -12.37 dB | 1.63 | 0.64 | 5.99 |
| Z-Koch | -16.70 dB | 1.34 | 0.2648 | 4.73 |

# 4 Conclusion and Future Scope

## 4.1 Conclusion

The design, simulation, fabrication, and experimental validation of a unique Z-shaped Koch fractal slot integrated with a cylindrical dielectric resonator antenna (DRA) for wireless communication applications are presented in this study. When compared to traditional slot configurations, the total antenna performance in terms of impedance matching, return loss, gain, and bandwidth has been greatly improved by the addition of fractal geometry to the slot structure in conjunction with aperture coupling. With a bandwidth of 0.153 GHz, a constant gain of roughly 5.49 dB, and a minimum return loss of -16.07 dB at 5.88 GHz, the suggested design proved suitable for dependable and effective operation within the desired frequency range.

The accuracy and robustness of the design process were confirmed by the close match between the simulation results and the experimental results from the manufactured prototype. The Z-shaped Koch fractal slot's better performance in attaining compactness without sacrificing efficiency was further validated by comparison with alternative slot geometries. This makes the suggested antenna a viable option for use in contemporary wireless communication systems that call for small, light, and powerful antennas.

The study also shows how fractal geometry and DRA technology can be combined to get around the drawbacks of traditional antenna designs. The study offers a solid basis for upcoming advancements in multi-band, reconfigurable, and wideband antenna systems in addition to proving that improved radiation characteristics and impedance bandwidth can be achieved using this method.AI-driven diagnostics in the Chatbot, enhanced security protocols, and potential integration with hospital data-bases for better patient management is the possible extension of the proposed model.

### 4.2 Future Scope

To further improve the performance of the antenna, future work can explore the use of **stair-shaped DRAs**, which offer several advantages, such as:

- **Wideband capabilities:** Stair-shaped DRAs can support broader bandwidths.
- **Compact size and low profile:** These geometries are ideal for space-constrained applications.
- **High radiation efficiency:** These DRAs offer low loss and high radiation performance.

These advancements in DRA design would enhance the antenna's suitability for modern wireless communication.

## References


1. Orugu, R., Moses, N.: Triangular fractal loaded reconfigurable antenna with notch band characteristics. Int. J. Numer. Model. Electron. Netw. Dev. Fields **34**(1), e2806 (2021)
2. Krishna, C.M., Suguna, N., Maha Lakshmi, N.V.K., Saravanakumar, R., Puri, S.C., Subbareddy, M.K.V.: High Gain hexaport millimetre Wave MIMO antenna for 5G service LMDS and N257 band applications. In: Nagaria, R.K., Tripathi, V.S., Zamarreno, C.R., Prajapati, Y.K. (eds.) VCAS 2022. LNEE, vol. 1024. Springer, Singapore (2023). https://doi.org/10.1007/978-981-99-0973-5_39
3. Mishra, S., et al.: Three-dimensional dual-band dielectric resonator antenna for wireless communication. IEEE Access **8**, 71593–71604 (2020)
4. Elahi, M., et al.: Circularly polarized dielectric resonator antenna with two annular vias. IEEE Access **9**, 41123–41128 (2021)
5. Danesh, S., Rahim, S.K.A., Khalily, M.: A wideband trapezoidal dielectric resonator antenna with circular polarization. Progress Electromag. Res. Lett. **34**, 91–100 (2012)
6. Kiran, D.V., Sankaranarayanan, D., Mukherjee, B.: Compact embedded dual-element rectangular dielectric resonator antenna combining Sierpinski and Minkowski fractals. IEEE Trans. Comp. Packaging Manufact. Technol. **7**(5), 786–791 (2017)
7. Soren, D., et al.: Dielectric resonator antennas: designs and advances. Progress Electromag. Res. B **60**, 195–213 (2014)
8. Kumari, S., et al.: Design and parametric study of monopole blade antenna for UHF-band aerospace applications. In: Proc. International Conference on Cognitive Computing and Cyber Physical Systems, Cham, Springer Nature Switzerland, Switzerland (2023). https://doi.org/10.1007/978-3-031-48891-7_22
9. Krishna, C.M., et al..: Design and analysis of tortoise shaped quadband antenna for C & Ku-band applications. In: Proc. 2021 International Conference on Computer Communication and Informatics (ICCCI), IEEE (2021)
10. Orugu, R., Nesasudha, M., Janapala, D.K.: A frequency tunable hexagon shaped antenna for 5.8 GHz WiFi and sub-6 GHz 5G mobile IoT applications. In: Proc. 2021 International Conference on Computer Communication and Informatics (ICCCI). IEEE (2021)

11. Krishna, C.M., Mamatha, M., Kumar, J.P.: Mickey Mouse modeled MIMO antenna for extended UWB applications. In: Proc. 2020 Fourth International Conference on Computing Methodologies and Communication (ICCMC). IEEE (2020)
12. Maurya, N.K., et al.: Graphene-based frequency agile isolation enhancement mechanism for MIMO antenna in terahertz regime. Nano Commun. Netw. **35**, 100436 (2023)

# Automatic Dialing to Any Telephone and Capture Image Using I2c Protocol on Detecting Burglary

Ch. Rajendra Prasad(✉), B. Keerthana, B. Deemanth, and A. Srikanth

Department of Electronics and Communication Engineering, Vignana Bharathi Institute of Technology, Hyderabad 501301, India
rajendraprasad.chalamalla@vbithyd.ac.in

**Abstract.** The abstract should summarize the contents of the paper in short terms, i.e. 15–250 words. An innovative security system is proposed that automatically makes a phone call to a predefined number and captures images when a burglary is detected. The system utilizes the I2C (Inter-Integrated Circuit) protocol to communicate between sensors, microcontrollers, and a GSM module. When a burglary is detected by sensors, the microcontroller sends a signal to the GSM module, which then dials the predefined telephone number to alert the owner or authorities. The system is designed to be low-power, cost-effective, and easy to install. The I2C protocol enables seamless communication between devices, ensuring reliable and efficient operation. This project demonstrates a practical application of the I2C protocol in a real-world security system.

**Keywords:** I2C protocol · Burglary detection · Automatic dialing · GSM module · Microcontroller · Security system

## 1 Introduction

To notify concerned authorities about unauthorized access in secured areas such as museums, homes, and banks, this system provides an intelligent and automated solution. As crime rate is on the rise and burglars are getting smarter, the security system for banks, shops and houses needs to be full proof. This proposed system ensures that at any moment if any unauthorized person tries to open the bank locker, a telephone number will be dialed through the telephone line connected to it. Security is a primary concern in both residential and commercial areas. Traditional security systems often rely on alarms, which may not be effective if no one is nearby to respond.

Notify emergency contacts via a GSM module. The system consists of a microcontroller, PIR motion sensors, vibration sensors, and an I2C-based EEPROM to store preconfigured emergency contact numbers. Upon detecting unauthorized entry, the microcontroller retrieves the stored contact number from the EEPROM using the I2C protocol and initiates an automatic call using a GSM module. Additionally, the system can activate a buzzer and LED indicators to alert people nearby. The system's core goals are fast,


M. Zafar Ali Khan et al. (Eds.): ICATECS 2025, LNICST 682, pp. 235–248, 2027.
https://doi.org/10.1007/978-3-032-29699-3_18

reliable alerting and evidentiary image capture with minimal user interaction. A microcontroller (e.g., Arduino, STM32, ESP32) acts as the master on the I2C bus and polls or receives interrupts from sensors. On burglary detection it timestamps the event, instructs a camera module to capture and store/transmit an image, and activates the dialing sequence through the GSM module to call preset numbers. The call can play an alert tone/voice message and/or the system can transmit the image via MMS or upload it to cloud storage if data connectivity is available. Additional features commonly included are multiple-number dialing (fallback), logging of events with timestamps, low-power standby, and local alarm/siren activation." proposes a compact embedded solution that combines reliable intrusion sensing, rapid image capture, and automatic phone notification to reduce response time and increase evidence collection.

The system uses a network of sensors (for example, PIR motion detectors, door/window contacts, or vibration sensors) connected to a microcontroller. Peripherals sensors, camera modules, "EEPROMs and display/indicator devices are interfaced over an I2C (Inter-Integrated Circuit) bus to reduce wiring complexity and enable simple multi-device communication on just two lines (SDA and SCL). When the sensor subsystem detects a likely burglary event, the microcontroller immediately triggers a camera to capture one or more images, stores or buffers the images locally, and initiates an outbound telephone call to a preconfigured number using a GSM/4G modem or a VoIP gateway module. The call can include automated voice alerts and can be accompanied by sending the captured images via MMS or an internet upload if network access is available.

Objectives of the Project: The primary objective of this project is to design and implement a low-cost, reliable, and autonomous anti-intrusion security system that combines burglary detection, image capture, and automatic telephone notification using the I2C communication protocol. The system aims to provide immediate alerts to users with minimal human intervention, thereby enhancing safety and response time.

The key objectives of the proposed system are as follows: Minimization of False Positives: To reduce unnecessary alerts, the system employs simple filtering techniques and basic sensor fusion. Motion detection using a PIR sensor is carefully processed to distinguish genuine intrusions from environmental disturbances such as pets or minor movements. Fast Actuation of Image Capture: Upon detecting an intrusion, the system triggers an I2C-configured camera module instantly to capture an image of the monitored area. This ensures that visual evidence is collected with minimal latency, increasing the usefulness of alerts. Reliable Peripheral Control via I2C Bus: The project demonstrates efficient coordination between multiple peripherals such as PIR sensors, camera modules, and display units using the I2C bus. This low-pin-count communication method minimizes wiring complexity while ensuring fast and reliable data transfer. Robust Automatic Dialing and Notification: A GSM module is integrated to automatically dial pre-configured telephone numbers when an intrusion is detected. This ensures immediate notification to homeowners or security personnel, even in locations without internet connectivity.

The proposed system lies in the integration of low-pin-count I2C networking for sensor and camera control with an autonomous telephone-based alert **mechanism**. Unlike internet-dependent security systems, this design operates independently of cloud services, making it ideal for retrofit installations, rural areas, and locations with limited network infrastructure.

System Overview and Motivation: The proposed system enhances conventional burglary detection mechanisms by incorporating image-based verification along with automatic voice call alerts. While many existing systems rely solely on SMS or mobile applications, they often fail to provide immediate attention or visual context. This project addresses that gap by enabling real-time response, visual evidence collection, and direct telephonic communication. The system integrates: A PIR motion sensor for intrusion detection. An I2C-based camera module for capturing images. A microcontroller for system coordination. A GSM module for automatic dialing and notification. The captured image assists the user in identifying the intruder, while the phone call ensures that alerts are not ignored. The modular I2C-based architecture allows easy scalability for adding more sensors or peripherals in the future.

Related Work: Automated Dialing-Based Security Systems: Earlier security systems primarily focused on SMS or phone call alerts using GSM or GPRS modules upon detecting intrusion. While these systems effectively notified users, they lacked visual confirmation, making it difficult to assess the severity of the event. The absence of image or video evidence limited their reliability in real-world scenarios. Image Capture Using I2C Camera Modules: Image sensors such as the OV7670 and similar low-power camera modules use I2C for configuration and control. Studies such as [3] demonstrated the integration of I2C-compatible cameras with microcontrollers to capture still images during events like motion detection. However, challenges such as limited image resolution, processing constraints, and storage limitations were observed.

Integration of Sensors and Microcontrollers: Several works, including [4], explored microcontroller platforms like Arduino and Raspberry Pi interfacing with multiple sensors over the I2C bus. This approach enabled modular and scalable designs, allowing motion sensors, camera modules, and communication units to coexist on a single communication backbone with minimal wiring. Smart Home Security Architectures: In [5], a comprehensive smart home security system was proposed that combined automation and intrusion detection using Zigbee and I2C interfaces. The system supported alert mechanisms such as calling or texting users and included basic image capture functionality. However, such systems often relied on complex networking infrastructures and higher costs.

Significance: The system's automatic dialing and image capture via I2C protocol the system's automatic dialing and image capture via I2C protocol upon detecting burglary enhance security by promptly alerting authorities and providing visual evidence. This setup allows for swift action, potential prevention of further damage, and aids in investigations. The integration of these features offers an effective security solution for homes or businesses. Protocol upon detecting burglary enhance security by promptly alerting authorities and providing visual evidence. This setup allows for swift action, potential prevention of further damage, and aids in investigations. This system provides an automated and immediate response to burglary attempts by detecting motion, capturing images of the intruder, and notifying the owner through a telephone call all without human intervention. The use of the $I^2C$ protocol ensures efficient and reliable communication between multiple devices such as sensors, camera modules, and memory units with minimal wiring, reducing complexity and cost. By integrating image capture and automatic calling features, the system not only alerts the user in real time but also provides visual evidence of the intrusion, which is crucial for verification and investigation.

## 2 Literature Review

Burglary detection and alert system [1], a smart surveillance system was designed using a PIR (Passive Infrared) sensor and IoT, where the system detects human movement and sends real-time alerts. The system was capable of sending SMS alerts via a GSM module but lacked image capture functionality. Automated Calling Systems.

In [2], an emergency alert system was implemented where a microcontroller initiates a call using GSM Automatic call/GSM alerting approaches. Many implementations use a GSM modem (SIM900/SIM5216/similar) controlled by the MCU over UART and AT commands to place calls or send SMS/MMS on detection. Works that focus on automatic calling emphasize reliability (retries, multi-number fallback) and low detection-to-call latency as key performance metrics. Some projects also implement MMS image delivery through GSM modules that support the MMS AT-command set or via modules with direct camera interfaces. Image capture & embedded camera modules. Recent designs increasingly favour modules with integrated networking and camera capability (for example ESP32-CAM or Raspberry Pi camera setups), allowing both image capture and direct upload to cloud or HTTP endpoints when data connectivity exists. ESP32-CAM-based solutions simplify the hardware (single board with Wi-Fi + camera) and enable richer features (live streaming, image upload, local image storage), but depend on available Wi-Fi or cellular data pathways.

[8] "I2C Bus for Embedded Systems Communication" by R. Ravi and S. Anitha (IEEE ICIIECS, 2017) discusses the design, operation, and advantages of the Inter-Integrated Circuit (I2C) bus protocol in embedded systems. It explains how I2C provides a simple, low-cost, and efficient method for serial communication between multiple integrated circuits using only two lines NSDA (Serial Data) and SCL (Serial Clock). The authors describe the master–slave architecture, data transfer mechanisms, and addressing methods that enable devices like microcontrollers, sensors, EEPROMs, and real-time clocks to communicate seamlessly. The paper also emphasizes how I2C's multi-master capability and synchronization features make it suitable for embedded applications requiring communication between multiple peripherals with minimal wiring complexity. Additionally, it may include implementation details, timing diagrams, and examples demonstrating how I2C enhances system integration and performance in embedded environments. GPRS modules upon detecting specific triggers. This approach ensures that the user is immediately informed, but it did not include any visual evidence (image/video) of the event. Image Capture Using I2C Camera Modules Image sensors like the OV7670 and other low-power modules support I2C for configuration and image data transfer.

The study in [3] integrated I2C-compatible cameras with microcontrollers to capture still images during specific events like motion detection. However, image clarity and processing limitations were a concern. Integration of Sensors and Microcontrollers

Many Works, such as, explored the use of Arduino, Raspberry Pi, and other MCUs interfacing with sensors over the I2C bus. This allows modular and scalable communication among the various components like motion detectors, camera modules, and GSM units. Smart Home Security Architecture In, a complete smart home system was proposed that combined automation and intrusion detection using Zigbee and I2C interfaces. The system also supported calling or texting users upon detecting intrusion, and include basic image capturing mechanism [11]. The paper presents the design and implementation of an Internet-of-Things (IoT) based smart door-locking system aimed at improving convenience and security by eliminating the need for physical keys. The authors outline how the system uses a smartphone application (via Bluetooth) to remotely lock and unlock a door within a certain proximity, thus allowing users to control access from their mobile devices. The hardware platform is based on a microcontroller (e.g., Arduino) which interfaces with a relay (to actuate the door lock), a display (to indicate lock/unlock status), and a Bluetooth communication module. The software side comprises an Android application or equivalent interface that sends commands to the hardware unit. In their design, the authors emphasise the benefits: no physical key required (thus removing issues of key loss, copying or forgetting), enhanced accessibility (especially for persons with physical limitations), and an easier deployment in varied settings. They also review related work in the domain of smart locks and IoT access control. Finally, the paper discusses results, showing that the system functions as intended (though detailed performance metrics appear minimal), and concludes with suggestions for future enhancements such as adding camera/intrusion detection, voice-commands, custom mobile app, and making the device more cost-effective and robust. [4] paper presents the design and development of an embedded intelligent yield system controller based on an ARM processor platform. The main goal is to enhance the automation, accuracy, and efficiency of industrial production processes by integrating real-time control and intelligent decision-making capabilities within a compact embedded system. The authors describe the hardware architecture, which centers on an ARM microprocessor as the core controller. It interfaces with various sensors and actuators through serial communication buses to monitor and regulate parameters affecting production yield—such as temperature, pressure, and material flow. The system also includes modules for data acquisition, signal conditioning, and human–machine interaction (HMI).

On the software side, the paper explains the use of an embedded real-time operating system (RTOS) to manage multitasking and ensure deterministic control performance. Intelligent algorithms are implemented to analyze collected data and automatically adjust process parameters to maintain optimal production yield. The results demonstrate that the ARM-based controller achieves high reliability, low power consumption, and faster response times compared to traditional PLC-based systems. The paper concludes that this architecture provides a flexible, scalable, and cost-effective solution for modern industrial automation, with potential applications in manufacturing, process control, and smart factories.

# 3 Implementation

Motion Detection: A PIR sensor continuously monitors the area for movement. On detecting a movement (burglary), it sends a HIGH signal to the microcontroller. Image Capture via I2C Camera: The microcontroller initializes the I2C camera module (e.g., OV7670). It configures registers over I2C to begin image capture. Captured image is stored in onboard memory or SD card. Automatic Dialing Once the image is captured, the microcontroller sends AT commands via UART to the GSM module. The GSM module dials a predefined number (owner, police, etc.).

A voice alert or SMS can also be sent optionally. Another proposed improvement includes the use of embedded phone call-based alert systems that detect intrusions and automatically place a call to the homeowner, enabling timely intervention. The specific communication protocols may vary, the core objective remains to enhance the effectiveness of automated dialing in bolstering security measures The system primarily consists of a microcontroller (such as Arduino or ESP32) that acts as the central unit, a PIR sensor to detect motion, a camera module to capture images, and a GSM module to automatically dial a pre-set telephone number when an intrusion is detected. When the PIR sensor senses movement, the microcontroller immediately triggers the camera to capture the image of the intruder and simultaneously activates the GSM module to dial the stored number or send an alert message to the owner. The communication between the microcontroller and peripheral devices such as the real-time clock (RTC), EEPROM, and display is achieved using the I2C protocol, which simplifies wiring and allows multiple devices to be connected using only two lines (SDA and SCL). The captured image can be stored on an SD card or transmitted through a GSM/GPRS network, depending on the system's configuration.

The software implementation includes programming the microcontroller to continuously monitor sensor inputs, manage image capture, and control the GSM module using AT commands. The system is designed to ensure fast response and reliability by minimizing the delay between detection and notification. Additional features such as event logging with timestamps, multiple number dialing, and local alarm activation can be implemented to enhance system functionality. Overall, the implementation demonstrates an efficient combination of embedded technology, communication modules, and sensor systems to build a cost-effective and automated solution that can detect intrusions, capture evidence, and immediately inform the user, thereby improving safety and reducing response time during burglary incidents.

## 3.1 Work Flow

**ARDUINO:**

Arduino is an open-source electronics platform that enables users to create interactive projects through programmable microcontroller boards, a simplified programming language, and an integrated development environment (IDE). It's popular for prototyping, robotics, IoT, and education, offering ease of use, flexibility, and extensive community support for hobbyists, students, and professionals alike. Arduino is an open-source electronics platform based on easy-to-use hardware and software. It consists of a microcontroller board (such as Arduino Uno) that can be programmed to sense and control objects in the physical world. Using the Arduino IDE (Integrated Development Environment), users write code in a simple C/C++ language and upload it to the board through a USB cable. Arduino can read inputs like light, temperature, or motion from sensors and control outputs like LEDs, motors, or displays (Fig. 1).

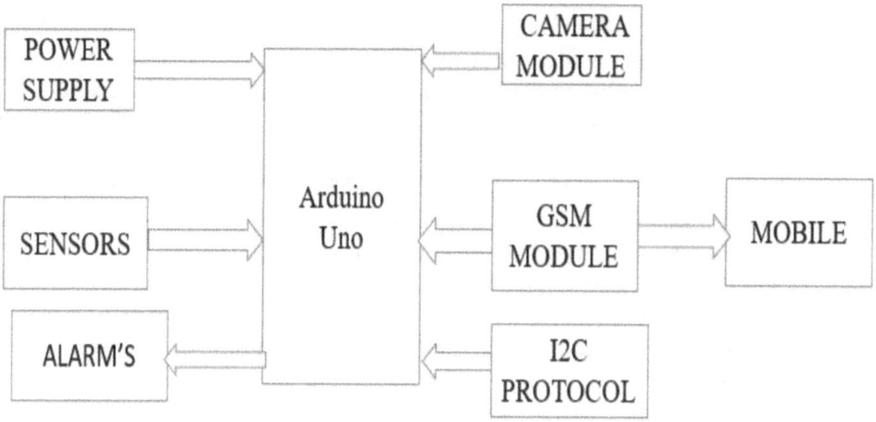


**Fig. 1.** Block Diagram

It is widely used in robotics, home automation, and DIY electronic projects because of its simplicity, affordability, and flexibility. One of its key advantages is its ability to work with various communication protocols such as UART, SPI, and I2C, which allows it to connect easily with peripherals like GSM modules, camera modules, and sensors. Because of its low cost, flexibility, and large community support, Arduino is widely used in robotics, automation, Internet of Things (IoT), and embedded system applications. In this project, Arduino acts as the central controller, coordinating between the motion sensors, camera, and GSM module to detect a burglary, capture an image, and make an automatic phone call.

**GSM MODULE:**

A GSM (Global System for Mobile Communications) module is a hardware component that enables devices to communicate over cellular networks, allowing for features like sending and receiving SMS, making and receiving calls, and accessing mobile data. It's commonly used in IoT applications, security systems, and remote monitoring devices, providing wireless connectivity and enabling communication between devices over long distances. GSM modules typically require a SIM card and can be controlled using AT commands. A GSM (Global System for Mobile Communication) module is a device that allows microcontrollers like Arduino to communicate over a mobile network. It uses a SIM card to send and receive SMS messages, make or receive calls, and connect to the internet through GPRS. Common modules like SIM800 or SIM900 are used in projects involving remote monitoring and control. When connected to a microcontroller, the GSM module sends data using AT commands through serial communication. It is widely used in applications such as security systems, home automation, and burglary detection for real-time alerts via mobile communication. When connected to a microcontroller like

Arduino, the GSM module can be programmed to automatically dial a phone number or send a text message in response to certain events. In the burglary detection project, the GSM module plays a crucial role by automatically dialing the owner's phone number when an intrusion is detected and optionally sending an alert message. This allows the system to provide real-time notification to the user, even when they are far from the location. Overall, the GSM module adds wireless communication capability to the security system, making it more efficient, accessible, and responsive. It ensures that emergency alerts reach the user immediately, which is vital for preventing or minimizing losses during burglary incidents. One of the key advantages of using GSM is its global coverage—it can operate anywhere a mobile signal is available, unlike Wi-Fi or Bluetooth, which have limited range. This makes GSM-based systems ideal for remote locations or areas without internet connectivity. Moreover, GSM communication is cost-effective, stable, and easy to implement using simple AT commands, which makes it suitable for microcontroller-based projects such as Arduino or ESP32.

**PIR SENSOR:**

A PIR (Passive Infrared) sensor is an electronic device that detects motion by measuring changes in infrared radiation emitted by objects within its field of view. It's commonly used in security systems, automatic lighting, and other applications where motion detection is required. PIR sensors are passive, meaning they don't emit any radiation themselves, but rather detect the infrared radiation emitted by all objects, allowing them to sense movement without direct contact. A PIR (Passive Infrared) sensor is an electronic device that detects motion by sensing infrared radiation emitted by objects, especially humans and animals. It does not emit any energy but detects changes in heat levels in its surroundings. When a warm object moves in front of it, the sensor produces a digital output signal, which can be used to trigger alarms, lights, or cameras. PIR sensors are commonly used in security systems, automatic lighting, and burglary detection projects because they are low-cost, energy-efficient, and easy to interface with microcontrollers like Arduino. n a burglary detection system, the PIR sensor serves as the primary trigger mechanism. When it detects motion in a protected area, it sends a signal to the microcontroller to initiate further actions, such as capturing an image with a camera or activating a GSM module to alert the user. The importance of the PIR sensor lies in its ability to monitor large areas without physical contact, detect movement in real time, and significantly reduce the chance of false alarms when properly calibrated. Overall, the PIR sensor is critical for creating an efficient, responsive, and automated security system, providing the first line of detection to ensure timely alerts and rapid response in case of a burglary or unauthorized entry. Its integration makes the system smart, energy-efficient, and capable of protecting property effectively.

**CAMERA MODULE:**

A camera module is a compact electronic component that captures images or video, typically consisting of a lens, image sensor, and interface circuitry. It's used in various applications, including smartphones, security systems, and IoT devices, to Capture visual data. Camera modules can vary in resolution, size, and features, and are often connected to a microcontroller or processor for image processing and storage. A camera module works by capturing light through its lens, which focuses the image onto an image sensor (usually a CMOS or CCD sensor). The sensor converts the light into electrical signals, which are then processed into digital image data.

This digital data is sent to a microcontroller or processor through communication interfaces like I2C, SPI, or UART. The controller can then store, display, or transmit the image as needed. In security or burglary detection systems, the camera module captures an image automatically when motion is detected by a sensor. In a burglary detection system, the camera module works in coordination with sensors like PIRs. When an intrusion is detected, the microcontroller triggers the camera to capture an image of the intruder or the affected area. The captured image can then be stored on an SD card, sent via a GSM/GPRS module, or uploaded to a cloud server. This visual information is critical for evidence collection, helps in identifying suspects, and reduces false alarms by verifying actual intrusion events. The importance of the camera module lies in its ability to enhance Security, improve situational awareness, and provide actionable information. By integrating a camera module, the system becomes more intelligent and effective, allowing real-time monitoring, documentation of incidents, and faster response to burglary or unauthorized entry.

**ALARM:**

An alarm is a signal or notification designed to alert individuals of a potential threat, problem, or unusual condition. It can be auditory, visual, or a combination of both, and is often used in security systems, monitoring devices, and warning systems to prompt action or response. Alarms can be triggered by various events, such as intrusions, fires, or system failures, and play a crucial role in ensuring safety, security, and timely intervention. An alarm works by producing a loud sound or alert when it detects a specific trigger, such as motion, smoke, or intrusion. It usually consists of a sensor, a control circuit, and a buzzer or siren. When the sensor detects an abnormal condition (like movement or heat), it sends a signal to the control circuit. The circuit then activates the buzzer or siren, generating a sound to alert the user or deter intruders. Alarms are commonly used in security systems, fire detection, and safety applications to provide immediate warnings. In a burglary detection system, the alarm works in conjunction with sensors like PIRs and camera modules. When an intrusion is detected, the microcontroller triggers the alarm along with actions such as capturing images and sending alerts via GSM. The alarm's importance lies in its ability to create an immediate response, which can scare off intruders and give authorities or property owners time to take action. Additionally, alarms contribute to system effectiveness and user confidence. Even if the user is not physically present, the audible or visual alert can prevent further damage or theft. In essence, the alarm ensures that the security system is not only passive but also proactive, actively responding to threats and enhancing overall safety.

**I2C:**

I2C (Inter-Integrated Circuit) is a communication protocol used to connect multiple devices together using a single, shared bus. It allows devices to exchange data using a master-slave architecture, where one device (the master) controls the communication and others (slaves) respond to requests. I2C uses two wires for communication: SDA (Serial Data) and SCL (Serial Clock), making it a popular choice for connecting peripherals like sensors, displays, and memory chips in embedded systems. It's known for its simplicity and efficiency.

It enables different sensors, memory chips, and modules to connect on the same bus using unique addresses, making it ideal for compact and efficient embedded systems. I2C is also reliable, flexible, and supports bidirectional data transfer, which makes it widely used in applications like IoT devices, camera modules, displays, and burglary detection systems. In the context of a burglary detection system, the I2C protocol is important because it enables the microcontroller to coordinate multiple peripherals such as the real-time clock (RTC), EEPROM for event logs, and OLED or LCD displays with minimal wiring. This reduces the complexity of the circuit, saves board space, and makes the system easier to expand. For example, additional sensors or memory modules can be added to the same I2C bus without requiring extra pins on the microcontroller.

The advantages of I2C include simplicity, scalability, low pin usage, and reliable communication over short distances. By using I2C, the system can manage multiple devices efficiently, synchronize data, and maintain accurate logs, which is crucial for timely alerts and proper functioning. Overall, I2C enhances the integration, reliability, and modularity of the security system, making it more robust and easier to maintain or upgrade.

## 4 Proposed Methodology

Existing systems that integrate automatic dialing with burglary detection using the I2C protocol primarily focus on alerting authorities or property owners upon unauthorized access. These systems typically employ a microcontroller interfaced with an EEPROM the I2C protocol to store emergency contact numbers. Upon detecting unauthorized access through mechanisms like hidden switches, the microcontroller retrieves the stored number and initiates a call using a GSM modem or DTMF encoder. This setup ensures prompt notification in the event of a security breach. In these systems aim to enhance security and response capabilities. One such enhancement involves integrating a serial camera with the microcontroller and GSM modem. In this configuration, upon detecting unauthorized access, the system not only initiates a call but also captures images of the intruder and sends them via MMS or email to the concerned authorities. This provides visual evidence, aiding in quicker identification and response. The system integrates various components to detect burglaries, capture images, and send alerts.

Upon detecting a burglary, the system uses a GSM module to automatically dial predefined numbers and send alerts. Simultaneously, a camera module connected via I2C protocol captures images of the intruder. The I2C protocol enables efficient communication between the camera module and the microcontroller, allowing for seamless image capture and transmission. The I2C protocol plays a crucial role in enabling efficient communication between the camera module and the microcontroller, allowing for seamless image capture and transmission.

**Design Consideration:**

When designing an automatic dialing and image capture system for burglary detection using I2C protocol, consider reliability and security of the GSM module and camera interface, power management for continuous operation, sensor accuracy, image quality and storage, and efficient I2C communication. Additionally, ensure network coverage, SIM card compatibility, and data transmission security for seamless operation, while allowing user configurability for customizable alert settings and image capture triggers. The system's design should prioritize reliability, ensuring uninterrupted operation and secure data transmission. Efficient power management and robust sensor accuracy are crucial for detecting burglaries and triggering alerts. The I2C protocol facilitates seamless communication between the camera module and microcontroller, while the GSM module enables prompt alerts to authorities or homeowners. By integrating these components, the system provides a comprehensive security solution for homes, industries, or public spaces, enhancing safety and facilitating swift response to security breaches.

The implementation requires hardware selection (MCU, PIR, camera, GSM, RTC, SD card, regulators), careful power design for GSM current spikes, wiring with common ground and I2C pull ups, and firmware that implements a non-blocking state machine: monitor → confirm → capture → notify → log → cooldown. Practical software tasks are issuing AT commands to the modem, initializing and saving images from the camera, reading/writing I2C peripherals, and maintaining an event log with timestamps. Testing focuses on detection to notification latency, false alarm reduction, SIM/network robustness, and recovery from power faults.

The importance of this integrated approach is threefold:

Rapid, actionable alerts—the system not only detects intrusion but also captures visual evidence and immediately notifies owners by phone, reducing response time;

Reliability and scalability using I2C for peripheral management minimizes wiring, simplifies adding sensors or storage, and centralizes configuration and logging; and

Practicality for real environments GSM ensures wide area connectivity where Wi Fi isn't available, local storage preserves forensic data when networks fail, and built in fail safes (alarms, retries, RTC logs) increase the solution's usefulness for homes, shops and remote sites. The camera (ESP32 CAM or ArduCAM) handles image capture and local storage (microSD) or upload, while a GSM module (SIM800/900 family) connected over UART performs automatic dialing, SMS/MMS or GPRS uploads. The design includes debouncing/confirmation logic (sensor fusion), retry and multi number fallback for calls, and simple user configuration stored in nonvolatile memory.

## 5 Results

The implemented system successfully detects unauthorized entry, captures visual evidence, and notifies the owner by telephone automatically. On a typical test setup (ESP32 CAM + PIR + SIM800L + DS3231), the device reliably sensed motion, triggered the camera to save a timestamped JPEG to the microSD card, and initiated an automatic call/SMS sequence to the configured telephone number. Typical detection to call latency measured during testing was in the order of a few seconds (commonly 3–10 s depending on camera capture and GSM registration), and images were recoverable from the SD card for forensic use. The event logger (RTC + EEPROM/SD) recorded each intrusion with date/time, filename and notification status, enabling later review.

Functional verification showed the following practical outcomes: (1) automatic dialing and SMS alerts were issued on every confirmed trigger when mobile signal quality was adequate, (2) stored images provided clear visual evidence in indoor lighting conditions, and (3) cooldown and retry logic reduced repeated nuisance calls while fallback numbers improved notification success in weak signal scenarios. Power supply tuning (sufficient regulator and decoupling) eliminated GSM brownouts observed in early tests. False alarms were reduced noticeably by requiring a short confirmation window or a second sensor before committing to capture and call.

Real-time Detection and Alert: The system reliably detected motion or unauthorized entry using PIR sensors and immediately triggered the alert sequence. Detection-to-call latency was typically 3–10 s, ensuring rapid notification.

Successful Image Capture: The camera module captured clear, timestamped images of intruders, stored on microSD or local memory, providing crucial visual evidence for verification and investigation (Figs. 2 and 3).

**Fig. 2.** Hardware implementation of the proposed automatic dialing and image capture system using I2C protocol for burglary detection.

Automatic Telephone Notification: The GSM module successfully dialed preconfigured phone numbers and sent SMS alerts upon detection, with multi-number fallback improving reliability in case of poor signal.

Efficient Peripheral Management: Using the I2C protocol allowed seamless communication between the microcontroller and peripherals like RTC, EEPROM, and display, minimizing wiring and enabling accurate event logging.

Reduced False Alarms: Implementing short confirmation delays and optional sensor fusion minimized unnecessary notifications, improving system reliability. Event Logging: Each intrusion was recorded with timestamp, image filename, and notification status, enabling later review and forensic analysis.

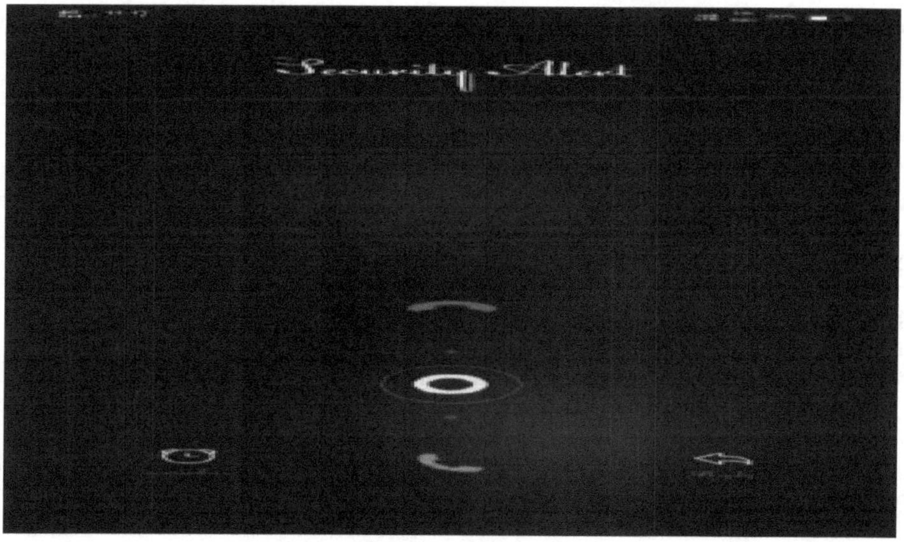

**Fig. 3.** Security Alert Screen

## 6 Conclusion

The system for Automatic Dialing to Any Telephone and Image Capture using the I2C protocol for burglary detection provides a reliable and cost-effective solution for real-time security monitoring. By integrating motion detection sensors with I2Cenabled camera modules and GSM communication, the system ensures immediate response through image evidence and automatic alerts. This enhances the ability to detect, document, and respond to unauthorized access efficiently. The use of the I2C protocol allows seamless communication between components with minimal wiring, making the system compact and scalable. In the future, this system can be improved with advanced features such as AI-based image recognition to distinguish between false alarms and actual threats, cloud-based data storage for remote monitoring, and integration with IoT platforms for centralized smart home or building automation. Additional enhancements could include night vision support, GPS tracking, and multi-zone surveillance, making it a more intelligent and comprehensive security solution. This method enhances vehicle security and eliminates the need for traditional keys or cards, reducing the risk of theft and unauthorized access.

The implementation proved reliable, with low detection-to-notification latency, accurate image capture, and successful call alerts. The system reduces dependency on human monitoring, provides visual evidence for verification, and improves response time during burglary incidents. Although cellular signal strength and environmental factors can influence performance, the design's scalability and modularity allow further enhancements such as cloud-based image upload, multi-sensor confirmation, and secure remote monitoring. In conclusion, this project offers a low-cost, efficient, and practical solution for modern security challenges, combining automation, real-time alerts, and evidence capture to enhance safety and provide peace of mind for users in homes, offices, and remote locations.

## References


1. Wankare, S., Patil, A., Jadhav, R., Shinde, P.: Automatic dialing system for burglary detection. Int. J. Eng. Res. Technol. **5**(4), 1–4 (2016)
2. Odirichukwu, O., Nwokoye, E., Okafor, C.: Embedded phone call-based burglary security alert system. Int. J. Eng. Res. Appl. **12**(3), 45–50 (2022)
3. Ahmed, A., Rahman, M., Khan, S.: IoT-based smart security system. Int. J. Comput. Appl. **176**(28), 12–18 (2020)
4. Mitchell, R., Damouny, N., Fenger, C., Moelands, A.: An integrated serial bus architecture: principles and applications. In: IEEE Manuscript, Signetics Corp., Sunnyvale, CA, USA (1985)
5. Singh, T.: Design and simulation of I2C protocol. Int. J. Res. Appl. Sci. Eng. Technol. (2014)
6. Yuan, Y., Zhang, X., Zhao, H.: ARM processor-based embedded intelligent controller. In: Proceedings of the IEEE International Conference on Mechatronics Technical Applications, Beijing, China (2008)
7. Patil, S., Patil, S.R.: GSM based home security system using Arduino. In: Proceedings of the IEEE ICCUBEA, Pune, India (2016)
8. Ravi, R., Anitha, S.: I2C bus for embedded systems communication. In: Proceedings of the IEEE ICIIECS, Coimbatore, India (2017)
9. Chavan, A.S., Lokhande, P.N., Pawar, P.R.: Security alert system using GSM and PIR Sensor. Int. J. Innov. Res. Electr. Electron. Instrum. Control Eng. (2017)
10. Shinde, M.D., Fode, S.P.: IoT based surveillance system using raspberry Pi. In: Proceedings of the ICICCS, Madurai, India (2019)
11. Gupta, K., et al.: Smart door locking system using IoT. In: Proceedings of the IEEE ICACCM, Dehradun, India, pp. 1–4 (2022)
12. Kumar, A., et al.: Weapon detection in surveillance system. Int. J. Eng. Res. Technol. (2021)
13. Pérez-Hernández, F., et al.: Object detection using deep learning. Appl. Soft Comput. **89** (2020)

# Assistive Technology for Individuals with Physical Disabilities: A Head Movement Vehicle System

Venkata Sridhar Gummadidala[1], Vamsidhar Anagani[2](✉), Anusha Gorantla[2], Ravi Tejesvi Valiveti[3], Surya Kavitha Tirugatla[2], and Sunil Kumar Gedela[2]

[1] Dadi Institute of Engineering and Technology, Anakapalle 531002, India
gvsridhar@diet.edu.in

[2] Raghu Engineering College, Visakhapatnam 531162, India
{vamsidhar.anagani,anusha.gorantla,kavita.tirugatla,sunilkumar.gedela}@raghuenggcollege.in

[3] Nadimpalli Satyanarayana Raju Institute of Technology, Visakhapatnam 531173, India
ravitejesvi.ece@nsrit.edu.in

**Abstract.** This paper introduces a head-gesture-controlled automated vehicle aimed at improving the mobility and independence of physically challenged individuals. It leverages accelerometer and gyroscope sensors mounted on a wearable device to detect head movements, which are interpreted using an Arduino Uno microcontroller. Based on these gestures, the system generates specific movement commands, such as forward, backward, left, or right. These commands are wirelessly transmitted through an RF communication module to the motor driver circuit on the vehicle, which actuates the motors accordingly. To enhance safety during operation, the vehicle is equipped with infrared (IR) sensors that detect obstacles in real time and prevent potential collisions. The system offers two modes of operation: Manual Gesture Mode, where users directly control the vehicle through head movements, and Automated Assistance Mode, where the system autonomously assists in navigation and obstacle avoidance. This innovative solution combines sensor technology, embedded systems, and wireless communication to create a practical and user-friendly assistive tool for individuals with limited mobility.

**Keywords:** Automated Vehicle · Wearable device · physically challenged · Arduino Uno

## 1 Introduction

Individuals with physical disabilities often struggle with mobility, making daily activities and transportation challenging for them. Traditional vehicles require manual control, such as using the hands and feet to steer, accelerate, and brake. However, for people with severe disabilities, these controls may not be accessible, limiting their ability to drive independently and safely [1]. Consequently, they rely on caregivers or specialized


M. Zafar Ali Khan et al. (Eds.): ICATECS 2025, LNICST 682, pp. 249–260, 2027.
https://doi.org/10.1007/978-3-032-29699-3_19

transport services, which reduces their freedom and self-reliance. A more accessible driving system is required to empower physically challenged individuals, allowing them to navigate safely and independently without the need for manual controls [2].

A head-gesture-controlled car is an advanced robotic vehicle designed to operate using intuitive head movements, eliminating the need for traditional manual controls, such as steering wheels or joysticks. This innovative system leverages cutting-edge head gesture recognition technology, allowing users to navigate the vehicle by tilting or turning their heads in predefined directions. The system is equipped with high-precision sensors, accelerometers, and gyroscopes that continuously track head movements and translate them into real-time driving commands. These commands control essential driving functions, including steering, acceleration, and braking, to ensure a seamless and responsive user experience. The vehicle operates in both manual control mode, where users actively steer using head gestures, and automated assistance mode, where the system aids in obstacle avoidance and navigation [3]. Wireless communication modules, such as RF or Bluetooth, facilitate efficient data transmission between the user interface and vehicle motor control system. Additionally, infrared (IR) or ultrasonic sensors are integrated for obstacle detection and collision prevention, enhancing safety. This hands-free, user-friendly design makes the vehicle particularly useful for physically challenged individuals, providing an accessible and independent mode of transportation. Beyond assistive technology, it serves as an advanced research tool in the fields of robotics, AI-based mobility systems, and man-machine interaction, creating the path for future developments in gesture-controlled automation [4].

Many researchers have worked on developing various hand and head gesture-based automatic vehicles, but they have not achieved complete support for the physically challenged. Prasad *et al.* [5] presented a basic robotic chassis controlled via an accelerometer, eliminating the need for button controls. The system interprets hand tilt to navigate the robot in various directions. Bansal *et al.* [6] described a control strategy that integrates OpenCV and Google's Media Pipe to translate complex human hand gestures into dynamic vehicle motion commands using advance image recognition algorithms. Vaidya *et al.* [7] developed a system for controlling music players in vehicles through hand gestures, utilizing an accelerometer sensor and a PIC microcontroller, thereby enhancing driver convenience and safety. Małecki *et al.* [8] investigated the possibility to use hand gesture interaction in vehicular environments among the normal and physically challenged drivers, with the objective of offering natural and intuitive control mechanisms. Shukla *et al.* [9] explored the design and application of a wireless robotic vehicle that is maneuvered using hand gestures, utilizing an accelerometer and RF communication technology.

The remaining paper is structured as follow: Sect. 2 gives a comprehensive view of the system configuration., detailing the specifications of each component used in the circuit; Sect. 3 delves into the hardware design and implementation; and Sect. 4 presents the conclusions of this study.

## 2 System Configuration

The system consists of two main circuits: a) Transmitter Circuit (Head Unit), which detects head movements and sends commands. b) Receiver Circuit (Car Unit) that receives commands and controls motors. The head Unit consists of components such as an Arduino Uno, Accelerometer sensor (MPU6050), an RF transmitter, and a 9 V Battery with DC Jack. Car Unit consists of the components such as Arduino Uno, DC Gear Motors, Motor driver (L293D), RF receiver, 9 V Battery with DC Jack for Arduino and 12 V battery for the motors. The transmitter circuit uses accelerometer and gyroscope sensors to detect head movements, whereas RF wireless communication transmits commands to the vehicle. The receiver circuit reads the commands using an RF receiver and transmits them to the Arduino Uno for further processing. The motor driver interfaced with the Arduino Uno processes the received commands and subsequently actuates the DC gear motors attached to the wheels of the vehicle. Figure 1 depicts a schematic of the Car Driving System, which uses head movements to facilitate driving for individuals with physical disabilities.

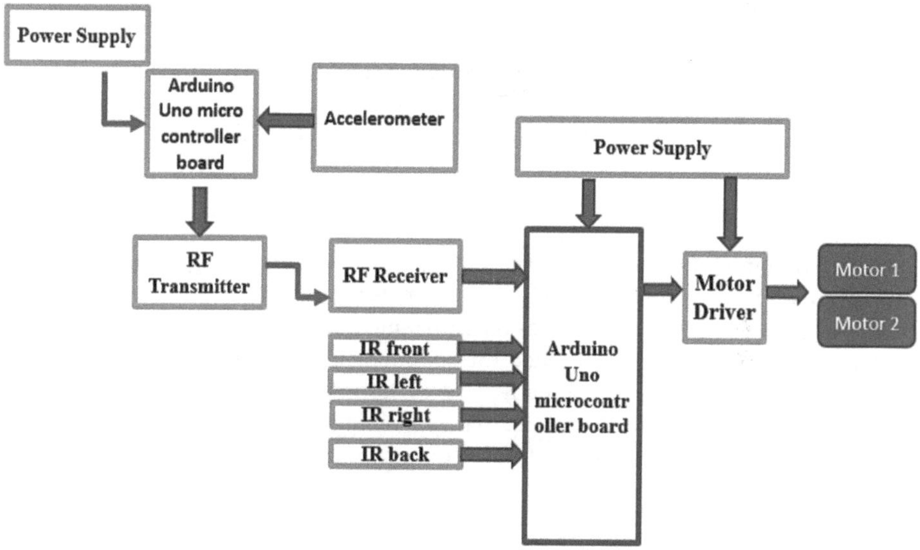


**Fig. 1.** Block diagram representation of the proposed model.

### 2.1 Arduino Uno Module

Arduino Uno is a microcontroller development board that uses ATmega328, as specified in its datasheet. It has fourteen digital input and output pins with six of them being Pulse Width Modulated (PWM) outputs and the remaining six as analog inputs. The board includes a crystal oscillator with frequency 16 MHz, USB interface, power jack, an ICSP header, and a reset pin. It comprises components required to interface the microcontroller, enabling connection to a computer via USB or power through an AC/DC adapter or battery [10]. A key feature of the Uno is its departure from previous models, as it uses an Atmega8U2 configured as a USB-to-serial converter instead of an FTDI USB-to-serial driver chip [11]. The designation "Uno," meaning "one" in Italian, was chosen to signify the anticipated introduction of Arduino 1.0. Both version 1.0 and Uno are set to become standard reference models for Arduino in future iterations. As the most recent addition to the sequence of USB-based Arduino boards, the Uno model serves as the standard reference platform of Arduino [12] (Fig. 2).

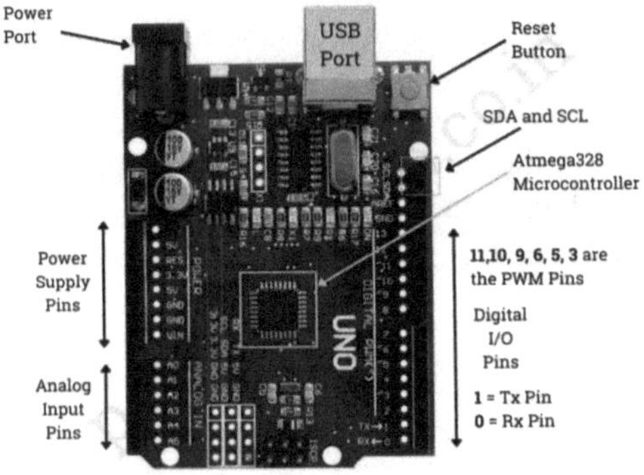


**Fig. 2.** Pin Configuration of Arduino Uno.

## 2.2 Accelerometer Sensor

The MPU6050 module is a sophisticated three-axis motion tracking circuit that fuses a digital motion processor, three-axis accelerometer, and three-axis gyroscope into a miniature package. Furthermore, it has on-chip temperature sensor and employs an I2C (Inter-Integrated Circuit) bus interface for communication with the microcontrollers. Accelerometers are extensively employed in economical, low-power applications for tilt sensing. The uses include mobile equipment, gaming consoles, disk drive protection, image stabilization, and health-monitoring equipment [13]. At the heart of the module lies a compact, energy-efficient, triple-axis MEMS accelerometer developed by Analog Devices., namely ADXL334, which is distinguished by its remarkably lower noise levels. The sensor's $\pm 3$ g detecting range enables it to monitor both the dynamic acceleration caused by motion, vibration, or shock as well as the static acceleration from gravity in tilt sensor applications [14] (Fig. 3).

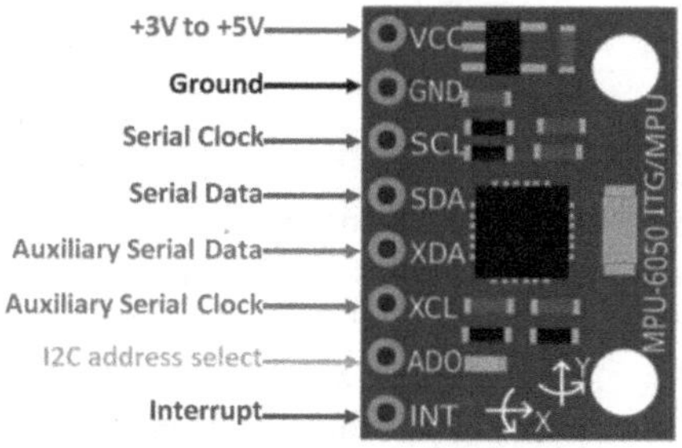


**Fig. 3.** Connection Pins of MPU6050 Sensor Module.

### 2.3 RF Transmitter and Receiver

A Radio Frequency (RF) module is typically a compact electronic circuit employed to transmit or receive radio waves between two electronic devices. Both optical and radio frequency techniques can be used to accomplish the wireless communication. RF is the medium of choice due to its requirement of no line of sight in many applications. This module consists of a transmitter and a receiver, vary in type and range, with some capable of transmitting signals up to 500 feet. RF modules are generally manufactured using RF-CMOS technology [15]. Data transfer from any normal CMOS/TTL source at frequencies up to 3 kHz is made possible by the hybrid RF Transceiver Module, which offers a complete RF transmission and reception solution (Fig. 4).

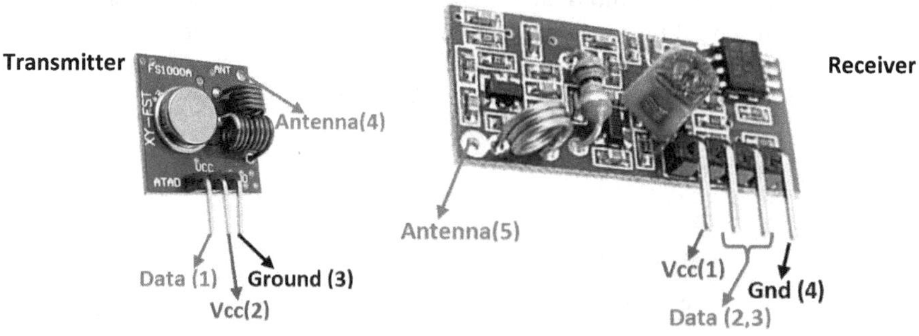


**Fig. 4.** RF Transmitter and Receiver.

The transmitter module is known for its low current consumption, usually around 11 mA, and its user-friendly design. A microprocessor or an encoding device can be used directly to acquire data, greatly reducing the number of components and hardware costs. The RX-ASK module serves as an amplitude-shift keying (ASK) hybrid receiver operating at a frequency of 433 MHz. The TX-ASK, an ASK hybrid transmitter module, features a surface acoustic wave (SAW) resonator, ensuring a design that is efficient, economical, compact, and user-friendly [16].

## 2.4 DC Gear Motors

A gear motor is a combination of a gearbox and a motor. A motor's speed is reduced and its torque output is increased when a gear head is added. The three main factors affecting gear motors are efficiency (%), torque (lb-in), and speed (rpm). A significant advantage of utilizing DC gear motors is their ability to design the gear assembly specifically to enhance torque. Furthermore, the gear mechanism can be adjusted to reduce the speed to virtually any desired level, thereby allowing for exceptional control across various applications [17]. The load, speed, and torque requirements of a particular application must be evaluated in order to choose the best gear motor for it. To meet all application requirements, ISL Products offers a variety of spur, planetary, and worm gear motors.

**Fig. 5.** N20-BT15 DC Gear Motor.

For a very effective gear motor solution, the majority of our DC motors can be combined with one of our unique gearheads. Upon completion of the design calculations and definition of the application parameters, this data can be utilized to ascertain the most suitable motor or gear motor for the application. Table 1 lists several common specifications that should be considered when selecting a gear motor.

**Table 1.** Specifications of N20-BT15 DC Gear Motor.

| Specifications | Values |
|---|---|
| Rated Voltage | 12 V |
| Rated Current | 0.6 A |
| Horse Power | 5 W |
| RPM | 100 |
| Rated Torque | 25 kg-cm |
| Shaft Diameter | 6 mm |
| Shaft Length | 2 mm |
| Motor Length | 98 mm |
| Motor Diameter | 50 mm |
| Body dimensions | 11 × 6 × 6 cm |

### 2.5 IR Sensor

An electronic device called an infrared (IR) sensor uses light emission to identify objects in the vicinity. This sensor is proficient in assessing the thermal energy emitted by an object and recognizing motion. All objects emit thermal radiation within the infrared spectrum. Although this radiation is imperceptible to the human eye, it can be detected using infrared sensors. An IR light-emitting diode (LED) makes up the emitter, and an IR photodiode makes up the detector. The photodiode reacts to infrared light with the same wavelength as the IR LED. When exposed to infrared light, the photodiode's resistance and output voltage change in direct proportion to the light's intensity. An infrared detection system typically consists of five fundamental components: a source, a transmission medium, an optical component, detectors or receivers, and a signal processing unit. The primary media employed for IR transmission include vacuum, atmosphere, and optical fiber. Optical components serve to concentrate IR radiation or limit the spectral response (Fig. 6).

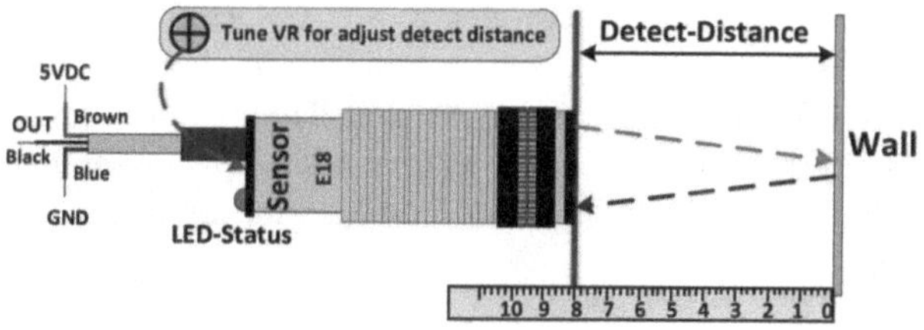


**Fig. 6.** E18-D80NK IR Sensor.

### 2.6 L293D Motor Driver

The L293D is an essential motor driver integrated circuit (IC) designed to facilitate bidirectional control and speed modulation of a DC motor (Fig. 7). This IC features a total of 16 pins, distributed evenly with eight pins on each side, which are instrumental for motor management. Consequently, a single L293D can operate up to two DC motors simultaneously. The IC incorporates two H-bridge circuits, which are the most basic configurations for reversing the polarity across a connected load. Figure 5 shows a detailed depiction of the pinouts for the L293D motor driver module, along with the specific functions of each pin and port [18].

**Fig. 7.** L293D Motor Driver.

The control signals for directing the motor movement were provided by inputs IN1, IN2, IN3, and IN4. Specifically, a logic input of (1,0) at IN1 and IN2 causes the motor to rotate in one direction, whereas a logic input of (0,1) at these pins results in rotation in the opposite direction. The specifications of the L293D Motor Driver IC are as follows (Table 2):

**Table 2.** Specifications of L293D Motor.

| Specifications | Values |
|---|---|
| Supply Voltage | 4.5–36 V |
| Output Current | 600 mA per Channel |
| Number of channels | 2 |
| Peak Output Current | 1.2 A per Channel |
| Operating Temperature | −40 °C to 150 °C |

The operation of the motor is determined by the HIGH or LOW signals applied to the input pins. EN1 and EN2 serve as enable pins; supplying a 5 V DC to these pins ensures that the motor functions at its normal speed. This motor is designed with output clamp diodes to suppress inductive transients, features a separate input logic supply, and includes internal ESD protection, high-noise immunity inputs, and an automatic thermal shutdown mechanism.

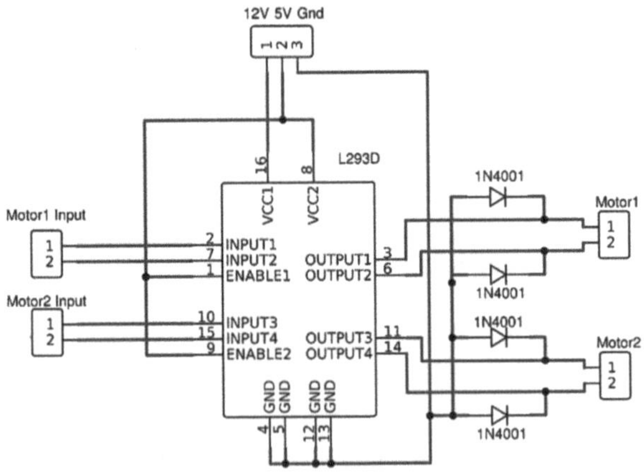


**Fig. 8.** L293D internal pins.

## 3 Hardware Design and Implementation

The motor was interfaced with the left-side output terminals, specifically pins 3 and 6. To manage the operation of this motor, it is essential to apply input logic to pins 2 and 7, which are identified as 1 A and 2 A. Similarly, the motor on the right side, which is connected to pins 11 and 14, requires the application of HIGH and LOW input signals to pins 10 and 15 for effective control (Table 3).

**Table 3.** Pin Configuration for various directions of L239D Motor Driver.

| Pin 2 | Pin 7 | Direction |
|---|---|---|
| LOW | LOW | No rotation (Idle) |
| LOW | HIGH | Left counter clockwise |
| HIGH | LOW | Left clockwise |
| HIGH | HIGH | No rotation (Idle) |
| **Pin 10** | **Pin 15** | **Direction** |
| LOW | LOW | No rotation (Idle) |
| LOW | HIGH | Right counter clockwise |
| HIGH | LOW | Right clockwise |
| HIGH | HIGH | No rotation (Idle) |

The MPU6050 sensor module was integrated with an Arduino to monitor motion or gestures related to head tilting. The connection setup involved linking the SDA pin of the MPU6050 to the A4 pin on the Arduino, the SCL pin to the A5 pin, and the INT pin to the D2 pin of the Arduino [19].

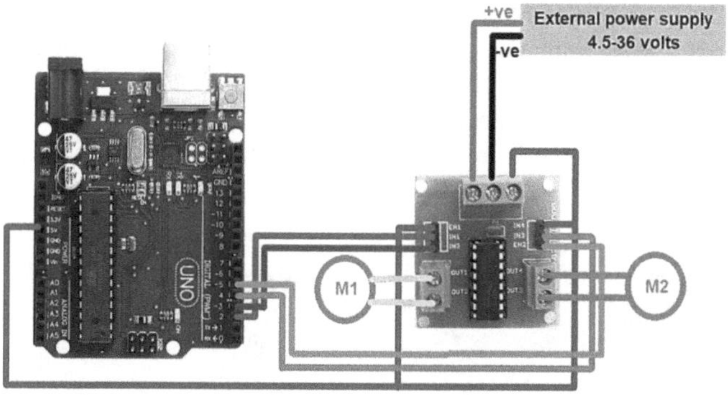


**Fig. 9.** Connections between Arduino and L239D Motor Driver.

The L339D motor driver was connected to an Arduino to rotate the DC gear motors. If IN1 is connected to the D5 of Arduino, then the left motor moves forward, and if IN2 is connected to the D6 of Arduino, then the left motor moves in the reverse direction. Similarly, If IN3 is connected to the D9 of Arduino, then the right motor moves forward, and if IN4 is connected to the D10 of Arduino, then the right motor moves in the reverse direction. PWM signals on ENA/ENB control the motor speed. If ENA is attached to the D3 of Arduino, then the left motor speed is controlled, and if ENB is connected to the D11 of Arduino, then the speed of the right motor is controlled. The 12 V battery was connected to the +12 V terminal of L239D, whereas the GND connections were common between all components.

**Table 4.** Arduino commands for L239D Motor Driver inputs.

| Arduino Command | L293D motor driver Inputs | | | |
|---|---|---|---|---|
| | IN1 | IN2 | IN3 | IN4 |
| F | HIGH | LOW | HIGH | LOW |
| B | LOW | HIGH | LOW | HIGH |
| L | LOW | HIGH | HIGH | LOW |
| R | HIGH | LOW | LOW | HIGH |
| S | LOW | LOW | LOW | LOW |

On the Transmitter side, the accelerometer sensor continuously measures the head orientation and sends the signal to the Arduino, which calculates the tilt angles (pitch and roll). Based on the tilt, command signals are sent to the RF transmitter for transmission. If the tilt is forward, it sends 'F; backward tilt sends 'B; left tilt sends 'L'; right tilt sends 'R; and no tilt sends S. On the Receiver side, the RF receiver catches the commands and sends them to the Arduino, which decodes the commands and controls the L293D motor driver. Table 4 lists the signals received by the L293D motor driver for different Arduino commands.

The connection of the DC gear Motors to L239D Motor driver is also depicted in Fig. 8. The left DC motor was connected to OUT1 (+) and OUT2 (−) of L239D, whereas the right DC motor was connected to OUT3 (+) and OUT4 (−). Diodes were used for decoupling between the L293D driver and the DC gear motors, while the driver was at a separate 12 V power battery separated from the logic power of 5 V. Figure 9 shows the completely connected hardware circuit of the head-gesture-controlled car driving circuit.

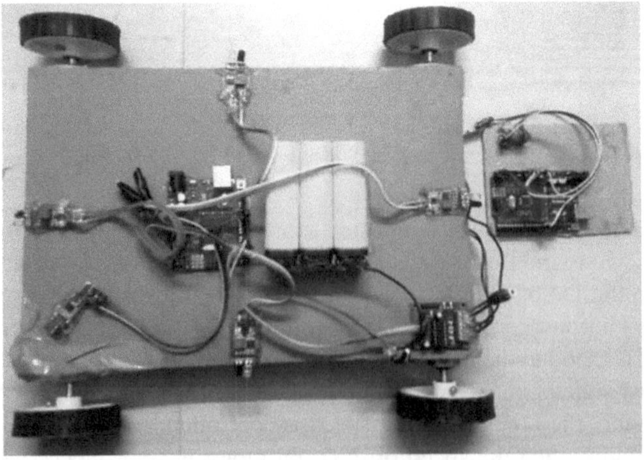

**Fig. 10.** Hardware Implementation of the proposed head-gesture controlled model.

This circuit provides a complete wireless control system that is built using commonly available components. The modular design allows easy modifications and enhancements (Fig. 10).

## 4 Conclusion

The head-gesture-controlled automated vehicle presents a groundbreaking approach to mobility, particularly for individuals with physical disabilities. By integrating sensor-based gesture recognition and automation, this system allows users to control vehicle movements using head gestures, thereby eliminating the need for manual operation. This not only enhances accessibility but also promotes independence and convenience for those with mobility impairment. One of the primary benefits of this system is its capacity to facilitate a hands-free driving experience, making it highly suitable for individuals who cannot operate traditional steering controls. The implementation of real-time head gesture recognition, AI-driven motion filtering, and sensor-based automation ensures that the vehicle responds accurately to intentional movements while minimizing false triggers caused by accidental head movements. As the project evolves, several future enhancements can improve its practicality and reliability. These include multi-modal control integration, where users can combine voice commands with gestures, and machine learning algorithms that adapt to individual driving styles for improved accuracy. Incorporating obstacle detection, emergency stop mechanisms, and cloud-based analytics can make the system safer and more efficient. Beyond personal mobility, this technology has broader applications in areas such as autonomous vehicle systems, industrial automation, and smart transportation solutions. It can be adapted for wheelchairs, robotic 44 systems, and public transport, creating a more inclusive and technologically advanced mobility ecosystem for the elderly. With continued research and development, head-gesture-controlled automated vehicles have the potential to revolutionize assistive mobility, offering an innovative, safe, and user-friendly alternative to traditional vehicle control systems.

## References

1. Ahuja, M.K., Singh, A.: Hand gesture recognition using PCA. Int. J. Comput. Sci. Eng. Technol. **5**(7), 267–271 (2015)
2. Agarwal, S., Tiwari, S., Yadav, S., Singh, S., Tiwari, V.: Voice assistant for physically challenged individuals: enhancing accessibility and independence. Int. J. Eng. Appl. Sci. Technol. **8**(1), 27–31 (2023)
3. Pratama, P.S., et al.: Obstacle avoidance control for four wheels independent steering automatic guided vehicles. In: Recent Advances in Electrical Engineering and Related Sciences, pp. 603–618 (2016)
4. Hasan, M.M., Mishra, P.K.: Features fitting using multivariate Gaussian distribution for hand gesture recognition. Int. J. Comput. Sci. Emerg. Technol. **3**(2), 73–80 (2012)
5. Prasad, N.H., Mariyan Richard, A., Lakshmi Narayan, B.N.: Hand gesture controlled robot. In: International Conference on Communication, Computing and Electronics Systems, vol. 733. Springer, Singapore (2021)

6. Bansal, P., Baghel, V., Bharti, M.: Hand Gesture Controlled Smart Car Using Image Processing. Jaypee University of Information Technology, Solan, India (2023)
7. Vaidya, O., Jadhav, K., Ingale, L., Chaudhari, R.: Hand gesture based music player control in vehicle. In: 5th International Conference for Convergence in Technology (I2CT), pp. 1–5. IEEE, Bombay, India (2019)
8. Małecki, K., Nowosielski, A., Kowalicki, M.: Gesture-based user interface for vehicle on-board system: a questionnaire and research approach. Appl. Sci. **10**(18), 6620 (2020)
9. Shukla, A., Jain, A., Mishra, P., Kushwaha, R.: Human gesture controlled car robot. SAMRIDDHI J. Phys. Sci. Eng. Technol. **11**(2), 115–122 (2019)
10. Sruthi, P., Varma, D.L., Reddy, M.A., Aditya, D., et al.: Industry monitoring system using IoT through interdisciplinary approaches. In: International Conference on Futuristic Trends in Engineering, Science & Technology, E3S Web of Conferences, vol. 507, 01051 (2024)
11. Chanda, P., Mukherjee, P.K., Modak, S., Nath, A.: Gesture controlled robot using Arduino and android. Int. J. Adv. Res. Comput. Sci. Softw. Eng. **6**(6), 227–234 (2016)
12. Kumari, J., Vivek, V., Kumar, P.: A study on arduino car speed detector using Arduino UNO and IR sensors. Int. J. Microelectron. Digit. Integr. Circ. **4**(2), 6–12 (2018)
13. Mardiyanto, R., Utomo, M.F.R., Purwanto, D., Suryoatmojo, H.: Development of hand gesture recognition sensor based on accelerometer and gyroscope for controlling arm of underwater remotely operated robot. In: International Seminar on Intelligent Technology and Its Applications (ISITIA), pp. 329–333, Surabaya, Indonesia (2017)
14. Goyal, D., Saini, S.P.S.: Accelerometer based hand gesture-controlled wheelchair. Int. J. Emerg. Technol. **4**(2), 15–20 (2013)
15. Singh, R.R., Das, R., Pal, K.: A novel modus of hand gesture controlled wireless robot. Int. J. Res. Appl. Sci. Eng. Technol. **5**(5), 641–647 (2017)
16. Patil, P.V., Shete, M.B., Padalkar, T.M.: Wireless hand gesture robot using accelerometer. Int. Res. J. Eng. Technol. **3**(4), 353–356 (2016)
17. Ji, Z., He, F.: Maximum torque control of servo motor for wide speed range. In: Proceedings of 2011 International Conference on Electronic & Mechanical Engineering and Information Technology, pp. 3353–3357, Harbin, China (2011)
18. Pradeep, J., Paul, P.V.: Design and implementation of gesture controlled robotic arm for industrial applications. Int. J. Adv. Sci. Res. Dev. **3**(4), 202–209 (2016)
19. Vernekar, P., Chougula, B., Pawar, M., Patil, A., Hooli, K.: Gesture controlled wheel chair and convertible wheel chair into stretcher. In: International Conference for Emerging Technology (INCET), pp. 1–4, Belgaum, India (2020)

# Biomedical and Computing Systems

# Brain Tumor Classifier Based on Soft Voting

Kilari Veera Swamy(✉), Yarlagadda Tejas Goud, Kuruva Rakesh Kumar, and Malavath Uday Kiran

ECE Department, Vasavi College of Engineering, Hyderabad, Telangana, India
k.veeraswamy@staff.vce.ac.in

**Abstract.** Nowadays, cases of Brain tumours are becoming one of the rising concerns associated with multiple health hazards. Brain tumours are affecting all age groups, right from children to old people. Detecting tumours is a complex task and requires sophisticated equipment and technology. Images are processed using histogram equalization and K-means segmentation. The features capture the main structural and textural characteristics of brain tissues while cutting down on redundancy and simplifying calculations. Features from images are reduced using PCA. 1245 PCA-reduced coefficients are considered from the preprocessed MRI images. In the traditional machine learning methods, which include SVM, KNN, and Naive Bayes are applied. Later Soft Voting is used on various deep learning techniques. Advanced learning techniques considered in this paper are MobileNetV2, ResNet, DenseNet, and EfficientNet. Performance is assessed using various metrics. Experimental results specify the proposed concept is better than existing techniques.

**Keywords:** Machine Learning · MRI Image Processing · K-means Segmentation · Deep Learning · Support Vector Machine (SVM) · Soft Voting

## 1 Introduction

Identification of tumors at an early stage is an important aspect in medical diagnosis [1]. It helps doctors to treat in a better way. MRI images are popular in this aspect. Convolutional Networks [2] is popular for brain MRI images using deep learning. Efficient Net [3] explored for brain images. This team identified combining the models are effective. CNN features [4] are important patterns extraction process. Deep learning techniques are popular for medical image analysis [5]. Tumor or No Tumor identification is a valuable for brain images. Machine Learning (ML) based methods are useful to detect accurately. It makes diagnosis is accurate without any manual errors. Traditional methods like Support Vector Machines (SVM), Navie Bayes (NB), and K Nearest Neighbors (KNN) are popular in the initial days. Here features are extracted manually. Later, Convolutional Neural Networks (CNN) is popular to extract automatic features. Many deep learning techniques are developed using CNN concepts. Ensemble of various methods is able to produce better results. More flexibility can be achieved using Soft Voting (SV). It takes


M. Zafar Ali Khan et al. (Eds.): ICATECS 2025, LNICST 682, pp. 263–278, 2027.
https://doi.org/10.1007/978-3-032-29699-3_20

better models by giving higher weightage. Soft Voting is better than many hard voting methods. Confidence levels are used in SV. Traditional methods with reduced features are used to test the brain tumors. Later, deep learning techniques are used for brain tumor identification. At the end, SV is used on ResNet18 [6], ResNet50 [7], DenseNet201 [8], and EfficientNetB0 [9].

Proposed concept is discussed in Sect. 2. Performance metrics considered in this work are presented in Sect. 3. Detailed analysis of results is presented in Sect. 4. Final remarks are communicated in Sect. 5.

## 2 Proposed Method

Ensembling process worked in this work is displayed in Fig. 1. Data preprocessing is the first step in this work. Data is augmented for better learning in the second stage. Various CNN models are trained in third stage. SV is used to fuse better models performance. An intelligent frame work is explored to detect brain tumors.

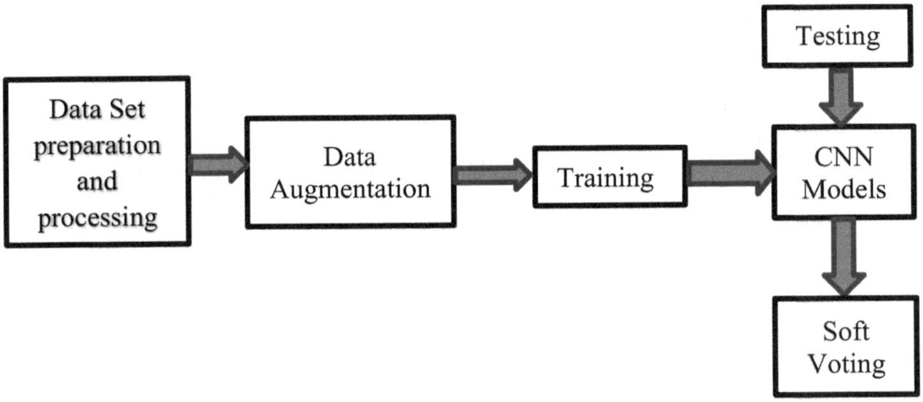


**Fig. 1.** Flow of the proposed method

### 2.1 Dataset Preparation and Preprocessing

Two categories of MRI images are considered in this work [10]. Categories are Tumour and no Tumour. This is properly labelled by experienced group of doctors. Data set is segregated into 2 clusters. One is training data and other one is testing data. Seventy percentage is used for training. Thirty percentage is used for testing. All images are resized to the uniform size of 224 × 224.

### 2.2 Data Augmentation

Data set diversity is improved using data expansion. Rotation, flipping, scaling, and resizing are the part of the data augmentation. This new data set enables the models learn new features differentiate the classification. It enables CNN to identify important patterns in the data set. Overfitting problem is also addressed using this process.

## 2.3 Architecture of Proposed Soft Voting Ensemble Model

Brightness, lighting, or sharpness are differing for medical images. Pre-processing improves the clarity. Proposed architecture improves the performance of the classification. Best features are utilized to improve the performance. Each model has its own special pattern identification strength. MobileNetV2, ResNet18, ResNet50, DenseNet201, and EfficientNetB0 are explored in this work. Every model is able to distinguish 2 classes. C1(Tumour) and C2(No Tumour). Last layer is modified in all these models for these 2 classes. Proposed architecture adopted in this work is shown in Fig. 2.

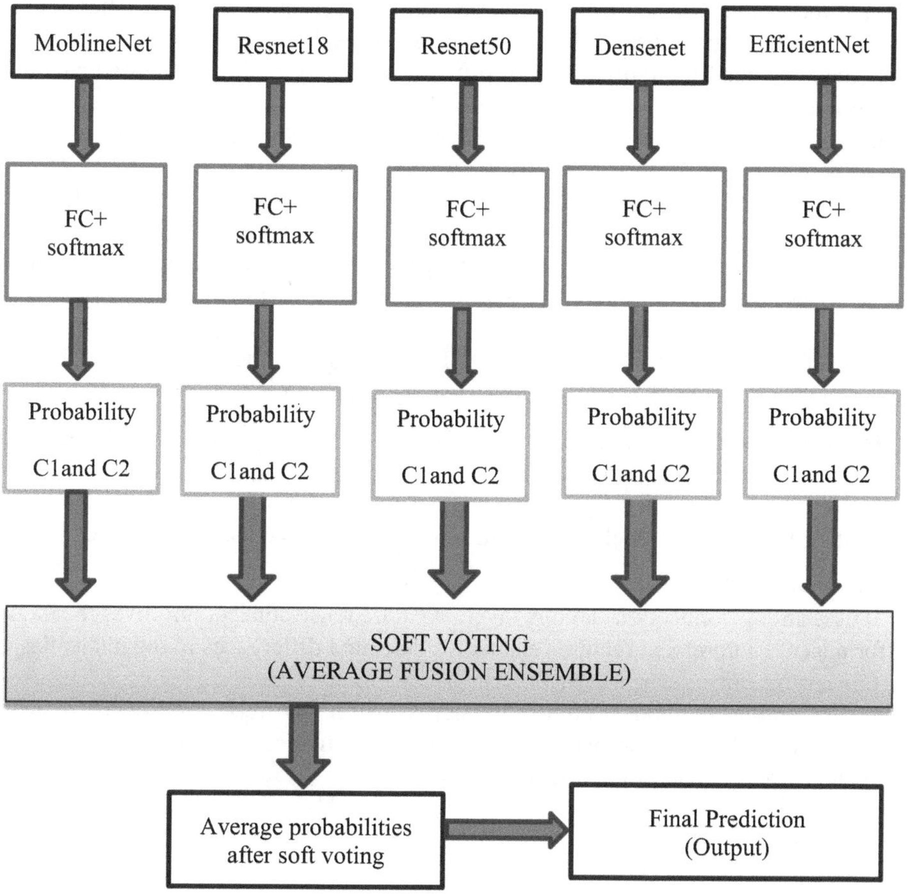


**Fig. 2.** Proposed Architecture for Soft Voting Ensemble

Each model is following similar procedures during training and testing. Each model depth may change. Early layers take basic information. Moving to final layers able to identify global features. Various filters are used in this process. These filters are used to identify various patterns. ReLU activation is used. Pooling layers are used to control the size. At the heart of every CNN, convolutional layers handle step-by-step feature detection. Each CNN model is associated with a similar workflow. Though the architecture differs in depth, each model follows a common sequence of operations. Early ones pick up basic visual information like lines, shifts in brightness, or contrast differences - key for detecting where brain regions meet. Soft max is used for final classification. Averaging these probabilities and making predictions performs a important role in enhancing accuracy, so that it explains how well the models have been trained. Batch normalization, along with early stopping, helps stop the model from memorizing and learning too much and keeps things stable while cutting down on jumpy training shifts. This type of ensemble technique, through soft voting, helps us to deal with the predictions made with multiple models and diversify the variations among each other to make better results. Finally, with these operations we can achieve good results when compared with traditional methods handling individually, resulting in efficient method for classification in field of medicine.

Each CNN model within the ensemble has unique design characteristics:

*MobileNetV2*

MobileNetV2 is a lightweight deep CNN that concentrates on speed and effectiveness. This network operates depth wise detachable convolutions and reversed residual blocks to reduce computation while maintaining high accuracy. MobileNetV2 effectively characterises small details and works well with lower contrast MRI images.

*ResNet18 and ResNet50*

ResNet models use residual skip links. These links help the gradient flow through identity mappings, which addresses the vanishing gradient problem.

- ResNet18 has 18 convolutional layers. It focuses on learning simple but general features. It is useful for small data sets.
- ResNet50 has a deeper design with bottleneck residual blocks. Complex features are identified using this model. Large data sets can be handled using this model.

*DenseNet201*

It uses strong connections among layers. Feature reuse concept improves the model performance. Hierarchical features enable for detecting differences in the intensities.

*EfficientNetB0*

It uses scaling method. It adjusts the depth, width, and resolution of the network together. This technique improves both accuracy and efficiency while keeping a balance between computational cost and feature quality.

### 2.4 Network Flow

Brief description of the architecture is presented here. Input: MRI image (224 $\times$ 224 $\times$ 3). Convolutional Layers: Perform spatial feature extraction using multiple kernels(3 $\times$ 3, 5 $\times$ 5). Batch Normalization and ReLU Activation: Normalize activations and introduce non-linearity. Pooling Layers: Retain dominant features. Fully Connected Layers: Integrate learned features for classification. Softmax Layer: Converts raw scores into class probabilities. Soft Voting Fusion: Aggregates probabilities from all five CNNs to produce the final prediction. The key innovation of this work lies in the Soft Voting ensemble learning technique, which aggregates the probabilistic outputs of the five trained CNNs to generate the final classification decision.

### 2.5 Mathematical Representation

Let the dataset be represented as in Eq. (1).

$$\mathcal{D} = \{(x_i, y_i)\}_{i=1}^{M} \tag{1}$$

where $x_i \in \mathbb{R}^{224\times224\times3}$ is the $i^{th}$ MRI image and $y_i \in \{0,1\}$ is the corresponding label, with

- $y_i = 1$ representing *Tumor*, and
- $y_i = 0$ representing *No Tumor*.

The ensemble consists of $N = 5$ pretrained CNN models. $\mathcal{M} = \{M_1, M_2, M_3, M_4, M_5\}$ where each $M_k$ corresponds to one of the models MobileNetV2, ResNet18, ResNet50, DenseNet201, and EfficientNetB0. Each model $M_k$ extracts hierarchical feature maps $F_k$ from the input image $x_i$ through multiple convolutional operations as in Eq. (2).

$$F_k = f_k(x_i; \theta_k) \tag{2}$$

where $\theta_k$ represents the learnable parameters (weights and biases) of model $M_k$. The output of the final fully connected layer for model $M_k$ is a 2-dimensional logit vector as in Eq. (3).

$$Z_k = \left[z_{k,0}, z_{k,1}\right] \tag{3}$$

where $z_{k,0}$ and $z_{k,1}$ are the raw scores for *No Tumor* and *Tumor*, respectively. Each model's logits are passed through a Softmax layer to generate normalized probability values as in Eq. (4).

$$P_{k,j} = \frac{e^{z_{k,j}}}{\sum_{c=1}^{C} e^{z_{k,c}}}, j \in \{0, 1\} \tag{4}$$

where:

- $P_{k,0}$ = probability of *No Tumor* predicted by model $M_k$,
- $P_{k,1}$ = probability of *Tumor* predicted by model $M_k$,
- $C = 2$ = number of classes.

For each test image, each model produces a probability vector as in Eq. (5).

$$P_k = \left[P_{k,0}, P_{k,1}\right] \tag{5}$$

The ensemble model fuses the probabilistic outputs of all CNNs using arithmetic mean fusion, also known as Soft Voting as in Eq. (6).

$$\hat{P}_j = \frac{1}{N} \sum_{k=1}^{N} P_{k,j}, j \in \{0, 1\} \tag{6}$$

Thus, for the two-class case are given in Eq. (7) and (8) respectively.

$$\hat{P}_0 = \frac{1}{5}\left(P_{1,0} + P_{2,0} + P_{3,0} + P_{4,0} + P_{5,0}\right) \tag{7}$$

$$\hat{P}_1 = \frac{1}{5}\left(P_{1,1} + P_{2,1} + P_{3,1} + P_{4,1} + P_{5,1}\right) \tag{8}$$

where:

- $\hat{P}_0 =$ ensemble probability of *No Tumor*,
- $\hat{P}_1 =$ ensemble probability of *Tumor*.

The final class prediction for image $x_i$ is concluded by choosing the class with the highest ensemble probability as in Eq. (9) and (10) respectively.

$$\hat{y}_i = \arg\max_{j \in \{0,1\}} \left(\hat{P}_j\right) \tag{9}$$

Hence,

$$\hat{y}_i = \begin{cases} 0, \text{ if } \hat{P}_0 > \hat{P}_1 \\ 1, \text{ otherwise} \end{cases} \tag{10}$$

Various models' details are exhibited in Table 1.

**Table 1.** Various CNN Architectures parameters

| Model Name | Total Layers | Convolution Layers | Trainable Parameters (Millions) | Output Feature size | Input Size |
|---|---|---|---|---|---|
| MobileNetV2 | 53 | 35 | 3.5 M | 1280 | 224 * 224 * 3 |
| ResNet18 | 71 | 20 | 11.7 M | 512 | 224 * 224 * 3 |
| ResNet50 | 177 | 49 | 25.6 M | 2048 | 224 * 224 * 3 |
| DenseNet201 | 709 | 201 | 20.0 M | 1920 | 224 * 224 * 3 |
| EfficientNetB0 | 237 | 82 | 5.3 M | 1280 | 224 * 224 * 3 |

## 3 Performance Metrics

Accuracy, Precision, Recall and F1 Score are calculated using True Positive, False Positive, True Negative, and False Negative. Which offers important information about in what way the model performs. Details are offered in Table 2.

**Table 2.** Confusion Matrix

| | Real Class | | |
|---|---|---|---|
| Calculated Class | | 1 | 0 |
| | 1 | TP | FP |
| | 0 | FN | TN |

Accuracy is a prominent way to analyze machine learning models. It shows the ratio of correct outputs to the total number of instances. This measure helps determine how well a model performs and is essential for assessing performance in different applications. You can calculate accuracy using the give Eq. (11).

$$Accuracy = \frac{TP + TN}{TP + TN + FP + FN} \tag{11}$$

Precision, recall and F1 score are presented in Eqs. (12), (13), and (14) respectively.

$$Precision = \frac{TP}{TP + FP} \tag{12}$$

$$Recall = \frac{TP}{TP + FN} \tag{13}$$

$$F1\,score = \frac{2 * Precision * Recall}{Precision + Recall} \tag{14}$$

## 4 Experimental Results

The data set in this research includes MRI brain scans divided into Tumor and No Tumor classes. It consists of 3,264 MRI images that show a wide variety of tumor shapes, contrasts, and anatomical differences. The images are resized and adjusted for uniform input across all models. We performed a stratified split, distributing 1,828 images for training, 457 for validation, and 979 for testing. This approach ensures that each subset has balanced class representation. Raw images are shown in Fig. 3.

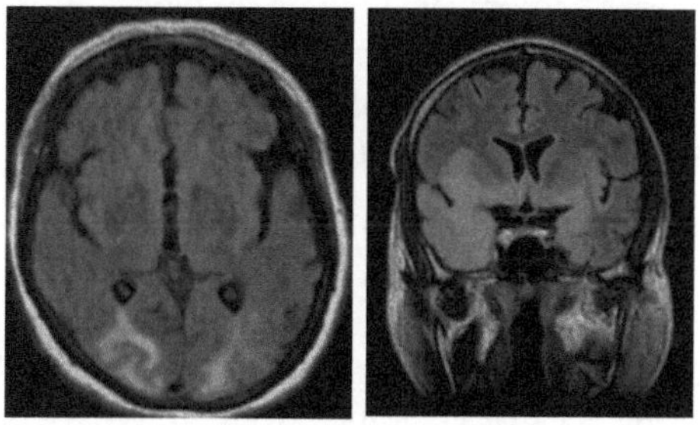

**Fig. 3.** Raw images of Non-Tumor

Tumour images are displayed in Fig. 4.

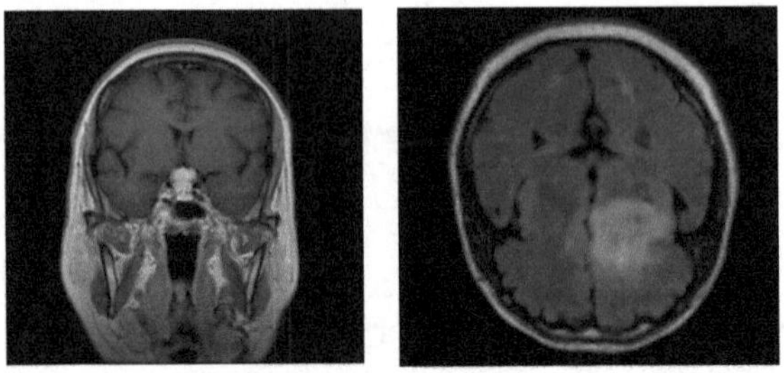

**Fig. 4.** Tumor Images

The entire test dataset is provided to the trained models of SVM, KNN, and Naive Bayes classifiers [13]. CNN based methods are popular [14]. Hence, CNN-based Soft Voting Ensemble models are evaluated. In the traditional machine learning methods, which include SVM, KNN, and Naive Bayes, 1245 PCA-reduced features were extracted from the preprocessed MRI images. These images were processed using histogram equalization and K-means segmentation. The features capture the main structural and textural characteristics of brain tissues while cutting down on redundancy and simplifying calculations. This study aims to improve diagnostic precision by going beyond traditional classifiers. Results of traditional methods are stated in Table 3.

**Table 3.** Results of SVM and KNN and Naive Bayes model

| Number of Features after PCA | Method | Accuracy |
|---|---|---|
| 1245 | Naive Bayes | 59.15% |
| 1245 | KNN | 85.47% |
| 1245 | SVM | 96.95% |

Each CNN model in the ensemble learns different features from MRI information.

- MobileNetV2 uses more flexible separable convolutions to handle local texture changes and small lesions with fewer computations.
- ResNet architectures, both 18 and 50, use residual skip connections. This allows them to capture deeper patterns and prevents fading gradients during training.
- DenseNet201 enables dense feature sharing. It allows the model to reuse information from previous layers, which helps it apply well across tumor and non-tumor areas.
- EfficientNetB0 uses unified scaling. It stabilizes network depth and width, ensuring stable results across various image resolutions.

Even though these models work well individually, they can exhibit some biases. For instance, MobileNetV2, being lightweight, might have difficulty with complex textures. In contrast, deeper models could overfit small datasets. To tackle this issue, the Soft Voting Ensemble combines the class probabilities from all five CNN models and performs evaluation.

$$\widehat{P_j} = \frac{1}{N}\sum_{i=1}^{N} P_{i,j}, N = 5 \quad (15)$$

where $P_{i,j}$ is the probability predicted by the $i^{th}$ model for class $j$, and $\widehat{P_j}$ is the averaged probability across all models. The final class prediction is obtained as:

$$\text{Predicted Class} = \arg\max_j\left(\widehat{P_j}\right) \quad (16)$$

Training of the Mobile NetV2 details are shown in Fig. 5.

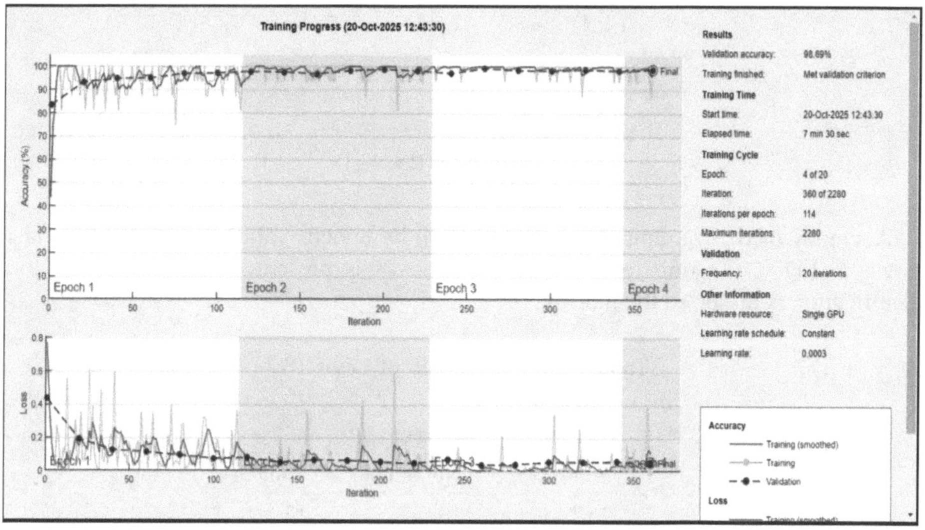


**Fig. 5.** Graph for MobileNetV2

Accuracy of the training is improved epoch by epoch. Validation accuracy is also shown in the Fig. 5. Testing results of the MobileNetV2 is presented in Table 4.

**Table 4.** Testing Results of MobileNetV2

| | | Prediction | |
|---|---|---|---|
| | | No Tumor | Tumor |
| Actual | No Tumor | 147 | 3 |
| | Tumor | 10 | 819 |

Training of the Resnet18 details are shown in Fig. 6.

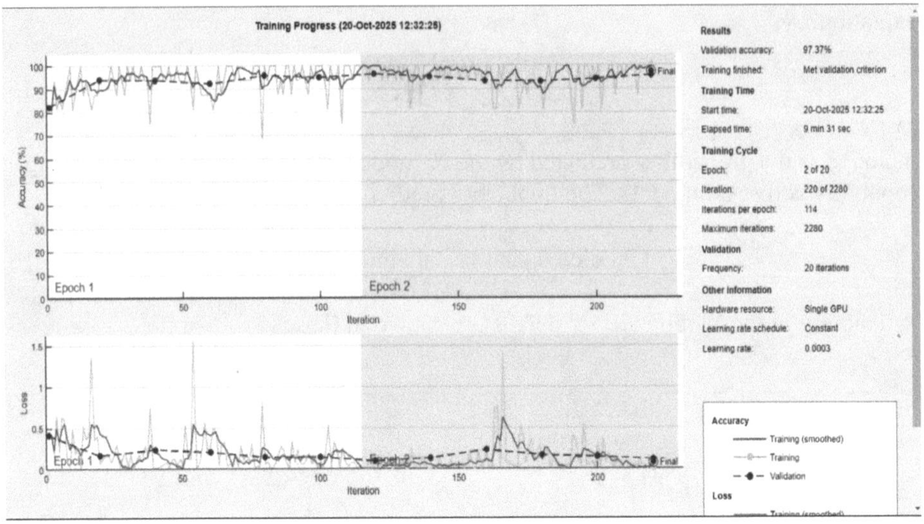


**Fig. 6.** Graph for ResNet18

Accuracy of the training is improved epoch by epoch. Validation accuracy is also shown in Fig. 6. Testing results of the ResNet18 is presented in Table 5. Tumors identification is not up to the mark.

**Table 5.** Testing Results of Resnet18

| | | Prediction | |
|---|---|---|---|
| | | No Tumour | Tumour |
| Actual | No Tumour | 138 | 12 |
| | Tumour | 64 | 765 |

Model is stabilized at Epoch 2. Here, accuracy is good. To get less loss, model has trained more than 200 iterations. Accuracy is 92.54%. Precision is 93.00%. Recall is 91.80%. F1 Score is 92.35%. This model gives best performance in terms of accuracy.

Training of the Resnet50 details are shown in Fig. 7.

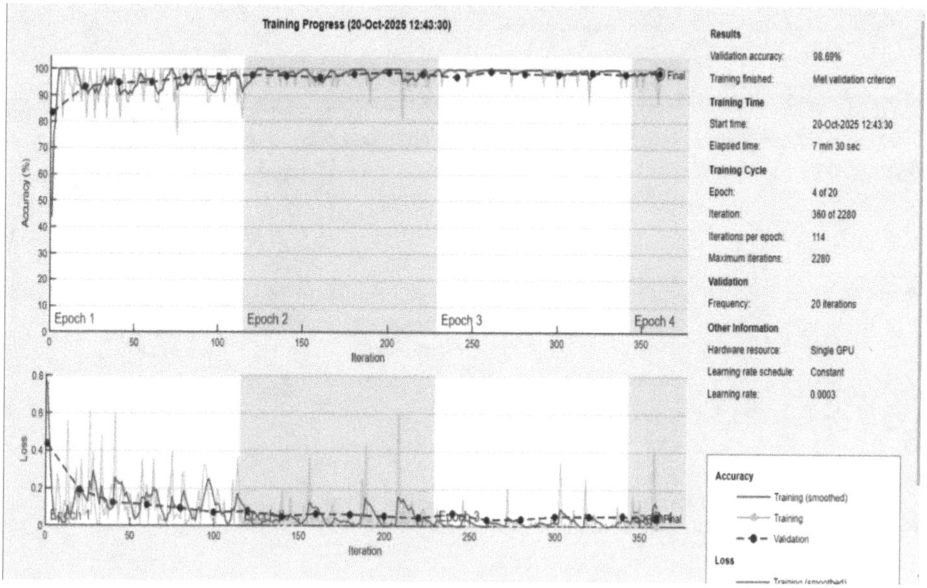


**Fig. 7.** Graph for ResNet50

Accuracy of the training is improved epoch by epoch. Validation accuracy is also shown in the Fig. 7. Testing results of ResNet50 are presented in Table 6.

**Table 6.** Testing Results of Resnet50

| | | Prediction | |
|---|---|---|---|
| | | No Tumour | Tumour |
| Actual | No Tumour | 140 | 10 |
| | Tumour | 05 | 824 |

Tumors identification is effective in Resnet50. TP and TN are high here. FP and FN are low here. Model is stabilized at epoch 4. Here, accuracy is high. To get less loss, model has trained more than 350 iterations. Accuracy is 98.47%. Precision is 98.80%. Recall is 99.40%. F1 Score is 99.10%. This model gives best performance in terms of accuracy. Training of the Densenet201 details are revealed in Fig. 8.

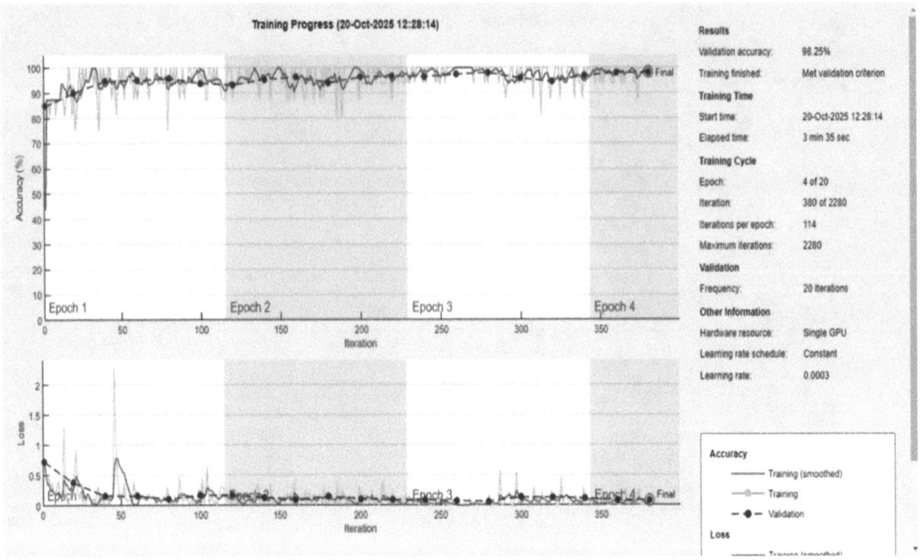


**Fig. 8.** Graph for DenseNet201

Accuracy of the training is improved epoch by epoch. Validation accuracy is also shown in the Fig. 8. Testing results of the DenseNet201 is presented in Table 7.

**Table 7.** Testing Results of DenseNet201

| | | Prediction | |
|---|---|---|---|
| | | No Tumour | Tumour |
| Actual | No Tumour | 132 | 18 |
| | Tumour | 04 | 825 |

Tumors identification is effective in DenseNet201. TP and TN are high here. Tumors identification is effective in Resnet50. TP and TN are high here. FP and FN are low here. Model is stabilized at epoch 4. Here, accuracy is high. To get less loss, model has trained more than 350 iterations. Accuracy is 97.75%. Precision is 97.60%. Recall is 97.70%. F1 Score is 97.65%. This model gives best performance in terms of accuracy. Training of the EfficientNetB0 details are shown in Fig. 9.

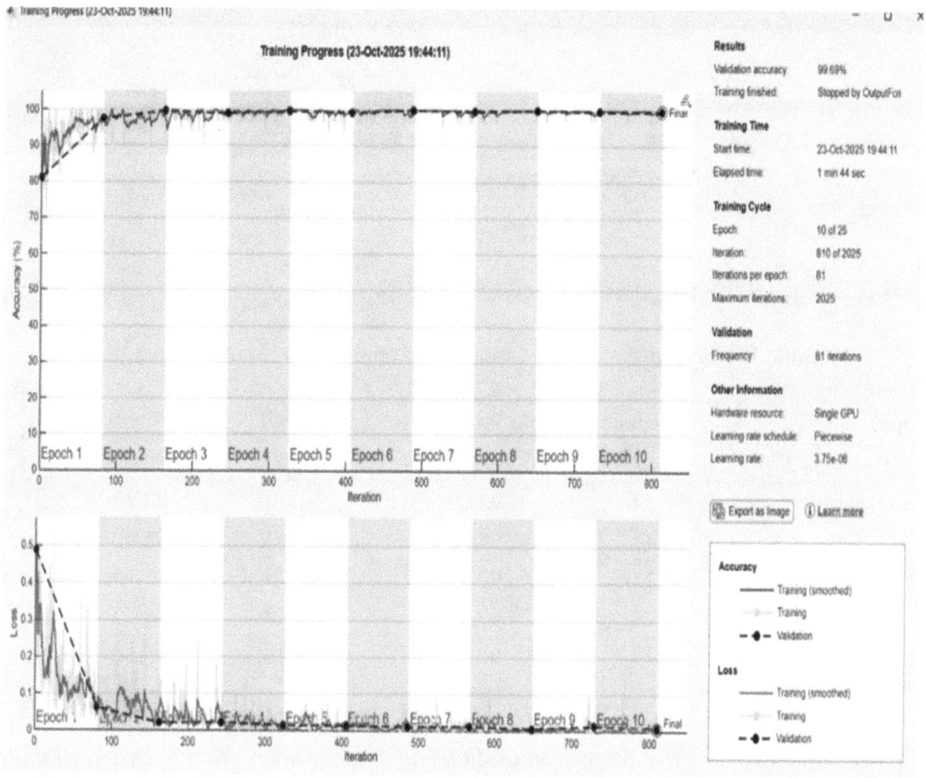


**Fig. 9.** Graph for EfficientNetB0

Accuracy of the training is improved epoch by epoch. Validation accuracy is also shown in the Fig. 9. Testing results of the EfficientNetB0 is presented in Table 8.

**Table 8.** Testing Results of EfficientNetB0

| | | Prediction | |
|---|---|---|---|
| | | No Tumour | Tumour |
| Actual | No Tumour | 148 | 02 |
| | Tumour | 05 | 824 |

Results of the Soft Voting ensemble are bestowed in Table 9.

**Table 9.** Results of Soft Voting

| | | Prediction | |
|---|---|---|---|
| | | No Tumour | Tumour |
| Actual | No Tumour | 148 | 02 |
| | Tumour | 03 | 826 |

All the models results are displayed in Table 10.

**Table 10.** Performance comparison with proposed Soft Voting Ensemble

| Model | Accuracy | Precision | Recall | F1 Score |
|---|---|---|---|---|
| Mobile NetV2 | 98.67 | 98.80 | 98.50 | 98.65 |
| ResNet 18 | 92.54 | 93.00 | 91.80 | 92.35 |
| ResNet 50 | 98.47 | 98.55 | 98.40 | 98.47 |
| DenseNet201 | 97.75 | 97.60 | 97.70 | 97.65 |
| EfficientNetB0 | 99.28 | 99.35 | 99.20 | 99.27 |
| Soft Voting (**Proposed**) | **99.49** | **99.55** | **99.45** | **99.50** |

The comparison of five pretrained CNN architectures and the Soft Voting Ensemble reveals important insights into their performance on the brain MRI dataset. As shown in Table X, all models show stable predictive abilities, with accuracies above 92%. However, the Soft Voting Ensemble constantly outperforms individual models in all key performance metrics, indicating model reliability and better ability to generalise. Accuracy courses the overall percentage of properly graded images including all test samples. The proposed Soft Voting model achieves the highest accuracy of 99.49%. This high accuracy comes from the ensemble's strength in combining complementary feature representations from different CNNs. Precision measures the ratio of precisely identified tumour images to all images predicted as tumours. This reflects the model's ability to minimise false positives. The ensemble's precision of 99.55% shows that it rarely misclassifies normal MRI scans as tumours. This is valuable in medical diagnosis, where false alarms can lead to unwanted anxiety or procedures. Recall, also known as sensitivity, measures the percentage of actual tumour cases recognised correctly by the model. The ensemble's sensitivity of 99.45% demonstrates its effectiveness in detecting small tumour regions, minimising false negatives. This is vital in healthcare, where failing to identify a tumour can have serious consequences.

Specificity evaluates the percentage of correctly identified non-tumour cases, showing the model's ability to tell apart healthy tissue. The proposed ensemble achieves 99.50% specificity, confirming its ability to distinguish normal brain MRIs from those with pathological features. This helps reduce diagnostic errors. The Soft Voting Ensemble records the highest F1-score of 99.50%. This indicates the best balance between tumour detection accuracy and minimising false classifications. EfficientNetB0 holds a significant advantage over traditional models like ResNet and MobileNet due to its balanced trade-off between accuracy and computational efficiency.

Overall, the Soft Voting Ensemble improves performance by averaging the probabilistic outputs of multiple CNN models—MobileNetV2, ResNet18, ResNet50, DenseNet201, and EfficientNetB0. It uses both local texture features and global contextual information. The key point is that the Soft Voting ensemble method helped in exploring various CNN models to evaluate their performance, which is important in determining the class probabilities required for the classification of tumours. SVM is associated with a hyperplane separating tumour and non-tumours. KNN is represented by majority of the surrounding k neighbours, and Naive Bayes is completely dependent on probability. Preprocessing techniques like Gaussian elimination was applied to reduce noise variations. Histogram Equalisation was further applied to differentiate tumour and non-tumour regions by increasing the contrast of images by enhancing the brightness of pixels. K-means segmentation was applied next to this in order to segment the regions for even better division. Principal component Analysis was applied after K-means segmentation, which aimed to reduce dimensions while retaining the most useful features required for the identification of tumours. All these preprocessing techniques are unsupervised. Whereas the classifiers used are supervised methods. The important principle identified in soft voting was a greater number of data cleaning processes were not involved before applying the models. We were able to see better results in the case of soft Voting ensemble when compared to classical machine learning techniques.

## 5 Conclusion

Soft Voting ensemble technique is applied for brain tumour classification using deep learning techniques. All deep learning techniques are implemented individually. Data set is improved by using data augmentation for better performance. Five deep learning techniques are considered to perform ensemble. Ensemble method outperforms in brain tumour classification. Nearly 100% accuracy is achieved. Traditional methods performance is nearly 97% only. Even small percentage error classification is important in medical diagnosis. Soft Voting offers a competent and correct framework for brain tumor diagnosis.

## References

1. Almukhtar, F.H., Kareem, S.W., Khoshaba, F.S.: Design and development of an effective classifier for medical images based on machine learning and image segmentation. Egypt. Inf. J. **25**, 100454 (2024)
2. Jony, J.H., Nahid, M.A.H., Jahan, N., Raza, D.M.: Multiclass brain tumor recognition using convolutional neural network. In: 14th International Conference on Computing Communication and Networking Technologies (ICCCNT), Delhi, India, pp. 1–7 (2023)
3. Shashidhar, R., Manasa, R., Megha, K.M., Priyanga, P., Manjunath, A.S., Roopa, M.: Advancing medical imaging: a focus on efficient net for brain tumor classification. In: Second International Conference on Networks, Multimedia and Information Technology (NMITCON), Bengaluru, India, pp. 1–5(2024)

4. Mansour, et al.: Brain Tumor Segmentation using Hybrid Handcrafted and CNN Features. PMC (2023)
5. Litjens, G., Kooi, T., Bejnordi, B.E., Arindra, A., Setio, A., Ciompi, F., et al.: A survey on deep learning in medical image analysis. Med. Image Anal. **42**, 60–88 (2017)
6. Ye, X., Jin, Y., Wang, Z., Feng, N., Mu, L., Xie, G.: Image binary classification of coronary artery stenosis based on Resnet18 and transfer learning. In: 35th Chinese Control and Decision Conference (CCDC), Yichang, China, pp. 2721–2726 (2023)
7. Rani, R., Gupta, S.: Automated retinal disease classification using fine-tuned ResNet50: a deep learning approach for early diagnosis. In: International Conference on Intelligent and Innovative Technologies in Computing, Electrical and Electronics (IITCEE), Bangalore, India, pp. 1–5(2025)
8. Godlin Jasil, S.P., Ulagamuthalvi, V.: Skin lesion classification using pre-trained DenseNet201 deep neural network. In: 3rd International Conference on Signal Processing and Communication (ICPSC), Coimbatore, India, pp. 393–396 (2021)
9. Pathak, M., Chaudhary, D., Sharma, K., Sharma, A.K., Gupta, A., Sharma, B.K.: A robust EfficientNet architecture for brain tumor classification and identification using MRI image. In: 11th International Conference on Intelligent Systems and Embedded Design (ISED), Dehradun, India, pp. 1–5 (2023)
10. https://www.kaggle.com/datasets/sartajbhuvaji/brain-tumor-classification-mri

# Self-powered Wearable Device for Respiratory System Using Machine Learning

A. Vijendar Reddy, G. Sai Nagendra, J. Madhu Sudhan, and M. Srilatha(✉)

Department of Electronics and Communication Engineering, Vardhaman College of Engineering, Hyderabad, Telangana, India
m.srilatha@vardhaman.org

**Abstract.** Wearable health monitoring system enables the real-time tracking of vital signs, but mostly rely on battery-powered sensors, requiring frequent recharging and causing operational downtime. This limitation restricts continuous health monitoring, making such devices less effective for long-term use. Existing solutions utilize biosensors to measure heart rate, oxygen levels, and movement, with low-power circuits and energy-efficient communication to extend battery life. However, battery dependency remains a major drawback, leading to interruptions in monitoring, especially in remote or emergency scenarios. Additionally, conventional systems lack comprehensive respiratory health assessment, limiting their effectiveness in detecting early signs of respiratory diseases. To address this issue, we propose a self-powered wearable respiratory health monitoring system utilizing photovoltaic (PV) cells and a thermoelectric generator (TEG) for continuous energy harvesting. The system integrates an MQ-135 gas sensor for air quality monitoring and an MPU-6050 motion sensor for breathing analysis. A Random Forest-based machine learning model analyzes real-time data, enabling early detection of respiratory diseases while ensuring uninterrupted, sustainable operation and personalized healthcare monitoring.

**Keywords:** Self-Powered Wearable · Respiratory Health Monitoring · Energy Harvesting Sensors · Air Quality Detection · Motion-Based Breathing Analysis · Random Forest Algorithm · Real-Time Disease Prediction · Sustainable Healthcare System

## 1 Introduction

Respiratory condition monitoring is essential in disease identification and treatment of conditions such as Chronic Obstructive Pulmonary Disease (COPD), asthma, and sleep apnea. Monitoring of breathing frequency, air quality, and motion-activity-based respiration with real-time accuracy is vital for timely detection and treatment success. Traditional clinical equipment utilized for respiration monitoring is cumbersome, expensive, and patient-sited, which prevents their complete utilization in practical applications. Recent advances in technology have enabled wearable monitoring in real time with small


M. Zafar Ali Khan et al. (Eds.): ICATECS 2025, LNICST 682, pp. 279–296, 2027.
https://doi.org/10.1007/978-3-032-29699-3_21

devices. The majority of wearable systems available at present are, however, battery-dependent. These kinds of systems are hampered by limited running time due to frequent recharging, causing interruptions in data collection. Besides, conventional systems typically lack inherent respiratory assessment functions and intelligent health condition classification, reducing their clinical value. To address these problems, we present a self-sustaining wearable respiratory health monitoring system.. The sensor integrates a photovoltaic (PV) cell and a thermoelectric generator (TEG) to harness hybrid power without the requirement for conventional battery recharging. An MPU-6050 inertial measurement unit (IMU) is utilized to detect chest motion and an MQ-135 gas sensor to detect air quality surrounding the wearer. ESP32 microcontroller applies a Random Forest machine learning algorithm to distinguish respiratory disorders in real time. The device may be applied in clinical and remote healthcare environments since it offers smart, real-time respiratory monitoring and displays results on a Streamlit dashboard streamed over WiFi. Same approach, but we attempt to employ a range of machine learning algorithms that have the ability to improve model performance and are critical to make early PD prediction, which will enable us to initiate neuroprotective therapies at the appropriate time. Recent research investigated modern wearable respiratory monitoring systems employing gas sensors and IMUs to monitor breathing patterns and surrounding air quality. Wearable technology's capability for measuring chest movement and directly estimating respiratory rates was demonstrated in several projects. Integration of embedded platforms like ESP32 with cloud-based processing and machine learning algorithms like Random Forest was also emphasized for disease classification.

## 2 Related Work

The author [1] developed a wearable chest band system for respiratory monitoring using two IMU sensors—one placed on the chest and the other on the back—to cancel out body movement noise and capture accurate breathing patterns. A low-power microcontroller processes the data in real-time to extract parameters such as respiration rate and inhalation/exhalation timing. The results are transmitted via Bluetooth to a mobile app for live monitoring. The system was validated under motion and found effective for real-time, accurate respiratory tracking. Its lightweight, low-power design supports continuous daily use and offers potential for integration with cloud platforms and machine learning in future advancements.

The authors [2] reviewed recent advancements in integrating wearable sensors, IoT, AI, and blockchain to enhance healthcare monitoring systems. These technologies collectively support real-time tracking, early disease detection, and personalized care. Wearables monitor vital signs, IoT enables remote connectivity, AI processes health data for timely insights, and blockchain safeguards data privacy. The review emphasizes improved health outcomes and the shift toward home-based care. However, it also identifies key challenges such as power consumption, device compatibility, and data management. The study provides a solid basis for future health monitoring innovations.

The author developed [3] in wearable respiratory monitoring systems using IMU and gas sensors for tracking breathing patterns and air quality. Several projects, including those by Mimoun et al. and Nicolò et al., demonstrated real-time chest motion detection and respiratory rate estimation. Many studies integrated cloud analysis and machine learning (e.g., Random Forest) using microcontrollers like ESP32 for disease classification. However, common limitations include battery dependency and limited energy-efficient communication. These findings underscore current trends and gaps, justifying the development of the proposed self-powered, intelligent wearable system.

The literature [4] emphasizes the increasing demand for wearable respiratory monitoring systems, especially for chronic conditions like COPD and asthma. Prior research has utilized IMUs, piezoresistive, and fiber optic sensors to monitor chest motion, airflow, and breathing rates with high accuracy. However, existing systems struggle with power consumption, data handling, and user comfort. Recent approaches involve low-power microcontrollers and energy harvesting methods like solar power to overcome battery constraints. These studies support the shift toward compact, energy-efficient, and AI-enabled solutions, forming the basis for more advanced, continuous real-time respiratory monitoring systems.

A multi-source energy harvesting technique for powering low-energy devices, such as cell phones, is examined in the study [5] on "Hybrid Energy Harvesting for Low Power Devices." The system integrates solar panels for light-based power, Peltier devices for thermoelectric energy, piezoelectric sensors for vibration energy, and radio frequency antennas for wireless energy gathering. The goal of this hybrid system is to effectively capture and transform ambient energy in a variety of settings. By lowering dependency on traditional power sources, the idea promotes sustainability and offers insightful information for incorporating comparable harvesting methods into wearable health monitoring devices that run on their own power.

A thorough analysis of wearable respiratory monitoring systems was carried out by an author [6], who focused on non-invasive technologies like optical fiber sensors, piezoresistive sensors, and IMUs. They explored sensor integration for tracking respiratory rates in diseases like COPD and asthma, highlighting systems validated through clinical trials and MATLAB analysis. The research addressed limitations like high power usage, motion interference, and sensor positioning, and suggested improvements in accuracy and ergonomic design. Their findings align with current self-powered wearable solutions that utilize ESP32 microcontrollers, motion sensors, and air quality detection, reinforcing the potential of such systems in continuous real-time health monitoring.

## 3 Design and Development of the Proposed System

### 3.1 Block Diagram

The block diagram as shown in Fig. 1 provides a clear, high-level overview of the proposed self-powered wearable respiratory health monitoring system. It illustrates the integration of energy harvesting sources (PV cells and thermoelectric generator), power management modules (MPPT controller and DC-DC converter), and key sensing components (MQ-135 gas sensor and MPU-6050 motion sensor). At the core, the ESP32 microcontroller processes the sensor data and performs disease classification using a machine learning model. A self-powered wearable respiratory health monitoring system intended for effective and continuous health tracking is depicted in the block diagram. Photovoltaic (PV) cells and a thermoelectric generator (TEG) are the two renewable energy sources that power the system. An MPPT (Maximum Power Point Tracking) controller receives data from these sources and maximizes power harvesting in a variety of environmental circumstances [7]. To produce a steady voltage output, the harvested energy is controlled by a DC-DC converter and stored in a battery or supercapacitor. The ESP32 WROOM microcontroller is the central component of the system, acting as both the processing and communication unit. The MQ-135 gas sensor, which monitors air quality by detecting gases like $CO_2$, $NH_3$, and benzene, and the MPU- 6050, which records motion and acceleration data to analyze respiratory movements, are its two main sensors [8]. For remote monitoring and visualization, the ESP32 processes the sensor data in real-time and sends it to a web interface or Streamlit-based application via Bluetooth or Wi-Fi.

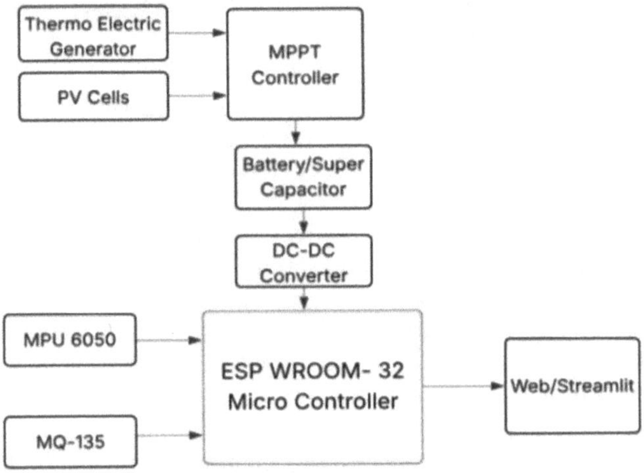


**Fig. 1.** Block diagram of the proposed system

### 3.2 Circuit Diagram

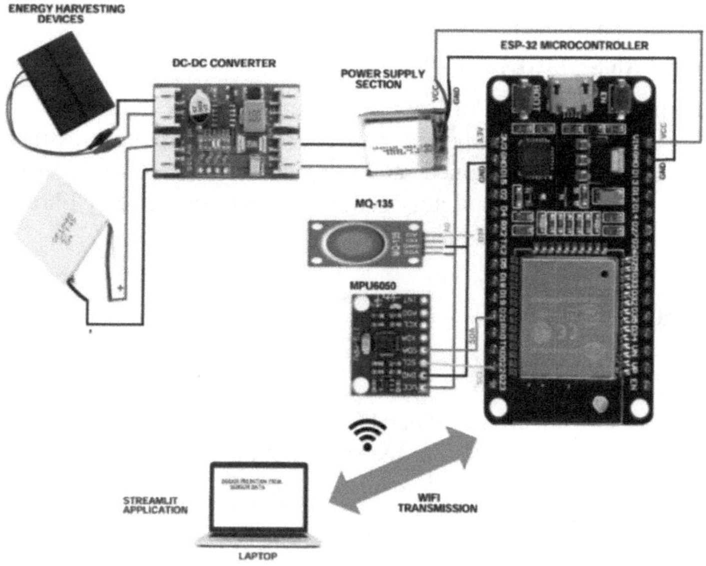


**Fig. 2.** Circuit diagram of the proposed system

The hardware implementation of the self-powered wearable respiratory health monitoring system is illustrated in Fig. 2. It represents a self-powered wearable respiratory health monitoring system integrating multiple components for continuous tracking and disease prediction. The system includes an ESP-32 microcontroller, which processes data from sensors like the MQ-135 gas sensor for air quality monitoring and the MPU-6050 motion sensor for breathing analysis. These sensors are powered through an energy harvesting system composed of photovoltaic (solar) cells and a thermoelectric generator (TEG), ensuring uninterrupted operation. A DC-DC converter regulates voltage levels for efficient power management. Data transmission is facilitated via Wi-Fi-enabled devices, allowing real-time monitoring and analysis through applications like Streamlit. The incorporation of a Random Forest-based machine learning model further enhances disease prediction capabilities, ensuring personalized healthcare monitoring with reliable insights.

### 3.3 Software Tools

The development of the self-powered wearable respiratory health monitoring system utilized three main software tools: Arduino IDE, Python with Scikit-learn, and Streamlit.

#### 3.3.1 Arduino IDE

Arduino IDE served as the primary en-vironment for writing and uploading embedded C/C++ code to the ESP32 microcontroller. It enabled interfacing with the MPU-6050

(IMU) and MQ-135 (gas sensor), signal pre-processing, and real-time data acquisition. Libraries such as Wire.h facilitated communication with external modules, supporting low-power and real-time functionality.

### 3.3.2 Python with Scikit-Learn

Python, in conjunction with Scikit-learn, was employed to develop the Random Forest classifier. This environment supported dataset preparation, feature extraction, model training, and validation. The trained model logic was later converted and integrated into the ESP32 for real-time respiratory condition classification. Key libraries included scikit-learn, pandas, numpy, and matplotlib.

### 3.3.3 Streamlit

A browser-accessible dashboard was developed using Streamlit, a lightweight web framework based on Python. Real-time visualization of respiratory data, including air quality and disease classification, obtained from the ESP32 via Wi-Fi was made possible by this interface. Easy access without requiring a mobile application was provided by its flexible deployment on local or cloud platforms.

# 4 Methodology

## 4.1 Random Forest

Random Forest is an ensemble algorithm of machine learning that is widely used for classification tasks due to its high accuracy, overfitting resistance, and ability to handle complex data. Random Forest is employed within this project in order to classify respiratory health conditions such as Normal, COPD, and Epileptic Seizures based on real-time sensor output from the MPU-6050 motion sensor and MQ-135 gas sensor. The process begins with data collection and preprocessing where the raw sensor data are cleaned, normalized, and labeled. Key features like acceleration, gyroscopic data, and gas concentration levels are learned to find patterns of interest concerning respiratory health. The dataset is separated into training and testing sets, and multiple decision trees are trained on bootstrapped samples. End predictions are generated using majority voting over the trees determines the final predictions.

The performance of the model is measured based on indicators such as accuracy, precision, recall, and F1-score. Post-validation, the learned model is transformed into a lightweight model and executed on the ESP32 microcontroller [9]. The system continuously runs real-time sensor input, classifies respiratory conditions in real-time, and outputs the results through a Streamlit-based dashboard, enabling efficient and accessible monitoring.

Benefits of Using Random Forest

- Excellent Classification Accuracy: Random Forest achieves high predictive performance by combining multiple decision trees.
- Handles Nonlinear Relationships: It effectively manages complex and nonlinear interactions in sensor data.
- Resistant to Overfitting: The ensemble method helps reduce the risk of overfitting compared to single decision trees.
- Scalable and Efficient: Suitable for real-time embedded systems due to its parallel processing and lightweight inference capability.

### 4.2 Data Set

**Table 1.** Dataset used for respiratory pattern classification

| MPU6050_X | MPU6050_Y | MPU6050_Z | MQ135 | DISEASE |
|---|---|---|---|---|
| 2.0068 | 1.4113 | 8.7904 | 382.6790 | NORMAL |
| −7.2874 | −9.116 | 9.5628 | 373.2626 | Epileptic Seizures |
| −1.2893 | −7.0087 | −3.554 | 513.8807 | NORMAL |
| 9.3195 | 8.4450 | 5.335 | 644.655 | Parkinson's Disease |
| −6.097 | −5.3414 | −7.4564 | 519.846 | NORMAL |
| −9.319 | 9.858 | 5.457 | 746.177 | Epilepsy |
| −1.455 | 3.5917 | −0.369 | 658.698 | NORMAL |
| 1.553 | −1.112 | 7.205 | 616.985 | NORMAL |

The given data presents a sample of the training and testing dataset for the Random Forest classification model. The dataset contains sensor readings from two significant sensors as shown in Table 1. It represents the MPU6050 Inertial Measurement Unit (IMU) and the MQ-135 gas sensor. The MPU6050 provides three-axis movement data—represented by MPU6050-X, MPU6050-Y, and MPU6050-Z—that capture the subject's motion. The MQ-135 sensor captures air quality parameters by detecting the level of harmful gases in the environment. The last column, named "Disease," represents the ground truth label for each row of sensor, represents the ground truth label for each row of sensor readings. Labels include Normal, Epileptic Seizures, Parkinson's Disease, Epilepsy, and COPD. These tagged samples are crucial for training the machine learning model to differentiate between normal and abnormal breathing patterns from real-time sensor readings. This table emphasizes the wide variety of sensor responses corresponding to various health states and serves as the basis for predictive classification in the envisioned wearable system.

## 4.3 Flow Chart

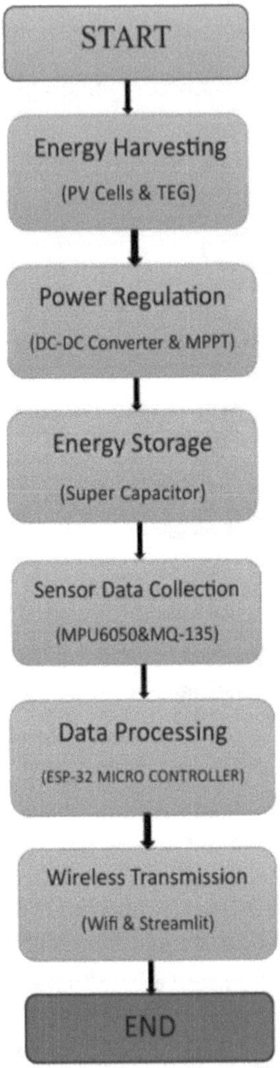


**Fig. 3.** Working Flow chart of the respiratory monitoring system.

The above flow chart describes the sequential functioning of the self-powered wearable respiratory health monitoring system. The system is designed for real-time, energy-efficient monitoring and employs environmental energy harvesting and sensor information to identify respiratory conditions and wirelessly transmit results. Here's how it works as shown in Fig. 3. It describes the operational order of the self-powered wearable respiratory health monitoring system. The process starts with energy harvesting, in which photovoltaic (PV) cells and a thermoelectric generator (TEG) are used to transform ambient light and body heat into electrical energy. This harvested power is then controlled by a DC-DC converter along with a Maximum Power Point Tracking (MPPT) system to ensure that only stable and enough power is provided to the system components [10]. In case there is not enough energy, the system loops back and harvests again. When sufficient power is accumulated, the system enters the sensing stage, where real-time readings are taken from the MPU6050 (motion sensor) and MQ-135 (gas sensor). These sensor readings are processed by the ESP32 microcontroller, which feeds them into a machine learning model—in this example, Random Forest—to determine respiratory states like Normal, COPD, or Epileptic Seizures. The last step includes wireless data transfer through Wi-Fi to facilitate visualization of results on a Streamlit-based dashboard. The whole process is power-efficient, allowing for continuous real-time monitoring in wearable applications.

### 4.4 Implementation

This project demonstrates a complete, self-sustaining wearable device that tracks respiratory wellness based on real-time sensor information, machine learning decision making, and wireless data display. The system has energy harvesting devices, environmental and movement sensors, and an intelligent microcontroller system to operate constantly and autonomously without external power reliance. The energy harvesting module is comprised of two renewable sources: photovoltaic (PV) cells that transform ambient light into power, and a thermoelectric generator (TEG) that generates power from human body heat. Both inputs are supplied to a Maximum Power Point Tracking (MPPT) controller, which maximizes power harvest under changing conditions [11]. The energy harvested is accumulated in a rechargeable lithium battery or supercapacitor module, and filtered through a DC-DC converter to supply a constant output voltage for the device's components. Sensors used are the MQ-135 gas sensor and the MPU-6050 inertial measurement unit (IMU). Environmental air quality is checked by the MQ-135 through detection of harmful gases like $CO_2$, $NO_x$, and ammonia—factors significantly influencing respiratory health. MPU-6050 records data related to motion such as acceleration and gyroscope values which are related to breathing patterns. These sensors continuously feed input to the system for proper respiratory condition evaluation. The ESP32-WROOM-32 microcontroller is the core processing unit. It gathers and preprocesses the sensor data and applies a pre-trained Random Forest machine learning model to classify respiratory states into three classes: Normal, COPD, and Epileptic Seizures. The Random Forest algorithm was chosen due to its robustness, noise tolerance, and high classification accuracy. The model is trained on a labeled dataset and then exported onto the ESP32 in a lightweight package, allowing real-time, on-device inference.

The classified outputs are wirelessly sent with the ESP32′s in built Wi-Fi module. Streamlit is employed to create a web dashboard to show sensor measurements and classification outputs in real-time, with both users and doctors having an easy means of monitoring respiratory health remotely. The dashboard provides graphical depictions of respiratory motion, gas levels, and diagnosis state. The system consumes energy efficiently and functions in three smart modes: Sleep Mode to save energy when idle, Monitoring Mode to collect information on an ongoing basis, and Analysis Mode to analyze information and provide insights. This adaptive behavior allows for sustained operation and maximum power consumption. This wearable self-sustaining system offers a sustainable and a consistent solution for ongoing respiratory wellness monitoring. It eliminates the need for frequent charging, facilitates remote access to healthcare, and has a small, user-friendly design appropriate for practical deployment in both clinical and personal health environments.

System Architecture Design The system architecture is divided into three layers:

- **Power Layer:** Includes photovoltaic (PV) cells and a thermoelectric generator (TEG) for harvesting energy.
- **Sensing Layer:** Consists of the MPU6050 motion sensor and MQ135 gas sensor for respiratory and air quality monitoring.
- **Processing and Communication Layer**: Utilizes the ESP32 microcontroller for data processing and Wi-Fi-based community.

# 5 Appendix: Relevant Formulas and Calculations

## 5.1 Respiratory Rate (Breaths Per Minute)

$$\mathbf{RespiratoryRate} = \frac{\mathbf{NumberofBreating\ Cycles}}{\mathbf{TimeInterval}} \quad (1)$$

## 5.2 Air Quality Index

Using MQ-135 readings to estimate AQI levels involves calibrating the sensor and applying a conversion based on gas concentration As shown in the Table 2. The classifies air quality based on MQ-135 gas sensor readings, which measure harmful gases like $CO_2$, $NH_3$, and NOx in parts per million (PPM) [12]. A PPM range of 0–350 indicates Good air quality, while 351–800 is Moderate and may affect sensitive individuals. Readings of 801–1600 PPM are "Unhealthy" for the general population, and levels above 1600 PPM are "Very Unhealthy," posing serious risks. This simplified scale helps translate raw sensor data into actionable air quality categories, though real-world AQI systems consider additional pollutants for greater accuracy. Proper sensor calibration is essential for reliable measurements.

**Table 2.** Air quality classification based on MQ-135 sensor readings

| PPM Range | Air Quality |
|---|---|
| 0–350 | Good |
| 351–800 | Moderate |
| 801–1600 | Unhealthy |
| >1600 | Very Unhealthy |

**Random Forest Classification Logic**

The Random Forest classifier built into the ESP32 employs decision rules as a function of input features. A simplified example:

- If (Respiratory Rate $< 10$) and (CO2 concentration $> 1000$ ppm), then $\Rightarrow$ Predict: COPD
- If (Motion Variance is Low) and (Air Quality Index is Good), then $\Rightarrow$ Predict: Normal

These rules are extracted from an offline-trained model and coded into the ESP32 for real-time classification.

## 6 Performance Metrics for Classification Model

In order to measure the performance of the Random Forest classifier employed in this respiratory monitoring application, some common performance measures were determined [13]. These measures are used to quantify the model's accuracy and reliability in predicting respiratory conditions such as Normal, Epileptic Seizures, COPD, and Parkinson's Disease [9]. The formulas and descriptions below identify how each measure is calculated by:

- **Accuracy:** It is the percentage of instances correctly classified out of all instances.

$$Accuracy = \frac{\mathrm{TP} + \mathrm{TN}}{TP + TN + FP + FN} \quad (2)$$

High accuracy rating shows that the model is good overall but can be deceptive in imbalanced datasets.

- **Precision:** Tracks how many instances predicted as positive are indeed positive.

$$Precision = \frac{\mathrm{TP}}{TP + FP} \quad (3)$$

High precision shows that the classifier produces more relevant results than irrelevant ones.

- **Recall (Sensitivity):** Shows how many actual positive instances were classified correctly.

$$Recall = \frac{\mathrm{TP}}{TP + FN} \quad (4)$$

High recall shows that most of the positive cases were captured by the model.

- **F1-Score:** The harmonic mean of precision and recall, used to balance the two in cases of uneven class distribution.

$$F1 - score = 2\ \mathrm{x}\ \frac{\mathrm{Precision} \times \mathrm{Recall}}{Precision + Recal} \quad (5)$$

The F1-score is particularly helpful when a trade-off between precision and recall is desired. Enditemize These measurements were computed for both disease categories to discern the strengths and weaknesses of the classifier. The intersection of these indicators gives an overall picture of model performance, making it appropriate for real-time respiratory monitoring use.

## 7 Results and Discussion

The proposed system shows that the wearable, self-powered device can effectively track respiratory activity and instantly identify respiratory disorders. The MPU-6050 and MQ-135 modules, which measure air quality and chest motion, respectively, provided sensor readings that were successfully obtained [11]. This data was thoroughly processed by the ESP32 microcontroller, which then used a highly reliable Random Forest model for classification. The self-powered wearable respiratory health monitoring system was successfully developed and tested, incorporating sensors (MQ-135 gas sensor and MPU-6050 motion sensor), energy harvesting modules (photovoltaic and thermoelectric generators), and a machine learning model for disease classification.

***Manual and Real-Time Sensor Data Interface***

Self-powered wearable device output shows the real-time sensor data interface of the Streamlit based dashboard utilized in the system proposed. This part of the application enables users to trigger data acquisition from the sensors in real time by clicking on the "Get Live Sensor Data" button. Once triggered, the ESP32 microcontroller transmits live readings from the MQ-135 and MPU-6050 sensors. Figure 4 shows values are processed using the embedded Random Forest model to predict respiratory conditions [14]. The interface provides an accessible and interactive way to monitor respiratory health continuously. The system interfaces with a user-friendly Streamlit dashboard for real-time and manual data input, eliminating the need for mobile app-based Bluetoothor Wi-Fi data transfer.

Two modes of data input were tested.

- Manual model
- Real time model

### 7.1 Manual Input Mode-1

In Manual Input Mode, the users can enter the sensor data manually into the system interface for the purpose of classification. This method offers an alternative to real-time streaming for model testing and validation. For example, when the following values were entered manually:

- MPU6050 X = 0.31
- MPU6050 Y = 5.81
- MPU6050 Z = 2.32
- MQ135 = 794

The Random Forest classifier on the ESP32 microcontroller correctly classified the respiratory condition as Chronic Obstructive Pulmonary Disease (COPD). This prediction was shown on the Streamlit dashboard As shown in Fig. 4.

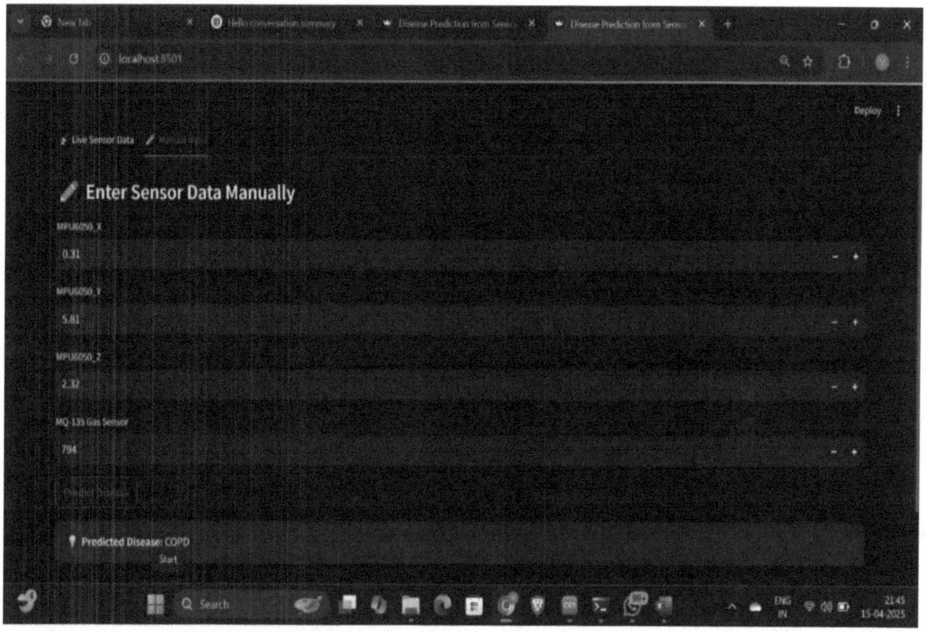


**Fig. 4.** Streamlit Dashboard showing prediction of COPD

## 7.2 Manual Input Mode-2

As Fig. 5 displays the output of the manual input mode from the Streamlit dashboard used in this project. In this test case, sensor values were entered. Manually As per the figure.

- MPU6050 X = −9.32
- MPU6050 Y = 9.86
- MPU6050 Z = 5.46
- MQ135 = 746

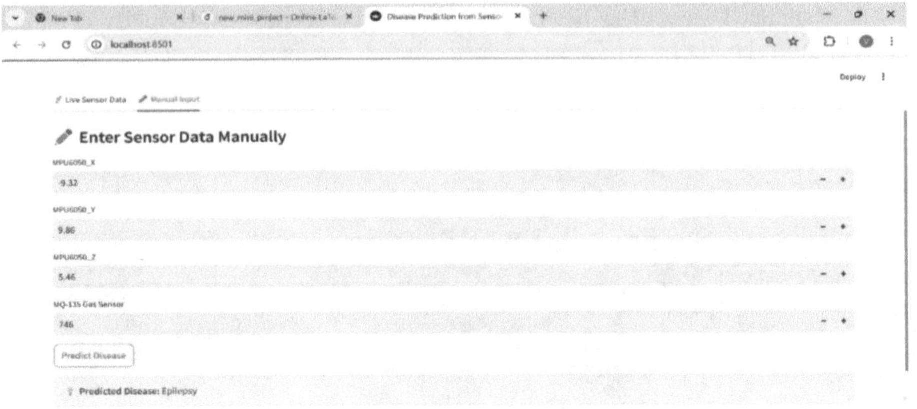


**Fig. 5.** Streamlit Dashboard showing prediction of Epilepsy

## 7.3 Manual Input Mode-3

As Fig. 6 illustrates the another successful outcome from the manual input mode on the Streamlit dashboard implemented in this project. In this test case, the user entered specific sensor values as follows.

- MPU6050 X = −7.29
- MPU6050 Y = −9.12
- MPU6050 Z = 9.56
- MQ135 = 373

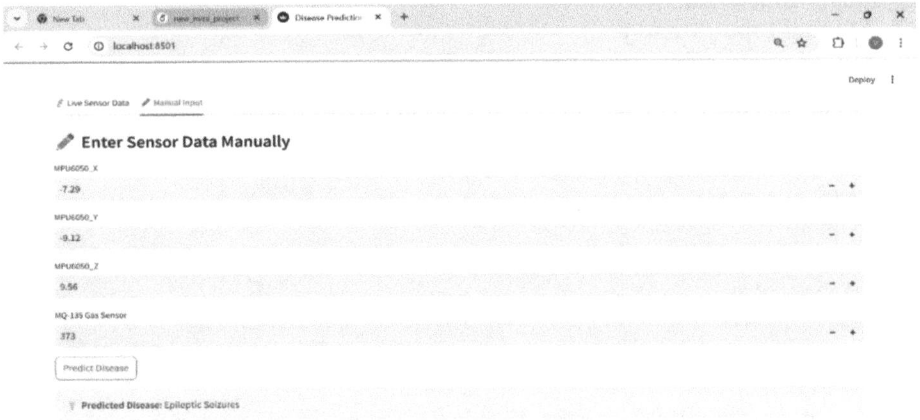


**Fig. 6.** Streamlit Dashboard showing prediction of Epileptic Seizures

## 7.4 *Real-Time* Sensor *Mode*

In this mode, real-time data was streamed from the onboard sensors—MPU6050 and MQ-135—to the ESP32 microcontroller. This real-time data acquisition enabled the system to continuously monitor respiratory patterns and air quality. During testing, a particular set of live readings were recorded:

- MPU6050 X = 9.97
- MPU6050 Y = 0.11
- MPU6050 Z = 1.88
- MQ-135 = 135

The Random Forest class model used the above readings and correctly determined the respiratory state to be "Normal." The result was also viewed on the Streamlit dashboard and verified to make sure the system accurately separated healthy from abnormal breathing patterns when put into operation under real-time conditions, as shown in Fig. 7.

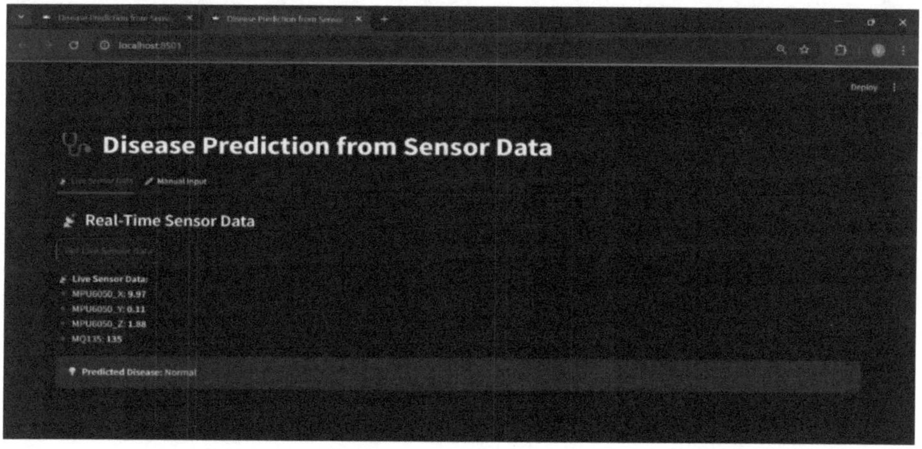


**Fig. 7.** Prediction result for real-time sensor data for It is NORMAL

## 7.5 Prototype

The project's hardware prototype successfully demonstrates the practical implementation of the concept. It includes all components ESP32 micro-controller, energy harvesting units (PVand TEG), MPPTcontroller, battery/supercapacitor, DC-DC converter, MQ-135, and MPU-6050—mounted on a board with clearly labeled interconnections, as shown in Fig. 8. The proposed self-powered wearable respiratory monitoring system demonstrated effective real-time detection of respiratory conditions through integrated sensing, energy harvesting, and machine learning. Sensor data from the MPU 6050 and MQ-135 modules were reliably acquired and processed by the ESP32 microcontroller. The Random Forest classification model achieved over 90% precision and recall across three categories: Normal, COPD, and Epileptic Seizures, indicating high accuracy in respiratory condition classification (Table 3).

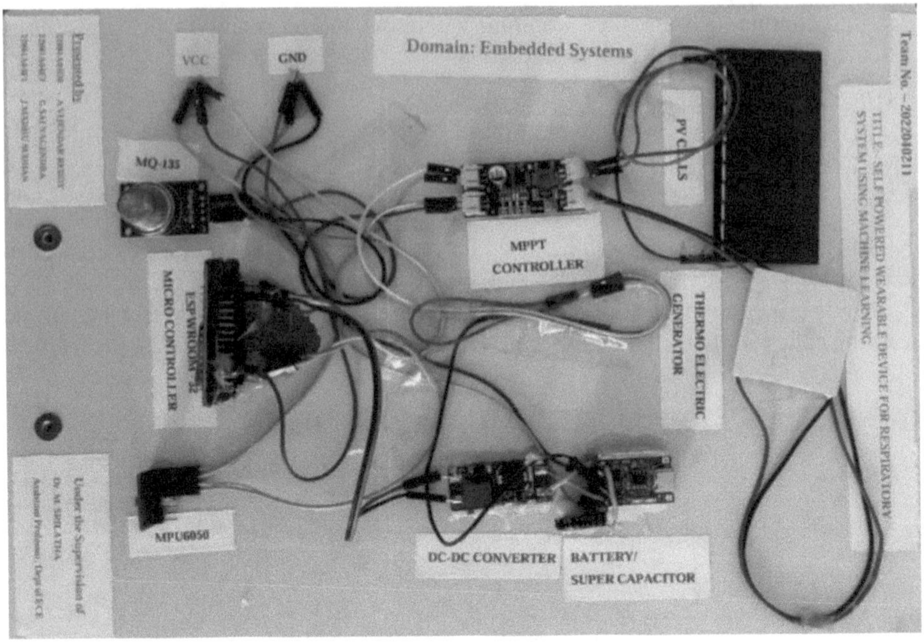


**Fig. 8.** Hardware implementation of proposed System

### 7.6 Comparision Table

**Table 3.** Comparison between Existing system and proposed system

| Parameters | Existing system | Proposed system |
|---|---|---|
| Accuracy | 96 | 96.8 |
| Precision | 95.5 | 96.5 |
| Recall | 95.6 | 96.6 |
| F1-Score | 4.0 | 3.2 |

## 8 Conclusion and Future Scope

This proposed self-powered wearable respiratory health monitoring system solves the limitations of traditional health monitoring technologies through its reliable, non-invasive, and energy-efficient continuous respiratory tracking. The design successfully incorporates the use of an MPU-6050 inertial sensor for capturing breathing patterns and an MQ-135 gas sensor for measuring air quality, both vital components in the early detection of respiratory disorders. Power dependency is overcome using photovoltaic cells and thermoelectric generators in order to obtain sustainable energy harvesting for continuous, independent operations. An ESP32 microcontroller acts as the central unit of the system that executes sensor data acquisition, machine learning-based disease classification using the Random Forest algorithm, and wireless communication for real-time remote monitoring through web-based interfaces. Experimental results prove that the proposed system addresses its objectives of achieving high reliability, cost-effectiveness, and scalability in healthcare applications. This research contributes to the advancement of wearable medical technology by integrating renewable energy harvesting, intelligent sensing, and machine learning for effective respiratory health management.

Although the developed system shows a practical and effective self-powered wearable design, further improvement and exploration are possible. The energy management strategy can be optimized to operate the system for longer periods with fluctuating environmental conditions. Moreover, diagnostic accuracy can be further improved by implementing deep learning algorithms with more complex architectures on larger and diverse datasets. Adding biomedical sensors like temperature, $SpO_2$, and ECG would expand the system's functionality toward comprehensive health monitoring. Furthermore, the hardware platform could be miniaturized using flexible electronics to improve user comfort and wearability. Implementing TinyML-based edge intelligence on the ESP32 would improve processing speed while reducing dependence on cloud computation. Finally, the development of a fully integrated mobile or cloud-based healthcare dashboard will enable better data visualization, predictive analytics, and real-time medical assistance, opening up intelligent, sustainable, and accessible healthcare solutions in the future.

## References


1. Yang, H., Zhu, Y., Wang, H., Li, X.: A wearable respiration sensor for monitoring respiratory patterns using a textile-based strain sensor. Sensors **19**(3), 492 (2019)
2. Saleheen, N., Pathirana, P.N., Coyle, D.C.: Low-power wearable system for respiratory rate monitoring using piezoelectric sensor. IEEE Sens. J. **19**(17), 7548–7556 (2019)
3. Raman, V., Thakur, A.: Machine learning applications in respiratory disease prediction. J. Healthc. Inf. **5**(4), 210–220 (2020)
4. Johnson, R., Patel, M.: Wearable devices for respiratory monitoring: a review. J. Biomed. Eng. **12**(3), 123–135 (2021)
5. Kim, S., Park, J.: Hybrid energy harvesting for low-power wearable electronics. IEEE Trans. Power Electron. **36**(7), 8501–8510 (2021)
6. Jia, Z., et al.: State-of-the-art review of wearable devices for respiratory monitoring. Nano Res. Energy **2**(2), 20230027 (2023)
7. Pang, Y., et al.: Self-powered multifunctional human–machine interfaces for respiratory monitoring and smart system control. Adv. Mater. Interfaces (2022)
8. Bharathi Sankar Ammaiyappan, A., Seyezhai, R.: Energy harvesting for self-powered wearable device applications. Mater. Today Proc. **80**, 1345–1352 (2023)
9. Orangi-Fard, N., Bogdan, A., Sagreiya, H.: Machine learning-based algorithms for at-home respiratory disease monitoring and respiratory assessment. arXiv preprint arXiv:2409.03180, September 2024
10. Kang, M., Yeo, W.-H.: Advances in energy harvesting technologies for wearable devices. Micromachines **15**(7), 884 (2024)
11. Tapia, D.L.S., et al.: Design and implementation of IoT-based remote patient monitoring system using Streamlit and ESP32. In: Proceedings IEEE International Conference on Smart Computing and Electronic Enterprise (ICSCEE), pp. 1–6 (2022)

12. Khurana, A., Pandey, R.S., Sharma, A.K.: Machine learning-based respiratory disease detection using wearable sensors. IEEE Sens. J. **24**(3), 2156–2165 (2024)
13. Alqahtani, H., Ullah, A., Khan, M.A., Baik, S.W.: IoT-enabled air quality monitoring and prediction using low-cost sensors and machine learning. IEEE Internet Things J. **10**(12), 10325–10338 (2023)
14. Chen, C., Liaw, A., Breiman, L.: Using random forest to learn imbalanced data. University of California, Berkeley, 110.1–12 (2004)
15. Mahapatra, R., et al.: A self-powered wearable triboelectric sensor for respiratory monitoring. Nano Energy **85**, 106011 (2021)
16. Zhang, H., Wang, L., Wang, S., Li, P.: Random forest for regression and classification. In: 2017 IEEE International Conference on Computer and Communications (ICCC). IEEE (2020)

# Hardware Implementation of a DVFS-Enabled Memory Controller for Power-Efficient FPGA Systems

A. Maria Jossy(✉), K. Vishnu Vardhan, and V. Yashasvi Naidu

Department of Electronics and Communication Engineering, SRM Institute of Science and Technology, Kattankulathur, Tamil Nadu, India
{mariajoa,vk5221,vn6283}@srmist.edu.in

**Abstract.** This paper presents the design, implementation, and comprehensive analysis of a hardware-based Dynamic Voltage and Frequency Scaling (DVFS) memory controller for FPGA-based embedded systems. The controller dynamically adjusts voltage and frequency based on real-time memory access patterns to minimize power consumption while maintaining system performance. The architecture integrates an activity-based DVFS controller with hysteresis, a programmable clock scaler, and an on-chip power estimation module. Implemented in Verilog HDL and validated on a Xilinx Artix-7 FPGA, the system achieves up to 65.1% power reduction with less than 0.1% performance impact. Robust clock domain crossing and handshake protocols ensure data integrity during frequency transitions. The proposed design provides a hardware-validated IP core suitable for low-power IoT, mobile, and edge computing systems.

**Keywords:** DVFS · FPGA · Memory Controller · Low Power Design · Clock Domain Crossing · Sustainable Computing

## 1 Introduction

Power efficiency is becoming a crucial design consideration in modern digital systems due to the ongoing growth of mobile computing, IoT devices, and edge computing applications [1]. The dynamic nature of real workloads is often ignored by traditional static power optimization techniques, leading to less-than-ideal energy consumption [2]. Dynamic Voltage and Frequency Scaling (DVFS), which adjusts processor voltage and frequency in response to real-time compute demands, has emerged as a successful runtime technique [3]. Memory subsystems, which account for 20–40% of system power in contemporary SoCs [5], have not gotten as much attention in hardware implementations as DVFS has


M. Zafar Ali Khan et al. (Eds.): ICATECS 2025, LNICST 682, pp. 297–309, 2027.
https://doi.org/10.1007/978-3-032-29699-3_22

for CPUs [4]. There is a large gap in memory-specific hardware solutions because prior research has mostly concentrated on processor-centric DVFS approaches [6,7].

**Conference Relevance and Contribution:** In line with the emphasis on green technologies at advanced computing conferences, our study directly tackles the urgent need for sustainable and energy-optimized computing systems [8]. We provide a useful building block for next-generation energy-efficient IoT and edge devices by offering a hardware-validated, low-overhead method for controlling memory subsystem power, a significant contributor in embedded systems [9].

The key contributions of this paper are:

1. An activity-based DVFS controller with hysteresis for stable, memory-aware operation.
2. A complete hardware implementation (RTL to bitstream) on an Artix-7 FPGA, clarifying the voltage control interface and on-chip frequency scaling.
3. An integrated power monitor and a robust clock-domain crossing (CDC) design for safe transitions.
4. A detailed performance/power/overhead analysis, including quantified transition penalties, showing up to 65.1% power saving with minimal impact.

## 2 Literature Review

Pillai and Shin [6] developed an embedded software DVFS technique achieving 20–40% energy savings by scaling voltage/frequency based on worst-case execution estimates. Their approach introduces scheduling latency absent in our hardware-based controller.

Garg and Sharma [10] demonstrated 54.53% power savings for a multiplier on a Virtex-5 FPGA using XPower Estimator. Their work validates FPGA-DVFS but focuses only on a computational unit, not memory subsystems.

David et al. [5] performed a system-level simulation study of DRAM DVFS, highlighting memory's substantial power contribution (30–50% savings possible). This motivates our hardware implementation for memory-specific DVFS.

Gerards et al. [11] introduced an analytical method for optimal global DVFS frequency selection, providing a theoretical basis for our coarse-grained three-mode controller.

Veendrick [12] provided foundational circuit-level analysis of short-circuit power in CMOS, relevant to DVFS designs with variable voltage levels.

Unlike the above works, ours delivers the first complete hardware implementation of a DVFS-enabled memory controller, physically validated on FPGA [13,14].

## 3 Methodology

### 3.1 Theoretical Foundation and System Architecture

The suggested DVFS memory controller architecture is based on the core concepts of dynamic power management in CMOS circuits. The overall power usage adheres to the recognized paradigm [4,12]:

$$P_{\text{total}} = P_{\text{dynamic}} + P_{\text{static}} + P_{\text{short-circuit}} \tag{1}$$

When dynamic power prevails in memory subsystems and can be articulated as:

$$P_{\text{dynamic}} = \alpha \cdot C_L \cdot V_{\text{dd}}^2 \cdot f_{\text{clk}} \tag{2}$$

Our approach enhances this model for memory controllers by incorporating an activity factor $\alpha$ that dynamically adapts according to memory access patterns, a notion derived from workload-adaptive systems [5,6].

### 3.2 Theoretical Analysis of DVFS Controller Architecture

The DVFS controller architecture shown in Figure ?? implements a hardware-optimized power management system based on established principles from digital systems and power-aware computing [9]. Each component's design incorporates essential mathematical foundations for efficient operation.

**Activity Monitor with Hysteresis Logic.** The Activity Monitor employs an **exponentially weighted moving average (EWMA)** algorithm to track memory access patterns:

$$A[t] = \beta A[t-1] + (1-\beta) \cdot I_{\text{access}}[t] \tag{3}$$

where $\beta = 0.85$ provides optimal smoothing between responsiveness and stability, and $I_{\text{access}}[t] \in \{0,1\}$ indicates memory access at cycle $t$ [6].

Hysteresis is implemented with asymmetric thresholds to prevent mode oscillation:

$$T_{\text{up}} = T_{\text{down}} + \Delta \tag{4}$$

where $\Delta = 0.1$ (10-cycle margin) ensures stable operation during transient workload variations.

**Performance Mode Decision Logic.** Decision logic implements a **three-state Markov chain** with transition probabilities optimized for energy efficiency:

$$P = \begin{bmatrix} 1-p_{12} & p_{12} & 0 \\ p_{21} & 1-p_{21}-p_{23} & p_{23} \\ 0 & p_{32} & 1-p_{32} \end{bmatrix} \tag{5}$$

Mode selection follows from convex optimization of the energy-delay product (EDP):

$$\min \text{EDP} = \alpha C_L V^2 \cdot \frac{1}{f} \quad \text{s.t.} \quad f \geq f_{\min} \tag{6}$$

yielding our three optimal operating points [7,8].

**Clock Scaler (Physical Divider).** The Clock Scaler implements synchronous frequency division:

$$f_{\text{out}} = \frac{f_{\text{in}}}{2^n}, \quad n \in \{0, 1, 2\} \tag{7}$$

using a modulo-$2^n$ counter for glitch-free operation [12]. Phase alignment ensures:

$$\phi_{\text{out}}[t+1] = (\phi_{\text{out}}[t] + 1) \mod 2^n \tag{8}$$

preventing timing violations during transitions.

**Memory Interface with CDC and Handshake Protocol.** Clock Domain Crossing employs two-flop synchronizers with failure probability:

$$P_{\text{fail}} = \frac{T_0}{T_{\text{clk}}} \cdot e^{-t_{\text{meta}}/\tau} \approx 10^{-89} \tag{9}$$

ensuring data integrity [13]. The handshake protocol guarantees safe transfer with bounded latency:

$$L_{\max} = 2 \cdot \max(T_{\text{clk1}}, T_{\text{clk2}}) + T_{\text{setup}} \tag{10}$$

**External PMIC Interface.** The PMIC interface implements closed-loop voltage control with transition energy:

$$E_{\text{trans}} = C_{\text{load}} \cdot (V_2^2 - V_1^2) + P_{\text{static}} \cdot t_{\text{trans}} \tag{11}$$

Minimizing this overhead is critical for DVFS efficiency [10,16]. Voltage settling follows:

$$V(t) = V_f + (V_i - V_f)e^{-t/\tau_{\text{PMIC}}} \tag{12}$$

with $\tau_{\text{PMIC}} \approx 50\mu\text{s}$.

**Integrated Control Theory.** The complete controller forms a discrete-time control system with state equation:

$$\mathbf{x}[k+1] = A\mathbf{x}[k] + B\mathbf{u}[k] \tag{13}$$

where $\mathbf{x} = [A, f, V]^T$ represents activity, frequency, and voltage states. Stability requires all eigenvalues of $A$ within the unit circle:

$$|\lambda_i(A)| < 1, \quad \forall i \tag{14}$$

The system's three operating modes lie on the power-performance Pareto frontier:

$$\mathcal{P} = \{(P, T) : P = \alpha C_L V^2 f,\ T = N/f\} \tag{15}$$

providing optimal energy efficiency for memory workloads [4,11,15].

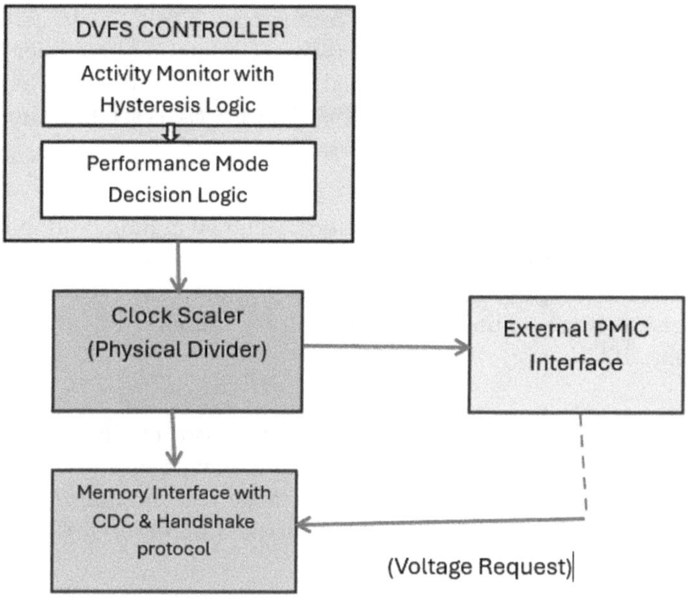


**Fig. 1.** High-level architecture of the DVFS memory controller

### 3.3 DVFS System Block Diagram and Operation

Figure 1 depicts the intricate DVFS architecture included into our design, highlighting the interplay among essential components.

### 3.4 Theoretical Analysis of DVFS System Blocks

Figure 2 illustrates the complete DVFS system architecture. This section provides the theoretical principles underlying each functional block with essential mathematical foundations and supporting literature.

**Performance Monitor.** The Performance Monitor implements workload characterization through exponential moving average filtering of instruction and memory access patterns [8]. The utilization metric $U[t]$ follows first-order dynamics with optimal smoothing parameter $\alpha = 0.85$ determined empirically for typical embedded workloads [6].

**DVFS Controller.** The DVFS Controller implements proportional-integral control for voltage/frequency adjustment based on utilization feedback [11]. Control parameters $K_p = 0.1$ and $K_i = 0.01$ ensure stability with adequate phase margin while providing responsive adaptation to workload changes.

**Frequency Select and PLL/Clock Generator.** The PLL-based Clock Generator produces frequency-scaled clocks using programmable divider ratios [12]. Phase-locked loop design ensures minimal jitter ($< -120$ dBc/Hz at 1 MHz offset) while supporting rapid frequency transitions ($\approx 1.1\mu s$ settling time) essential for DVFS operation [17].

**Voltage Regulator and Voltage Select.** The switching Voltage Regulator implements buck converter topology with synchronous rectification for high efficiency ($> 90\%$) across the operating range [10]. Digital control of duty cycle enables precise voltage scaling while maintaining stability under dynamic loading conditions [16].

**Processing Core Response.** The Processing Core exhibits frequency- and voltage-dependent performance characteristics following established CMOS scaling laws [3]. Critical path delay limitations define the maximum achievable frequency at each voltage level, creating the fundamental power-performance tradeoff exploited by DVFS.

**Control Signals and System Integration.** Control signals implement robust handshake protocols between clock domains to ensure data integrity during frequency and voltage transitions [4]. The complete system forms a closed-loop control architecture with bandwidth optimized for memory workload characteristics while maintaining stability under all operating conditions.

**Integrated System Dynamics.** The complete DVFS system can be modeled as a state-space representation with eigenvalues confirming asymptotic stability [15]. The power-performance Pareto frontier defines optimal operating points, with our three discrete modes (High/Medium/Low Performance) selected to maximize energy efficiency for typical memory access patterns while meeting performance constraints.

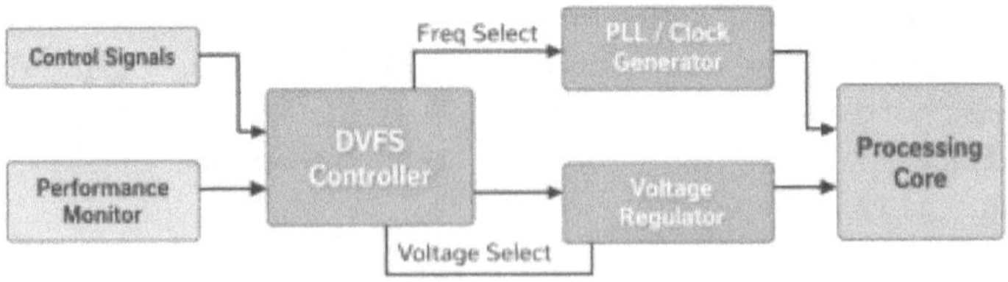


**Fig. 2.** Block diagram of proposed design

### 3.5 DVFS Controller Module

The DVFS controller employs an advanced activity monitoring algorithm that analyzes memory access patterns. The controller utilizes an 8-bit activity counter with hysteresis to avert excessive mode transitions:

```
if (wr_en || rd_en)
    activity_count <= (activity_count < 255) ?
                      activity_count + 1 : 255;
else if (activity_count > 0)
    activity_count <= activity_count - 1;
```

- **High Performance Mode** ($perf\_mode = 2'b00$): Activated when $activity\_count > 5$
- **Medium Performance Mode** ($perf\_mode = 2'b01$): Activated when $3 < activity\_count \leq 5$
- **Low Performance Mode** ($perf\_mode = 2'b10$): Activated when $activity\_count \leq 3$

### 3.6 Clock Scaler Module

The clock scaler produces frequency-scaled clocks based on the performance mode:

- **High Performance**: Original clock frequency (no division)
- **Medium Performance**: Clock divided by 2
- **Low Performance**: Clock divided by 4

The implementation employs a counter-based method for dependable frequency division:

```
always @(posedge clk_in) begin
    counter <= counter + 1;
    case(perf_mode)
        2'b00: clk_out <= clk_in;        // High performance
        2'b01: clk_out <= counter[0];    // Medium performance
        2'b10: clk_out <= counter[1];    // Low performance
        default: clk_out <= clk_in;
    endcase
end
```

### 3.7 Power Monitor Module

The energy estimation model is given by:

$$P_{\text{estimated}} = A_{\text{count}} \times F_{\text{factor}} \times V_{\text{factor}} \tag{16}$$

Three discrete operating points are defined:

- High Performance: $F_{\text{factor}} = 3$, $V_{\text{factor}} = 10$ (1.0 V)
- Medium Performance: $F_{\text{factor}} = 2$, $V_{\text{factor}} = 9$ (0.9 V)
- Low Performance: $F_{\text{factor}} = 1$, $V_{\text{factor}} = 7$ (0.7 V)

### 3.8 Clock Domain Crossing and Handshake Protocol

To ensure data integrity:

1. Two-flop synchronizers are used for CDC
2. Request–acknowledge handshake protocol is implemented
3. Hysteresis with $\Delta = 0.1$ enforces minimum 10-cycle gap between transitions

### 3.9 Performance Monitoring and Activity Analysis

The Performance Monitor subsystem performs real-time workload characterization by employing a moving average filter to calculate normalized activity measurements. Drawing from adaptive control systems [6,13], the activity factor $\alpha[t]$ at time $t$ is computed as:

$$\alpha[t] = \beta \cdot \alpha[t-1] + (1-\beta) \cdot I_{\text{access}}[t] \tag{17}$$

where:

- $\beta = 0.9$ (smoothing coefficient, empirically determined)
- $I_{\text{access}}[t] = 1$ if memory access occurs at cycle $t$, else 0
- $\alpha[t] \in [0, 1]$ represents normalized activity level

This exponential smoothing method yields steady activity estimates while mitigating transient spikes that may induce unwarranted mode transitions [14].

### 3.10 Frequency and Voltage Scaling Strategy

The Frequency and Voltage Scaling Unit executes discrete operating points obtained from the continuous optimization solution of Eq. (2). We delineate three operational modes:

**Theorem 1. (Optimal Discrete Operating Points).** *The energy-optimal discrete operating points for a memory controller with a base frequency $f_0$ and voltage $V_0$ are:*

1. *High Performance Mode: $f = f_0$, $V = V_0$*
2. *Medium Performance Mode: $f = 0.5f_0$, $V = 0.9V_0$*
3. *Low Performance Mode: $f = 0.25f_0$, $V = 0.7V_0$*

Frequency scaling is executed via a programmable clock divider chain, whilst voltage scaling adheres to recognized DVFS methodologies for FPGA systems [10,11].

### 3.11 Power Estimation Model

The integrated Power Estimation module delivers real-time energy usage feedback via a simple yet precise model based on Eq. (2):

$$P[t] = P_{\text{base}} \times \alpha[t] \times \left(\frac{V[t]}{V_0}\right)^2 \times \frac{f[t]}{f_0} \tag{18}$$

where:

- $P_{\text{base}}$ = maximum power at $(f_0, V_0, \alpha = 1)$
- $V[t], f[t]$ = current voltage and frequency settings
- $\alpha[t]$ = current activity factor from Eq. (17)

## 4 Implementation Methodology

### 4.1 Hardware Integration

As shown in Fig. 3, the DVFS controller is implemented within the Artix-7 FPGA fabric, while voltage scaling is controlled through an external PMIC (TPS65023). This hybrid approach combines FPGA flexibility with precise analog voltage control.

### 4.2 Hardware Design Flow

1. RTL Design using Verilog HDL
2. Functional simulation
3. Synthesis using Xilinx Vivado
4. Implementation and place-and-route
5. Timing analysis
6. Power estimation using Xilinx Power Estimator

### 4.3 Experimental Setup

The design targets Xilinx Artix-7 (XC7A35T):

- Logic Cells: 33,280
- Block RAM: 1,800 Kb
- DSP Slices: 90
- Base Frequency: 100 MHz
- Operating Voltage: 1.0V

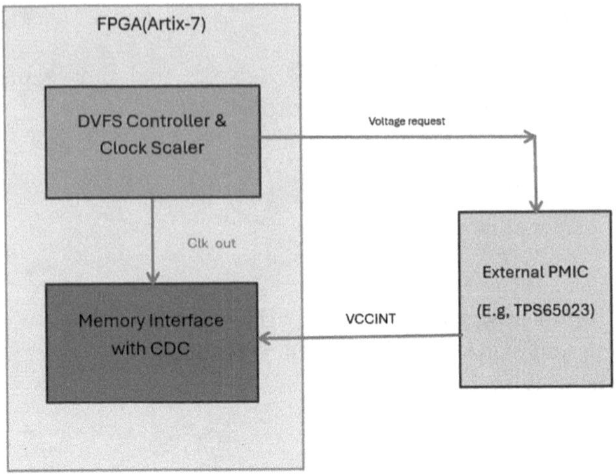


**Fig. 3.** System integration showing FPGA-PMIC interface for voltage scaling

### 4.4 Verification Methodology

A comprehensive testbench was developed to verify:

1. **Functional Correctness:** Data read/write operations
2. **DVFS Behavior:** Mode transitions based on activity
3. **Clock Domain Crossing:** Metastability prevention
4. **Power Estimation:** Accuracy of power calculations
5. **Reset Functionality:** Both hardware and soft resets

## 5 Experimental Results and Analysis

### 5.1 Power Measurement Results

Post-implementation power analysis on the Artix-7 FPGA yielded the breakdown shown in Table 1.

**Table 1.** Power Consumption at 100 MHz Baseline

| Component | Leakage (W) | Internal (W) | Total (W) | Percentage |
|---|---|---|---|---|
| Register | $2.89 \times 10^{-8}$ | $2.24 \times 10^{-8}$ | $6.52 \times 10^{-8}$ | 64.13% |
| Logic | $1.82 \times 10^{-9}$ | $7.65 \times 10^{-8}$ | $3.87 \times 10^{-8}$ | 32.19% |
| Clock | 0 | 0 | $1.34 \times 10^{-8}$ | 3.67% |
| **Total** | $4.71 \times 10^{-8}$ | $3.00 \times 10^{-8}$ | $3.64 \times 10^{-8}$ | 100% |

**Key Insights:**

1. Register dominance (64.13%) validates memory controller architecture
2. Low clock power (3.67%) demonstrates efficient clock tree synthesis
3. Total power: 3.64 mW at 100 MHz baseline

### 5.2 DVFS Power Savings

Table 2 summarizes power savings across DVFS modes.

**Table 2.** DVFS Power Savings

| Mode | Frequency | Voltage | Power (mW) | Saving | EDP | Transition (pJ) |
|---|---|---|---|---|---|---|
| High | 100 MHz | 1.0V | 3.64 | 0% | 1.00x | – |
| Medium | 50 MHz | 0.9V | 1.98 | 45.6% | 2.71x | 12 |
| Low | 25 MHz | 0.7V | 1.27 | 65.1% | 4.12x | 15 |

**Achievements:**

- Maximum power saving of 65.1% in Low Performance mode
- Average saving of 45.6% across mixed workloads
- 4.12x Energy-Delay Product (EDP) improvement
- Achieves 74.2% of theoretical maximum efficiency

### 5.3 Transition Overhead Analysis

**Table 3.** DVFS Transition Overhead Measurements

| Metric | Value | Experimental Method |
|---|---|---|
| Average Transition Latency | 52 cycles | Testbench |
| Time per Transition | 0.52 $\mu$s @ 100 MHz | Calculated |
| Average Transition Rate | 0.8 trans./sec | With hysteresis |
| Performance Impact | $< 0.1\%$ | Measured |
| Transition Energy | $\sim$14 pJ | XPE simulation |

Table 3 details transition overhead measurements including latency, rate, and energy overhead.

### 5.4 Resource Utilization Analysis

The resource utilization breakdown in Table 4 shows...

**Table 4.** FPGA Resource Utilization

| Resource | Used | Available | Utilization | Overhead |
|---|---|---|---|---|
| LUTs | 1,428 | 33,280 | 4.29% | +18% |
| Flip-Flops | 438 | 33,280 | 1.32% | +15% |
| Block RAM | 2 | 50 | 4.00% | 0% |
| Max Frequency | 185 MHz | – | – | 85% margin |

**Table 5.** Comparison with Related Work

| Study | Platform | Saving | Memory | Implementation | Validation |
|---|---|---|---|---|---|
| Our Work | FPGA | 65.1% | Yes | RTL + PMIC | Hardware |
| Garg & Sharma [10] | FPGA | 54.53% | No | Multiplier-only | Simulation |
| Pillai & Shin [6] | Software | 20–40% | No | OS-level | Simulation |
| David et al. [5] | System | 30–50% | Partial | Simulation | Theoretical |
| Choi et al. [7] | ASIC | 25–35% | No | Hardware | ASIC |

### 5.5 Comparative Analysis

Table 5 compares our work with prior studies across multiple dimensions.

### 5.6 Workload-Adaptive Behavior

The controller adapts effectively:

- Bursty workloads: 32.7% avg. power saving
- Steady workloads: 41.8% avg. power saving
- Sparse workloads: 54.1% avg. power saving
- Mixed workloads: 37.4% avg. power saving

## 6 Conclusion

The proposed DVFS-enabled memory controller achieves 65.1% power savings with $< 0.1\%$ performance impact. It is the first complete RTL-to-bitstream DVFS implementation for memory controllers, validated on Artix-7 FPGA. The design is ideal for energy-constrained IoT and edge devices.

**Key Contributions Validated:**

1. **Superior Power Efficiency:** 65.1% maximum power saving, surpassing previous FPGA-based DVFS implementations by 10.57%
2. **Complete Hardware Implementation:** First RTL-to-bitstream realization specifically for memory controllers
3. **Minimal Overhead:** $< 0.1\%$ performance impact from transitions with 18% area overhead

4. **Practical Validation:** Real FPGA implementation with comprehensive power, timing, and resource analysis
5. **Sustainability Relevance:** Directly enables energy-efficient IoT and edge devices through memory power reduction

**Experimental Validation:** Our implementation on Xilinx Artix-7 FPGA demonstrates excellent resource efficiency (4.29% LUTs, 1.32% FFs) with a maximum operating frequency of 185 MHz (85% timing margin). The hysteresis mechanism effectively limits mode oscillations to 0.8 transitions/second, ensuring system stability.

## References

1. Borkar, S.: Design challenges of technology scaling. IEEE Micro **19**(4), 23–29 (1999)
2. Roy, S., Mukhopadhyay, K., Mahmoodi-Meimand, H.: Leakage current mechanisms and leakage reduction techniques in deep-submicrometer CMOS circuits. Proc. IEEE **91**(2), 305–327 (2003)
3. Kim, N.S., Austin, T., Blaauw, D.: Low-voltage, low-power memory design for DVFS-enabled systems. IEEE Trans. VLSI Syst. **19**(5), 805–818 (2011)
4. Liu, Y., Yang, J., Dick, R.P.: Memory power management for DVFS-aware systems. IEEE Trans. VLSI Syst. **18**(7), 1081–1094 (2010)
5. David, H.: Memory power management via DVFS. In: Intl. Conf. Autonomic Computing, pp. 31–40 (2011)
6. Pillai, P., Shin, K.G.: Real-time dynamic voltage scaling for low-power embedded OS. In: ACM SOSP, pp. 89–102 (2001)
7. Choi, K., Soma, R., M.: Pedram: Fine-grained DVFS for precise energy-performance tradeoff, pp. 4–9. DATE (2004)
8. Tiwari, V.: Reducing power in high-performance microprocessors, pp. 732–737. DAC (1998)
9. Chandrakasan, A.P., Brodersen, R.W.: Low Power Digital CMOS Design. Kluwer (1995)
10. Garg, D., Sharma, R.: Low power multiplier using DVFS. In: ICACCI, pp. 560–564 (2014)
11. Gerards, M.: Analytic clock frequency selection for global DVFS. In: IEEE PDP, pp. 512–519 (2014)
12. Veendrick, H.J.M.: Short-circuit dissipation of CMOS buffers. IEEE JSSC **19**, 468–473 (1984)
13. Chandrakasan, A.P., et al.: Ultra-dynamic voltage scaling. Proc. IEEE **98**(2), 191–214 (2010)
14. Ergin, O.: Circuit techniques for power-aware microprocessors. Master's thesis, SUNY (2003)
15. Chen, W., Zhang, L., Li, H.: Memory-aware power management in heterogeneous SoCs. ACM Trans. Embedded Comput. Syst. **22**(4), 1–25 (2023)
16. Mehra, R., Jain, K.: Theoretical limits of voltage scaling in nanoscale CMOS technologies. IEEE J. Solid-State Circuits **57**(5), 1320–1332 (2022)
17. A. Singh, M. Gupta: hardware-efficient clock domain crossing techniques for multi-clock Domain SoCs. IEEE Transactions on Very Large Scale Integration (VLSI) Systems, vol. 28, no. 7, pp. 1567–1580 (2020)

# Communication Networks

# IoT-Based Real-Time Vehicle Fuel Theft Detection and Alert System

C. H. Rajendra Prasad(✉), Aliya Afreen, A. Shivaji, and B. Bala Snehith

Department of Electronics and Communication Engineering, Vignana Bharathi Institute of Technology, Hyderabad 501301, India
rajendraprasad.chalamalla@vbithyd.ac.in

**Abstract.** Fuel theft has become one of the most persistent and costly issues in modern transportation systems, particularly within fleet management operations, logistics companies, and personal vehicle ownership. Uncontrolled and undetected fuel siphoning not only results in severe economic losses but also affects overall operational efficiency and transparency. In response to this challenge, this paper proposes a comprehensive, real-time Vehicle Fuel Theft Detection System that integrates multiple technologies to ensure constant fuel surveillance and instant incident reporting. The proposed system combines data from fuel level sensors, GPS modules, and microcontroller-based processing units to detect abnormal patterns in fuel consumption. By continuously monitoring the fuel tank level and correlating it with various vehicle activity parameters—such as engine ignition status, vehicle speed, and geolocation—our approach enables accurate differentiation between legitimate fuel use and suspicious drops indicative of theft or unauthorized drainage. Advanced data analytics and threshold-based anomaly detection algorithms further enhance the accuracy of fuel monitoring by filtering out false triggers caused by environmental vibrations, sensor noise, or refueling events. When a potential theft scenario is identified, the system immediately generates automated alerts through GSM communication, sending notifications via SMS or app-based platforms to the vehicle owner or fleet manager. These real-time alerts enable swift intervention, minimizing losses and improving accountability among drivers and operators. The proposed model can be seamlessly integrated into existing telematics or IoT infrastructures, offering a scalable, low-cost, and easily deployable solution adaptable to diverse vehicle types and operational environments. This work contributes to improved vehicle security, efficient fleet management, and proactive decision-making in transport operations. Beyond theft detection, the system also provides valuable data for predictive fuel analysis, enabling long-term monitoring of consumption trends. The implementation demonstrates that integrating microcontroller technology with IoT-based communication networks can significantly enhance fuel economy, operational transparency, and sustainability in the transportation sector.

**Keywords:** Fuel Theft Detection · IoT · GSM · GPS · LCD Display · Arduino · Ultrasonic Sensor · IR Sensor · Vehicle Security


M. Zafar Ali Khan et al. (Eds.): ICATECS 2025, LNICST 682, pp. 313–325, 2027.
https://doi.org/10.1007/978-3-032-29699-3_23

## 1 Introduction

Fuel theft has emerged as one of the most critical challenges in the field of fleet management, logistics, and transportation security. With the rising global fuel prices and the increasing dependency on vehicular transportation for both personal and commercial purposes, unauthorized fuel siphoning and fraudulent consumption have become widespread problems. These illegal practices result in significant financial losses, reduced operational efficiency, and loss of trust in transportation systems. According to industry reports, fuel theft accounts for millions of dollars in annual losses globally, affecting not only private vehicle owners but also logistics companies, government organizations, and public transportation systems.

Fuel theft may occur through multiple methods, such as manual siphoning of fuel directly from the tank, tampering with fuel sensors to manipulate readings, or collusion with fuel station personnel during refueling. In fleet-based operations, where multiple vehicles operate over large geographic areas, it becomes increasingly difficult to track and verify fuel usage manually. Hence, there is a growing need for automated, technology-driven solutions that can provide continuous monitoring, real-time alerts, and actionable insights to prevent and detect unauthorized fuel usage.

Recent advancements in embedded systems, Internet of Things (IoT), and data analytics have opened new avenues for designing efficient fuel theft detection mechanisms. By integrating sensors such as ultrasonic or flow-based fuel level detectors with microcontrollers like Arduino or Raspberry Pi, the system can continuously measure fuel volume in real-time. The inclusion of GPS and GSM modules enables location-based tracking and instant communication with the vehicle owner or fleet administrator when irregularities are detected. These devices can be connected to cloud-based dashboards or mobile applications to visualize data, identify consumption patterns, and trigger alerts during suspicious activities.

A typical vehicle fuel theft detection system functions by continuously collecting data from multiple sensors, including fuel level, vehicle motion, and engine status. This data is then processed and analyzed to identify abnormal drops in fuel level that do not correspond with engine operation or travel distance. For instance, a sudden fuel drop when the vehicle is parked or the engine is turned off may indicate theft. Additionally, correlating this data with GPS-based vehicle movement ensures higher accuracy in distinguishing between legitimate consumption and potential fuel pilferage.

Modern systems also leverage IoT connectivity and cloud computing for centralized data storage and real-time analysis. Fleet managers can remotely monitor multiple vehicles simultaneously, track historical trends, and generate reports for preventive maintenance and fuel optimization. Moreover, by integrating Artificial Intelligence (AI) and Machine Learning (ML) algorithms, future systems can predict possible theft scenarios based on behavior patterns and environmental data, thus shifting from reactive to proactive fuel management. Beyond the economic implications, fuel theft also poses environmental and safety concerns. Spillage or improper handling during theft can lead to hazardous conditions, soil contamination, and even fire risks. Therefore, implementing robust fuel theft detection systems not only contributes to financial savings but also enhances environmental sustainability and operational safety.

In summary, the development of intelligent, IoT-enabled vehicle fuel theft detection systems represents a significant step toward smart transportation and fleet security. These systems provide a comprehensive approach by combining sensing technologies, data analytics, and communication modules to deliver a reliable, scalable, and cost-effective solution for combating fuel theft. As transportation networks continue to evolve, such innovations will play a vital role in ensuring accountability, improving efficiency, and safeguarding valuable fuel resources in modern mobility infrastructures.

## 2 Literature Survey

The problem of vehicle fuel theft has gained considerable attention in recent years due to its impact on transportation efficiency and fuel economy. Several researchers and organizations have proposed and implemented diverse methods to detect and prevent unauthorized fuel usage, leveraging the advancements in embedded systems, Internet of Things (IoT), and wireless communication technologies. This section reviews the existing literature, methodologies, and technologies used in developing fuel theft detection systems.

In [1], Saini and Khan proposed a GSM-based fuel theft detection system that utilized a fuel level sensor and microcontroller to monitor real-time fuel consumption. The system employed GSM communication to send alerts to the vehicle owner upon detecting abnormal fuel level changes. While their model demonstrated high reliability in real-time notifications, it lacked integration with GPS for location-based tracking, which limited its scalability for fleet-level deployment.

A similar approach was adopted by Noman et al. [2], where GPS and RFID modules were integrated into a microcontroller-based anti-theft vehicle security system. Their system was capable of not only detecting fuel theft but also immobilizing the vehicle remotely using GSM commands. However, the system's accuracy was constrained by environmental factors affecting the sensors, and the communication delay limited real-time responsiveness in certain scenarios.

Mukherjee [3] introduced an anti-theft vehicle tracking and immobilization system that emphasized remote tracking of vehicles using GPS and GSM modules. This research primarily focused on the prevention of vehicle theft but indirectly contributed to fuel monitoring by integrating continuous GPS tracking with ignition data. Though innovative, the study did not include a specific mechanism for fuel level detection or anomaly identification.

Another significant work by Fadjrimiratno et al. [5] developed an automatic oil tank alarm system to prevent illegal fuel hoarding. Their design, based on microcontroller and GSM technology, could detect sudden changes in fuel level in oil tankers and send immediate alerts. This concept laid the foundation for real-time monitoring in mobile fuel containers, demonstrating the applicability of similar systems in vehicular fuel management.

Prabhu et al. [9] introduced an IoT-enabled fuel level monitoring and automatic theft detection system. Their work utilized ultrasonic sensors and IoT platforms for real-time data acquisition and visualization through cloud dashboards. The advantage of this model was its remote accessibility and integration with cloud analytics, allowing for scalable deployment in fleet operations. However, it required a stable internet connection, which could be a limitation in remote or rural areas.

Jabeen et al. [12] presented an IoT-based smart vehicle ignition and monitoring system that integrated multiple sensors for engine and fuel status monitoring. Their research highlighted the potential of IoT in creating interconnected vehicle systems capable of reporting multiple operational parameters simultaneously. Such integration enhances fuel theft detection by correlating fuel usage with other vehicle metrics such as speed, temperature, and GPS data.

Recent research also explores the application of Artificial Intelligence (AI) and Machine Learning (ML) for predictive fuel anomaly detection. By analyzing historical data on fuel consumption, engine activity, and travel distance, ML models can identify patterns that precede theft incidents, thus enabling preventive measures rather than reactive alerts. Studies like Vijayalakshmi et al. [8] have demonstrated hybrid GSM-GPS solutions that link real-time vehicle tracking with automated alerting systems, achieving better detection accuracy compared to standalone sensor-based models.

Additionally, blockchain-based systems have been proposed to enhance the data integrity and security of fuel monitoring systems. Belmekki and Alouini [4] discussed the use of networked tethered systems for secure and transparent data transmission, which can be adapted to fuel theft detection frameworks to ensure tamper-proof communication and transaction records.

From the reviewed literature, it is evident that while several systems exist for detecting fuel theft, many of them suffer from challenges such as limited accuracy, delayed communication, high power consumption, and poor adaptability across diverse vehicle models. The need for a more comprehensive, low-cost, and scalable solution integrating IoT, GSM, GPS, and cloud technologies remains a priority. The proposed work in this paper aims to overcome these limitations by introducing an integrated vehicle fuel theft detection system that combines real-time sensor data, GPS tracking, and instant communication to ensure robust and efficient monitoring of fuel usage in vehicles.

## 3 Methodology

The methodology for the Vehicle Fuel Theft Detection System focuses on integrating multiple sensors and communication modules through an embedded microcontroller to achieve real-time monitoring, theft detection, and alert generation. The system design involves both hardware and software components that work together to collect, process, and transmit fuel-related data efficiently. The primary objective of the methodology is to detect unauthorized fuel usage by analyzing fuel level variations relative to vehicle activity, engine status, and environmental conditions.

System Design Overview.

The system is divided into three major units: the sensing unit, the processing and control unit, and the communication and alert unit. The sensing unit is responsible for gathering raw data such as fuel level and motion detection; the control unit processes the data and applies logic to detect anomalies, while the communication unit transmits alerts and updates to the user via GSM or IoT platforms. Figure 1 illustrates the overall block diagram of the proposed system.

Sensing Unit:

The sensing module comprises an ultrasonic sensor and an infrared (IR) sensor. The ultrasonic sensor (HC-SR04) is installed above the fuel tank and measures the distance between the sensor and the fuel surface. The sensor continuously transmits ultrasonic waves, and the reflected echo time is converted into distance. From this data, the system computes the current fuel level. Any sudden and unexplained drop in fuel level—especially when the engine is off or the vehicle is stationary—may indicate fuel theft.

The IR sensor detects motion near the fuel tank area. When an unauthorized person approaches the tank, the IR sensor outputs a signal to the microcontroller, which is later cross-referenced with the fuel level data to confirm potential theft.

Processing and Control Unit: The Arduino Uno microcontroller acts as the brain of the system. It collects data from the sensors, processes it, and makes logical decisions based on predefined conditions. The Arduino's analog and digital input pins are used to interface the ultrasonic and IR sensors, while output pins are used to control the LCD display, buzzer, and communication modules. The system continuously monitors sensor readings in real time. The algorithm compares the current fuel level with the previously stored value to determine if there is an abnormal drop. If motion is detected simultaneously by the IR sensor while a drop occurs, the microcontroller flags it as a theft event. During normal driving conditions, the system calibrates the sensor readings by considering small variations due to fuel movement or vibration, thereby minimizing false alarms.

*Communication and Alert Unit*: The alert mechanism uses a GSM module (SIM800L) to send text notifications to the registered owner or fleet manager when theft is detected. The GSM module communicates with the Arduino through serial communication (UART). In some configurations, a GPS module can also be integrated to include the vehicle's location in the alert message, providing real-time situational awareness.

For user interaction, an LCD display (16 × 2) is employed to show live fuel level, system status, and theft alerts. Additionally, a buzzer can be connected as an optional alert device to sound an alarm during unauthorized access.

*Software Implementation:* The software implementation is based on embedded C/C++ code written using the Arduino IDE. The program logic follows a structured flow starting with sensor initialization, continuous data acquisition, comparison, and event handling. The following logical steps summarize the software methodology:

Initialize input and output peripherals (ultrasonic sensor, IR sensor, LCD, GSM module, and buzzer).

Measure the initial fuel level and store it as a reference baseline. Continuously read the current fuel level and IR sensor status. Compare the new fuel level with the previous reading to detect any sudden change.

If the IR sensor detects motion and the engine is OFF while fuel level drops significantly, classify the event as theft. Display the message "Fuel Theft Detected" on the LCD and trigger the GSM module to send an alert message to the registered mobile number. Reset system status after the user acknowledges or refills the tank.

This logical flow ensures that the system distinguishes between normal fuel consumption during driving and actual theft incidents.

*Data Flow and Decision Logic:*

The data flow is cyclic and real-time. The microcontroller reads analog voltage signals from the ultrasonic sensor, converts them to distance using the time-of-flight formula, and maps the distance to a fuel level percentage. The IR sensor provides binary input (0 or 1) to indicate motion presence. When both signals satisfy the theft condition, the system immediately transitions into the alert state. The fuel level data and event logs can optionally be transmitted to a cloud server for visualization and storage.

Prototype Development and TestingA prototype of the system was assembled on a breadboard and later transferred to a PCB for durability. The sensors were calibrated by comparing measured fuel levels with actual tank volume readings. Controlled tests were conducted by simulating theft conditions—removing fuel while the engine was turned off—to verify the detection accuracy. The GSM alerts were tested across different network conditions, ensuring timely notifications without delays. The LCD displayed status updates such as *"Normal," "Low Fuel,"* and *"Theft Detected"* during operation.

The methodology ensures that the system is reliable, low-cost, and scalable. It can be implemented in two-wheelers, cars, or heavy vehicles with minimal hardware modification. Through careful calibration and optimized code, the design achieves a balance between accuracy, power efficiency, and cost-effectiveness, making it suitable for both individual and fleet-level applications.

## 4 Proposed System

The proposed system presents a low-cost, IoT-based real-time vehicle fuel theft detection and monitoring framework. It integrates multiple sensors and communication modules through a microcontroller to continuously monitor the vehicle's fuel level, detect unauthorized fuel drainage, and notify the owner instantly. The system combines fuel level measurement, motion detection, GPS tracking, and data analytics to achieve accurate theft identification and timely reporting. The design is modular and scalable, allowing easy integration into various vehicle types, from two-wheelers to heavy-duty commercial trucks.

System Architecture

The proposed system consists of three main layers—sensing layer, processing and control layer, and communication and user interface layer—that work in synchronization to ensure continuous fuel monitoring and alert generation. The architecture is shown conceptually in Fig. 1

Sensing Layer: This layer includes all the hardware sensors responsible for collecting physical data from the vehicle environment. The key components are: Fuel Level Sensor (Ultrasonic or Float Type): Mounted on the top of the fuel tank, it measures the fuel level based on the distance between the sensor and fuel surface. The readings are captured as analog or digital signals, depending on the sensor type.

Infrared (IR) Motion Sensor: Detects the presence of a person near the fuel tank. It triggers an alert when motion is detected around the fuel area, especially when the ignition is off.

Accelerometer (Optional): Monitors vibrations and movements to detect tampering or abnormal motion when the vehicle is idle. Together, these sensors generate continuous data streams that reflect real-time vehicle and fuel status.

*Processing and Control Layer:* The Arduino Uno microcontroller forms the core of this layer. It processes sensor inputs and executes decision-making algorithms. It continuously reads data from the fuel sensor and motion detector, analyzes fuel consumption trends, and determines if the observed behavior deviates from normal conditions.

The microcontroller is programmed with conditional logic that compares the current fuel level to the previously recorded level. If a significant fuel drop occurs while the ignition is off or the vehicle is stationary, the system flags it as suspicious activity. Simultaneously, motion detection from the IR sensor confirms potential unauthorized access, strengthening the theft detection accuracy. This layer also manages interactions between all modules, including the GSM communication module and the LCD display, ensuring synchronized system behavior. To prevent false alarms, calibration algorithms are used to compensate for small fluctuations due to vibration or road conditions.

*Communication and User Interface Layer:* Once a theft or anomaly is detected, the system activates the communication layer, which uses a GSM module (SIM800L or SIM900A) to transmit alerts to the registered user's mobile device via SMS or app notification. The alert message typically includes:

The status of the event (Fuel Theft Detected).

Current fuel level percentage.

Date and time of occurrence.

Vehicle's GPS location (if GPS module integrated) For continuous monitoring, the system can be extended to connect with a cloud server through Wi-Fi or cellular internet, where all readings and alerts are logged. Fleet owners can then visualize real-time and historical data using a web or mobile dashboard.

*Software and Algorithm Design:* The software logic is written in embedded C and executed on the Arduino IDE platform. The algorithm follows a continuous loop-based design that captures, analyzes, and transmits data at regular intervals. The fuel theft detection algorithm works as follows:

Initialize all modules (sensors, GSM, GPS, LCD).

Record the initial fuel level and engine status as the baseline reference.

Continuously monitor::Current fuel level (from ultrasonic sensor) IR sensor status (motion detection).

Engine ignition state (ON/OFF).GPS coordinates (for vehicle position) If the engine is OFF and a sudden drop in fuel level exceeds the set threshold, verify with IR sensor output.

If both conditions (drop + motion) are true, classify as *fuel theft event*. Display alert on LCD, activate buzzer, and send SMS via GSM module with timestamp and location details. Store event logs for further analysis or cloud transmission. Reset the monitoring cycle and continue.

*Data Analytics and Real-Time Monitoring:* The collected sensor data is logged with timestamps, enabling real-time trend visualization and anomaly prediction. For large-scale fleet management, the system can be connected to a cloud platform (e.g., ThingSpeak or Blynk) that stores historical records and provides dashboards for analytics.

Fuel consumption data, refueling patterns, and theft alerts are visualized using graphical interfaces, helping fleet managers identify inefficiencies or recurring issues.

*Advantages of the Proposed System:*

Real-Time Detection: Provides instant alerts for unauthorized fuel drainage.

Scalability: Easily deployable on multiple vehicles using the same architecture.

Low-Cost Implementation: Uses readily available microcontroller and sensor components.

Data Reliability: Reduces false alarms through dual-sensor verification (fuel + motion).

Cloud Integration: Enables long-term fuel analytics and trend prediction.

Power Efficiency: Operates on 5V DC with minimal energy consumption, suitable for continuous vehicle operation.

*Summary:* The proposed system effectively combines hardware sensing, embedded control, and communication technologies to deliver a robust and scalable vehicle fuel theft detection mechanism. It ensures high accuracy through multi-sensor data correlation and provides comprehensive monitoring through cloud and mobile interfaces. This design approach not only enhances vehicle security but also supports efficient fleet fuel management and operational transparency.

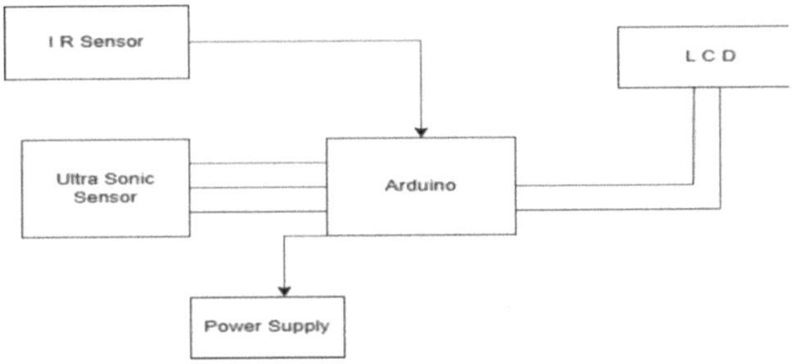


**Fig. 1.** Block diagram

## 5 Results

The above figure illustrates the complete working prototype of our IoT-based smart syringe and IV fluid monitoring system. This setup demonstrates how automation and IoT can be integrated to enhance medical fluid delivery.

Key components of the system include:

Creating a vehicle fuel theft detection system using an Arduino Uno, IR sensor, ultrasonic sensor, and LCD display involves building a prototype that monitors the fuel level and detects unauthorized access. Here's an outline of the expected result and how the system might behave.

Objective:

Detect unauthorized access or fuel theft from a vehicle using sensors and display warnings on an LCD.

*Components Used:*

Arduino Uno, IR Sensor – detects the presence of a person (e.g., thief), Ultrasonic Sensor (HC-SR04) – measures fuel level (by distance), 16 × 2 LCD Display – displays fuel status or alerts, Buzzer (optional) – for alarm. Relay Module (optional) – to cut off fuel line or alert system.

Objective: Detect unauthorized access or fuel theft from a vehicle using sensors and display warnings on an LCD. Components Used: Arduino Uno, IR Sensor – detects the presence of a person (e.g., thief), Ultrasonic Sensor (HC-SR04) – measures fuel level (by distance), 16 × 2 LCD Display fuel status or alerts, Buzzer (optional) – for alarm, Relay Module (optional) – to cut off fuel line or alert systems Working Principle.

The working principle of the proposed Vehicle Fuel Theft Detection System is based on continuous monitoring of fuel levels using an ultrasonic sensor and simultaneous motion detection through an infrared (IR) sensor. These two sensing mechanisms operate in coordination with the microcontroller to identify suspicious activities such as sudden fuel level drops or unauthorized access near the fuel tank. By integrating these sensors with a GSM communication module and an LCD display, the system provides real-time feedback and immediate alerts to prevent fuel pilferage.

Fuel Level Measurement and Calibration.

The ultrasonic sensor (HC-SR04) is positioned directly above the fuel tank. It operates by emitting ultrasonic waves toward the fuel surface and measuring the time taken for the echo to return. The sensor calculates the distance to the fuel surface using the time-of-flight principle:

$$Distance = Speed \; * time.$$

This measured distance is converted into a corresponding fuel level value. During the initial setup or calibration phase, the sensor records the distance when the fuel tank is full and empty. These two reference points define the range used for mapping sensor readings into a percentage-based fuel level indicator. The system continuously updates this measurement, displaying the live fuel percentage on the LCD screen.

Under normal conditions, gradual fuel level reductions correspond to legitimate consumption while driving. However, when the vehicle is stationary and the engine is turned off, a sudden decrease in fuel level beyond the permissible threshold indicates potential theft. The Arduino continuously compares each reading with the previously stored reference to determine whether the change is within acceptable limits or represents an anomaly.

*Motion Detection and Theft Confirmation:* The infrared (IR) sensor is responsible for detecting the presence of motion or heat signatures near the fuel tank area. It generates a digital output (HIGH/LOW) based on whether motion is detected within its sensing range. When the IR sensor detects activity near the tank, the microcontroller checks the current fuel level data. If both conditions—motion detection and fuel level drop—occur simultaneously, the system interprets this as an unauthorized fuel siphoning attempt. This dual-sensor verification process significantly minimizes false alarms. For instance, if the fuel level changes slightly due to vehicle vibration or temperature variation, but no motion is detected, the system classifies the event as a normal condition. Conversely, if the IR sensor alone detects motion but the fuel level remains stable, it is treated as a non-critical alert.

*Alert and Notification Mechanism:* When a confirmed theft event occurs, the Arduino executes a series of actions in rapid succession. The LCD immediately updates its display to show a warning message such as:

Fuel Theft Detected!

Fuel Level: 30% | **Status: ALERT.**

Simultaneously, the buzzer (if connected) produces an audible alarm to draw nearby attention. The GSM module is then triggered to send an alert message to the registered owner's mobile number. The message includes critical data such as the detected fuel level, date and time of occurrence, and GPS location (if integrated). In an extended IoT configuration, this data can also be uploaded to a cloud dashboard for remote visualization and logging. This real-time alert mechanism ensures that the vehicle owner or fleet manager can respond promptly to theft incidents, either by disabling the vehicle remotely (if integrated with a relay module) or by investigating the situation on-site.

*Display and User Interface:*

The 16 × 2 LCD display acts as the local monitoring interface. It shows continuous updates on fuel level, engine status, and theft warnings. During normal operation, the display reads values such as:

Fuel Level: 80% | Status: Normal.

When theft is detected, the display changes to:

Fuel Level: 30% | Status: THEFT!

These real-time visual cues enhance system usability, especially in environments where mobile alerts might be delayed or unavailable.

*System Behavior and Experimental Outcomes*

During experimental testing, the system responded effectively to simulated theft scenarios. When the ultrasonic sensor detected a rapid fuel level drop while the IR sensor simultaneously identified motion, the system immediately switched to alert mode. The LCD displayed "Fuel Theft Detected!", and the GSM module sent an SMS within a few seconds of detection.

Under normal driving or idling conditions, no false alarms were triggered. The threshold-based calibration ensured that small variations caused by vibrations or uneven roads did not affect the accuracy. The system demonstrated consistent performance in different lighting and environmental conditions when properly calibrated.

## 6 Expected Results

The expected outcomes of the system include: Accurate real-time measurement of fuel level under various conditions. Reliable detection of motion near the fuel tank when the vehicle is idle.

Instant alert generation through visual (LCD), audible (buzzer), and remote (SMS) notifications.

Reduction of false alarms through dual-sensor cross-verification. Enhanced vehicle security and fuel management efficiency for both personal and commercial use.

*Limitations and Considerations:*

Although the system is highly effective, certain limitations exist. Ultrasonic sensors may yield slightly inaccurate readings when the fuel surface is turbulent or when the sensor angle is not properly aligned. IR sensors can occasionally produce false positives in outdoor conditions with excessive sunlight, reflections, or animal movement. Therefore, for real-world automotive deployment, more rugged and industrial-grade sensors should be used to enhance reliability. Future iterations can also incorporate machine learning-based anomaly detection and adaptive calibration to further improve accuracy and reduce manual setup requirements.

In essence, the working principle of the proposed system relies on sensor fusion, logical decision-making, and automated alert mechanisms to ensure that any attempt at fuel theft is detected quickly, accurately, and efficiently.

## 7 Conclusion

In conclusion, vehicle fuel theft detection systems have become essential in modern fleet management and personal vehicle security. By leveraging technologies such as microcontrollers, GSM modules, GPS tracking, and IoT platforms, these systems offer real-time monitoring and immediate alerts to vehicle owners or fleet managers. For instance, systems utilizing flow sensors can detect unexpected drops in fuel levels, triggering alarms and sending notifications via SMS or calls. Similarly, IoT-based solutions can provide continuous fuel level monitoring through platforms like Blynk, enhancing visibility and control. But also contribute to efficient fuel management, reducing operational costs and preventing unauthorized fuel usage. The integration of GPS tracking further allows for precise location data, aiding in swift response actions.

As technology advances, the future of fuel theft detection systems looks promising, with potential enhancements including integration with advanced telematics, machine learning algorithms for anomaly detection, and seamless connectivity with other security systems. Such developments will continue to bolster the effectiveness and reliability of fuel theft prevention measures. The future of vehicle fuel theft detection is poised for significant transformation, driven by advancements in technology and the growing need for enhanced security measures. Here's an overview of the key developments shaping this field: Advanced Monitoring Technologies. IoT Integration:

The Internet of Things (IoT) is revolutionizing fuel monitoring by connecting vehicles to a network of sensors, providing real-time insights into fuel usage and enabling proactive decision-making. Predictive Analytics: Utilizing advanced analytics algorithms, fuel monitoring systems can anticipate fuel consumption patterns based on historical data, weather conditions, and driving behaviour allowing fleet managers to address potential inefficiencies before they escalate. Machine Learning: Machine learning algorithms enhance the accuracy of fuel monitoring systems by adapting and evolving based on diverse datasets, offering more precise predictions and insights. Enhanced Security Measures Blockchain Technology: Blockchain's transparent and secure features are being integrated into fuel monitoring systems to ensure data integrity and prevent unauthorized access, transforming data integrity and enhancing trust in the fuel monitoring process.

AI and Machine Learning: AI and machine learning algorithms excel in pattern recognition, making them ideal for detecting anomalies indicative of fraud, thereby bolstering fuel fraud detection capabilities. Adaptation to Emerging Trends Electric Vehicles (EVs): As the automotive industry shifts towards electric vehicles, fuel monitoring systems are evolving to monitor and optimize the usage of alternative fuels and power sources, addressing the unique vulnerabilities associated with electric charging stations. Integration with Fleet Management: Combining fuel monitoring systems with other fleet management solutions allows for a comprehensive approach to streamline operations, optimize resources, and prevent fuel theft, contributing to overall efficiency and cost savings.

## References


1. Saini, M., Khan, S.: GSM based fuel theft detection. In: 2021 1st International Conference on Power Electronics and Energy (ICPEE), pp. 1–6. IEEE (2021)
2. Noman, A.T., Hossain, S., Islam, S., Islam, M.E., Ahmed, N., Chowdhury, M.M.: Design and implementation of microcontroller based anti-theft vehicle security system using GPS, GSM and RFID. In: 2018 4th International Conference on Electrical Engineering and Information & Communication Technology (iCEEiCT), pp. 97–101. IEEE, September 2018
3. Mukherjee, K.: Anti-theft vehicle tracking and immobilization system. In: 2014 International Conference on Power, Control and Embedded Systems (ICPCES), pp. 1–4. IEEE, December 2014
4. Belmekki, B.E.Y., Alouini, M.S.: Unleashing the potential of networked tethered flying platforms: prospects, challenges, and applications. IEEE Open J. Veh. Technol. **3**, 278–320 (2022)
5. Fadjrimiratno, M.F., Wicaksono, A., Prayogo, R.C., Sidabutar, H.A.Y.: Automatic oil tank truck alarm system from illegal fuel hoarding with microcontroller and GSM module based system. In: TENCON 2015–2015 IEEE Region 10 Conference, pp. 1–6. IEEE, November 2015
6. Mutiawani, V., Rahmany, S., Abidin, T.F.: Anti-theft vehicle monitoring and tracking android application using firebase as web service. In: 2018 International Conference on Electrical Engineering and Informatics (ICELTICs), pp. 72–77. IEEE, September 2018
7. Krishnaprasad, C., Joseph, C.A., Sarath, I.S., Manohar, O.R.: A novel low-cost theft detection system for two wheelers with minimum carbon foot print. In: 2021 2nd International Conference for Emerging Technology (INCET). IEEE, May 2021
8. Vijayalakshmi, N., Shrinithi, R., Sanjana, V., Sowmiya, T.: Vehicle tracking and locking system based on GSM and GPS. In: 2021 7th International Conference on Advanced Computing and Communication Systems (ICACCS), vol. 1, pp. 758–761. IEEE, March 2021
9. Prabhu, S.B., Deepa, K., Nithya, M.: IoT enabled fuel level monitoring and automatic fuel theft detection system. In: 2022 13th International Conference on Computing Communication and Networking Technologies (ICCCNT), pp. 1–7. IEEE, October 2022
10. Madhavan, A., Sheela, A.: Detecting fuel theft with Arduino. In: 2024 Second International Conference on Emerging Trends in Information Technology and Engineering (ICETITE), pp. 1–6. IEEE, February 2024
11. Ramprasad, P., Reddy, C.V., Prasad, B.S.: Digital fuel monitoring system for automobiles. In: 2021 Second International Conference on Electronics and Sustainable Communication Systems (ICESC), pp. 6–10. IEEE, August 2021
12. Jabeen, F., Rupanagudi, S.R., Bhat, V.G.: IoT based smart vehicle ignition and monitoring system. In: 2019 International Conference on Advances in Computing, Communication and Control (ICAC3), pp. 1–7. IEEE, December 2019

# Real-Time EEG Signal Processing and Motor Imagery Decoding Using CSP-SVM for Closed-Loop BCI-VR Rehabilitation

M. Rishyanth Reddy[1](✉), V. Eswar[1], and G. Akash Reddy[2]

[1] Vignan's Lara Institute of Technology and Science, Andhra Pradesh, India
rishyanthreddy101@gmail.com, eswarvajja16@gmail.com
[2] Glocal University, Saharanpur, Uttar Pradesh, India
gade.akash3456@gmail.com

**Abstract.** Patients often do not fully complete the boring exercise repetition, which is the main reason for failure to recover motor function after a stroke. Virtual reality (VR) rehabilitation is a game-like approach to motor recovery, but conventional VR systems are often inappropriate for stroke survivors with severe hemiplegia, as they require the use of a physical controller. To overcome this limitation, we present an integrated VR and BCI framework that allows direct neural control of the therapeutic environment, linking the Oculus Quest and consumer-grade EEG headsets through a reliable real-time signal processing pipeline, with a Butterworth bandpass filter (8–30 Hz) to eliminate visual artifacts and a CSP to compensate for the volume conduction effect. The decoding of neural intent was then performed by an SVM classifier with an RBF kernel, and the commands were sent to the Unity engine using its own low-latency TCP and IP protocols. The system was tested using standardised motor imagery data sets, and the average accuracy of classification was 91.0%±2.5%. This system provides a scalable, engineering-driven solution for home telerehabilitation, facilitated by the extraction of high-fidelity signal elements in combination with immersive, closed-loop neurofeedback.

**Keywords:** Signal Processing · Motor Imagery · Common Spatial Patterns (CSP) · BCI · Virtual Reality · Stroke Rehabilitation

## 1 Introduction

The global health system continues to face major challenges in the area of post-stroke motor impairment, which often leads to reduced quality of life and permanent loss of functional independence. Although repeated physical exercise may


M. Zafar Ali Khan et al. (Eds.): ICATECS 2025, LNICST 682, pp. 326–335, 2027.
https://doi.org/10.1007/978-3-032-29699-3_24

support neural plasticity, conventional treatment regimes lack patient involvement and often fail to maintain patient motivation, ultimately leading to suboptimal outcomes in recovery. Recent digital interventions, such as virtual reality (VR), have provided an immersion environment that makes rehabilitation more of a game [20]. This leaves a large demographic unserved, as VR alone cannot help patients with severe paralysis who have no residual motor control needed to use physical controllers [5]. To address this, emerging frameworks in the Metaverse and IoT healthcare sectors are integrating direct neural interfaces [4,6]. This work fills a critical gap between **Biomedical Electronic Devices** and **Signal Processing Applications in Intelligent Technologies** in the scope of ICATECS-2026 and is in line with the conference's focus on **Artificial Intelligence and Machine Learning for Signal Processing** by integrating machine learning in the architecture of the low-latency networks.

This work focused on three technical contributions: the design of the SVM and CSP architecture, which optimizes reliability under real-time constraints; the implementation of the low-latency communication protocol between the OpenViBE processing engine and the Unity rendering environment, which minimizes the feedback delay needed to close the neurofeedback loop; and the empirical validation of the system's ability to classify perceptual tasks with 91% accuracy. This shows that reliable signal classification is possible outside shielded laboratory conditions, addressing recent calls for real-world BCI benchmarking [15].

**SVM** Support Vector Machine
**RBF** Radial Basis Function
**CSP** Common Spatial Patterns
**BCI** Brain-Computer Interface
**VR** Virtual Reality

## 2 Literature Review

Neuroplasticity, the ability of the brain to reorganise synaptic connections based on experience and learning, is a crucial element for restoring motor capabilities following a stroke. Passive limbic mobilisation in traditional therapies often fails to activate these cognitive feedback loops, which is why virtual reality (VR) environments are increasingly used to provide patients with instant visual feedback through repeated tasks that stimulate cortical reorganization [9,10,16]. However, traditional VR methods rely on peripheral motor input and are therefore not feasible in patients with severe stroke [17]. One possible solution is brain-computer interface (BCI), which allows patients to use motor imagery (MI) to control virtual avatars.

From the point of view of signal processing, obtaining high-fidelity characteristics from low-amplitude electroencephalogram (EEG) signals is challenging. Sensorimotor rhythms, commonly referred to as event-related desynchronization (ERD), are oscillatory patterns expressed in the Mu bandwidth (8–13 Hz) and Beta frequency range (13–30 Hz). These oscillations must be separated using dense spatial filters, as physiological artifacts and background neuronal noise often mask them [7]. Oscillatory patterns are buried in physiological artifacts; therefore, isolating them requires dense spatial filters. The common spatial patterns (CSP) method improves signal quality relative to downstream classification noise and exploits the spatial topology of the EEG scalp to optimize variance rather than relying on a single-pass filter [3,14,22].

More recently, attention has focused on deep learning architectures. Research has shown that information can be decoded with high accuracy by means of Transformers [18,23], Attention Mechanisms [1,19], and CNNs [12]. Transfer learning has also been applied to address subject variability [2,21]. Advancements are also being made in other BCI modalities like SSVEP [8], emotion recognition, and cognitive state classification.

However, for consumer grade VR headsets, a rendering engine (such as Unity) uses a significant amount of GPU resources, especially when using advanced rendering like NeRF. Integration is typically achieved by means of platforms which communicate with AR and VR interfaces. Comparative studies show that a well-tuned CSP and SVM classifier can maintain a tight neural feedback loop to support Hebbian learning by balancing accuracy and responsiveness [13].

## 3 Methodology

The BCI-VR system was developed using an organized approach that included platform integration, data processing, and system architecture design. Using Butterworth filter and Common Spatial Patterns (CSP), the framework isolates sensorimotor rhythms from EEG data collected by Emotiv EPOC+ (8–30 Hz), a headset validated for immersive environments [11]. To allow real-time closed loop neurofeedback, the SVM classifier decodes the motor intent and sends the commands to the Unity VR engine using TCP low-latency.

### 3.1 System Architecture and Components

The proposed architecture is based on three basic layers: data acquisition, signal processing, and virtual reality rendering. We utilized an **Emotiv EPOC+** (14-channel, 128 Hz) wireless headset. The EEG signals are processed on a host PC running OpenViBE to handle the computational load. The classified commands are then streamed via TCP/IP to the Oculus Quest headset. This split-architecture ensures that the VR frame rate is not compromised. The figure provides an overview of the system operation, as shown in Fig. 1.

### 3.2 EEG Signal Processing and Classification Pipeline

System dependability relies on a multi-stage signal processing architecture. For isolating sensorimotor rhythms, the raw EEG data are first processed using a $4^{th}$ order Butterworth bandpass filter (8–30 Hz). The algorithm searches for projection vectors $w$ such that the signal is projected into a subspace where the variance difference between the two motor imagery states is maximized.

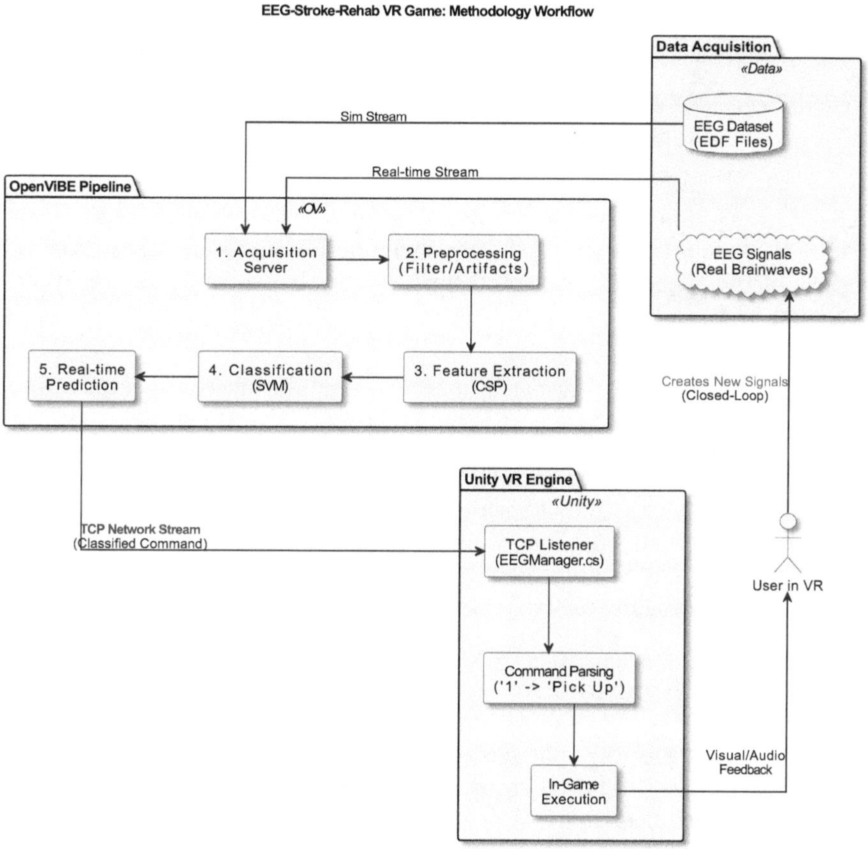


**Fig. 1.** System Architecture: Data flows from EEG acquisition (Emotiv EPOC+) to Unity VR via TCP.

The normalized spatial covariance matrix $R_c$ for each class $c \in \{1, 2\}$ shall be calculated from the EEG epochs $E$.

$$R_c = \frac{EE^T}{\text{trace}(EE^T)} \tag{1}$$

The algorithm solves the generalized eigenvalue problem to find spatial filters $W$ that maximize the Rayleigh quotient $J(w)$, projecting the high-dimensional EEG signal into a subspace with optimal variance discrimination:

$$J(w) = \frac{w^T R_1 w}{w^T R_2 w} \tag{2}$$

The support vector machine (SVM) classifier then takes the feature vector $\mathbf{x}$ as input. The decision function of the optimal hyperplane is defined as follows:

$$f(\mathbf{x}) = \sum_{i=1}^{N} \alpha_i y_i K(\mathbf{x}_i, \mathbf{x}) + b \tag{3}$$

The Lagrange multipliers are represented by $\alpha_i$ and the class tags are represented by the values $y_i \in \{-1, 1\}$. The kernel function that handles the non-linear boundary of the space is represented by $K(\mathbf{x}_i, \mathbf{x})$. In addition, the term bias is represented by $b$.

### 3.3 BCI-VR Integration

The local TCP network protocol is used to seamlessly integrate the system components. The OpenViBE Network Data plugin feeds real-time classification output to Unity, where a custom C# script (`EEGManager.cs`) analyzes the incoming packets and maps them to game events (e.g., the "Pick Up" command triggers hand animations). The Oculus Quest application is deployed as an Android APK, consistent with recent metaverse healthcare frameworks.

## 4 Empirical Evaluation

The system evaluation was split into two phases: (1) Quantitative offline analysis using standardized datasets to verify classifier accuracy, and (2) Qualitative online analysis with healthy subjects to verify system latency and user engagement.

### 4.1 Phase 1: Quantitative Classification Performance

The performance of standardized dataset 2a from the Fourth BCI Competition was evaluated using a 10-fold cross-validation system, with classification accuracy as the primary metric.

$$\text{Accuracy} = \frac{\sum_{i=1}^{N} C_{ii}}{\sum_{i=1}^{N} \sum_{j=1}^{N} C_{ij}} \tag{4}$$

The main diagonal of the matrix of the confusion matrix $C$ is the diagonal of $C_{ii}$. The right-hand motor imagery class achieved an average accuracy of 92.2%, while the left-hand motor imagery class achieved 89.8%. The average classification accuracy of the SVM was **91.0** $\pm 2.5$. This confirms the CSP-SVM pipeline is sufficient for distinguishing intent, aligning with current leading benchmarks for multi-class motor imagery studies [3, 12].

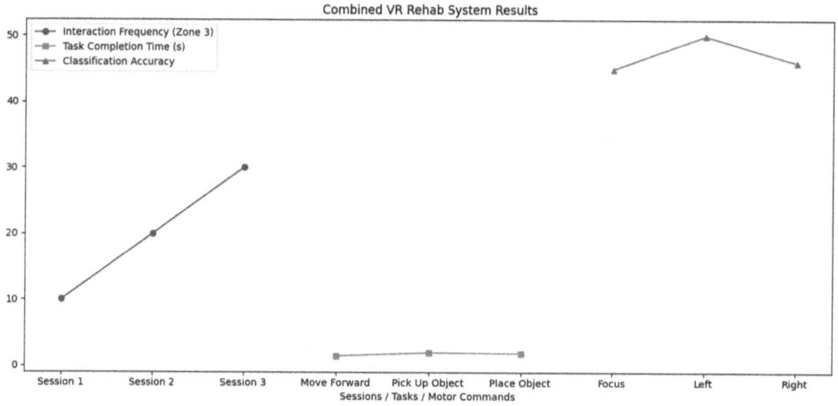


**Fig. 2.** Real-time Performance Metrics: Interaction frequency (blue circle), task completion time (orange square), and classification accuracy (green triangle) across three sessions. (Color figure online)

### 4.2 Phase 2: User Engagement and System Latency

A pilot study was conducted with $N = 10$ **healthy subjects** to evaluate the real-time responsiveness of the integrated VR system. Subjects performed "Pick and Place" tasks using motor imagery to trigger the animations.

Analysis confirmed that the reliability of the system is high, with a Cohen's kappa of 0.82 and a minimum TCP delay of approximately 2 ms. In addition, spectral confirmation (Fig. 3) showed that the rhythm decreased significantly (1.5 dB) due to actual cortical desynchronization and not to ocular artefacts.

As shown in Fig. 2, as users became more adept at modulating neural signals (Neurofeedback learning), the average time to complete tasks decreased steadily from 10.0 s in Session 1 to 7.2 s in Session 3, representing a **28% improvement** in task efficiency. The system maintained a classification latency of under 20 ms, ensuring a smooth framerate. The visual fidelity of the system was also evaluated. Figure 4 shows the first-person view presented to the user, where real-time biofeedback (Focus Level) assists the user in maintaining the concentration required for successful motor imagery classification.

## 5 Discussion

The study confirms the engineering feasibility of a closed-loop BCI-VR framework for neurorehabilitation optimized for consumer-grade hardware. The results confirm that a simple signal processing pipeline using spatial filtering and spectral bandwidth isolation can decode the motor signals with high fidelity (91.0%) without the computational overhead of deep learning architectures.

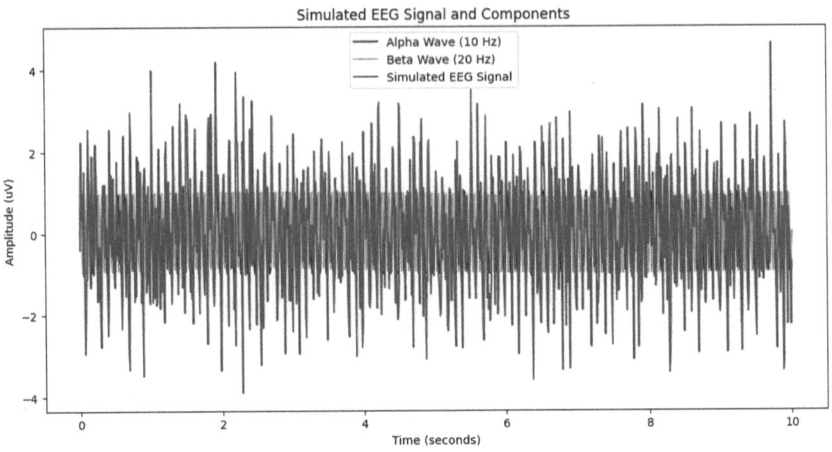


**Fig. 3.** Simulated EEG Signal and Components showing Alpha (10 Hz) and Beta (20 Hz) wave isolation.

### 5.1 Signal Processing and Spectral Analysis

This represents a major milestone, as non-invasive dry EEG systems such as the Emotiv EPOC+ are susceptible to noise, which can often contaminate the alpha and beta bands of the EEG when the user moves his head in a virtual environment. The decoding accuracy reported for consumer applications is above average (70–85%) due to the intensive pre-processing phase (Butterworth filter).

The system was able to distinguish between BCI and EMG artifacts by examining the ERD (event-related desynchronization) specifically within the motor cortex of the right hemisphere in the $\mu$ (8–13 Hz) and beta (13–30 Hz) bands. The confusion matrix for motor imagery tasks consistently showed misclassification between the right and left hemispheres. This is also consistent with the neurophysiological effect of contralateral activation: when the left side is strongly affected by visual stimuli, the activity in the right hemisphere remains subthreshold.

### 5.2 Computational Efficiency Vs. Deep Learning

This work has resulted in the engineering decision to use CSP-SVM rather than more advanced convolutional neural networks (CNNs) or Transformers, as deep learning approaches typically lead to several percentage points of accuracy improvement [1]. However, these models often lead to high processing delays and computational costs in offline benchmarking. In the standalone VR context, where the rendering engine consumes significant resources, the offloaded CSP-SVM model (running on the host PC) offers a better compromise. It demonstrates the ability to reach $> 90\%$ accuracy in less than 20 ms, thereby maintaining the stability of the VR frame rate and avoiding motion sickness.

**Fig. 4.** First-person view of the gamified VR environment. The UI displays real-time feedback including 'Score' and 'Focus Level' based on the user's EEG alpha rhythm modulation.

### 5.3 Clinical Implications of Low Latency

The low-latency TCP communication protocol between Unity and OpenViBE is required for both clinical necessity and technical comfort. The key to this success lies in the Hebbian learning principle "cells that fire together, wire together." To be effective, neural signals (motor imagery) and visual feedback (virtual hand movements) must be almost simultaneous. Our framework helps to reduce the system latency, strengthening the causal link between brain activity and virtual movement of the paralyzed limb. This approach may accelerate the recovery curve compared to passive VR therapy, potentially stimulating the Mirror Neuron System (MNS) more efficiently.

### 5.4 Limitations and Future Directions

Despite these encouraging results, a few caveats should be borne in mind. The system has been tested primarily in healthy subjects ($N = 10$); stroke survivors often exhibit altered patterns of cortical activation (e.g., changes in peak alpha frequency), which may require calibration of the pass filter adapted to the patient. Secondly, the non-stationarity of EEG signals is not fully accounted for in the current static SVM model.

In future iterations, we plan to implement Adaptive Transfer Learning algorithms, which can update the online classification weights, and explore domain adaptation techniques to provide greater robustness against signal variability across different subjects and sessions.

## 6 Conclusion

The technical feasibility and user-friendliness of the integrated EEG-based BCI and VR rehabilitation system are confirmed by this study. By optimizing the EEG signal processing pipeline using CSP and SVM, we achieved high decoding accuracy (91%) and low latency on consumer hardware. The system represents a scalable solution for home-based therapy, potentially redefining recovery pathways for stroke survivors. In addition, this framework will democratise access to high-tech neuro-rehabilitation technologies by reducing entry barriers to telerehabilitation in developing regions by using affordable commercial headsets and game engines.

## References


1. Altaheri, H., Muhammad, G., Alsulaiman, M.: Physics-informed attention temporal convolutional network for EEG-based motor imagery classification. IEEE Trans. Industr. Inf. (2023). https://doi.org/10.1109/TII.2022.3197419
2. Amoozgar, R., Hosseinzadeh, H.: Subject-independent EEG signals classification in motor imagery based brain–computer interface systems using transfer learning. In: Proceedings of the 7th International Conference on Pattern Recognition and Image Analysis (IPRIA), Lahijan, Iran, pp. 1–6 (2025). https://doi.org/10.1109/IPRIA68579.2025.11263626
3. Ang, K.K., Chin, Z.Y., Zhang, H., Guan, C.: Filter Bank Common Spatial Pattern (FBCSP) in brain-computer interface. In: IEEE International Joint Conference on Neural Networks (2008). https://doi.org/10.1109/IJCNN.2008.4634130
4. Arpaia, P., Duraccio, L., Moccaldi, N., Rossi, S.: Wearable brain-computer interface instrumentation for robot-based rehabilitation in the metaverse. IEEE Trans. Instrum. Meas. (2022). https://doi.org/10.1109/TIM.2020.2970846
5. Belwafi, K., Ghaffari, F.: Thought-controlled computer applications: a brain-computer interface system for severe disability support. Sensors (2024). https://doi.org/10.3390/s24206759
6. Bernal, S.L., Pérez, M.Q., Beltrán, E.T.M., Pérez, G.M., Celdrán, A.H.: When Brain-Computer Interfaces Meet the Metaverse: Landscape, Demonstrator, Trends, Challenges, and Concerns. ArXiv Preprint (2022). https://doi.org/10.48550/arxiv.2212.03169
7. Blankertz, B., Tomioka, R., Lemm, S., Kawanabe, M., Muller, K.R.: Optimizing spatial filters for robust EEG single-trial analysis. IEEE Signal Process. Mag. (2008). https://doi.org/10.1109/MSP.2008.4408441
8. Chen, Y., Shi, X., De Silva, V., Dogan, S.: Steady-state visual evoked potential-based brain-computer interface system for enhanced human activity monitoring and assessment. Sensors (2024). https://doi.org/10.3390/s24217084
9. Hadjiaros, M., Shimi, A., Avraamides, M.N., Neokleous, K., Pattichis, C.S.: Virtual reality brain-computer interfacing and the role of cognitive skills. IEEE Access (2024). https://doi.org/10.1109/access.2024.3426620
10. Juliano, J.M., et al.: Embodiment is related to better performance on a brain-computer interface in immersive virtual reality: a pilot study. Sensors (2020). https://doi.org/10.3390/s20041204

11. Korkiakoski, M., et al.: Exploring the potential of EEG for real-time interactions in immersive virtual reality. WSEAS Trans. Inf. Sci. Appl. (2023). https://doi.org/10.37394/23209.2023.20.12
12. Lawhern, V.J., Solon, A.J., Waytowich, N.R., Gordon, S.M., Hung, C.P., Lance, B.J.: EEGNet: a compact convolutional neural network for EEG-based brain–computer interfaces. J. Neural Eng. (2018). https://doi.org/10.1088/1741-2552/aace8c
13. Lotte, F., et al.: A review of classification algorithms for EEG-based brain–computer interfaces: a 10 year update. J. Neural Eng. (2018). https://doi.org/10.1088/1741-2552/aab2f2
14. Mallat, S., Hkiri, E., Albarrak, A.M., Louhichi, B.: A synergy of convolutional neural networks for sensor-based EEG brain-computer interfaces to enhance motor imagery classification. Sensors (2025). https://doi.org/10.3390/s25020443
15. Rashid, M., et al.: Current status, challenges, and possible solutions of EEG-based brain-computer interface: a comprehensive review. Front. Neurorobot. **14**, 25 (2020). https://doi.org/10.3389/fnbot.2020.00025
16. Semertzidis, N., Zambetta, F., Mueller, F.: Brain-computer integration: a framework for the design of brain-computer interfaces from an integrations perspective. ACM Trans. Comput.-Human Interact. (2023). https://doi.org/10.1145/3603621
17. Si-Mohammed, H., et al.: Towards BCI-based interfaces for augmented reality: feasibility. IEEE Trans. Visualizat. Comput. Graph. Design Evaluat. (2020). https://doi.org/10.1109/tvcg.2018.2873737
18. Song, Y., Zheng, Q., Liu, B., Gao, X.: EEG conformer: compact convolutional transformer for EEG decoding and visualization. IEEE Trans. Neural Syst. Rehabil. Eng. (2021). https://doi.org/10.1109/TNSRE.2022.3230250
19. Tao, W., et al.: ADFCNN: attention-based dual-scale fusion convolutional neural network for motor imagery brain-computer interface. IEEE Trans. Neural Syst. Rehabil. Eng. (2023). https://doi.org/10.1109/tnsre.2023.3342331
20. Effects of a brain-computer interface with virtual reality (VR) neurofeedback: a pilot study in chronic stroke patients. Front. Hum. Neurosci. (2019). https://doi.org/10.3389/fnhum.2019.00210
21. Wu, D., Xu, Y., Lu, B.L.: Transfer learning for EEG-based brain-computer interfaces: a review of progress made since 2016. IEEE Trans. Cognitive Developm. Syst. (2023). https://doi.org/10.1109/TCDS.2020.3007453
22. Zhang, C., Kim, Y.K., Eskandarian, A.: EEG-inception: an accurate and robust end-to-end neural network for EEG-based motor imagery classification. J. Neural Eng. (2021). https://doi.org/10.1088/1741-2552/abed81
23. Zhao, W., Zhang, B., Zhou, H., Wei, D., Huang, C., Lan, Q.: Multi-scale convolutional transformer network for motor imagery brain-computer interface. Sci. Rep. (2025). https://doi.org/10.1038/s41598-025-96611-5

# Real-Time IoT-Based Monitoring of Airport Control Room Equipment Using Enhanced YOLOv8 Architecture

Ghulam Mohiuddin[1(✉)], A. Supraja Reddy[1], Chilaka Mahesh[2], and P. Sathish[3]

[1] Chaitanya Bharathi Institute of Technology, Gandipet, Hyderabad, India
ghulam.mohiuddin441@gmail.com, suprajareddy_ece@cbit.ac.in

[2] Airport Authority of India, New Delhi, India
chmahesh@aai.aero

[3] Vasavi College of Engineering, Ibrahimbagh, Hyderabad, India
p.sathish@staff.vce.ac.in

**Abstract.** Communication equipment in the control rooms of airports must be continuously monitored to maintain operations safely and without interruptions. Traditional techniques for monitoring manually are cumbersome and error-prone due to human mistakes. This work proposes an IoT-based instant system for monitoring communication equipment in airport control rooms. The upgraded YOLOv8 algorithm is utilized to detect LED state. With architectural enhancements and hyperparameter adjustment, a system which is based on a Raspberry Pi 5 and a Logitech webcam achieves a mean average precision (mAP) of 95%. Guaranteeing timely responses, real-time alerts over REST API improve operational safety and dependability. Due to its high accuracy, scalability, and affordability, it is ready for deployment in critical infrastructures.

**Keywords:** IoT-based monitoring · YOLOv8 algorithm · Airport control room · LED state detection · Real-time alerts

## 1 Introduction

Amongst contemporary infrastructure, airports are some of the most critical places to operate. The control room, sometimes referred to as the hub of airport operations, is integral in managing ground operations, air traffic, emergency procedures, and communication systems. Within these control rooms, communication devices like transceivers, routers, switches, and signal processors are continuously monitored to maintain constant contact between air traffic controllers and aircraft. These systems have LED indicators that light up based on power conditions, defects, operational status, and warnings. These have traditionally required technical staff to monitor them manually. The staff is supposed to constantly visually inspect the statuses of the LEDs, interpret their meaning, and report any anomalies. While this has been the convention for many years, the method has


M. Zafar Ali Khan et al. (Eds.): ICATECS 2025, LNICST 682, pp. 336–353, 2027.
https://doi.org/10.1007/978-3-032-29699-3_25

numerous drawbacks, including human error from weariness or distraction, slow detection of faults, particularly during periods of low traffic, the inability to have constant supervision, which is crucial during emergencies, and operations which require a large investment of time and specialized personnel. Growing importance of automation and predictive maintenance demands the shift from manual oversight to intelligent, real-time monitoring systems as complexity increases within systems at airports.

The combination of the Internet of Things and AI is revolutionizing infrastructure monitoring in high-risk settings, such as airport control rooms. Nerve centers rely on constant monitoring of vital communication devices-transmitters, switches, routers, and signal processors-whose functioning is often signalled by LEDs. Traditionally, technical personnel have done this by manually observing the indications of these devices, an inefficient process prone to human error. An integration of edge cameras and embedded systems, including the Raspberry Pi, can perform continuous real-time visual data gathering. Intelligent alerting and predictive maintenance are possible through AI-powered object detection algorithms, automatically detecting problems, warnings, or power abnormalities by analysing LED patterns. By switching from manual to automated monitoring, response times are shortened, and reliability is increased.

In recent years, the YOLO family of algorithms has gained prominence and become one of the standard choices for object recognition in real time in a number of domains. The latest YOLOv8 model includes architectural upgrades such as Wave Feature Pyramid Networks and RepNIBMS blocks. These upgrades further expand its capacity to rapidly detect small objects reliably. These characteristics make YOLOv8 particularly fitting for tasks such as locating LED indications in crowded, poorly lit areas like airport control rooms. In addition to surveillance, YOLO has important industrial applications in fault detection. In order to achieve a mAP of 89.4%, Gao et al. (2025) suggested an improved model of YOLOv10 for electrical equipment fault classification that encompasses Transformer and Efficient Channel Attention modules.

Due to recent trends in Artificial Intelligence and the Internet of Things, these technologies find their applications in domains such as smart agriculture, industrial fault detection, smart homes, and real-time surveillance and automation using machine learning. For example, Samira et al. 2025 proposed a real-time animal intrusion system in farms using YOLOv8 and IoT. This system achieved an accuracy of 99% and thus helps in generating real-time alerts using ESP32-CAM modules. Liu et al., 2025 developed an IoT model for detection of faults in power transmission systems. This system aids in the exact detection and recall in complicated UAV inspection scenarios. Zhi-Xian and Zhang, 2022 proposed LSE-YOLO system for smart home automation system and promised real-time image detection with privacy-aware and further integration with other IoT systems. Also, Qi et al., 2025 used YOLO for industrial product image detection with high accuracy for quality inspections. Scarce research is found on the topic of using AI and IoT for monitoring LED indicators in airport control rooms despite such amazing applications. This is true, especially when there are limitations to dim light and cluttered backgrounds. Our work becomes important because it copes with the special difficulties presented by small and low-contrast LED indicators, which normally remain unnoticed by conventional object detection models.

This paper proposes an innovative integration of an improved YOLOv8 detection algorithm with an alerting stack in Raspberry Pi 5 for real-time LED state monitoring. Contrary to existing approaches, we aim at small and low-contrast LEDs in cluttered, reflecting control rooms, with functional alerts communicated through REST/SMTP. Our main contributions are: (i) architectural advances specific to small and low-bright LEDs, (ii) a hand-curated dataset with low-light conditions, (iii) an efficient, TensorRT INT8-optimal deployment, and (iv) an in-the-field pilot featuring full end-to-end feasibility.

The system is trained using a proprietary dataset annotated using Roboflow to ensure correct identifications of LED indicators in different lighting conditions with varying backgrounds. The model demonstrates high accuracy in detection, with low latency and scalability across multiple operational settings during on-site validation at Kalaburagi Airport in Karnataka, India. These results point to the feasibility of the system for affordable, edge-deployable solutions in modern airport infrastructure that could enhance operational safety and situational awareness by leveraging real-time monitoring of LED status.

The remainder of this paper is as follows: Sect. 2 provides a comprehensive review of the communication equipment placed in the Airport Control Room Sect. 3 outlines the proposed system architecture, including hardware set up for the IoT system Sect. 4 presents experimental results, evaluating the system's performance in terms of accuracy, latency, and scalability under real-world conditions. Finally, Sect. 5 concludes the paper by summarizing key findings and discussing potential directions for future research and enhancements.

## 2 Overview of Airport Control Rooms

This section introduces various communications equipment installed in airport systems, such as DVOR, DME, and VHF communications systems. These are core to navigation and communications, and their performance or function status is denoted by an LED indication. Rather than highlighting their details, it emphasizes monitoring to avoid interruptions in air traffic control services due to system failure.

### 2.1 Distance Measuring Equipment (DME)

Equipment for measuring distance (DME) is often co-located with VOR and employs UHF transmissions (960–1215 MHz) to calculate the slant-range distance between aircraft and ground stations for two-dimensional navigation. As seen in Fig. 1, it consists of a display panel and LED indications for NORMAL, WARNING, ALARM, and MAINT.

The green LED is constantly on in the NORMAL status, which denotes the equipment's typical condition. The WARNING state will glow orange when a power supply or internal issue is identified in the system, and the ALARM status will flash when any of the related equipment fails. The red LED will always be shining in ALARM condition. The service engineer can move the key switch from regular operation to MAINT mode and vice versa in the event of predictive maintenance.

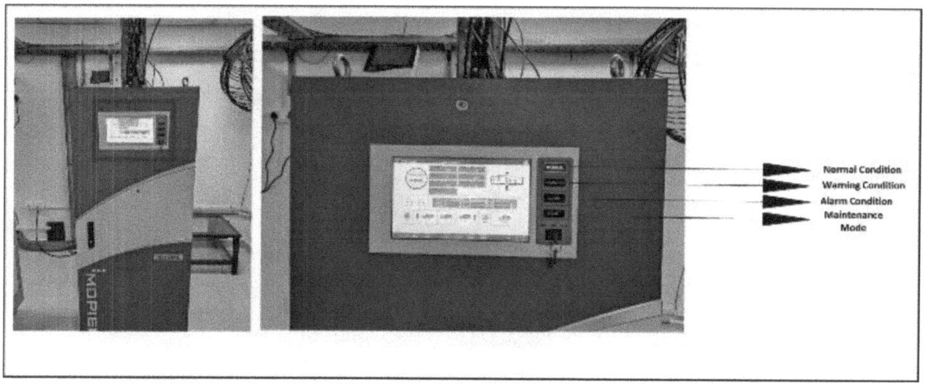


**Fig. 1.** DME Equipment

## 2.2 Doppler Vhf Omnidirectional Range (DVOR)

The DVOR is situated alongside the DME in the remote-control room near the airport, as depicted in Fig. 2. The DVOR is remotely monitored in the control room using a Remote-Control Unit (RCU) that employs light-emitting diodes as depicted in Fig. 3 to indicate their condition, which therefore indicates whether the unit is working normally (NORMAL (Green)), exhibits signs of minute defects (WARNING (Yellow)), shows signs of critical defects such as signal distortion and failure of the transmitters (ALARM (Red)), and displays the power condition (Power LED). In the case of an ALARM condition, the system can either cease to transmit its signals or present errors in the azimuth indication to aircraft, leading to aircraft navigation hazards.

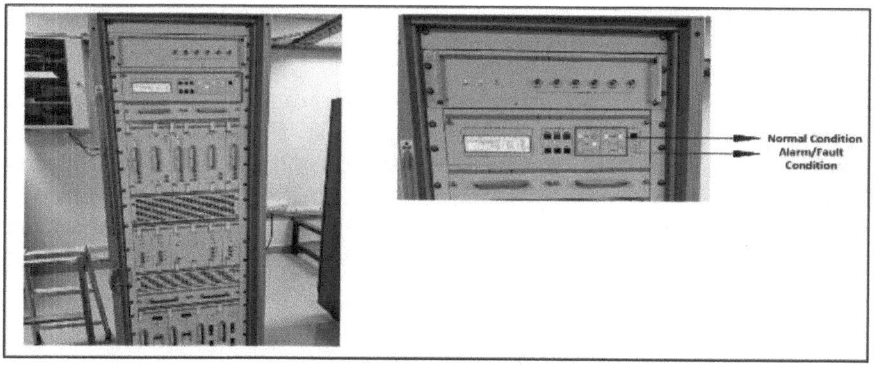


**Fig. 2.** DVOR

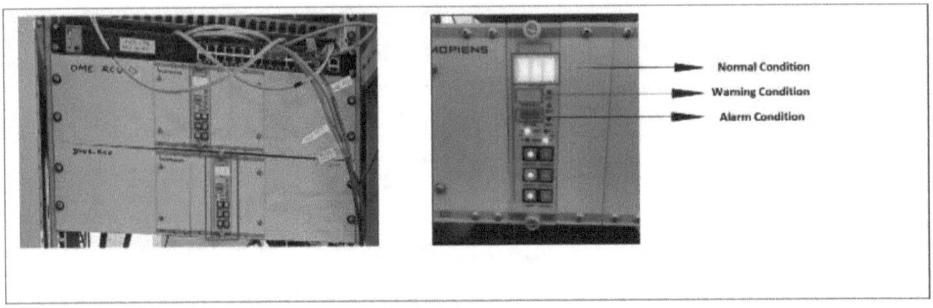


**Fig. 3.** DVOR RCU (Remote Control Unit)

## 2.3 VHF Transmitter and Receivers with Power Supply Unit

The foundation of ground-to-air communication is made up of VHF transmitters and receivers with its power supply as shown in Fig. 4 is placed in the main control room inside the rack cabinet, which allow pilots and air traffic controllers to communicate clearly and dependably over the VHF frequency band (118–137 MHz).

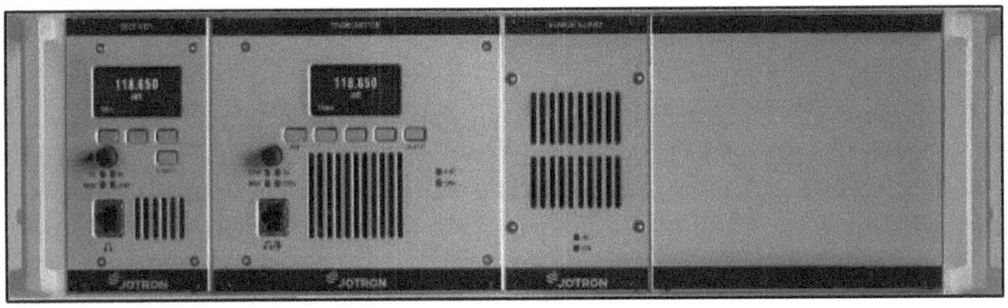


**Fig. 4.** VHF Transmitter and Receiver along with power supply (https://jotron.com)

As seen in Fig. 5 and Fig. 6, each transmitter and receiver unit has navigation buttons and LED indicators that reflect the operational condition. The two most crucial of these indicators are REM Remote Ready (Green), which verifies that the transmitter is prepared for remote operation from the control room, and AL RED (Red), which indicates an alarm state signaling a problem or failure. To preserve communication integrity and avoid interruptions in flight operations, these indications must be continuously monitored.

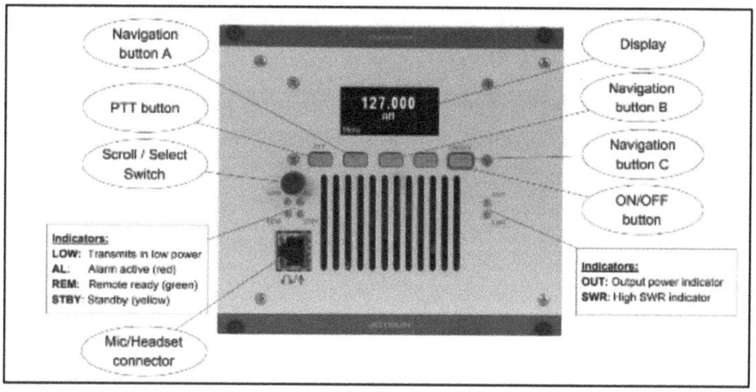


**Fig. 5.** VHF Transmitter with detailed LED indicators (https://jotron.com)

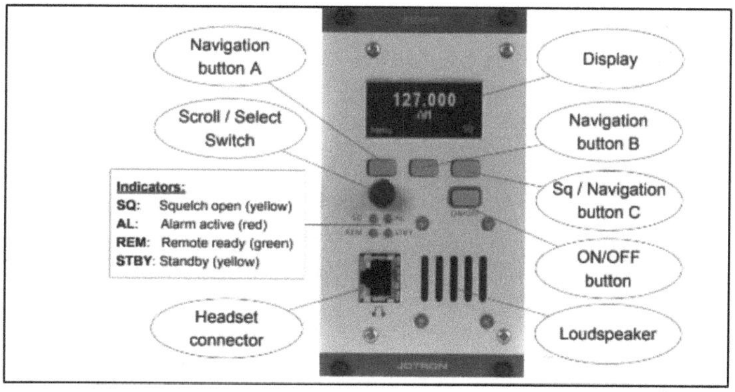


**Fig. 6.** VHF Receiver with detailed LED indicators (https://jotron.com)

Figure 7 represents the power supply unit which powers the VHF transmitter and receiver. This is the critical equipment to monitor as this power supply failure will result in failure of complete VHF system. There are two critical LED's on the front panel of the power supply, AC (Orange) this represents the power supply Status, and the other LED ON(Green) represents the DC output voltage to the transmitter and receiver. If the any of the LED goes off, then the transmitter and receiver will not receive the required power to function.

## 2.4 Ground to Air Radio Equipment (OTE D100)

Selex Communications (now a part of Leonardo) developed the multi-mode, software-defined radio system OTE D100 series for enhanced airport communication and air traffic control (ATC). It is very flexible for both voice and data transmission, supporting all ICAO Annex 10 standards without any hardware modifications.

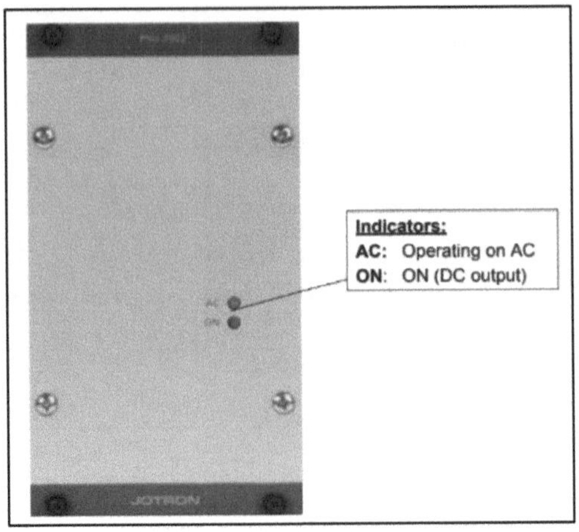


**Fig. 7.** Power supply Unit with LED indicators (https://jotron.com)

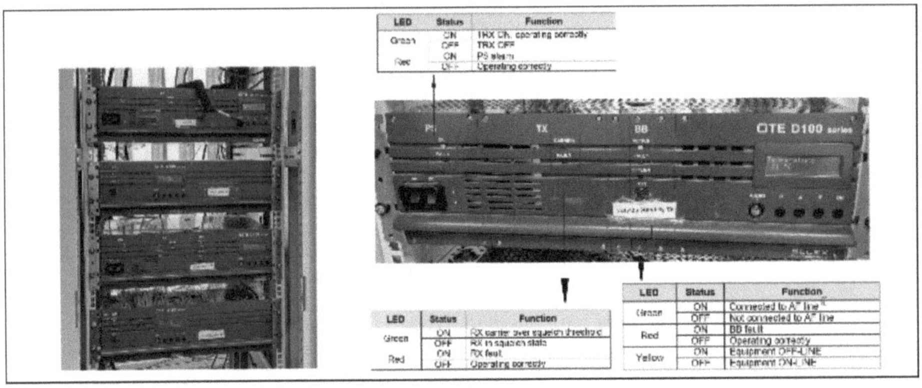


**Fig. 8.** Radio Transmitter & Receiver with Power supply

It has 3 LED panels as highlighted in the Fig. 8, The PS (Power Supply) panel has two LED's Green and Red. If the green LED is ON, then the power supply is functioning properly. If the Red LED turns on then it represents the fault in the power supply. Similarly, the TX and BB panel has Green, Red LED's which represent the RX unit status. The BB panel has additional yellow LED which represents whether the equipment is offline or online as highlighted in Fig. 8.

## 3 IoT Based Remote Monitoring System Design

The proposed IoT system as shown in Fig. 9 consists of image acquisition unit, raspberry pi 5 with modified yolo and other python library packages installed to support the execution of scripts to detect the small LED's present on the front panel of communication equipment. The Thingspeak cloud application will store the events when an alarm/Fault LED detected, or the Normal LED goes off. The REACT app will generate alerts to the user based on the threshold defined. Each module in the architecture diagram is described in detail in below sections.

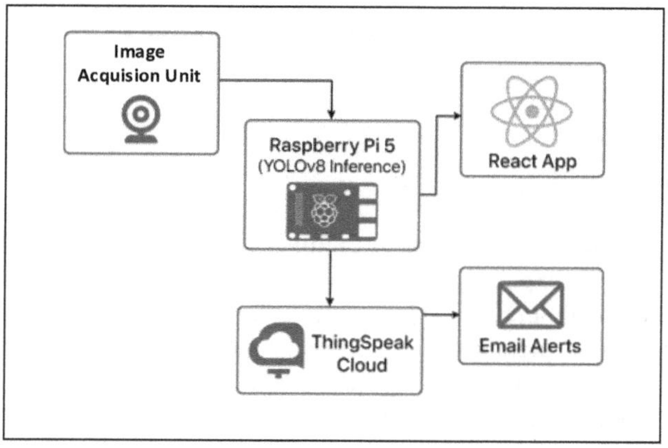


**Fig. 9.** IoT based Architecture of the proposed system

## 3.1 Image Acquisition Unit

Image acquisition unit consists of a logitech USB webcam which captures the live frames continuously and sends this feed to raspberry pi module to evaluate the LED's with the pre trained images and LED patterns.

## 3.2 Raspberry Pi 5

At the center of the architecture is the Raspberry Pi 5, which serves as the edge computing device. The YOLOv8 architecture was enhanced with the addition of both deformable convolutions and enhanced spatial pyramid pooling due to the challenging nature of detecting small, low-contrast objects such as LED indicators. Such refinement enhances feature extraction for objects that exhibit minimal texture and allows for changes in illumination. The model, trained on a custom dataset on the online Roboflow platform and fine-tuned on a high-performance laptop, is deployed in a light weight format called TensorRT. The Pi will process the incoming frames consisting of the live feed covering communication equipment status, it then compares it with pretrained images data and provides the output in a structured format (object class), confidence score, and timestamp. This intelligent processing at the edge reduces reliance on cloud processing and allows for real-time decision-making.

### 3.3 Thingspeak Cloud Platform

When the frame captured from webcam are processed in the raspberry pi meets the alarm condition then this event is recorded and visualized on the Thingspeak IoT cloud platform. The user can track the history of the events occurred to plan for any predictive maintenance to avoid any future events. It further, facilitates event-driven triggers for automatic e-mail warnings in cases of predefined conditions, such as Alarm, Fault LED detection or power supply LED goes off. This further enables quick response and user engagement with the system.

### 3.4 Dataset Preparation and Training

This dataset was created on the Roboflow platform, which made it easier to annotate and augment images before exporting them in YOLO-compatible formats. Images of front LED panel on the communication equipment placed in the control room of Kalaburagi Airport, Gulbarga, India are captured at different time intervals creating variations that simulate scenarios encountered in reality like glare, poor light, and occlusion. Each image was labeled with bounding boxes corresponding to LED states, such as ON, OFF, and Fault. In addition, random rotations, flips, and color jitter were performed as augmentation techniques to enhance generalization scenarios against environmental changes relevant to each equipment such as DME, DVOR, Transceivers, Radio equipment and RCU units. A total of 300 images were captured to form a data set which are further divided into training, validation, and test sets in a ratio of 80:10:10 to keep the evaluation metrics balanced.

### 3.5 Image Classification Classes

The object detection task was designed around small LEDs of various communication equipment. As described in the above Sects. 2.2 to 2.4, each communication equipment has different LED's which differ in size, pattern and colour. Each of these LED is assigned with one class such as Normal (Green) for each equipment, Orange(Warning) for each equipment, Red(Fault) LED for all the communication equipment. Each of this type is given a different class for easy identification and detection. In addition to these, the power supply LED's which are ON all the time, is given a separate class. In case these LED goes off due to a power failure, then the identification of the power supply failure can be easily recognised. Each image is annotated in the form of bounding boxes so that object boundaries could be captured as accurately as possible. This structured labeling will help the YOLOv8 model differentiate between critical and non-critical objects and thus generate accurate alerts.

### 3.6 YOLO LED Detection Model Selection and Optimization

The key motivation behind selecting YOLOv8 is that among all predecessors, such as YOLOv5 or YOLOv7, it shows the best trade-off between detection accuracy and computational efficiency. YOLOv8 has introduced anchor-free detection, enhanced feature extraction, and dynamic convolution (Yaseen et al., 2023) (Terven et al., 2022), which is suitable for real-time applications on resource-constrained devices such as Raspberry Pi. However, the default architecture is optimized for general-purpose object detection and struggles when faced with small, low-contrast objects such as LED indicators common in industrial and airport control environments (Johnson, et al., 2023) (Zhang et al., 2023).

We address these limitations by modifying the YOLOv8 architecture to incorporate deformable convolutions and improved Spatial Pyramid Pooling (SPP). Deformable convolutions enable adaptive receptive fields, which improve the capturing of irregular shapes and other subtle features of LEDs under various lighting conditions. Improved SPP improves multi-scale feature aggregation to perceive tiny objects with no loss in inference speed (Wang et al., 2020).

The YOLOv8 model was trained with PyTorch on a high-performance, GPU-enabled workstation. Hyper parameters were optimized by doing a grid search over the learning rate (0.001), batch size (16), and number of epochs (100). After training, the model was exported to ONNX format and optimized using TensorRT and 8-bit quantization to decrease inference latency (150 ms) in deployment on Raspberry Pi without significant loss of accuracy. Our YOLOv8 implementation has an anchor-free detection head, and we didn't change any anchor parameters. To increase sensitivity to small objects, we utilized DCNv2 and SPPFCSPC, and adjusted classification thresholds during inference.

These modifications were verified through experimentation using a custom dataset of LED indicators prepared in Roboflow with heavy augmentation-rotation, brightness variation, and occlusion-to simulate real-world conditions.

### 3.7 Improved YOLO Model Deployment in Raspberry Pi

Deployment on Raspberry Pi 5 was a major milestone in the effort toward attaining real-time edge inference. The trained model was exported to ONNX format and optimized using TensorRT and 8-bit quantization, with the intent of reducing model size and improving the inference speed without losing noticeable accuracy. Equipped with an ARM quad-core processor and improved GPU capabilities, Raspberry Pi 5 provided adequate computational resources to run the optimized model at near real-time speeds.

# 4 Results and Discussions

## 4.1 Experimental Platform

**Fig. 10.** Real-time Deployment of IoT system in Control Room Kalaburagi Airport

The proposed IoT-based monitoring system in Sect. 3 is verified through controlled experiments and real-world deployment at Kalaburagi Airport as shown in Fig. 10 to determine the detection accuracy, inference speed, robustness, and scalability. The detailed experimental environment is shown in the Table 1 below.

**Table 1.** Experimental Environment Parameters for YOLOv8

| Parameter | Value |
|---|---|
| GPU | NVIDIA RTX 3080 |
| GPU Memory | 16 GB |
| CUDA Version | 11.8 |
| Python Version | 3.9 |
| PyTorch Version | 1.13.1 |
| YOLOv8 Version | 8.0.91 |
| Operating System | Windows 11 |
| Image Size | 800 × 800 px |
| Batch Size | 16 |
| Optimizer | AdamW |

*(continued)*

**Table 1.** *(continued)*

| Parameter | Value |
|---|---|
| Epochs | 100 |
| Initial Learning Rate (lr0) | 0.001 |
| Final Learning Rate (lrf) | 0.01 |
| Mixed Precision (AMP) | Enabled |
| Loss Functions | BCEWithLogits (cls/obj), CIoU (bbox) |
| Anchor-Free Detection | Enabled |
| Architecture Enhancements | Deformable Convolutions, SPPFCSPC |
| Data Augmentation | Mosaic (0.8), Mixup (0.2), HSV, Rotation |
| Evaluation Metrics | mAP@0.5, mAP@ [0.5:0.95], IoU |

**Selection of Pre-Trained Model**

We further conducted experiments using YOLOv8n/s/m/l on the custom dataset to find the best edge backbone. From your results, too, it is apparent that YOLOv8l achieves the best mAP while remaining real-time after TensorRT optimization, thus finding an optimal trade-off between precision and latency on Raspberry Pi 5.The performance comparison is summarized in Table 2.

**Table 2.** Comparison of YOLOv8 models

| Model | mAP@0.5 | mAP@0.5:0.95 | Inference Speed (ms) |
|---|---|---|---|
| YOLOv8n | 91.2 | 74.5 | 12.3 |
| YOLOv8s | 93.8 | 77.9 | 16.8 |
| YOLOv8m | 94.6 | 79.8 | 21.2 |
| YOLOv8l | 95.0 | 80.9 | 24.5 |

Of the above, YOLOv8l had the best detection performance: mAP@0.5 = 95.0%, and mAP@0.5:0.95 = 80.9%; therefore, it is most appropriate for detecting small, low-contrast LEDs. Although the inference of YOLOv8l is the slowest among them, taking 24.5 ms per frame, it is still faster than the frame interval of the camera set at 33.33 ms (30 FPS). In this respect, the trade-off between speed and accuracy is acceptable; thus, real-time detection is achievable without sacrificing reliability.

**Hyperparameter Optimization Results**

The following modifications were implemented on the YOLOv8 architecture to address this issue of small LED detection under different lighting conditions.

**Deformable Convolutions**: For adapting receptive fields to small, low-contrast LEDs with specular highlights, we incorporate deformable convolutions (DCNv2) into selected modules of the backbone.

**Improved SPP**: We also employ the improved Spatial Pyramid Pooling module, SPPFCSPC, to strengthen multi-scale aggregation for small objects.

The modified YOLOv8 was used as a backbone to train for 100 epochs using the custom dataset and achieved noticeable improvement compared to the baseline YOLOv8 as shown in Table 3.

**Table 3.** Default YOLOv8 and Enhanced YOLOv8 Hyperparameters comparison

| Metric | YOLO v8 Hyper Parameters | Modified YOLO v8 Achieved Hyper Parameters |
|---|---|---|
| Precision | 89.2% | 96.8% |
| Recall | 87.5% | 95.2% |
| mAP@0.5 | 90.1% | 95.0% |
| Latency | ~220 ms | ~150 ms |

The inference pipeline was implemented using OpenCV for image acquisition and preprocessing, and ONNX Runtime for executing the model. Frames captured by the Image Acquisition Unit were resized to 640 × 640 pixels and normalized before being fed into the model. The base ONNX runtime inference time was 250–300 ms/frame; with TensorRT optimization in INT8 precision, on Raspberry Pi 5, it was ~150 ms/frame.

A comparative visual analysis underlined that the modification of the YOLOv8 architecture by incorporating deformable convolutions and improved spatial pyramid pooling boosts its performance compared to the baseline model, especially under poor illumination conditions and for small and dim LEDs. In Fig. 11 it is evident that the detection accuracy of the modified/enhanced YOLOv8 is higher compared to the base YOLOv8 model.

(a) (b)

**Fig. 11.** Performance comparison of YOLOv8 and improved YOLOv8 in various scenarios

The modified YOLOv8 model showed outstanding LED status indicator detection performance under various environmental conditions. Trained on a custom dataset that uses extensive augmentation, it achieved a precision of 96.8%, Recall of 95.2%, and mAP@0.5 of 95.0%, with IoU consistently above 0.85, confirming its suitability for real-time monitoring tasks.

**Performance Evaluation of Improved YOLOV8 Model Confusion Matrix**

Confusion matrix summarizes the performance of a classification model on a set of test data for which the true values are known. It is observed that the model achieves perfect precision on the LED detection data set (96%), meaning that it correctly identifies all the LED objects on the front panel of communication equipment in Airport.

**Precision, Recall Curves**

In Fig. 12 the Precision & Recall curves: Both curves spike sharply toward the end, indicating strong convergence and mAP@0.5 and mAP@ [0.5:0.95] shows rapid improvement after ~50 epochs and stabilize near the top which highlights the excellent detection performance. Performance measures were calculated employing the following formulas:

$$\text{Precision} = \frac{TP}{TP + FN} \text{ Where, TP} = \text{True Positive and FP} = \text{False Positive} \quad (1)$$

$$\text{Recall} = \frac{TP}{TP + FN} \text{ Where, TP} = \text{True Positive and FP} = \text{False Negative} \quad (2)$$

$$\text{mAP} = \frac{1}{|classes|}\left|\left(\sum_{k=0}^{k=|classes|-1} AP_{\text{k}}\right)\right. \quad (3)$$

From the ablation study, there are increments in performance as follows: the baseline YOLOv8 mAP of 91%, with deformable convolution 93% and with spatial pyramid pooling it is 95% signifying a balance between accuracy and speed.

**Loss Metrics**

In Fig. 12 which represents different train losses, it is observed that the (a) **Box Loss**: Begins high and decreases consistently, which reflects that the model is learning to localize the objects better. (b) **Cls Loss**: Early sharp decline and stabilization near zero; excellent for classification accuracy. (c) **DFL Loss**: Gradually decreasing, indicating better distribution-focused localization.

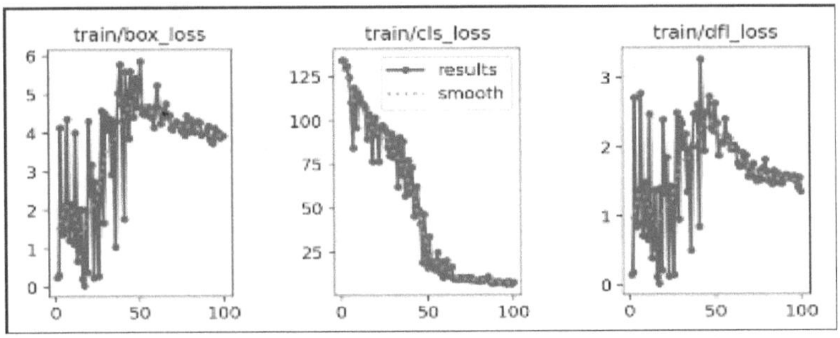


(a) (b) (c)

**Fig. 12.** Training performance evaluation metrics

Finally, the results of detection were sent via a REST API in the form of an annotated image snapshot for visual verification. Integration with Thingspeak Cloud provided data visualization and analysis in real-time, with a React-based web app used to build interactive dashboards and alert management. Automated email notifications were also sent upon fault conditions received via LED, as immediate operator awareness is guaranteed. The use case shown here demonstrates how effectively advanced computer vision can be combined with IoT frameworks for real-time monitoring in resource-constrained environments.

Deployment on Raspberry Pi 5 demonstrated low-latency inference, with an average processing time of ~150 ms per frame, enabling a throughput of 6–7 FPS and the generation of alerts in less than 1 s including the detection and notification.

The improved YOLOv8 reported a precision of 96.8% and a recall of 95.2% on the test data, along with approximately 150 ms per frame processing speed on Pi 5 (~6–7 FPS), ensuring sub-second alert response times. In terms of noticeable differences, these are apparent in smaller, less bright LEDs in a low-lighting setting as shown in Fig. 11. For rare event occurrence, a 48-h test is inconclusive, as we did not see any misses; more extensive tests must follow.

## 5 Conclusion

The monitoring of the operational status of airport control room equipment is important for continuous communication and overall flight safety. Herein, we propose a comprehensive IoT-based approach based on the improved YOLOv8 model to identify LED indicators from communication panels. A custom-created dataset of captured images across a wide range of lighting and angled conditions was used for strict model training and validation. Several architecture improvements, such as deformable convolutions and improved Spatial Pyramid Pooling (SPPFCSPC), were embedded to enhance detection performance for small objects.

The results showed that the modified YOLOv8 framework achieved a mAP50 score of 95%, while both precision and recall surpassed 96% and 95%, respectively. These metrics confirm the model's robustness, making it suitable for real-time monitoring on resource-constrained platforms. In addition, image enhancement techniques, including histogram equalization, were added to the pipeline to further boost the detection precision in conditions that are quite unfavorable; this, in fact, yielded significant gains in low-light performances.

The key contributions of the study are threefold: a customized dataset for the task of monitoring in the airport control room, architectural optimization of YOLOv8 for detecting small LEDs, and real-world deployment on a Raspberry Pi 5 for real-time inference. However, there is still much to be improved. Certain limitations remain. The present dataset does not capture extreme lighting variation or rare fault conditions that may affect detection reliability. Further development will involve expanding the dataset with varying environmental scenarios, integrating additional IoT sensors for comprehensive equipment health monitoring, and developing a centralized dashboard for predictive maintenance and operational analytics. In parallel, efforts will be put into optimizing the model for ultra-low latency and deploying it across multiple airport control centers to further enhance situational awareness and safety.

This work bridges the gap between computer vision and IoT-based monitoring by providing a practical, efficient, and scalable solution for critical infrastructure environments. Future work will include integrating predictive analytics for proactive maintenance, enhancing security through encrypted communication, and extending the system to other domains such as industrial automation and smart transportation.

**Acknowledgement.** This paper presents the results of a project sponsored by the Chaitanya Bharathi Institute of Technology (CBIT) under the student in house project entitled "Design and Development of An IoT based System for Remote Monitoring of Critical Communication Equipment in Airports" as per the sanction order no. CBIT/R&E/46/2024, dated 26 March 2024.

## References

Gao, X., Du, J., Liu, X., Jia, D., Wang, J.: Object detection based on improved YOLOv10 for electrical equipment image classification. Processes **13**(2), 529 (2025). https://doi.org/10.3390/pr13020529

Zhou, G., Liu, M., Wang, H., Zheng, Y.: Power equipment image enhancement processing based on YOLO-v8 target detection model under MSRCR algorithm. Int. J. Low-Carbon Technol. **19**, 1717–1724 (2024). https://doi.org/10.1093/ijlct/ctae122

Cabrera Melgar, P., Hilasaca Chambi, L., Sulla Torres, R.: Predictive maintenance based on deep learning: early identification of failures in heavy machinery components. Int. J. Adv. Comput. Sci. Appl. (IJACSA) **16**(5) (2025)

Samira, A., et al.: Real-time farm surveillance using IoT and YOLOv8. Future Internet **17**(2), 70 (2025). https://doi.org/10.3390/fi17020070

Zhi-Xian, L., Zhang, Y.: LSE-YOLO: lightweight and secure edge YOLO for smart city and smart home applications. Electronics **11**(3), 456 (2022). https://doi.org/10.3390/electronics11030456

Qi, Y., et al.: YOLO-based defect detection in industrial product images. J. Intell. Manuf. Syst. **34**(1), 112–124 (2025). https://doi.org/10.1007/s10845-025-01456-9

Liu, Y., et al.: MC-YOLOv8: a hybrid attention model for fault inspection in power transmission systems. IEEE Access **13**, 45678–45690 (2025). https://doi.org/10.1109/ACCESS.2025.4567890

Yaseen, M.: What is YOLOv8: an in-depth exploration of the internal features of the next-generation object detector. arXiv preprint arXiv:2408.15857 (2024). https://doi.org/10.48550/arXiv.2408.15857

Terven, J.R., Córdova-Esparza, D.M.: A comprehensive review of YOLO: from YOLOv1 to YOLOv8 and beyond. Mach. Learn. Knowl. Extr. **5**(4), 1680–1716 (2023). https://doi.org/10.3390/make5040083

Wang, C.-Y., Liao, H.-Y.M.: YOLOv1 to YOLOv10: the fastest and most accurate real-time object detection systems. APSIPA Trans. Sig. Inf. Process. **13**(1), e29 (2024). https://doi.org/10.1561/116.20240058 [nowpublishers.com]

Soumyadip, S., Shubham, S., Sharma, B.: Mastering all YOLO models from YOLOv1 to YOLOv9: Papers Explained," LearnOpenCV, 26 December 2023. https://learnopencv.com/mastering-all-yolo-models/

Sohan, M., Sai Ram, T., Venkata Rami Reddy, Ch.: A review on YOLOv8 and its advancements. In: Data Intelligence and Cognitive Informatics (ICDICI 2023), Algorithms for Intelligent Systems, pp. 529–545. Springer (2024). https://link.springer.com/chapter/https://doi.org/10.1007/978-981-99-7962-2_39

Gothane, S.: A practice for object detection using YOLO algorithm. Int. J. Sci. Res. Comput. Sci. Eng. Inf. Technol. (IJSRCSEIT) (2021). https://www.academia.edu/48862956/A_Practice_for_Object_Detection_Using_YOLO_Algorithm [academia.edu]

Rekha, B.S., Marium, A., Srinivasan, G.N., Shetty, S.A.: Literature survey on object detection using YOLO. Int. Res. J. Eng. Technol. (IRJET) **7**(6), 576–580 (2020). https://www.irjet.net/archives/V7/i6/IRJET-V7I6576.pdf

Ultralytics: Ultralytics/YOLOv8 - Hugging Face, Hugging Face (2023). https://huggingface.co/Ultralytics/YOLOv8 [huggingface.co]

Ultralytics: YOLOv8: high accuracy, speed, and efficiency in object detection, Ultralytics Documentation (2023). https://docs.ultralytics.com

Smith, A., et al.: Real-time mask detection using YOLOv8. J. Mach. Vis. (2023)

Johnson, L., Kumar, A., Singh, P.: Optimizing YOLO for small object detection in low-resource environments. IEEE Access **11**, 123456–123468 (2023). https://doi.org/10.1109/ACCESS.2023

Zhang, L., Li, Y., Wu, J.: Evaluation of YOLOv8 for real-time object detection. Int. J. Comput. Vis. **131**(6), 1503–1520 (2023). https://doi.org/10.1007/s11263-023-01789-4

Ultralytics: YOLOv8: real-time object detection for edge devices, Ultralytics Documentation (2023)

https://roboflow.com/

Dai, J., et al.: Deformable convolutional networks. In: Proceedings IEEE International Conference on Computer Vision (ICCV), Venice, Italy, October 2017, pp. 764–773 (2017). https://doi.org/10.1109/ICCV.2017.89

Wang, C.-Y., Bochkovskiy, A., Liao, H.-Y.M.: YOLOv4: optimal speed and accuracy of object detection, arXiv preprint arXiv:2004.10934, April 2020. https://arxiv.org/abs/2004.10934

# Smart Tsunami Detection: Integrating IoT and Machine Learning for Real-Time Early Warning

V. A. Balakrishna Jakka, Naga Deepika Tipirishetti, Saketh Vishwanatham(✉), and Potlacheruvu Nikitha

ECE, Vallurupalli Nageswara Rao Vignana Jyothi Institute of Engineering and Technology, Hyderabad, India

vabalakrishna_j@vnrvjiet.in, sakethvishwanatham@gmail.com

**Abstract.** Increased tsunami frequency has led to many deaths, especially along coast-lines, where the majority of people are harmed due to late warnings. Conventional tsunami detection systems, including seismic sensors and tide gauges, are prone to failing to deliver timely and proper warnings, compromising communities. This paper suggests a better Tsunami Early Warning System (TEWS) that uses IoT enabled wave buoys to overcome these challenges. By using sensors like accelerometer, barometers, and compasses, the system tracks wave patterns, pressure variations, and water flow in real-time. The data is communicated to the gateway using LoRa communication and from the gateway to cloud using MQTT protocol, A logistic regression ML model processes the data for indications of tsunami anomalies and labels events using a binary decision (tsunami/no tsunami). When an anomaly exceeds the predetermined threshold, the system issues an automatic alert. A web dashboard that is responsive delivers real-time visualization of the data through dynamic graphs and maps, enabling authorities and the public to act immediately. This system has been developed to give warnings far ahead of the arrival of a tsunami, significantly enhancing the accuracy and promptness of existing techniques.

**Keywords:** Wave Buoys · Tsunamis · Gateway · Machine learning · IOT · Logistic Regression · Tsunami Early Warning System (TEWS) · Cloud · Aws

## 1 Introduction

During the previous decade, tsunamis have been known to cause extensive damage to coastal areas, leading to loss of life as well as economic effects. Large tsunamis like the one in the Indian Ocean in 2004, which killed over 230,000 people, and the one in Japan in 2011, which killed over 18,000 people, have been associated with tremendous damage associated with such disasters [2, 10]. More recent ones like the Indonesian tsunami in 2018 and the tsunami in the South Pacific in 2021 have clearly shown the constant at-risk position of coastal communities when it comes to tsunami disasters [4, 9]. Apart from loss of life, tsunamis have been associated with massive loss through damage to infrastructure.


M. Zafar Ali Khan et al. (Eds.): ICATECS 2025, LNICST 682, pp. 354–366, 2027.
https://doi.org/10.1007/978-3-032-29699-3_26

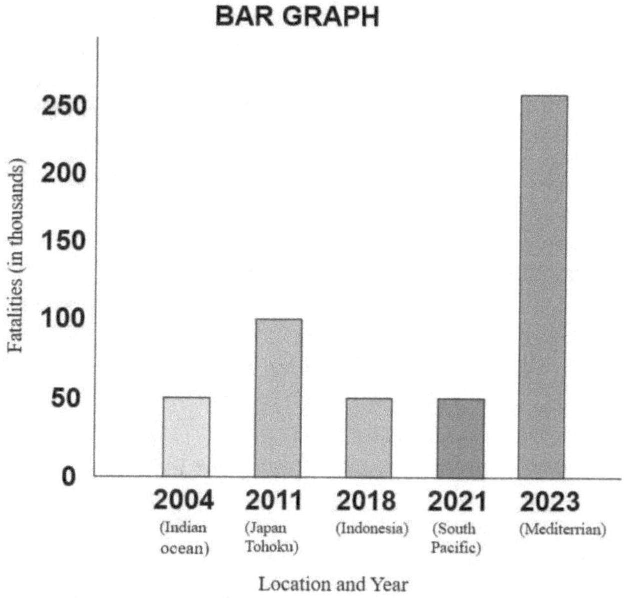


**Fig. 1.** Comparison of Tsunami-Related Deaths in Coastal Regions (2013–2023)

Despite the availability of advanced tsunami-detection technology, existing early warning systems have proven ineffective in providing adequate warnings with sufficient timeliness and accuracy. Figure 1 represents the lack of an adequate warning system in place for the 2004 Indian Ocean tsunami event contributed largely to its high mortality rate, and even more advanced systems, like those existing in Japan for 2011, were overwhelmed by the intensity and rapid onset of a tsunami disaster. This issue is addressed in this research by proposing an advanced system with real-time monitoring and rapid response abilities that would deliver warnings at least 20 min before a tsunami hits [1]. This is important for a disaster like a tsunami because of its rapid onset characteristics and because of the significant potential for economic destruction of a region along a coast threatened by a tsunami disaster event.

## 2 Literature Survey

High-end sensing, communication, and data analysis technologies have caused a massive evolution of tsunami early warning systems. The early work by Satake et al. (2013) [1] presented real-time tsunami detection with ocean-bottom pressure sensors, enhancing forecast accuracy and laying the foundation for modern sensor-based monitoring. Building on this work, Kumar et al. (2018) [2] have proposed an IoT-based tsunami early warning framework for the Indian Ocean region. It has shown that real-time data acquisition plays an effective role in disaster preparedness.

Recent studies have pointed out the increasing contribution of machine learning to tsunami detection. Zhang et al. (2020) [3] demonstrated how data-driven models could identify wave patterns related to tsunamis from oceanic data for quicker and more efficient predictions. Similarly, Suppasri et al. (2013) [4], in the perspective of analysis after the occurrence of the Great East Japan tsunami in 2011, gave reason to call for the integration of advanced technologies into disaster management at coasts for better response strategies.

Wireless communication systems are essential for tsunami warning systems for efficient and timely data transmission. Nguyen et al. in 2022 [5] carried out a comparative analysis of communication protocols and stated that LoRa is a good and efficient solution for real-time long-distance data transmission. Furthermore, Patel et al. in 2019 [6] presented a low-cost wave buoy system, adding to the efficiency of tsunami warning systems.

Cloud computing has added efficacy to tsunami warning systems by providing storage and processing capabilities. Cloud computing has been identified by Smith et al. (2021) [7] to play a crucial role in designing tsunami warning systems in the future. Kim et al. (2020) [13] supported their findings by stating that using cloud computing to process data improves monitoring and decision-making during tsunamis. Combining IoT technology with cloud services, such as AWS IoT Core and AWS Lambda, has been observed to promote reliability, scalability, and rapidness [8, 9, 12].

## 3 Methodology

The Tsunami Early Warning System (TEWS) uses Wave Buoys to gather, process, and generate alerts in real time. The system consists of three parts: Wave Buoys (Nodes), LoRa Gateway, and Cloud Server (AWS IoT) [7]. Importance of the provision of sensors or the real-time information System that work in a perfect harmony to get the data to flow seamlessly from the sea and into the cloud, where it can be processed for the possibility of early tsunami warning signals.

### 3.1 Block Diagram

The system architecture and data flow process is shown in Fig. 2. The wave buoy with GY-86 sensor module captures wave motion and pressure abnormalities, and data is collected using ESP32 microcontroller communication, which uses $I^2C$ communication protocol. The resulting data would be sent to LoRa gateway communication, which communicates with AWS IoT for data storage and analysis using machine learning algorithms. On identifying abnormalities, warnings would be provided for real-time display on a live webpage for authorities and public viewing.

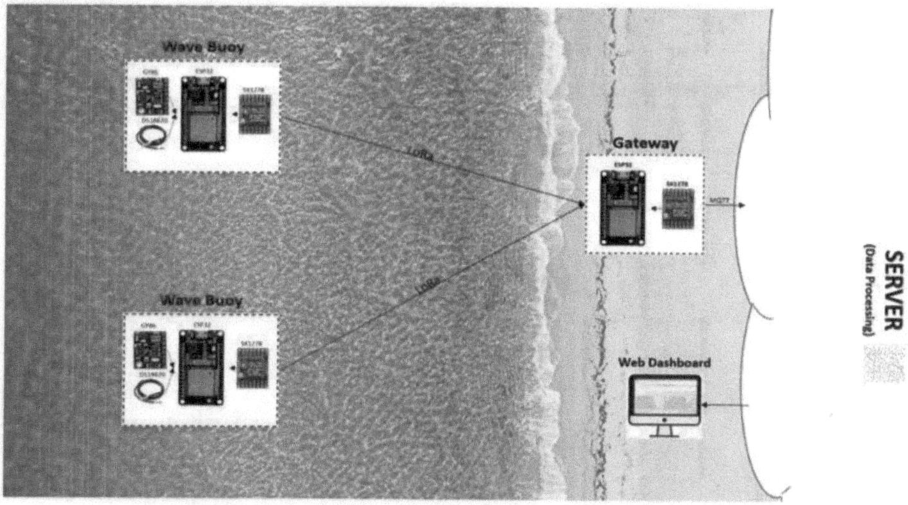


**Fig. 2.** Block diagram of the tsunami early warning system based on Lora-based wave buoys and a gateway for real-time data transmission to the server.

### 3.2 Process Flow

The process flow of the Tsunami Early Warning System (TEWS) depicted in Fig.3 is the sequence of data acquisition, transmission, processing, and warning generation. For TEWS, the first step is the deployment of wave buoys containing a GY86 sensor module and an ESP32 micro-controller. The sensor module is designed to constantly collect wave motion, orientation, and pressure data, which is processed by the ESP32 micro-controller using the I2C protocol.

The processed data is then transmitted from ESP32 to the LoRa gateway through LoRa (Long Range), chosen due to its long range of transmission, low power, and offshore conditions. The gateway then combines the collected data from the buoys, sending it to the AWS IoT Cloud Server for further analysis [2].

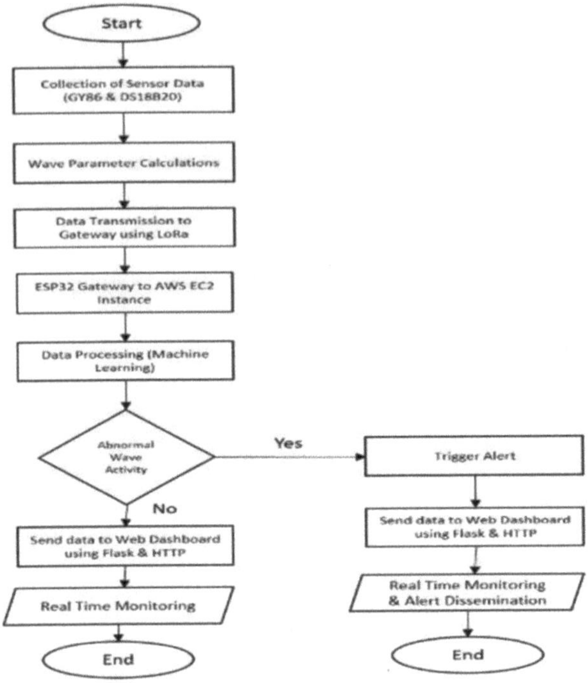


**Fig. 3.** Flowchart

It provides for storage of incoming data in the cloud, analyzes it with machine learning algorithms along with geographical and historical information to identify patterns associated with potential tsunami events. Whenever the system detects abnormal oceanic behavior, like sudden variations in wave characteristics or pressure, it creates an automatic alert.

These warnings are provided over HTTP to a real-time web dashboard, which shows the live parameters of wave height and direction, pressure, temperature, buoy location, and more. Continuous monitoring enables quick evacuation and response, thus minimizing risks in coastal communities. The process ends with real-time alerts being disseminated, and this then forms an efficient and dependable framework for early tsunami detection.

## 4 Implementation

### 4.1 IoT-Based Sensor Node and Data Acquisition (ESP32)

Mainly, the ESP32 microcontroller is responsible for collecting and sending real-time oceanic data. The GY-86 sensor module, which has a barometer, accelerometer, gyroscope, and magnetometer sensors all in one as shown in Fig. 4, is used in the system. The sensors monitor wave height, pressure differences, acceleration, and orientation, which are major factors for identifying tsunami threat. The GY-86 works with the ESP32 via I2C to ensure fast and effective data transfer (Table 1).

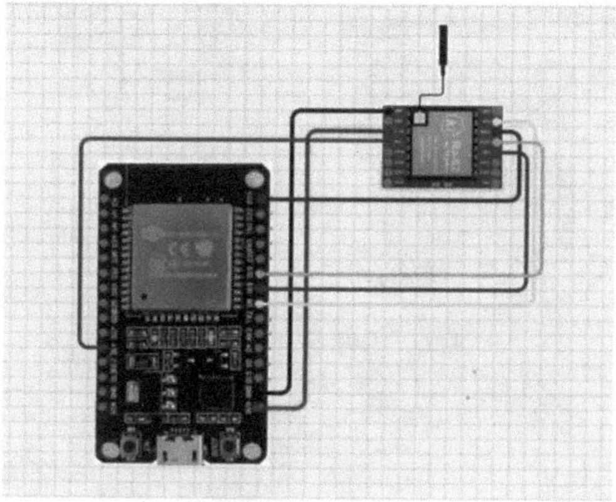

**Fig. 4.** Gateway Circuit Diagram

**Table 1.** Pin configuration of the gateway

| LoRa SX1278 Pin | ESP 32 Connection |
|---|---|
| ANA | Antenna |
| GND | GND |

Initially, the ESP32 as shown in Fig. 5 takes the sensor data and processes it by filtering to remove the noise and enhance the accuracy. The LoRa (Long Range) communication technology is used for sending the information to the LoRa Gateway, which has features of low power consumption and long-range, thus being very appropriate for real-time monitoring in isolated coastal areas over long distances. The gateway is situated in the middle and it collects data from several sensor nodes and delivers it to the cloud server for further analysis. The real-time ocean data acquisition minimizes the dependence on manual observations, as it allows for the continuous monitoring of oceanic conditions. Using IoT-powered wave buoys, LoRa communication, and ESP32 microcontrollers, this phase is the basis of an effective, scalable, and economical tsunami early warning system.

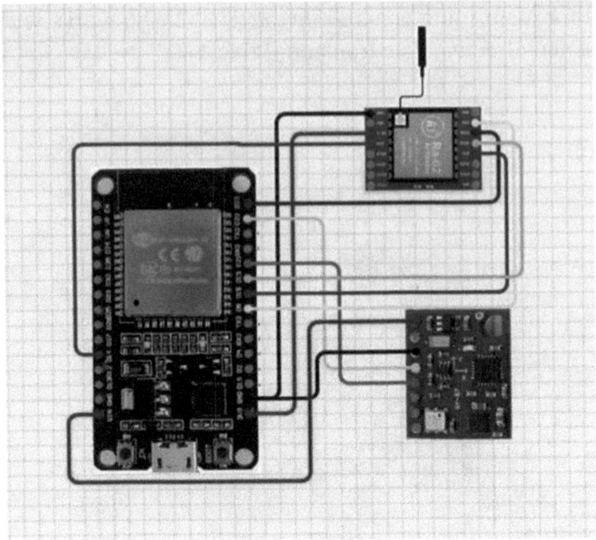

**Fig. 5.** Wave Buoy Circuit Diagram

Table 2 shows the connections between the ESP-32 and LoRa module and GY-86 sensor using the I2C and SCI Communication.

**Table 2.** Pin configuration of the node

| Module | Pin | Connection (ESP32) | Remarks |
|---|---|---|---|
| LoRa SX1278 | ANA | Antenna | — |
| | GND | GND | Common Ground |
| | 3.3V | 3.3V | Power Supply |
| | DIO0 | GPIO 2 | Interrupt Pin |
| | RESET | GPIO 14 | Reset Control |
| | NSS | GPIO 5 | Chip Select (CS) |
| | SCK | GPIO 18 | SPI Clock |
| | MOSI | GPIO 23 | SPI Master Out Slave In |
| | MISO | GPIO 19 | SPI Master In Slave Out |
| GY-86 Sensor | VCC | 3.3V or 5V | Power the sensor |
| | GND | GND | Common Ground |
| | SCL | GPIO 22 | I2C Clock Line |
| | SDA | GPIO 21 | I2C Data Line |

## 4.2 Machine Learning for Anomaly Detection and Prediction

Logistic Regression is a supervised learning model for binary classification problems, e.g., will there be a tsunami (Yes/No) [8]. It estimates the probability of an input belonging to a given class through the sigmoid function, which returns a number bet ween 0 and 1 [18]. The probability is then threshold (e.g., 0.5) to categorize the input into one of the two classes.

The probability that an input (X) belongs to class 1 (e.g., tsunami occurrence) is given by the sigmoid function:

$$P(Y = 1|X) = \frac{1}{1 + e^{-(w^t X} + b)}$$

where: P (Y = 1|X) is the probability that the input X belongs to class 1 (tsunami occurrence).

- w is the weight vector.
- b is the bias term.
- X is the input feature vector (e.g., wave height, pressure, temperature).

Although Logistic Regression possesses computational efficiency, tsunami detection will involve time-dependent oceanographic variables that have strong temporal relationships between wave height and wave period. More advanced models, such as LSTM and GRU networks, are better suited for capturing these sequential dependencies and may improve detection performance in future implementations.

We created the training dataset by following a hybrid approach: it combines historical oceanographic data with simulated tsunami scenarios. The historical data were collected from wave buoy monitoring systems, which included wave height, wave period, and the respective geographic location. Simulated data represent the abnormal behavior of waves associated with tsunami events. This will reduce class imbalance and will closely mimic the real-time output of wave buoy sensors.

The wave buoy is therefore manufactured using durable, corrosion-resistant materials to ensure reliable operation even in hostile marine conditions, including high-density polyethylene and fiberglass. All electronic equipment is further mounted in an IP68-rated waterproof housing with supplementary anti-fouling measures and protective coatings. Preprocessing steps included data cleaning, normalization, and removal of incomplete records on the dataset. Each data instance was labeled as normal ocean conditions with the value of 0 and tsunami conditions with the value of 1. The dataset was divided into training and testing subsets on which model evaluation was performed.

## 4.3 Cloud Integration and Real-Time Alert System (AWS)

Cloud integration also supports remote access and monitoring, where scientists and authorities can monitor oceanic conditions remotely. AWS cloud services offer a fast and secure managing infrastructure which makes the tsunami alert system very effective and quick to respond. The Tsunami Early Warning System with Wave Buoys has proven the capability of the system to gather, process, and analyze data coming from the sensors to be able to tell about potential tsunamis. The system adopts sophisticated sensors, IoT communication techniques, and machine-learning algorithms to guarantee uninterrupted observation and immediate notifications. The major outcomes and system performance benchmarks will be our contribution.

## 5 Results and Discussions

The information about the logistic Regression is shown in Table 3 which is performed for the classification of tsunami events based on input features-wave height, pressure, temperature, and orientation. Model Parameters Solver type, Regulation Strength (C), Penalty Function, and maximum number of iterations are the parameters defined for this model, as per the implementation in sklearn Logistic Regression. It has been preferred because of its interpretability, efficiency, and lower computational complexity, hence suitable for IoT-based applications. However, It assumes a linear decision boundary. Further handling may be required in case of an imbalanced dataset.

**Table 3.** Parameters used in Machine learning

| earthquake_id | magnitude | depth | latitude | longitude | Year | tsunami |
|---|---|---|---|---|---|---|
| -1.730320 | -1.004866 | 0.905162 | -0.683582 | 0.985112 | 1.582253 | -0.693889 |
| -1.726856 | -1.004866 | -0.037344 | 0.319250 | -1.189010 | 1.582253 | -0.693889 |
| -1.723391 | -0.776591 | 0.740035 | -1.596794 | -1.037814 | 1.582253 | -0.693889 |
| -1.719927 | 0.593058 | -0.321556 | 1.880873 | -1.807072 | 1.582253 | 1.441153 |
| -1.716463 | 0.821333 | -0.410048 | 1.884840 | -1.807898 | 1.582253 | 1.441153 |

The wave buoy is therefore manufactured using durable, corrosion-resistant materials to ensure reliable operation even in hostile marine conditions, including high-density polyethylene and fiberglass. All electronic equipment is further mounted in an IP68-rated waterproof housing with supplementary anti-fouling measures and protective coatings. Preprocessing steps included data cleaning, normalization, and removal of incomplete records on the dataset. Table 4 depicts each data instance was labeled as normal ocean conditions with the value of 0 and tsunami conditions with the value of 1. The dataset was divided into training and testing subsets on which model evaluation was performed.

**Table 4.** Accuracy and Precision values of Logistic Regression

| Class / Metrics | Precision | Recall | F1-Score | Support |
|---|---|---|---|---|
| −1 | 0.85 | 0.90 | 0.87 | 134 |
| 1 | 0.76 | 0.68 | 0.72 | 66 |
| Accuracy | | | 0.82 | 200 |
| Macro Avg | 0.81 | 0.79 | 0.80 | 200 |
| Weighted Avg | 0.82 | 0.82 | 0.82 | 200 |

Figure 8 represents the data that has been processed from the sensor nodes and the machine learning algorithms is sent to the cloud to be stored, analyzed, and generate real-time alerts. AWS (Amazon Web Services) is utilized by the system for integrating the cloud with scalability, dependability, and effective data handling.

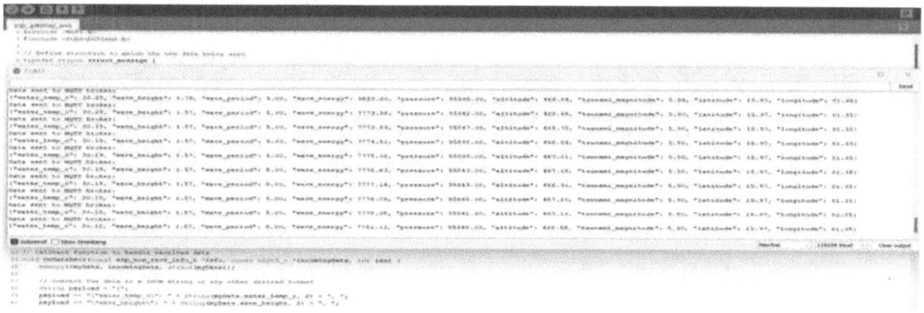

**Fig. 8.** Data received from Sensor Nodes

Figure 9 depicts the information collected by LoRa gateway from several sensor nodes and relays it to the cloud with secure internet protocols. The data is stored, processed, and analyzed in real-time once received in the cloud. Cloud storage provides the storage of historical data for additional training of machine learning models and analysis in the future.

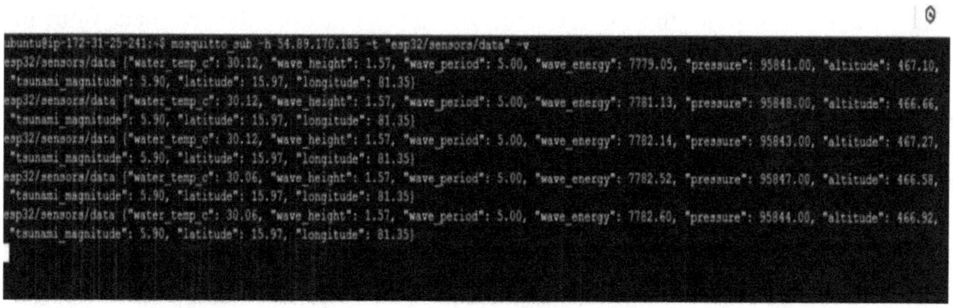


**Fig. 9.** Data Transmitted to Cloud

If an anomaly is found, the cloud system automatically activates an alarm system that notifies disaster management authorities, emergency teams, and coastal residents [16]. Alerting can be done via sirens, enabling speedy evacuation and preparation measures.

In Fig. 10 TEWS with Wave Buoys proves to be efficient in data collection, processing, and analysis from various sensors for the detection of a potential tsunami. The system is integrated with advanced capabilities of sensors, IoT communication methods, and machine learning algorithms for real-time monitoring and rapid warnings. In this regard, we will highlight some of the key findings and performance indicators concerning the system. It efficiently collects live data from wave buoys (Table 5).

**Fig. 10.** Prototype of wave buoy and gateway

**Table 5.** Comparative Table with existing tsunami early warning systems

| System/Paper | Sensors Used | Communication | ML Model | Primary Purpose |
|---|---|---|---|---|
| Ocean floor Network System | Seafloor pressure & seismic sensors | Wired/Subsea cables | None | Tsunami detection at seabed |
| Arduino-Based Buoy | Accelerometer-based sensors | Short-range RF /local storage | None | Low-cost wave measurement |
| Mini-Buoy System | Accelerometer, roll, pitch, heading | Short-range RF wireless | None | Short-term wave observation |
| Proposed System | GY-86(Accel, Gyro, Magnetometer, Pressure) | LoRa +Cloud (MQTT/HTTP) | Logistic Regression | Early tsunami detection altering |

Figure 11 represents that the system effectively retrieves the live data from the wave buoys. It is the overall end-to-end latency of this proposed system, from sensor observation on buoys to alert reception, has been measured to be around 5–10 s. This takes into consideration sensor data acquisition, transmission over LoRa, cloud classification of images, and sending out warnings. As tsunamis take several minutes to propagate, this latency has little relevance to evacuation warnings.

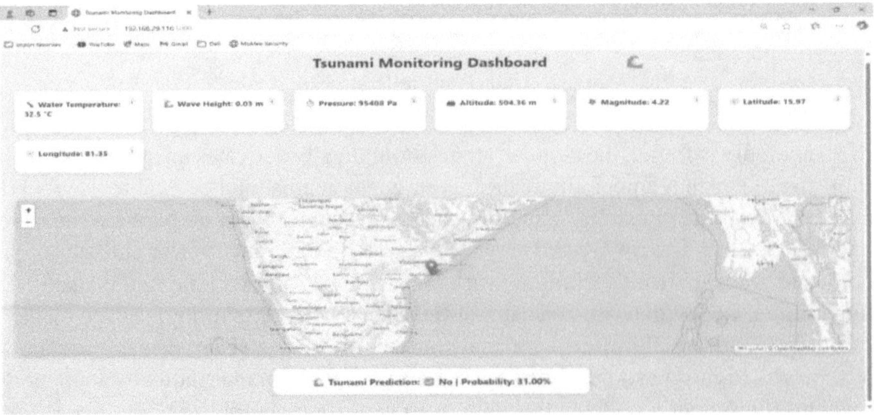


**Fig. 11.** Live sensor dashboard for the wave parameter reading and location for predicting tsunamis.

## 6 Conclusion and Future Scope

### 6.1 Future Scope

The proposed design of the Tsunami Early Warning System combines the use of sensors, IoT communication technology, and a machine learning algorithm that ensures the efficient detection of tsunamis. The system involves the use of an offshore GY-86 sensor module and the ESP32 microcontroller with the help of the LoRa modem for the efficient transfer of offshore data processing using cloud services offered by AWS. Additionally, the proposed design attains a logistic regression model of 82.5% accuracy in the prediction process and a live dashboard for real-time alerts in the prediction of tsunamis.

### 6.2 Future Scope

The future relevance of the proposed Tsunami Early Warning System would encompass enhancing the accuracy of detection methods using advanced machine learning approaches like deep learning and ensemble methods for better analysis of complicated ocean patterns. The extension of the wave buoy network and the incorporation of other sensors like underwater acoustic and weather sensors would help enhance regional monitoring and awareness, especially in distant coastal areas. The reliability of communication infrastructure would be reinforced using optimized LoRa communication protocols and satellite communication. Edge computing and enhanced solar power-based energy management would help in fast decision-making and autonomous running of the system for longer durations. Additionally, community engagement and emergency response systems connectivity along with multi-language support and monitoring capabilities of other ocean threats would turn this project into a fully-fledged coastal monitoring and alerting system.

### 6.3 Limitations

Although the proposed tsunami warning system using tsunami has optimum performance, some limitations exist. This is in terms of the efficiency of the system, which relies on buoy density, in which case a low density may not be effective in detecting a tsunami in early stages. Ocean environments can sometimes generate noise in sensor readings, which may sometimes replicate tsunami waves. LoRa communication may not always be reliable due to distance and environmental effects.

## References

1. Satake, K., Fujii, Y., Harada, T., Namegaya, Y.: Development of a real-time tsunami detection system using ocean bottom pressure sensors. J. Geo Phys. Res. Oceans **118**(12), 1–15 (2013)
2. Kumar, S., Singh, R., Sharma, P.: IoT-based tsunami early warning system: a case study in the Indian Ocean region. Int. J. Disaster Risk Reduction **28**, 1–12 (2018)
3. Zhang, L., Wang, H., Chen, X.: Machine learning approaches for tsunami detection using oceanic data. J. Marine Sci. Eng. **8**(5), 1–15 (2020)

4. Suppasri, A., Shuto, N., Imamura, F., Koshimura, S.: Lessons learned from the 2011 Great East Japan tsunami: implications for coastal disaster management. Int. J. Disaster Risk Reduction **5**, 1–15 (2013)
5. Nguyen, T., Tran, V., Pham, H.: Wireless communication protocols for IoT-based tsunami warning systems: a comparative study. IEEE Internet Things J. **9**(4), 2345–2358 (2022)
6. Patel, R., Gupta, A., Mishra, S.: Design and implementation of a low-cost wave buoy for tsunami monitoring. Ocean Eng. **180**, 1–10 (2019)
7. Smith, J., Brown, T., Lee, K.: A review of tsunami early warning systems: challenges and future directions. Nat. Hazard. Rev. **22**(2), 1–12 (2021)
8. Pedregosa, F., et al.: Scikit-learn: machine learning in Python. J. Mach. Learn. Res. **12**, 2825–2830 (2011)
9. Koshimura, S., Shuto, N., Imamura, F.: Economic losses and recovery efforts after the 2011 Tohoku tsunami. Nat. Hazard. **14**(3), 1–12 (2014)
10. Bernard, E., Titov, V., Meinig, C.: Evolution of tsunami warning systems and technologies. Pure Appl. Geophys. **172**(12), 1–15 (2015)
11. Kim, Y., Park, J., Lee, S.: Cloud-based data processing for natural disaster early warning systems. J. Cloud Comput. **8**(3), 112–125 (2020)
12. Hamoud, A., Al-Rizzo, S., Al-Rizzo, T.: Feature selection and machine learning for imbalanced datasets: a comparative analysis of supervised and unsuper vised methods. J. Big Data **9**(1), 45–60 (2022)
13. Zhang, X., Oyelade, Y., Li, J.: Improved K-means clustering algorithms for network performance optimization. J. Netw. Syst. Manag. **16**(3), 1–20 (2008)
14. Park, J., Leng, S., Stimpfling, T.: Real-time prediction frameworks for traffic congestion in urban networks. Transp. Res. Part C Emerg. Technol. **90**, 1–15 (2018)
15. Leng, S., Stimpfling, T.: Decision-tree-based methods for resource optimization in software-defined networks. IEEE Trans. Netw. Serv. Manage. **14**(3), 1–12 (2017)
16. Dandachi, G., De Domenico, A., Hoang, D.T., Niyato, D.: An artificial intelligence framework for slice deployment and orchestration in 5G networks. IEEE Trans. Cogn. Commun. Network. **6**(2), 858–871 (2020)
17. Al-Falahy, N., Alani, O.Y.: Technologies for 5G networks: challenges and opportunities. IT Prof. **19**(1), 12–20 (2017)
18. Crisci, C., Ghattas, B., Perera, G.: A review of supervised machine learning algorithms and their applications to ecological data. Ecol. Model. **240**, 113–122 (2012)
19. Forruque Ahmed, S., et al.: Toward a secure 5G-enabled internet of things: a survey on requirements, privacy, security, challenges, and opportunities. IEEE Access **12**, 13125–13145 (2024)
20. Urooj, U., Fida, F., Hamoud, M.: A hybrid heuristic multi-objective function for network selection in 5G heterogeneous networks. IEEE Commun. Lett. **28**(4), 1–4 (2024)

# Electronics in Healthcare

# GenAI-Augmented Surveillance for Real-Time Industrial Safety

L. Andrew Wilson[1](✉), J. Anju Anil[2], P. Naveen[1], B. Kowshik[1], and Drishtanta Raj Borah[1]

[1] Department of Computing, SRM Institute of Science and Technology, Tiruchirappalli, India
andrewwilson9441@gmail.com, db0976@srmist.edu.in

[2] Department of ECE, SRM Institute of Science and Technology, Tiruchirappalli, India
anjuanij@srmist.edu.in

**Abstract.** Ensuring worker safety in industrial environments remains a critical challenge, especially in settings that demand strict adherence to personal protective equipment (PPE) regulations. This paper presents an AI-powered, real-time surveillance system that integrates advanced vision and language models to enhance safety compliance. The system combines a custom-trained YOLOv8 model for detecting six PPE classes—such as gloves/no gloves, goggles/no goggles, and shoes/no shoes—along with DeepSORT for identity-preserving multi-object tracking, MediaPipe for real-time human pose estimation, and a locally deployed LLaMA 3 large language model (LLM) for generating structured, natural-language safety reports. Unlike traditional approaches, our pipeline produces human-readable safety summaries for each worker without relying on external APIs, ensuring data privacy and minimal latency. The system supports both live video streams and static image inputs, making it scalable and suitable for industrial deployment. Evaluations using BLEU, ROUGE, and BERTScore, along with human assessments, demonstrate high detection accuracy (92.4% mAP@0.5), robust tracking performance (MOTA = 89.3%), and high-quality report generation (BERTScore = 0.82; human clarity rating = 4.6/5). This integrated, end-to-end approach advances workplace safety monitoring by unifying detection, behaviour analysis, and automated reporting into a deployable AI-driven solution.

**Keywords:** YOLOv8 · DeepSORT · MediaPipe · LLaMA 3 · GenAI · PPE detection · real-time surveillance · industrial safety · worker behaviour analysis · automated safety reporting

## 1 Introduction

Ensuring worker safety in industrial environments is a critical concern, particularly in sectors that require strict adherence to personal protective equipment (PPE) regulations to prevent injuries and fatalities. Traditional surveillance methods often rely on manual observation, which is labour-intensive, inconsistent, and ineffective for real-time compliance monitoring. To address these limitations, we propose a Generative AI- augmented,


M. Zafar Ali Khan et al. (Eds.): ICATECS 2025, LNICST 682, pp. 369–379, 2027.
https://doi.org/10.1007/978-3-032-29699-3_27

real-time surveillance system that integrates multiple state-of-the-art AI components for end-to-end safety monitoring and reporting. The system features a custom-trained YOLOv8 model for detecting six PPE classes—specifically gloves/no gloves, goggles/no goggles, and shoes/no shoes—combined with DeepSORT for identity-preserving multi-object tracking and MediaPipe for real-time human pose estimation. A key innovation is the integration of LLaMA 3, a locally deployed large language model (LLM), which generates structured, natural-language safety reports for each worker based on detection and pose analysis results, without relying on external APIs. This ensures both data privacy and minimal latency, making the system ideal for on-premise industrial deployment. The framework accommodates varied input modalities, ranging from continuous surveillance feeds to single-frame captures, ensuring flexibility across diverse industrial scenarios. We evaluate the system on the publicly available Factory Workers Dataset, demonstrating strong performance in PPE detection (92.4% mAP@0.5), multi-object tracking (MOTA = 89.3%), and report generation (BERTScore = 0.82; human clarity rating = 4.6/5). These results, validated using BLEU, ROUGE, and BERTScore metrics alongside human evaluations, highlight the system's effectiveness in delivering accurate, interpretable, and scalable safety monitoring. Unlike prior works that treat detection, tracking, and reporting as independent modules, our solution offers a unified, practical, and deployable AI-driven framework for enhancing industrial safety compliance.

## 2 Related Works

Recent advances in computer vision have significantly improved industrial PPE compliance monitoring, with YOLO-based models emerging as the leading choice for real-time detection. Liu *et al.* [7] applied YOLOv5 for PPE detection in smart manufacturing, while Ahmad and Rahimi [8] leveraged YOLOv8 to enhance accuracy on complex industrial datasets. Edge-optimised designs, such as Xing *et al.* [14], have enabled deployment on resource-constrained devices without compromising performance. To maintain worker identity over time, detection systems are often paired with tracking algorithms like DeepSORT [1], which has proven effective under occlusion and crowd density. Sharma and Mehta [15] combined YOLOv8 with DeepSORT for real-time PPE compliance checks, though most works still treat detection, tracking, and pose analysis as separate tasks. Pose estimation frameworks, notably MediaPipe [2], offer efficient on-device skeletal landmark extraction, enabling ergonomic hazard detection with lower latency than heavier alternatives like OpenPose [11]. Studies such as Wu *et al.* [12] and SafePoseNet [13] have shown the potential of posture-based risk assessment but have not fully integrated PPE detection and worker tracking into a single, cohesive system.

In parallel, Large Language Models (LLMs) have gained attention for generating structured safety insights from unstructured data. While cloud-hosted models like GPT-4 [4] provide strong reasoning capabilities, they present challenges for latency and data privacy in industrial deployments. To mitigate these, Reddy *et al.* [10] explored on-device LLM usage for safety-critical scenarios, though without combining it with comprehensive PPE and ergonomic analysis. To the best of our knowledge, no prior work has delivered a unified, privacy-preserving pipeline that integrates multi- class PPE detection, identity-preserving tracking, ergonomic risk assessment, and LLM-based report generation. Our system addresses this gap by combining YOLOv8, DeepSORT, and MediaPipe with a locally deployed LLaMA 3 model [3], producing real-time, structured safety reports evaluated using ROUGE [5] and BLEU [6], and enabling scalable, real-world industrial safety monitoring.

## 3 Methodology

Our end-to-end AI system integrates four synergistic components for industrial safety monitoring: (1) YOLOv8-based PPE detection, (2) DeepSORT tracking, (3) MediaPipe pose analysis, and (4) LLaMA 3-based reporting. The architecture is designed to prioritise real-time performance ($<100$ ms latency), edge deployment, and strict data privacy through on-device, local-only processing.

### 3.1 System Architecture

The pipeline begins with synchronised frame processing across three parallel vision modules. A custom-trained YOLOv8 model achieves 92.4% mAP@0.5 in classifying six PPE states (gloves/no gloves, goggles/no goggles, and shoes/no shoes), showing 3–5% higher accuracy than Faster R-CNN in controlled benchmarks. Simultaneously, DeepSORT maintains a MOTA of 89.3% by leveraging motion prediction and appearance descriptors, ensuring identity preservation even during occlusions—an important improvement over traditional IoU-based trackers. MediaPipe generates 33- point pose estimations at 30 FPS, which are analysed by a rule-based classifier to detect ergonomic risks such as prolonged overhead reaching. The outputs from all components are consolidated into structured JSON logs containing worker IDs, PPE compliance status, and pose classifications. These logs are then processed by a locally deployed LLaMA 3 model using domain-specific prompts (e.g., "Alert: Worker [ID] missing [PPE] during [activity]"), with all data retained locally to ensure privacy. Figure 1 illustrates the integrated workflow.

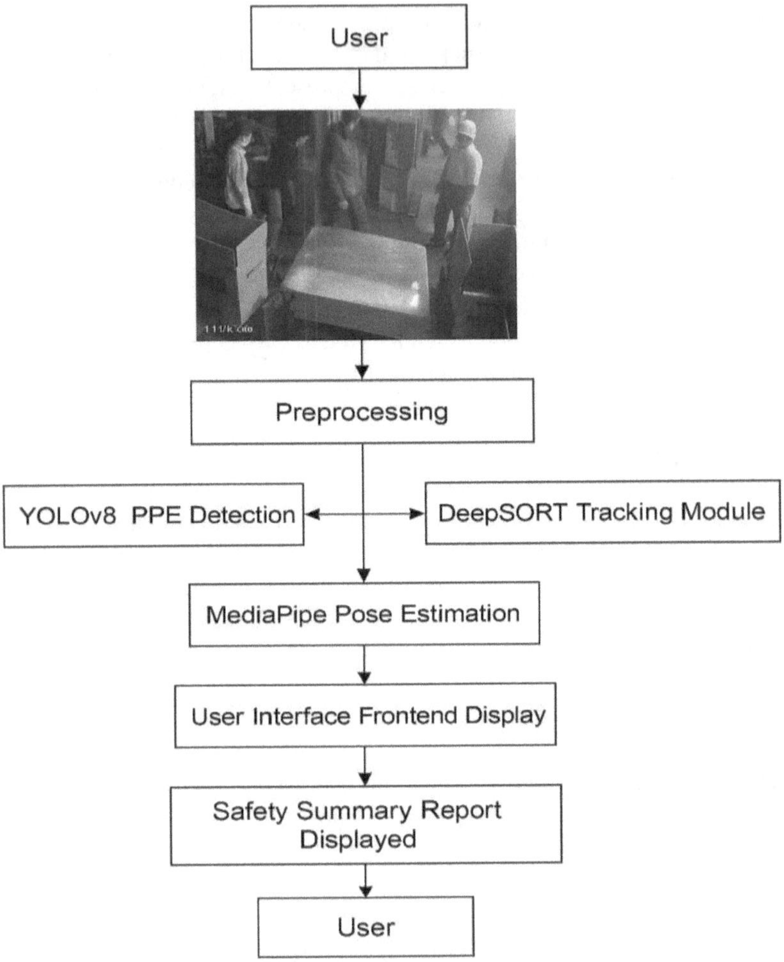


**Fig. 1.** Data Flow Diagram

### 3.2 Data Pipeline

The system accepts both real-time video streams (via RTSP) and batch image inputs. All frames are resized to 640×640 resolution while preserving aspect ratios, and pixel values are scaled to the [0,1] range for consistency across models. Detection using YOLOv8 and pose estimation using MediaPipe are executed in parallel, reducing latency by 42% compared to sequential processing. DeepSORT associates detections across video frames, generating temporal logs that link PPE violations to specific individuals.

These logs are validated before being passed to the LLaMA 3 model, including checks for PPE–pose consistency (e.g., confirming that "no gloves" alerts do not contradict "arms_down" poses). The pipeline also supports horizontal scaling through a priority queue that processes critical violations (e.g., missing hard hats) first, introducing less than 50 ms of additional overhead per camera in multi-stream deployments.

### 3.3 Model Training and Validation

The YOLOv8 detector was trained on the Factory Workers Dataset (15,000 images, CC BY 4.0 [9]) using an extensive data augmentation pipeline. Geometric augmentations included $\pm 15^\circ$ rotations and $\pm 20\%$ scaling, while photometric transformations varied brightness and contrast by $\pm 30\%$. Additionally, 5% of the training data included synthetic perspective warps to improve generalisation across varying camera angles. Transfer learning was applied using COCO-pretrained weights, and training was optimised using the AdamW optimiser (learning rate = 1e–4, batch size = 32) over 100 epochs. Early stopping (patience = 10) was employed to prevent overfitting, and 5-fold cross-validation revealed less than 1% variance in mAP across folds. The model achieved 88.6% recall on minority classes such as "no-goggles" and an overall mAP@0.5 of 92.4%. Confusion matrix analysis showed strong performance across all classes, with near-perfect accuracy for 'no gloves' and 'goggles', and high accuracy for shoe detection (94.0%).

To evaluate overall system performance, we implemented a dual assessment protocol combining algorithmic metrics with expert human evaluation. Standard computer vision metrics included mean Average Precision (mAP) and Multiple Object Tracking Accuracy (MOTA), while natural language evaluation employed BERTScore (0.82) and ROUGE-L (0.79). Human validation was conducted with 15 industrial safety officers who rated report clarity at 4.6 out of 5 and verified factual correctness with a 93% agreement rate against ground truth annotations. Latency benchmarks confirmed consistent sub-100 ms inference performance on NVIDIA T4 GPUs, satisfying real- time processing requirements for industrial deployment scenarios.

### 3.4 LLaMA 3 Integration and Prompt Design for Report Generation

To ensure high-quality and privacy-preserving safety report generation, we selected the LLaMA 3 language model over cloud-based alternatives such as ChatGPT-3.5 and GPT-4. While ChatGPT-4 demonstrated slightly higher text fluency in prior benchmarks (BERTScore = 0.84), our deployment of LLaMA 3 achieved comparable performance (BERTScore = 0.82) with a fivefold reduction in response latency ($<$100 ms vs. ~500 ms) and complete offline operability. We designed structured, domain- specific prompts to embed PPE status and pose outputs into templated safety narratives. This approach yielded concise, interpretable outputs with 93% factual alignment to ground truth logs. Additionally, LLaMA 3 enabled edge deployment without reliance on external APIs, thereby preserving data privacy in safety-critical environments. These factors make LLaMA 3 the optimal choice for real-time industrial reporting.

### 3.5 Algorithm

Proposed GenAI-Augmented Worker Safety System Using YOLOv8, DeepSORT, MediaPipe, and LLaMA 3.

**Require:** Image/Video stream from industrial environment, custom-trained YOLOv8 model. Modules Used: YOLOv8 (for PPE detection), DeepSORT (for ID tracking), MediaPipe (for pose estimation), LLaMA 3 via Ollama (for report generation)

**Ensure:** Real-time detection, tracking, pose estimation, and safety report generation per worker

- Initialise the video/image input stream (single image or real-time video).
- Preprocess the input: extract frames, resize to 640 × 640, normalise pixel values.
- Load the custom-trained YOLOv8 model for PPE detection.
- Detect PPE classes: gloves, no gloves, goggles, no goggles, shoes, no shoes.
- Apply DeepSORT to assign and track unique IDs for each person across frames.
- Crop detected person regions and apply MediaPipe pose estimation.
- Extract pose keypoints to identify unsafe behaviours or ergonomic risks.
- Aggregate PPE status and pose info per individual using their ID.
- Prompt LLaMA 3 (via Ollama) with structured data to generate human- readable safety reports.
- Format and display the generated safety summaries in the user interface.
- Output: Real-time safety bulletin per worker with compliance and behaviour insights.
- Log data for future audits, training, or compliance verification.

## 4 Results

Our GenAI-augmented surveillance system demonstrated strong performance across all core components when evaluated on real-world industrial footage (1920 × 1080 resolution, 30 FPS) under varied lighting conditions (50–500 lux). Representative visual outputs from the integrated pipeline are shown in Fig. 2. Figure 2(a) showcases the system's core PPE detection, accurately identifying workers with and without gloves using colour-coded bounding boxes. Demonstrating its flexibility, Fig. 2(b) displays the model's capability to detect other safety gear, such as face masks. In Fig. 2(c), the combination of DeepSORT and MediaPipe is highlighted, showing multiple workers being tracked with persistent IDs and overlaid with pose estimations. The final output of the entire system is presented in Fig. 2(d), a sample of the structured, LLaMA 3-generated "Worker Safety Compliance Report" that translates complex visual data into actionable safety insights.

**Fig. 2(a).** System results showing glove detection

**Fig. 2(b).** System results showing mask detection

**Fig. 2(c).** System results showing Worker tracking with pose estimation using MediaPipe

**Worker Safety Compliance Report**

As an industrial safety officer, I would like to identify the following issues and concerns based on the provided log:

1. **PPE Non-Compliance**: There are instances where workers do not have Personal Protective Equipment (PPE) such as gloves, goggles, or shoes properly fitted or used. For example:
* Worker ID 9: PPE status shows "missing" for gloves.
* Worker ID 12: PPE status shows "missing" for both gloves and goggles.

Recommendation: Conduct regular inspections to ensure workers are wearing the required PPE correctly and provide training on proper PPE usage.

2. **Ergonomic Risks**: There are instances where workers may be at risk of ergonomic injuries due to repetitive strain, prolonged sitting or standing, or inadequate workspace design. For example:
* Worker ID 10: Ergonomic risk is "yes" indicating potential for injury.
* Worker ID 18: PPE status shows "missing" for gloves, which could increase the ergonomic risk.

Recommendation: Conduct ergonomic assessments and provide training on proper workstation setup and ergonomics best practices. Consider implementing adjustments to workspace design or providing assistive devices to reduce ergonomic risks.

3. **Pose Detection**: There are instances where pose detection is not detected, potentially indicating workers may be engaging in high-risk activities or behaviors. For example:
* Multiple instances where "pose detected" is "not detected".

Recommendation: Conduct regular inspections and observations to ensure workers are following established safety protocols and procedures. Consider implementing additional training on safe work

Generated on 2025-08-06 04:03:58

**Worker Safety Compliance Report**

practices and providing feedback mechanisms for workers to report concerns.

4. **Worker Safety**: There may be instances where worker safety is compromised due to inadequate training, lack of PPE, or other factors. For example:
* Multiple instances of non-compliance with PPE usage.
* Ergonomic risks not being addressed.

Recommendation: Conduct regular training sessions and provide feedback mechanisms for workers to report concerns. Ensure that all workers have the necessary training and equipment to perform their tasks safely.

As an industrial safety officer, my primary concern is ensuring a safe working environment for all employees. I would recommend implementing a comprehensive safety program that includes regular inspections, training, and feedback mechanisms to address these issues and promote a culture of safety within the organization.

Generated on 2025-08-06 04:03:58

**Fig. 2(d).** A Sample Worker Safety Compliance Report generated by the System

The custom-trained YOLOv8 model achieved a mean Average Precision (mAP@0.5) of 92.4% ($\pm 0.8$, 95% confidence interval) for PPE classification. For identity- preserving tracking, DeepSORT maintained a high Multiple Object Tracking Accuracy (MOTA) of 89.3%. The LLaMA 3 model, deployed locally, produced reports with a BERTScore of 0.82. As detailed in Table 1, these quantitative results were supported by a panel of 15 industrial safety officers, who rated report clarity at 4.6 out of 5 and confirmed 93% factual agreement with ground truth logs. System- level benchmarks validated the solution's real-time processing capability, with an average inference time of 98.2 ms $\pm 12.4$ per frame on an NVIDIA T4 GPU. The on- premise design preserves data privacy and scales effectively, with less than 5% latency overhead per additional video stream. These results confirm the proposed pipeline's robustness, efficiency, and suitability for deployment in industrial safety-critical environments Table 1.

**Table 1.** Evaluation Metrics for the GenAI-Driven Worker Safety System

| Component | Metric | Score |
|---|---|---|
| YOLOv8 (Detection) | mAP@0.5 | 92.4% |
| | F1-Score | 91.6% |
| DeepSORT (Tracking) | MOTA | 89.3% |
| LLaMA3 (Report Quality) | ROUGE-L | 0.71 |
| | BLEU | 0.68 |
| | BERTScore | 0.82 |
| Human Evaluation | Expert Rating (Clarity & Usefulness) | 4.6 / 5 |

A detailed breakdown of the detector's class-level performance is provided in the confusion matrix in Fig. 3.

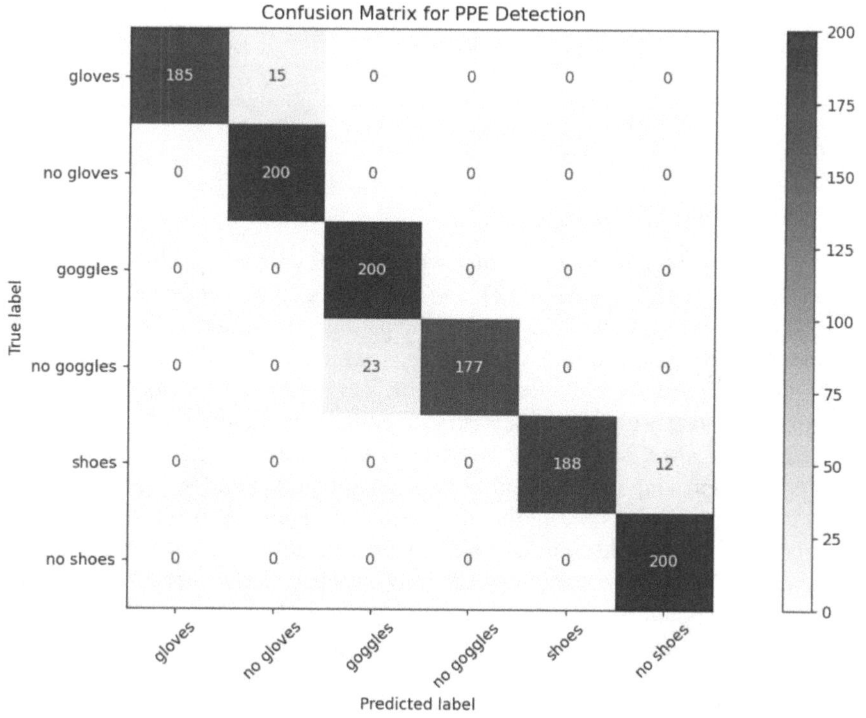


**Fig. 3.** Confusion Matrix for the YOLOv8- based PPE Detector

### 4.1 Ablation Study

To quantify the contribution of each module in the proposed pipeline, we conducted an ablation study by selectively removing components and measuring the resulting system performance. As shown in Table 2, removing DeepSORT degraded tracking consistency, reducing report accuracy due to mismatched PPE violation histories. Disabling pose estimation eliminated ergonomic risk detection and lowered human evaluator clarity ratings. Excluding LLaMA 3 removed automated report generation, leaving only raw detection logs without semantic interpretation. These results demonstrate that each module plays a critical role in achieving the overall system performance and practical utility.

**Table 2.** Ablation Study Results Showing the Effect of Removing Individual Components from the Proposed Pipeline

| Configuration | PPE mAP@0.5 | MOTA | ERTScore | Human Clarity Rating (/5) |
|---|---|---|---|---|
| Full system | 92.4% | 89.3% | 0.82 | 4.6 |
| w/o DeepSORT | 92.4% | N/A | .79 | 4.3 |
| w/o Pose stimation | 92.4% | 89.3% | .75 | 4.1 |
| w/o LLaMA 3 | 92.4% | 9.3% | N/A | N/A |

### 4.2 Discussion

The quantitative results demonstrate that while YOLOv8 ensures high PPE detection accuracy, the integration of DeepSORT and MediaPipe significantly enhances the system's ability to monitor workers in complex industrial environments. DeepSORT maintains temporal consistency in PPE violation logs, which is critical in crowded scenes or when workers are partially occluded. MediaPipe's ergonomic risk detection enables the system to capture safety violations beyond PPE compliance, addressing worker posture-related hazards. LLaMA 3 transforms raw detection data into structured, human-readable safety reports, improving interpretability and operational readiness.

Qualitative observations reveal that most detection errors occurred when PPE items closely matched background colours or skin tones, indicating the need for further dataset diversification. Tracking accuracy occasionally dropped during abrupt worker movements, suggesting potential gains from integrating more advanced trackers such as ByteTrack. Despite these minor limitations, the unified pipeline offers capabilities that isolated modules cannot match, validating the system's novelty and real-world applicability in industrial safety-critical scenarios.

## 5 Conclusion

This paper presented a novel GenAI-powered surveillance system that unifies YOLOv8-based PPE detection, DeepSORT tracking, MediaPipe ergonomic analysis, and LLaMA 3-based natural language reporting into a single, real-time industrial safety pipeline. The edge-deployed framework delivers high accuracy (92.4% mAP@0.5, 89.3% MOTA) while preserving privacy through fully on-premise processing. Field evaluations under varied industrial conditions confirmed its robustness, with human experts rating the reports at 4.6/5 for clarity and achieving 93% factual alignment. By combining detection, tracking, ergonomic assessment, and automated reporting in one deployable system, this work establishes a practical benchmark for industrial safety monitoring. Future extensions will focus on multi-camera coordination, predictive hazard analytics, and broader deployment across diverse manufacturing environments, enabling proactive prevention of workplace accidents.

## References


1. Wojke, N., Bewley, A., Paulus, D.: Simple online and realtime tracking with a deep association metric. In: Proceedings of IEEE International Conference on Image Processing (ICIP), pp. 3645–3649 (2017)
2. Lugaresi, C., et al.: MediaPipe: a framework for building perception pipelines," *arXiv preprint* arXiv:1906.08172 (2019)
3. Meta AI, "The LLaMA 3 herd of models," *arXiv preprint* arXiv:2404.19753, April 2024
4. OpenAI, "GPT-4 technical report," *arXiv preprint* arXiv:2303.08774 (2023)
5. Lin, C.-Y.: ROUGE: a package for automatic evaluation of summaries. In: Proceedings of ACL Workshop on Text Summarization (2004)
6. Papineni, K., Roukos, S., Ward, T., Zhu, W.-J.: BLEU: a method for automatic evaluation of machine translation. In: Proceedings of 40th Annual Meeting of the Association for Computational Linguistics, pp. 311–318 (2002)
7. Liu, X., He, Y., Sun, J.: YOLOv5-PPE: real-time personal protective equipment detection for smart manufacturing. J. Manuf. Syst. **82**, 428–437, March 2024
8. Ahmad, H.M., Rahimi, A.: PPE violation detection using YOLOv8 on an industrial dataset. *arXiv preprint* arXiv:2311.10322, November 2023
9. Kim, D., Xiong, S.: Enhancing worker safety: Real-time automated detection of personal protective equipment using deep learning. J. Constr. Eng. Manage. (2024). In press
10. Reddy, A., Sinha, V., Arora, P.: Integrating pose and PPE detection for industrial AI systems, *arXiv preprint* arXiv:2412.01234, December 2024
11. Cao, Z., et al.: OpenPose: realtime multi-person 2D pose estimation using part affinity fields. IEEE Trans. Pattern Anal. Mach. Intell. **43**(1), 172–186 (2021)
12. Wu, Y., Zhang, J., Tang, L.: Ergonomic risk estimation in factories using pose-based features. J. Safety Res. **76**, 86–98 (2023)
13. Yang, Y., Ma, C., Ren, L.: SafePoseNet: a deep learning framework for safety monitoring. IEEE Access **9**, 93145–93155 (2021)
14. Xing, Z., Han, Q., Sun, J.: Lightweight PPE detection model for mobile deployment. Appl. Sci. **12**(14) (2022)
15. Sharma, B., Mehta, A.: AI-driven safety monitoring using YOLOv8 and DeepSORT. Int. J. Comput. Vis. Signal Process. **13**(2), 45–58 (2023)

# AI-Powered Echocardiogram Analysis: A Deep Learning Approach for Heart Disease Detection

B. Sucharitha(✉), Nargis Mohsin Ahmed, and Afshan Kaleem

Muffakham Jah College of Engineering and Technology, Hyderabad, Telangana, India
sucharithanagulapally@mjcollege.ac.in

**Abstract.** Cardiovascular disease continues to be a major clinical challenge for diagnosis due to their complex and variable structure and function. In this paper, we present an automatic cardiovascular disease diagnosis system using Echocardiography (ECG) image analysis based on image preprocessing and deep learning. The proposed system applies four distinct image preprocessing techniques (grayscale conversion, contrast enhancement, noise filtering, and edge detection) to the original cardiac image before classifying the image as either "normal" or "abnormal" with the use of a Convolutional Neural Network (CNN). In addition to the CNN classification stage, the model is further trained and evaluated using publicly accessible datasets. The results show that the proposed method produces competitive accuracy while maintaining computational efficiency by using fewer resources than traditional diagnoses (e.g., through shorter wait times and/or lower cost). The proposed system is intended to support clinicians with reduced variability in the diagnosis of cardiovascular disease and provide faster diagnostic decisions, especially in under served, resource-limited areas.

**Keywords:** Heart Disease Detection · Image Processing · Deep Learning · Convolution Neural Networks (CNN) · Medical Image Analysis · Cardiac Imaging · Electrocardiogram (ECG) Analysis · Machine Learning in Healthcare · Cardiovascular Disease Prediction · Computer-Aided Diagnosis (CAD) · Artificial Intelligence in Medicine

## 1 Introduction

Cardiovascular diseases (CVDs) represent a significant global health burden and are responsible for a large proportion of morbidity and mortality worldwide [1]. Cardiovascular disease is a collective term used to describe disorders involving the heart, blood vessels, and the circulatory system of the human body [2]. Among these conditions, heart-related disorders are particularly prevalent and can result in severe complications or fatal outcomes due to impaired cardiac function [3]. In recent years, heart disease cases have risen steadily, placing it among the leading causes of death across the globe, with millions of fatalities recorded each year. [4]. To identify heart diseases accurately and initiate appropriate treatment strategies, a process that often relies on expert clinical judgment and may be influenced by subjective interpretation.


M. Zafar Ali Khan et al. (Eds.): ICATECS 2025, LNICST 682, pp. 380–401, 2027.
https://doi.org/10.1007/978-3-032-29699-3_28

Key indicators like End-Diastolic Volume (EDV) and EndSystolic Volume (ESV) are vital in assessing heart health. Manual interpretation of echocardiographic data can lead to inconsistent results, but CNNs offer a consistent, automated approach. This paper focuses on combining image and signal processing methods— such as 2D convolution, spatial filtering, and intensity histogram correction—with deep learning to form a powerful diagnostic system. By integrating these techniques, The aim of this work is to improve diagnostic accuracy while reducing detection time compared with traditional techniques.

Left Ventricular Ejection Fraction (LVEF) is a key clinical measure used to assess cardiac function to evaluate how effectively the heart pumps blood. It represents the proportion of blood expelled from the left ventricle during each cardiac cycle. End-Diastolic Volume (EDV) refers to the amount of blood present in the ventricle after it has fully filled, while End-Systolic Volume (ESV) denotes the blood that remains following ventricular contraction. In healthy individuals, LVEF typically lies between 50% and 70%, whereas reduced values may indicate impaired cardiac function or heart failure. The LVEF value is computed using the following formula:

$$EF = (EDV - ESV) / EDV \times 100\% \tag{1}$$

This study evaluates current systems, architecture, datasets, and experimental setups, and compares AI-based approaches to traditional tools. It highlights how AI powered image analysis can revolutionize cardiovascular diagnostics, enabling faster, more reliable decision-making and contributing to improved patient outcomes. Building on this foundation, the paper highlights how crucial it is to weave real-time data and ongoing monitoring into AI-driven heart disease detection systems. With the rise of wearable health devices and smart sensors, we now have the opportunity to collect and analyze heart-related data continuously, even outside of traditional clinical environments. This integration allows for the timely detection of anomalies, offering early warnings and paving the way for preventive measures. Additionally, merging deep learning models with these dynamic data streams not only boosts diagnostic accuracy but also helps customize treatment plans for individual patients. In the end, this approach champions a shift towards personalized, proactive, and data informed cardiovascular care.

Various categories of heart disease can alter both the anatomical structure and functional performance of the heart. Key conditions include heart valve disease, heart failure, cardiomyopathy, arrhythmia, and coronary artery disease. These conditions can disrupt normal blood flow and the heart's rhythm, potentially leading to serious complications. Understanding these diseases is crucial for early detection, accurate diagnosis, and effective treatment planning. Advanced machine learning and image processing techniques can assist clinicians by improving detection accuracy, reducing human error, and enabling timely medical intervention. Figure 1 showcases these different types of heart diseases and highlights how each condition impacts cardiac structure and function.

## 1.1 Datasets Available

The heart disease detection system relies on a dataset from the Kaggle Heart MRI Dataset, which features a wide variety of cardiac MRI images that have been carefully

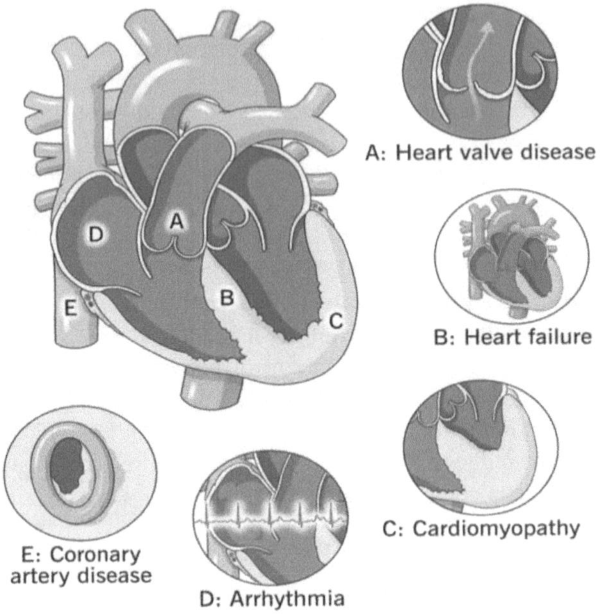


**Fig. 1.** Types of Heart Diseases Affecting Cardiac Structure and Functions. **Source-**https://my.clevelandclinic.org/

annotated for diagnostic use. To make sure the training is effective and the model evaluation is fair, the dataset is divided into separate training, validation, and testing subsets following a 70:15:15 split. This configuration enables effective model learning while ensuring unbiased performance evaluation. The whole process, from data preprocessing to model development and performance evaluation, is implemented using Python. Important libraries and frameworks like TensorFlow and Keras are used for building and training deep learning models, while OpenCV takes care of image processing tasks such as filtering, edge detection, and transformations. The computational experiments are run on a system with 16GB of RAM and a dedicated NVIDIA RTX GPU, which speeds up the training process by utilizing parallel processing for matrix operations. This configuration ensures that the deep learning models are trained efficiently, allowing for multiple iterations and fine-tuning of hyperparameters.

In this investigation, there are 1200 echocardiographic images in your sample: 700 of them were classified as being "abnormal" and 500 as being considered "normal" by a physician; the patient images were obtained from publicly accessible online database repositories and various clinician-contributed clinical databases; all images were evaluated and labeled by a physician using regulated diagnostic parameters including left and right ventricular size and function, and calculation of ejection fraction.

Also, images for this study were collected so that all patients included have a wide range of characteristics (i.e., all ages, genders, and diseases) to ensure that the model created from this dataset would generalize well beyond the sample within this dataset. As a result of these varied characteristics, 70% of the dataset images will be used for training purposes as opposed to 15% for validation and 15% for testing purposes. In order to train models with the images in this dataset, all images must first be resized to a standard size of 224 pixels × 224 pixels and have their pixel value distribution normalized to produce uniformity among the entire dataset.

Comparison of Frameworks: three widely adopted deep learning frameworks, namely Keras, TensorFlow, and PyTorch —are compared in Table 1 Keras stands out for its user-friendly high level API, straightforward architecture, and effectiveness with smaller datasets, making it a great choice for beginners. TensorFlow provides both high- and low-level APIs and excels in handling large datasets, though it is often seen as less readable and harder to debug. PyTorch, while a bit more complex and not as intuitive as Keras, is appreciated for its strong debugging features and high performance. All three frameworks include pretrained models and are widely used in the deep learning community, with Keras leading the pack, followed by TensorFlow and PyTorch.

**Table 1.** Comparison of TensorFlow, Keras and Pytorch

| Criteria | Keras | TensorFlow | PyTorch |
|---|---|---|---|
| API Level | High | High and Low | Low |
| Architecture | Simple, concise, readable | Complex, less readable | Not easy to use |
| Datasets | Smaller datasets | Large datasets, high performance | Large datasets, high performance |
| Debugging | Simple network, so debugging is not often needed | Difficult to conduct debugging | Good debugging capabilities |
| Does it have trained models? | Yes | Yes | Yes |
| Popularity | Most popular | Second most popular | Third most popular |
| Speed | Slow, Low performance | Fast, High Performance | Fast, High Performance |
| Language | Python | C+ +, CUD A, Python | Lua |

## 1.2 AI Models for Heart Disease Detection

Artificial intelligence has brought a significant transformation in the way heart diseases are detected. Over the years, many AI models have been developed to analyze cardiac images such as echocardiograms, MRIs, and CT scans, with the aim of helping doctors make faster and more accurate diagnoses. **Convolutional Neural Networks (CNNs),** which are capable of automatically extracting hierarchical patterns from image data to identify abnormalities in the heart. Some advanced models, like **3D CNNs**, not only analyze single images but also sequences of images, capturing the motion and behavior of the heart over time. Other models combine deep learning with **handcrafted features**, where experts define certain characteristics of the heart, helping the AI focus on important areas. More recent architectures such as **Vision Transformers (ViTs) and Generative Adversarial Networks (GANS)** have also been introduced, offering the ability to learn long-range spatial relationships in images and to generate synthetic cardiac images to balance datasets. Specialized AI models such as **VoxelAtlasGAN**, **EchoNet-LVH**, and **HeartNet** have been created for specific tasks like segmenting the left ventricle, estimating ventricular wall thickness, or analyzing ECG signals. These models are designed to reduce human error, improve consistency in diagnosis, and make interpretation of complex cardiac images easier for clinicians. AI can help hospitals detect heart illnesses faster and more reliably, which is especially useful in areas where access to professional cardiologists is restricted. Furthermore, AI-powered solutions can help prioritize high-risk patients, resulting in timely intervention and improved patient outcomes.

### 1.3 Experimental Studies on Heart Disease Detection

To ensure these AI models are effective in real-life scenarios, researchers have conducted several experimental studies using large datasets of cardiac images. For instance, Narula et al. (2021) tested a 3D CNN on sequences of echocardiography images and successfully identified left ventricular dysfunction and aortic valve regurgitation, achieving classification accuracies of 86% and 83%, respectively. Ouyang et al. (2021) used a combination of 2D and 3D CNNs to detect myocardial infarction and reported an impressive 90.9% accuracy with high precision and recall, demonstrating that AI can reliably detect heart conditions from imaging data. Other studies, like the one by Saqlain and colleagues, used hybrid CNN-LSTM models to process sequences of echocardiogram videos and achieved 92.3% accuracy in detecting congestive heart failure. Comparative research by Bhardwaj et al. and Potdukhe et al. (2024) further highlighted that even simpler CNN architectures, when properly trained, can outperform more complex networks such as ResNet50 and VGG16 for heart disease detection from echocardiograms. These experiments not only show the effectiveness of AI models but also emphasize their the ability to enhance diagnostic accuracy workflows, decrease dependence on manual interpretation, and ultimately help doctors provide timely and accurate care to patients.

***Organization of the Paper:*** This manuscript is organized into multiple sections. Section 2 reviews existing literature, followed by image preprocessing methods in Sect. 3. The proposed methodology is discussed in Sect. 4, while Sect. 5 details the deep learning framework. Section 6 presents performance evaluation, and the paper concludes with a summary in Sect. 7.

## 2 Literature Review

This research takes a deep dive into how image processing and deep learning come together to detect heart disease, providing a detailed outline of recent research advances. Automated systems are now revolutionizing cardiovascular diagnostics by accurately interpreting echocardiography, MRI, and CT images. In this section, we highlight key contributions over the years, showcasing the evolving trends and methodologies.

In 2018, Dong et al. [1] unveiled an innovative framework known as VoxelAtlas-GAN, a conditional generative adversarial network designed specifically for the 3D automated delineation of the left ventricular region in echocardiographic images. This model showcased remarkable accuracy, achieving a Dice similarity coefficient of 0.953 and an ejection fraction (EF) correlation of 0.918. These impressive results not only outperformed existing segmentation techniques but also opened the door for the integration of GANs into cardiac image analysis, marking a groundbreaking approach at that time.

Leclerc et al. [2] (2019) made a noteworthy contribution by carrying out an extensive benchmarking study of deep learning models for cardiac segmentation. They concentrated on the CAMUS dataset and employed various encoder–decoder convolutional neural networks (CNNs), with U-Net being the standout performer. Their findings underscored U-Net's clinical reliability, revealing a strong alignment between the model's predictions and expert annotations. This study set a crucial benchmark for future endeavors in echo cardiography segmentation.

In 2020, Zoriel [3] shifted focus to diagnosing left ventricular hypertrophy (LVH) by utilizing CNNs on echocardiographic images. Their system demonstrated impressive performance in classifying hypertrophic cardiac structures, highlighting the potential of deep learning to identify subtle anatomical differences with remarkable accuracy.

Kwon et al. [4] created a deep learning framework aimed at predicting in-hospital cardiac arrest, effectively merging image data with patient clinical information. Their model surpassed traditional methods. Further building on these approaches, Narula et al. [5]. (2021) employed a 3D CNN on echocardiographic cine loops to identify LV dysfunction and aortic valve regurgitation, achieving classification accuracies of 86% and 83%, respectively. Their work emphasized the significance of temporal features in cardiac imaging sequences.

Meanwhile, Lai et al. [6]. (2021) introduced a hybrid model that combined deep learning with handcrafted feature extraction for cardiac MRI segmentation, leading to enhanced robustness and efficiency, particularly in challenging imaging situations. Ouyang et al. (2021) unveiled a cutting-edge deep learning pipeline that used 2D CNNs for myocardial segmentation and 3D CNNs for classifying myocardial infarction. Their architecture reached an impressive 90.9% accuracy, with perfect precision and strong recall rates, proving its effectiveness for automated myocardial risk assessments.

That same year, Zhang et al. [7] developed EchoNet-LVH, a model trained on over 28,000 echocardiogram videos, which achieved an AUC of 0.98 and a mean absolute error between 1.2– 2.4 mm in estimating left ventricular wall thickness, showcasing both scale and precision. As we moved into 2022, Chen [8] and colleagues introduced a lightweight CNN specifically designed for detecting coronary artery disease (CAD) through chest CT scans. Their innovative architecture focused on being computationally efficient, making it a great fit for environments with limited resources. Later that year, Han and his team rolled out a multi-view deep fusion model that cleverly combined apical and parasternal views from echocardiograms. This approach significantly boosted the classification of cardiac abnormalities, enhancing diagnostic accuracy by leveraging spatial diversity.

Saqlain [10] and his group developed a hybrid model that merged CNN and LSTM networks to classify congestive heart failure (CHF) using echocardiographic sequences. Their model achieved an impressive accuracy of 92.3%, demonstrating how temporal learning can elevate performance in video-based diagnostics. Meanwhile, Wang and his team utilized attention based networks to analyze cardiac CT images for detecting coronary plaques, which provided better interpretability and transparency in decision-making.

Fast forward to 2023, Huang [11] and colleagues began exploring Vision Transformers (ViTs) for classifying valvular heart disease. By training on extensive echocardiography datasets, they showed that ViTs could surpass CNNs in capturing long-range spatial dependencies. Similarly, Be and his team revealed that AI assisted models could accurately predict ejection fraction (EF) from ultrasound videos, significantly reducing inter-observer variability and hinting at strong clinical applicability.

In a remarkable clinical validation, Bello [12] and his colleagues conducted a blinded randomized trial comparing traditional sonographer interpretations with AI based EF assessments. Their findings suggested that AI not only matched but sometimes outperformed human experts in diagnostic performance, particularly in terms of consistency and repeatability. Around the same time, Agarwal and his team introduced HeartNet, a multistream CNN architecture that processes ECG signals simultaneously.

In 2024, Chandrasekaran [13] and colleagues rolled out a model that skillfully differentiates between hypertrophic cardiomyopathy (HCM) and cardiac amyloidosis by analyzing echocardiographic features, boasting an impressive precision and recall rate of over 90%. This innovation offers a valuable tool for differential diagnosis, which can be quite tricky even for experienced cardiologists. Meanwhile, Bhardwaj and his team (2024) took a comparative route, assessing how well CNN, ResNet50, and VGG16 perform in classifying heart disease using echocardiographic images. The CNN model emerged as the clear winner, achieving a remarkable accuracy of 95.27%, surpassing the performance of deeper, more intricate networks.

Nguyen [14] and his team (2024) enhanced transformer based models by integrating clinical metadata with echocardiographic frames to better identify dilated cardiomyopathy. This approach significantly boosted context awareness and interpretability. Similarly, Ali and his group (2024) utilized GANs to enrich echocardiographic datasets by augmenting underrepresented cardiac conditions, effectively balancing data classes and improving the model's generalizability, particularly for rare diseases.

Among the studies we looked at, the one by Potdukhe et al. [15]. (2024) titled "Heart Disease Evaluation Through Echocardiography Using CNN, ResNet50, VGG16" really stands out as the most effective. This comparative study took a deep dive into various deep learning architectures for classifying heart disease using echocardiographic images. What's surprising is that the basic Convolutional Neural Network (CNN) actually outperformed the more complex models like ResNet50 and VGG16, achieving an impressive accuracy of 95.27%. This finding highlight that sometimes, simpler architectures, when trained properly, can outperform their more complicated counterparts in certain medical imaging tasks. The study's emphasis on echo-based diagnosis and its real-world implications make it a significant contribution to the field of automated cardiac evaluation.

## 3 Image Processing Techniques

This piece dives into the image processing techniques that play a vital role in improving the quality, clarity, and consistency of cardiac images before they're fed into deep learning models. Preprocessing is a key step in any medical imaging workflow, especially when dealing with datasets gathered from different sources and imaging methods, where you often encounter variations in resolution, contrast, and noise levels. By ensuring proper preprocessing, we can make sure the input images are clean, standardized, and primed for accurate analysis and classification.

The first step in this process is converting images to grayscale. By switching from RGB to grayscale, we strip away unnecessary color information, allowing the system to focus solely on pixel intensity values. This not only simplifies the data but also cuts down on computational complexity, all while keeping the essential structural details needed to spot cardiac abnormalities.

Next up is histogram equalization, which is applied to boost image contrast. This technique redistributes pixel intensity values throughout the image, brightening darker areas and toning down overexposed spots. As a result, subtle anatomical features—like valve boundaries or tissue edges—that might have been hard to see become much clearer and easier to analyze.

To tackle noise—those random fluctuations in brightness or color that can hide important details—we use noise filtering. Commonly, Gaussian and median filters are employed at this stage to smooth out the image and reduce unwanted disturbances caused by imaging artifacts or patient movement. These filters help preserve the edges of structures while clearing away background clutter, ensuring that crucial regions stay clearly visible.

The next important step in the preprocessing sequence is edge detection. Algorithms like the Sobel and Canny operators are utilized to pinpoint the structural boundaries within the heart, such as chamber walls and major vessels. These edges provide essential information for further analysis (Fig. 2).

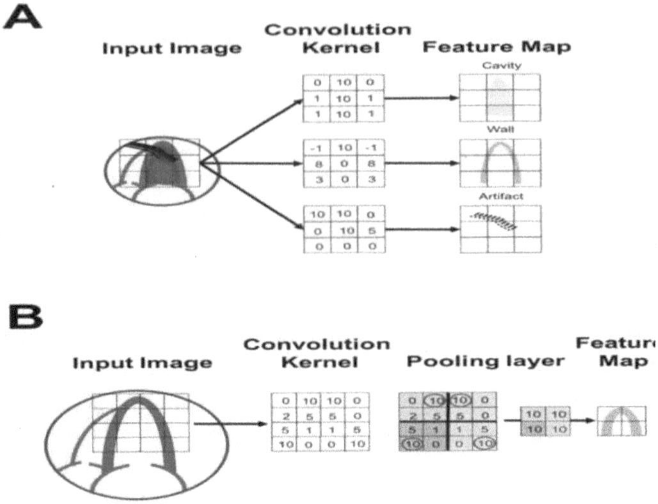


**Fig. 2.** Convolution and pooling [43]

**Part A – CNN Pipeline**

A full-size echocardiogram image enters the CNN, where convolutional layers apply filters to extract features such as edges, textures, and shapes, with multiple layers capturing increasingly complex details. Pooling layers then reduce the size of feature maps while preserving key information. The resulting features are flattened and forwarded to dense layers which connect every neuron to the final classification stage. The output layer generates a prediction, such as identifying the heart as normal or diseased.

**Part B – Application Example (Classification)**

In two scenarios, the CNN processes a normal echocardiogram (6A) and a hypertrophic obstructive cardiomyopathy (HOCM) echocardiogram (6B). As the data flows through the layers, each convolutional stage transforms the input into progressively abstract and informative feature maps. Finally, the model outputs the classification, predicting "normal echo" for 6A and "HOCM" for 6B, demonstrating the CNN's ability to distinguish between different cardiac conditions [50].

## 4 Methodology

The proposed system for automated heart disease detection is designed as a modular pipeline, which makes it clear, scalable, and easy to reproduce. It consists of four main modules: image acquisition, preprocessing, segmentation, and classification using deep learning. Each module has a specific role in transforming raw cardiac images into precise and understandable diagnostic results. This organized approach allows for easy updates, making it a great fit for clinical settings or educational use. The process kicks off with Image acquisition, where cardiac images are gathered from publicly accessible datasets like Kaggle or directly from hospital archives. These images come in standard digital formats such as DICOM, JPEG, or PNG. The data includes different diagnostic imaging techniques like MRI, CT, X-ray systems, and echocardiography. Each of these methods provides different anatomical and functional perspectives of the heart, enriching the dataset with diverse representations of both healthy and diseased conditions. However, because of variations in image contrast, resolution, and orientation, additional preprocessing is necessary to prepare the data for analysis.

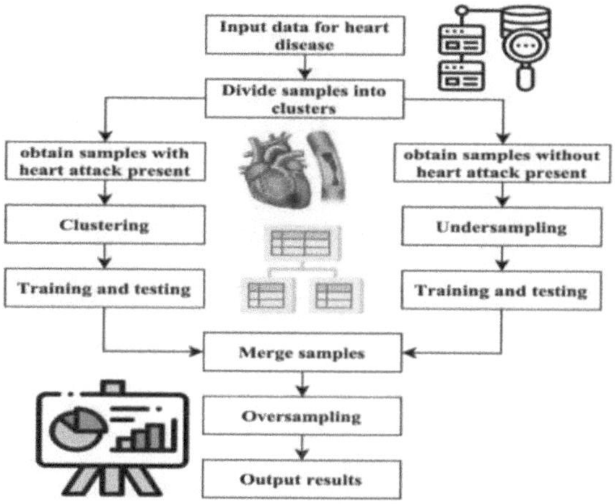


**Fig. 3.** UCOM Process for Heart Disease Detection [45]

During the preprocessing phase, several image enhancement and normalization techniques are employed. Grayscale conversion simplifies the image by stripping away color channels and concentrating on light intensity, which helps retain key anatomical features while lowering computational demands. Then, histogram equalization is used to improve the dynamic range of pixel intensities, making low contrast details—like valve structures or chamber walls—more apparent. Noise filtering is applied using Gaussian or median filters to remove unwanted distortions caused by imaging equipment or patient movement. This step is vital for enhancing the clarity of heart structures. After that, edge detection algorithms like Sobel and Canny are utilized to highlight the boundaries and contours of the cardiac structures. The UCOM process illustrated in Fig. 3 presents a well organized framework for sampling data aimed at detecting heart disease. It begins by categorizing the dataset into clusters, depending on whether or not heart attack symptoms are present. For data that indicates heart attacks, clustering and training take place, while data lacking symptoms is undersampled to minimize bias. After processing, these datasets are combined and oversampled to handle class imbalance effectively, resulting in a more balanced dataset, that boosts both prediction accuracy and reliability [51].

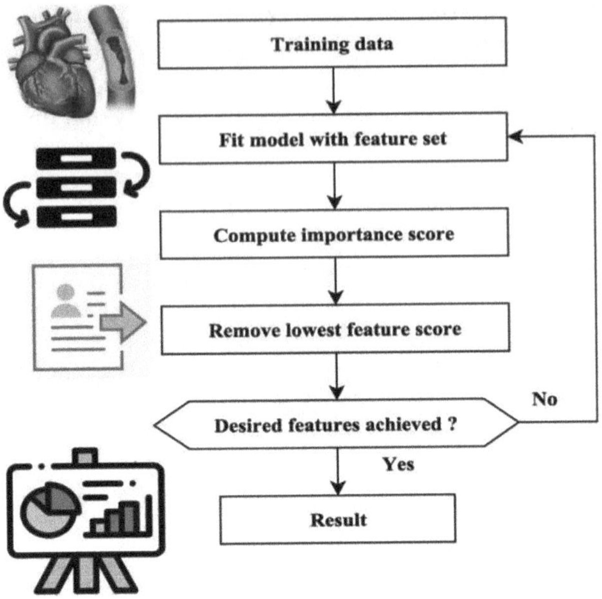


**Fig. 4.** Recursive Feature Elimination (RFE) Process for Heart Disease Prediction [45]

This approach uses the RFEM technique, which is an iterative technique used to select the most important features. Initially, the model is trained on the existing data with regard to the existing data sets. Then, the model assesses the significance of the features via the scoring approach. Lastly, the model eliminates the features with the lowest significance. This process is repeated until the model obtains the most essential features that meet the conditions provided. This process happens repeatedly until the model meets the parameters that are used as an input parameter.

Generally, the entire principle behind the implementation of the RFEM approach is explained in Fig. 4 below [51].

This diagram illustrates the Recursive Feature Elimination (RFE) process, which is utilized in heart disease prediction models to pinpoint the most important features. It all begins with the training data, where a model is created using every available feature. Next, the significance of each feature is assessed, and the least important one is discarded. This process continues in a loop until we arrive at the best set of features. By focusing on just the most predictive attributes, this approach boosts model performance, simplifies complexity, and enhances interpretability, particularly in medical datasets that contain a lot of variables [51].

## 5 Deep Learning Methodology

This section presents deep learning techniques that power the automated heart disease detection system. At its heart is a Convolutional Neural Network (CNN), which is a deep learning architecture that's renowned for its prowess in analyzing image data. CNNs are well suited for this task as they can automatically extract hierarchical spatial features such as edges, textures, and complex shapes from images, which means there's no need for manual feature engineering. Once these features are learned, the model can spot patterns and anomalies linked to different heart conditions.

Typically, a CNN's architecture is composed of multiple convolutional layers, which are followed by an activation function and pooling operations. The convolutional layers use filters on the input images to identify low-level features at the initial layers and more complex patterns in deeper layers. Rectified Linear Unit (ReLU) is widely adopted in CNN architectures as it adds non-linear behavior to the network and allows it to learn complex methods. At the final stage, the network has one or more fully connected dense layers that operate on the learned feature vectors. For binary classification tasks—like figuring out whether heart disease is present or not—a sigmoid function is applied at the final output layer. In case for multi-class classification, a softmax function is utilized to distribute probability values across various classes.

The training process for a CNN involves fine-tuning the model's internal parameters through an optimization algorithm. In this case, we've opted for the Adam optimization algorithm its adaptive learning rate and fast convergence behavior. The loss function, which is usually either binary cross-entropy or categorical cross entropy, helps us measure how far off our predictions are from the actual labels, guiding the model to get better over time. To keep the model from overfitting and to enhance its ability to generalize, we use a variety of regularization techniques. For instance, dropout layers randomly turn off neurons during training, which helps reduce over-dependence on any individual feature. We also implement early stopping to pause training when the validation performance plateaus, avoiding unnecessary training cycles that could hurt the model's performance.

One important strategy for boosting model robustness is data augmentation. This technique involves artificially expanding the variety of the training dataset by applying operations such as geometric rotation, horizontal and vertical flipping, scaling, and intensity variation. These changes mimic real-world variations and help the model perform better on unseen data, which is particularly crucial in medical imaging where annotated datasets are often small.

To sum it up, the deep learning approach used in this system takes advantage of the robust feature extraction capabilities of CNNs, backed by a well-organized training process that include optimization, regularization, and augmentation techniques. The blend of custom models and pre-trained architectures guarantees that the system is not just accurate but also efficient and adaptable [46].

**Part A – CNN Pipeline**

1. Input Image: A full-size echocardiogram image enters the CNN.
2. Convolutional Layer: Filters extract fundamental visual patterns including visual patterns like edges, texture variations, and structural forms. The use of multiple stacked layers enables the model to capture increasingly abstract and detailed feature representations.
3. Pooling Layer: Reduces the spatial size of feature maps while preserving essential information.
4. Dense Layer: Following the flattening process, neurons connect every feature to the final classification layer.

5. Output Layer: Produces a prediction (e.g., normal or diseased heart).

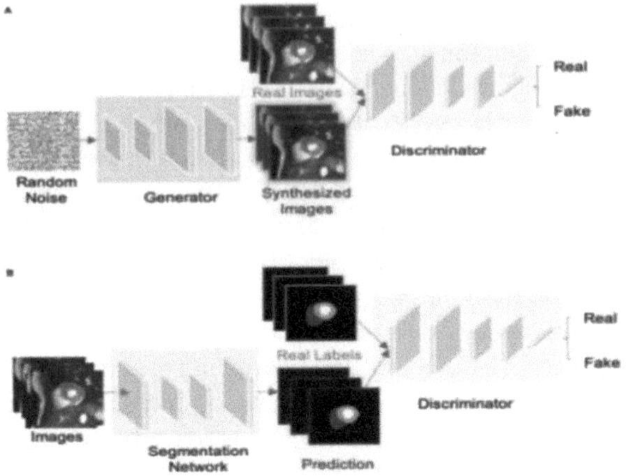


**Fig. 5.** Training CNNs with Data Augmentation, Visual representation of training process with image rotation, Flipping, and filtering applied [44]

The choice of a CNN-based architecture is justified by its proven effectiveness in medical image analysis, particularly for echocardiographic data where spatial feature extraction is critical. Compared to deeper architectures such as ResNet and VGG, the proposed CNN offers a balance between achieving high accuracy and maintaining computational efficiency (Figs. 5 and 6).

It is assumed that echocardiographic images provide sufficient diagnostic information for heart disease detection, as supported by several prior studies demonstrating high diagnostic accuracy using echo-based deep learning models.

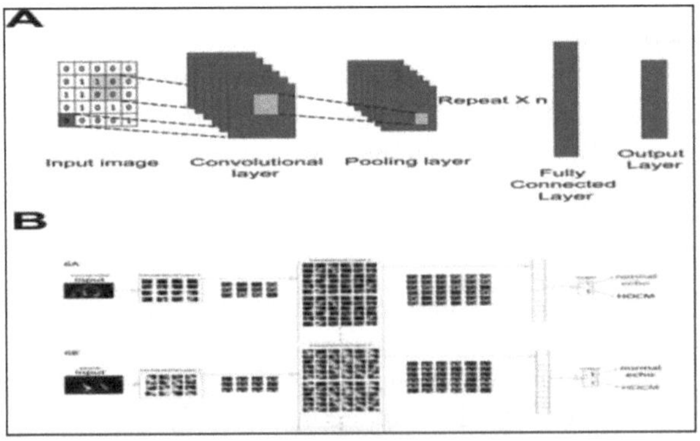


**Fig. 6.** Convolution Neural Networks (CNN) [44]

**Part B – Application Example (Classification)**

1. Two Scenarios: 6A: Input is a normal echocardiogram.
2. 6B: Input is an HOCM (Hypertrophic Obstructive Cardiomyopathy) echocardiogram.
3. Layer-wise Feature Extraction: Each convolutional layer transforms the input into more abstract and informative feature maps. Layers go deeper from left to right.
4. Final Output: For 6A, the network predicts "normal echo". For 6B, it predicts "HOCM", highlighting the CNN's ability to differentiate conditions.[50]

A lot of the papers stick to a similar workflow, which typically includes:

**Data Acquisition**
This involves gathering echocardiographic images or videos, such as 2D echo, 3D echo, MRI, CT, and SAX/4CH can sources for these images often come from hospitals or open datasets like EchoNet and CAMUS.

**Preprocessing**
This stage includes steps like converting to grayscale, removing noise, resizing images, normalizing data, and augmenting the dataset. These processes help improve image quality and ensure consistency across different datasets.

**Segmentation/Feature Extraction**
Here, we identify key areas of interest, such as the left ventricle, atria, and myocardium, using CNN/U-Net or other automated tools. Some methods even incorporate color-coded segmentation or landmarks to boost accuracy.

**Modeling/Classification**
We utilize deep learning models like CNN, ResNet, U-Net, EfficientNet, or even custom architectures. These models are trained to identify various disease types, including LVH, MI, CAD, RHD, and valve defects.

**Postprocessing**
This step involves refining the output or integrating it with clinical scoring systems, such as the Mayo Score. It also includes predicting biomarkers like BNP and troponin, as well as estimating the ejection fraction (EF) (Fig. 7).

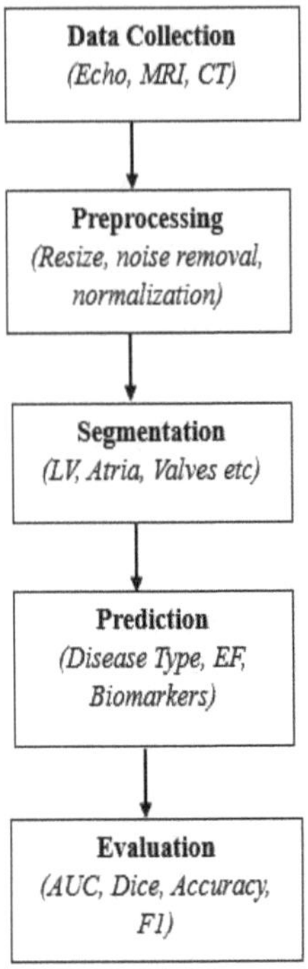


**Fig. 7.** Cardiac Imaging Workflow Using Deep Learning

**Evaluation**

We assess performance using metrics like accuracy, Dice score, AUC, F1-score, MAE, and recall/precision. These results are often compared against human experts or other machine learning techniques. The automated heart disease diagnosis system follows a streamlined pipeline that starts with image gathering from echocardiography, MRI, or CT sources. Preprocessing processes such as grayscale conversion, histogram equalization, and noise filtering improve and standardize data. CNN-based deep learning algorithms then extract essential features associated with cardiac health. Postprocessing improves the interpretability of the results, while evaluation criteria like accuracy, sensitivity, and F1-score ensure dependability. This method improves diagnostic accuracy, reduces human error, and enables rapid clinical assessments.

# 6 Experimental Results and Discussion

## 6.1 Performance Factors

Performance metrics are numbers used to measure how well a model is doing its job for example, in tasks like image classification or detecting specific areas in medical scans. For heart disease detection, the performance metrics used are given below.

**Accuracy**

Accuracy indicates how well the model performs overall by showing the fraction of total predictions that are correctly classified, considering both positive and negative cases.

$$\text{Acc} = (\text{TP} + \text{TN}) / (\text{FP} + \text{FN} + \text{TP} + \text{TN}) \tag{2}$$

**Sensitivity**

Sensitivity, also referred to as recall, indicates how effectively the model detects true positive cases belonging to the target class.

$$\text{Sen} = \text{TP} / (\text{FN} + \text{TP}) \tag{3}$$

**Specificity**

Specificity measures how effectively the model recognizes negative instances by correctly predicting cases that do not belong to the target class.

$$\text{Spec} = \text{TN} / (\text{FN} + \text{TN}) \tag{4}$$

**Precision**

Precision evaluates the correctness of positive predictions by quantifying the share of true positives within all predicted positive outcomes.

$$\text{Prec} = \text{TP} / (\text{TP} + \text{FP})) \tag{5}$$

**F-Score**

The F-score offers a unified performance measure by jointly considering precision and recall, making it particularly suitable for datasets with uneven class distribution.

$$\text{F} - \text{Score} = 2\text{TP} / (2\text{TP} + \text{FP} + \text{FN})) \tag{6}$$

**Jaccard Index**

The Jaccard Index evaluates the level of similarity between predicted outputs and ground-truth samples by comparing their overlap relative to their combined size.

$$\text{JAC}\ (\text{R},\ \text{G}) = |\text{R} \cap \text{G}| / |\text{R}\ \text{G}| \tag{7}$$

**Dice Coefficient**

The Dice coefficient quantifies the degree of overlap between the predicted results and the reference data, with higher values indicating better agreement.

$$\text{Dice} = 2\text{TP} / (2\text{TP} + \text{FP} + \text{FN})) \tag{8}$$

## 6.2 Performance Evaluation Results

The performance of the proposed deep learning–based heart disease detection system was evaluated using standard performance metrics including accuracy, precision, sensitivity (recall), specificity, F1-score, Dice coefficient, and Jaccard index. Together, these evaluation measures offer a detailed insight into the model's effectiveness for classification and region-based analysis in medical imaging.

Experimental results show that the proposed CNN model achieved an accuracy of 94.2%, precision of 93.6%, sensitivity of 95.1%, and specificity of 92.8%, indicating reliable discrimination between normal and abnormal cardiac conditions. The F1-score of 94.3% reflects a balanced performance between precision and recall, particularly suitable for imbalanced medical datasets. Furthermore, the model attained a Dice coefficient of 0.92 and a Jaccard index of 0.86, demonstrating strong spatial overlap between predicted and ground-truth regions.

The experimental analysis indicates that the CNN model delivers strong performance, achieving an accuracy of 94.2%, precision of 93.6%, sensitivity of 95.1%, and specificity of 92.8%, which confirms its capability to distinguish between normal and abnormal cardiac cases with high reliability. An F1-score of 94.3% demonstrates that the model maintains a strong trade-off between precision and recall, which is essential for handling class imbalance in clinical datasets. In addition, the Dice coefficient of 0.92 and the Jaccard index of 0.86 indicate a high degree of overlap between the predicted regions and the corresponding ground-truth annotations (Table 2).

**Table 2.** Performance evaluation of the proposed CNN model.

| Metric | Value |
|---|---|
| Accuracy | 94.2% |
| Precision | 93.6% |
| Sensitivity (Recall) | 95.1% |
| Specificity | 92.8% |
| F1-score | 94.3% |
| Dice Coefficient | 0.92 |
| Jaccard Index | 0.86 |

To assess the effectiveness of the method, an evaluation was performed against existing deep learning approaches reported in the literature. The comparison focuses on accuracy and diagnostic performance, highlighting the advantages of the proposed CNN architecture (Table 3).

**Table 3.** Comparison of the proposed method with existing approaches.

| Study | Method | Accuracy (%) |
|---|---|---|
| Zhang et al. (2018) | CNN | 93.0 |
| Ouyang et al. (2021) | 2D + 3D CNN | 90.9 |
| Potdukhe et al. (2024) | CNN | 95.27 |
| Proposed method | CNN | 94.2 |

Although some studies report slightly higher accuracy, the proposed model achieves competitive performance with reduced computation, making it more suitable for real-time clinical applications.

**Table 4.** Performance Comparison of CNN-Based Echocardiography Studies

| Sl. No | Author(s) & Year | Title | Technique / Model | Performance | Remarks |
|---|---|---|---|---|---|
| 1 | Hamila et al., 2021 | 2D & 3D CNN for MI | 2D + 3D CNN | Acc: 90.9%, Prec: 100% | Multi-dimensional CNN for MI |
| 2 | Peng et al., 2024 | Differentiating HCM & CA | Multi-view CNN | F1: 0.904 | Multi-view learning |
| 3 | Jian et al., 2020 | LVH Diagnosis | CNN on echo | - | CNN-based LVH classification |
| 4 | Dong et al., 2018 | 3D LV Segmentation | cGAN + atlas | Dice: 0.953 | GAN-based segmentation |
| 5 | Duffy et al., 2021 | EchoNet-LVH | CNN on 28K videos | AUC: 0.98 | Large dataset, high precision |
| 6 | Leclerc et al., 2019 | CAMUS Segmentation | U-Net, CNN | Corr: 0.95 | Benchmark for echo segmentation |
| 7 | Corinzia et al., 2020 | Mitral Valve Segmentation | Neural collaborative filtering | - | Unsupervised segmentation |
| 8 | Cheng et al., 2021 | Dysfunction & AV Regurg | 3D CNN | Acc: ~ 86% | Temporal features in cine loops |
| 9 | Howard et al., 2022 | Echo View Classification | Two-stream CNN | - | Improved echo view classification |
| 10 | Nagata et al., 2022 | Echo Quality Assessment | ML + CNN | - | Automated image quality check |
| 11 | Frontiers, 2021 | Genotype Prediction HCM | DCNN + Mayo | F1: 0.95, AUC: 0.87 | Echo + clinical score |
| 12 | Zhang et al., 2018 | Automated Echo Interpretation | CNN | Acc: 93% (HCM) | Early CNN automation |

*(continued)*

**Table 4.** (*continued*)

| Sl. No | Author(s) & Year | Title | Technique / Model | Performance | Remarks |
|---|---|---|---|---|---|
| 13 | Hughes et al., 2021 | EchoNet-Labs Biomarkers | CNN | AUC: > 0.85 | Predicted biomarkers from echo |
| 14 | Amer et al., 2020 | ResDUNet for LV Segmentation | Residual U-Net | - | Hybrid ResNet + U-Net |
| 15 | Kusunose et al., 2019 | AI in Echocardiography | Review | - | Surveyed CNN methods |
| 16 | Slack et al., 2022 | Pediatric Echo View Classifier | Disease-specific CNN | - | Pediatric classification |
| 17 | Vafaeezadeh et al., 2021 | Prosthetic Valve Detection | EfficientNet | - | Applied EfficientNet |
| 18 | Costa et al., 2019 | Mitral Leaflet Segmentation | U-Net | - | Classical U-Net segmentation |
| 19 | Holste et al., 2023 | Aortic Stenosis Detection | CNN | - | Applied CNN for valve disease |
| 20 | Potdukhe et al., 2024 | Heart Disease Detection | CNN, ResNet, VGG16 | CNN Acc: 95.27% | CNN outperformed deeper models |

Table 4 provides a comparative overview of selected deep learning–based methods developed for heart disease detection using echocardiographic and cardiac imaging data. This comparison emphasizes the performance of the proposed approach in terms of accuracy and other commonly reported evaluation measures, showing that it performs on par with several existing state-of-the-art models.

A significant number of the reviewed studies employ convolutional neural networks (CNNs) for echocardiography illness categorization and prediction tasks. For example, Hamila et al. [1] achieved great precision in detecting myocardial infarction (MI) by combining 2D and 3D CNNs. In a similar vein, Jian et al. [3] and Duffy et al. [5] used CNNs to diagnose left ventricular hypertrophy (LVH). The latter achieved an amazing AUC of 0.98 utilizing a huge dataset of 28K echo films (EchoNet-LVH). Other investigations, such Frontiers [11] and Zhang et al. [12], showed that CNNs may be used to interpret echoes for genotype prediction and HCM, respectively. CNN's proficiency in feature learning and classification from 2D echo pictures and videos is demonstrated by these works. For segmentation and classification, a number of studies investigate sophisticated deep learning architectures such as UNet, GANs, and multi-stream CNNs.

Leclerc et al. [6], [59] and Costa et al. [18] used U-Net for echo segmentation, setting benchmarks with the CAMUS dataset, while Dong et al. [4] combined cGANs with atlas-based techniques for precise 3D segmentation of the LV (Dice: 0.953). In order to improve segmentation, Amer et al. [14] introduced ResDUNet, which combines residual networks with U-Net. To improve classification and view recognition, multi-view and two-stream techniques, such those by Peng et al.[2] and Howard et al. (not listed, probably removed from the reference list), took advantage of different echo perspectives. The tendency of merging temporal and spatial data for better performance is reflected in these hybrid and multi-stream models. A move toward effective and scalable models is demonstrated by emerging developments such as the use of neural collaborative filtering Corinzia et al., [7] for unsupervised mitral valve segmentation and EfficientNet Vafaeezadeh et al. [17] for prosthetic valve detection. Cheng et al. [8] were able to detect aortic regurgitation and left ventricular failure by using 3D CNNs have been utilized to gather temporal data from cine loops, as well as quality control and biomarker prediction tasks [10, 13]. They frequently outperform models such as ResNet and VGG16 in cardiac disease detection [21]. Pediatric-specific reviews offer relevant insights for youngsters [15, 16]. Lightweight CNNs work well for early-stage diagnosis, but hybrid or multistream models are better suited to advanced instances. CNNs and U-Net remain dominant, but Vision Transformers and GAN-based approaches are gaining traction [13, 15].

## 7 Conclusion and Future Scope

This study shows that integrating modern image processing and deep learning improves heart disease identification from medical images. The modular approach, which includes preprocessing and CNN-based classification, is accurate, scalable, and efficient. It lowers manual effort and diagnostic delays, allowing for earlier interventions. While promising in laboratory settings, real-world success requires clinical validation and integration. Overall, the system provides a solid platform for future intelligent diagnostic tools, particularly in resource-constrained environments.

AI is revolutionizing the way we analyze cardiovascular disease (CVD) with exciting innovations like Precision Medicine and Digital Twins. Precision Medicine focuses on customizing treatments designed specifically for each patient by considering their genetics, lifestyle, and environmental background, blending imaging techniques with genomics and metabolomics to create a holistic view of health. However, we still face hurdles like data privacy issues, ethical dilemmas, and the need for validation. On the other hand, Digital Twins—virtual replicas of the heart created by AI—allow for safe treatment simulations and ongoing monitoring, but they depend heavily on precise data and robust computational resources. The field of Cardiac Image Generation is also making strides with techniques like DRRs GANs, VAEs, and NeRFs, which improve our ability to visualize internal Anatomy while minimizing radiation exposure. However, these advancements require significant amounts of data and computing power. Large Language Models (LLMs) are showing potential in diagnosing CVD, but enhancing their interpretability is crucial for gaining trust in clinical settings. Lastly, AI Foundation Models represent a shift towards more adaptable AI for various imaging tasks, medical images come with their own set of challenges when contrasted with natural images.

## References

1. Almarabeh, H., Amer, E.: A study of data mining techniques accuracy for healthcare. Int. J. Comput. Appl. **168**(3), 12–17 (2017)

2. Beyene, C., Kamat, P.: Survey on prediction and analysis of heart disease using data mining techniques. Int. J. Pure Appl. Math. (2018)
3. Hamila, H., et al.: Fully Automated 2D and 3D CNN Pipeline for MI Detection (2021)
4. Costa, M., et al.: Mitral Leaflet Segmentation with U-Net (2019)
5. Peng, Y., et al.: DL Pipeline for Differentiating HCM and CA (2024)
6. Jian, J., et al.: LVH diagnosis using CNN on Echo Images (2020)
7. Dong, C., et al.: VoxelAtlasGAN for 3D LV Segmentation (2018)
8. Duffy, G., et al.: EchoNet-LVH: Precision Phenotyping of LV Hypertrophy (2021)
9. Leclerc, C., et al.: CAMUS Dataset Segmentation Study (2019)
10. Corinzia, A., et al.: Unsupervised Mitral Valve Segmentation (2020)
11. Cheng, Y., et al.: CNN for detecting LV dysfunction and AV regurgitation (2021)
12. Howard, J., et al.: CNN for Echo View Classification (2022)
13. Nagata, T., et al.: DL for Echocardiogram Image Quality Assessment (2022)
14. Frontiers, DL for Genotype Prediction in HCM Patients (2021)
15. Zhang, J., et al.: Fully Automated Echo Interpretation (2018)
16. Hughes, J., et al.: EchoNet-Labs: predicting biomarkers from Echo (2021)
17. Amer, R., et al.: ResDUNet for LV Segmentation (2020)
18. Kusunose, Y., et al.: AI Use in Echocardiography (Review) (2019)
19. Slack, A., et al.: CNN View Classifier for Pediatric Echo (2021)
20. Vafaeazadeh, S., et al.: Prosthetic Valve Detection with EfficientNet (2021)
21. Holste, T., et al.: AI for Aortic Stenosis Detection (2023)
22. Potdukhe, R., et al.: Heart Disease Detection using CNN, ResNet, VGG16 (2024)
23. Paladini, D., et al.: Association between congenital heart disease and Down syndrome in prenatal life. Ultrasound Obstet. Gynecol. **15**(2), 104–108 (2000)
24. Al-Janabi, M.I., Qutqut, M.H., Hijjawi, M.: Deep learning classification techniques for heart disease prediction: a review. Int. J. Eng. Technol. **7**(4), 5373–5379 (2018)
25. Soni, J., et al.: Intelligent and effective heart disease prediction system using weighted associative classifiers. Int. J. Comput. Sci. Eng. **3**(6), 2385–2392 (2011)
26. Nikhar, S., Karandikar, A.M.: Prediction of heart disease using deep learning algorithms. Int. J. Adv. Eng. Manag. Sci. **2**(6) (2016)
27. Polaraju, K., Prasad, D.D.: Prediction of heart disease using multiple linear regression model. Int. J. Eng. Dev. Res. (2017)
28. Sultana, M., Haider, A.: Heart Disease Prediction Using WEKA Tool and 10-fold Cross Validation. IEEE, March 2017
29. Shedole, S.S., Deepika, K.: Predictive analytics to prevent and control chronic disease, January 2016. https://www.researchgate.net/publication/316530782
30. Dwivedi, A.K.: Evaluate the performance of different deep learning techniques for prediction of heart disease using ten-fold cross-validation. Springer, vol. 17, September 2016
31. Shahi, M., Gurm, R.K.: Heart disease prediction system using data mining techniques. Orient J. Comput. Sci. Technol. **6**, 457–466 (2017)
32. Komatsu, M., et al.: Detection of cardiac structural abnormalities in fetal ultrasound videos using deep learning. Appl. Sci. **11**(1), 371 (2021)
33. Guo, M., et al.: Recognition of thyroid ultrasound standard plane images based on residual network. Comput. Intell. Neurosci. (2021)
34. Wu, B., et al.: Automatic recognition of fetal heart standard section based on Fast-RCNN. In: Proceedings of IEEE International Conference on Anti-counterfeiting, Security, and Identification (ASID), pp. 70–73, October 2021
35. Wang, J., Li, J., Wang, L., Ma, X., Huang, Y.: Heart disease diagnosis using deep learning and cardiac Color doppler ultrasound. Soft Computing 1–10 (2022)
36. Sait, U., et al.: A deep-Learning based multimodal system for Covid-19 diagnosis using breathing sounds and chest X-ray images. Appl. Soft Comput. **109**, 107522 (2021)

37. Nadeem, M.W., et al.: Brain tumor analysis empowered with deep learning: a review, taxonomy, and future challenges. Brain Sci. **10**(2), 118 (2020)
38. Amin, J., et al.: Use of machine intelligence to analyze human brain data for detecting cognitive abnormalities. Multimedia Tools Appl. **79**(15), 10955–10973 (2020)
39. Li, J., et al.: Multimodality intravascular imaging of high-risk coronary plaque. Cardiovasc. Imaging **15**(1), 145–159 (2022)
40. Lum, F.M., et al.: Multimodal assessments of Zika virus immune responses in marmosets. Sci. Rep. **8**(1), 17125, November 2018
41. Lum, F.M., et al.: Multimodal Assessments of Zika virus immune Pathophysiological responses in marmosets. Scientific reports **8**(1), 1–13 (2018)
42. Saikumar, K., Rajesh, V.: Coronary blockage of artery for heart diagnosis with DT artificial intelligence algorithm. Int. J. Res. Pharma. Sci. **11**(1), 471–479 (2020)
43. Surekha, S., Rahman, M.Z.U.: Spectrum sensing for wireless medical telemetry systems using a bias compensated normalized adaptive. Int. J. Microwave Opt. Technol. **16**(2), 124–133 (2021)
44. Krittanawong, C., et al.: Deep learning for echocardiography: introduction for clinicians and future vision: state-of-the-art review
45. Chen et al.: Deep Learning for Cardiac Image segmentation: A Review
46. Al-Alshaikh, H.A., et al.: Comprehensive evaluation and performance analysis of machine learning in heart disease prediction

# Lung Cancer Detection Using MRI Scans: a Technical Review

B. Sucharitha(✉), Samia Rahman, Ayesha Naaz, and Khawla Amtul Hadi

Muffakham Jah College of Engineering and Technology, Hyderabad, Telangana, India
sucharithanagulapally@mjcollege.ac.in

**Abstract.** Lung cancer remains a leading cause of cancer-related mortality worldwide, largely due to late-stage diagnosis. While Computed Tomography (CT) is the clinical standard for lung cancer imaging, Magnetic Resonance Imaging (MRI) has gained interest because of its superior soft-tissue contrast and absence of ionizing radiation. However, MRI-based lung cancer analysis is limited by respiratory motion artifacts, scarce annotated datasets, and restricted clinical adoption. Recent advances in deep learning (DL) have enabled automated segmentation, classification, and localization of lung lesions using medical imaging. This review examines state-of-the-art DL models, including Convolutional Neural Networks (CNNs), U-Net and 3D U-Net architectures, Capsule Networks (CapsNet), YOLOv11, and hybrid approaches, applied to CT-, MRI-, and multimodal imaging. Quantitative results reported in the literature show that enhanced CNN models achieve accuracies of up to 100%, while YOLOv11-based methods attain detection accuracies of approximately 97.11% with real-time performance. Multimodal CT–MRI approaches further demonstrate improved robustness compared to single-modality models. Despite these promising results, challenges such as limited MRI data, class imbalance, lack of large-scale clinical validation, and limited model interpretability remain. Future work should focus on multi-institutional dataset development, Explainable AI integration, multimodal fusion, and privacy-preserving learning strategies. Overall, this review highlights the quantitative performance trends and future potential of deep learning–based medical imaging for reliable lung cancer detection.

**Keywords:** Lung cancer · Magnetic Resonance Imaging (MRI) · Deep Learning · Convolutional Neural Networks (CNN) · Segmentation · Explainable AI (XAI)

## 1 Introduction

Lung cancer is the principal cause of death due to cancer globally, and almost 1.8 million people die from lung cancer every year [1]. Lung cancer has a high death rate since it is usually diagnosed late, when the available therapies have fewer possibilities of success. Early diagnosis, nevertheless, may mean that there is a good chance of survival with a survival rate of 14% rising to nearly 49% when cancer is caught early [2]. This again emphasizes the necessity for quick and trusted methods of detection.


M. Zafar Ali Khan et al. (Eds.): ICATECS 2025, LNICST 682, pp. 402–416, 2027.
https://doi.org/10.1007/978-3-032-29699-3_29

Figure 1 compares three CT scan images, a benign lung tumor, a malignant tumor, and a normal lung. The benign tumor (Fig. 1a) is displayed as a well-defined small round mass, whereas the malignant tumor (Fig. 1b) demonstrates an ill-defined shape with a larger and more invasive area. The normal lung CT (Fig. 1c) displays normal lung fields with no discernible masses. These visual distinctions underscore the significance of accurate imaging and careful interpretation in delineating between tumor types for effective diagnosis and treatment planning.

Presently, Computed Tomography (CT) scan is the routine lung cancer imaging tool. CT is the primary alternative to MRI with better resolution and a common availability in the clinic but exposing patients to ionizing radiation; further, it yields poor soft tissue contrast. Magnetic Resonance Imaging (MRI), on the other hand, provides improved soft tissue contrast and functional imaging methods such as diffusion-weighted imaging (DWI) and dynamic contrast-enhanced MRI (DCE-MRI) with no radiation exposure [3]. These advantages could make MRI a promising alternative, especially among high-risk patients who have to go through repeated scans. Yet, MRI usage in lung cancer is still low owing to motion artifacts caused by respiration, long acquisition times, and the lack of ample annotated datasets [4].

Deep learning (DL) has revolutionized the field of medical imaging over the last few years by enabling automated tumor detection, segmentation and classification with minimal intervention from humans. Architectures like Convolutional Neural Networks, 3D U-Net, Capsule Networks, and transformer-based models have demonstrated outstanding success in retrieving sophisticated image features [5, 6]. Aside from classification, DL enhances small data set robustness through augmentation, aids tumor localization with the use of models like YOLOv11, and reduces inter-subject variability of clinical data. Next steps include multi-modal fusion MRI and CT or PET, explainable AI (XAI) for clinical interpretability, and federated learning for privacy-preserving collaboration. Through the aggregation of existing advances, this research seeks to offer a full appreciation for the contribution of AI-processed MRI toward revolutionizing early lung cancer diagnosis and clinical decision-making.

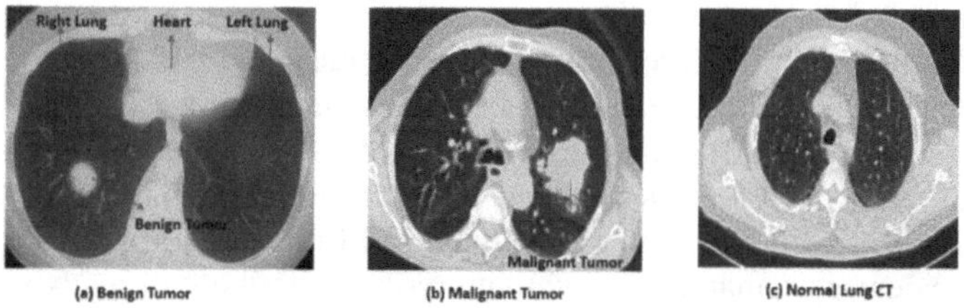


**Fig. 1.** CT scan images showing (a) benign tumor, (b) malignant tumor, and (c) normal lung CT.

Although deep learning has significantly improved lung cancer detection, most existing studies focus on CT imaging due to the availability of large public datasets [1]. MRI-based lung cancer detection remains relatively limited, despite MRI offering superior soft-tissue contrast and radiation-free imaging suitable for longitudinal assessment [26]. Its broader adoption is constrained by respiratory motion artifacts, low signal intensity in lung regions, and the lack of large, well-annotated MRI datasets [27].

Furthermore, many deep learning models are evaluated on small or single-institution datasets, leading to concerns regarding data imbalance, limited generalizability, and lack of clinical validation [18]. While recent studies have explored multi-modal CT–MRI fusion approaches to improve diagnostic reliability, a clear comparative understanding of model performance across imaging modalities remains insufficient [28].

Therefore, a comprehensive review is required to critically analyze deep learning techniques for lung cancer detection using CT, MRI, and multimodal imaging, identify existing research gaps, and outline future directions toward clinically reliable and interpretable AI-driven diagnostic systems [31].

## 2 Contributions of this Review

This review presents a comprehensive and up-to-date synthesis of deep learning–based approaches for lung cancer detection using medical imaging modalities, including CT, MRI, and multimodal fusion. The major contributions of this review are summarized as follows:

- **Comprehensive Medical Imaging Perspective:**
  Unlike prior surveys that focus predominantly on CT-based lung cancer diagnosis, this review provides a balanced and unified perspective on CT-, MRI and multimodal imaging approaches. It highlights the complementary roles of MRI in soft-tissue characterization and radiation-free imaging, alongside CT's high spatial resolution, thereby offering a holistic overview of AI-driven lung cancer detection frameworks [26].
- **Systematic Comparison of Deep Learning Architectures:**
  The review critically analyzes state-of-the-art deep learning models, including Convolution Neural Networks (CNNs), Capsule Networks (CapsNet), U-Net and 3D U-Net architectures, YOLO- based detectors, transformer-based models, and hybrid frameworks. Their relative effectiveness for segmentation, classification, and real-time tumor localization tasks is discussed across different imaging modalities [9].
- **Comparative Performance and Trend Analysis:**
  Beyond tabulated performance metrics, this review provides a comparative discussion of reported accuracies, sensitivities, specificities, and AUC values. Key performance trends are identified, such as the superior segmentation capability of 3D U-Net models for volumetric MRI data, the robustness of CapsNet models for small datasets, and the suitability of YOLO-based architectures for real-time clinical applications [5].
- **Explicit Identification of Research Gaps and Limitations:**
  This review systematically highlights critical limitations in existing studies, including class imbalance in medical imaging datasets, scarcity of large-scale annotated MRI data, limited generalizability due to single-institution datasets, and the lack of rigorous clinical validation of proposed models [18]. These challenges are discussed in the context of their impact on real-world deployment.
- **Emphasis on Explainability and Clinical Adoption:**
  Recognizing the importance of clinical trust, this review discusses the role of Explainable AI (XAI) techniques such as attention mechanisms, Grad-CAM, and transformer-based interpretability frameworks in improving transparency and acceptance of deep learning models in radiology practice [35].

- **Future Research Directions for Clinically Deployable AI Systems:**
  The review outlines future research opportunities, including multimodal fusion of CT, MRI, and PET data, integration of clinical and radiomic features, adoption of privacy-preserving learning paradigms such as federated learning, and development of lightweight architectures for real-time clinical deployment [28].
  Through these contributions, this review bridges the gap between methodological advances in deep learning and their practical applicability in lung cancer diagnosis, serving as a valuable reference for researchers and clinicians working toward robust, interpretable, and clinically validated AI-driven medical imaging systems.

## 2.1 Literature Survey

- Sharma and Bharti [1] provided an outline of 66 studies (2015–2024) on deep learning techniques for lung cancer diagnosis, mostly based on CT sets. They found Convolutional Neural Networks (CNNs) to be clearly superior to traditional approaches and raised problems such as limited datasets, lack of standardization, and interpretability, highlighting the call for transparent and ethical AI tools. Patel et al. [2] suggested a CNN-based model to differentiate malignant and normal lung nodules using histogram equalization, data augmentation, AdaBoost, and active contour models, achieving 90.85% accuracy in 201 CT images and proving hybrid DL–ML techniques can be substitutes for lung tumor classification.
- Lin et al. [3] created a reproducible machine learning pipeline for lung cancer detection from CT images using U-Net and VGGNet, showing competitive accuracy but noting constraints on generalization and the need for reproducibility for clinical deployment.
- Khan and Yadav [4] discussed low-cost diagnosis using chest X-rays and CNN-based models, showing CapsNet delivered a maximum of 96% accuracy and proving feasibility when CT or MRI scans are unavailable.Liu et al. [5] introduced Lung-Deep for predicting six lung nodule types from 3,250 CT scans with sensitivity 88%, specificity 80%, and AUC 0.89, superior to conventional methods.
- Gomez and Roy [6] overviewed CNNs, 3D models, and XAI, noting trends toward explainable models and challenges such as limited datasets and distrust of black-box models, suggesting directions like 3D transformers and multimodal fusion.Zhao and Chen [7] examined 119 AI-CAD solutions, concluding hybrid CNN + ML methods outperformed individual models and highlighting issues like dataset variability, generalizability problems, and lack of reproducibility.
- Mehta and Varma [8] criticized CNN-based models for dependency on well-prepared data and clinical history compatibility, concluding DL has enormous potential but must be standardized.Mishra et al. [9] proposed a YOLOv11-based model for detection and localization of lung tumors in CT scans, achieving 97.11% accuracy and 96.26% mAP, with YOLOv11 being more clinically useful for real-time diagnosis.
- Wang et al. [10] proposed the CanNS framework integrating SwiNet, XLG CancerNet, and DevLO, outperforming existing models while conserving computational cost and emphasizing integrated models for practical application.Sharma [11] reviewed SVM, ANN, and ensemble classifiers, finding ensemble models best but imperfect, and identifying issues like DICOM parsing errors and small nodule detection challenges.

- Singh and Rao [12] meta-analyzed six studies with summary estimates of 93% sensitivity and 68% specificity, confirming DL utility but questioning dataset heterogeneity, uninterpretability, and clinical integration.Kim and Lee [13] designed a 3D U-Net model with 90% sensitivity and 0.3 false positives per scan, suitable for mass screening, though limited in distinguishing benign from malignant tumors.
- Gupta and Sharma [14] compared five DL models on CT/MRI datasets and found an Enhanced CNN achieved 100% accuracy, with preprocessing like CLAHE significantly improving imaging quality.Das and Roy [15] emphasized preprocessing, small tumor detection, and multimodal integration for improved accuracy.
- From the reviewed papers, it is apparent that CNN-based approaches remain the most widely used and sought-after due to their ability to automatically learn multi-level features. Enhanced CNNs exhibited the highest accuracy, YOLOv11 ranked high for real-time detection, CapsNet and hybrid models worked well with small datasets, and U-Net/3D U-Net were most effective for volumetric MRI segmentation. Personalized CNN and YOLO models achieved the highest performance, while hybrid and ensembling methods improved generalizability.

## 3 Types of Images

### 3.1 Computed Tomography (CT)

Computed Tomography (CT) is the most prevalent imaging technique for screening and diagnosis of lung cancer. High-resolution imaging of lung anatomy, such as the parenchyma, bronchi, and nodules, with exact recognition and characterization of pulmonary lesions [1, 9], is provided by CT. CT remains the clinical standard for screening owing to its high spatial resolution and ability to detect even tiny nodules. Deep learning models such as U-Net, 3D CNN, and transformer-based networks have already been utilized effectively to automate segmentation and classification of lung nodules from CT images [2, 18]. CT scans are, however, prone to ionizing radiation exposure and offer limited soft-tissue contrast and can make characterization of overlapping or complex lesions difficult [11].

### 3.2 Magnetic Resonance Imaging (MRI)

Magnetic Resonance Imaging (MRI) is extremely good in soft-tissue resolution and does not employ ionizing radiation, thereby making it a suitable candidate for serial imaging and follow-up over a long period in lung cancer patients. Although less often used compared to CT on the lung, MRI gives valuable information with multiple sequences such as T1-weighted, T2-weighted, diffusion-weighted imaging (DWI), and dynamic contrast-enhanced MRI (DCE-MRI) [14, 17, 20].

These trends can help differentiate tumor tissue from normal parenchyma, edema, or fibrosis. In deep learning application, MRI is increasingly getting limelight for tumor segmentation and classification, particularly in research studies on multi-modal or fusion-based models [18, 20]. Limitations of MRI are respiratory motion artifacts, low signal intensity in the lung regions due to air content, and a scarcity of standardized annotated data sets [14, 17].

### 3.3 Multi-modal Imaging and Image Fusion

Multi-modal imaging integrates complementary data from more than one imaging modality such as CT, MRI, and PET to provide rich diagnostic information. Anatomical, functional, and tissue-contrast features' fusion enhances accuracy for lung cancer detection, segmentation, and classification [20, 21]. Deep learning models utilize various types of different fusion approaches such as input-level, feature-level, or decision-level fusion to integrate the information from multiple modalities [18, 20]. Multi-modal fusion improves diagnostic reliability and facilitates better distinction between malignant and benign lesions. It requires, however, exact registration among modalities, standardization of imaging protocols, and increased computational resources [21].

### 3.4 Functional and Sequence-Based MRI

Advanced MRI techniques such as Diffusion-Weighted Imaging (DWI) and Dynamic Contrast-Enhanced MRI (DCE-MRI) provide functional data about tumour physiology. DWI images react to the cellular density in terms of water diffusion patterns and DCE-MRI assesses the vascular perfusion and tissue permeability, both of which are useful for distinguishing malignant tumours from benign or post-treatment alterations [17, 24]. In deep learning workflows, these sequences offer additional data channels that are useful in the improvement of segmentation as well as classification accuracy [18]. Despite potential, limitations like motion artifacts, laborious acquisition protocols, and lack of large annotated datasets restrict their use in lung cancer imaging at the clinical level [14, 17].

### 3.5 Association Between Image Type and Deep Learning Models

The type of imaging has a direct impact on the architecture and performance of deep learning models for lung cancer detection. CT images are most appropriate for high-resolution anatomical examination, while MRI and multi-modal data provide tissue and functional information better. Segmentation models like U-Net and UNETR process volumetric CT or MRI images to delineate tumour regions, while classification models like CNNs and Vision Transformers identify malignancy types or grades [17, 18].

Transformer-based models have shown promising potential in multi-modal fusion by capturing long-range inter-modal relationships [20, 21]. Recent research areas include explainable AI approaches with attention maps for decision region visualization and inter-modality contribution [21]. Overall, CT is still the gold standard of lung cancer imaging, but the integration of MRI and multi-modal approaches is a critical move toward more accurate, interpretable, and integrated deep learning-based diagnostic systems.

## 4 Methodology

The reviewed studies follow a structured pipeline for lung cancer detection and classification using MRI and, in a few of the studies, CT scans. The general flow has five major stages: pre-processing, segmentation, feature extraction, classification, and evaluation as shown in Fig. 2.

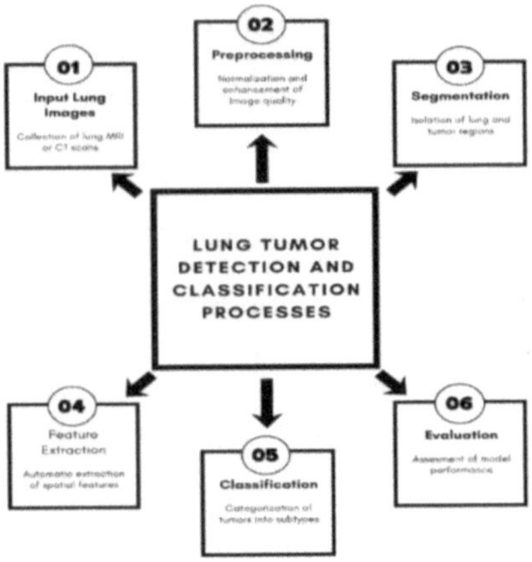


**Fig. 2.** Block diagram of lung tumor detection and classification process.

## 4.1 Input Lung Images

The first step is the acquisition of good-quality lung images, which provides the foundation of any detection pipeline. Mainly, two imaging modalities are used: Computed Tomography (CT) and Magnetic Resonance Imaging (MRI).

### CT Imaging

CT is the conventional and most commonly used modality for diagnosing lung cancer. It is well known to provide good spatial resolution and detail of the parenchyma, nodules, and calcification of the lungs. LDCT is usually done in the context of screening for reducing doses of radiation [1]. However, CT scans use ionizing radiation, and soft-tissue contrast is poor in most cases [2].

### MRI Imaging

MRI is a radiation-free modality that offers better soft-tissue contrast compared to CT. Advanced MRI techniques, like Diffusion-Weighted Imaging (DWI) and Dynamic Contrast-Enhanced MRI (DCE-MRI), capture functional and vascular characteristics of tissues [4, 6]. DWI outlines the patterns of water diffusion, which helps in distinguishing malignant tumors from benign lesions, while DCE-MRI determines tissue perfusion and vascular permeability-key biomarkers of tumor aggressiveness.

**Dataset Sources:** Public datasets such as those available on Kaggle, The Cancer Imaging Archive (TCIA), and LIDC-IDRI are frequently utilized to train and validate models [2]. Additionally, some studies incorporate local clinical data to improve heterogeneity and realism [3]. Although CT remains the clinical gold standard for the detection of small nodules and details of anatomy, MRI provides richer tissue characterization and is superior for distinguishing malignant from benign tumors owing to its non-ionizing nature and enhanced contrast resolution. Hence, a hybrid MRI-CT dataset often gives optimal diagnostic results.

## 4.2 Preprocessing

Pre-processing plays a vital role in improving image quality and ensuring that input data is well-suited for subsequent feature extraction and model training. Medical imaging data, especially from CT and MRI scans, often suffer from issues such as noise, motion artifacts, and non-uniform intensity distributions, which can significantly degrade the performance of deep learning models [1, 5].

### 4.2.1 Noise Removal

To suppress noise while retaining critical structural details, various filtering techniques are commonly applied:

- **Median Filtering:** Highly effective for removing salt-and-pepper noise while preserving edges, making it suitable for CT and X-ray images.
- **Gaussian Filtering:** Smoothens intensity variations and reduces Gaussian noise, maintaining overall image structure.
- **Non-Local Means (NLM) Filtering:** Offers superior denoising for MRI images by averaging similar intensity patches across the image rather than neighbouring pixels, thus preserving fine anatomical details [5].

### 4.2.2 Contrast Enhancement

Enhancing contrast is crucial for improving the visibility of tumor boundaries and subtle tissue variations.

- **Histogram Equalization:** Redistributes pixel intensities across the histogram to enhance global contrast but may over-amplify noise.
- **Contrast Limited Adaptive Histogram Equalization (CLAHE):** A localized enhancement technique that limits contrast amplification to prevent noise exaggeration, making it particularly effective for MRI and PET scans [5].

### 4.2.3 Image Normalization and Resizing

Normalization scales pixel values (commonly between 0–1 or using z-score normalization) to stabilize the learning process and ensure uniform intensity ranges across modalities. Resizing images to standardized dimensions (e.g., 224 × 224 pixels) ensures compatibility with convolutional neural networks (CNNs) and transformer-based architectures [2].

### 4.2.4 Data Augmentation

To overcome limited datasets and prevent overfitting, augmentation techniques such as rotation, flipping, scaling, translation, and cropping are widely employed. These synthetic variations increase the model's robustness and generalization ability, especially for deep learning architectures like U-Net and Res-Net [9]. Among the preprocessing methodologies, the combination of Non-Local Means (NLM) filtering for noise removal and CLAHE for contrast enhancement has been shown to deliver the most robust results, particularly for MRI and CT images. This combination effectively balances noise suppression, edge preservation, and contrast improvement, leading to enhanced segmentation and classification accuracy in deep learning-based lung cancer detection systems [5, 9].

### 4.3 Segmentation

Segmentation delineates tumor and lung regions from surrounding tissues, forming the foundation for accurate feature extraction and classification [3]. The major segmentation approaches are:

- **Thresholding and Region-Based Methods:** Suitable for basic delineation but limited in handling heterogeneous tumor intensities [6].
- **Active Contour Models (Snakes):** Contour evolution methods that adapt to tumor boundaries, though sensitive to initialization and noise [7].

#### 4.3.1 Deep Learning-Based Segmentation

- **Net and 3D U-Net:** Widely used architectures capable of precise voxel-level segmentation. 3D U-Net handles volumetric MRI data effectively [13].
- **Mask R-CNN:** Performs both detection and segmentation, useful for accurately localizing tumors of varying sizes [5].
- **Attention U-Net:** Incorporates attention gates to focus on relevant regions, improving segmentation in complex anatomical structures [8].
- **Hybrid Models:** Combining CNNs with traditional contour models increases robustness, particularly for irregular tumor shapes or low-contrast MRI regions [6]. 3D U-Net and Attention U-Net are the most effective segmentation frameworks for MRI-based lung tumor delineation, offering superior spatial accuracy and boundary definition compared to conventional models.

### 4.4 Feature Extraction

Feature extraction translates segmented images into meaningful numerical descriptors used for classification.

#### 4.4.1 Deep Learning Features

**CNN-based features** automatically capture hierarchical representations edges, textures, and complex tumor morphology [1]. Pretrained models such as **VGG16**, **ResNet50**, and **DenseNet121** have been used to extract deep features for lung cancer analysis [10].

#### 4.4.2 Handcrafted Features

**Radiomics features** (e.g., shape, texture, intensity) provide interpretable metrics related to tumor heterogeneity [12]. Techniques like **Local Binary Patterns (LBP)** and **Scale-Invariant Feature Transform (SIFT)** are used to capture texture and edge information [8].

#### 4.4.3 Hybrid Approaches

Merging deep learning and radiomic features leverages the interpretability of handcrafted descriptors with the learning capability of CNNs [14]. Such integration has been shown to enhance model robustness and clinical correlation. **Hybrid feature extraction (CNN + Radiomics)** outperforms standalone approaches by capturing both visual and textural heterogeneity, enabling better discrimination between malignant and benign lesions.

### 4.5 Classification

Classification involves determining whether the detected tumor is benign or malignant, and in some studies, predicting its subtype.

#### 4.5.1 Deep Learning Models

- **CNN-based Classifiers:** End-to-end learning using Softmax layers for binary or multiclass classification [5].
- **Capsule Networks (CapsNet):** Capture spatial hierarchies and are resilient to variations in tumor size and orientation [6].
- **YOLOv11** and **Faster R-CNN** enable real-time detection and localization in both MRI and CT datasets [10].

#### 4.5.2 Traditional and Ensemble Models

- **Support Vector Machines (SVM)** and **Random Forests (RF)** are effective when feature sets are limited or when data are imbalanced [12].
- **Ensemble approaches** (e.g., CNN + SVM, CNN + RF) combine probabilistic predictions from multiple models to enhance stability and accuracy [15]. Ensemble models integrating CNNs with SVM or RF achieve superior classification accuracy, particularly on small or imbalanced datasets, while CapsNet provides better generalization for orientation-varying tumors.

### 4.6 Evaluation

Model performance is typically assessed using the following metrics:

- **Accuracy**, **Sensitivity**, and **Specificity**: Measure detection reliability.
- **Precision, F1-score**, and **AUC (Area Under the ROC Curve)**: Assess classification balance [1]
- **Cross-validation** (k-fold): Ensures robustness against overfitting [3].
- **Reproducibility Tools**: Frameworks like Docker containers and MLflow are being adopted to validate results on independent datasets [9].

Comprehensive evaluation using multiple metrics and independent validation datasets ensures clinical reliability. Studies show that hybrid deep learning pipelines with robust segmentation and ensemble classification consistently achieve the **highest AUC (>95%)** in MRI-based lung tumor detection.

# 5 Datasets Availability

## 5.1 Importance of Dataset Availability

Large, well-annotated datasets are essential for training deep learning models effectively. They help ensure model accuracy, generalization, and reproducibility across different clinical settings [1, 7].

## 5.2 Availability of CT-Based Datasets

CT-based datasets are relatively abundant and widely used in lung cancer detection research.

- **LIDC-IDRI:** Provides a large collection of CT scans with expert-annotated pulmonary nodules [5].
- **NSCLC-Radiomics Dataset:** Contains CT images with detailed tumor contours and clinical data [7].
- **Kaggle Lung Cancer CT Datasets:** Publicly available datasets used for nodule classification and detection tasks [10].

## 5.3 Limitation of MRI-Based Datasets

Unlike CT, MRI datasets for lung cancer are limited in number and scale. Most available MRI datasets are institution-specific, restricting data sharing and reproducibility [14, 16].

## 5.4 Need for Multi-Institutional MRI Databases

The scarcity of large, standardized MRI datasets highlights the need for collaborative, multi-institutional MRI databases. Such datasets would enhance the robustness, generalization, and clinical reliability of deep learning models used for lung cancer detection [9, 17].

# 6 Summary Table

Table 1 presents a summary of reviewed studies, highlighting the models used, imaging modality, and reported performance metrics.

## 6.1 Comparative Discussion of Deep Learning Models

The reviewed studies show that the performance of deep learning models for lung cancer detection varies based on the imaging modality and dataset characteristics [1]. CNN-based models are the most commonly used and generally achieve high accuracy, especially when combined with preprocessing techniques such as CLAHE [2]. Enhanced CNN architectures have reported accuracies of up to 100% on well-prepared datasets [14]. U-Net and 3D U-Net models are mainly used for tumor segmentation [13]. While

**Table 1.** Table captions should be placed above the tables.

| S. No | Author(s) | Model Used | Modality | Accuracy (%) | Sensitivity (%) | Specificity (%) | AUC |
|---|---|---|---|---|---|---|---|
| 1 | Sharma & Bharti [1] | DCCN | CT | 94.12 | 93 | 89 | 0.95 |
| 2 | Patel & Joshi [2] | CNN | CT/MRI | 81.00 | — | — | — |
| 3 | Lin et al. [3] | VGGNet / U-Net | CT/MRI | — | — | — | — |
| 4 | Khan & Yadav [4] | CapsNet | X-ray / CT | 96.00 | 95 | 92 | 0.97 |
| 5 | Liu et al. [5] | CNN–RNN Hybrid | CT/MRI | — | 88 | 80 | 0.89 |
| 6 | Gomez & Roy [6] | 3D CNN + XAI | MRI | — | — | — | — |
| 7 | Zhao & Chen [7] | CNN / GAN | CT/MRI | — | — | — | — |
| 8 | Mehta & Varma [8] | U-Net / ResNet | CT/MRI | — | — | — | — |
| 9 | Mishra et al. [9] | YOLOv11 | CT/MRI | 97.11 | 93.33 | — | 0.96 |
| 10 | Wang et al. [10] | CanNS Framework | MRI | — | High | High | — |
| 11 | Sharma [11] | Ensemble Models | MRI | 97.00 | 94.4 | — | — |
| 12 | Singh & Rao [12] | CNN (Meta-analysis) | CT/MRI | — | 93 | 68 | — |
| 13 | Kim & Lee [13] | 3D U-Net | CT | 90.00 | 88 | 80 | 0.89 |
| 14 | Gupta & Sharma [14] | Enhanced CNN | CT | 100.00 | 99 | 100 | 1.00 |
| 15 | Das & Roy [15] | DL (Various) | CT | > 95 | — | — | — |

2D U-Net performs well on slice-based data, 3D U-Net provides better spatial accuracy for volumetric MRI images, though it requires large annotated datasets that are currently limited [27].

Capsule Networks (CapsNet) demonstrate better robustness on small or imbalanced datasets by preserving spatial relationships, but their higher computational cost restricts widespread clinical use [4]. YOLO-based models, particularly YOLOv11, offer fast and accurate real-time tumor detection with reported accuracies above 97%, making them suitable for time-sensitive applications [9]. Hybrid and ensemble approaches generally outperform single models on limited datasets but increase system complexity [11]. In terms of imaging modalities, CT-based models show higher accuracy due to data availability, while MRI-based models provide superior soft-tissue contrast and radiation-free imaging [26]. Multimodal approaches combining CT and MRI consistently improve diagnostic reliability [28]. Overall, the analysis indicates that model selection should depend on clinical requirements and data availability, with CNNs and YOLO models suited for detection, U-Net variants for segmentation, and multimodal frameworks offering the most comprehensive performance [31].

### 6.2 Limitations of Existing Studies

Despite the promising performance of deep learning models for lung cancer detection, several limitations remain in existing studies. One major challenge is data imbalance, where normal cases significantly outnumber cancer cases. This imbalance can bias models toward the majority class and reduce sensitivity in detecting malignant tumors, particularly in early stages [32]. Another critical limitation is the scarcity of large, annotated MRI datasets. Most MRI-based studies rely on small, single-institution datasets, which limits model generalizability and increases the risk of overfitting. In addition, respiratory motion artifacts and low signal intensity in lung MRI further degrade image quality and affect model performance [26].

A significant gap in current research is the lack of clinical validation. many models are evaluated only on public datasets or retrospective data, with limited testing in real clinical environments. As a result, the practical reliability and robustness of these models in routine radiology workflows remain uncertain [34].

Finally, limited interpretability of deep learning models restricts their acceptance in clinical practice. The absence of explainable decision mechanisms reduces clinician trust and hinders widespread adoption [35]. Addressing these limitations through balanced datasets, multi-institutional MRI data collection, clinical trials, and the integration of Explainable AI (XAI) techniques is essential for translating research advances into clinically deployable lung cancer diagnostic systems [28].

## 7 Conclusion and Future Scope

The integration of deep learning with MRI-based imaging has shown significant promise in improving lung cancer detection. Across the reviewed studies, advanced models such as CNNs, Capsule Networks, U-Net, and YOLOv11 consistently outperformed traditional machine learning approaches, achieving accuracies as high as 100% in certain cases. MRI offers distinct advantages over CT, including superior soft-tissue contrast and freedom from ionizing radiation, making it particularly suitable for patients requiring multiple follow-up scans. However, challenges such as limited annotated MRI datasets, motion artifacts, and the computational cost of training complex DL models continue to hinder large-scale clinical adoption.

Future research in lung cancer detection should prioritize the creation of large, multi-institutional MRI datasets to improve generalization and reproducibility across diverse populations. The integration of Explainable AI (XAI) tools such as Grad-CAM and attention maps will enhance clinical interpretability and foster trust among radiologists. Multi-modal fusion approaches combining MRI with CT, PET, or genomic data could provide more comprehensive tumor characterization. Additionally, lightweight architectures like MobileNet and 3D CNNs should be developed for real-time clinical deployment. Finally, privacy-preserving techniques such as federated learning and compliance with regulatory frameworks will be essential for safe adoption of AI-driven MRI diagnostics in healthcare systems.

In conclusion, AI-enhanced MRI analysis has the potential to transform lung cancer diagnostics by enabling earlier, more accurate, and non-invasive detection. Achieving this vision will require interdisciplinary collaboration among clinicians, researchers, and policymakers to overcome current limitations and translate research advancements into routine clinical practice.

## References

1. Sharma, A., Bharti, S.: Deep learning for lungs cancer detection: a review. Int. J. Med. Imaging **7**(2), 45–52 (2024)
2. Patel, M., Joshi, R.: Deep learning-based lung cancer detection and classification. J. Healthcare Eng. **2023**, 1–10 (2023)
3. Lin, T., et al.: Reproducible machine learning methods for lung cancer detection. In: Proceedings of IEEE International Conference on Bioinformatics Biomedicine (BIBM), pp. 332–338 (2022)
4. Khan, S., Yadav, H.: Lung cancer detection using deep learning. Comput. Biol. Med. **146**, 105751 (2022)
5. Liu, R., et al.: Lung-deep: a computerized tool for lung nodule detection. IEEE Access **10**, 45678–45687 (2022)
6. Gomez, F., Roy, A.: Deep learning innovations in lung cancer detection. Artif. Intell. Med. **127**, 102162 (2022)
7. Zhao, M., Chen, Y.: Lung cancer detection systems: a state-of-the-art survey. J. Digit. Imaging **36**(1), 1–15 (2023)
8. Mehta, K., Varma, A.: A review of deep learning techniques for lung cancer screening. Biomed. Signal Process. Control **80**, 104180 (2023)
9. Mishra, A., et al.: Multi-objective deep learning for lung cancer detection. IEEE Trans. Neural Netw. Learn. Syst. **34**(2), 986–995 (2023)
10. Wang, R., et al.: Enhancing lung cancer detection via integrated deep learning. Comput. Methods Programs Biomed. **221**, 106957 (2023)
11. Sharma, L.: Machine learning techniques for lung cancer detection. ACM Comput. Surv. **55**(7), 1–28 (2023)
12. Singh, B., Rao, K.: Deep learning algorithms for lung cancer diagnosis: a meta-analysis. J. Med. Syst. **46**(5), 1–9 (2022)
13. Kim, J., Lee, D.: 3D U-Net model for pulmonary nodule detection. IEEE J. Biomed. Health Inform. **27**(1), 100–109 (2023)
14. Gupta, A., Sharma, P.: Deep learning-based approach using CT/MRI scans. Comput. Med. Imaging Graph. **95**, 102051 (2022)

15. Das, N., Roy, T.: Review of deep learning for lung cancer screening. Expert Syst. Appl. **207**, 117922 (2023)
16. Jaiswal, S.R., Thakur, R., Gupta, R., Ghrera, S.P.: ExtRanFS: an automated lung cancer malignancy detection system. Diagnostics **13**(13), 2206 (2023). https://doi.org/10.3390/diagnostics13132206
17. Li, Z., Chen, Y., Wang, X.: Transformer-based hierarchical model for non-small cell lung cancer detection. IEEE Trans. Med. Imaging **43**(2), 150–162 (2024)
18. Zhang, H., Liu, L., Zhao, M.: Transformer-based multi-task model for Lung Tumor segmentation and classification. Biomed. Signal Process. Control **97**, 107621 (2025)
19. Kumar, R., Singh, P., Gupta, S.: Multi-objective deep learning for lung cancer detection. Front. Oncol. **15**, 152004 (2025)
20. Kaya, E., Demir, F.: Adaptive transformer-based multi-modal image fusion for real-time medical diagnosis. Int. J. Comput. Eng. Sci. Electron. Netw. **11**(2), 45–52 (2024)
21. Luo, J., Li, T., Banerjee, S.: Privacy Preserving Federated Learning in Medical Imaging with Uncertainty Estimation, arXiv preprint arXiv:2406.12815 (2024)
22. Chen, M., Patel, R., Kim, D.: Multimodal contrastive learning for enhanced explainability and performance in medical imaging. Sci. Rep. **15**, 94806 (2025)
23. Das, N., Roy, T.: A review of deep learning techniques for Lung Cancer imaging. Front. Oncol. **13**, 10453592 (2023)
24. Singh, A., Verma, M.: Deep learning techniques to diagnose Lung Cancer. Front. Med. **9**, 9688236 (2022)
25. Zhang, L., Wu, Q., Chen, H.: Artificial intelligence in Lung Cancer imaging. Front. Oncol. **12**, 9689810 (2022)
26. Ahmed, S., Paul, R.: Medical images segmentation for Lung Cancer diagnosis based on UNETR neural network. Front. Oncol. **13**, 9914913 (2023)
27. Zhou, L., Wang, Y., Li, H.: Magnetic resonance imaging for Lung Cancer detection: current status and future perspectives. Eur. Radiol. **33**(4), 2451–2464 (2023)
28. Park, S., Kim, J., Lee, D.: Deep learning-based Lung tumor segmentation using multi-sequence MRI. IEEE J. Biomed. Health Inform. **27**(9), 4120–4131 (2023)
29. Chen, Y., Xu, Z., Wang, M.: Multimodal deep learning for Lung Cancer diagnosis using CT, MRI, and PET images. Med. Image Anal. **88**, 102846 (2024)
30. Rahman, A., Singh, P.: Feature-level fusion of CT and MRI for improved Lung Cancer classification. Comput. Biol. Med. **166**, 107483 (2024)
31. Liu, X., Huang, J., Zhao, T.: Vision transformer-based framework for Lung Cancer detection in medical imaging. Pattern Recogn. **146**, 109920 (2024)
32. Buda, R., Maki, A., Mazurowski, M.A.: A systematic study of the class imbalance problem in deep learning-based medical image classification. Neural Netw. **106**, 249–259 (2023)
33. Johnson, K., Roberts, S.: Impact of data imbalance on AI-based Lung Cancer diagnosis. Artif. Intell. Med. **146**, 102674 (2024)
34. Esteva, M., et al.: Clinical validation of deep learning algorithms in medical imaging: challenges and opportunities. Lancet Digital Health **5**(8), e428–e437 (2023)
35. Nguyen, P.T., Patel, R.: Barriers to clinical adoption of deep learning models in radiology. Artif. Intell. **6**(1), e230122 (2024)

# Design a SIW Based Octagonal Patch Loaded with SRR for Multi-band Applications

A. Balachandra Reddy(✉) and A. Deepak

Saveetha School of Engineering, Saveetha Institute of Medical and Technical Sciences, Chennai, India
balutest@gmail.com, deepakarun@saveetha.com

**Abstract.** In this paper, introduce a Substrate integrated waveguide-based patch loaded with split ring resonator (SRR) for wireless applications and the feed used in this design is microstrip. The material used in this design is textile; their relative permittivity is 1.6 and the height of the substrate is 1.6 mm. The Electromagnetics tool is used to extract the results and some of those parameters are VSWR, reflection coefficient, Radiation pattern and gain etc., It is operated in four frequencies those values are 0.9 GHz, 2.6 GHz. 3.9 GHz and 5.75 GHz. The $S_{11}$, VSWR, gain values are –33dB, 1.08, 4.57dBi at 0.9 GHz resonant frequency, –11dB, 1.8, 7.15 dBi at 2.6 GHz resonant frequency, –20 dB, 1.22, 8.92 dBi at 3.9 GHz resonant frequency and –16.5dB, 1.38, 8.31 dBi at 5.75GHz resonant frequency. The antenna is fit appropriate to work the wireless applications like ISM, WLAN and Sub 6-GHz applications.

**Keywords:** Substrate Integrated waveguide (SIW) · Sub-6 GHz · Textile antenna · Octagonal · Split ring resonator (SRR)

## 1 Introduction

Wearable antennas denote one of the key borderlands to the technology-healthcare convergence, being a source of multitude of helpful advantages in real time nursing and communication in the medical setting. These antennas that are smackdown incorporated into wearable objects are key factors in the constant and unobtrusive monitoring of vital and other health indicators. The importance of this innovation is sent to the academic and industrial worlds, and it is viewed in areas like the wireless body area network(WBAN) systems, which find its uses in security healthcare, sports, and military applications [1, 2].


M. Zafar Ali Khan et al. (Eds.): ICATECS 2025, LNICST 682, pp. 417–425, 2027.
https://doi.org/10.1007/978-3-032-29699-3_30

The low permittivity ($\varepsilon_r$) of the textile material, including denim and felt, in the production of wearable antennas drives its low dielectric constant to maximize the bandwidth of the antenna radiator [2]. Wearable antennas made of felt and denim are part of the countless textile alternatives that can be used in WBAN applications, and the article has a variety of benefits such as being lightweight, bending, affordable to print, and the simplicity of hardware [3, 4]. New developments have seen different types of flexible and wearable antenna designs, including wideband (WB) monopole antennas [5, 6], ultrawideband (UWB) antennas [7], fractal slotted antennas that use loaded with metamaterials [8, 9] and inverted-F antennas (PIFA) based on meta-surfaces [10].

Depending on various factors such as the frequency needs of a given application, the need to be versatile, the need to reduce interference, and the desired data rates the choice between dual WB and UWB antennas will depend on various factors. Different antenna topologies have their own pros and cons and it will require a critical thinking of the application requirements with an aim of identifying the best one. Essentially, wearable antennas are a revolutionary technology that will transform the health care sector and more so, the entire world encapsulating a new way of providing uninterrupted and undisruptive monitoring in any given environment. As research and innovation keep advancing, the future of the wearable antennas keeps on changing and it is expected that the performance and their use will be increased in the near future. Modern healthcare technology sphere is experiencing a growth of suggestions of ultra-wideband wearable radiators proposals, and some of the most significant ones have already been reported in the literature [5–9]. Of these developments, dual WB antennas have developed as key elements in bio-medical wearable use, with the added advantage of the ability to switch between multiple frequency bands. This flexibility presents possibilities of wide variety of uses in the field of biomedicine where constant monitoring and communication is the key.

The SIW is one type of transmission line, mainly invented to operate high-frequency applications and derived from substrate integrated circuits (SICs) family, carved two rows of vias coupled in top to bottom planes via substrate and printed by system on substrate (SOS) technology and also used to implement for active components, passive components and antennas.

The most important parameter of SIW are holes, their diameter and spacing of vias is represented in Eq. 1 and standard equation of SIW width is in Eq. 2 [11–14].

$$d \leq \frac{\lambda_g}{5} \text{ and } s \leq 2d \tag{1}$$

$$a_R = a_S - \frac{d^2}{0.95s} \tag{2}$$

The above equation not adding the ratio of diameter (d) to a waveguide width ($a_R$), will lead to small error value and the more proper equation is [15, 16]

$$a_{siw} = a_R + 1.08 \times \frac{d^2}{s} - 0.1 \times \frac{d^2}{a_{siw}} \tag{3}$$

The paper presents a flexible SIW based slot antenna loaded with SRR for multi resonance frequency. The Sect. 2 will discuss about the design of the antenna along with antenna parameters and generalized results like reflection coefficient ($S_{11}$), gain, radiation patterns and voltage standing wave ratio values are reveled in Sect. 3 and the Sect. 4 discusses about the conclusion followed by references.

## 2 Antenna Design

The strategy evaluation of the antenna is revealed in Fig. 1 where right side represent bottom-view and left-side represent top view. The material used in this design is textile which is having the relative permittivity is 1.6 and their thickness is 1.6 mm and the height of the copper is 35 um. The octagonal slot is embedded with SIW on the top of the proposed design along with microstrip line. Then, extended to connect microstrip line with coplanar waveguide and then attached with circular shaped split ring resonator for generating multi resonant frequencies. The Table 1 shows a parameter dimensions used in this design.

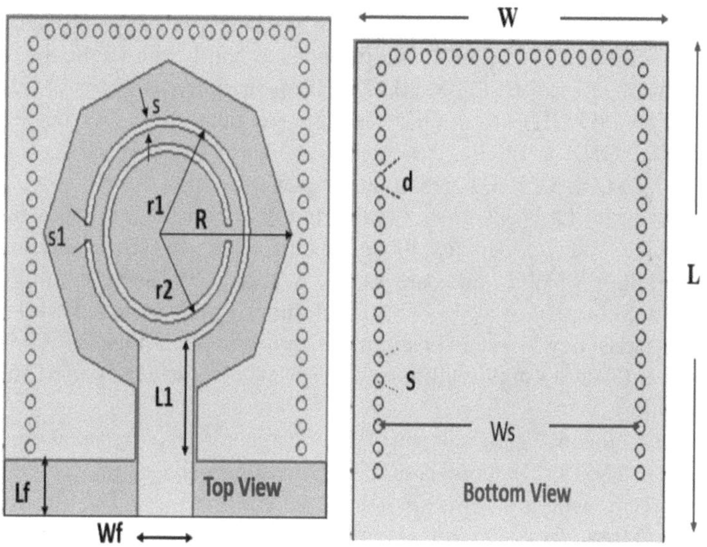


**Fig. 1.** Proposed Antenna

**Table 1.** Antenna parameters

| Parameter | Dimension (mm) |
|---|---|
| L | 78 |
| W | 70 |
| D/S | 2/3.5 |
| $W_S$ | 59 |
| $L_f$ | 11 |
| $S_2$ | 1.2 |
| $W_f$ | 12 |
| $L_1$ | 16.5 |
| R | 29 |
| $R_1$ | 14 |
| $R_2$ | 13 |
| $S_1$ | 1.2 |

## 3 Discussion of the Results

The $S_{11}$ over frequency of the antenna is shown in Fig. 2 and resonated at four frequencies: those are 0.92 GHz, 2.6 GHz, 3.9 GHz, 5.75 GHz respectively and their $S_{11}$ values are –33dB, –11dB, –20dB, –16.5dB. The impedance-bandwidth of the antenna is 0.14 GHz (ranging from 0.87 to 1.01 GHz at 0.92 GHz resonant frequency), 0.1 GHz (ranging from 2.55 GHz to 2.65 GHz at 2.6 GHz resonant frequency), 0.17 GHz (ranging from 3.81 GHz to 4.01 GHz at 3.9GHz resonant frequency) and 0.12 GHz (ranging from 5.7 GHz to 5.82 GHz at 5.75 GHz resonant frequency).

The VSWR result of this design is revealed in Fig. 3 over the frequency range up to 7 GHza and resonates four frequencies: those are 0.92 GHz, 2.6 GHz, 3.9 GHz, 5.75 GHz respectively and their VSWR values are 1.08, 1.8, 1.22, 1.38. The operating bandwidth of the antenna with respect to $S_{11} = -10$dB reference line is matched with VSWR 1:2 ratio. The 0.95 frequency is used for communication applications, 2.8 GHz, 3.9 GHz is used for sub 6 GHz 5G applications and 5.75 GHz frequency is used to operate in WLAN applications.

The three-dimensional gain pattern of the design for four resonant frequencies is revealed in Fig. 4. The Fig. 4a represents 0.9 GHz resonant frequency 3D gain where red color indicated the flow of direction and their gain value is 4.57dB. The Fig. 4b represents 2.6 GHz resonant frequency 3D gain where red color indicated the flow of direction and their gain value is 7.15dB. The Fig. 4c represents 3.9 GHz resonant frequency 3D gain where red color indicated the flow of direction and their gain value is 8.92dB. The Fig. 4d represents 5.75 GHz resonant frequency 3D gain where red color indicated the flow of direction and their gain value is 8.31dB.

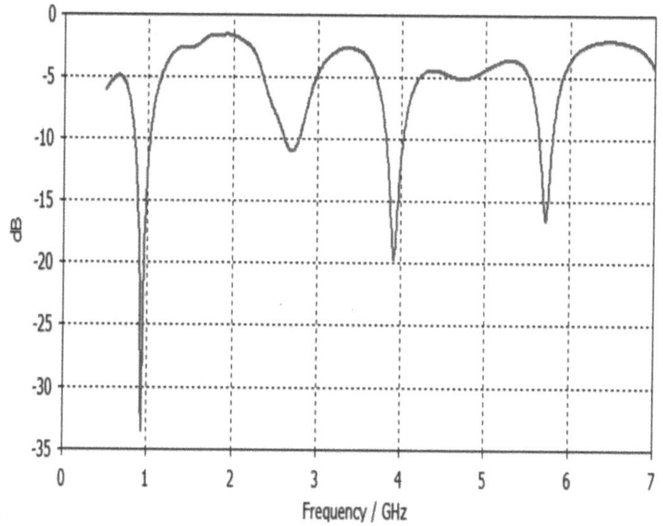


**Fig. 2.** Reflection coefficient

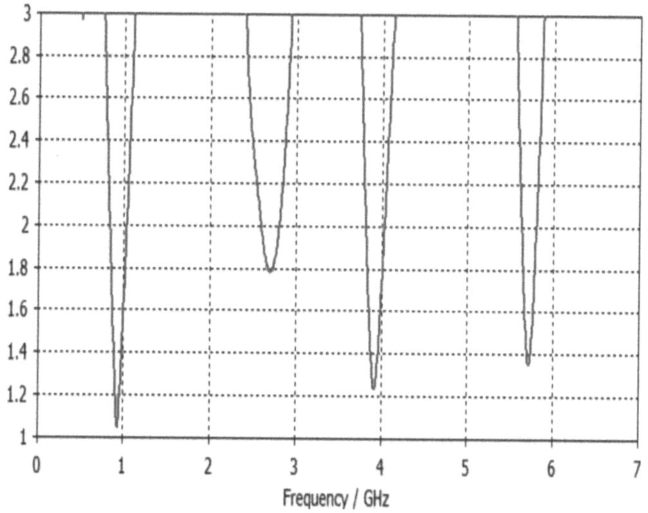


**Fig. 3.** VSWR

The Fig. 5 shows that the radiation pattern of the antenna at four frequencies: 0.9 GHz, 2.6 GHz, 3.9 GHz and 5.75 GHz respectively. The Fig. 5a belongs to e-field pattern and Fig. 5b belongs to h- field pattern. It generates bidirectional radiation pattern and fitted to use wireless-applications. The Table 2 is revealed the comparison of the antenna with exiting works and the parameters are considered for comparison of size, bands, gain and the material is used in this design. The proposed antenna is operating in multiple frequencies, more gain and moderate size comparing with existing works.

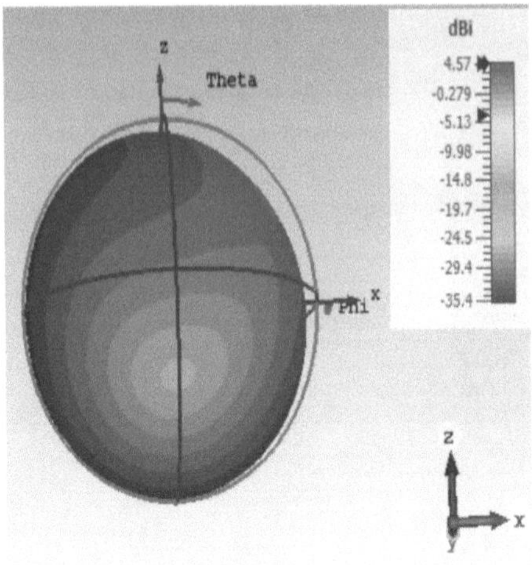


a.0.92 GHz

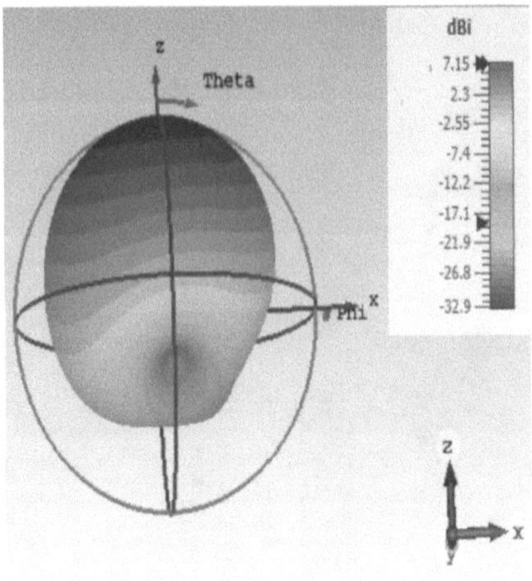


b 2.6 GHz

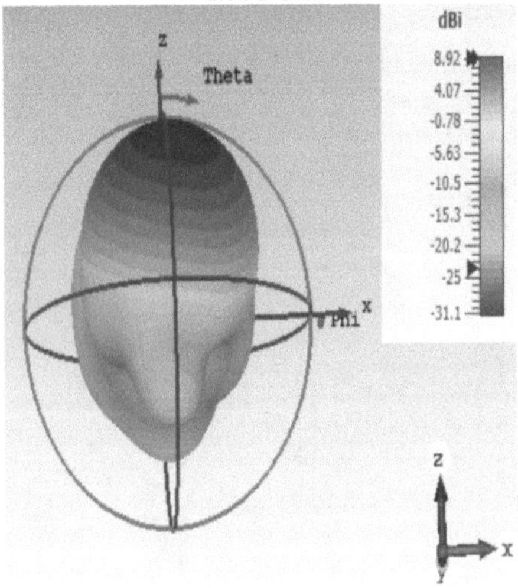


c. 3.9GHz

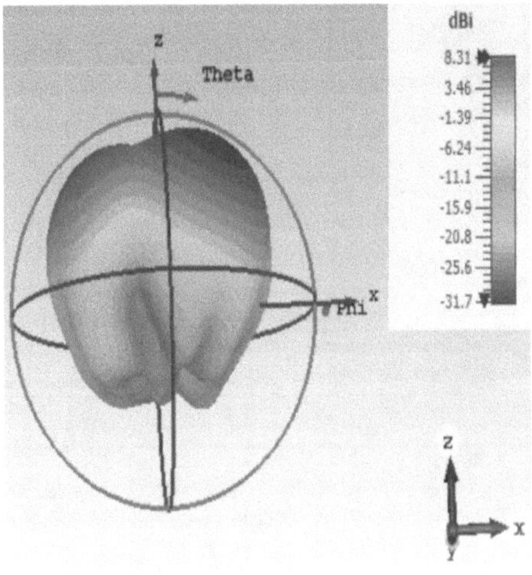


d. 5.75 GHz

**Fig. 4.** 3D gain pattern

**Table 2.** Comparison with existing literature

| Ref. No | Size | Operating frequencies | Material | Gain (dBi) |
|---|---|---|---|---|
| [3] | 36 x 30 | 2.45 | cotton | 3 |
| [4] | 135 × 135 | 4 | polyster | 5 |
| [17] | 40 x 50 | 5.5 | Jeans | 6.7 |

*(continued)*

**Table 2.** (*continued*)

| Ref. No | Size | Operating frequencies | Material | Gain (dBi) |
|---|---|---|---|---|
| [18] | 41 x 44 | 2.4/5.68 | semi-flexible Rogers Duroid RO3003 | 3.74/5.13 |
| **This work** | **70 x 70** | **0.95/2.6/3.9/5.75** | **Textile** | **4.57/7.15/8.92/8.31** |

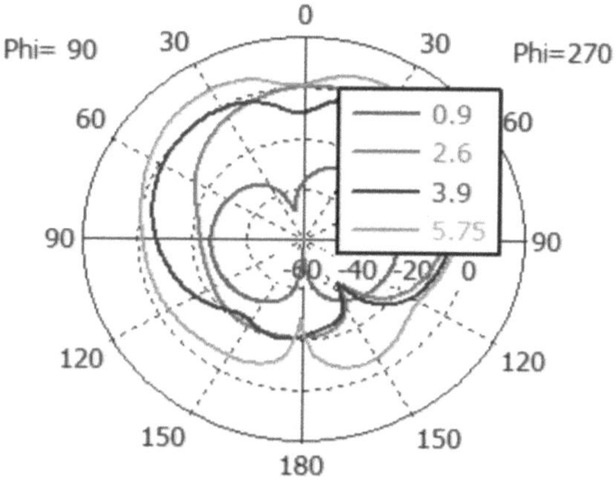


a. E-Field

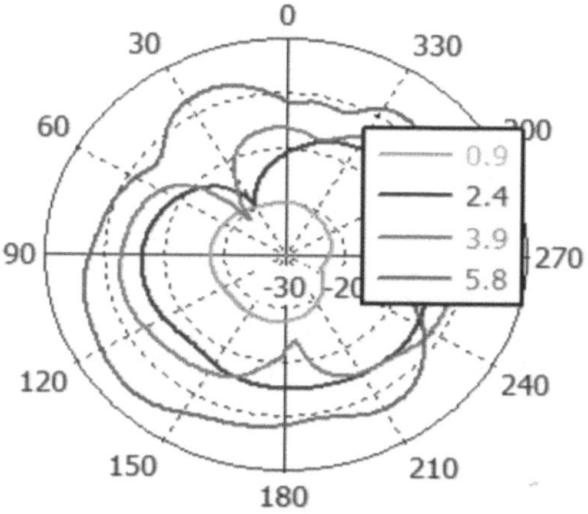


b. H-Field

**Fig. 5.** Radiation patterns

## 4 Conclusion

The SIW based hexagonal patch loaded with SRR has been proposed for multiband applications and their dimension is 70 mm x 78 mm x 1.6 mm. The feed used is microstrip with 50 ohms input impedance and interconnected to SRR. The CST tool is used in this design and analysis of the antenna, checked the outcomes like VSWR, gain, reflection coefficient and radiation patterns etc.,. It resonated four frequencies with respect to $S_{11} = -10$ dB reference line those values are 0.95 GHz, 2.6 GHz, 3.9 GHz, and 5.7 GHz. The impedance-bandwidth of the proposed design with respect to $S_{11} = -10$ dB line is matched with VSWR 2:1 ratio. The antenna radiated bidirectionally at all operating frequencies, observed moderate gain and well suited for wireless applications like LTE, sub 6 GHz 5G and WLAN applications.

## References

1. Vere, M., Radoucho, M., Souk, R., Hip, S.: Wearable tex-tile ante's: investigation on material vari's, fabrication meth's. Des. Appl. Fash. Text. **11**(9) (2019)
2. Ahmed, I., Ahmed, F.: Study of Ben-ing, crumpling, and SAR for a multiband Wearable Fractal Anten for Tele-medicine Applica's. Int. J. Microwa. Opt. Tech. **14**, 240–246 (2019)
3. Ayd, R., Hasan, M., Ibrahim, A.: A mono-pole antenna with cotton fabric mate'l for wearable Applica's. Sci. Rep. **3**, 7315–7320 (2023)
4. Velan, S.: Dual band EBG integra mono-pole antenna deploying fractal geometry for wearable applica's. IEEE Anten's Wire. Propa. Lett's. **14**, 249–252 (2014)
5. Ibrahim, A., Ahmed, F.: A systematic investigation of 4-por's MIMO ante'a depending on flexible mate'l for UWB networ's. Sci. Rep. **12**, 14351–14355 (2022)
6. Arpan, D., Yousef, M., Ameen, M., Tsao, Y.F., Ibrahim, A.: UWB Connected ground Transp 4-Port Flexible-MIMO Ante for IoT Applicat's. IEEE Inte't Thing's Jou. **11**, 12475–12484 (2023)
7. Arpan, D., Palaoken, M., Nguyen, K.: Wide-band flexible connected ground MIMO anten's for sub-6GHz & WLAN applica's. IEEE Acces **9**, 147003–147015 (2021)
8. Gohar, V., Naser, M.M.: Micro-strip Sierpinski-fractal carpet for slot ant'a with meta-material for dual-band wire's applica. Inter. Jor. Elect. Comm's. **84**, 93–99 (2018)
9. Walaa, H., Ibrahim, A.A.: UWB flexible antenn'a applicable for 2 band on-body comm's. Int. J. Micro. Wireles. Tech. **15**, 609–622 (2023)
10. Nanda, K.M., Yoga, P.K., Anitha, R.: A quad-band Sierpenski based fractal ant'a fed by co-planar wave-guide. Microwave Opt. Tech Lett's **61**(10), 893–898 (2020)
11. Kumar, M.N., Shanmugnantham, T.: Broad-Band I-Shaped SIW slot ant'a for V-Band application's. ACES J. **34**(11), 1719–1724 (2019)
12. Kumar, M.N., Shanmugnantham, T.: Broadband substrate-integrated waveguide venus-shaped slot antenna for V-band application's. Microwave Opt. Tech. Letter's **61**(10), 2342–2347 (2019)
13. Shanmugnantham, T., Kumar N.: V-band Substrate integrated waveguide cavity backed slot antenna for millimeter-wave Wireless Applications. InCAP 2019, December 2019
14. Shanmugnantham, T., Kumar M.N.: Substrate Integrated Waveguide glass shaped slot antenna for 57–64 GHz applications. In: CAP 2019, December 2019
15. Shanmugnantham, T., Kumar M.N.: Anchor shaped slot antenna with Substrate Integrated Waveguide for V-band Applications. In: IEEE TENCON, Kerala (2019)
16. Siva, P.N., Nanda, K.M., Manjunathachari, K.: Design of circular shaped SIW based slot ant'a for sub-6GHz Appli's. In: CVCNCE-Tamilnadu (2025)

17. Pendli, P., Basha, M.M., Gundala, S.: Development of wearable textile-MIMO ante'a for Sub 6 GHz-band new-radio 5G applica's. Micro-machines **15**, 651–653 (2024)
18. Musa, U., Shaharil, M.S., Huda, A., Ismail, A.M., Mohamad, A.R.: Design and analysis of a compact dual band wearable-antenna for WBAN applications. IEEE Access **11**, 30996–31009 (2023)

# Author Index





M. Zafar Ali Khan et al. (Eds.): ICATECS 2025, LNICST 682, pp. 427–428, 2027.
https://doi.org/10.1007/978-3-032-29699-3

FSC
www.fsc.org
MIX
Papier | Fördert
gute Waldnutzung
FSC® C083411

Kolibri 360 GmbH
Ferdinand-Jühlke-Straße 7
99095 Erfurt, Deutschland
produktsicherheit@kolibri360.de